TAKING◉SIDES

Clashing Views in

Business Ethics and Society

TENTH EDITION

TAKING SIDES

Clashing Views in

Business Ethics and Society

TENTH EDITION

Selected, Edited, and with Introductions by

Lisa H. Newton
Fairfield University

and

Maureen M. Ford
Fairfield University

Boston   Burr Ridge, IL   Dubuque, IA   New York   San Francisco   St. Louis
Bangkok   Bogotá   Caracas   Kuala Lumpur   Lisbon   London   Madrid   Mexico City
Milan   Montreal   New Delhi   Santiago   Seoul   Singapore   Sydney   Taipei   Toronto

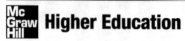

Higher Education

TAKING SIDES: CLASHING VIEWS IN BUSINESS ETHICS AND SOCIETY, TENTH EDITION

Published by McGraw-Hill, a business unit of The McGraw-Hill Companies, Inc., 1221 Avenue of the Americas, New York, NY 10020. Copyright © 2008 by The McGraw-Hill Companies, Inc. All rights reserved. Previous edition(s) 1990–2006. No part of this publication may be reproduced or distributed in any form or by any means, or stored in a database or retrieval system, without the prior written consent of The McGraw-Hill Companies, Inc., including, but not limited to, in any network or other electronic storage or transmission, or broadcast for distance learning.

Some ancillaries, including electronic and print components, may not be available to customers outside the United States.

Taking Sides® is a registered trademark of the McGraw-Hill Companies, Inc.
Taking Sides is published by the **Contemporary Learning Series** group within the McGraw-Hill Higher Education division.

 This book is printed on recycled, acid-free paper containing 10% postconsumer waste.

1 2 3 4 5 6 7 8 9 0 DOC/DOC 0 9 8 7

MHID: 0-07-352727-0
ISBN: 978-0-07-352727-7
ISSN: 95-83859

Managing Editor: *Larry Loeppke*
Production Manager: *Faye Schilling*
Senior Developmental Editor: *Susan Brusch*
Editorial Assistant: *Nancy Meissner*
Production Service Assistant: *Rita Hingtgen*
Permissions Coordinator: *Lori Church*
Senior Marketing Manager: *Julie Keck*
Marketing Communications Specialist: *Mary Klein*
Marketing Coordinator: *Alice Link*
Project Manager: *Jane Mohr*
Design Specialist: *Tara McDermott*
Senior Administrative Assistant: *DeAnna Dausener*
Senior Operations Manager: *Pat Koch Krieger*
Cover Graphics: *Maggie Lytle*

Compositor: Hurix Systems Private Limited
Cover Image: Comstock/PictureQuest

Library of Congress Cataloging-in-Publication Data
Main entry under title:
Taking sides: clashing views in business ethics and society/selected, edited, and with introductions by Lisa H. Newton and Maureen M. Ford—10th ed.

Includes bibliographical references.
1. Business ethics, I. Newton, Lisa H., *comp*. II. Ford, Maureen., *comp*.
174.4

www.mhhe.com

Preface

From the very beginning of critical thought, we find the distinction between topics susceptible of certain knowledge and topics about which uncertain opinions are available. The dawn of this distinction, explicitly entertained, is the dawn of modern mentality. It introduces criticism.

Alfred North Whitehead
Adventures of Ideas (1933)

This volume contains 42 selections, presented in a pro and con format, that debate a total of 21 different controversial issues in business ethics. In this book we ask you, the reader, to examine the accepted practices of business in the light of human needs, justice, rights, and dignity. We ask you to consider what moral imperatives and values should be at work in the conduct of business.

This method of presenting opposing views on an issue grows out of the ancient learning method of *dialogue*. Two assumptions lead us to seek the truth in a dialogue between opposed positions. The first assumption is that the truth is really out there and that it is important to find it. The second is that no one of us has all of it (the truth). The way to reach the truth is to form our initial opinions on a subject and give voice to them in public. Then we let others with differing opinions reply, and while they are doing so, we listen carefully. The truth that comes into being in the public space of the dialogue—literally, the space in between the two disputants—becomes part of our opinions on all related matters. We now have more informed opinions, and they are reliably based on the reasoning that emerged in the course of airing those views.

Each issue in this volume has an issue *introduction* that sets the stage for the debate as it is argued in the YES and NO selections. Each issue concludes with a *postscript* that makes some final observations and points the way to other questions related to the issue. The introductions and postscripts do not preempt what is the reader's own task: to achieve a critical and informed view of the issue at stake. In reading an issue and forming your own opinion, you should not feel confined to adopt one or the other of the positions presented. There are positions in between the given views, or totally outside them, and the *suggestions for further reading* that appear in each issue postscript should help you to continue your study of the subject. At the back of the book is a listing of all the *contributors to this volume,* for further information on the varied backgrounds of the writers represented in this book.

Changes to this edition   This edition represents a substantial revision. There are six completely new issues: Is It a Mistake to Urge Corporate Managers to Be Moral? (Issue 4); Is Privatizing Social Security Good Business? (Issue 5); Should the States Regulate Appropriate Business Behavior? (Issue 6); Is Employer

Monitoring of Employee E-Mail Justified? (Issue 10); Is Direct-to-Consumer Advertising of Pharmaceuticals Bad for Our Health? (Issue 14) and Should the World Continue to Rely on Oil as a Major Source of Energy? (Issue 21). Most of the rest have been updated. New selections accompany some of the issues, with an especially good new selection on the problems of CEO compensation and Wal-Mart's profits gained at the expense of its workers and the public.

A word to the instructor   An *Instructor's Resource Guide with Test Questions* (multiple choice and essay) is available through the publisher for the instructor using *Taking Sides* in the classroom. A general guidebook, *Using Taking Sides in the Classroom,* which discusses methods and techniques for integrating the pro-con approach into any classroom setting, is also available. An online version of *Using Taking Sides in the Classroom* and a correspondence service for *Taking Sides* adopters can be found at http://www.mhcls.com/usingts/.

   Taking Sides: Clashing Views on Controversial Issues in Business Ethics and Society is only one title in the *Taking Sides* series. If you are interested in seeing the table of contents for any of the other titles, please visit the *Taking Sides* website at http://www.mhcls.com/takingsides/.

Acknowledgements   Praise and thanks are due to God and our families, without whose patience and support this volume would never have been completed. Special thanks go to those who responded to the questionnaire with specific suggestions for the ninth edition.

Lisa H. Newton
Fairfield University

Maureen M. Ford
Fairfield University

Correlation Guide

The Taking Sides series presents current issues in a debate-style format designed to stimulate student interest and develop critical thinking skills. Each issue is thoughtfully framed with an issue summary, an issue introduction, and a postscript. The pro and con essays—selected for their liveliness and substance—represent the arguments of leading scholars and commentators in their fields.

Taking Sides: Clashing Views in Business Ethics and Society, 10/e is an easy-to-use reader that presents issues on important topics such as corporate social responsibility, CEO compensation, and environmental policy. For more information on Taking Sides and other McGraw-Hill Contemporary Learning Series titles, visit www.mhcls.com.

This convenient guide matches the units in Taking Sides: Business Ethics and Society, 10/e with the corresponding chapters in two of our best-selling McGraw-Hill Business Ethics textbooks by Hartman/DesJardins and Ghillyer.

Taking Sides: Business Ethics and Society, 10/e	Business Ethics: Decision-Making for Personal Integrity & Social Responsibility, 1/e by Hartman/DesJardins	Business Ethics, 1/e by Ghillyer
Issue 1. Can Capitalism Lead to Human Happiness?	Chapter 1. Ethics and Business Chapter 3: Philosophical Ethics and Business Chapter 5: Corporate Social Responsibility	Chapter 1: Understanding Ethics Chapter 2: Defining Business Ethics Chapter 4: Corporate Social Responsibility Chapter 10: Making it Stick: Doing What's Right
Issue 2. Can Restructuring a Corporation's Rules Make a Moral Difference?	Chapter 1: Ethics and Business Chapter 3: Philosophical Ethics and Business Chapter 4: The Corporate Culture Chapter 5: Corporate Social Responsibility	Chapter 2: Defining Business Ethics Chapter 3: Organizational Ethics Chapter 4: Corporate Social Responsibility Chapter 5: Corporate Governance Chapter 9: Ethics & Globalization Chapter 10: Making it Stick: Doing What's Right
Issue 3. Should Corporations Adopt Policies of Corporate Social Responsibility?	Chapter 1: Ethics and Business Chapter 5: Corporate Social Responsibility	Chapter 3: Organizational Ethics Chapter 4: Corporate Social Responsibility Chapter 9: Ethics & Globalization
Issue 4. Is It a Mistake to Urge Corporate Managers to Be Moral?	Chapter 1: Ethics and Business Chapter 2: Ethical Decision-Making: Personal and Professional Contexts Chapter 3: Philosophical Ethics and Business Chapter 4: The Corporate Culture	Chapter 3: Organizational Ethics Chapter 5: Corporate Governance Chapter 6: The Role of Government Chapter 7: Blowing the Whistle

Taking Sides: Business Ethics and Society, 10/e	Business Ethics: Decision-Making for Personal Integrity & Social Responsibility, 1/e by Hartman/DesJardins	Business Ethics, 1/e by Ghillyer
Issue 14. Is Direct-to-Consumer Advertising of Pharmaceuticals Bad for Our Health?	Chapter 5: Corporate Social Responsibility Chapter 8: Ethics and Marketing	Chapter 4: Corporate Social Responsibility Chapter 5: Corporate Governance Chapter 6: The Role of Government
Issue 15. Was Ford to Blame in the Pinto Case?	Chapter 2: Ethical Decision-Making: Personal and Professional Contexts Chapter 5: Corporate Social Responsibility Chapter 6: Ethical Decision-Making: Employer Responsibilities and Employee Rights Chapter 8: Ethics and Marketing	Chapter 4: Corporate Social Responsibility Chapter 5: Corporate Governance Chapter 6: The Role of Government Chapter 8: Ethics & Technology
Issue 16. Should We Require Labeling for Genetically Modified Food?	Chapter 3: Philosophical Ethics and Business Chapter 5: Corporate Social Responsibility	Chapter 3: Organizational Ethics Chapter 4: Corporate Social Responsibility Chapter 8: Ethics & Technology
Issue 17. Are Multinational Corporations Free from Moral Obligation?	Chapter 1: Ethics and Business Chapter 5: Corporate Social Responsibility Chapter 6: Ethical Decision-Making: Employer Responsibilities and Employee Rights	Chapter 2: Defining Business Ethics Chapter 3: Organizational Ethics Chapter 5: Corporate Governance Chapter 7: Blowing the Whistle Chapter 8: Ethics & Technology Chapter 9: Ethics & Globalization
Issue 18. Should Patenting Life Be Forbidden?	Chapter 1: Ethics and Business Chapter 3: Philosophical Ethics and Business	Chapter 1: Understanding Ethics Chapter 4: Corporate Social Responsibility Chapter 8: Ethics & Technology
Issue 19. Do Environmental Restrictions Violate Basic Economic Freedoms?	Chapter 5: Corporate Social Responsibility Chapter 9: Business, the Environment, and Sustainability	Chapter 4: Corporate Social Responsibility Chapter 5: Corporate Governance Chapter 9: Ethics & Globalization Chapter 10: Making it Stick: Doing What's Right
Issue 20. Is Bottling Water a Good Solution to Problems of Water Purity and Availability?	Chapter 9: Business, the Environment, and Sustainability	Chapter 8: Ethics & Technology Chapter 9: Ethics & Globalization Chapter 10: Making it Stick: Doing What's Right
Issue 21. Should the World Continue to Rely on Oil as a Major Source of Energy?	Chapter 9: Business, the Environment, and Sustainability	Chapter 5: Corporate Governance Chapter 6: The Role of Government Chapter 8: Ethics & Technology Chapter 9: Ethics & Globalization

Contents In Brief

Contents

Business leaders now recognize, Hay and Gray argue, that in the long run, business will only be successful if it is directed to the needs of the society—and if it chooses to ignore that advice, government regulation is likely to fill the gap between business operations and the welfare of the people the government is sworn to protect. Friedman argues that businesses have neither the right nor the ability to fool around with "social responsibility;" they serve employees and customers best when they do their work with maximum efficiency.

John Boatright, Baumhart Professor of Business Ethics at Loyola College, argues that corporate managers already have a moral duty—to carry out their role as steward of the resources of the corporation—and that if we want more ethical business practices, we should structure our markets to bring business incentives in line with ethics. Jack Guynn, President and CEO of the Federal Reserve Bank of Atlanta, insists that the moral foundation of the market system is not law and courts, but individual trustworthiness and willingness to act morally.

Altig and Gokhale are participants in the conservative Cato Project on Social Security Privatization, convinced that there is "growing support for privatizing the retirement program" as its "problems become more apparent." Thomas Bethell, on the contrary, finds nine alternatives which would avoid both punishing taxation and cuts in benefits, without giving the money to the private sector.

Eliot Spitzer, then Attorney General (now Governor) of New York State, points out that the business community has been consistent in its opposition to transparency, disclosure, and obligation to the public, and especially to all law, rule, or prosecution that aims to obtain those. Under the circumstances, enforced law is necessary to protect the public. Alan Yuspeh,

that attempting to stop unethical company activities exemplifies, not challenges, company loyalty.

DePree and Jude acknowledge the resentment of the monitored, but contend that corporations are liable for the communications of their employees and therefore have not only the right but the duty to monitor e-exchanges. The Reuters report calls attention to the fact that e-monitoring is not only unprecedented, but also unregulated and potentially unlimited, and without the worker's consent seems to be seriously wrong.

Richard Epstein defends the "at-will" contract as an appropriate expression of autonomy of contract on the part of both employee and employer, and as a means to the most efficient operations of the market. John McCall argues that the defense of the Employment-At-Will doctrine does not take account of its economic and social consequences, and is in derogation of the very moral principles that underlie private property and freedom of contract.

Ira Kay, a consultant on executive compensation for Watson Wyatt Worldwide, argues that in general the pay of the CEO tracks the company's performance, so in general CEOs are simply paid to do what they were hired to do–bring up the price of the stock to increase shareholder wealth. Edgar Woolard, a former CEO himself, holds that the methods by which CEO compensation is determined are fundamentally flawed, and suggests some significant changes.

in knowing the processes by which our foods arrived on the table, and the demand for a label for bioengineered foods is entirely legitimate. Addressing the U.S. Senate, Joseph Levitt points out that as far as the law is concerned, only the nutritional traits and characteristics of foods are subject to safety assessment.

Ethicist Manuel Velasquez argues that since any business that tried to conform to moral rules in the absence of enforcement would cease to be competitive, moral strictures cannot be binding on such companies. John E. Fleming asserts that multinational corporations tend to deal with long-term customers and suppliers in the goldfish bowl of international media and must therefore adhere to moral standards or lose business.

Jeremy Rifkin charges that if the trend to patenting life continues, all the genes in our bodies will belong no longer to us but to the global pharmaceutical firms that own the patents. William Domnarski finds Rifkin's attacks shrill, misdirected, and generally out of touch with the reality of genuine progress in the fields of genetic engineering.

John Shanahan, vice president of the Alexis de Tocqueville Institution in Arlington, Virginia, argues that many government environmental policies are unreasonable and infringe on basic economic freedoms. Environmental scientists Paul R. Ehrlich and Anne H. Ehrlich argue that many objections to environmental protections are self-serving and based in bad or misused science.

The commonly available information on bottled water certainly conveys the impression that it is purer and better than mere tap water; all the ads conjure up a vigorous and healthy outdoor lifestyle amid forests, lakes, and pure flowing springs. Brian Howard argues that bottling water is environmentally disastrous, because of the huge drains on scarce aquifers and the haphazard disposal of the plastic bottles, and that tap water is often superior to bottled in purity.

Red Cavaney, president and CEO of the American Petroleum Institute, argues that recent revolutionary advances in technology will yield sufficient quantities of available oil for the foreseeable future. James Howard Kunstler, author of *The Long Emergency/2005,* suggests that simply passing the all-time production peak of oil and heading toward its point of depletion will result in a global energy predicament that will seriously change our lives.

Introduction

An Essay on the Background of Business Ethics: Ethics, Economics, Law, and the Corporation

Philosophy is a conversation; philosophical ethics is a conversation about conduct, the doing of good and the avoiding of evil. Business ethics is a conversation about right and wrong conduct in the business world. This book is aimed at an audience of students who expect to pursue careers in business, who know that there are knotty ethical problems out there, and who want a chance to confront them ahead of time. The method of confronting them is an invitation to join in a debate, a contest of contrary facts and conflicting values in many of the major issues of the millennium. This introductory essay, in effect a short text on the major components of business theory, should make it easier to join in the argument. Managing ethical policy problems in a company takes a wide background—in ethics, economics, law, and the social sciences—that the book cannot hope to provide. But since some background assumptions in these fields are relevant to several of the problems we take on, we will sketch out very briefly the major understandings that control them. There is ultimately no substitute for thorough study of the rules of the game and years of experience and practice; but an overview of the playing field may at least make it easier for a novice to understand the object and limitations of the standard plays.

Business ethics was generally known as the world's most famous oxymoron (a term that contradicts itself into impossibility) until the last thirty years. Then came the alarming newspaper headlines. Foreign bribes, scandals on Wall Street, exploding cars, conflicts over whistleblowers and civil rights in the workplace suddenly came into the headlines and would not go away. Now we know that value questions are never absent from business decisions, and that moral responsibility is the first requirement of a manager in any business. Out of all this has emerged a general consensus that a thorough grounding in ethical reasoning is essential preparation for a career in business.

This book will not supply the substance of a course in ethics. For that you are directed to any of several excellent texts in business ethics (see the suggested readings at the end of this essay), or to any general text in ethics. *Taking Sides* teaches ethics from the issue upward, rather than from the principle downward. You will, however, come upon much of the terminology of ethical reasoning in the course of considering these cases. For your information, the terms and reasoning most commonly used in this book are found in the following chart:

Economics: the Capitalist Background

Capitalism as we know it is the product of the thought of Adam Smith (1723–1790), a Scottish philosopher and economist, and a small number of his European contemporaries. The fundamental "capitalist act" is the *voluntary exchange*: two adults, of sound mind and clear purposes, meet in the marketplace, to which each repairs in order to satisfy some felt need. They discover that each has that which will satisfy the other's need—the housewife needs flour, the miller needs cash—and they exchange, at a price such that the exchange furthers the interest of each. The *marginal utility* to the participant in the free market of the thing acquired must exceed that of the thing traded, or else why would he make the deal? So each party to the voluntary exchange walks away from it richer.

Adding to the value of the exchange is the *competition* of dealers and buyers; because there are many purveyors of each good, the customer is not forced to pay exorbitant prices for things needed (it is a sad fact of economics, that to the starving man, the marginal value of a loaf of bread is very large, and a single merchant could become unjustly rich). Conversely, competition among the customers (typified by an auction) makes sure that the available goods end in the hands of those to whom they are worth the most. So at the end of the market day, not only does everyone go home richer (in real terms) than when he came—the voluntariness of the exchange ensures that—but also, as rich as he could possibly be, since he had available all possible options of goods or services to buy and all possible purchasers of his goods or services for sale.

Sellers and buyers win the competition through *efficiency*, through producing the best quality goods at the lowest possible price, or through allotting their scarce resources toward the most valuable of the choices presented to them. It is to the advantage of all participants in the market, then, to strive for efficiency, that is, to keep the cost of goods for sale as low as possible while keeping the quality as high as possible. Adam Smith's most memorable accomplishment was to recognize that the general effect of all this self-interested scrambling would be to make the most possible goods of the best possible quality available at the lowest possible price. Meanwhile, sellers and buyers alike must keep an eye on the market as a whole, adjusting production and purchasing to take advantage of fluctuations in *supply and demand*. Short supply will make goods more valuable, raising the price, and that will bring more suppliers into the market, whose competition will lower the price, to just above the cost of manufacture for the most efficient producers. Increased demand for any reason will have the same effect. Should supply exceed demand, the price will fall to a point where the goods will be bought. Putting this all together, Smith realized that in a system of free enterprise, you have demonstrably the best possible chance of finding for sale what you want, in good quantity and quality, at a reasonable price. Forget benevolent monarchs ordering things for our good, he suggested; in this system we are led as by an *"invisible hand"* to serve the common good even as we think we are being most selfish.

Adam Smith's theory of economic enterprise and the "wealth of nations" emerged in the Natural Law tradition of the eighteenth century. As was the fashion for that period, Smith presented his conclusions as a series of iron laws: the Law of Supply and Demand, that links supply, demand, and price; the law that links efficiency with success; and ultimately, the laws that link the absolute freedom of the market with the absolute growth of the wealth of the free market country.

To these laws were added others, specifying the conditions under which business enterprise would be conducted in capitalist countries. The laws of *population* of Thomas Malthus (1766–1834) concluded that the supply of human beings would always reach the limits of its food supply, ensuring that the bulk of humanity would always live at the subsistence level. Since Smith had already proved that employers will purchase labor at the lowest possible price, it was a one-step derivation for David Ricardo (1772–1823) to conclude that workers' *wages* would never exceed the subsistence level, no matter how prosperous industrial enterprise should become. From these capitalist theorists alone proceeded the nineteenth-century assumption that society would inevitably divide into two classes, a tiny minority of fabulous wealth and a vast majority of subsistence-level workers.

These laws, like the laws of physics advanced at that time by Sir Isaac Newton (1642–1727), and laws of psychology and government advanced at that time by Dr. John Locke (1632–1704), were held to be immutable facts of nature, true forever and not subject to change. No concept of progress, or of historical fitness of system to society, was allowed to enter the Heavenly City of rigorously derived Natural Law.

The Marxian Critique

Only within the last century and a half have we learned to think historically. The notion of progress, the vision of a better future, and even the very idea that we might modify that future, in part by the discernment of historical trends, are unknown to the ancients and of no interest to the medieval chroniclers. For Western political philosophy, history emerged as a factor in our understanding only with the work of the nineteenth-century philosopher G. W. F. Hegel (1770–1831), who traced the history of the Western world as an ordered series of ideal forms, evolving one from another in logical sequence toward an ideal future. A young German student of Hegel's, Karl Marx (1818–1883), concluded from his study of economics that Hegel had to be wrong: the phases of history were ruled not by ideas, but by the *material conditions* of life, and their evolution one from another came about as the ruling class of each age generated its own revolutionary overthrow.

Marx's theory, especially as it applies to the evolution of capitalism, is enormously complex; for the purposes of this unit, it can be summarized simply. According to Marx, the *ruling class* in every age is the group that *owns the means of production* of the age's product. Through the seventeenth century, the product was almost exclusively agricultural, and the means of production was almost exclusively agricultural land: landowners were the aristocrats and rulers. With the coming of commerce and industry, the owners of the factories joined the ruling class and eventually dominated it. It was in the nature of such capital-intensive industry to concentrate within itself more capital: its greater efficiency would, as Adam Smith had proved, drive all smaller labor-intensive industry out of business, and its enormous income would be put to work as more capital, expanding the domain of the factory and the machine indefinitely (at the expense of the cottage and the human being). Thus would the wealth of society concentrate in fewer and fewer hands, as the owners of the factories expanded their enterprises without limit into mighty industrial empires, dominated by machines and by the greed of their owners.

Meanwhile, all this wealth was being produced by a new class of workers, the unskilled factory workers. Taken from the ranks of the obsolete peasantry, artisans and craftsmen, this new working class, the "proletariat," expanded in numbers with the gigantic mills, whose "hands" they were. Work on the assembly line demanded no education or skills, so the workers could never make themselves valuable enough to command a living wage on the open market. They survived as a vast underclass, interchangeable with the unemployed workers (recently displaced by more machines) who gathered around the factory gates looking for jobs, *their* jobs. As Ricardo had demonstrated, they could never bargain for any wage above the subsistence level—just enough to keep them alive. As capitalism and its factories expanded, the entire population, excepting only the wealthy capitalist families, sank into this hopeless pauperized class.

So Marx took from Ricardo the vision of ultimate division of Western society under capitalism: into a tiny group of fabulously wealthy capitalists and a huge mass of paupers, mostly factory workers. The minority would keep the majority in strict control by its hired thugs (the state: the army and the police), control rendered easier by thought control (the schools and the churches). The purpose of the "ideology" taught by the schools and the churches—the value structure of capitalism—was to show both classes that the capitalists had a right to their wealth (through the sham of liberty, free enterprise, and the utilitarian benefits of the free market) and a perfect right to govern everyone else (through the sham of democracy and equal justice). Thus the capitalists could enjoy their wealth in good conscience and the poor would understand their moral obligation to accept the oppression of the ruling class with good cheer.

Marx foresaw, and in his writings attempted to help bring about, the disillusionment of the workers: there will come a point when they will suddenly ask, *why* should we accept oppression all our lives? and the search for answers to this question will show them the history of their situation, expose the falsehood of the ideology and the false consciousness of those who believe it, show them their own strength, and lead them directly to the solution that will usher in the new age of socialism—the revolutionary overthrow of the capitalist regime. Why, after all, should they not undertake such a revolution? People are restrained from violence against oppression only by the prospect of losing something valuable, and the industrialized workers of the world had nothing to lose but their chains.

As feudalism had been swept away, then, by the "iron broom" of the French Revolution, so capitalism would be swept away by the revolt of the masses, the irresistible uprising of the vast majority of the people against the tiny minority of industrial overlords and their terrified minions—the armed forces, the state, and the church. After the first rebellions, Marx foresaw no lengthy problem of divided loyalties in the industrialized countries of the world. Once the scales had fallen from their eyes, the working-class hirelings of army and police would quickly turn their guns on their masters, and join their natural allies in the proletariat in the task of creating the new world.

After the revolution, Marx predicted, there would be a temporary "dictatorship of the proletariat," during which the last vestiges of capitalism would be eradicated and the authority to run the industrial establishment returned to the workers of each industry. Once the economy had been decentralized, to turn each factory into an industrial commune run by its own workers and each landed estate into an agricultural commune run by its farmers, the state as such would simply wither away. Some central authority would certainly continue to exist, to coordinate and facilitate the exchange of goods within the country (one imagines a giant computer, taking note of where goods are demanded, where goods are available, and where the railroad cars are, to take the goods from one place to the other). But with no ruling class to serve, no oppression to carry out, there will be no need of state to rule *people*; what is left will be confined to the administration of *things*.

Even as he wrote, just in time for the Revolution of 1848, Marx expected the end of capitalism as a system. Not that capitalism was evil in itself; Marx did not presume to make moral judgments on history. Indeed, capitalism was necessary as an economic system, to concentrate the wealth of the country into the industries of the modern age. So capitalism had a respectable past, and would still be necessary, for a while, in the developing countries, to launch their industries. But that task completed, it had no further role in history, and the longer it stayed around, the more the workers would suffer and the more violent the revolution would be when it came. The sooner the revolution, the better; the future belonged to communism.

As the collapse of the Communist governments in Eastern Europe demonstrates, if demonstration were needed, the course of history has not proceeded quite as Marx predicted in 1848. In fairness, it might be pointed out that no other prophets of the time had any more luck with prognostication; the twentieth century took all of us by surprise. But there is much in Marx's analysis which is rock solid, possibly for reasons, especially ethical reasons, that he himself would have rejected. In any case, since Marx wrote, all participants in the debate on the nature and future of capitalism have had to respond to his judgments and predictions.

Law: Recovering for Damages Sustained

Life is full of misfortune. Ordinarily, if you suffer misfortune, you must put up with it, and find the resources to deal with it. If your misfortune is my fault, however, the law may step in and make me pay for those damages, one way or another. Through the *criminal law*, the public steps in and demands punishment for an offense that is serious enough to outrage public feeling and endanger public welfare. If I knock you on the head and take your wallet, the police will find me, restore your wallet to you, and imprison or otherwise punish me for the crime. Strictly speaking, you should recover from me not only your wallet, but the money to sew up your head and damages for the fright and insult. But the average street criminal does not have the money to make full restitution to his victims; in fact, you'll be lucky to get your wallet back.

Through the *civil law*, if I do you damage through some action of mine, you may take me to civil court and ask a judge (and jury) to determine whether I have damaged you, if so by how much, and how I should pay you back for that damage. There are a number of forms of action under which you may make your claim; the most common for business purposes are *contract* and *torts*. If you and I agree to (or "contract for") some undertaking, and I back out on it, after you have relied on our agreement to commit your resources to the undertaking, you have a right to recover what you have lost. In torts, if I simply injure you in some way, hurting you in health, life or limb, or destroying your property, I have done you a wrong ("tort," in French), and I must pay for the damage I have done. How much I will have to pay will depend (as the jury will determine), on (1) the amount of the damage that has been caused, (2) the extent to which I knew or should have known that my action or neglect to act would cause damage (my *culpability*), and (3) the extent to which *you* contributed to the damage, beyond whatever I did (*contributory negligence*).

In the debates that follow, one (on the Pinto automobile) has to do with suits at law alleging *negligence*, a tort, on the part of a company, in that it made and put up for sale a product known to be defective, and that the defect injured its users. To establish negligence, civil or criminal, four elements must be demonstrated: First, there must have been a *duty*: the party accused of negligence must have had a preexisting duty to the plaintiff. Second, there must have been a *breach*, or failure to fulfill, that duty. Third, the plaintiff must have suffered an *injury*. And fourth, the breach of the duty must have been the *proximate cause* of the injury, the thing that actually brought it about. Where negligence is alleged in a product liability case, it must be established that the manufacturer had a duty to make a product that could not do certain sorts of harm; that the duty was breached, the harm caused, that nothing else was to blame, and that the manufacturer therefore must compensate the victim for the damage done.

There are very similar allegations in other cases here, even when no lawsuit is at issue. In all of these cases one set of claims amounts to an accusation of deliberately damaging innocent consumers, placing them in harm's way for the sake of profit; the other set counters that the company did not know and could not have known that the product was dangerous, and/or that the freely chosen behavior of the consumers contributed in some way to the damage that was done, so the company cannot be held totally responsible. In all cases, *risk* and *responsibility* are the central issues: when a small car explodes and burns when hit by a much larger van, to what extent is the company responsible for the flimsiness of the car and to what extent did the consumer assume the risk of that happening when she bought a small, economical car? (And whatever happened to the responsibility of the driver of the van?) Should companies be ultimately responsible for any harm that comes from the use of the products they so profitably marketed and sold? Or should consumers be content to bear the responsibility for risks they have freely accepted? Our ambivalence on this question as a society mirrors, and proceeds from, the ambivalence of the individual at the two poles of material-ization of risk: when we are in a hurry, short of cash, or in need of a cigarette, then risky behavior looks to us to be our right, and we are resentful of the busybodies who would always be having us play it safe and wear our rubbers when it rains. But when the risk materializes—when the accident or the disease happens—the perception of that risk (and the direction of that resentment) change drastically. From the perspective of the hospital bed, it is crystal clear that the behavior was not worth the risk, that we never realized the behavior was risky, that we would never have engaged in the behavior if we had known how risky it was, that we should have been warned about the risks, and that it was someone's duty to warn us. In that instantaneous change of perspec-tive, three elements of negligence come into view: duty, breach, and injury. No wonder product liability suits are so common.

Yet the suit is a relatively recent phenomenon, because of a peculiarity in the law. Until the twentieth century, a judge faced with a consumer who had been injured by a product (physically or financially) had to apply the principle of *caveat emptor*—Let the Buyer Beware—and could ask the seller to pay damages only to the original buyer, and only if the exact defect in the product could be proven. For example, a defective kerosene lamp might explode and burn five people, but the exact defect (broken seam or shoddy wick) had to be brought into court or the case would be thrown out. In addi-tion, the buyer could sue only the seller, not the manufacturer or designer, for the right to collect damages rested on the law of *contract*, not torts, and upon the warrant of merchantability implied in the contractual relationship between buyer and seller. The cause of the action was understood to be a breach in that contract.

There matters stood until 1916, when an American judge allowed a buyer to sue the manufacturer of a product. A Mr. MacPherson had been injured when his car collapsed under him due to a defect in the wood used to build one of the wheels, and MacPherson went to court against the Buick Motor Company. The judge reasoned that the action was in torts, specifi-cally negligence, and not in contract, for a manufacturer is under a duty to make carefully any product that could be expected to endanger life, and this duty existed irrespective of any contract. So if MacPherson, or any future user of the product, was injured because the product was badly made, he could collect damages even if he had never dealt with the manu-facturer in any way.

In the 1960s the automobile was still center stage in the arguments over the duties of manufacturers. Ralph Nader's book *Unsafe at Any Speed* (1966) spearheaded the consumer rights movement with its scathing attack on General Motors and its exposé of the dangerous design of the Corvair. In response to the consumer activism resulting from that movement, Congress passed the Consumer Product Safety Act in 1972 and empowered the Consumer Product Safety Commission, an independent federal agency, to set safety standards, require warning labels, and order recalls of hazardous products. When three girls died in a Ford Pinto in 1978, the foundations of consumer rights against careless manufacturers were well established. What is new in the Ford Motor Company case is the allegation of *criminal* negligence—in effect, criminal homicide.

At present, product liability suits are major uncharted reefs in the navigational plans of American business. If a number of people die in a fire in a hotel, for instance, their families will often sue not only the hotel, for culpable negligence, but the manufacturers of the furniture that burned, alleging that it should have been fire-retardant; the manufacturers of the cushions on the furniture, alleging that they gave off toxic fumes in the fire; and the manufacturers of the chemicals that went into those cushions, alleging that there was no warning to the consumers on the toxicity of those chemicals in fire conditions. The settlements that can be obtained are used to finance the suit, and the law firm that is managing it, for the years that it will take to exhaust all the appeals. This phenomenon of unlimited litigation is relatively new on the American scene, and we are not quite sure how to respond to it.

The Corporation

The human being is a social animal. We exist in the herd, and depend for our lives on the cooperation of those around us. Who are they? Our anthropologists tell us that originally we traveled in extended families, then settled down into villages of intensely interlocked groups of families. With the advent of the modern era, we have found our identities in family, village, church, and nation. Yet in the great transformation of the obligations of the Western world (see Henry Maine [1822–1888] *From Status to Contract*), we have abandoned the old family-oriented care systems and thrown ourselves upon the mercy of secondary organizations: club, corporation, and State. The French sociologist Emil Durkheim (1858–1917) suggested (in his classic work, *Suicide*) that following the collapse of the family and the church, the corporation would be the association, in the future, that would supply the social support that every individual needs to maintain the moral life.

Can the corporation do that? Or is the corporation merely the organization that implements Adam Smith's self-interested pursuit of the dollar, with no purpose but to maximize return on investment to the investors while protecting them from unlimited liability? The issue of "meaningful work" raises this question in particularly direct form. On the other hand, once formed, and having become a major community figure and employer, does the corporation have a right to exist that transcends at least the immediate pursuit of money? The issue of "hostile takeovers" sends us back to the purpose and foundation of business enterprise in America. Let us review: When an entrepreneur gets a bright idea for how to make money, he secures the capital he will need to run the business from investors (venture capitalists), uses that capital to buy the land, buildings, and machinery he will need to see it through, hires the labor needed to do the work, and goes into production. As the income from the enterprise comes in, he pays the suppliers of raw materials, pays the workers, pays the taxes, rent, mortgages, and utility bills, keeps some for himself (salary), and then divides up the rest of the income ("profit") among the investors (probably including himself) in proportion to the capital they invested. Motives of all parties are presupposed: the entrepreneur wants money, the laborers want money, so do the landlords, and so, of course, do the investors, who are the shareholders in the company. The investors thought that this enterprise would yield them a higher return on their capital than any other investment available to them at the time; that's why they invested. Meanwhile, this is a free country, and people can move around. If the worker sees a better job, he'll take it; if the landlord can rent for more, he'll terminate the lease; and if the investors see a better place to put their capital, they'll move it. The determiner of the flow of capital is the rate of return, no more and no less. "Loyalty to the company," faithfulness to the corporation for the sake of the association itself, is not on anyone's agenda—not on the worker's, certainly not on the landlord's, and *most* certainly not on the shareholder's.

The shareholders are represented by a board of directors elected by them to see that the company is run efficiently—that is, that costs are kept down and income up, to yield the highest possible return. The board of directors hires management—the cadre of corporate officers headed by the president/chief executive officer to do the actual running of the company. The corporate officers thus stand in a *quasi-fiduciary* relationship to the shareholders: that is, they are forbidden by the understandings on which the corporation is founded to do anything at all except that which will protect and enhance the interests of the shareholders. That goes for all the normal business decisions made by the management; even the decision not to break the law can be seen as a prudent estimate of the financial costs of lawbreaking.

Yet our dealings with the business world, as citizens and as consumers, have always turned on recognition and support of the huge, reliable corporations in established industries: not just coal and steel, which had certain natural limitations built into their consumption of natural resources, but the automobile companies, the airlines, the consumer products companies, even the banks. Companies had "reputations," "integrity," cultivated (and bought and sold) "good will," consumers cooperated with the companies that catered to them in developing "brand loyalty." And, most importantly, those working in business cooperated with their employers in developing "company loyalty," which became a part of their lives as loyalty to one's tribe or nation was part of the lives of their ancestors. Is the company that sought our loyalty—and got it—just a scrap of paper, to disappear as soon as return on investment falls below the nearest competition? What part do we want our corporations to play in our associative life? If we want them to be any more than profit maximizers for the investors, what sorts of protections would we have to offer them, and what sorts of limitations should we put on their not-for-profit activities?

Current Issues

Business ethics ultimately rests on a base of political philosophy, economics, and philosophical ethics. As these underlying fields change, new topics and approaches will surface in business ethics. For example, "hostile takeovers" did not take place very often in the regulatory climate that obtained prior to the Reagan administration. The change in political philosophy introduced by his administration resulted in new business practices, which resulted in new ethical problems. Also the work of John Rawls, a professor of philosophy at Harvard, profoundly influenced our understandings of distributive justice, and therefore our understanding of acceptable economic distribution in the society. The work currently being done in "postmodern" philosophy will change the way we see human beings generally, and hence the activity of business.

No single work can cover all the issues of ethical practice in business in all their range and particularity, especially since, as above, we are dealing with a moving target. Our task here is much more limited. The purpose of this book is just to allow you to grapple with some of the ethical issues of current business practice in the safety of the classroom, before they come up on the job where human rights and careers are at stake and legal action looms outside the boardroom, or factory, door. We think that rational consideration of these issues now will help you prepare for a lifetime of the types of problems that naturally arise in a complex and pluralistic society. You will find here no dogmas, no settled solutions to memorize. These problems do not have preset answers, but require, as Whitehead insisted, that you use your mind, to balance the values in conflict and to work out acceptable policies in each issue. To do business ethics, you must learn to think critically, to look beyond short-term advantage and traditional ways of doing things, to become an innovator. The exercise provided by these debates should help you in this learning.

There is no doubt that businesspersons think that ethics is important. Sometimes the reasons why they think ethics is important have to do only with the long-run profitability of business enterprise. Greater employee honesty and diligence will improve the bottom line, strict attention to environmental and employee health laws is necessary to preserve the company from expensive lawsuits and fines. But ethics goes well beyond profitability, to the lives that we live and the persons we want to be. What the bottom line has taught us is that the working day is not apart from life. We must bring the same integrity and care to the contexts of factory and office that we are used to showing at home and among our friends. The third imperative of business ethics is to make of your business life an opportunity to become, and remain, the person that you know you ought to be—and as far you can, to extend that opportunity to others.

We attempt, in this book, to present in good, debatable form some of the issues that raise the big questions—of justice, of rights, of the common good—in order to build bridges between the workaday world of employment and the ageless world of morality. If you will enter into these dialogues with an open mind, a willingness to have it changed, and a determination to master the skills of critical thinking that will enable you to make responsible decisions in difficult situations, you may be able to help build the bridges for the new ethical issues that will emerge in the century to come. At the least, that is our hope.

Suggested readings for the ethics background for business ethics:

DeGeorge, Richard T. *Business Ethics*, Third Edition. New York: Macmillan, 1990.

Hoffman, W. Michael, and Jennifer Mills Moore. *Business Ethics: Readings and Cases in Corporate Morality*, Fourth Edition. New York: McGraw Hill, 2001.

Donaldson, Thomas, and Patricia H. Werhane. *Ethical Issues in Business: A Philosophical Approach*, Third Edition. Englewood Cliffs, NJ: Prentice Hall, 1988.

Beauchamp, Tom L., and Norman E. Bowie. *Ethical Theory and Business*, Third Edition. Englewood Cliffs, NJ: Prentice Hall, 1988.

Shaw, William, and Vincent Barry, *Moral Issues in Business*, Fourth Edition. Belmont, CA: Wadsworth Pub. Co., 1989.

Velasquez, Manuel. *Business Ethics: Concepts and Cases*, Second Edition. Englewood Cliffs, NJ: Prentice Hall,

Matthews, John, Kenneth Goodpaster, and Laura Nash, *Policies and Persons: A Casebook in Business Ethics*, Sixth Edition. New York: McGraw Hill, 2006.

Internet References . . .

Business Ethics Resources on WWW

Sponsored by the Centre for Applied Ethics, site of business ethics resources links to corporate codes of ethics, business ethics institutions and organizations, and online papers and publications, as well as other elements.

http://www.ethics.ubc.ca/

International Business Ethics Institute

The International Business Ethics Institute offers professional services to organizations interested in implementing, expanding, or modifying business ethics and corporate responsibility programs. Its mission is to foster global business practices that promote equitable economic development, resource sustainability, and democratic forms of government.

http://www.business-ethics.org/

Capitalism and the Corporation

*G*iven *the behavior of the highest officials of the most profitable enterprises in the country in recent years, we might wonder if there is such a thing as ethical business! Where are moral standards to be found in the business enterprise—in the actions of the managers? In the policies, internal and external, of the corporation? Or in the capitalist system itself? How can business itself be encouraged to adopt higher ethical standards than we have seen in operation recently?*

- Can Capitalism Lead to Human Happiness?
- Can Restructuring a Corporation's Rules Make a Moral Difference?
- Should Corporations Adopt Policies of Corporate Social Responsibility?
- Is It a Mistake to Urge Corporate Managers to Be Moral?

ISSUE 1

Can Capitalism Lead to Human Happiness?

YES: Adam Smith, from *An Inquiry Into the Nature and Causes of the Wealth of Nations*, vols. 1 and 2 (1869)

NO: Karl Marx and Friedrich Engels, from *The Communist Manifesto* (1848)

ISSUE SUMMARY

YES: If we will but leave self-interested people to seek their own advantage, Adam Smith (1723–1790) argues, the result, unintended by any one of them, will be the greater advantage of all. No government interference is necessary to protect the general welfare.

NO: Leave people to their own self-interested devices, Karl Marx (1818–1883) and Friedrich Engels (1820–1895) reply, and those who by luck and inheritance own the means of production will rapidly reduce everyone else to virtual slavery. The few may be fabulously happy, but all others will live in misery.

T he confrontation of capitalism and communism dominated the twentieth century. In these selections we have the classic defense of the free market and its most powerful opposition. The rationale of capitalism portrays it as an unintended coordination of self-interested actions into the production of the greatest welfare of the whole. The argument is elegant and powerful: As a natural result of free competition in a free market, quality will improve and prices will decline without limit, thereby raising the real standard of living of every buyer. To protect themselves in competition, sellers will be forced to innovate, discover new products and new markets, thereby raising the real wealth of the society as a whole. Products improve without limit, wealth increases without limit, and society prospers.

But how fares the Common Man—the "least advantaged" members of society, as John Rawls would characterize them? Not very well. Only when free competition *fails,* because the economy is expanding so rapidly that it runs out of labor, can the working man's wages rise in a free market. For the most efficient factory will be the one that hires its workers at lowest cost, and if all industry is accomplished by essentially unskilled labor, and every worker can therefore be replaced by any other, there is no reason to pay any worker beyond the subsistence wage. Fortunately for the capitalist, according to the theory, such a market imbalance—too few workers and therefore "artificially" high wages—will rapidly disappear, as greater prosperity causes more of the working-class babies to survive to adulthood and entry into the workforce. Smith and eighteenth-century economists Thomas Malthus and David Ricardo were in agreement: As the society as a whole approaches maximum efficiency, all except the capitalists, the owners, approach the subsistence level of survival. So all the accumulated "wealth" of the nation actually ends up in the hands only of the employers, the factory owners, who enjoy the low prices of bread themselves, and save the money they would have to spend to keep their workers alive if the bread were more expensive. Another way of putting that point: Adam Smith was absolutely correct if he is taken to be describing capital *formation*; but when it comes to the *distribution* of the wealth the free market has created, his mechanisms have no way of ensuring justice.

This is where Karl Marx comes in. He focuses not on the making of the wealth—Adam Smith is quite correct on how wealth is created and accumulated. Instead he asks how the wealth is distributed—who gets it, and gets to enjoy it, when it has been generated by the capitalist process. There is no reason under Heaven that all that money has to languish in the bank accounts of the super-rich, or decorate their houses and their poodles. The welfare of the nation as a whole would be vastly increased if it could be shared systematically with the workers, to allow them to join their employers as consumers of the manufactured goods of the society. Lord John Maynard Keynes would later point out that such distribution would be an enormous spur to the economy; Marx was more concerned that it would be a great gain in justice.

Yes, but if the controllers of the wealth, the capitalists, are required to share it with the workers who produced it, will they not lose motivation to put that money at risk in such productive enterprises? This is one of the empirical questions that surround the issue of social justice in a free market society, often arising when CEO salaries are under discussion. It may seem counterintuitive that CEOs whose salary is reduced from $46.2 million per annum to $24.3 million per annum would suffer a serious loss of incentive to keep working, but that has been argued. Other questions concern entitlement—are not those who control the capital entitled to the entire return on it?—the justice of combination (Adam Smith also had to deal with unions), and the relative importance of liberty and equality as political values. Other questions concern the possibility of "pure" capitalist endeavors. Adam Smith's arguments surely work for small factories and farms, where no producer is big enough to influence the market. These were the only business enterprises he knew. But does it apply to technology-created monopolies and oligopolies? And does it contemplate speculating millions of dollars in foreign currency? Keep in mind, as you read these selections, that the controversy is not bounded by the historical understandings of Marx and his opponents, but goes to the core of our notions of entitlement, social welfare, and justice.

3

YES

Adam Smith

An Inquiry Into the Nature and Causes of the Wealth of Nations

Of the Division of Labour

The greatest improvement in the productive powers of labour, and the greater part of the skill, dexterity, and judgment with which it is anywhere directed or applied, seem to have been the effect of the division of labour.

The effects of the division of labour, in the general business of society, will be more easily understood by considering in what manner it operates in some particular manufactures. It is commonly supposed to be carried furthest in some very trifling ones; not perhaps that it really is carried further in them than in others of more importance: but in those trifling manufactures which are destined to supply the small wants of but a small number of people, the whole number of workmen must necessarily be small; and those employed in every different branch of the work can often be collected into the same work-house, and placed at once under the view of the spectator. In those great manufactures, on the contrary, which are destined to supply the great wants of the great body of the people, every different branch of the work employs so great a number of workmen, that it is impossible to collect them all into the same workhouse. We can seldom see more, at one time, than those employed in one single branch. Though in such manufactures, therefore, the work may really be divided into a much greater number of parts than in those of a more trifling nature, the division is not near so obvious, and has accordingly been much less observed.

To take an example, therefore, from a very trifling manufacture, but one in which the division of labour has been very often taken notice of, the trade of the pin-maker; a workman not educated to this business (which the division of labour has rendered a distinct trade), nor acquainted with the use of the machinery employed in it (to the invention of which the same division of labour has probably given occasion), could scarce, perhaps, with his utmost industry, make one pin in a day, and certainly could not make twenty. But in the way in which this business is now carried on, not only the whole work is a peculiar trade, but it is divided into a number of branches, of which the greater part are likewise peculiar trades. One man draws out the wire, another straights it, a third cuts it, a fourth points it, a fifth grinds it at the top for receiving the head; to make the head requires two or three distinct operations;

From Adam Smith, *An Inquiry Into the Nature and Causes of the Wealth of Nations*, vols. 1 and 2b (1869). Notes omitted.

to put it on is a peculiar business, to whiten the pins is another; it is even a trade by itself to put them into the paper; and the important business of making a pin is, in this manner, divided into about eighteen distinct operations, which in some manufactories are all performed by distinct hands, though in others the same man will sometimes perform two or three of them. I have seen a small manufactory of this kind where ten men only were employed, and where some of them consequently performed two or three distinct operations. But though they were very poor, and therefore but indifferently accommodated with the necessary machinery, they could, when they exerted themselves, make among them about twelve pounds of pins in a day. There are in a pound upwards of four thousand pins of a middling size. Those ten persons, therefore, could make among them upwards of forty-eight thousand pins in a day. Each person, therefore, making a tenth part of forty-eight thousand pins, might be considered as making four thousand eight hundred pins in a day. But if they had all wrought separately and independently, and without any of them having been educated to this peculiar business, they certainly could not each of them have made twenty, perhaps not one pin in a day; that is, certainly, not the two hundred and fortieth, perhaps not the four thousand eight hundredth part of what they are at present capable of performing, in consequence of a proper division and combination of their different operations. . . .

This great increase of the quantity of work, which, in consequence of the division of labour, the same number of people are capable of performing, is owning to three different circumstances: first, to the increase of dexterity in every particular workman; secondly, to the saving of the time which is commonly lost in passing from one species of work to another; and lastly, to the invention of a great number of machines which facilitate and abridge labour, and enable one man to do the work of many. . . .

It is the great multiplication of the productions of all the different arts, in consequence of the division of labour, which occasions, in a well-governed society, that universal opulence which extends itself to the lowest ranks of the people. Every workman has a great quantity of his own work to dispose of beyond what he himself has occasion for: and every other workman being exactly in the same situation, he is enabled to exchange a great quantity of his own goods for a great quantity, or, what comes to the same thing, for the price of a great quantity of theirs. He supplies them abundantly with what they have occasion for, and they accommodate him as amply with what he has occasion for, and a general plenty diffuses itself through all the different ranks of the society.

Observe the accommodation of the most common artificer or day-labourer in a civilised and thriving country, and you will perceive that the number of people of whose industry a part, though but a small part, has been employed in procuring him this accommodation exceeds all computation. The woollen coat, for example, which covers the day-labourer, as coarse and rough as it may appear, is the produce of the joint labour of a great multitude of workmen. The shepherd, the sorter of the wool, the wool-comber or carder, the dyer, the scribbler, the spinner, the weaver, the fuller, the dresser, with many others, must all join their different arts in order to complete even this homely production. How many merchants and carriers, besides, must have been employed in transporting the materials from some of those workmen to others who often live in a very distant part of the country! How much commerce and navigation in particular, how many ship-builders, sailors, sail-makers, rope-makers, must have been employed in order to bring together the different drugs made use of by the dyer, which often come from the remotest corners of the world! What a variety of labour too is necessary in order to produce the tools of the meanest of those workmen! To say nothing of such complicated machines as the ship of the sailor, the mill of the fuller, or even the loom of the weaver, let us consider only what a variety of labour is requisite in order to form that very simple machine, the shears with which the shepherd clips the wool. The miner, the builder of the furnace for smelting the ore, the feller of the timber, the burner of the charcoal to be made use of in the smelting-house, the brickmaker, the bricklayer, the workmen who attend the furnace, the mill-wright, the forger, the smith, must all of them join their different arts in order to produce them. Were we to examine, in the same manner, all the different parts of his dress and household furniture, the coarse linen shirt which he wears next his skin, the shoes which cover his feet, the bed which he lies on, and all the different parts which compose it, the kitchen-grate at which he pre-pares his victuals, the coals which he makes use of for that purpose, dug from the bowels of the earth, and brought to him perhaps by a long sea and a long land carriage, all the other utensils of his kitchen, all the furniture of his table, the knives and forks, the earthen or pewter plates upon which he serves up and divides his victuals, the different hands employed in preparing his bread and his beer, the glass window which lets in the heat and the light and keeps out the wind and the rain, with all the knowledge and art requisite for preparing that beautiful and happy invention, without which these northern parts of the world could scarce have afforded a very comfortable habitation, together with the tools of all the different workmen employed in producing those different conveniences; if we examine, I say, all these things, and consider what a variety of labour is employed about each of them, we shall be sensible that without the assistance and co-operation of many thousands, the very meanest person in a civilised country could not be provided, even according to, what we very falsely imagine, the easy and simple manner in which he is commonly accom-modated. Compared, indeed, with the more extravagant luxury of the great, his accommodation must no doubt appear extremely simple and easy; and yet it may be true, perhaps, that the accommodation of an European prince does not always so much exceed that of an industrious and frugal peasant, as the accommodation of the latter exceeds that of many an African king, the abso-lute master of the lives and liberties of ten thousand naked savages.

Of the Principle Which Gives Occasion to the Division of Labour

This division of labour, from which so many advantages are derived, is not originally the effect of any human wisdom, which foresees and intends that general opulence to which it gives occasion. It is the necessary, though very slow and gradual consequence of a certain propensity in human nature which has in view no such extensive utility; the propensity to truck, barter, and exchange one thing for another.

Whether this propensity be one of those original principles in human nature, of which no further account can be given; or whether, as seems more probable, it be the necessary consequence of the faculties of reason and speech, it belongs not to our present subject to inquire. It is common to all men, and to be found in no other race of animals, which seem to know neither this nor any other species of contracts. . . . But man has almost constant occasion for the help of his brethren, and it is in vain for him to expect it from their benevolence only. He will be more likely to prevail if he can interest their self-love in his favour, and show them that it is for their own advantage to do for him what he requires of them. Whoever offers to another a bargain of any kind, proposes to do this. Give me that which I want, and you shall have this which you want, is the meaning of every such offer; and it is in this manner that we obtain from one another the far greater part of those good offices which we stand in need of. It is not from the benevolence of the butcher, the brewer, or the baker, that we expect our dinner, but from their regard to their own interest. We address ourselves, not to their humanity but to their self-love, and never talk to them of our own necessities but of their advantages. Nobody but a beggar chooses to depend chiefly upon the benevolence of his fellow-citizens. Even a beggar does not depend upon it entirely. The charity of well-disposed people, indeed, supplies him with the whole fund of his subsistence. But though this principle ultimately provides him with all the necessaries of life which he has occasion for, it neither does nor can provide him with them as he has occasion for them. The greater part of his occasional wants are supplied in the same manner as those of other people, by treaty, by barter, and by purchase. With the money which one man gives him he purchases food. The old clothes which another bestows upon him he exchanges for other old clothes which suit him better, or for lodging, or for food, or for money, with which he can buy either food, clothes, or lodging, as he has occasion.

. . . Each animal is still obliged to support and defend itself, separately and independently, and derives no sort of advantage from that variety of talents with which nature has distinguished its fellows. Among men, on the contrary, the most dissimilar geniuses are of use to one another; the different produces of their respective talents, by the general disposition to truck, barter, and exchange, being brought, as it were, into a common stock, where every man may purchase whatever part of the produce of other men's talents he has occasion for. . . .

Of Restraints Upon the Importation From Foreign Countries of Such Goods as Can Be Produced at Home

. . . The general industry of the society never can exceed what the capital of the society can employ. As the number of workmen that can be kept in employment by any particular person must bear a certain proportion to his capital, so the number of those that can be continually employed by all the members of a great society, must bear a certain proportion to the whole capital of that society, and never can exceed that proportion. No regulation of commerce can increase the quantity of industry in any society beyond what its capital can maintain. It can only divert a part of it into a direction into which it might not otherwise have gone; and it is by no means certain that this artificial direction is likely to be more advantageous to the society than that into which it would have gone of its own accord.

Every individual is continually exerting himself to find out the most advantageous employment for whatever capital he can demand. It is his own advantage, indeed, and not that of the society, which he has in view. But the study of his own advantage naturally, or rather necessarily, leads him to prefer that employment which is most advantageous to the society.

First, every individual endeavours to employ his capital as near home as he can, and consequently as much as he can in the support of domestic industry; provided always that he can thereby obtain the ordinary, or not a great deal less than the ordinary, profits of stock.

Thus, upon equal or nearly equal profits, every wholesale merchant naturally prefers the home trade to the foreign trade of consumption, and the foreign trade of consumption to the carrying trade. In the home trade his capital is never so long out of his sight as it frequently is in the foreign trade of consumption. He can know better the character and situation of the persons whom he trusts, and, if he should happen to be deceived, he knows better the laws of the country from which he must seek redress. In the carrying trade, the capital of the merchant is, as it were, divided between two foreign countries, and no part of it is ever necessarily brought home, or placed under his own immediate view and command. The capital which an Amsterdam merchant employs in carrying corn from Konigsberg to Lisbon, and fruit and wine from Lisbon to Konigsberg, must generally be the one half of it at Konigsberg and the other half at Lisbon. No part of it need ever come to Amsterdam. The natural residence of such a merchant should either be at Konigsberg or Lisbon, and it can only be some very particular circumstance which can make him prefer the residence of Amsterdam. The uneasiness, however, which he feels at being separated so far from his capital, generally determines him to bring part both of the Konigsberg goods which he destines for the market of Lisbon, and of the Lisbon goods which he destines for that of Konigsberg, to Amsterdam; and though this necessarily subjects him to a double charge of loading and unloading, as well as to the payment of some duties and customs, yet for the sake of having some part of his capital always under his own view and command, he willingly submits to this extraordinary charge; and it is in this manner that every country which has any considerable share of the carrying trade, becomes always the emporium, or general market, for the goods of all the different countries whose trade it carries on. The merchant, in order to save a second loading and unloading, endeavours always to sell in the home market as much of the goods of all those different countries as he can, and thus, so far as he can, to convert his carrying trade into a foreign trade of consumption. A merchant, in the same manner, who is engaged in the foreign trade of consumption, when he collects goods for foreign markets, will always be glad, upon equal or nearly equal profits, to sell as great a part of them at home as he can. He saves himself the risk and trouble of exportation, when, so far as he can, he thus converts his foreign trade of consumption into a home trade. Home is in this manner the centre, if I may say so, round which the capitals of the inhabitants of every country are continually circulating, and towards which they are always tending, though by particular causes they may sometimes be driven off and repelled from it towards more distant employments. But a capital employed in the home trade, it has already been shown, necessarily puts into motion a greater quantity of domestic industry, and gives revenue and employment to a greater number of the inhabitants of the country, than an equal capital employed in the foreign trade of consumption; and one employed in the foreign trade of consumption has the same advantage over an equal capital employed in the carrying trade. Upon equal, or only nearly equal profits, therefore, every individual naturally inclines to employ his capital in the manner in which it is likely to afford the greatest support to domestic industry, and to give revenue and employment to the greatest number of people of his own country.

Secondly, every individual who employs his capital in the support of domestic industry, necessarily endeavours so to direct that industry, that its produce may be of the greatest possible value.

The produce of industry is what it adds to the subject or materials upon which it is employed. In proportion as the value of this produce is great or small, so will likewise be the profits of the employer. But it is only for the sake of profit that any man employs a capital in the support of industry; and he will always, therefore, endeavour to employ it in the support of that industry of which the produce is likely to be of the greatest value, or to exchange for the greatest quantity either of money or of other goods.

But the annual revenue of every society is always precisely equal to the exchangeable value of the whole annual produce of its industry, or rather is precisely the same thing with that exchangeable value. As every individual, therefore, endeavours as much as he can both to employ his capital in the support of domestic industry, and so to direct that industry that its produce may be of the greatest value, every individual necessarily labours to render the annual revenue of the society as great as he can. He generally, indeed, neither intends to promote the public interest, nor knows how much he is promoting it. By preferring the support of domestic to that of foreign industry, he intends only his own security; and by directing that industry in such a manner as its produce may be of the greatest value, he intends only his own gain, and he is in this, as in many other cases, led by an invisible hand to promote an end which was no part of his intention. Nor is it always the worse for the society that it was no part of it. By pursuing his own interest he frequently promotes that of the society more effectually than when he really intends to promote it. I have never known much good done by those who affected to trade for the public good. It is an affectation, indeed, not very common among merchants, and very few words need be employed in dissuading them from it.

What is the species of domestic industry which his capital can employ, and of which the produce is likely to be of the greatest value, every individual, it is evident, can, in his local situation, judge much better than any statesman or lawgiver can do for him. The statesman, who should attempt to direct private people in what manner they ought to employ their capitals, would not only load himself with a most unnecessary attention, but assume an authority which could safely be trusted, not only to no single person, but to no council or senate whatever, and which would nowhere be so dangerous as in the hands of a man who had folly and presumption enough to fancy himself fit to exercise it.

To give the monopoly of the home market to the produce of domestic industry, in any particular art or manufacture, is in some measure to direct private people in what manner they ought to employ their capitals, and must, in almost all cases, be either a useless or a hurtful regulation. If the produce of domestic can be brought there as cheap as that of foreign industry, the regulation is evidently useless. If it cannot, it must generally be hurtful. It is the maxim of every prudent master of a family, never to attempt to make at home what it will cost him more to make than to buy. The tailor does not attempt to make his own shoes, but buys them of the shoemaker. The shoemaker does not attempt to make his own clothes, but employs a tailor. The farmer attempts to make neither the one nor the other, but employs those different artificers. All of them find it for their interest to employ their whole industry in a way in which they have some advantage over their neighbours, and to purchase with a part of its produce, or, what is the same thing, with the price of a part of it, whatever else they have occasion for.

What is prudence in the conduct of every private family, can scarce be folly in that of a great kingdom. If a foreign country can supply us with a commodity cheaper than we ourselves can make it, better buy it of them with some part of the produce of our own industry, employed in a way in which we have some advantage. The general industry of the country, being always in proportion to the capital which employs it, will not thereby be diminished, no more than that of the above-mentioned artificers, but only left to find out the way in which it can be employed with the greatest advantage. It is certainly not employed to the greatest advantage, when it is thus directed towards an object which it can buy cheaper than it can make. The value of its annual produce is certainly more or less diminished, when it is thus turned away from producing commodities evidently of more value than the commodity which it is directed to produce. According to the supposition, that commodity could be purchased from foreign countries cheaper than it can be made at home. It could, therefore, have been purchased with a part only of the commodities, or, what is the same thing, with a part only of the price of the commodities, which the industry employed by an equal capital would have produced at home, had it been left to follow its natural course. The industry of the country, therefore, is thus turned away from a more to a less advantageous employment, and the exchangeable value of its annual produce, instead of being increased, according to the intention of the lawgiver, must necessarily be diminished by every such regulation.

By means of such regulations, indeed, a particular manufacture may sometimes be acquired sooner than it could have been otherwise, and after a certain time may be made at home as cheap or cheaper than in the foreign country. But though the industry of the society may be thus carried with advantage into a particular channel sooner than it could have been otherwise, it will by no means follow that the sum total, either of its industry or of its revenue, can ever be augmented by any such regulation. The industry of the society can augment only in proportion as its capital augments, and its capital can augment only in proportion to what can be gradually saved out of its revenue. But the immediate effect of every such regulation is to diminish its revenue, and what diminishes its revenue is certainly not very likely to augment its capital faster than it would have augmented of its own accord, had both capital and industry been left to find out their natural employments.

Though for want of such regulations the society should never acquire the proposed manufacture, it would not, upon that account, necessarily be the poorer in any one period of its duration. In every period of its duration its whole capital and industry might still have been employed, though upon different objects, in the manner that was most advantageous at the time. In every period its revenue might have been the greatest which its capital could afford, and both capital and revenue might have been augmented with the greatest possible rapidity.

The natural advantages which one country has over another in producing particular commodities are sometimes so great, that it is acknowledged by all the world to be in vain to struggle with them. By means of glasses, hot-beds, and hot-walls, very good grapes can be raised in Scotland, and very good wine too can be made of them, at about thirty times the expense for which at least equally good can be brought from foreign countries. Would it be a reasonable law to prohibit the importation of all foreign wines, merely to encourage the making of claret and burgundy in Scotland? But if there would be a manifest absurdity in turning towards any employment thirty times more of the capital and industry of the country than would be necessary to purchase from foreign countries an equal quantity of the commodities wanted, there must be an absurdity, though not altogether so glaring, yet exactly of the same kind, in turning towards any such employment a thirtieth or even a three-hundredth part more of either. Whether the advantages which one country has over another be natural or acquired, is in this respect of no consequence. As long as the one country has those advantages and the other wants them, it will always be more advantageous for the latter rather to buy of the former than to make. It is an acquired advantage only which one artificer has over his neighbour who exercises another trade; and yet they both find it more advantageous to buy of one another than to make what does not belong to their particular trades.

**Karl Marx and
Friedrich Engels**

Manifesto of the Communist Party

Aspectre is haunting Europe—the spectre of Communism. All the powers of old Europe have entered into a holy alliance to exorcise this spectre; Pope and Czar, Metternich and Guizot, French Radicals and German police-spies.

Where is the party in opposition that has not been decried as communistic by its opponents in power? Where the opposition that has not hurled back the branding reproach of Communism, against the more advanced opposition parties, as well as against its reactionary adversaries?

Two things result from this fact.

I. Communism is already acknowledged by all European Powers to be itself a Power.

II. It is high time that Communists should openly, in the face of the whole world, publish their views, their aims, their tendencies, and meet this nursery tale of the Spectre of Communism with a Manifesto of the party itself.

To this end, Communists of various nationalities have assembled in London, and sketched the following manifesto, to be published in the English, French, German, Italian, Flemish and Danish languages.

Bourgeois and Proletarians

The history of all hitherto existing society is the history of class struggles.

Freeman and slave, patrician and plebeian, lord and serf, guild-master and journeyman, in a word; oppressor and oppressed, stood in constant opposition to one another, carried on an uninterrupted, now hidden, now open fight, a fight that each time ended, either in a revolutionary re-constitution of society at large, or in the common ruin of the contending classes.

In the early epochs of history, we find almost everywhere a complicated arrangement of society into various orders, a manifold graduation of social rank. In ancient Rome we have patricians, knights, plebeians, slaves; in the Middle Ages, feudal lords, vassals, guild-masters, journeymen, apprentices, serfs; in almost all of these classes, again, subordinate gradations.

The modern bourgeois society that has sprouted from the ruins of feudal society, has not done away with class antagonisms. It has but established new classes, new conditions of oppression, new forms of struggle in place of the old ones.

Our epoch, the epoch of the bourgeoisie, possesses, however, this distinctive feature; it has simplified the class antagonisms. Society as a whole

From Karl Marx and Friedrich Engels, *The Communist Manifesto* by (1848).

is more and more splitting up into two great hostile camps, into two great classes directly facing each other: Bourgeoisie and Proletariat.

From the serfs of the Middle Ages sprang the chartered burghers of the earliest towns. From these burgesses the first elements of the bourgeoisie were developed.

The discovery of America, the rounding of the Cape, opened up fresh ground for the rising bourgeoisie. The East-Indian and Chinese markets, the colonization of America, trade with the colonies, the increase in the means of exchange in commodities, generally, gave to commerce, to navigation, to industry, an impulse never before known, and thereby, to the revolutionary element in the tottering feudal society, a rapid development.

The feudal system of industry, under which industrial production was monopolized by closed guilds, now no longer sufficed for the growing wants of the new markets. The manufacturing system took its place. The guild-masters were pushed on one side by the manufacturing middle-class; division of labor between the different corporate guilds vanished in the face of division of labor in each single workshop.

Meantime the markets kept ever growing, the demand, ever rising. Even manufacturing no longer sufficed. Thereupon, steam and machinery revolutionized industrial production. The place of manufacture was taken by the giant, Modern Industry, the place of the industrial middle-class, by industrial millionaires, the leaders of whole industrial armies, the modern bourgeoisie.

Modern Industry has established the world-market, for which the discovery of America paved the way. This market has given an immense development to commerce, to navigation, to communication by land. This development has, in its turn, reacted on the extension of industry; and in proportion as industry, commerce, navigation, railways extended in the same proportion the bourgeoisie developed, increased its capital, and pushed into the background every class handed down from the Middle Ages.

We see, therefore, how the modern bourgeoisie is itself the product of a long course of development, of a series of revolutions in the modes of production and of exchange.

Each step in the development of the bourgeoisie was accompanied by a corresponding political advance of that class. An oppressed class under the sway of the feudal nobility, an armed and self-governing association in the medieval commune, here independent urban republic (as in Italy and Germany), there taxable "third estate" of the monarchy (as in France), afterwards, in the period of manufacturing proper, serving either the semi-feudal or the absolute monarchy as a counterpoise against the nobility, and in fact, cornerstone of the great monarchies in general, the bourgeoisie has at last, since the establishment of Modern Industry and of the world-market, conquered for itself, in a modern representative State, exclusive political sway. The executive of the modern State is but a committee for managing the common affairs of the whole bourgeoisie.

The bourgeoisie, historically, has played a most revolutionary part.

The bourgeoisie, wherever it has got the upper hand, has put an end to all feudal, patriarchal, idyllic relations. It has pitilessly torn asunder the motley feudal ties that bound man to his "natural superiors," and has left remaining no other nexus between man and man than naked self-interest, than callous "cash payment." It has drowned the most heavenly ecstasies of religious fervor, of chivalrous enthusiasm, of philistine sentimentalism, in the icy water of egotistical calculation. It has resolved personal worth into exchange value, and in place of the numberless indefeasible chartered freedoms, has set up that single, unconscionable freedom—Free Trade. In one word, for exploitation, veiled by religious and political illusions, it has substituted naked, shameless, direct, brutal exploitation.

The bourgeoisie has stripped of its halo every occupation hitherto honored and looked up to with reverent awe. It has converted the physician, the lawyer, the priest, the poet, the man of science, into its paid wage-laborers.

The bourgeoisie has torn away from the family its sentimental veil, and has reduced the family relation to a mere money relation.

The bourgeoisie has disclosed how it came to pass that the brutal display of vigor in the Middle Ages, which Reactionists so much admire, found its fitting complement in the most slothful indolence. It has been the first to show what man's activity can bring about. It has accomplished wonders far surpassing Egyptian pyramids, Roman aqueducts, and Gothic cathedrals; it has conducted expeditions that put in the shade all former Exoduses of nations and crusades.

The bourgeoisie cannot exist without constantly revolutionizing the instruments of production, and thereby the relations of production, and with them the whole relations of society. Conservation of the old modes of production in unaltered form, was, on the contrary, the first condition of existence for all earlier industrial classes. Constant revolutionizing of production, uninterrupted disturbance of all social conditions, everlasting uncertainty and agitation distinguish the bourgeois epoch from all earlier ones. All fixed, fast-frozen relations, with their train of ancient and venerable prejudices and opinions, are swept away, all newly-formed ones become antiquated before they can ossify. All that is solid melts into air, all that is holy is profaned, and man is at last compelled to face with sober senses, his real conditions of life, and his relations with his kind.

The need of a constantly expanding market for its products chases the bourgeoisie over the whole surface of the globe. It must nestle everywhere, settle everywhere, establish connections everywhere.

The bourgeoisie has through its exploitation of the world-market given a cosmopolitan character to production and consumption in every country. To the great chagrin of Reactionists, it has drawn from under the feet of industry the national ground on which it stood. All old-established national industries have been destroyed or are daily being destroyed. They are dislodged by new industries, whose introduction becomes a life and death question for all civilized nations, by industries that no longer work up indigenous raw material, but raw material drawn from the remotest zones; industries whose products are consumed, not only at home, but in every quarter of the globe. In place of the old wants, satisfied by the productions of the country, we find new wants, requiring for their satisfaction the products of distant lands and climes. In place of the old local and national seclusion and self-sufficiency, we have intercourse in every direction, universal inter-dependence of nations. And as in material, so also in intellectual production. The intellectual creations of individual nations become common property. National one-sidedness and narrow-mindedness become more and more impossible, and from the numerous national and local literatures there arises a world-literature.

The bourgeoisie, by the rapid improvement of all instruments of production, by the immensely facilitated means of communication, draws all, even the most barbarian, nations into civilization. The cheap prices of its commodities are the heavy artillery with which it batters down all Chinese walls, with which it forces the barbarians' intensely obstinate hatred of foreigners to capitulate. It compels all nations, on pain of extinction, to adopt the bourgeois mode of production; it compels them to introduce what it calls civilization into their midst, i.e., to become bourgeois themselves. In a word, it creates a world after its own image.

The bourgeoisie has subjected the country to the rule of the towns. It has created enormous cities, has greatly increased the urban population as compared with the rural, and has thus rescued a considerable part of the population from the idiocy of rural life. Just as it has made the country dependent on the towns, so it has made barbarian and semibarbarian countries dependent on the civilized ones, nations of peasants on nations of bourgeois, the East on the West.

The bourgeoisie keeps more and more doing away with the scattered state of the population, of the means of production, and of property. It has agglomerated population, centralized means of production, and has concentrated property in a few hands. The necessary consequence of this was political centralization. Independent, or but loosely connected provinces, with separate interests, laws, governments and systems of taxation, became lumped together in one nation, with one government, one code of laws, one national class-interest, one frontier and one customs-tariff.

The bourgeoisie, during its rule of scarce one hundred years, has created more massive and more colossal productive forces than have all preceding generations together. Subjection of Nature's forces to man, machinery, application of chemistry to industry and agriculture, steam-navigation, railways, electric telegraphs, clearing of whole continents for cultivation, canalization of rivers, whole populations conjured out of the ground—what earlier century had even a presentiment that such productive forces slumbered in the lap of social labor?

We see then: the means of production and of exchange on whose foundations the bourgeoisie built itself up, were generated in feudal society. At a certain stage in the development of these means of production and of exchange, the conditions under which feudal society produced and exchanged, the feudal organization of agriculture and manufacturing industry, in one word, the feudal relations of property became no longer compatible with the already developed productive forces; they became so many fetters. They had to be burst asunder; they were burst asunder.

Into their places stepped free competition, accompanied by a social and political constitution adapted to it, and by the economical and political sway of the bourgeois class.

A similar movement is going on before our own eyes. Modern bourgeois society with its relations of production, of exchange and of property, a society that has conjured up such gigantic means of production and of exchange, is like the sorcerer, who is no longer able to control the powers of the nether world whom he has called up by his spells. For many a decade past the history of industry and commerce is but the history of the revolt of modern productive forces against modern conditions of production, against the property relations that are the condition for the existence of the bourgeoisie and of its rule. It is enough to mention the commercial crises that by their periodical return put on trial, each time more threateningly, the existence of the entire bourgeois society. In these crises a great part not only of the existing products, but also of the previously created productive forces, are periodically destroyed. In these crises there breaks out an epidemic that, in all earlier epochs, would have seemed an absurdity—the epidemic of overproduction. Society suddenly finds itself put back into a state of momentary barbarism; it appears as if a famine, a universal war of devastation had cut off the supply of every means of subsistence; industry and commerce seem to be destroyed; and why? Because there is too much civilization, too much means of subsistence, too much industry, too much commerce. The productive forces at the disposal of society no longer tend to further the development of the conditions of bourgeois property; on the contrary, they have become too powerful for these conditions, by which they are fettered, and so soon as they overcome these fetters, they bring disorder into the whole of bourgeois society, endangering the existence of bourgeois property. The conditions of bourgeois society are too narrow to comprise the wealth created by them. And how does the bourgeoisie get over these crises? On the one hand by enforced destruction of a mass of productive forces; on the other, by the conquest of new markets, and by the more thorough exploitation of the old ones. That is to say, by paving the way for more extensive and more destructive crises, and by diminishing the means whereby crises are prevented.

The weapons with which the bourgeoisie felled feudalism to the ground are now turned against the bourgeoisie itself.

But not only has the bourgeoisie forged the weapons that bring death to itself; it has also called into existence the men who are to wield those weapons—the modern working-class—the proletarians.

In proportion as the bourgeoisie, i.e., capital, is developed, in the same proportion is the proletariat, the modern working-class, developed, a class of laborers, who live only so long as they find work, and who find work only so long as their labor increases capital. These laborers, who must sell themselves piecemeal, are a commodity, like every other article of commerce, and are consequently exposed to all the vicissitudes of competition, to all the fluctuations of the market.

Owing to the extensive use of machinery and to division of labor, the work of the proletarians has lost all individual character, and, consequently, all charm for the workman. He becomes an appendage of the machine, and it is only the most simple, most monotonous, and most easily acquired knack that is required of him. Hence, the cost of production of a workman is restricted, almost entirely, to the means of subsistence that he requires for his maintenance, and for the propagation of his race. But the price of a commodity, and also of labor, is equal to its cost of production. In proportion, therefore, as the repulsiveness of the work increases, the wage decreases. Nay more, in proportion as the use of machinery and division of labor increases, in the same proportion the burden of toil also increases, whether by prolongation of the working hours, by increase of the work enacted in a given time, or by increased speed of the machinery, etc.

Modern Industry has converted the little workshop of the patriarchal master into the great factory of the industrial capitalist. Masses of laborers, crowded into the factory, are organized like soldiers. As privates of the industrial army they are placed under the command of a perfect hierarchy of officers and sergeants. Not only are they the slaves of the bourgeois class, and of the bourgeois State, they are daily and hourly enslaved by the machine, by the over-looker, and, above all, by the individual bourgeois manufacturer himself. The more openly this despotism proclaims gain to be its end and aim, the more petty, the more hateful and the more embittering it is.

The less the skill and exertion or strength implied in manual labor, in other words, the more modern industry becomes developed, the more is the labor of men superseded by that of women. Differences of age and sex have no longer any distinctive social validity for the working class. All are instruments of labor, more or less expensive to use, according to their age and sex.

No sooner is the exploitation of the laborer by the manufacturer so far at an end, that he receives his wages in cash, than he is set upon by the other portions of the bourgeoisie, the landlord, the shopkeeper, the pawnbroker, etc.

The low strata of the middle class—the small trades-people, shopkeepers, and retired tradesmen generally, the handicraftsmen and peasants—all these sink gradually into the proletariat, partly because their diminutive capital does not suffice for the scale on which Modern Industry is carried on, and is swamped in the competition with the large capitalists, partly because their specialized skill is rendered worthless by new methods of production. Thus the proletariat is recruited from all classes of the population.

The proletariat goes through various stages of development. With its birth begins its struggle with the bourgeoisie. At first the contest is carried on by individual laborers, then by the workpeople of a factory, then by the operatives of one trade, in one locality, against the individual bourgeois who directly exploits them. They direct their attacks not against the bourgeois conditions of production, but against the instruments of production themselves; they destroy imported wares that compete with their labor, they smash to pieces machinery, they set factories ablaze, they seek to restore by force the vanished status of the workman of the Middle Ages.

At this stage the laborers still form an incoherent mass scattered over the whole country, and broken up by their mutual competition. If anywhere they unite to form more compact bodies, this is not yet the consequence of their own active union, but of the union of bourgeoisie, which class, in order to attain its own political ends, is compelled to set the whole proletariat in motion, and is moreover yet, for a time, able to do so. At this stage, therefore, the proletarians do not fight their enemies, but the enemies of their enemies, the remnants of absolute monarchy, the landowners, the non-industrial bourgeoisie, the petty bourgeoisie. Thus the whole historical movement is concentrated in the hands of the bourgeoisie; every victory so obtained is a victory for the bourgeoisie.

But with the development of industry the proletariat not only increases in number, it becomes concentrated in great masses, its strength grows, and it feels that strength more. The various interests and conditions of life within the ranks of the proletariat are more and more equalized, in proportion as machinery obliterates all distinction of labor, and nearly everywhere reduces wages to the same low level. The growing competition among the bourgeoisie, and the resulting commercial crises, make the wages of the worker ever more fluctuating. The unceasing improvement of machinery, ever more rapidly developing, makes their livelihood more and more precarious, the collisions between individual workmen and individual bourgeois take more and more the character of collision between two classes. Thereupon the workers begin to form combinations (Trades Unions) against the bourgeoisie; they club together in order to keep up the rate of wages; they found permanent associations in order to make provision beforehand for these occasional revolts. Here and there the contest breaks out into riots.

Now and then the workers are victorious, but only for a time. The real fruits of their battles lie, not in the immediate result, but in the ever expanding union of the workers. This union is helped on by the improved means of communication that are created by modern industry, and that place the workers of different localities in contact with one another. It was just this contact that was needed to centralize the numerous local struggles, all of the same character, into one national struggle between classes. But every class struggle is a political struggle. And that union, to attain which the burghers of the Middle Ages, with their miserable highways, required centuries, the modern proletarians, thanks to railways, achieve in a few years.

This organization of the proletarians into a class, and consequently into a political party, is continually being upset again by the competition between the workers themselves. But it ever rises up again, stronger, firmer, mightier. It compels legislative recognition of particular interests of the workers, by taking advantage of the divisions among the bourgeoisie itself. Thus the ten-hour bill in England was carried.

Altogether collisions between the classes of the old society further, in many ways, the course of development of the proletariat. The bourgeoisie finds itself involved in a constant battle. At first with the aristocracy; later on, with those portions of the bourgeoisie itself, whose interests have become antagonistic to the progress of industry; at all times, with the bourgeoisie of foreign countries. In all these battles it sees itself compelled to appeal to the proletariat, to ask for its help, and thus, to drag it into the political arena. The bourgeoisie itself, therefore, supplies the proletariat with its own elements of political and general education, in other words, it furnishes the proletariat with weapons for fighting the bourgeoisie.

Further, as we have already seen, entire sections of the ruling classes are, by the advance of industry, precipitated into the proletariat, or are at least threatened in their conditions of existence. These also supply the proletariat with fresh elements of enlightenment and progress.

Finally, in times when the class-struggle nears the decisive hour, the process of dissolution going on within the ruling class, in fact, within the whole range of old society, assumes such a violent, glaring character, that a small section of the ruling class cuts itself adrift, and joins the revolutionary class, the class that holds the future in its hands. Just as, therefore, at an earlier period, a section of the nobility went over to the bourgeoisie, so now a portion of the bourgeoisie goes over to the proletariat, and in particular, a portion of the bourgeois ideologists, who have raised themselves to the level of comprehending theoretically the historical movements as a whole.

Of all the classes that stand face to face with the bourgeoisie today, the proletariat alone is a really revolutionary class. The other classes decay and finally disappear in the face of Modern Industry; the proletariat is its special and essential product. . . .

In the conditions of the proletariat, those of old society at large are already virtually swamped. The proletarian is without property; his relation to his wife and children has no longer anything in common with the bourgeois family-relations; modern industrial labor, modern subjugation to capital, the same in England as in France, in America as in Germany, has stripped him of every trace of national character. Law, morality, religion, are to him so many bourgeois prejudices, behind which lurk in ambush just as many bourgeois interests.

All the preceding classes that got the upper hand, sought to fortify their already acquired status by subjecting society at large to their conditions of appropriation. The proletarians cannot become masters of the productive forces of society, except by abolishing their own previous mode of appropriation, and thereby also every other previous mode of appropriation. They have nothing of their own to secure and to fortify; their mission is to destroy all previous securities for, and insurances of, individual property.

All previous historical movements were movements of minorities, or in the interests of minorities. The proletarian movement is the self-conscious, independent movement of the immense majority, in the interest of the immense majority. The proletariat, the lowest stratum of our present society, cannot stir, cannot raise itself up, without the whole superincumbent strata of official society being sprung into the air.

Though not in substance, yet in form, the struggle of the proletariat with the bourgeoisie is at first a national struggle. The proletariat of each country must, of course, first of all settle matters with its own bourgeoisie.

In depicting the most general phases of the development of the proletariat, we traced the more or less veiled civil war, raging within existing society, up to the point where that war breaks out into open revolution, and where the violent overthrow of the bourgeoisie lays the foundation for the sway of the proletariat.

Hitherto, every form of society has been based, as we have already seen, on the antagonism of oppressing and oppressed classes. But in order to oppress a class, certain conditions must be assured to it under which it can, at least, continue its slavish existence. The serf, in the period of serfdom, raised himself to membership in the commune, just as the petty bourgeois, under the yoke of feudal absolutism, managed to develop into a bourgeois.

The modern laborer, on the contrary, instead of rising with the progress of industry, sinks deeper and deeper below the conditions of existence of his own class. He becomes a pauper, and pauperism develops more rapidly than population and wealth. And here it becomes evident that the bourgeoisie is unfit any longer to be the ruling class in society, and to impose its conditions of existence upon society as an over-riding law. It is unfit to rule, because it is incompetent to assure an existence to its slave within his slavery, because it cannot help letting him sink into such a state that it has to feed him, instead of being fed by him. Society can no longer live under this bourgeoisie, in other words, its existence is no longer compatible with society.

The essential condition for the existence, and for the sway of the bourgeois class, is the formation and augmentation of capital; the condition for capital is wage-labor. Wage-labor rests exclusively on competition between the laborers. The advance of industry, whose involuntary promoter is the bourgeoisie, replaces the isolation of the laborers, due to competition, by their revolutionary combination, due to association. The development of Modern Industry, therefore, cuts from under its feet the very foundation on which the bourgeoisie produces and appropriates products. What the bourgeoisie therefore produces, above all, are its own grave-diggers. Its fall and the victory of the proletariat are equally inevitable.

POSTSCRIPT

Can Capitalism Lead to Human Happiness?

As a society, Americans have always prized liberty over equality. We have always believed what we thought followed from Smith—that the wealth of the society as a whole was the only legitimate goal of economic enterprise as a whole, and that distribution for the sake of equity, or charity, was a side issue, best left to churches and private charity. We Americans have resisted any attempts at socializing such basic needs as medicine, communications (the telephone companies), and economic security for the old, young, and infirm. We have always enjoyed characterizing our business system as one where, as far as your personal income is concerned, "the sky's the limit." We point to the failures of "socialism" in England and Sweden, and cite with particular satisfaction the fall of communism in Eastern Europe and Russia.

We have built some safety nets: Social Security, Medicare and Medicaid, Aid to Dependent Children, and the like. But these and all the other elements of the welfare system have become a major problem and political issue for both parties. People in that system complain about its failure to provide adequately for those in the most need, babies and the infirm elderly. Meanwhile, conservative members of Congress complain that even these modest subsidies are costing the taxpayer too much, and recent modifications to these programs have put firm time limits on our ability to access them.

Why should subsidies to the poor bother us so? We provide price supports to farmers, corporate welfare (bailouts) to businesses, subsidized water and grazing land at public expense to ranchers and farmers, and access to minerals on public land for miners. We have allowed even foreign companies to come into the national forests, to mine and forest for their own profit, even when they leave tailings and barren land for us as taxpayers to clean up and restore. Why, it might be asked, should we subsidize the rich in our tender public compassion, while resenting the poor?

In most of the redistributive activities of the economy, we see the very visible hands of the CEOs and the Wall Street analysts. Where, in all of this, is the Invisible Hand of Adam Smith? Or does the whole arrogant parade of conspicuous billionaires force us to consider the alternatives to Adam Smith? Was Marx's political philosophy persuasive? Should we work to redistribute the productive assets of the country? The last two decades of economic reform have seen a steady redistribution in the other direction, as the richest persons in the country absorb more and more of the wealth and income, as the poorest get poorer. How can this be right?

Suggested Reading

For more information on this subject the following readings may be of help:

John D. Bishop, "Adam Smith's Invisible Hand Argument," *Journal of Business Ethics* March 1995, vol. 14, no. 3, pp. 165–80.

Robert L. Heilbroner, *The Worldly Philosophers*, fifth edition (New York: Touchstone, 1980).

David Korten, "The Difference Between Money and Wealth: How Out-of-Control Speculation is Destroying Real Wealth," *Business Ethics* January/February 1999, p. 4.

Karl Marx, *Communist Manifesto*, A Gateway Edition (Chicago Ill.: Henry Regnery Company, 1954).

Donald McCloskey, "Bourgeois Virtue," *American Scholar* 63 (1994).

Richard John Neuhaus, "The Pope Affirms the 'New Capitalism,'" *The Wall Street Journal* (May 2, 1991).

M.G. Piety, "The Long Term: Capitalism and Culture in the New Millennium," *Journal of Business Ethics*, vol. 51, no. 2, May 2004.

David Schweickart, *Against Capitalism* (Cambridge: Cambridge University Press, 1993).

"The Search for Keynes: Was He a Keynesian?" *The Economist* Dec. 26, 1992, pp. 108–10.

Adam Smith, *The Wealth of Nations* (Clarendon Press, 1976).

Patricia H. Werhane, *Adam Smith and His Legacy for Modern Capitalism* (New York: Oxford University Press, 1991).

ISSUE 2

Can Restructuring a Corporation's Rules Make a Moral Difference?

YES: Josef Wieland, from "The Ethics of Governance," *Business Ethics Quarterly* (January 2001)

NO: Ian Maitland, from "Distributive Justice in Firms: Do the Rules of Corporate Governance Matter?" *Business Ethics Quarterly* (January 2001)

ISSUE SUMMARY

YES: Can moral values be attributed to organizations (as well as to individual persons)? Josef Wieland, director of the German Business Ethics Network's Centre for Business Ethics, argues that they can. After carefully developing a concept of governance ethics for corporations, he argues that the incorporation of moral conditions and requirements into the structures of the firm is the precondition for lasting beneficial effects of the virtues of the individuals within it. We can only be moral persons at work when the workplace, too, is moral.

NO: Ian Maitland, professor of Business, Government and Society at the University of Minnesota's Carlson School of Management, here plays his favorite role as Business Ethics Curmudgeon. Changing the rules will have no effect whatsoever on the moral work of the corporation (taking as his example the justice of the distributive mechanisms of the firm) and will only succeed, if taken seriously, in impairing its efficiency.

$\mathbf{A}$s Wieland points out, the question of whether an organization of some sort, as opposed to its human members, may assume the status of moral agent has been around for a very long time. (It actually goes back to Aristotle, who took up in the *Politics* the question of the conditions under which a government is morally obligated to pay the debts incurred by its predecessor. It is more difficult with organizations than with humans to tell when you're dealing with "the same" entity that undertook the obligation.) New in Wieland's approach is the use of recent economic theory (referred to as "the

New Economics of Organization"). Readers not exposed to the language of this theory may find it rough going at first, but the attempt to reach almost mathematical precision in the language of organizational ethics is a very useful intellectual stretch. We have left out section 4 as peripheral to our purposes; we trust that no confusion will result.

His thesis, again traceable to Aristotle, is perpetually fascinating. To what extent is my ability and inclination to act morally ("cooperate" with others) dependent on the institutional atmosphere, the communication from the highest levels that moral behavior is approved? Approval of being nice won't do it. What the moral agent in the corporation needs is a strong message that moral behavior will be rewarded even if it entails falling short on numerical goals set by the management—even if it cuts into return on investment and the increase of shareholder wealth. That's the only message that matters.

Or does it matter? Ian Maitland addresses himself to a different group of corporate reformers, those who hold that restructuring corporate rules to signal a new concern with morality can make the corporation more willing to take into account stakeholders other than the shareholders—the employees, for instance, or the natural environment. Rules are neutral, Maitland argues, at least as far as morality goes. But they can do a beautiful job of fouling up the corporate enterprise's efficiency, as people who should be worrying about how to get their job done faster and with less consumption of resources find themselves worrying instead about how to create a more moral world.

You'll note that Wieland and Maitland are aiming at slightly different targets, so it should not surprise you if their arrows seem often to fly past each other. Often Maitland sounds simply mischievous, which he is, and often Wieland's article reads like translated German, which it is. But the fundamental conflict is right there, and it is just the conflict that defines business ethics. Should we expect moral behavior of the corporation? Should we hold our corporations to moral standards? Should we engage in moral criticism of the corporation? Or should we recognize, as Milton Friedman, Adam Smith, and so many others have argued, that the corporation is by right and by law no more than a legal device for turning money into money, and to be held to account only insofar as the law specifically requires it to operate within the bounds of the public interest?

Ask yourself, as you read these selections, whether Wieland's conviction that the corporation can be a moral agent, and can make itself more moral if it chooses to, is helped by the theory he brings to bear; ask yourself if Maitland is not simply right in his skepticism about the uselessness of the enterprise.

YES

Josef Wieland

The Ethics of Governance

Introduction: Organization and Ethics

In this [selection] I want to pursue two questions. The first of these is as follows: what is the subject and scope of business ethics?[1] The second question is this: in what way does it make sense to talk about the ethics of the firm-as-an-organization?

The topic of this [selection]—the Ethics of Governance—already implies a connection between corporate governance and business ethics; that is, between the management, governance, and control regimes of a firm and its ethics as an organization. In practice these are interrelated: codes of ethics, ethics management systems, and corporate ethics programs can be understood as governance structures by which firms control, protect, and develop the integrity of their transactions. The theoretical investigation and integration of these ethical systems has hitherto been developed only to a limited extent and has been confined to individual aspects, as far as I can see. There are reasons for this.

The theoretical explanation and integration of codes of ethics, ethics management systems, and other organizational measures for the implementation of moral claims in organizational contexts requires a conceptual distinction between the moral values of an individual person (value ethics), the values of an individual person in a given function or role (management ethics), and the moral values of an organization (governance ethics). This distinction would provide the basis for a better understanding of the trade-offs, conflicts, and dilemmas contained in those distinct levels of business ethics.

In the following discussion I would like to focus my own investigation on just one of the aspects mentioned—i.e., on the moral characteristics of an organization as a distinct moral actor. There has been a lengthy, extensive, and controversial debate on this issue. Its focus is the question of the attribution of moral responsibility to collective actors.[2] Differing viewpoints revolve around the issue as to whether firms as corporate actors are independent action systems or subjects, or whether their status as action systems or subjects is derived from individual actors. Although this discussion has yielded important insights for research on business ethics, the issue remains unresolved. I believe the reason for this deadlock is to be found in the individualistic notion of action that grounds all the arguments. This emphasis is in full

Josef Wieland, "The Ethics of Governance", *Business Ethics Quarterly*, vol. 11, no. 1, January 2001, pp. 73–85. Copyright © 2001 by Business Ethics Quarterly. Reprinted by permission of The Philosophy Documentation Center, publisher of Business Ethics Quarterly. References omitted.

accordance with philosophical tradition. However, business ethics questions are questions about ethics in the context of a functional structure: they cannot be developed by analogy with the ethics of a person, but must be developed out of the characteristics and conditions of the structure itself. Is it then possible to develop a type of business ethics that does not resort to an action-theoretic notion of the person? In the following sections I will argue that this question can be answered affirmatively, and that its answer requires the substitution of the notion of person by that of governance, and of that of action by that of cooperation. . . .

Form and Process of the Organization

In this section, the notions of governance and governance ethics that so far have been introduced in a more intuitive way will be located in theoretical terms and further developed. In accordance with the discussion so far, only one particular form of governance will be the object of this endeavor: governance of the firm. Of course, rules and orders at the level of the state also are governance structures. However, for reasons of precision and simplicity they will not be dealt with systematically here.

Questions regarding the ethics of the firm are questions with regard to an organization. From the point of view of the institutionalist New Economics of Organization,[3] which this [selection] regards as normative, these are questions about the moral characteristics of a governance structure for the execution of economic transactions.

Governance structures are formal and informal arrangements for the "steering" of the different codes of a system or organization. They are a matrix within which distinct transactions are negotiated and executed, completely if possible.[4] For the purposes of this investigation it is useful to distinguish between global and local governance structures. Global governance structures refer to the constitutional parameters of an organization or a system; local governance structures to the micropolitical governance of transactions. State, market, and firms, frameworks, corporate charters, and ethical codes of conduct are global governance structures in this sense. In pursuing the question of business ethics I will interpret global governance structures as firm-specific assets (structures, resources, competences, skills) for the identification and processing of moral problems in the economy. Local governance structures are standard operating procedures, organizational structures, rites, and moral values within the firm that can constitute transaction-specific assets for the identification and processing of problem issues.

Governance structures differ with regard to their ability to support the efficient execution of a given transaction. Efficiency in the context of governance is defined as adaptive efficiency, that is, as comparison of at least two governance structures with regard to their capacity to cope with the uncertainties and contingencies that can occur during the process of transaction. Since such structures usually consist of formal and informal codes of practice, moral ambitions and values can without too much difficulty be interpreted as elements of the governance of economic transactions.

The above argument implies that business ethics is not about the moral standards and behavior of entrepreneurs, management teams, or employees. Those are personal virtues that can be attributed to acting persons, but not to the normativity of organizations. There seems to be general consensus in the literature that the moral constitution of an organization has to be different from the sum of the moral convictions of its members. However, it remains to a large extent unclear how the phenomenon of a structural ethics can be approached at all.[5] In the following I will develop my own views on this topic and locate them in the notion of governance ethics.

First of all it is important to introduce the convention that regarding their normativity organizations are contractually constituted systems of institutionalized behavioral constraints and thus also represent behavioral options.[6] In other words, business ethics cannot be developed based on the notion of action, but must be premised on the characteristics of a global governance structure for economic transactions that limits (and extends) behavioral options. The investigation into the theoretical problems this disposition entails must begin with a differentiated notion of the organization itself. We differentiate as follows: organization denotes the general *process* of organizing, and also the specific *form* within which this process takes place.

The introduction of this distinction between process and form has far-reaching consequences; these can be demonstrated by using the example of the distinction between market and hierarchy[7] common in economic theory. Market and hierarchy represent different global governance structures. As options for the execution of a transaction, e.g., a long-term employment relationship, they are equivalent. But as concrete "form" under whose regime this employment relationship takes place, they are not equivalent. It is precisely because markets and hierarchies have at their disposal different characteristics and capabilities for the governance of economic processes that the problem of cost-efficient assignments of transactions to the most efficient governance structure arises. In the case of a long-term employment relationship governance is optimally organized not via the market but via the hierarchical form of "firm."

The difference between process and form that is inherent in the notion of organization can be used for the theoretical construction of an institutional business ethics. Insofar as the process of organizing involves individual action, virtues and vices matter. But the organizational form within which this process is taking place—the firm—stands outside the realm of traditional value ethics. This decoupling of form and process is rooted in different temporal characteristics. The processual character of the organization called "firm" can in principle be set to infinite duration by the form character of the same organization to the extent that form is based on the exclusion of "human beings," "individuals," or "persons."[8] Because of this, business ethics—if we take the label seriously—has to refer constitutively to the form of a "firm" as a governance structure. It can be systematically developed as governance ethics only under conditions where individual virtues can and must have their effect.

Of course, the analysis and design of governance structures is part of institutional theory. However, it is important to realize that in the theoretical design developed here the notions of "governance" and "institution" are not synonyms. The notion of institution aims at directing behavior via formal or informal behavioral constraints and incentives (utility maximizing). In contrast, the notion of governance emphasizes the integration and interaction of formal and informal constraints with regard to any given problem and focuses on the problem of adaptivity, i.e., the reflexivity and recursiveness of structures. From a governance-theoretic perspective, whereas the notion of institution is more static (goal-oriented directing of behavior via narrowing of options), the notion of governance is dynamic (goal-oriented directing of behavior via adaptivity).

Two conclusions emerge from the foregoing discussion. First, business ethics needs to be developed as governance ethics. Second, the relationship between value ethics and governance ethics is as follows: whereas management virtues belong to the process of the firm, the proper locus of governance ethics is the form of the firm.

Governance Ethics: Contract and Organization

The foregoing argument leads to the consideration that the "shape" of business ethics has to be developed based on the characteristics of a particular form, i.e., that of the firm as organization. The New Economics of Organization, an institutionalist and simultaneously interdisciplinary research program, captures this form in descriptive and explanatory terms in two dimensions—contract and organization.

Contract

From an organization-economic perspective the firm constitutes itself as economic form by means of a constitutional contract, the corporate charter.[9] This establishes not only the goals and policies of the firm, but also the identity of its stakeholders.[10] The process of constitution can be reconstructed in contract-theoretical terms as a "nexus of contracts" between individual resource owners.[11] According to this theoretical architecture, the constituting process of the enterprise (or team) is taking place because the gains of each individual resource owner attainable by cooperation are above the level that could be reached by each alone. The motive for founding the firm is thus not profit making,[12] but the realisation of a cooperation rent. This rent from cooperation, although an organizational collective good, gives a strictly individualist and self-interested motive for the formation of a team.

Now the decisive question is: how can it be possible that actors who are exclusively self-oriented can bind themselves together permanently in an organization in order to produce this collective good? The answer is: by entering into chosen long-term and adaptively designed contractual arrangements in which all partners to the contract commit themselves to agreed contractual provisions. On the one hand they thereby agree to constraints on their present and future behavioral options: only in this way can teamwork among strictly self-interested actors become possible. On the other hand, however, the partners to a contract opt to combine their particular resources and capabilities and thus extend the range of their respective individual behavioral options in a way that is by definition not precisely spelled out by the terms of the contract, but is indicative of the adaptivity of the contractual arrangements. The initial sets of resources of all partners to the contract are not reciprocally known completely, since it is impossible to measure them precisely, nor can future learning processes and the appropriation of implicit knowledge be anticipated. This might be a disadvantage from the performance measurement and marginal productivity point of view. But in this disadvantage lies also the dynamic and adaptive potential of a team.

It is thus the systematic incompleteness of contracts, desired by the contracting parties because of its potential for innovation, that initially leads to a problem of adaptation to newly arising situations and contingencies in the market and organizational environment of a firm. For reasons of adaptivity discretionary behavior has to be acceptable. It would be easy to interpret discretionary behavior as shirking.[13] However, the potential for innovation and productivity, organizational learning, and implicit knowledge; the resources, competences, and skills of an organization and its members for the realization of competitive advantage—all of these can be practically activated and theoretically reconstructed only if incompleteness and uncertainty are allowed to exist in contractual relations. It is the problem of adaptivity that is the source of entrepreneurial dynamic and the origin of novelty. Thus, via incompleteness and uncertainty we reconstruct the firm in contract-theoretic terms as a bundle of resources, skills, and competencies[14] the activation of which is based on implicit contracts.[15]

It is precisely these trade-offs between constraint and extension, performance control and development, contract and resource that characterise the form "firm" as a contractually constituted organization. The constitution of a firm as a network of explicit and implicit contracts codifies behavioral constraints and justified expectations, and thus creates cooperative behavioral options and resource use possibilities. In other words, it is the agreed explicit and implicit contracts of individual resource owners that constitute the collective actor "firm" as a cooperation project, and demarcate the form "firm" from firm-as-process. This interpretation of the form "firm" as a set of constitutional (corporate charter, standards of conduct) and postconstitutional (employment contracts) explicit and implicit contracts between resource owners defines a first interface for questions of morality.

Those questions can be developed on the basis of the problem of cooperation; more precisely, the values "willingness to cooperate" and "capability to cooperate." "Willingness to cooperate" signifies an ability to cooperate successfully, given that cooperation benefits at least one of the partners. The notion thus captures both a resource dimension and a behavioral dimension. The "capability to cooperate" signifies those mental factors that activate the willingness to cooperate. Thus we can formulate more precisely: long-term contracts for the foundation of a cooperation project in and between firms are incomplete[16] regarding the willingness and capability to cooperate, and are therefore characterized by ambiguity and contingency. Their fulfillment thus always raises moral questions. The basis of those moral questions lies in the fact that self-interested actors have a strong incentive to exploit contractual incompleteness, ambiguity, and contingency in an opportunistic way whenever they can do so in a cost-efficient manner. Such behavior by its very nature represents a suspension of the willingness to cooperate and a destruction of the capability to cooperate. On the other hand, the rejection of such behavior on moral grounds and the productive use of incompleteness have the contrary effect. Both types are determinants of the realization of a cooperation rent by the actors, with inverted signs.[17] The governance-theoretic development of questions of morality thus makes it possible to approach business ethics via the values "willingness to cooperate" and "capability to cooperate" as the immanent problematic of the form of a cooperation project.

Organization

It follows from the foregoing that cooperation of self-interested economic actors can attain duration and stability only if conflict, dependence, and order in an organization and between organizations can be balanced and communicated in an appropriate way. In order to generate this balance economic incentive systems and organizational processes and controls are fundamental. However, during the last couple of years the discussion of corporate culture and an "economics of atmosphere"[18] has increasingly made clear that the management of "soft facts," atmosphere, and values is also of crucial importance. The integration of these economic and non-economic incentives and factors is the theoretical and practical core of the ethics of governance.

(i) Conflict in organizations initially and inevitably develop because of the self-interest and opportunism of team members, because of disagreements over the distribution of the cooperation rent, and because of differences in priorities given to the realization of tasks. Technical (procedure, control) and economic (incentives) methods of avoiding or overcoming such conflicts are aggravated by the bounded rationality of actors under conditions of informational, personal, and situational uncertainty and imperfect information. Shared moral values can make a contribution to the handling of conflict.

(ii) Dependency is a basic element in cooperative relationships. It arises from the fact that the success potential of actor A depends on the resources and behavior of actor B and vice versa. If resources were dependent but behavior-predictable, there would be no problem. If resources were independently controlled and behavior-unpredictable there would also be no problem. The problem consists in the exploitability of asymmetric dependencies between the actors by one of the actors via the collective cooperation rent that can be achieved only via this dependency. Shared moral values can make a contribution to containing opportunism.

(iii) Order is manifest in constitutions, standard operating procedures, management principles, guidelines, organizational charts, codes of ethics, ethics management systems, and implicit expectations of performance and behavior, all of which constitute the matrix of globally and locally effective governance structures. For this reason, cooperation projects can be described and analyzed as specific sets of rules and values. In doing so, we must distinguish between performance values (competence), interaction values (loyalty), and moral values (justice) that only together can enable economic cooperation of resource owners and that cannot be reduced to each other. Performance values, interaction values, and moral values form the basis of the two guiding values of firms as cooperation projects, i.e., the "willingness to cooperate" and the "capability to cooperate," and thus determine the number of the chances for cooperation a firm can attain.

(iv) Firms are communication systems. The significance of the role of formal and informal communication in production and cooperation has generated much organizational research in recent years.[19] For our topic it is important to note that firms are polylingual systems. Unlike the market, which has to code every event in prices in order to be able to communicate it, firms have to be able to simultaneously or selectively evaluate and process relevant events in many different "language games"—economy, technology, law, process, morality. The economic code—expenditure/return or cost/profit—has a lead function in the overall bundle of the polylingual resources of the firm when it comes to decisions; this reflects the fact that it is the market system that structures the environment of the firm. Firms are organizations of the economic system: everything relevant in firms has economic relevance or consequence. But not everything in the firm is economic.

We can draw three conclusions from the polylingual character of the firm. In the first place, firms have to build up a comprehensive incentive management that cannot be reduced to economic incentives.[20] In other words, moral values do matter. Secondly, an ethics that aims to achieve something in the firm can be incentive-sensitive and management-oriented without having to become economics. Thirdly, an ethics that seeks to protect itself against this and wants to be undertaken for its own sake is irrelevant in the real-life firms of the economy.

These conclusions follow from the polylingual character of economic cooperation projects, but they also have another basis. From an organizational point of view profits—as mentioned already—are not a maximization goal of firms as cooperation projects, but the inevitable limitation of the relevance of all language games in firms. In other words, profits are the most important, but not the only behavioral constraint of a firm. This methodological rearrangement of profit from a maximization function to a behavioral constraint is an immediate consequence of the rearrangement of the object of the discussion from "firms" to "governance structures for specific transactions." Whereas in the first case the focus of interest is the goal or purpose of the firm, in the second case the focus is on its capacity for adaptivity. A governance structure that would have "profit" as its only adaptive criterion would be inefficient with regard to its adaptive capability.

Moral Communication and Moral Incentives

We must now clarify the status of moral communication in firms. The "moral" does not structure the market environment of the firm, nor is it a behavioral constraint constituting the market. However, via the aspect of comprehensive incentive management and the polylingual character of organization, we have assigned it the status of a behavioral constraint and a resource for firms. Obviously it is relevant to take into account the management context and the way it functions when analyzing behavioral constraints and resources. But what is the role of moral communication in decisions of the firm as a cooperation project? In the economic literature this question often involves a focus on the social and informal character of moral rules and values.[21] These develop in an evolutionary way, exist in society, may well contain both threat and promise, and through these affect decisions of economic actors to a greater or lesser extent. We can accept this analysis, but we do not want to take on the implicit value-ethical interpretation of business ethics that comes with it. We prefer to focus on the ambiguity of evolutionary-derived and non-codified, that is, informal, social moral values. By doing so an interesting characteristic of moral values is exposed. Although in principle it is clear what is meant by moral values, in practice borders between the intended and the approved become fuzzy. Moral values are held in stock communicatively in society, but not in a form that is use-specific.[22] There is thus considerable demand for definition, control, and enforcement of those values that can be met on the level of persons, organizations, and social institutions. Personal societies such as ancient Europe found their moral base in the virtue of actors. Institutionalised societies such as modern Europe make use of specific governance structures for this purpose, e.g., the state or firms.

When firms design an explicit code of ethics,[23] they are attempting to transform moral ambiguity in their environment into organizational self-commitment by rules and values. Those codified rules and values then are firm-specific constitutional global governance structures, idiosyncratic moral resources, competences and capabilities of the organization.[24] From a transaction-cost economics perspective this represents an investment in "asset specificity,"[25] which I would designate "atmospheric specificity" for the execution of transactions. To the extent to which a firm invests in moral specificity and thus builds up a competency for the execution of transactions, it is committed to this investment. The factor-specific implications of moral communication in the firm are thus organizational identity as an economic and moral actor, transparency of claims to action and behavior, and the degree to which these are binding. Furthermore, the moral commitment involved is also an encouragement to a similar commitment on the part of organizational stakeholders (team members, customers, partners, suppliers). The ultimate intention is to attain stable behavioral expectations and control over the organizational and social environment of the firm by committing oneself and thus creating incentives for others to commit themselves as well. Self-commitment and commitment by others thus are the reasons for specific investments in the atmospheric parameters of a transaction.

At this point the significance of genuine moral incentives in polylingual organizations becomes obvious. Firms have economic incentives at their disposal, the relevance and effectiveness of which derive from the economic lead code of organizational systems. However, these have to be distinguished from moral incentives, which cannot be reduced to or transformed into economic incentives. But what do we know about moral incentives? In this investigation we implicitly distinguish between social, personal, and organizational moral incentives. Social moral incentives spring from enculturated moral convictions sanctioned by the majority of the members of society, which are thus intrinsically "intended." Virtues and notions of justice belong to this category. An example of personal moral incentives are lived virtues and credible role model behavior (moral character, charisma) by managers and leaders. Organizational moral incentives are, for instance, codes of ethics, ethics management systems, and ethics audit systems. Neither this characterization nor the examples cited are theoretically elaborated or complete. Their common characteristic, however, seems to be that their relevance depends on the fact that they are valued in themselves and because of their implications. It would be the task of a "theory of moral incentives"—which still needs to be written—to work out and account for these matters in detail.

We now proceed to investigate the specific efficiency of the governance mechanism of moral values. The investigation so far has led to the following conclusions: the economic lead code has a direct and long-acting effect on the cooperation rent achievable in firms via the expenditure/return and cost/profit conditions. The moral encoding works via organizational self-commitment (identity, transparency, binding nature) on the cooperation lead values "willingness to cooperate" and "capability to cooperate," and in this way on the cooperation chances of a firm. Moral self-commitment is activated selectively via reputation capital when transactions can affect this capital. This scheme explains firstly why governance ethics is not and should not be in demand by all firms; after all, manufacturers of screws have a different demand from social service providers. The scheme explains secondly why moral communication always carries a promise of performance that is contingent on self-commitment. We have already explained this in terms of the characteristics of firm- and transaction-specific investments in "atmosphere," but in this context we would like to point out that speech act theory in philosophy has arrived at similar results, in that it has shown that moral communication does have a performative character.[26] Those who talk about morality or codify moral values do not talk about facts but implicitly promise performance. Firms that have codes of ethics are not making statements about existent facts, but promising self-commitment to and self-organization of a performance promise. A firm thus commits itself through its moral communication and the communication's organization in a specific fashion, and thus creates behavioral expectations and behavioral standards for itself and others. If these expectations are disappointed this leads not only to the moral disregard of the collective actors, but also to costs due to loss of reputation or motivation or to political intervention. The reduction of cooperation chances has immediate effects on the level of the cooperation rent attainable.

Economic and moral values and incentives thus, in their own distinctively specifiable ways, have an effect on the willingness to cooperate, the capability to cooperate, and the cooperation chances of a firm. Economic and moral values and incentives lose their respective identities only in the cooperation rent.

Definition of Governance Ethics

The differentiation of form- and process-determination of the firm and the ensuing differentiation of the form of the firm in the contract- and organizational relations of a cooperation project has enabled us to develop a view of business ethics on the basis of the governance characteristics of the firm itself. Business ethics, seen systemically, is neither external correction of negative external effects nor external enlightenment of economic stubbornness and blindness. It is rather a constitutive element of the firm itself, mediated by rules and values, governance ethics, and as such it is in every sense part of the economic problem of making possible the cooperation of self-interested actors in and via firms. "In every sense" implies that the economic and organizational relevance of the moral factor parallels its embeddedness in the economic and organizational context.

In conclusion we would like to draw consequences from the theoretical viewpoint outlined here which may be helpful in defining the role of an institutionalist business ethics as governance ethics.

1. The elements of governance ethics are the moral resources and behavioral constraints and extensions deriving from organizational rules and values as well as their communication in and via cooperation projects. Accordingly, it is not the notion of action, but of governance which is its point of reflexion. Governance structures are sets or matrices of communicated formal and informal rules and values that constitute the cooperative actor as constraints and furnish him or her with explicit and implicit rules of the game for contractual and organizational relations for the realisation of specific transactions.
2. Analytically, governance ethics investigates those global and local, formal and informal structures of a firm that constitute and transaction-specifically govern the moral behavior of the individual and collective actors in an organization (intrafirm-relations), between organizations (interfirm-relations), and between organizations and society (extrafirm-relations). The unit of analysis is thus a specific transaction in the context of and in its interaction with the governance structures surrounding it.
3. Methodologically, business ethics compares different structures for the governance of separate economic transactions; it asks which moral and immoral rules; values and incentives they reflect and which kind of economic behavior they reward. It explains the presence, relevance, and the change of moral preferences in the context of the economic and moral incentive structure of a given organization and its economic and social environment. Business ethics as governance ethics thus is a comparative research program.

4. In normative terms business ethics as governance ethics proposes the development and implementation of such ethical systems (e.g., ethics management systems, ethics audit systems[27]) in and by way of organizations. Those organizations—as governance structures for transactions—foster the willingness to cooperate, the capability to cooperate, and the cooperation chances of economic actors. It does this by creating economic and moral certainty of expectations through providing self-commitment and indirect commitment of others. What is prioritised here is not profit maximization, but rents from the economizing of cooperation.

5. In conclusion: the governance ethics of the firm is the theory of the comparative analysis of a moral-sensitive design and communication of governance structures for specific economic transactions via cooperation.

Notes

1. For the translation of this essay I wish to thank Markus Becker. The original German term is *Unternehmensethik*, which carries the connotation of "corporate ethics."

2. Cf. Donaldson (1982), French (1984), Donaldson/Werhane (1988), Werhane (1985).

3. This research program was initiated by Williamson. For the interdisciplinary intentions connected to it cf. for example Williamson (1990, 1993). In this paper we will make use of contract-based, transaction-cost-based, and organizational (resource-based, economics of competencies; cf. Dosi/Teece 1998; Teece/Pisano/Shuen 1997) considerations in explaining the role of "soft factors" (culture, communication, morality) in firms. With this, we are continuing our efforts of building an economic theory which is integrating these "soft factors" without dissolving them in the process. Cf. Wieland 1996a.

4. Cf. Williamson 1985, and the 1996 volume edited by Williamson with the telling title *The Mechanisms of Governance*.

5. Contemporary philosophy/ethics has never heard of organization, or at best accepts it as a peripheral phenomenon amongst several other issues. This ignorance as to a central societal actor and addressee of ethical claims is one of the conceptual problems of applied ethics that is blocking its theoretical development in a major way.

6. Cf. Vanberg 1992 and Gifford 1991. For the distinction of the notions of system, institution, and organization cf. Wieland 1997, pp. 62ff. It was Schmoller who made the first institutionalist inspired proposition for a distinction between institution and organization. Whereas institution for him is "the firm container of the action of generations" (Schmoller 1901, p. 61), organization is "the personal side of the institution" (ibid). Organizations are combinations of commodities and persons for a specific purpose. In this distinction, all the problems of contemporary institutionalist theory are already present, i.e., a static notion of institutions and a neglect of the normativity of organizations.

7. Cf. Williamson 1975.

8. In our understanding this insight presents a substantial contribution of German institutionalism to the theory of the firm. Cf. only Sombart (1902–1927/1987, pp. 101ff.), where he states that "the elevation of an independent economic organism over the individual economic human beings is guaranteeing its

continual existence over time." Barnard (1938/1968) has shown in systems theoretic terms why precisely it is the exclusion of actors that represents the essence of the firm.

9. This, by the way, is one of the weaknesses of resource based organization theory. It does not treat the process of the constitution of the firm. At this point, contract-based theories are indispensable.

10. For the connection between the management of morality and stakeholders cf. Donaldson/Preston 1995.

11. For an early contribution to that insight cf. Schmoller (1901, pp. 414, 428f, 453). For the relevance of a differentiation of various types of contracts for a theory of the firm cf. Williamson 1991.

12. Of course the resignation from the profit motive is not a new idea, but commences with the development of an independent theory of the firm, independent of the Walrasian equilibrium model and price theory. For this part of the history of ideas cf. the interesting investigation by Krafft/Ravix (1998).

13. Shirking respectively the trade off between performance and control are the central problem of that branch of the theory of the firm that is oriented towards property rights. The classical text is Alchian/Demsetz 1972. However, they already emphasize the potential importance of moral values for the containing of shirking.

14. Cf. Dosi/Teece 1998. They do not take into consideration such a reformulation. They distinguish between theories of firms as production function, as optimal contract, and as organization. As long as this tripartite distinction will remain, there indeed is not much hope for theoretical integration. But contract theories have more to offer than optimal contracts. The theories of incomplete and implicit contracts (cf. Wieland 1996a, pp. 120ff., 158ff.) open the possibility of treating organizational phenomena in organizational terms, and to their own advantage.

15. For an overview cf. Bull 1983.

16. In Wieland 1998 we have pointed out the central sociological and managerial importance of cooperation and a theoretical notion capturing this aspect. This importance forms the basis for the arguments developed here.

17. Hobbes (1651/1914, pp. 68ff.) has described this particularity of contractual cooperation as a game-theoretic dilemma, the only escape from which is represented by rational calculation of advantage plus the power of the state to enforce plus implicit contracts (the covenant in the contract).

18. For the economics of atmosphere cf. Wieland 1996b and the literature referenced there.

19. Cf. Casson 1997 as well as Wieland 1999.

20. This connection has been clear since Xenophon, who in his *Oikonomikos* is building his human resource management and development theory for the *oikos* on this foundation. Cf. Wieland 1989, pp. 196ff.

21. This, by the way, is true for Williamson as well (1985, pp. 44, 271). In this way he is losing the option of a theory-endogenous parameter against opportunism.

22. The ancient Europe has attempted to cope with this characteristic of social moral communication by casuistry with approved exceptions. In functionally differentiated and abstract societies, however, the experience that now exceptions are more or less the rule has led to the situation that moral values have to be kept in stock in an abstractly justified way.

23. For this phenomenon cf. Weaver 1993 as well as Wieland 2001.

24. Cf. the already mentioned paper by Dosi/Teece (1998) as well as Barney 1991.

25. Cf. Williamson 1985, pp. 84ff., which distinguished site specificity, physical assets, human assets, and dedicated assets specificity. We propose an extension of this distinction to the notion of atmospheric specificity. In this way soft factors like culture, communication, and morals can be integrated into the theoretical framework of transaction cost theory.

26. Cf. in particular Searle 1969, chap. 8, and for the pertaining condition of sincerity Searle 1979, pp. 21ff.

27. Cf. the contributions of Center for Business Ethics (1992), Paine (1994), and Weaver/Trevino/Cochran (1999).

Ian Maitland

 **NO**

Distributive Justice in Firms: Do the Rules of Corporate Governance Matter?

Can we achieve greater fairness by reforming the corporation? Some recent progressive critics of the corporation argue that it is possible to achieve greater social justice both inside and outside the corporation by simply rewriting or reinterpreting corporate rules to favor non-stockholders over stockholders. But the progressive program for reforming the corporation rests on a critical assumption, which I challenge in this [selection],[1] namely that the rules of the corporation matter, so that changing them can effect a lasting redistribution of wealth from stockholders to non-stockholders (for convenience I will refer to non-stockholders as "stakeholders"[2]). This [selection] uses a critique of the progressive reform program to make the case that the rules of the corporation are distributively neutral. The corporation as we know it isn't rigged against stakeholders, and changing its rules will not improve the bargaining power of stakeholders. However, the [selection] will show that while the rules may be epiphenomenal from the standpoint of distributive justice, they can have substantial impacts on the corporation's efficiency. As a result, the proposed reforms of the corporation may hurt its capacity to generate benefits for all the parties concerned.

The Progressive Program for Reforming the Corporation

This [selection] examines some recent "progressive" scholarship on the corporation and proposals for its reform.[3] In many respects, the progressive reformers advocate a model of the corporation strikingly similar to what business ethicists call the "stakeholder corporation." They favor rewriting the rules that govern the relations between stockholders and stakeholders to eliminate what they see as built-in biases in favor of stockholders. And they propose to use reform of the corporation as a vehicle for greater social justice in the work place and the marketplace. They view the rules of a corporation simultaneously as an embodiment of capitalist privilege and as a potential point of leverage for redistributing wealth and power.[4]

It is a key premise of the progressive critique of the corporation that its rules are not neutral between the different constituencies of the corporation. Thus David Millon argues that the important rules that govern the relations between stockholders and stakeholders are systematically biased in favor of stockholders. The rules of the corporation do not simply mirror background inequalities in society but actually create and reinforce those inequalities. As Joseph Singer puts it, "[t]he current legal rules created that imbalance of power [between workers and corporations in the market], and they can be altered to equalize it."[5]

Some of these rules are rules of corporate law, and some are not. As examples of the former, Millon cites voting rights in the corporation, limited liability, and management's fiduciary duty to run the corporation in the exclusive interest of stockholders (the "stockholder primacy principle"). Employment-at-will, on the other hand, is a common law doctrine. All of these rules confer powers and immunities on stockholders while imposing disadvantages on stakeholders or exposing them to certain contingencies or costs.

However, this non-neutrality cuts both ways. If the rules of the corporation are rigged in favor of stockholders, then that bias can be eliminated by simply changing the rules. But why stop there? The reformers want to structure the rules of the corporation to advance the progressive agenda of redistributing power and wealth in the broader society. If the relative power of stockholders and stakeholders is a function (in part) of the current legal rules, then those rules can be rewritten to redress that imbalance or even to tip the scales in favor of stakeholders.

> To a large extent, it is contract and property law that will determine [the parties'] relative bargaining power. If we want to protect the most vulnerable party to the relationship in times of economic stress, we have no alternative but to make them less vulnerable. This means systematically interpreting and changing property and contract principles in ways that effectively redistribute power and wealth to workers.[6]

In summary, the progressives claim that rules matter. Accordingly, the rules furnish a point of leverage for altering the outcomes of the corporation so that they favor stakeholder groups and thereby redistributing power and wealth in society.

Neutrality Thesis

In opposition to the progressive view, this [selection] argues that the rules don't matter. The null hypothesis, or neutrality thesis, proposed here, is that the corporation is distributively neutral. Appearances notwithstanding, the rules don't systematically favor stockholders, and they cannot be manipulated so as to favor stakeholder groups like employees. The corollary is that proposals to change the rules to favor stakeholders will not have any systematic effect on the distributive impacts of the corporation.

This does not mean that existing outcomes are in some way equitable or in conformity with distributive justice. It is simply to say that the rules are neutral, in the sense that they passively pass along or mirror pre-existing inequalities of resources (where resources are to be broadly conceived as wealth, energy, skill, cunning, etc.).

This [essay] does not present a fully rounded or comprehensive account of the progressive critique of the corporation but instead focuses on certain propositions concerning the impact of corporate rules on distributive justice inside the corporation.

The Rules of Corporate Governance

The case for the neutrality of the corporation is rooted in the observation that the rules of corporate governance are essentially voluntary. This claim may seem odd, given the fact that the rules are prescribed by law. But, although we refer to "corporate law," as if the rules were commanded by legislatures or by common law, the reality is that the rules of the corporation are more accurately viewed as being self-imposed. The law does not mandate the rules. Instead, it provides a framework or template of "default" rules, which the parties or groups making up the corporation (stockholders, employees, etc.) remain free to modify or waive by agreement.

Thus nothing in the law stops corporations from accepting unlimited liability for any debts they may incur or from agreeing to override the law's presumption of at-will employment. Nor does the law prevent representatives of employees from sitting on the board of the corporation or from bargaining for the right to have management owe them fiduciary duties. Many progressive scholars concede this point. Millon notes that, "It is true that . . . the affected parties can reverse the assignment of benefit and burden specified by the rule should they choose to do so. Thus, of course, a creditor can bargain for unlimited stockholder liability or for voting rights."[7] Another critic of the corporation, Margaret Blair, notes that, "[b]ecause U.S. corporation law, contract law, and securities law readily accommodate most experiments in new organizational forms, many new governance structures are emerging on their own. This is one of the strengths of the U.S. system."[8]

If the rules are voluntary, then what purpose is served by state law codes or common law rules of corporate governance? The standard answer is that such laws reduce the costs of contracting (or "transaction costs") for the parties by providing a standard contract for governing their relations. That way the parties do not need to re-invent the corporation by explicitly negotiating the whole set of rules from scratch. "[S]hareholders typically contract with management by entering into the standard-form agreement applied by the relevant state law code and corpus of common law. This 'off-the-rack' contract includes a collection of terms that stockholders would typically prefer, so including them greatly reduces transaction costs."[9] Many (though not all) can be modified by express contract if the stockholders so choose.

The fact that the corporate form of organization—with its familiar structure of entitlements and obligations—is the dominant one in our economy may leave the impression that it is somehow mandatory. But the law provides other organizational forms to choose from. These include sole proprietorships, partnerships, cooperatives, trusts, and non-firm relational contracts, such as franchises and long-term supply contracts. In addition, there is an almost infinite variety of arrangements that the parties might conceivably fashion by agreement. Of course, not only are the parties free to take or leave the rules provided by the law, but also nothing prevents them from choosing not to contract with a corporation at all, or from limiting their business to other types of business organization.[10] On this account, then, the corporation is essentially a voluntary association. It exists only because the parties that make it up choose it as a means of governing their relationships.

If the corporation is voluntary, why would some groups agree to terms that seem so clearly inequitable? Why would employees accept, say, rules providing for employment at will or exclusion from voting rights in the corporation? Answers to this question make up the heart of the financial or contractarian theory of the firm developed by Fama and Jensen and others.[11] I won't try to summarize that extensive literature here. But the gist of it is that rights in the firm (say, voting rights) go to the highest bidders. That leaves the question of why stockholders would consistently outbid other groups for management's fiduciary loyalty and for voting control. Contractarian theorists explain that stockholders have the greatest stake in the outcome of corporate decision making because they occupy a peculiarly vulnerable position in the corporation. As "residual claimants" they differ from other groups in that they are not entitled to a guaranteed return. Their share is what is left over (if anything) after every other groups' contractually specified claims have been met. That gives stockholders a special interest in the efficient management of the corporation. If efficiency is maximized, then, over the long run, the corporation is better able to provide benefits for all participants.

On this view of the firm, the distribution of rights in the corporation is the outcome of bargaining between the different groups or parties. Since nothing in the law bars it, employees might (and indeed frequently do) contract for protection from arbitrary dismissal. But they have to "buy" that protection with lower wages. Conversely, if stockholders value the right to lay off employees at will more than employees value their job security, they may buy that right with higher wages.

Interestingly, the progressive scholars largely accept the contractarian account of the corporation. Nevertheless they argue that the corporation is rigged against stakeholders. They charge that the corporation does not merely reproduce existing imbalances of social power and wealth but creates and reinforces them. This charge is difficult (if not impossible) to reconcile with the contractarian view of the firm as a voluntary association. It would mean that stakeholders are consistently duped or manipulated by stockholders into accepting bargains that are inferior to the ones they could have achieved.

The thesis of this [selection] is that the rules of the corporation are distributively neutral. If that is the case, then we should observe two things: (a) that existing rules don't discriminate against stakeholders, and (b) that proposed changes in the rules won't make non-stockholders better off. The next section examines specific rules and proposed changes to those rules in order to see if these two predictions hold.

Progressive Proposals for Changing the Rules of the Corporation

Extending Fiduciary Duties

One perennially popular rule change would extend management's fiduciary duties to other parties, like employees. Management would no longer operate the corporation in the exclusive interests of the stockholders but would be required by law to balance the interests of stockholders with those of employees and other stakeholders.[12]

What would be the distributive effects of such a rule change? There could be a once-for-all expropriation of current stockholders. That is, if the law was introduced, enacted, and signed overnight, stockholders would wake up the next day to find that they were no longer the sole beneficiaries of management's fiduciary obligations. They would (literally) be poorer because the anticipated lower returns and increased risk would be reflected in a lower stock market valuation of their shares.

But any benefit to employees would be short-lived as investors would hesitate to buy corporations' shares, would hold off investing, and/or would demand a premium to reflect the added risk and lower return. Investors cannot be compelled to supply capital to American corporations. They can instead buy real estate, gold, Treasury bonds or shares in Japanese corporations, or they can invest in orchards,[13] to mention a few examples. If the risk-adjusted return from owning shares in U.S. corporations falls below that from alternative investments, then we should expect a flight of capital to alternative investments.[14]

In such circumstances, in order to attract the capital necessary to finance their operations, corporations would be forced to take steps to increase the prospective return to stockholders. That would likely require cutting wages, raising prices, laying off workers, etc. In short, it would require changes that would defeat the purpose of changing the fiduciary rule in the first place. Of course, those actions might be complicated—if not barred altogether—by management's new fiduciary duties to stakeholders. In that case, corporations might simply be unable to raise new capital. In due course, this would mean that corporations would find it difficult to expand their operations, there would be a drastic reduction in business start-ups relying on equity capital, and employment would suffer. All the parties to the corporation would be losers from the resulting economic disruptions.[15]

Employment-at-Will

David Millon argues that the employment-at-will rule favors stockholders over employees. It "confers freedom of action on stockholders while imposing costs on employees that would not be present if the default rule were a presumption of employment security."[16] Millon admits that, like other corporate rules, the employment-at-will rule is an optional or default rule, but he claims that even "mere" default rules have distributive consequences. Thus, by replacing the employment-at-will rule by an employment-security rule, we can increase the bargaining leverage of employees and enable them to capture a greater share of the benefits of the corporation. If we reverse the existing biases, "starting points will differ, and outcomes therefore will too."[17]

According to Millon, "a rule like the employment-at-will doctrine makes stockholders wealthier than an employment-security doctrine would." Under employment-at-will, if employees want protection against arbitrary dismissal, they have to *pay* stockholders for it. By contrast, if the rule were reversed, "stockholders would either have to compensate employees following termination of employment or would have to bribe them into giving up a property right in their job. The bias . . . has the potential to affect significantly the respective wealth of stockholders and stakeholders."[18]

Employees are also disadvantaged by the employment-at-will rule in cases where transaction costs prevent the parties from agreeing on trading a wage reduction for job security. There may be substantial, and sometimes prohibitive, costs associated with negotiating and drafting a satisfactory agreement. These "transaction costs" may prevent employees from reaching an agreement even if both sides would gain from it. In such a case, the default rule, viz., employment-at-will, will hold, and employees will find themselves stuck with the *status quo,* namely no job protection.

But Millon's scenario can't withstand close scrutiny. For simplicity, suppose that there are two types of firms, ones that provide job security to their employees and ones that do not. Under an employment-at-will regime, it is reasonable to assume that, other things (like employee characteristics) equal, firms that provide job security pay lower wages than firms that do not. (Otherwise, firms providing job security would have higher labor costs and/or risks which would over time lead to their failure).

Now suppose that we adopt Millon's proposal to replace employment-at-will with employment security as our default rule. Under the new rule, firms that don't provide job security will be required to start doing so *or* to compensate their employees for giving up their right to job security. (Firms that already provide job security will be unaffected.) Recall, however, that firms without job security were *already* paying higher wages. As a result of the rule change, such firms will be faced with a choice between (a) providing job security (*and* continuing to pay the higher wage) or (b) giving employees an additional wage increase (on top of the original premium they enjoy) in return for the right to dismiss at will. In either case, such firms will have unsustainably higher labor costs. Consequently, they will be forced to reduce wages to competitive levels or to go out of business. In either case, of course, there will be no lasting redistribution of wealth from stockholders to employees.

However, while the distributive effect of the initial default rules will be nonexistent or trivial, the real-world efficiency effects might be substantial. By "real-world," I mean that we reintroduce transaction costs into the example. Suppose employees value employment-security guarantees less than stockholders disvalue them, then a rule that provides for employment-security will—in the presence of significant transaction costs—make both stockholders and employees worse off. If the parties are unable to reach an agreement to override the employment-security guarantees in exchange for higher wages, then they will both be poorer than if the rule had been employment-at-will.

This example illustrates why (as economists urge) it is mutually beneficial if default rules are set to reflect the outcomes that the parties *would have* (but for transaction costs) agreed on. That way they can help the parties economize on transaction costs "by supplying standard contract terms the parties would otherwise have to adopt by [expensive] express agreement."[19] In other words, Millon's proposal, by trying to correct an imaginary bias in the rules, will likely make it more difficult for parties to reach a mutually advantageous bargain. As a result, the proposal to flip the rules so that they favor stakeholders may actually wind up hurting the very people it is intended to help.[20]

Limited Liability

Millon also charges that limited liability "benefit[s] stockholders while having a correspondingly negative effect on creditors, who . . . lose a degree of financial security that a rule of unlimited liability would otherwise provide."[21] The rule "limit[s] stockholders' liability to corporate creditors to their capital contribution, leaving creditors to bear the risk of corporate insolvency."[22]

That account is accurate as far as it goes. But Millon is mistaken in thinking that limited liability has any distributive implications. That is because, as Posner has pointed out, creditors are paid to bear this risk. "The lender is fully compensated for the risk of default by the higher interest rate that the corporation must pay lenders by virtue of its limited liability."[23] Furthermore, creditors are "also free to insist as a condition of making the loan that the stockholders personally guarantee the corporation's debts, or insert in the loan agreement other provisions limiting the lender's risk. Any resulting reduction in the risk of default will of course reduce the interest rate."[24]

One risk facing creditors is the possibility of nonpayment because of limited liability. Another risk, according to Easterbrook and Fischel, is the "prospect, common to all debtor-creditor relations, that after the terms of the transaction are set the debtor will take increased risk, to the detriment of the lender."[25] However, as they go on to note,

> As long as these risks are known, the firm pays for the freedom to engage in risky activities. Any creditor can get the risk-free rate by investing in T-bills or some low-risk substitute. The firm must offer a better risk-return combination to attract investment. If it cannot make credible promises to refrain from taking on excessive risks, it must pay higher interest rates (or, when the creditors are employees and trade creditors, higher prices for the work or goods delivered on credit). Although managers may change the riskiness of the firm after borrowing, debt must be repaid; this drives the firm back to the credit market, where it must pay a rate of interest appropriate to the soundness and risk of its current projects. . . . Voluntary creditors receive compensation in advance for the chance that

the firm will step up the risk of its projects and later be unable to meet its obligations.[26]

Of course, creditors, too, enjoy limited liability. What is more, in the event of bankruptcy their claims on the corporation's assets outrank the claims of stockholders. Finally, lenders are not compelled to extend credit to the corporation. If limited liability is such a bargain, they are free to use their funds to purchase stock in the corporation instead.

Legal Obligation Arising out of Interdependence

Another proposed reform would change the rules of the corporation to recognize a legally enforceable right to job security arising out of longstanding and/or dependent relationships. Marleen O'Connor advocates that the courts should recognize a right to job security in cases of long-run employment. Joseph Singer proposes that the courts should recognize employees' property rights in longstanding relationships on which they have come to depend. He says "It is morally wrong for the owner to allow a relationship of dependence to be established and then cut off the dependent party."[27]

What would be the distributional impacts of such a rule change? Stockholders would likely be able to defeat or circumvent such a rule or, failing that, shift its cost back to employees. In that event, employees would find themselves forced to purchase a right (job security or severance pay) which they value less than what they would give up (wages and employment opportunities) in exchange for it.[28]

The set of possible responses by stockholders is limited only by the imagination. One obvious move would be to write into all employment contracts a disclaimer by which employees expressly waived their right to such job protection. Of course, the courts might choose to ignore or override such disclaimers.[29] That would still leave stockholders with many options which they might use singly or in combination to get around the rule.

If courts chose to ignore waivers of job security, then stockholders' specific responses would depend on how the rule was framed or interpreted. If courts relied on employees' length of service to determine whether they were owed job security, then the rule would perversely encourage stockholders to dismiss employees shortly before their claims to job security vested. Alternatively, if the courts relied on some measure of dependency or intimacy, stockholders might avoid such relationships with their employees.

Alternatively corporations might develop a two-tier work force with a core of highly skilled workers (who would enjoy job security) and a peripheral floating population of casual or temporary or contract workers (without job security).[30] Only the first would qualify for the legal privileges that come with a long-term relationship with the corporation. In any case, corporations would be cautious about expanding employment because of the legal barriers in the way of lay-offs in the event of a downturn in business. Therefore they would likely respond to increased demand for their products by increasing overtime, speeding up the line or working employees more intensively.

Another possibility is that stockholders might try to offset the expected costs of job security by reducing wages or (if that was impractical) by granting smaller wage increases and/or cutting back on any discretionary benefits (subsidized lunches or parking, pension contributions, etc.). If payroll costs could not be stabilized in this way, stockholders would shift to more capital-intensive production methods, and would reduce employment or increase it more gradually.[31] If the real wages of workers were increased by the implicit cost of greater job security, the stockholders would find it unprofitable to hire "marginal" workers because the value of their marginal product would be less than the cost of employing them.

In the short run, it might be possible for stockholders to pay the higher real wages and pass their cost along to consumers in the form of higher product prices. However, such price increases would not be sustainable in the long run. Of course, any reduced demand as a result of the price increases would mean lower employment. If the stockholders found themselves unable to pass the increased real wages along to consumers or employees, the resulting lower rates of return would eventually cause firms to exit the industry and/or would reduce the flow of investment capital to the industry, thus limiting employment growth. If companies expect to face heavy costs if they have to close a plant, they are going to be more reluctant to open new plants, knowing that the penalty for misjudging the market will be more severe.

One of the ironies of such a rule is that it would impose an implicit "tax" on the very behaviors we would generally wish to encourage—long-term employment relationships, the hiring of marginal workers, and so on. In self-defense, stockholders would avoid relationships with employees that might lock them into an onerous commitment.

Employee Rights in Cases of Plant Closure

The same objections apply to Joseph Singer's proposal to rewrite the rules to give employees a right to purchase their plant for its "fair market value" in the event that the stockholders declare their intention to close it down.

Singer acknowledges that employees might not choose to exercise their right, under such a rule, to buy their plant and keep it in operation. But he says that the rule would be a useful bargaining chip for employees: "[I]f we . . . give workers a right to assert an ownership interest in the plant when the company wants to close it or when the company fails to manage the plant well, then the company would have to offer the workers more than the workers would ask to give up this right. Because the workers would *own* this right, their wealth would be dramatically higher than if the company had the legal liberty to destroy the plant."[32]

As I have noted, employees would get the right to purchase the plant at its "fair market value." That is what Singer says, but it doesn't seem to be what he means. Nothing in the current rules stops employees from banding together and offering to buy the plant. If their bid is higher than the next best alternative bid, then stockholders will presumably accept their offer. That is, employees appear already to enjoy the right that Singer wants to confer on them. What's more, if the employees acquire the plant at its market value, there is no transfer of wealth.

A transfer of wealth from stockholders to employees would happen only if the rules permitted employees to buy the plant at *less* than its market value. But a rule that permitted employees to buy the plant at less than what other bidders might pay for it would predictably lead stockholders to take certain actions in their self-defense.[33] Employees would presumably be paid less than they would absent the law. Stockholders would in effect withhold an implicit insurance "premium" from each worker's wage. They might attempt to mitigate the possible additional expense of closure by renting rather than buying plant and equipment. Macey's observations on compulsory plant closing notification apply *a fortiori* to Singer's rule. He says that "if a legislature unilaterally gives rank-and-file workers a right to prior notification of a layoff or a plant closing, the workers will benefit only if, to retain that right, they will not have to give up something worth more than the right itself. The price of the forced 'purchase' of a right to notification may take the form of lower wages, reduced pension benefits, or a reduction in the overall size of the work force."[34]

That is not all. The added difficulty or expense of closing down a money-losing plant would likely make corporations more wary of opening new plants in the first place—especially in marginal areas where alternative employment opportunities are few. As Richard McKenzie has said, restrictions on plant closings are restrictions on plant openings.[35]

In summary, Singer's rule would not have any obvious redistributive effects. But, once again, it might worsen the lot of *both* stockholders and stakeholders by putting obstacles in the way of their agreeing on the optimal contract terms.

Courts as Guardians of Employees' Interests

Some progressive critics of the corporation suggest that the courts should aggressively interpret the law in favor of stakeholders. Singer says that "means systematically interpreting and changing property and contract principles in ways that effectively redistribute power and wealth to workers."[36] O'Connor favors using an expansive interpretation of management's fiduciary duty to tip the scales in favor of the vulnerable. She says that the "courts can use the fiduciary duty to prevent opportunistic behavior even where the terms of the contract explicitly allow the stronger party to engage in this type of conduct."[37] She would have courts to set aside contracts or override contract terms on grounds of distributive justice or "common morality." Although O'Connor invokes supposed "implicit contracts" between stockholders and employees, it is clear that she intends the courts to disregard the actual intentions of the parties (whether express or implicit). The content of the corporations' duties to employees would no longer be defined by the parties' explicit or implicit agreements but by some external standard of social justice or the conscience of the court.

But it is doubtful whether such judicial activism could actually help stakeholders vis-à-vis stockholders. Once again, the crucial point is that investors are not compelled to invest their capital in corporations. If the courts deliberately tilted in favor of stakeholders, then to attract equity capital stakeholders would have to try to devise safeguards to reassure investors.

It is impossible to imagine exactly what forms such safeguards might take. If investors anticipate that the courts will systematically discriminate against them, and disregard the agreements they strike with stakeholders, then they have various (non-mutually exclusive) options. First, they might demand compensation from stakeholders for the additional risk they would have to bear. Second, they might insist on bypassing the courts and resolving their disputes by means of arbitration. (There would be an incentive for workers to band together in "firms" which would seek to acquire a reputation for *not* resorting to the courts in order to opportunistically renege on their agreements with stockholders. That reputation would permit them to lower the cost of capital to themselves.) Third, if it is too costly or impractical for investors to protect themselves by these means (or others), they might simply decide that it is pointless to invest in the stock of U.S. corporations. In that case, all the parties would forgo the benefits that the corporation might have created.

The point is that stockholders and stakeholders alike *need* the courts as a guarantor and/or impartial arbiter of their agreements with one another. Otherwise those (mutually advantageous) agreements may be too risky to enter into in the first place. Consequently, both sides are the losers when the courts define their mission as achieving their own conceptions of social justice in place of giving effect to the intent of the parties. As Easterbrook and Fischel have noted, "future contracting parties, viewing the court's selective enforcement of the present contract, will try to take steps to avoid the disappointment of having their contract selectively enforced. But these steps will cause the parties to incur additional contracting costs, additional over which they would be if the act simply enforced perfect contracts."[38]

Conclusion: How Liberty Upsets Patterns

This [selection] has shown that, on close examination, many corporate rules that appear to be biased in favor of stockholders prove to be neutral and nondiscriminatory. That should not come as a surprise since the rules are essentially voluntary. What would have been surprising would have been the discovery that parties continued to do business with the corporation on terms that are manifestly disadvantageous.

Moreover, precisely because the corporation is a voluntary association, an externally mandated rule change that is intended to achieve greater distributive justice is bound to fail. The parties themselves, including the supposed beneficiaries of the rule, are likely to collude to defeat it, because they all have a stake in maintaining the corporation as a going concern. A rule change that redistributes benefits and costs among the parties without regard to their contributions jeopardizes the carefully constructed bargain on which the corporation is based. If the party that loses from the rule change is not compensated for its loss, then its contribution to the corporation will exceed its benefits, and it will look outside the corporation for returns commensurate with its contribution. Meanwhile, the beneficiary of the rule change will enjoy benefits that exceed its contribution, and it will have to compensate the loser(s) from the rule change in order to retain its cooperation.

Contractarian theorists call the firm a nexus of contracts. If the totality of contracts that make up the corporation (including mandated contract terms or rules) does not accurately value the contributions made respectively by employees, creditors, suppliers, etc. then it is likely to be unstable. In that case, the rules of the corporation cannot be rigged to favor stockholders—or to favor stakeholders either. Therefore the rules can't furnish the point of leverage the progressive reformers of the corporation want in order to implement their program of social reform.

Notes

1. I would like to thank Thomas L. Carson, Alexei Marcoux and Patricia H. Werhane for their comments on an earlier draft of this paper.

2. Strictly, of course, stockholders are stakeholders too, along with employees, customers, vendors, lenders, and, sometimes, local communities.

3. Some of this work is usefully collected in Lawrence E. Mitchell, ed., *Progressive Corporate Law* (Boulder, Col.: Westview Press, 1995). See also Amitai Etzioni, "A Communitarian Note on Stakeholder Theory," *Business Ethics Quarterly* 8 (1998): 679–691.

4. Stakeholder theories also invoke distributive justice. See Thomas Donaldson and L. E. Preston, "The Stakeholder Theory of the Corporation: Concepts, Evidence, and Implications," *Academy of Management Review* 20 (1995): 84.

5. Joseph William Singer, "The Reliance Interest in Property," *Stanford Law Review* 40 (1983): 729.

6. Singer, "Reliance Interest," p. 723.

7. David Millon, "Communitarianism in Corporate Law: Foundations and Law Reform Strategies," in Mitchell, *Progressive Corporate Law,* p. 24.

8. Margaret M. Blair, *Ownership and Control* (Washington, D.C.: Brookings, 1995), p. 277.

9. Millon, "Communitarianism," p. 3.

10. "[N]o one is forced to use the corporate form of organization. . . . Thus, we do not observe all economic activity being carried on through one type of economic activity. Instead, we observe millions of organizations of many types, sizes, and structures" (Henry N. Butler and Larry E. Ribstein, *The Corporation and the Constitution* [Washington, D.C.: AEI Press, 1995], p. 4).

11. Eugene F. Fama and Michael C. Jensen, "Separation of Ownership and Control," *Journal of Law and Economics* 26 (1983): 301–325; Michael C. Jensen and William H. Meckling, "Theory of the Firm: Managerial Behavior, Agency Costs and Ownership Structure," *Journal of Financial Economics* 3 (1976): 305–360. See also Frank H. Easterbrook and Daniel R. Fischel, *The Economic Structure of Corporate Law* (Cambridge, Mass.: Harvard University Press, 1991).

12. Kenneth E. Goodpaster terms this a "multi-fiduciary" theory of managerial responsibility in "Business Ethics and Stakeholder Analysis," *Business Ethics Quarterly* 1 (1991): 53–73. See also Etzioni: "The stakeholder argument . . . accepts the legitimacy of the claim that shareholders have . . . rights and entitlements, but maintains that the same basic claim should be extended to all those

who invest in the corporation. This often includes employees (especially those who worked for a corporation for many years and loyally); the community . . . ; creditors . . . ; and, under some conditions, clients" (Etzioni, "Stakeholder Theory," p. 682, emphasis omitted); and John Orlando, "The Fourth Wave: The Ethics of Corporate Downsizing," *Business Ethics Quarterly* 9 (1999): 295–313.

13. "When we adjust for the risks involved and for various other factors that influence the return to an activity, we see that the returns most firms earn are not excessive compared to what the same resources could have earned in such manifestly non-exploitative alternatives as tree growing" (Robert Frank, *Choosing the Right Pond* [New York: Oxford University Press, 1985], p. 39). See also Easterbrook and Fischel, *Corporate Law,* p. 213.

14. This would not take the form of a "capital strike," as suggested by Lindblom, but would be the result of uncoordinated actions of millions of investors each acting in rational self-defense (Charles E. Lindblom, *Politics and Markets* [New York: Basic, 1977]).

15. The cost of the rule change would be borne by its beneficiaries. "Any legal regime that 'protects' workers by making them the 'beneficiaries' of fiduciary duties will, by definition, make those same workers less valuable (in monetary terms) to their employers. . . . Since workers generally prefer to receive compensation in the form of cash wages rather than in other ways, even the workers themselves will prefer that fiduciary duties not be imposed on employers since such duties will, at the margin, result in lower cash compensation to workers" (Jonathan R. Macey, "An economic analysis of the various rationales for making shareholders the exclusive beneficiaries of corporate fiduciary duties," *Stetson Law Review* 21 (1991): 37–38).

16. Millon, "Communitarianism," p. 24.

17. Ibid., p. 31.

18. Ibid., p. 28.

19. Richard A. Posner, *Economic Analysis of Law* (Boston: Little, Brown and Co., 1977), p. 396.

20. Note that an employment-security rule might be more efficient than an employment-at-will rule. This essay is agnostic on that point. However, the rule change would be neutral from the standpoint of distributive justice.

21. Millon, "Communitarianism," p. 26.

22. Ibid., p. 23.

23. Posner, *Economic Analysis,* p. 395. Posner suggests various reasons why creditors (rather than stockholders) might be better placed to bear the risk of business failure. Assume the lender is a bank. The bank might be in a better position to appraise the risk than is the individual investor who may know little or nothing about the business he has invested in. Then, also, the stockholder is likely to be more risk-averse than the bank.

24. Ibid.

25. *Corporate Law,* p. 50.

26. Ibid., p. 51. "Equity investors and managers have incentives to make arrangements that reduce risk and thus reduce the [interest rate] premium they must pay to debt claimants" (p. 51). The parties may also purchase insurance. As Easterbrook and Fischel say, "The ability of potential victims to protect themselves against loss through insurance is a strong reason for disregarding distributional concerns in choosing among liability rules" (p. 52).

27. Singer, "Reliance Interest," p. 667. See also Marleen A. O'Connor, "Promoting Economic Justice in Plant Closings: Exploring the Fiduciary/Contract Law

Distinction to Enforce Implicit Employment Agreements," in Mitchell, *Progressive Corporate Law,* pp. 224 *et seq.* According to Etzioni, "[a] fair number of court decisions recognize employees' rights to employment by the corporation for which they have been working, based on good faith implied by continuous satisfactory service" ("Stakeholder theory," p. 684).

28. Otherwise why would employees not already have purchased this right in return for lower wages? Or, what is probably the more usual case, why would they have chosen employment in a firm that insisted on its right to dismiss at will?

29. Millon, "Communitarianism," p. 10.

30. New jobs in Europe tend to be temporary or casual owing to the difficulty of firing regular staff. Moreover, in Europe "those out of work for more than a year account for one-third of the unemployed" (Gary Becker, "Unemployment in Europe and the United States," *Journal des Economistes et des Etudes Humaines,* 7 [1996]: 101. Cited by David Schmidtz in Schmidtz and Robert E. Goodin, *Social Welfare and Individual Responsibility* [New York: Cambridge University Press, 1996]).

31. "Laws in many European countries, including Germany, Italy, and France, make it all but impossible to fire people. So companies don't hire—they invest in equipment instead." Thomas K. Grose, "Labor, Social Costs, Taking Toll on Governments," *USA Today,* September 19, 1996, pp. B–1, 2. Cited in Schmidtz and Goodin, *Social Welfare.*

32. Singer, "Reliance Interest," pp. 722–723. See also Orlando, "The Fourth Wave."

33. It also assumes *employees* won't change their behavior. But, as Jonathan R. Macey has pointed out, if employees can acquire the plant at *less* than fair market value, then they will be tempted to sabotage its operations and drive it into bankruptcy. See "Symposium: Fundamental Corporate Changes: Causes, Effects, and Legal Responses: Externalities, Firm-specific Capital Investments, and the Legal Treatment of Fundamental Corporate Changes," *Duke Law Journal,* February 1989, p. 193.

34. Macey, "Symposium," p. 180.

35. Ian Maitland, "Rights in the Workplace: A Nozickian Argument," *Journal of Business Ethics,* 1989, p. 953; Richard B. McKenzie, "The Case for Plant Closures," *Policy Review* 15 (1981): 122.

36. Singer, "Reliance Interest," p. 723.

37. O'Connor, "Plant Closings," p. 233.

38. Easterbrook and Fischel, *Corporate Law,* p. 231.

POSTSCRIPT

Can Restructuring a Corporation's Rules Make a Moral Difference?

Can the corporation live a moral life? For that matter, can *I* live a moral life? This is not the kind of question one can answer in a day, or a week after reading some contrary views on the subject. But it must be answered somehow, and the less we think about it, the more definitively will it be answered by our actions. Corporations have often developed corporate "codes of conduct" or "vision statements," affirming a fundamental recognition of the importance of ethical behavior in business, but just as often they have left us in doubt about the motivation for the code. Was the intention of the "code" to help people live more ethical lives for their own sake? Was it a public relations ploy, to impress neighbors and regulators or to get more favorable treatment from the local zoning board and inspectors? Was it intended as a legal lever, to put corporate officers in a position to fire employees whose aggressive business practices become an embarrassment to the firm, or to get credit for an "ethics program" under the federal sentencing guidelines? Sometimes, corporate executives extol the moral life only, as they will tell us, to keep the lowest-paid workers honest. Where do you stand on the issue?

Suggested Reading

You might want to follow up on this topic, in company with the new literature on the corporate code. The following sources may be of interest:

Amar Bhide and Howard H. Stevenson, "Why Be Honest if Honesty Doesn't Pay?" *Harvard Business Review* (September–October 1990).

D.M. Messick and M.H. Bazerman, "Ethics for the 21st Century: A Decision Making Perspective," *Sloan Management Review* (1996).

R. Murray Lindsay, Linda M. Lindsay, and V. Bruce Irvine, "Instilling Ethical Behavior in Organizations: A Survey of Canadian Companies," *Journal of Business Ethics*, vol. 15, no. 4 (April 1996).

James C. Wimbusch, Jon M. Shepard, and Steven E. Markham, "An Empirical Examination of the Relationship Between Ethical Climate and Ethical Behavior from Multiple Levels of Analysis," *Journal of Business Ethics*, vol. 16, no. 16 (December 1997).

O. Scott Stovall, John D. Neill, and David Perkins, "Corporate Governance, Internal Decision Making, and the Invisible Hand," *Journal of Business Ethics*, vol. 51, No. 2, May 2004.

Tracey C. Rembert, "CSR in the Crosshairs: A Broad Counter-Attack Against Corporate Reform Is Growing. (Could That Be a Sign of Progress?)" from *Business Ethics*, vol. 19, no. 1, Spring 2005.

ISSUE 3

Should Corporations Adopt Policies of Corporate Social Responsibility?

YES: Robert D. Hay and Edmund R. Gray, from "Introduction to Social Responsibility," in David Keller, man. ed., *Ethics and Values: Basic Readings in Theory and Practice* (Pearson Custom Publishing, 2002)

NO: Milton Friedman, from "The Social Responsibility of Business Is to Increase Its Profits," in Thomas Donaldson and Patricia H. Werhane, eds., *Ethical Issues in Business: A Philosophical Approach,* 4th ed. (Prentice Hall, 1993)

ISSUE SUMMARY

YES: Business leaders now recognize, Hay and Gray argue, that in the long run, business will only be successful if it is directed to the needs of the society—and if it chooses to ignore that advice, government regulation is likely to fill the gap between business operations and the welfare of the people the government is sworn to protect.

NO: In this classic defense of *laissez-faire,* Milton Friedman argues that businesses have neither the right, in law or morals, nor the ability in fact, to mess around with "social responsibility": customers, employees, and the general public are best served when the company simply does its job with maximum efficiency.

Should a company think past the bottom line, and try to do good (or at least avoid evil) in this world? This question, probably the first one asked in the infant discipline of business ethics a quarter of a century ago, has received many answers along the spectrum between yes and no; this spectrum is one of the arcs along which the political pendulum swings. In the 1950s, what Friedman argues was taken as gospel truth, and those who agreed with Hay and Gray were regarded as churchy do-gooders who understood nothing of business. During the 1970s, in a very rapid switch brought on by the consumer movements of the 1960s, the pendulum moved to Hay and Gray's position. By the 1970s, when he wrote the article reproduced here, Friedman was regarded as an interesting dinosaur. In the Reagan-Bush administrations, the pendulum swung back, to the point where at present Friedman is regarded as a prophet and Hay and Gray's orientation a knowledgeable and good-hearted "variant perspective." Nothing is certain in this debate, save that the pendulum will swing the other way after a while.

And so it should. There are widely differing opinions on the costs and benefits of an economic regime oriented to liberty rather than protection, but the American consensus has always been, following Smith, that the free market is good, individual liberty to pursue self-interest in economic matters is good, and that if everyone pursues self-interest exclusively—if business increases profits, to the exclusion of all other goals—in the end we will all, even the poorest of us, be better off. Whenever possible, we adhere to the free-market ideology. But it isn't really true—even Smith did not think it was really true—unless it is balanced by a strong legal regime prohibiting the uses of force and fraud, banning toxins and other dangers invisible to the consumer, and actively intervening in business's endemic tendency to create monopolies, combinations designed to thwart the market for the greater profit of the combiners. When that regime fails, businesses turn into predators, citizens are robbed, poisoned, and impoverished, and eventually they become outraged. Then the government is re-empowered to defeat—arrest, jail, fine, banish—the "malefactors of great wealth," and a period of protection and rehabilitation of the poor succeeds the period of liberty for the corporations. It has happened often, and will happen again—the only thing that changes is the sophistication of the technology.

Underlying the image of a political pendulum is a fixed structure of partnership. Society retains the right to seek the maximum happiness; we can't just leave the poor behind, they are our neighbors. Nor would it be in accordance with justice to abandon the economy to the businesses: after all, the public granted the rights that the corporations have exercised to make their profits, protected their operations at taxpayer expense, and created and maintained the infrastructures (roads, water, power, sanitation) that the corporations depend upon.

Ask yourself, as you read these selections, what balance between the freedom of the entrepreneur and the protection of the rest of the citizenry would be appropriate to a free and affluent society. How much of the responsibility for the citizenry should be taken on by corporations themselves?

YES

**Robert D. Hay and
Edmund R. Gray**

Introduction to Social Responsibility

It was Jeremy Bentham, late eighteenth century English philosopher, who espoused the social, political, and economic goal of society to be "the greatest happiness for the greatest number." His cardinal principle was written into the Declaration of Independence as "the pursuit of happiness," which became a societal goal of the American colonists. Bentham's principle was also incorporated into the Constitution of the United States in the preamble where the goal was stated "to promote the general welfare."

The economic-political system through which we in America strive to achieve this societal goal emphasizes the economic and political freedom to pursue individual interests. Adam Smith, another English political economist of the late eighteenth century, stated that the best way to achieve social goals was as follows:

> Every individual is continually exerting himself to find out the most advantageous employment for whatever capital he can command. It is his own advantage, indeed, and not that of the society, which he has in view. But the study of his own advantage naturally, or rather necessarily, leads him to prefer that employment which is most advantageous to the society. . . .
>
> As every individual, therefore, endeavors as much as he can both to employ his capital in the support of domestic industry, and so to direct that industry that its produce may be of the greatest value, every individual necessarily labours to render the annual revenue of the society as great as he can. He generally, indeed, neither intends to promote the public interest, nor knows how much he is promoting it. By preferring the support of domestic to that of foreign industry, he intends only his own security; and by directing that industry in such a manner as its produce may be of the greatest value, he intends only his own gain, and he is in this, as in many other cases, led by an invisible hand to promote an end which was not part of his intention. Nor is it always the worse for the society that it was no part of it. By pursuing his own interest he frequently promotes that of the society more effectually than when he really intends to promote it. I have never known much good done by those who affected to trade for the

From *Business and Society, 2nd Ed.* by Robert D. Hay and Edmund R. Gray, pp. 198–205, 1981. Reprinted with permission of South-Western, a division of Thomson Learning. www.thomasrights.com. Fax 800 730-2215.

public good. It is an affectation, indeed, not very common among merchants, and very few words need be employed in dissuading them from it.

Adam Smith's economic values have had an important influence on American business thinking. As a result, most business people for the first hundred and fifty years of our history embraced the theory that social goals could be achieved by pursuing individual interests.

By 1930 American values were beginning to change from that of the individual owner ethic to that of the group or social ethic. As part of this changing mood, it was felt that Smith's emphasis on owner's interests was too predominant at the expense of other contributors to a business organization. Consequently, a new philosophy of management took shape which stated that the social goals could be achieved by balancing the interests of several groups of people who had an interest in a business. It was stated by Charles H. Percy, then president of Bell and Howell, in the 1950s as follows:

> There are over 64 million gainfully employed people in the United States. One half of these work directly for American corporations, and the other half are vitally affected by business directly or indirectly. Our entire economy, therefore, is dependent upon the type of business management we have. Business management is therefore in many respects a public trust charged with the responsibility of keeping America economically sound. We at Bell & Howell can best do this by keeping our own company's program on a firm foundation and by having a growing group of management leaders to direct the activities of the company.
>
> Management's role in a free society is, among other things, to prove that the real principles of a free society can work within a business organization.
>
> Our basic objective is the development of individuals. In our own present program we are doing everything conceivable to encourage, guide, and assist, and provide an opportunity to everyone to improve their abilities and skills, thus becoming more valuable to the company and enabling the company to improve the rewards paid to the individual for such additional efforts.
>
> Our company has based its entire program for the future on the development of the individual and also upon the building of an outstanding management group. This is why we have emphasized so strongly the supervisory training program recently completed by all Bell & Howell supervisors, and why we are now offering this program to others in the organization training for future management responsibilities.
>
> But a company must also have a creed to which its management is dedicated. I hope that we can all agree to the following:
>
> We believe that our company must develop and produce outstanding products that will perform a great service or fill a need for our customers.
>
> We believe that our business must be run at an adequate profit and that the services and products that we offer must be better than those offered by competitors.
>
> We believe that management must serve employees, stockholders, and customers, but that we cannot serve the interests of any one group at

the undue expense of the other two. A proper and fair balance must be preserved.

We believe that our business must provide stability of employment and job security for all those who depend on our company for their livelihood.

We believe that we are failing in our responsibility if our wages are not sufficiently high to not only meet the necessities of life but provide some of the luxuries as well. Wherever possible, we also believe that bonus earning should be paid for performance and output "beyond the call of duty."

We believe that every individual in the company should have an opportunity for advancement and growth with the organization. There should be no dead-end streets any place in an organization.

We believe in the necessity for constantly increasing productivity and output. Higher wages and greater benefits can never be "given" by management. Management can only see that they are paid out when "earned."

We believe in labor-saving machinery. We do not think human beings should perform operations that can be done by mechanical or electronic means. We believe in this because we believe in the human dignity and creative ability of the individual. We are more interested in the intellect, goodwill, initiative, enthusiasm, and cooperativeness of the individual than we are in his muscular energy.

We believe that every person in the company has a right to be treated with the respect and courtesy that is due a human being. It is for this reason that we have individual merit ratings, individual pay increases, job evaluations, and incentive pay; and it is why we keep every individual fully informed—through The Finder, through our annual report, through Family Night, and through individual letters—about the present program of the company and also about our future objectives.

We believe that our business must be conducted with the utmost integrity. We may fight the principle of confiscatory taxation, but we will pay our full share. We will observe every governmental law and regulation, local, state, and national. We will deal fairly with our customers, we will advertise our product truthfully, and we will make every attempt to maintain a friendly relationship with our competitors while at the same time waging the battle of free competition.

Some business leaders, on the one hand, preach the virtues of the free enterprise, democratic system and, on the other hand, run their own business in accordance with autocratic principles—all authority stemming from the top with little delegation of responsibility to individuals within the organization. We believe in democracy—in government and in our business.

We hope that every principle we believe in is right and is actually being practiced throughout the company as it affects every individual.

Then in the late 1960s American business leaders began to take another look at the problems of society in light of the goal of "the greatest happiness for the greatest number." How could people be happy if they have to breathe foul air, drink polluted water, live in crowded cities, use very unsafe products, be misled by untruthful advertising, be deprived of a job because of race, and face many other problems? Thus, another philosophy of management emerged. It was voiced by several American business leaders:

> Business must learn to look upon its social responsibilities as inseparable from its economic function. If it fails to do so, it leaves a void that will quickly be filled by others—usually by the government. (George Champion, Chase National Bank, 1966.)
>
> I believe there is one basic principle that needs to be emphasized more than ever before. It is the recognition that business is successful in the long term only when it is directed toward the needs of the society. (Robert F. Hansberger, Boise Cascade, 1971.)
>
> The actions of the great corporations have so profound an influence that the public has come to judge them not only by their profit-making record, but by the contribution of their work to society as a whole. Under a political democracy such as ours, if the corporation fails to perceive itself and govern its action in essentially the same manner as the public at large, it may find itself in serious trouble. (Louis B. Lundborg, Bank of America, 1971.)

With these remarks we can see that there has been a shift in managerial emphasis from owners' interests to group interests, and finally, to society's interests. Managers of some American businesses have come to recognize that they have a social responsibility.

Historical Perspective of Social Responsibility

The concept of the social responsibility of business managers has in recent years become a popular subject of discussion and debate within both business and academic circles. Although the term itself is of relatively recent origin, the underlying concept has existed as long as there have been business organizations. It rests on the logical assumption that because the firm is a creation of society, it has a responsibility to aid in the accomplishment of society's goals. In the United States concepts of social responsibility have moved from three distinct phases which may be labeled Phases I, II, and III.

Phase I—Profit Maximizing Management

The Phase I concept was based on the belief that business managers have but one single objective—maximize profits. The only constraint on this pursuit was the legal framework within which the firm operated. The origin of this view may be found in Adam Smith's *Wealth of Nations*. As previously noted, Smith believed that individual business people acting in their own selfish interest would be guided by an "invisible hand" to promote the public good. In other words, the individual's drive for maximum profits and the regulation of the competitive marketplace would interact to create the greatest aggregate wealth for a nation and therefore the maximum public good. In the United

States this view was universally accepted throughout the nineteenth century and the early part of the twentieth century. Its acceptance rested not only on economic logic but also on the goals and values of society. America in the nineteenth and first half of the twentieth centuries was a society of economic scarcity; therefore, economic growth and the accumulation of aggregate wealth were primary goals. The business system with its emphasis on maximum profit was seen as a vehicle for eliminating economic scarcity. In the process employee abuses such as child labor, starvation wages, and unsafe working conditions could be tolerated. No questions were raised with regard to using up the natural resources and polluting streams and land. Nor was anyone really concerned about urban problems, unethical advertising, unsafe products, and poverty problems of minority groups.

The profit maximization view of social responsibility also complemented the Calvinistic philosophy which pervaded nineteenth and twentieth century American thinking. Calvinism stressed that the road to salvation was through hard work and the accumulation of wealth. It then logically followed that a business person could demonstrate diligence (and thus godliness) and accumulate a maximum amount of wealth by adhering to the discipline of profit maximization.

Phase II—Trusteeship Management

Phase II, which may be labeled the "trusteeship" concept, emerged in the 1920s and 30s. It resulted from structural changes in both business institutions and in society. According to this concept, corporate managers were responsible not simply for maximizing the stockholders' wealth but rather for maintaining an equitable balance among the competing claims of customers, employees, suppliers, creditors, and the community. In this view the manager was seen as "trustee" for the various contributor groups to the firm rather than simply an agent of the owners.

The two structural trends largely responsible for the emergence of this newer view of social responsibility were: (1) the increasing diffusion of ownership of the shares of American corporations, and (2) the development of a pluralistic society. The extent of the diffusion of stock ownership may be highlighted by the fact that by the early 1930s the largest stockholders in corporations such as American Telephone and Telegraph, United States Steel, and the Pennsylvania Railroad owned less than one percent of the total shares outstanding of these companies. Similar dispersion of stock ownership existed in most other large corporations. In such situations management typically was firmly in control of the corporation. Except in rare circumstances, the top executives were able to perpetuate themselves in office through the proxy mechanism. If an individual shareholder was not satisfied with the performance of the firm, there was little recourse other than to sell the stock. Hence, although the stockholder's legal position was that of an owner—and thus a principal-agent relationship existed between the stockholder and the managers—the stockholder's actual position was more akin to bondholders and other creditors of the firm. Given such a situation it was only natural to ask, "To whom is management responsible?" The "trusteeship" concept provided an answer. Management was responsible to all the contributors to the firm—that is, stockholders, workers, customers, suppliers, creditors, and the community.

The emergence of a largely pluralistic society reinforced the logic of the "trusteeship" concept. A pluralistic society has been defined as "one which has many semi-autonomous and autonomous groups through which power is diffused. No one group has overwhelming power over all others, and each has direct or indirect impact on all others. From the perspective of business firms this translated into the fact that exogenous groups had considerable impact upon and influence over them. In the 1930s the major groups exerting significant pressure on business were labor unions and the federal government. Today the list has grown to include numerous minority, environmental, and consumer groups among others. Clearly, one logical approach to such a situation is to consider that the firm has a responsibility to each interested group and that management's task is to reconcile and balance the claims of the various groups.

Phase III—Quality of Life Management

Phase III, which may be called the "quality of life" concept of social responsibility, has become popular in recent years. The primary reason for the emergence of this concept is the very significant metamorphosis in societal goals which this nation is experiencing. Up to the middle part of this century, society's principal goal was to raise the standard of living of the American people, which could be achieved by producing more goods and services. The fact that the U.S. had become the wealthiest nation in the world was testimony to the success of business in meeting this expectation.

In this process, however, the U.S. has become what John Kenneth Galbraith calls an "affluent society" in which the aggregate scarcity of basic goods and services is no longer the fundamental problem. Other social problems have developed as direct and indirect results of economic success. Thus, there are pockets of poverty in a nation of plenty, deteriorating cities, air and water pollution, defacement of the landscape, and a disregard for consumers to mention only a few of the prominent social problems. The mood of the country seems to be that things have gotten out of balance—the economic abundance in the midst of a declining social and physical environment does not make sense. As a result, a new set of national priorities which stress the "Quality of life" appear to be emerging.

Concomitant with the new priorities, societal consensus seems to be demanding that business, with its technological and managerial skills and its financial resources, assume broader responsibilities—responsibilities that extend beyond the traditional economic realm of the Phase I concept or the mere balancing of the competing demands of the sundry contributors and pressure groups of the Phase II concept. The socially responsible firm under Phase III reasoning is one that becomes deeply involved in the solution of society's major problems.

Personal Values of the Three Styles of Managers

Values are the beliefs and attitudes which form one's frame of reference and help to determine the behavior which an individual displays. All managers have a set of values which affect their decisions, but the values are not the same for each manager; however, once values are ingrained in a manager, they do not change except over a period of time. It is possible to group these values into a general pattern of behavior which characterizes three styles of managers—the profit-maximizing style, the trusteeship style, and the "quality of life" style of management.

Phase I Managers

Phase I, profit-maximizing managers have a personal set of values which reflects their economic thinking. They believe that raw self-interest should prevail in society, and their values dictate that "What's good for me is good for my country." Therefore, Phase I managers rationalize that making as much profit as is possible would be good for society. They make every effort to become as efficient as possible and to make as much money as they can. To them money and wealth are the most important goals of their lives.

In the pursuit of maximum profit the actions of Phase I managers toward customers are reflected in a *caveat emptor* philosophy. "Let the buyer beware" characterizes decisions and actions in dealing with customers. They are not necessarily concerned with product quality or safety, or with sufficient and/or truthful information about products and services. A profit-maximizing manager's view toward employees can be stated as, "Labor is a commodity to be bought and sold in the marketplace." Thus, chief accountability lies with the owners of the business, and usually the Phase I manager is the owner or part owner of the organization.

To profit maximizers technology is very important. Machines and equipment rank high on their scale of values, therefore, materialism characterizes their philosophy.

Social values do not predominate the thinking of Phase I managers. In fact, they believe that employee problems should be left at home. Economics should be separate from societal or family concerns. A Phase I manager's leadership style is one of the rugged individualist—"I'm my own boss, and I'll manage my business as I please." Values about minority groups dictate that such groups are inferior, so they must be treated accordingly.

Political values are based on the doctrine of laissez faire. "That government is best which governs the least" characterizes the thinking of Phase I managers. As a result anything dealing with politicians and governments is foreign and distasteful to them.

Their beliefs about the environment can be stated, "The natural environment controls one's destiny; therefore, use it to protect your interests before it destroys you. Don't worry about the physical environment because there are plenty of natural resources which you can use."

Aesthetic values to the profit maximizer are minimal. In fact, Phase I managers would say, "Aesthetic values? What are they?" They have very little concern for the arts and cultural aspects of life. They hold musicians, artists, entertainers, and social scientists in low regard.

The values that a profit-maximizing manager holds were commonly accepted in the economic textbooks of the 1800s and early 1900s although they obviously did not apply to all managers of those times. It is easy to see how they conflict with the values of the other two styles of management.

Phase II Managers

Phase II, trusteeship managers have a somewhat different set of values. They recognize that self-interest plays a large role in their actions, but they also recognize the interests of those people who contribute to the organization—the customers, employees, suppliers, owners, creditors, government, and community. In other words, they operate with self-interest plus the interests of other groups. They believe that "What is good for my company is good for the country." They balance profits of the owners and the organization with wages for employees, taxes for the government, interest for the creditors, and so forth. Money is important to them but so are people, because their values tells them that satisfying people's needs is a better goal than just making money.

In balancing the needs of the various contributors to the organization, Phase II managers deal with customers as the chief providers of revenue to the firm. Their values tell them not to cheat the customers because cheating is not good for the firm.

They are concerned with providing sufficient quantities of goods as well as sufficient quality for customer satisfaction. They view employees as having certain rights which must be recognized and that employees are more than mere commodities to be traded in the marketplace. Their accountability as managers is to owners as well as to customers, employees, suppliers, creditors, government, and the community.

To the trusteeship-style manager, technology is important, but so are people. Innovation of technology is to be commended because new machines, equipment, and products are useful to people to create a high standard of living. Materialism is important, but so is humanism.

The social values held by trusteeship managers are more liberal than those held by profit maximizers. They recognize that employees have several needs beyond their economic needs. Employees have a desire for security and a sense of belonging as well as recognition. Phase II managers see themselves as individualists, but they also appreciate the value of group participation in managing the business. They view minority groups as having their place in society. But, a trusteeship manager would add: "Their place is usually inferior to mine; they are usually not qualified to hold their jobs but that's not my fault."

The political values of Phase II managers are reflected in recognizing that government and politics are important, but they view government and politics as necessary evils. They distrust both, recognizing that government serves as a threat to their existence if their firms do not live up to the laws passed since the 1930s.

The environmental beliefs of trusteeship managers are stated as follows: "People can control and manipulate their environment. Therefore, let them do it for their own benefit and incidentally for society's benefit."

Aesthetic values are all right to the trusteeship manager, but "they are not for our firm although someone has to support the arts and cultural values."

Phase III Managers

In contrast to profit maximizers and trustee managers, "quality of life" managers believe in enlightened self-interest. They agree that selfishness and group interests are important, but that society's interests are also important in making decisions. "What's good for society is good for our company" is their opinion. They agree that profit is essential for the firm, but that profit in and of itself is not the end objective of the firm. As far as money and wealth are concerned, their set of values tells them that money is important but people are more important than money.

In sharp contrast to *caveat emptor* in dealings with customers, the philosophy of Phase II managers is *caveat venditor*, that is, let the seller beware. The company should bear the responsibility for producing and distributing products and services in sufficient quantities at the right time and place with the necessary quality, information, and services necessary to satisfy customers' needs. Their views about employees are to recognize the dignity of each, not treating them as a commodity to be bought and sold. Their accountability as managers is to the owners, to the other contributors of the business, and to society in general.

Technological values are important but people are held in higher esteem than machines, equipment, computers, and esoteric products. A "quality of life" manager is a humanist rather than a materialist.

The social values of "quality of life" managers dictate that a person cannot be separated into an economic being or family being. Their philosophy is, "We hire the whole person including any problems that person might have." Phase III managers recognize that group participation rather than rugged individualism is a determining factor in an organization's success. Their values about minority groups are different from the other managers. Their view is that "A member of a minority group needs support and guidance like any other person."

The political values of "quality of life" managers dictate that government and politicians are necessary contributors to a quality of life. Rather than resisting government, they believe that business and government must cooperate to solve society's problems.

Their environmental beliefs are stated as, "A person must preserve the environment, not for the environment's sake alone, but for the benefit of people who want to lead a quality life."

As far as aesthetic values are concerned, Phase III managers recognize that the arts and cultural values reflect the lives of people whom they hold in high regard. Their actions support aesthetic values by committing resources to their preservation and presentation.

Milton Friedman  **NO**

The Social Responsibility of Business Is to Increase Its Profits

When I hear businessmen speak eloquently about the "social responsibilities of business in a free-enterprise system," I am reminded of the wonderful line about the Frenchman who discovered at the age of 70 that he had been speaking prose all his life. The businessmen believe that they are defending free enterprise when they declaim that business is not concerned "merely" with profit but also with promoting desirable "social" ends; that business has a "social conscience" and takes seriously its responsibilities for providing employment, eliminating discrimination, avoiding pollution and whatever else may be the catchwords of the contemporary crop of reformers. In fact they are—or would be if they or anyone else took them seriously—preaching pure and unadulterated socialism. Businessmen who talk this way are unwitting puppets of the intellectual forces that have been undermining the basis of a free society these past decades.

The discussions of the "social responsibilities of business" are notable for their analytical looseness and lack of rigor. What does it mean to say that "business" has responsibilities? Only people can have responsibilities. A corporation is an artificial person and in this sense may have artificial responsibilities, but "business" as a whole cannot be said to have responsibilities, even in this vague sense. The first step toward clarity in examining the doctrine of the social responsibility of business is to ask precisely what it implies for whom.

Presumably, the individuals who are to be responsible are businessmen, which means individual proprietors or corporate executives. Most of the discussion of social responsibility is directed at corporations, so in what follows I shall mostly neglect the individual proprietors and speak of corporate executives.

In a free-enterprise, private-property system, a corporate executive is an employee of the owners of the business. He has direct responsibility to his employers. That responsibility is to conduct the business in accordance with their desires, which generally will be to make as much money as possible while conforming to the basic rules of the society, both those embodied in law and those embodied in ethical custom. Of course, in some cases his employers may have a different objective. A group of persons might establish a corporation for an eleemosynary purpose—for example, a hospital or a school. The manager of such a corporation will not have money profit as his objective but the rendering of certain services.

In either case, the key point is that, in his capacity as a corporate executive, the manager is the agent of the individuals who own the corporation or establish the eleemosynary institution, and his primary responsibility is to them.

Needless to say, this does not mean that it is easy to judge how well he is performing his task. But at least the criterion of performance is straightforward, and the persons among whom a voluntary contractual arrangement exists are clearly defined.

Of course, the corporate executive is also a person in his own right. As a person, he may have many other responsibilities that he recognizes or assumes voluntarily—to his family, his conscience, his feelings of charity, his church, his clubs, his city, his country. He may feel impelled by these responsibilities to devote part of his income to causes he regards as worthy, to refuse to work for particular corporations, even to leave his job, for example, to join his country's armed forces. If we wish, we may refer to some of these responsibilities as "social responsibilities." But in these respects he is acting as a principal, not an agent; he is spending his own money or time or energy, not the money of his employers or the time or energy he has contracted to devote to their purposes. If these are "social responsibilities," they are the social responsibilities of individuals, not of business.

What does it mean to say that the corporate executive has a "social responsibility" in his capacity as businessman? If this statement is not pure rhetoric, it must mean that he is to act in some way that is not in the interest of his employers. For example, that he is to refrain from increasing the price of the product in order to contribute to the social objective of preventing inflation, even though a price increase would be in the best interests of the corporation. Or that he is to make expenditures on reducing pollution beyond the amount that is in the best interests of the corporation or that is required by law in order to contribute to the social objective of improving the environment. Or that, at the expense of corporate profits, he is to hire "hard-core" unemployed instead of better qualified available workmen to contribute to the social objective of reducing poverty.

In each of these cases, the corporate executive would be spending someone else's money for a general social interest. Insofar as his actions in accord with his "social responsibility" reduce returns to stockholders, he is spending their money. Insofar as his actions raise the price to customers, he is spending the customers' money. Insofar as his actions lower the wages of some employees, he is spending their money.

The stockholders or the customers or the employees could separately spend their own money on the particular action if they wished to do so. The executive is exercising a distinct "social responsibility," rather than serving as an agent of the stockholders or the customers or the employees, only if he spends the money in a different way than they would have spent it.

But if he does this, he is in effect imposing taxes, on the one hand, and deciding how the tax proceeds shall be spent, on the other.

This process raises political questions on two levels: principle and consequences. On the level of political principle, the imposition of taxes and the expenditure of tax proceeds are governmental functions. We have established elaborate constitutional, parliamentary and judicial provisions to control these functions, to assure that taxes are imposed so far as possible in accordance with the preferences and desires of the public—after all, "taxation without representation" was one of the battle cries of the American Revolution. We have a system of checks and balances to separate the legislative function of imposing taxes and enacting expenditures from the executive function of collecting taxes and administering expenditure programs and from the judicial function of mediating disputes and interpreting the law.

Here the businessman—self-selected or appointed directly or indirectly by stockholders—is to be simultaneously legislator, executive and jurist. He is to decide whom to tax by how much and for what purpose, and he is to spend the proceeds—all this guided only by general exhortations from on high to restrain inflation, improve the environment, fight poverty and so on and on.

The whole justification for permitting the corporate executive to be selected by the stockholders is that the executive is an agent serving the interests of his principal. This justification disappears when the corporate executive imposes taxes and spends the proceeds for "social" purposes. He becomes in effect a public employee, a civil servant, even though he remains in name an employee of a private enterprise. On grounds of political principle, it is intolerable that such civil servants—insofar as their actions in the name of social responsibility are real and not just window dressing—should be selected as they are now. If they are to be civil servants, then they must be elected through a political process. If they are to impose taxes and make expenditures to foster "social" objectives, then political machinery must be set up to make the assessment of taxes and to determine through a political process the objectives to be served.

This is the basic reason why the doctrine of "social responsibility" involves the acceptance of the socialist view that political mechanisms, not market mechanisms, are the appropriate way to determine the allocation of scarce resources to alternative uses.

On the grounds of consequences, can the corporate executive in fact discharge his alleged "social responsibilities"? On the other hand, suppose he could get away with spending the stockholders' or customers' or employees' money. How is he to know how to spend it? He is told that he must contribute to fighting inflation. How is he to know what action of his will contribute to that end? He is presumably an expert in running his company—in producing a product or selling it or financing it. But nothing about his selection makes him an expert on inflation. Will his holding down the price of his product reduce inflationary pressure? Or, by leaving more spending power in the hands of his customers, simply divert it elsewhere? Or, by forcing him to produce less because of the lower price, will it simply contribute to shortages? Even if he could answer these questions, how much cost is he justified in imposing on his stockholders, customers and employees for this social purpose? What is his appropriate share and what is the appropriate share of others?

And, whether he wants to or not, can he get away with spending his stockholders', customers' or employees' money? Will not the stockholders fire him? (Either the present ones or those who take over when his actions in the name of social responsibility have reduced the corporation's profits and the price of its stock.) His customers and his employees can desert him for other producers and employers less scrupulous in exercising their social responsibilities.

This facet of "social responsibility" doctrine is brought into sharp relief when the doctrine is used to justify wage restraint by trade unions. The conflict of interest is naked and clear when union officials are asked to subordinate the interest of their members to some more general purpose. If the union officials try to enforce wage restraint, the consequence is likely to be wildcat strikes, rank-and-file revolts and the emergence of strong competitors for their jobs. We thus have the ironic phenomenon that union leaders—at least in the U.S.—have objected to Government interference with the market far more consistently and courageously than have business leaders.

The difficulty of exercising "social responsibility" illustrates, of course, the great virtue of private competitive enterprise—it forces people to be responsible for their own actions and makes it difficult for them to "exploit" other people for either selfish or unselfish purposes. They can do good—but only at their own expense.

Many a reader who has followed the argument this far may be tempted to remonstrate that it is all well and good to speak of government's having the responsibility to impose taxes and determine expenditures for such "social" purposes as controlling pollution or training the hard-core unemployed, but that the problems are too urgent to wait on the slow course of political processes, that the exercise of social responsibility by businessmen is a quicker and surer way to solve pressing current problems.

Aside from the question of fact—I share Adam Smith's skepticism about the benefits that can be expected from "those who affect to trade for the public good"—this argument must be rejected on grounds of principle. What it amounts to is an assertion that those who favor the taxes and expenditures in question have failed to persuade a majority of their fellow citizens to be of like mind and that they are seeking to attain by undemocratic procedures what they cannot attain by democratic procedures. In a free society, it is hard for "evil" people to do "evil," especially since one man's good is another's evil.

I have, for simplicity, concentrated on the special case of the corporate executive, except only for the brief digression on trade unions. But precisely the same argument applies to the newer phenomenon of calling upon stockholders to require corporations to exercise social responsibility (the recent G.M. crusade for example). In most of these cases, what is in effect involved is some stockholders trying to get other stockholders (or customers or employees) to contribute against their will to "social" causes favored by the activists. Insofar as they succeed, they are again imposing taxes and spending the proceeds.

The situation of the individual proprietor is somewhat different. If he acts to reduce the returns of his enterprise in order to exercise his "social responsibility," he is spending his own money, not someone else's. If he wishes to spend his money on such purposes, that is his right, and I cannot see that there is any objection to his doing so. In the process, he, too, may impose costs on employees and customers. However, because he is far less likely than a large corporation or union to have monopolistic power, any such side effects will tend to be minor.

Of course, in practice the doctrine of social responsibility is frequently a cloak for actions that are justified on other grounds rather than a reason for those actions.

To illustrate, it may well be in the long-run interest of a corporation that is a major employer in a small community to devote resources to providing amenities to that community or to improving its government. That may make it easier to attract desirable employees, it may reduce the wage bill or lessen losses from pilferage and sabotage or have other worthwhile effects. Or it may be that, given the laws about the deductibility of corporate charitable contributions, the stockholders can contribute more to charities they favor by having the corporation make the gift than by doing it themselves, since they can in that way contribute an amount that would otherwise have been paid as corporate taxes.

In each of these—and many similar—cases, there is a strong temptation to rationalize these actions as an exercise of "social responsibility." In the present climate of opinion, with its widespread aversion to "capitalism," "profits," the "soulless corporation" and so on, this is one way for a corporation to generate goodwill as a by-product of expenditures that are entirely justified in its own self-interest.

It would be inconsistent of me to call on corporate executives to refrain from this hypocritical window-dressing because it harms the foundations of a free society. That would be to call on them to exercise a "social responsibility"! If our institutions, and the attitudes of the public make it in their self-interest to cloak their actions in this way, I cannot summon much indignation to denounce them. At the same time, I can express admiration for those individual proprietors or owners of closely held corporations or stockholders of more broadly held corporations who disdain such tactics as approaching fraud.

Whether blameworthy or not, the use of the cloak of social responsibility, and the nonsense spoken in its name by influential and prestigious businessmen, does clearly harm the foundations of a free society. I have been impressed time and again by the schizophrenic character of many businessmen. They are capable of being extremely far-sighted and clearheaded in matters that are internal to their businesses. They are incredibly short-sighted and muddle-headed in matters that are outside their businesses but affect the possible survival of business in general. This short-sightedness is strikingly exemplified in the calls from many businessmen for wage and price guidelines or controls or income policies. There is nothing that could do more in a brief period to destroy a market system and replace it by a centrally controlled system than effective governmental control of prices and wages.

The short-sightedness is also exemplified in speeches by businessmen on social responsibility. This may gain them kudos in the short run. But it helps to strengthen the already too prevalent view that the pursuit of profits is wicked and immoral and must be curbed and controlled by external forces. Once this view is adopted, the external forces that curb the market will not be the social consciences, however highly developed, of the pontificating executives; it will be the iron fist of government bureaucrats. Here, as with price and wage controls, businessmen seem to me to reveal a suicidal impulse.

The political principle that underlies the market mechanism is unanimity. In an ideal free market resting on private property, no individual can coerce any other, all cooperation is voluntary, all parties to such cooperation benefit or they need not participate. There are no values, no "social" responsibilities in any sense other than the shared values and responsibilities of individuals. Society is a collection of individuals and of the various groups they voluntarily form.

The political principle that underlies the political mechanism is conformity. The individual must serve a more general social interest—whether that be determined by a church or a dictator or a majority. The individual may have a vote and say in what is to be done, but if he is overruled, he must conform. It is appropriate for some to require others to contribute to a general social purpose whether they wish to or not.

Unfortunately, unanimity is not always feasible. There are some respects in which conformity appears unavoidable, so I do not see how one can avoid the use of the political mechanism altogether.

But the doctrine of "social responsibility" taken seriously would extend the scope of the political mechanism to every human activity. It does not differ in philosophy from the most explicitly collectivist doctrine. It differs only by professing to believe that collectivist ends can be attained without collectivist means. That is why, in my book *Capitalism and Freedom*, I have called it a "fundamentally subversive doctrine" in a free society, and have said that in such a society, "there is one and only one social responsibility of business—to use its resources and engage in activities designed to increase its profits so long as it stays within the rules of the game, which is to say, engages in open and free competition without deception or fraud."

POSTSCRIPT

Should Corporations Adopt Policies of Corporate Social Responsibility?

Why should a business be moral? This question is different from the original question of ethics, that is, why should I (or any human being) be moral? We should be moral as individuals because we are social animals (like dogs), and we cannot fulfill our nature unless we recognize, honor, and work to protect the community that enfolds us. The corporation is different. It is an artificial person, chartered by the state, for the sole purpose of enriching its owners. Corporations then have no interest but self-interest, in that respect; they are solitary animals (like cats), and they violate their nature if they try to live for others. As the selections show, the essential difference between the social-responsibility theorist and the increase-profit theorist is one of long-range or short-range planning. The intelligent corporate officer knows that in the long run, government, customers, and the press will make life intolerable for his company unless he takes care of the community's needs as conscientiously as he does the corporation's. Friedman, on the other hand, is a college professor. With tenure.

Suggested Reading

If you're interested in following up on this subject, you might find the following selections interesting:

John K. Galbraith, *The Affluent Society* (New York: Random House, 1971).

George A. Steiner, *Business and Society* (New York: Random House, 1971).

Manuel G. Velasquez, *Business Ethics* (Englewood Cliffs, N.J.: Prentice-Hall, 1982 and later editions).

Peter A. French, *Collective and Corporate Responsibility* (New York: Columbia University Press, 1984).

R. Edward Freeman, "Fixing the Ethics Crisis in Corporate America" *Miller Center Report* (vol. 18, no. 4, Fall 2002, pp. 13–17).

Bennett Daviss, *The Futurist,* March 1999.

Adam Smith, *The Wealth of Nations* (Oxford: Clarendon Press, 1976).

Thomas Donaldson and L.E. Preston, "The Stakeholder Theory of the Corporation: Concepts, Evidence and Implications." *Academy of Management Review* (vol. 20: 65–91).

ISSUE 4

Is It a Mistake to Urge Corporate Managers to Be Moral?

YES: John R. Boatright, from "Does Business Ethics Rest on a Mistake?" *Business Ethics Quarterly* (October 1999)

NO: Jack Guynn, from "Ethical Challenges in a Market Economy: Do the Right Thing When Nobody Is Looking," Delivered to the Scott Symposium on Business Ethics (April 11, 2005)

ISSUE SUMMARY

YES: In his presidential address to the Society for Business Ethics, John Boatright presents an ingenious argument to the effect that the duty of stewardship of the investor's money, entrusted to the corporation to manage, trumps all other moral duties that might be suggested for the corporation.

NO: Echoing Adam Smith, Jack Guynn argues that beneath all the self-interest pursued in the market system, certain basic virtues, especially trustworthiness and moral integrity, are essential for its viability. The true measure of business success is found in what is done when no one is looking.

It's a curious match: John Boatright, Ph.D., one of the most respected of the distinguished line of presidents of the Society for Business Ethics, ascends the podium to deliver his presidential address, and proceeds to demonstrate, with a persuasiveness and purity of logic that brings tears to the eyes, that this academic field, as generally understood, really doesn't exist. See, it's simple. The corporation is the product of an agreement of investors, to pool their money on an enterprise in order to make more money. The manager is hired to make their money grow, not to water the flowers or do good works. He is a moral manager when he does his job. No point urging him to engage in corporate charity or environmental responsiveness or whatever, or at least no point urging him on moral grounds. He has no choice but to steer the company along the lines of the financial incentives that the society has placed before him. If you want a better world, work on the structure of the incentives (to create moral markets), not the moral action of the manager.

Since "business ethics" is all about "new social contracts" that require, in the ethicist's imagination, constant managerial deviations from that straight path, constant actions in derogation of the manager's responsibility to the shareholders, business ethics must be seriously mistaken. Goodbye, business ethics.

Then Jack Guynn, president and chief executive officer of the Federal Reserve Bank in Atlanta, argues to the opposite conclusion from financial facts, not philosophical logic—starting with the astronomical financial and criminal penalties brought down on their own heads and the heads of many others by the reckless senior executives of the companies that failed in the recent scandals. Consider the managers themselves, and the companies that dealt with them as bankers and auditors: the executives are dead, in jail, or headed that way, and the SEC has obtained huge judgments against Wall Street and the accounting firms (one of them, Arthur Andersen, was put out of business in the fallout). Consider the investors: Enron was no scam, and many sophisticated investors put their money into it, only to watch a loss of market capitalization of some $66 billion before the bankruptcy; in WorldCom's case, it was $177 billion. Not all of the investors were millionaire financial sorts: most of us have our pensions invested in securities. Consider the employees: laid off, their pension money gone with the same cold wind that chilled Wall Street, destroying their faith in the American dream and investors' faith in the market in the same blow. We will never trust the market again, not in the same way. We were betrayed, and betrayal causes intense anger. So it is no surprise that everyone was willing to see punitive regulations slapped down on the financial industry; Sarbanes-Oxley passed overwhelmingly. Yet in its very administration there are more costs to be borne by business and the public. Guynn's conclusion is as simple as Boatright's, but on the opposite tack: Be ethical. We can't afford the bottom-line consequences of profit-driven unethical behavior. It's just too expensive. Stay close, business ethics.

This dispute is not new: for Boatright's philosophical background, see the selections from Adam Smith and Milton Friedman, above. For Guynn's conclusions, Adam Smith is also good background. Smith argued consistently that without virtues, specifically the virtues of honesty, transparency, promise-keeping and fairness, the business system would never survive. Guynn surveys some of the threats to its survival, and goes on to consider the rewards of truly good behavior, characterized by honesty and integrity. Keep in mind, as you read these selections, that managers must always walk a fine line between rigid adherence to the motive of profit and responsibility to the shareholders on the one hand, and responsiveness to the community on the other.

YES

John R. Boatright

Does Business Ethics Rest on a Mistake?

Presidential addresses before professional societies are often appraisals of the state of the field—to successes achieved, to failures (if any), and to the challenges that lie ahead. By any measure, the academic field of business ethics is prospering. We can take pride in our accomplishments, including the growth of business ethics courses, the profusion of books and articles, an unending round of academic conferences (that could inspire David Lodge to write a sequel to *Small World*), and the development of journals and societies (especially our own Society for Business Ethics and the journal *Business Ethics Quarterly*).

But what of our impact on business practice? Much of the support for business ethics derives from the public's expectation that our academic activities will trickle down to the real world. In headier moments, we picture ourselves as high-minded missionaries, engaged in an arduous struggle to convert a heathen mass from their idolatrous worship of the bottom line. If we are engaged in a battle, the reports from the front are not very encouraging.

- *Newsweek* columnist Robert Samuelson announced in 1993 that the "good corporation" that provided job security and generous benefits is dead.[1] Among its successors is the "virtual corporation" made up of temporary alliances among small firms and individuals around the world.[2]
- Financially driven mergers and restructurings are the order of the day, creating ever-larger firms that transcend national boundaries and shed layers of unneeded employees in their relentless march to greater share-holder value.
- Even giant corporations and nation-states are at the mercy of the world currency market that (like the Internet) is controlled by no one.
- It is safe once again in corporate America for CEOs to declare that their job is to serve only the shareholders. "Chain Saw Al" Dunlap's proud advocacy of "mean business" is very much in vogue (even if "Chain Saw Al" himself has been felled with his own favored implement).[3]
- As "baby boomers" save feverishly for retirement, they have come to expect 25 percent annual gains in their pension accounts, regardless of the consequences. As Pogo said, "We have met the enemy and he is us."

John Boatright, "Does Business Ethics Rest on a Mistake?", *Business Ethics Quarterly*, vol. 9, issue 4, 1999, pp. 583–591. Copyright © 1999 by Business Ethics Quarterly. Reprinted by permission.

Whether we in the field of business ethics have had any beneficial impact depends very much on what counts as an improvement. Exactly what is it that we are trying to achieve? Although each of us would probably give a slightly different answer to this question, there is a rough consensus. We tend to focus in our teaching and research on the high-level corporate manager, typically a CEO, who shapes the environment of an organization and makes the key strategic decisions. On the conventional view, this manager acts on competitive market considerations within the limits set by law. The objective is clear: Make as much money as you can without breaking the law! Or perhaps the objective is: Make as much money as you can and still get away with it!

The field of business ethics offers a counterview—that ethics ought to be incorporated into management decision making and organizational design. Managers ought to consider ethics along with law and profits, and they should create organizations in which ethics plays a vital role.

I could cite many expressions of this view, but let me single out just one. Ken Goodpaster labels the conventional view, in which ethics is merely a systemic constraint, Type 2 thinking.[4] The aim of business ethics, he claims, is to move managers to Type 3 thinking, in which ethics is an "authoritative guide." Profit and law are not ignored in Type 3 thinking, he says, but "respect for the rights and concerns of all affected parties is given independent force in the leader's operating consciousness."[5]

The view that I am describing has no name, so let's call it the Moral Manager Model. On this model, the moral manager is not one who merely *acts* morally but who *thinks* morally—that is, who actively includes moral considerations in business decision making. And the goal of business ethics is to turn out moral managers, that is, skilled moral reasoners.

Since I am gomg to throw stones at this view, let me admit that I am not without sin. In the first chapter of my textbook *Ethics and the Conduct of Business*, I introduce the economic, legal, and moral points of view and recommend the integration of all three.[6] What I call an "integrated approach" closely resembles Goodpaster's Type 3 thinking and the Moral Manager Model.

I now think that this view is mistaken—or at least in need of substantial qualification. If the Moral Manager Model captures what business ethics is all about, then, I contend, business ethics rests on a mistake. But what's wrong with this view? It is so deeply ingrained in the business ethics literature that its truth might seem obvious. And what is the alternative? What should business ethics be about if not this?

First, if the Moral Manager Model describes the aim of business ethics, then we are fighting a losing battle. The most admired corporate executives fit the conventional view of the hard-headed, business-savvy decision maker. And the reports from the front do not describe trends that favor the Moral Manager Model.

The Moral Manager Model has its exemplars. Aaron Feuerstein of Malden Mills (who was our keynote speaker at last year's meeting) and Robert Haas of Levi Strauss are successful business leaders who explicitly incorporate ethical values in their decision making. Many of us teach the Principled Reasoning

Approach that Levi Strauss used in deciding whether to continue sourcing in China.[7] (I will not comment on the recent reversal of their initial decision to withdraw.) We need to ask, however, whether Aaron Feuerstein and Robert Haas are role models for all corporate chiefs, or whether their management styles are to be recommended only under certain circumstances. Do they represent an *option* or a moral *dictate*?

Second, the Moral Manager Model applies primarily to high-level decision makers in large business organizations. Most people in business are Indians, not chiefs. The vast majority of people in this country are employed in small- and medium-sized firms, many in non-business organizations, including government. Many people are self-employed or joined in ventures. The Moral Manager Model does not speak to their situation.

Third, we all engage in *business activity*, not only as employees but as consumers, investors, and in a variety of other roles. Each one of us runs a small business, known as a household. The word *economics*, as we all know, derives from the Greek term for household management. In thinking about the Moral Manager Model, I have paused to reflect on how I conduct my own life. I consider myself to be a reasonably good, ethical person and a pretty good ethical reasoner. Yet, I realize that I conduct business activity mainly as a typical *homo economicus*. As the manager of a household, I employ maintenance and repair workers; I buy groceries and other supplies; I borrow money from lenders. In each instance, I act and think as a market participant who strives to obtain the best value. Faced with this realization, I have to ask myself: If this is how I conduct my life, why should I expect the manager of a business organization to act differently? What's wrong with managers being primarily economic actors? Why should they be moral philosophers as well?

The Moral Manager Model rests, I believe, on the assumption that the business *organization* is the fundamental unit of analysis for business ethics and that a business organization is directed by its top executives. As a result, the central task of business ethics becomes how to introduce ethics into corporate decision making, which is to say the thought processes of managers.

This focus on the organization and its leaders is exemplified by the cases that have powerfully shaped our conception of business ethics, such as the success stories of James Burke at Johnson & Johnson and Roy Vagelos at Merck, or the cautionary tales provided by the Ford Pinto and Nestlé infant formula episodes. These kinds of cases suggest that the introduction of ethics into business must overcome two main obstacles. One is the logic of *bureaucracy*, which has been explored in business ethics by John Ladd and Robert Jackall in influential works.[8] The other is the logic of the *marketplace*.

Bureaucracies and markets each have an ideal of rationality. In the face of these two "logics," the fundamental problem of business ethics underlying the Moral Manager Model can be further characterized as introducing ethics into organizations that already embody two powerful ideals of rationality. The rationality of ethics needs to be combined somehow with the logic of bureaucracy and the logic of the marketplace.

What's the alternative to the Moral Manager Model? The alternative is a conception of business ethics that focuses on individuals acting in a marketplace.

Markets rather than organizations would be the focus of business ethics. And the fundamental problem is how to create moral markets.

Of course, the justification of market activity is the point of Adam Smith's famous "invisible hand" argument. By seeking personal gain in market exchanges, a person "is led by an invisible hand to promote an end which was no part of his intention." We point out to our students that this argument presupposes efficient markets and effective regulation. And many ethical problems in business arise from market and regulatory failures. Many of the leading questions for business ethics ask how best to overcome these failures.

The Moral Manager Model places the responsibility on the leaders of business organizations and seeks to influence their discretionary decision-making authority. The model I propose—let's call it the Moral Market Model— would place responsibility on all of us to improve the business system. That is, to create more efficient markets and more effective regulation.

Let me illustrate the Moral Market Model and contrast it with the Moral Manager Model by briefly considering three prominent themes in business ethics, namely responsibility, participation, and relationships.

One recurrent theme in business ethics is that individual responsibility has been lost in the modern business system and ought to be restored. Robert Jackall, in his analysis of corporations, documents the myriad ways in which individual responsibility is diffused and evaded.[9] Ambrose Bierce in *The Devil's Dictionary* defines a corporation as "An ingenious device for obtaining individual profit without individual responsibility."[10]

Echoing Bierce, Alan Wolfe describes the corporation, on the standard economic view, as "*a device through which human beings, who have moral obligations, come together for the purpose of ridding themselves of their capacity to exercise moral obligations.*"[11] The corporation, he adds, is a "mechanism of responsibility displacement," and, he continues, "If chimpanzees could be trained to count, they would be just as good, if not better, managers than human beings."[12]

The Moral Manager Model reflects these sentiments and offers a corrective. A moral manager is one who takes individual responsibility and thereby becomes more fully human, more than a counting chimpanzee.

The Moral Market Model does not dismiss individual responsibility as unimportant but stresses the importance of role responsibility in economic organizations. In order to enjoy the benefits of joint production, we commit ourselves to certain roles and bind others to their roles. And we expect everyone, ourselves included, to fulfill their obligations in those roles. Without a system of role responsibility, large-scale business organizations and a global market system would be impossible. On the Moral Market Model, individual responsibility enters into the picture at the beginning, when we create roles and commit ourselves to them. Once these roles are assumed, individual responsibility has limited scope.

The Moral Market Model's emphasis on role responsibility encourages a market system and a system of corporate governance that minimizes individual discretion and favors rules. William Baumol in his book *Perfect Markets and Easy Virtue: Business Ethics and the Invisible Hand*, observes: "The invisible hand does not work by inducing business firms to pursue the goals of society as a matter of conscience and goodwill. Rather, when the rules are designed properly it gives management no other option.[13] Instead of "Increase responsibility," the motto of the Moral Market Model, then, might be "Reduce options."

Two examples can serve to illustrate the different approaches of the two models with respect to responsibility. First, the American Law Institute's proposed Principles of Corporate Governance includes a controversial section 201 (b) that would permit managers to "take into account ethical considerations that are reasonably regarded as appropriate to the responsible conduct of business." In short, managers should have the freedom to act responsibly! Who could possibly oppose this? This section is perfectly in accord with the Moral Manager Model. However, from a Moral Market perspective, the adoption of the ALI proposal would free managers from their role responsibility. And that would make them not more responsible but less so. The danger of section 201(b) is that it would upset the carefully defined system of rules that keeps managers restrained, to serve society's interests.

Second, the Federal Sentencing Guidelines (also known as the Ethics Consultant Full Employment Act) has been criticized because it makes the adoption of ethics programs a matter of expediency rather than conviction. The Moral Manager Model would have managers institutionalize ethics because that is the right thing to do, not because it provides legal protection. The approach of the Federal Sentencing Guidelines is right in line with the Moral Market Model, however, because of its emphasis on creating market incentives.

Turning now to the theme of participation, the Moral Manager Model recognizes that business organizations are undemocratic but insists nonetheless that every group has a right to participate in decisions that affect them. In the absence of effective participation in decision making, managers should at least consider each group's interests. This kind of consideration is an essential component of Goodpaster's Type 3 thinking and also of stakeholder theory.

The Moral Manager model encourages participation *in corporate decision making*. By contrast, the Moral Market Model emphasizes participation *in markets*. Not only do we participate actively in markets as consumers and investors, and perhaps as providers of goods or services, but business organizations themselves are a kind of market in which we participate as employees.

The two models offer differing prescriptions for increasing participation. The Moral Manager Model favors more inclusive decision making. Thus it applauds wider representation on boards of directors, other constituency statutes, and the like. Despite this call for greater inclusiveness, the Moral Manager Model is still highly paternalistic. In contrast, the Moral Market Model would remove areas of decision making from managers and place them in other hands. Meaningful participation on this model is the opportunity for each group to achieve its own ends through participation in a market system.

Dan Gilbert makes this point in a critique of Goodpaster's proposal for Type 3 thinking. Although Goodpaster's project is motivated by the attempt to introduce respect for persons into the corporation, Gilbert charges (correctly, I believe) that it reflects a "profound disrespect" for persons as beings capable of pursuing their own ends.[14] The alternative for Gilbert is a conception of the corporation in which individuals become independent by bargaining with others. This I interpret as something akin to the Moral Market Model.

Let me offer two quick illustrations of the differences between the two models with regard to participation. Traditional corporate pension plans place control in the hands of managers and thereby create an obligation for them to act responsibly. This is in accord with the Moral Manager Model. With the increasing availability of portable, fully vested pension plans, employees are now freed from a reliance on the good will of management and given the power to control their own funds. This latter approach, I suggest, is more in keeping with the Moral Market Model.

In a similar vein, secure employment in the American workplace has been giving way to the concept of employability, whereby employees and employers alike have an obligation to maintain marketable skills. Making secure employment a corporate objective accords with the Moral Manager Model by putting responsibility in the hands of management. By contrast, enabling people to manage their own careers presents a Moral Market Model solution.

Finally, I come to the theme of relationships. Business ethicists have rightly seized upon the importance of relationships in business and the role that integrity, trust, and care play in developing and sustaining relationships. By so doing, the field of business ethics has been able to make a significant contribution, primarily because of the neglect of relationships in neo-classical economic theory and the practice of American management.

The Moral Market Model does not neglect relationships but regards them differently. First, some business ethicists appear to regard relationships in business as having inherent value. We value relationships in our private lives because they are essential to our search for meaning and fulfillment. To have relationships is essential for being human. It does not follow, however, that relationships have the same value in business.

In some parts of the world, relationships are essential for doing business. This sometimes takes the form of "crony capitalism," and we see the fruits of this today in the wreckage of some Asian economies. An often-praised feature of the Japanese economy is the close relationships that consumers develop with retailers. The corner gas station provides solicitous, personal service for the price of an expensive fill-up. In recent years, however, Japanese consumers have shown that they don't want a relationship with the corner gas station. They prefer cheap fuel in a quick, impersonal market exchange. You may recall the time when Alice, in the Dilbert comic strip, was scheduling Saturday morning meetings because she didn't have a life outside work and wanted the human contact.

On the Moral Market Model, the ideal business relation is not an open-ended relationship but a fully-defined contractual relation. Unfortunately, completely planned business relations are not possible for many reasons, the prime ones being the complexity of business situations, incomplete knowledge, and uncertainty about the future. A major challenge for business is to structure relationships that compensate for the inability to write precise contracts. This task is the central concern of agency theory.

Two points should be observed here. First, on the Moral Market Model, relationships are best avoided. They exist—or should exist—only to the extent that precise contracts cannot be written. Second, many means exist for structuring business relationships where precise contracts are not possible. Integrity, trust, and other ethical supports for relationships may be effective in some situations, but they are not always essential to business relationships nor the most effective means available.

These two perspectives on relationships have very practical implications for regulation. Both self-regulation and government regulation have ranged between two sets of polar opposites. The two poles in self-regulation are informal and formal modes of social control. And government regulation in the United States has alternated between the two poles of trust and contract approaches.

Sociologists have observed that as societies become more complex, they move from informal social control based on personal relations to formal controls based on impersonal contracts.[15] Whereas simpler natural communities tend to restrain self-interest by developing social bonds, more complex artificial societies attempt to channel self-interest in socially beneficial ways. The history of American regulation reveals two opposing approaches to regulation. One is a trust approach, which makes managers trustees or fiduciaries whose conduct is bound by social norms. The other is regulation by means of contractual relations that operate by market rules.[16]

In general, the Moral Manager Model involves a preference for informal modes of social control and a trust approach to regulation, whereas the Moral Market Model favors formal modes of social control and a contract approach to regulation.

I would like to conclude by speculating on the motivation for the Moral Manager Model. Why has it dominated thinking in the field of business ethics? I see two motivating forces. One is a distrust of markets and a belief in the need for a guiding hand. The moral manager is thus a part of Alfred Chandler's "visible hand" that complements the invisible hand of Adam Smith.[17] The other motivating force is the communitarian impulse, which resists the movement toward mass society, in which personal and informal relationships are replaced by impersonal, contractual relations. Communitarianism stresses the themes of responsibility, participation, and relationships that I have discussed.

Finally, it has been observed that the depiction of a corporation as a community that reflects the values of its top executives is an application of the policy framework developed at the Harvard Business School.[18] The dominance of the Moral Manager Model, therefore, might be attributed to the influence of Harvard. The Moral Market Model, on the other hand, reflects more the thinking of the Chicago school of economics. The Moral Market Model which I am proposing, is in an early stage of development. I cannot describe it fully. But I invite each of you, now sitting comfortably here in San

Diego, to join me in moving away from Boston in the direction of Chicago. In doing so, you will be taking an exciting intellectual journey that promises to change the direction of the field of business ethics.

Notes

This paper was presented as the Presidential Address to the Society for Business Ethics, at the Annual Meeting in San Diego, California, August 8, 1998.

1. Robert J. Samuelson, "R.I.P.: The Good Corporation," *Newsweek*, July 5, 1993, p. 41.
2. See William H. Davidow and Michael S. Malone, *The Virtual Corporation* (New York: HarperBusiness, 1992).
3. Albert J. Dunlap, *Mean Business* (New York: Random House, 1996).
4. Kenneth E. Goodpaster, "Ethical Imperatives and Corporate Leadership," in *Business Ethics: The State of the Art*, ed. R. Edward Freeman (New York: Oxford University Press, 1991).
5. Goodpaster, "Ethical Imperatives and Corporate Leadership," p. 97.
6. John R. Boatright, *Ethics and the Conduct of Business*, 2nd ed. (Upper Saddle River, N.J.: Prentice Hall, 1997), p. 19.
7. "Levi Strauss and Co.: Global Sourcing (A)," Harvard Business School, 9-395-127.
8. John Ladd, "Morality and the Ideal of Rationality in Formal Organizations," *Monist* 54 (1970); Robert Jackall, "Moral Mazes: Bureaucracy and Managerial Work," *Harvard Business Review*, September–October 1983.
9. Robert Jackall, *Moral Mazes: The World of Corporate Managers* (New York: Oxford University Press, 1988.
10. Ambrose Bierce, *The Devil's Dictionary* (New York: World, 1911).
11. Alan Wolfe, "The Modern Corporation: Private Agent or Public Actor?" *Washington and Lee Law Review* 50 (1993): 1686.
12. Wolfe, "The Modern Corporation," p. 1686.
13. William Baumol, *Perfect Markets and Easy Virtue: Business Ethics and the Invisible Hand* (Oxford: Blackwell, 1991), p. 53.
14. Daniel R. Gilbert, Jr., "Respect for Persons, Management Theory, and Business Ethics," in *Business Ethics: The State of the Art*, ed. R. Edward Freeman (New York: Oxford University Press, 1991), p. 116.
15. For an example, see E. A. Ross, *Social Control* (New York: Macmillan, 1901).
16. The distinction is due to Adolf A. Berle, Jr., and Gardiner C. Means, *The Modern Corporation and Private Property* (New York: Macmillan, 1932).
17. Alfred D. Chandler, *The Visible Hand: The Managerial Revolution in American Business* (Cambridge: Belknap Press, 1977).
18. Gilbert, "Respect for Persons, Management Theory, and Business Ethics," p. 113.

Ethical Challenges in a Market Economy: Do the Right Thing When Nobody is Looking

Thank you, Phil, [Stone] for the nice introduction and for inviting me to be your speaker this evening for the Scott Symposium on Business Ethics. You have been a gracious host, and I can certainly sense why Bridgewater College has become even more special under your leadership.

As Dr. Stone mentioned, I grew up near Staunton, so it's always a pleasure to come back to the Shenandoah Valley. My roots are here, and this is also where I got my first lessons in right and wrong. My parents were both public school teachers, and as I was growing up I had the sense that they were always looking for "teachable moments"—chances to give to their students, along with my brothers Jimmy, Doug and me, lessons in life to go with their academic teaching.

I'm not sure where I heard it—maybe from a teacher or a Scout leader—but somewhere along the way in my early life I heard a simple test of ethical behavior that has stuck with me for all these years. And that is "Do the right thing when nobody's looking."

That phrase was in the back of my mind as I went off for my freshman "rat" year to Virginia Tech. At that time, Tech was run like a military academy, and when a member of the corps of cadets broke the ethics code in a serious way he was "drummed out." The drumming-out ritual was chilling. In the middle of the night, every cadet was rousted out of bed and marched in formation to the courtyard. With an eerie drum roll, we were commanded to turn our backs to the offending cadet as someone recited his honor code violations. It was an experience one never forgets.

Just as I learned many important lessons during my years at Virginia Tech, I am sure that those of you who are Bridgewater students will reap many benefits from your education in this very special place. To make it to the top in today's very competitive workplace, you'll need a broad understanding of how the business world works. But if you want to stay there and remain successful over the long term, then you'll need something even more important: a solid ethical foundation.

Now, that may seem like a surprising statement because, as I'm sure you're aware, the picture of business ethics that has emerged over the past few

From The Scott Symposium on Business Ethics at Bridgewater College, Bridgewater, Virginia, April 11, 2005.

years isn't very pretty. It seems like every week we hear another story about corporate dishonesty, deception, or self-serving acts. Sometimes, it seems like we have a business culture that is ethically challenged.

Let me say up front that I'm no expert on the academic study of business or economic ethics, and I certainly don't want to place myself or my organization on an ethical pedestal. In my role at the Federal Reserve, our nation's central bank, however, I interact with a wide cross section of business leaders. And in my role as a monetary policymaker, I have become especially sensitive to the health and integrity of our United States financial system. Let me emphasize that I believe that corruption in business is still the exception and not the norm. But I have seen how just a few instances of unethical behavior can seriously undermine our market economy and our broader society.

It's from this perspective that I'm going to argue today that the ability to provide leadership in ethics is more important than ever—for current and future business managers.

To make my case about the importance of ethics, let me start by assessing the scope of the problem and the damage caused by recent lapses in business ethics. Then I'll turn to some potential reasons for these problems, and finally share some thoughts on what steps we need to take as a society and as individuals to address today's challenges to business ethics.

The Scope of the Problem

Between 2002 and the end of last year, the U.S. Securities and Exchange Commission brought more than 1,300 civil cases against businesses and obtained orders for penalties in excess of $5 billion. Those numbers are higher than for any comparable period in the agency's history.

For many of us, the list of fallen corporate stars in recent times probably began with Enron. Then there was WorldCom, Tyco, Adelphia, and HealthSouth, to name just a few of the most notable companies that have been subjected to SEC enforcement actions. In addition, some of the top names in the mutual fund industry have settled SEC enforcement actions. And in October 2003, ten of the biggest firms on Wall Street paid a $1.4 billion settlement related to conflicts of interest between research and investment banking.

The nature of the ethical breaches has varied widely. Many cases involved accounting tricks used to inflate earnings and to protect the value of a company's stock. Some cases involved efforts to defraud investors through misleading advice or schemes that broke the rules, such as after hours trading of mutual funds. And in other cases, the motive was to directly benefit the personal wealth and ego of the top executive—for instance, spending millions of dollars of company money on personal art work, lavish parties or home improvements. And according to a news story last week, a senior corporate executive may have used company money to pay for an expensive kennel for his hunting dogs. I would argue that whatever the motive, all are examples of greed, hubris and poor ethical conduct. And while all such actions may or may not be illegal, unethical behavior often imposes a cost not only on the victim and the wrongdoer, but also on countless others including, I expect, many of us in this room.

As we saw with Enron and WorldCom a few years ago, many long-time employees lost their jobs and their retirement pensions as well. Shareholders also have taken a beating in the aftermath of corporate scandals, and many of the investors who were burned were highly sophisticated. Going back to peak valuations, shareholders saw a loss of market capitalization of some $66 billion in the case of Enron and $177 billion in the case of WorldCom.

But it's not just deep-pocketed investors and institutions that have suffered. Today, nearly half of all adult Americans participate in the stock market. That's compared with only about 6 percent in 1952. Millions of households invest in employer-sponsored plans and in mutual funds. In the aftermath of recent scandals, I've heard a number of young people express skepticism about investing in equities. Given the huge losses in recent years, it's understandable that folks are being more cautious in how they allocate their hard-earned savings.

In 2002, when many ethical scandals were coming to the surface, stock market investors saw years of gains vanish in a matter of months, in some cases in just days and weeks. In one survey taken in November 2003, 77 percent of investors reported they were less confident in the trustworthiness of corporate management, with 59 percent less confident in the safety of financial markets overall. These numbers jibe with my gut sense that the overall level of trust in businesses and financial markets has taken a big hit.

Moreover, we can't ignore the costs of new regulations that I believe were necessary to prevent such malfeasance in the future. In 2002, Congress overwhelmingly passed the Sarbanes-Oxley Act, a new law that is designed to tighten standards for accounting and require more disclosure on the part of public companies. The law also provides for much tougher penalties for executives and even directors who participate in or enable fraudulent behavior.

When it passed three years ago, only three votes were cast against this sweeping and complex legislation. That decisive congressional action is a testament to the public outcry for reform in corporate governance.

But the legislation brings a very substantial cost. A top executive of a large company with annual revenues of about $37 billion told me recently that his company estimated that Sarbanes-Oxley had added approximately $16 million a year to expenses. Another executive with a company with about $12 billion in annual revenues put the added costs at about $40 million annually. And it's not possible to quantify other indirect costs as senior executives shift their attention and resources from growing their businesses and creating new jobs to regulatory compliance. But based on anecdotal reports, I do have the sense that the extraordinary attention devoted to the new corporate governance rules very likely delayed strategic business decisions and capital investment decisions that we would have seen earlier as the economy recovered from the 2001 recession.

Clearly, corporate governance reform—while necessary—has been expensive. And that burden is being carried by the vast majority of businesses in our country that have always played by the rules. The money to pay for improved corporate governance comes out of corporate profits and represents another price we are all paying for corporate fraud and deception.

Reasons for Ethical Lapses

As we evaluate these costs, I think it's important to explore the underlying factors in the recent spate of business scandals. You can't blame it all on greed and hubris; these fundamental human flaws have been with us forever.

So what's new? Well, I believe one difference is the complexity of many of today's businesses. In the past decade or so, new technologies have spurred the evolution of our financial markets. New and innovative financial products enable transactions to occur more rapidly and efficiently than ever. The bad news is that this new automation has the potential to open new avenues for fraud.

Take Enron, for example. With the help of Wall Street investment bankers, accountants, and complex derivative instruments, Enron engaged in transactions that were nearly impossible to understand and untangle. In fact, a special investigative committee of Enron's board reviewed 430,000 pages of documents and interviewed scores of people about the so-called special purpose entities that were part of the Enron corporate hierarchy. Even with that intense level of scrutiny, I've read that they still haven't gotten to the bottom of everything Enron was doing. If boards of directors and experienced financial analysts couldn't figure out what's going on, how were novice individual investors supposed to understand these transactions?

A second factor that I believe makes ethical behavior more challenging is the intense competitive pressure of today's global marketplace. The temptation to cheat rather than fail is timeless, but in recent years this ethical dilemma may have become even more widespread.

Our most recent economic boom and bust cycle demonstrates how these pressures can play out and lead to a series of business scandals. During the late 1990s, people were investing huge sums of money based on extremely optimistic assumptions that rapid economic growth and market appreciation of corporate stock values would continue indefinitely.

It's true that the late 1990s saw great technological innovation and productivity gains that brought real value to our economy. The potential of the Internet and other technologies generated great excitement on Wall Street, and analysts fueled the fire by hyping dot-com companies and other hot stocks. They predicted sharply rising profits, quarter after quarter. But then the market got ahead of itself as investors poured money into undisciplined businesses, which were then held to improbable short-term targets. In the end, businesses and entire industries imploded.

Looking back at this climate of unrealistic expectations, we can see how these problems unfolded. Executives who were unable to meet their targets began to make use of confusing financial reporting, which helped to hide their actual performance. In some cases, businesses that reported clear and accurate numbers were actually at a competitive disadvantage.

The term "creative accounting" became a popular euphemism for nonstandard accounting practices involving novel ways of characterizing income, assets and liabilities. Enron touted its own accounting wizardry, and even some business schools were reported to be teaching creative accounting—something I trust you never taught here at Bridgewater.

A third factor contributing to the erosion of business ethics involves lapses in corporate governance. Starting at the top, businesses are designed with checks and balances to ensure management accountability and above-board operations, since in the modern corporation managers are distinct from owners, or stockholders.

If you're a member of a board of directors, it's your fiduciary duty to ask tough questions and intervene in questionable practices. But as businesses have become more complex and competitive, as I discussed a moment ago, these protections have not always sufficed and in some cases have broken down completely.

Aside from the additional analytical challenges, too many directors fell short on their core responsibilities. In some cases, there were conflicts of interest because directors had major deals pending with the businesses they were supposed to be overseeing on behalf of shareholders. In other cases, management gave themselves and their directors significant privileges and perks. As Abraham Lincoln once said, "Knavery and flattery are blood relations."

The structure of executive compensation also has led to problems and in some cases is now being rethought. For the past decade or so, many directors have been granting stock options as an incentive for management to run their businesses in a way that increases the company's stock price. While it makes sense to align performance with compensation, stock options have not always been carefully structured. In the worst cases, stock options actually motivated managers to do the wrong thing, such as manipulate short-term earnings to meet bonus targets or cash in on insider knowledge.

So, in addition to age-old traits such as fear of failure, greed, and pride, modern-day ethical challenges in business have been exacerbated by technologies that have spawned increasingly complex financial products and accounting techniques. Fierce global competition and more complex and demanding governance responsibilities are other factors. Since the underlying characteristics of these new developments are positive, we don't want to attack them. But we also can't ignore systemic flaws that lead to ethical lapses.

Society's Prescriptions

I would like to spend my last few moments thinking with you about what I believe we can do to bolster the ethical foundation of our economy. As I noted earlier, after the initial flare-up of corporate scandals a few years ago, Congress overwhelmingly passed the Sarbanes-Oxley Act to demand greater business accountability. So as a society, we've already taken steps to address some of the most glaring ethical weaknesses in our economy.

Despite the expense of the legislation that I described to you earlier, I believe Sarbanes-Oxley has led to some positive developments in business. In my view, stricter and more uniform accounting standards were needed, and I applaud the work of former New York Fed President Bill McDonough, who is now in charge of the Public Company Accounting Oversight Board, an authority created by Sarbanes-Oxley.

With tougher oversight and penalties on the books, today's boardroom culture seems to be changing. Corporate governance reform has weeded out some of the most egregious conflicts of interest.

As investors and board members become more skeptical and assertive, chief executives face more tough questions. In recent months, boards have "drummed out" several CEOs and senior executives for ethical lapses. I am optimistic that business leaders are becoming more accountable and are getting the message about ethics.

Moreover, there is evidence that with of all the attention devoted to fraud and the risks in the marketplace, investors are doing more homework. In the same survey from November 2003 that I mentioned before, 79 percent of investors report being more interested in how corporations are governed, with 68 percent more likely to seek financial and accounting information about investments.

I am encouraged that investors now seem to be getting more savvy. Markets are extremely sensitive to information flows, and they work best in a climate of accountability and transparency. With human nature as it is, secrecy is the enemy of ethical behavior. But transparency is an iterative process, not one that occurs all at once. Financial and commercial corporations are actively working on transparency and ethical behavior, and I believe they are making good progress to get it right.

As more information pours into the marketplace, we as individuals have obligations as well. It's up to each one of us to take advantage of this new openness and bear more responsibility for our investments. Read the footnotes, check multiple sources of information and use common sense to recognize that higher returns generally entail higher risk. As they say, if something sounds too good to be true, then it probably is too good to be true.

Next Steps—Individual Actions

Clearly, as a society we've taken forceful measures to address recent corporate scandals. But make no mistake: It takes everybody acting in a spirit of trust to make markets work effectively. That's why a strong ethical foundation is so important. Albert Einstein summed it up pretty well when he said, "Every kind of peaceful cooperation among men is primarily based on mutual trust and only secondarily on institutions such as courts of justice and police."

Of course we are a society of laws, and if you commit a corporate crime, you stand a high probability of getting caught and going to jail. That is certainly an incentive to behave ethically. But ethics requires obeying not just the letter of the law, but also the spirit of the law. As Federal Reserve Chairman Alan Greenspan has observed, our economy functions smoothly in large part because we can generally rely on trust.

Our first line of defense in preserving trust in our market economy should be a culture of ethics in all our organizations. Ethical behavior is good business, and it needs to take place on a day-to-day basis. Formal controls that foster ethical behavior on the part of every employee are part of the process. Ethics needs to become a habit.

All CEOs have to set the right tone at the top. But management cannot see and do everything, and lofty words can only do so much to foster good ethical behavior. In fact, many if not most of the companies now being prosecuted had high-minded vision statements, and their executives made eloquent speeches about corporate values. But in addition to just talking about ethics from time to time, we have to instill ethics throughout the workplace culture and up and down the whole organization, day after day and year after year.

Summing It All Up

This evening, I have tried to think with you about some of the reasons behind the recent flare-up in corporate scandals. I also have tried to convey a sense of the costs that fraud and corruption have imposed on all of us.

In closing, let me say again that we are fortunate to live in a competitive free-market economy that thrives on self-interest and the pursuit of maximum profit. As the Scottish economist and philosopher Adam Smith observed back in the late 18th century, "It is not from the benevolence of the butcher, the brewer, or the baker that we expect our dinner, but from their regard to their own interest."

But just as we are free to pursue our self-interests, individuals sometimes do bad things. And we live in a representative society where the public demands accountability and a reasonable degree of fairness. We have to acknowledge this tension between public and private interests without restraining the forces that make our economy strong. Above all, we must continually strengthen, and, when necessary, repair our ethical foundation to ensure trust in our financial markets and business enterprises.

Unless I miss my bet, as I was thinking out loud earlier in my remarks about some of my own growing up experiences that occurred just down the road from here, you were thinking about your own ethical issues. To the students here, I would suggest that your ethical challenges will only become tougher as you move into the workforce and gain more responsibilities. Having a strong ethical foundation will serve you well throughout your life. To the faculty here, I encourage you to continue to look for those teachable moments when you can underscore the importance of how one achieves results. And to the business and civic leaders, I challenge you to make a culture of ethics one of your high-priority objectives not just in 2005 but every year.

One of the things that I learned growing up in the Valley is the value of your word and your name. Living in a small community, you see one another most every day, and I expect it's still true that in many personal and business deals a handshake around here is as good as a notarized contract.

Now, I know things are more complex in our fast-paced global economy. You have to watch your back, read the footnotes, and be realistic about balancing risk and reward. But I still think we'll all be more successful, and ultimately happier with ourselves, if we practice that advice someone gave me many years ago somewhere along the way: "Do the right thing when nobody is looking."

POSTSCRIPT

Is It a Mistake to Urge Corporate Managers to Be Moral?

The manager's behavior is not predetermined; he has a range of discretion for the exercise of which he is responsible, within which he can set the company on more or less fruitful courses. Where do you come down: on the side of the pure business theory and the equally pure management imperatives, or on the side of common sense and flexibility?

Suggested Reading

For further reading:

Lisa Newton, *Permission to Steal,* (Malden, Mass.: Blackwell, 2006).

Internet References . . .

STAT-USA/Internet

This site, a service of the U.S. Department of Commerce, provides one-stop Internet browsing for business, trade, and economic information. It contains daily economic news, frequently requested statistical releases, information on export and international trade, domestic economic news and statistical series, and databases.

`http://www.stat-usa.gov/stat-usa.html`

PhRMA: America's Pharmaceutical Companies

PhRMA membership represents approximately 100 U.S. pharmaceutical companies that have a primary commitment to pharmaceutical research. Information on the effects of pharmaceutical price controls on research spending is one of the many topics covered at this site.

`http://www.phrma.org`

NumaWeb

This Numa Financial Systems site calls itself "the Internet's home page for financial derivatives." This site includes a reference index, a discussion forum, and links to many related sites.

`http://www.numa.com/index.htm`

Current Business Issues

*M*uch *as we like profitable businesses, and the benefits and taxes that they bring us, there is always the possibility that the pursuit of profit will go "too far" and negatively affect other valuable parts of our lives—our environment, our future security, the morals of our children (and neighbors), and the reliability of our public utilities. Where is government regulation and limitation of business enterprise needed? appropriate? inappropriate?*

- Is Privatizing Social Security Good Business?
- Should the States Regulate Appropriate Business Behavior?
- Is Wal-Mart a Good Model for Retail Sales?
- Does the Enron Collapse Show that We Need More Regulation of the Energy Industry?

ISSUE 5

Is Privatizing Social Security Good Business?

YES: David Altig and Jagadeesh Gokhale, from "Social Security Privatization: One Proposal," *Cato Institute*, www.Cato.org/pubs/ssps

NO: Thomas N. Bethell, from "What's the Big Idea?" *AARP Bulletin* (April 2005)

ISSUE SUMMARY

YES: David Altig and Jagadeesh Gokhale argue persuasively that the Social Security system, as presently running, cannot keep going indefinitely and that drastic solutions (involving radical cuts in benefits) may soon be the only way out of its deepening crisis. Their suggestion for privatization may be the best alternative to systemic collapse.

NO: Thomas Bethell does not share their alarm. The system can easily be kept solvent for the remainder of the century if we raise the payroll tax rate and make cuts in benefits. But there are at least nine other ways that the system can be kept above water without doing either of these.

The outlines of the dispute are clear enough: Social Security was initiated in 1935 to provide old age and survivors disability insurance; it was a mandatory government-administered fund, paid into by all workers, to take care of them when they were no longer able to work. In theory, it was like a collective bank account, that little bit of savings our fathers were always urging us to take out of each week's income for when we were old, in this case added to with a matching contribution from the employer; only it was mandatory, since by the Depression we knew that workers could not and would not accumulate sufficient personal savings to cover their retirement. In theory, you could only take out of the fund what you (and your employer) put into it. But the manifest unfairness of depriving all currently old and disabled persons of such income, when they were obviously very poor and had had no chance to pay into any such fund themselves, immediately changed Social Security into an old-age welfare program, funded not by the receivers but by the next generation of workers. Retirements weren't expensive then, or for a while, and workers seemed to have no objection to periodic increases in their Social Security contributions; the system did what it was supposed to do, and workers now had a good prospect of passing their post-work years in some semblance of dignity and comfort.

Except the money didn't stay where it was supposed to stay. In theory, the funds paid into Social Security each year, in excess of what was needed that year, were to have been put into a trust fund, the sole purpose of which was to fund the retirements of all eligible Americans. In practice, the excess was simply dropped into the general fund and spent for any purpose that seemed good at the time. Surpluses continued; even after adding Medicare to Social Security expenditures, more money has been coming in than has been going out.

But America is aging: as medical care improves, people live longer and longer, drawing down their Social Security entitlement; full-time, full-benefit jobs are leaving the country and being replaced by part-time and contract positions that do not contribute to the fund. The birth rate is dropping, and the surpluses will not continue forever. As a matter of fact, they'll stop by 2018, on current projections. If none of the fund money that has been spent on other programs is put back into Social Security, and if in fact we continue, in these last years of surplus, to treat Social Security funds as a free-for-all-purposes piggy bank, at the current rate of collection, there will not be enough money to pay benefits for all the new retirees—the Baby Boomers, the healthiest generation in history, expected to live to 100. What should we do about this looming crisis?

One popular suggestion is to create mechanisms by which Social Security levies could be redirected from the government to the capital markets—to Wall Street, for investment, where returns are ordinarily higher than in public investments. Altig and Gokhale have a proposal which has attracted some respect; note, however, that it has to be implemented almost immediately to do any good. Two major objections to this and to any such proposal have to be considered: First, there is the objection that Wall Street investments tend to serve the banks and the brokers first and mainly, leaving little for the retirees. It is not always so clear that money invested privately in the capital markets will have a higher yield than government securities; we have to pick our periods of comparison very carefully. Second, there is the objection that any scheme to hand over public money for private parties to use for their own profit is seriously flawed from the standpoint of justice, and that some alternative should be found. The question turns on trust: do we, as Americans, trust the private sector more than the public sector? Our traditions suggest that we do.

YES

David Altig and
Jagadeesh Gokhale

Social Security Privatization: One Proposal

Executive Summary

As Social Security's problems become more apparent, there is growing support for privatizing the retirement program. As the debate intensifies, it becomes more important to move beyond generalizations and provide detailed proposals for accomplishing privatization. Without endorsing any specific proposal, the Cato Project on Social Security Privatization will present a number of possible privatization scenarios.

In this study, David Altig and Jagadeesh Gokhale offer a proposal based on the following key elements:

- Workers under age 32 would be allowed to divert up to 46 percent of their payroll taxes to individually owned, privately invested accounts, similar to individual retirement accounts or 401(k) pension plans. The remainder of the payroll tax would be used to continue to provide benefits for the currently retired and those who will retire soon.
- Assuming private investment returns below historic averages, individuals in the privatized system would receive retirement benefits equal to or greater than those currently promised by Social Security. However, individuals would receive no recognition of or benefits based on past payroll taxes paid.
- During the early years of the transition, the government would issue new debt to supplement revenues from the continuing portion of the payroll tax. Once benefits to current and soon-to-be retirees had been paid, the continuing portion of the payroll tax would be used to service and retire the debt.
- No new taxes are required to finance the transition.

The authors make the important point that the window of opportunity for such a privatized system is narrow. For example, if the system were implemented immediately, workers under the age of 32 could shift to the privatized system, diverting 46 percent of their payroll taxes to individual accounts. However, if privatization were delayed until 2011, only individuals under the

From *Cato Journal*, May 29, 1997. Copyright © 1997 by Cato Institute. Reprinted by permission.

age of 20 could move to the new system, and those individuals could divert only 22.1 percent of their payroll taxes. Therefore, moving to a privatized Social Security system takes on a new urgency.

Introduction

The U.S. Social Security system, now more than 60 years old, has grown from a small program designed to provide retirement security to a massive and complex system that transfers resources between different demographic groups. Concern about how to reform Social Security to meet future needs is likely to intensify as the oldest members of the baby-boom generations (those born from the mid-1940s through the mid-1960s) begin to retire and collect their Social Security benefits in the year 2008—just 11 years from now. The strain of maintaining the existing system in the face of changing demographics has the potential to provoke significant conflict between the interests of the young and those of the old. Indeed, maintaining the current system will inevitably require either substantial increases in the tax burden on younger workers or reductions in the benefit levels of retirees.

Under current contribution and benefit rules, the program is expected to provide today's workers with rates of return that are much lower than the average returns obtainable by investing in private capital markets. Even worse, projections of Social Security finances under those rules suggest that the system will enter financial insolvency by the year 2012 (instead of by 2029 as officially recognized by the Social Security Administration). The strategy of restoring the current system's long-range solvency by reducing benefits or by increasing worker contributions has several drawbacks, not the least of which is a further deterioration in the returns for young workers.

Our position is that, under reasonable economic and demographic assumptions, it may be possible to reform Social Security in a manner that avoids the stark choice of abrogating promised benefits or escalating tax burdens, while at the same time placing the retirement of current and future generations on a sound economic foundation. Like other advocates of reform, we propose moving toward a mandatory privatized retirement system. Unlike many others, however, our proposal follows the "no harm, no foul," principle: the benefits of older generations are preserved while the young obtain the same or better benefits (on average) by investing a major part of their current payroll contributions in private capital markets.

At its core, our proposal hinges on the fact that returns to private capital exceed the growth rate of the wage-income tax base, which has been diminished by both slow growth of labor productivity and unfavorable demographic developments. In essence, we ask the following question: taking current rates of payroll contributions as given, is it feasible to (a) shift those below some specific age to a privatized system, (b) finance the benefits promised to those over that age under the current system, and (c) provide retirement resources to participants under the new system that are no smaller than what they could reasonably expect under the status quo? Using a straightforward generational accounting exercise based on official population projections and reasonable assumptions about rates of return, we conclude that the answer to that question is yes.[1]

The approach we outline contains several desirable elements. First, it establishes a defined contribution system for young generations, thus tightening the link between contributions and benefits and thereby improving work incentives. In addition, the plan gradually eliminates the ongoing intergenerational redistribution of resources, a major cause of the sustained decline in U.S. saving. Furthermore, economic theory suggests that the economic distortions of financing the transition to a privatized system can be minimized if, after adjusting for rising incomes due to growth, the burden of benefit obligations to older generations is spread across all future generations via a proportional (flat) tax.[2] Our plan incorporates that feature, thus reinforcing incentives for work, saving, and investment.

Second, unlike other plans that may require additional nonpayroll taxation to pay off or service debt created during the transition to a private system, our plan has as its foundation the current payroll tax structure and existing payroll tax rates. Hence, it will not introduce ancillary saving disincentives for individuals—due to, for instance, additional income taxation—that can mitigate the beneficial macroeconomic effects of privatization. In the broader context of fiscal reform more generally, this feature may be particularly important: recent research by economists Alberto Alesina and Roberto Perotti indicates that higher payroll taxes (or personal income taxes more generally) are typically associated with unsuccessful reform efforts.[3]

Finally, and perhaps most important, our plan meets the requirements that any reform proposal be economically sustainable and politically feasible. It is economically sustainable because it provides for the retirement security of all future generations. It is politically feasible because it preserves the benefits to older generations while offering the promise of the same or better retirement security for younger generations.

After a general discussion of the trends and issues that motivate our proposal, we present the basic plan, but first a preview: under our baseline assumptions we calculate that immediate implementation of a "no harm, no foul" privatization scheme would involve shifting all workers below age 32 to a defined contribution private pension plan with the following provisions: (a) workers shifted to the privatized system forfeit all claims to accrued Social Security benefits; (b) mandated total "contributions" remain at existing levels; and (c) roughly 46 percent of the contributions in the privatized system are allocated to approved private saving vehicles, and the balance is dedicated to financing the acquired benefits of all those aged 32 and older (who remain in the existing system).

An important aspect of the calculations reported in this paper is that a reform of the nature we propose has a limited window of opportunity. Specifically, as the retirement date of the last of the baby boomers grows nearer, the tax burden on current and future workers required to finance the benefits of retired cohorts at current levels increases, and the net return to those shifted to the privatized system is diminished. In fact, given our assumptions, the type of privatization we envision would not be technically feasible beyond the year 2011.

The practical consequence of the limited window of opportunity is that the cutoff age becomes lower, and the necessary tax portion of total contributions becomes larger, as the date of the plan's implementation is pushed further into the future.

A final note before proceeding: we focus our attention solely on the implied liabilities of the current system and a plan to honor those obligations while shifting to a mandatory privatized pension scheme. Our proposal intentionally omits fiscal strategies for supporting current and prospective non-Social Security government expenditures that are financed from surplus Social Security contributions.

The Current Status of the U.S. Social Security System

The U.S. Social Security program was created in 1935 during the aftermath of the Great Depression. Although motivated by the desire to provide assistance to the needy elderly of the time, it was not established as a short-term welfare program. Rather, its founders' objective was to create a long-lasting system for ensuring economic security during retirement. The program was expanded in 1939 to provide survivors' benefits to the spouses and children of covered workers and yet again in 1956 to provide disability insurance. Hence, the program is known as Old-Age and Survivors and Disability Insurance (OASDI).

People become eligible for various benefits by paying money into the system when they are working. Frequent rate hikes since the 1940s have increased the fraction of wages that workers pay into the system.[4] Social Security benefits have also increased rapidly as a result of far-reaching changes in both the scope and the generosity of the system. At its inception, Social Security was essentially a funded system. Only workers *under* age 65 in commerce and industry (except railroad employees and agricultural and domestic workers) were covered. However, persistent poverty among the elderly forced an abandonment of any pretense of full funding. In 1939 Congress extended coverage to those *over* age 65, regardless of their previous contributions to the system, thus firmly anchoring the system in a pay-as-you-go (PAYGO) framework involving intergenerational transfers. Additional extensions progressively brought an ever larger fraction of the population under compulsory Social Security coverage. Moreover, the benefit formulas were amended on several occasions to increase benefit payments.[5]

The broadening of Social Security's coverage across additional demographic groups has brought about a sizable (and ongoing) *intra*generational transfer of resources: in addition to old age insurance, the system provides protection against financial destitution as a result of widowhood, child and spousal dependency, divorce, and disability. For that reason, Social Security treats married couples and women more favorably than single individuals and men. Although that redistribution is motivated by social considerations, from an economic standpoint it breaks the link between the amount that different groups pay into the system and the benefits that they receive from it. Because of that, many workers may be viewing Social Security payments as taxes rather than pension contributions meant to secure their own retirement. The Social

Security payroll "tax" thus adds to marginal income tax rates and worsens individual incentives to work.

Further, the expansion of PAYGO Social Security benefits (along with the growth in health benefits via Medicare and Medicaid) occasions an ongoing transfer of resources across generations—from young and unborn generations to older retirees. Because older individuals consume a much larger fraction of their available lifetime resources than do young and unborn generations (the latter of whom have zero current consumption), some observers have identified such *inter*generational resource transfers as the chief cause of the dramatic and sustained decline in U.S. national saving since the mid-1970s.[6]

Judging the long-term financial prospects of Social Security is tricky business. Taken at face value, official projections of the Social Security Administration suggest that the system will remain financially solvent for another 33 years. Through 2018 the system is expected to generate annual surpluses of income (including interest) over expenditures. Thereafter, the excess of projected outgo over income will require the redemption of the trust fund's government bonds. Trust fund holdings of those bonds will decline rapidly after 2018 and are expected to be exhausted by the year 2029 (Figure 1). However, those numbers tell only part of the story. The trust fund's finances are intimately related to those of the rest of the government, and analyzing them independently can create an unwarranted illusion of security.

Figure 1

Projected Income, Outgo, and End-of-Period Assets under Intermediate Assumptions

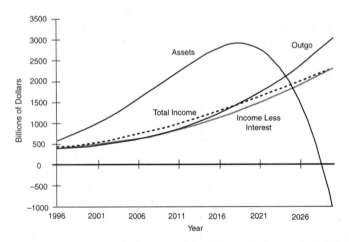

Source: 1996 Annual Report of the Board of Trustees of the Old Age, Survivors, and Disability Trust Funds (Washington: Government Printing Office, 1996), Table III.B3. Detailed data provided by the Social Security Administration.

Note: Income includes income from payroll contributions, taxation of benefits, payments from the general fund of the Treasury, and interest earnings. Outgo includes benefit payments, administrative expenses, and payments to the Railroad Retirement system. These are the Social Security Administration's calendar year projections based on intermediate economic and demographic assumptions.

The key feature that irrevocably links the Social Security trust fund to the government's general budget is the statutory requirement that any surplus be invested in Treasury securities. The requirement that trust fund surpluses be invested in government bonds makes those funds available for current government expenditure. Hence, almost all current contributions are consumed, either by retirees or by the government.[7] Indeed, that implies that most worker contributions *to date* have been consumed rather than invested in real assets (real capital in the form of plants, equipment, and structures).[8] Therefore, almost all contributions represent an investment, not in tangible income-generating assets, but in the willingness and ability of future workers to contribute to the system. In other words, the Social Security trust fund is merely an accounting device that creates the illusion of a "funded" system, whereas in reality it is completely "unfunded." As a consequence, judgment about the long-term solvency of the system should be based on when income from payroll contributions plus taxation of benefits begins to exceed outgo, not on the reported magnitude of accumulated trust fund surpluses.

According to the official projections, outgo will exceed the sum of payroll contributions and revenue from benefit taxation in the year 2012. Therefore, the cost of honoring benefit obligations will spill over to other tax revenue sources. Because the first wave of baby boomers will begin to retire in 2008, the inevitable conclusion is that the current system is incapable of meeting its benefit obligations to those workers and future generations.

Related to the solvency issue is the fact that, given the anticipated decline in the number of working-age individuals relative to retirees—and recognizing that the effects of that decline are not likely to be offset by an acceleration in wage growth—the return that future retirees can expect to realize from Social Security is significantly lower than what could be earned from private pension contributions.

As can be seen in Figure 2, the inflation-adjusted rate of return for future beneficiaries of the system is projected to fall well below 2 percent, which is much lower than, say, the rate of return on long-term government securities. In fact, the outlook is even worse than that implied by Figure 2, which calculates expected returns on the basis of gross benefits. As discussed in the previous section, the need to reduce benefits or increase contributions will drive the net return to Social Security even lower, possibly even negative. Simply put, the existing public PAYGO pension system is a bad deal for both current and future workers.

Options for the Future

In the future, a policy of imposing sizable benefit cuts is likely to come up against several hurdles. First, benefit reductions will become increasingly difficult as the number and political power of retirees and near-retirees grow progressively greater relative to the rest of the population. Second, although Congress has the authority to change Social Security's tax and benefit rules, the system has so far encouraged the sentiment that retirees have *earned* the

Figure 2

Real Internal Rates of Return for OASDI

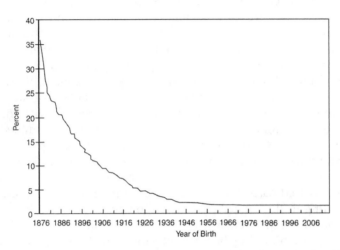

Source: Dean Leimer, "Cohort-Specific Measures of Lifetime Net Social Security Transfers," Working paper 59, Office of Research and Statistics, Social Security Administration, pp. 84–89.

right to benefits by virtue of their past contributions. Hence, although small benefit reductions may be feasible, *significant* benefit reductions will be perceived as an unfair abrogation of that right. In the worst case, the effects of major benefit reductions could be similar to those of repudiating (explicit) government debt—a loss of confidence in public policies and a reduction of the government's ability to engage in future borrowing. Third, substantial benefit cuts may jeopardize the living standards of a sizable fraction of those already retired or close to retirement—those with little time or ability left for amassing adequate retirement savings on their own.

Other proposals for reducing benefits include accelerating and extending the scheduled increase in normal retirement ages after the year 2000 and altering the inflation-indexing formula for benefit payments. We perceive those "solutions" as no less problematic than explicit reductions. Postponing retirement may involve economic hardship for some individuals if an extended life span does not coincide with an extended ability to work or to find gainful employment at an older age. Changing cost-of-living adjustments represents a marginal fix that will push the date of financial insolvency forward by only a few years. In either case, those proposals are thinly disguised benefit cuts at best and subject to all of the criticisms of explicit cuts noted above.

The option of increasing contribution rates to meet benefit obligations also poses problems: According to the official projections, a 2.19 percent increase in the contribution rate will restore Social Security's long-term solvency.[9] Such an increase, however, will further exacerbate the ongoing inter- and intragenerational redistribution of resources that produces bad saving outcomes and creates disincentives to work. In addition, that approach preserves the system's structural deficiencies that cause most current contributions to be consumed rather than invested in tangible physical capital assets.

A Simple Proposal for Privatizing Social Security

The basic point of the foregoing discussion is that the current structure of Social Security has several shortcomings: it detracts from incentives to work, contributes to declining national saving, and represents a bad deal for young workers. The current system is not sustainable, and the usual remedies of cutting benefits or increasing payroll taxes will only worsen the economic position of all generations—current retirees and soon-to-be retirees, as well as young and future generations.

The question, therefore, is whether there exists an economically and politically viable solution that avoids the shortcomings of the current system. Economic viability requires that the program be sustainable. Political viability implies that the system is acceptable to current (and future) participants. Any reform that would leave all participants at least as well off under the new program as under the current one would satisfy those conditions.

Does such an alternative exist? Our analysis suggests that it does. In the rest of this paper, we outline a reform proposal for privatizing the system by shifting future and some current young generations into a defined contribution plan for retirement saving. This is simply the outline of a privatization plan. It does not attempt to answer all the questions surrounding the regulation, design, and implementation of a privatized Social Security system. Rather, it provides a simple framework for calculating a strategy for financing the transition.

Under our proposal, workers below a specified cutoff age would be allowed to divert a portion of their Social Security payroll tax to an individually owned, privately invested account, similar to an individual retirement account or 401(k) pension plan. The remainder of the payroll tax would continue to be paid into the current system to finance benefits to current beneficiaries and those above the cutoff age. Workers in the new system would receive no recognition or accrued benefits for past taxes paid into the Social Security system. In addition, individuals in the privatized system would be responsible for using a portion of their returns to purchase private life and disability insurance, replacing Social Security's survivors' and disability benefits.

The reform we suggest applies only to future generations and current generations below a specified cutoff age. All current participants above the cutoff age remain under the existing system. Their benefits are financed by the payroll contributions of all current and future workers who are shifted to the privatized system. Despite the diversion of a part of their payroll contributions to meeting benefit obligations to older generations, the enhanced returns available from investments in private capital markets allow the retirement resources of young and future generations to be preserved or increased, on average. This plan satisfies both the economic viability and political feasibility conditions by adhering to the "no harm, no foul" principle: Because it preserves or improves the retirement resources of young and future generations, it is economically sustainable. Because it guarantees the retirement benefits of current retirees and those close to retirement, it is politically feasible.

Why would privatization be viewed as an attractive alternative for at least some current participants? Many of the benefits of privatization that we have discussed are primarily macroeconomic in nature. Although it may be clear how the economy as a whole might benefit, political support for privatization will emerge only if young workers can be shown that privatization is likely to provide them better retirement resources than can be provided under the existing regime, even after accounting for the taxation required to honor the benefit obligations to older workers and retirees. As suggested above, the case is supported by a comparison of the rates of return obtainable in PAYGO systems and those obtainable in defined contribution or "funded" systems. In the former, because each period's benefits are directly paid out of that period's contributions, the rate of return on contributions is ultimately tied to the growth rate of labor compensation. Real compensation approximately equals the sum of the rates of growth of labor productivity and the size of the working population. The growth rate of labor productivity averaged about 2.8 percent during 1950–69 but only 1.5 percent in the following 25 years.[10] Unfortunately, perhaps because of lower saving and investment in the 1970s and 1980s, growth in real compensation fell even more sharply, averaging only 0.67 percent during 1970–94 compared to 3.0 percent in the 1950–69 period.

In contrast to the feasible rate of return in a PAYGO system, we estimate that the after-tax rate of return on private-sector (for-profit) capital assets has averaged 8.2 percent since 1970.[11] Exploiting the disparity in the rates of return available from a PAYGO retirement scheme and one based on investment in private capital is the basis of most reform proposals, including those contained in the recently released report of the 1994–96 Advisory Council on Social Security (henceforth referred to as the ACSS report).[12] The novel insight provided by our calculations is that high private rates of return provide sufficient scope for a privatization plan that leaves all parties at least as well off as they would be under the status quo.

Before proceeding, we emphasize that by privatization we mean mandated contributions to approved private saving plans. Examples of such plans are the standard 401(k) plans. The essential element of such plans is that they are of the defined contribution type. Returns are not fixed but are tied to claims on private capital. It should be noted that our proposal does not permit the government to directly participate in private asset markets on behalf of participants. In particular, our proposal does not involve (nor do we recommend) the trust fund's Treasury securities being replaced by a portfolio of private stocks to be managed by the government, as is contemplated, for instance, under option 1 of the ACSS report. Such a swap of government obligations for private stocks would, in our opinion, perversely affect the incentives facing the government and private agents. In particular, it might provide the government with the incentive and the leverage to pursue industrial policy or otherwise try to influence private resource allocations.[13] Such ancillary agendas would probably undermine confidence in the plan and inhibit acceptance of a transition to a privatized system even in light of the superior returns that it can deliver relative to the current PAYGO scheme.

The "no harm, no foul" principle prescribes two conditions that must be satisfied in going to a private system. First, as noted, our rule requires that benefit obligations to retirees and those close to retirement who stay under the current system (those above the cutoff age) be met under the new plan. A portion of those obligations can be financed from the contributions of preretirees themselves. The remainder must be met out of the contributions of younger workers who participate in the new privatized system.

However, the second condition of the "no harm, no foul" principle is that the present value of returns in the privatized plan (net of the amount devoted to paying older generations' benefits) must at least equal the present value of benefits young workers would receive under the current Social Security system. The central issue to be resolved in our proposal is how to determine an appropriate cutoff age below which workers are shifted to the privatized plan and above which all participants who remain in the existing unfunded system receive the same benefits they could anticipate without the reform.

One key to the feasibility of our reform proposal is the fact that the rate of return in the privatized system will exceed that under the current PAYGO system. However, if the chosen cutoff age is too high, some workers will not have enough remaining years to exploit the increased private returns, leaving them worse off than before. A lower cutoff age provides younger generations with more time to accumulate plan contributions at the higher private rate of return. However, that must be traded off against the fact that the liabilities to those remaining under the current system (which increase as the cutoff age is lowered) must be partly financed out of the contributions of those who are shifted to the new plan (whose numbers decrease as the cutoff age is lowered). Choosing the appropriate cutoff age and the fraction of young workers' contributions to be devoted to paying off the liabilities to older generations requires balancing those concerns.

Calculations using the current distributions of Social Security benefits by age and sex suggest that 32 is the appropriate cutoff age.[14] If age 32 was the dividing line, about 54 percent of young workers' contributions would be adequate to provide older generations with benefits at least equal to those received under the current system. Furthermore, given our assumptions, future retirement resources for workers younger than 32 would be *greater* than those offered by the current system because those workers' contributions would reap the higher private rate of return for a longer period of time.

Our estimated cutoff age and share of contributions dedicated to financing existing benefits do, of course, depend on our specific assumptions. Those assumptions include the appropriate discount rate applied to

Table 1

Sensitivity Analysis of Cutoff Age for Shift to Privatized System

Private Capital Rate of Return	Benefit Discount Rate			
	5%	6%	7%	8%
6%	26	26	26	27
7%	30	29	29	30
8%	33	**32**	32	32
9%	35	34	34	34
10%	37	36	36	36

Note: The **bold** figure represents the benchmark case. Calculations assume an 8 percent annual return to private capital and a 6 percent rate of discount applied to Social Security benefits.

Table 2

Percentage of Contribution Dedicated to Financing Current Benefit Obligations

Private Capital Rate of Return	Benefit Discount Rate			
	5%	6%	7%	8%
6%	49.1	50.7	50.1	49.8
7%	49.9	52.5	53.3	54.0
8%	49.8	**53.5**	55.4	56.0
9%	49.5	53.8	56.2	57.4
10%	48.8	53.6	56.5	58.3

Note: The **bold** figure represents the benchmark case. Calculations assume an 8 percent annual return to private capital and a 6 percent rate of discount applied to Social Security benefits.

Social Security benefits and the return to private capital. Tables 1 and 2 provide information on how those estimates change given different choices for the values. In particular, the tables show that assuming lower average rates of return on private capital does not alter the results substantially. For example, with a 6 percent rate of return on private capital and the same rate of discount on benefit payments, the cutoff age falls to 26 and the fraction of young workers' contributions that must be devoted to paying older generations' benefits becomes 51 percent.[15] We emphasize that our essential message at this point is not so much that a particular cutoff age or "contribution tax" is the right one but that, given sensible parameters, the type of reform that we propose is feasible.

Debt, Taxes, and the Transition to a Private System

When discussing privatization of Social Security, some economists have expressed concern about the costs of transition from the current to a new, privatized system.[16] Under some proposals such a transition involves sizable increases in fiscal deficits and debt for financing the benefit payments to older generations, which means that the economic impact of privatization depends crucially on how the additional debt is serviced. For example, using higher income taxes to service the debt may harm saving incentives. The lower saving and investment may, at least temporarily, lead to slower economic growth. In contrast, the proposal outlined in this paper does not involve any taxation over and above payroll contributions at the current rate. Because our plan calls for paying full benefits under current law to older generations, but devoting only a part of current young workers' contributions to that end, the gap between benefit payouts and revenue earmarked for that purpose must be met by the creation of additional public debt. Debt creation on this account is temporary. Thereafter, the share of future generations' payroll contributions that is devoted to "paying off" benefit liabilities would be devoted to servicing the debt created along the transition path to the fully privatized system.

It is important to emphasize that debt creation associated with privatization imposes no additional liability on current and future generations. The role of debt in the plan is to implement an equal (growth-adjusted) distribution of the burden of benefit payments to current older generations that remain in the existing system. Diverting an equal (flat) proportion of young and future generations' wages to pay current retirees' benefits or to service the debt created by doing so makes possible an intergenerational sharing of costs for honoring promises to those who remain under the current Social Security program.

Truth in Advertising: Some Caveats and Complications

The calculations used to support our proposal are partial equilibrium in nature. That is, they do not take into account feedback from changes in the macroeconomy that would result from implementation of the privatization scheme that we advocate. For example, the fact that today the rate of return on capital is greater than the growth rate of the economy suggests that the U.S. economy is undercapitalized. Over time, privatization may be expected to increase saving and investment, thereby increasing the capital-labor ratio. That would reduce the rate of return on capital and increase the rate of labor compensation. All else being equal, a decline in the return to capital will tend to offset some of the higher returns to the privatized system. But all else will not be equal. The closer linkage between contributions and benefits inherent in a defined contribution plan is likely to improve incentives to work, increase labor-force participation, and dampen the increase in the capital-labor ratio. Moreover, the better work incentives and added saving and investment will probably mean that the fraction of young and future workers' contributions required for financing older generations' benefits will be lower than 54 percent.

A fully satisfactory examination of the proposal would require formal analysis in a general equilibrium context. We note, however, that the results reported in Tables 1 and 2 can be used to provide some sense of whether general equilibrium effects would overturn the feasibility of our privatization scheme. For example, in his recent work on Social Security privatization, Laurence Kotlikoff employs a model that implies a prereform annual posttax rate of return to capital of about 8 percent, identical to the assumed rate of return in our benchmark calculations.[17] In his analysis, a "cold-turkey" privatization that maintains some "no harm, no foul" provisions would cause the return to fall by about 16 percent. As seen in Tables 1 and 2, a change of such magnitude—which is quite large—would still leave us within the feasibility range for our proposal.

We have adopted the position that, at its core, Social Security is a pension system. That is an admittedly restrictive view, as the system in the United States also plays a role in redistributing income within given age groups and providing public insurance against macroeconomic shocks across generations.[18] We treat those goals as separate from the central purpose of Social Security and assume that, to the extent they are desirable, they can be met through alternative fiscal programs. Doing so may, of course, entail additional taxation and expenditure policies, with corresponding effects that we have not factored into this analysis. It is our position, however, that those should be treated as distinct from the pension issue, which is at the center of the Social Security system, as both an intellectual and a practical matter.[19]

One potential drawback to the type of privatized plan we describe is that a defined contribution scheme shifts market risk to contributors, thus mitigating its attractiveness. We respond to that argument in three ways: First, the issue of increased risk will arise to some degree in any reform scheme that has a defined contribution element, which is to say, most of them. Second, given the history of Social Security legislation and the questionable viability of the current system, benefits under the status quo are far from certain. Third, the magnitude of the spread between implied returns for current workers under Social Security and those available from investments in private capital over long horizons is sufficiently large to compensate for the greater uncertainty of the latter, even for people who are quite risk averse.[20]

Because our plan redirects all future contributions into private investments via private individually managed defined contribution plans, there remains the issue of how the government will finance that part of current spending paid for by the trust fund's annual surpluses. In this context, it is important to remember that the so-called trust fund—if its obligations are honored—amounts to nothing more than government bonds and the promise to increase taxes in the future. We view that spending as independent of the public pension system per se and believe that the nonpension aspects of fiscal policy should, in practice, be separated from the Social Security program, be it public or private in nature. Our preference would be to respond to the elimination of temporary Social Security surpluses by reductions in spending; we believe that there is value in an approach to reform that directly and exclusively addresses the need to provide retirement security without commingling the system designed for that purpose with other fiscal programs.

Nevertheless, the reality of the current situation forces consideration of how public spending currently being financed by Social Security's annual surpluses would be paid for under our proposal. We evaluate the impact of adding that spending to the liabilities to old generations in the privatized system proposed here. Doing so reduces the cutoff age to 30 and increases the fraction of payroll revenues devoted to paying off liabilities to 60 percent under our benchmark assumptions. Tables 3 and 4 show the results based on other discount rate combinations.[21] Thus, factoring into our calculations the cost of government spending that is now being financed by annual Social Security surpluses does not eliminate the economic and political feasibility of our plan.

Table 3

Sensitivity Analysis of Cutoff Age for Shift to Privatized System with Replacement of Surplus-Financed Government Expenditures

Private Capital Rate of Return	Benefit Discount Rate			
	5%	6%	7%	8%
6%	23	23	33	24
7%	28	27	27	27
8%	31	**30**	30	29
9%	34	33	32	32
10%	36	35	34	34

Source: 1996 Annual Report of the Board of Trustees of the Old-Age and Survivors Insurance and Disability Insurance Trust Funds (Washington: Government Printing Office, 1996), Table III.B3. Detailed data provided by the Social Security Administration.

Note: The **bold** figure represents the benchmark case.

Table 4

Percentage of Contribution Dedicated to Financing Current Benefit Obligations

Private Capital Rate of Return	Benefit Discount Rate			
	5%	6%	7%	8%
6%	54.4	56.9	57.0	57.1
7%	55.2	58.8	60.5	60.8
8%	55.0	**59.6**	62.1	62.7
9%	54.3	59.6	62.7	64.5
10%	53.5	59.3	62.9	65.2

Source: 1996 Annual Report of the Board of Trustees of the Old-Age and Survivors Insurance and Disability Insurance Trust Funds (Washington: Government Printing Office, 1996), Table III.B3. Detailed data provided by the Social Security Administration.

Note: The **bold** figure represents the benchmark case.

Some concern has been raised about the potential administrative costs of a privatized system, which by most accounts would exceed those of the current public system. That skepticism has been fueled in particular by the relatively high costs realized under the privatized plan implemented by Chile, which is often held out as a possible model for U.S. reform.[22] Because administrative costs will reduce the effective rate of return on private investment portfolios, the issue is important.

Ultimately, the administrative costs of a privatized system will depend on the exact nature of the plan, including whether benefits are annuitized or paid out in lump sums, the number and types of assets to which individual savers have access, and how much flexibility investors have in choosing among the available options. However, a sense of the probable magnitude of the administrative costs of the type of system we have described can be gleaned from a recent comprehensive study by Olivia Mitchell, who examined the typical costs of a variety of managed retirement saving vehicles.[23]

At one extreme, Mitchell finds that representative 401(k) plans—which have significant flexibility in payout and contribution options, among other features—have expenses that range from 0.84 to 1.88 percent of total assets.[24] At the other end of the spectrum, the costs of administering a simple stock index fund are in the area of only about 0.3 percent of assets. The College Retirement Equity Fund, an existing plan that has a large asset base and falls in between the other two alternatives with respect to flexibility and number of investment options, has expense ratios in the neighborhood of those of the simple index funds.

In fact, we think of the CREF structure as a reasonable model for the type of privatized plan we are espousing. Nonetheless, as the calculations in Tables 1–4 indicate, our plan would remain viable even at the relatively high expense ratios associated with existing 401(k) plans.

Conclusion

The plan described here suggests that it is indeed possible to restructure Social Security in a way that is economically viable and politically feasible, to place it on a secure and sustainable economic foundation for the long term while simultaneously honoring benefit obligations to current retirees and preretirees. The calculations we provide suggest that the most ambitious of privatized schemes, such as option 3 of the ACSS report, can be implemented without reducing benefits or increasing payroll taxes. Our specific numbers may, of course, be susceptible to additional refinement. However, the basic argument provides a sensible framework for addressing one of the most important fiscal challenges facing the nation in the next few decades.

Privatizing Social Security will, in addition to rendering the system sustainable, confer other benefits. Current tax and benefit rules generate a redistribution of resources both within and across generations, weakening the link between contributions and benefits. Further, the current system results in consumption of worker contributions rather than their investment in real capital assets. Hence, the current system harms work incentives and reduces

Table 5

The "Window of Opportunity"

Year of Reform Implementation	Cutoff Age	"Contribution Tax" Rate
1995	32	54.0
2000	30	57.4
2005	27	63.5
2010	22	74.3
2011	20	77.9
2012	Not feasible	Not Feasible

national saving. A transition to a privatized system would restore the link between contributions and benefits and would gradually reduce the ongoing redistribution of resources from young and unborn generations to older ones. It would thereby improve work effort, saving, and ultimately national output.

As a final point, we emphasize again that the window of opportunity for exploiting the benefits of a plan like the one we have proposed is relatively narrow. Table 5 gives, for different years of implementation, the cutoff ages and share of contributions that would have to be used to finance the benefits of those who are not shifted to the private plan. Deferring implementation reduces the former and increases the latter. Our plan would be economically infeasible if not implemented in or before 2011.

Given the rapid rise in the "contribution tax" necessary to honor the obligations to those who remain under the current system, political infeasibility may result well before that date. The type of Social Security privatization described here has several favorable features in comparison with other plans and is likely to hold up under a variety of alternative assumptions about the economic environment. Given that the window of opportunity is in fact narrow, we believe that our framework deserves careful consideration in current debates on Social Security reform.

Notes

The authors wish to thank Stuart Dorsey, Larry Kotlikoff, Randy Mariger, Bill Niskanen, Kent Smetters, and Carolyn Weaver for helpful comments. We are especially indebted to Michael Tanner for detailed discussions and input. All errors remain our own.

1. For a description of the general methodology of generational accounting, see Alan Auerbach, Jagadeesh Gokhale, and Laurence Kotlikoff, "Generational Accounting: A Meaningful Way to Evaluate Fiscal Policy," *Journal of Economic Perspectives* 8, no. 1 (Winter 1994): 73–94.

2. We make the usual assumption that nondistortionary lump-sum taxation is precluded.

3. Alberto Alesina and Roberto Perotti, "Fiscal Adjustment in OECD Countries: Composition and Macroeconomic Effects," IMF Working Paper WP/96/70, 1996.

4. Initially, the contribution rate was 2 percent applicable to wages up to $3,000, and the contribution per worker was limited to $60. Today the contribution rate exceeds 10.5 percent and is applicable to wages below $62,700. As a result, the *average* contribution per worker stood at $2,500 in 1994. The last figure is obtained by multiplying the average wage for 1994 ($23,753) by the contribution rate applicable in that year (10.52 percent).

5. Coverage was extended to seamen and bank and loan-association employees in 1939; to farm workers, domestic workers, and public workers not already covered under a government program in 1950; to the self-employed in 1954; and to employees of the uniformed services in 1956. Benefits were increased in 1950 and again in 1972. In 1975 they were indexed to the Consumer Price Index to keep pace with inflation.

6. See Jagadeesh Gokhale, Laurence Kotlikoff, and John Sabelhaus, "Understanding the Postwar Decline in US National Saving: A Cohort Analysis," *Brookings Papers on Economic Activity* 1 (1996). In addition, payment of Social Security benefits in the form of regular monthly checks until death (rather than in the form of a lump-sum distribution at retirement) provides insurance against life-span uncertainty. Although access to annuitized resources improves retirees' welfare by enabling them to consume their resources at a faster rate, annuitization may also constitute a reason for the decline in U.S. saving. Recent research suggests that the growth of entitlement and pension programs increased the annuitized share of the resources of the elderly from under 20 percent in the early 1960s to just under 50 percent in the late 1980s. See Alan Auerbach et al., "The Annuitization of Americans' Resources: A Cohort Analysis," National Bureau of Economic Research Working Paper no. 5089, 1995.

7. Most current payroll tax revenue is directly handed over to retirees and is consumed. In 1995, for example, of total revenue of $400 billion, $333 billion (83 percent) was paid out as OASDI benefits.

8. It is difficult to estimate precisely the fraction of trust fund assets that may be viewed as having been invested via government spending. At one extreme, all government spending may be called investment since government operations enable the private economy to function efficiently. At the other extreme, all government spending may be called consumption because it does not result in income-generating assets for the government. In any event, the essential issue is whether, at the margin, the return to government spending in terms of expanding the wage-tax base is higher or lower than the return to investment in private capital. The evidence appears to be ambiguous, but some recent studies suggest that, with the possible exception of spending on education, government investment expenditures do not add to private productivity. See Paul Evans and Georgios Karras, "Are Government Activities Productive? Evidence from a Panel of U.S. States," *Review of Economics and Statistics* 76, no. 1 (February 1994): 1–11; Douglas Holtz-Eakin, "Public Sector Capital and the Productivity Puzzle," *Review of Economics and Statistics* 76, no. 1 (February 1994): 12–21; and Kevin Lansing, "Is Public Capital Productive? A Review of the Evidence," Federal Reserve Bank of Cleveland Economic Commentary, March 1, 1995.

9. See *1995 Annual Report of the Board of Trustees of the Old-Age Survivors Insurance and Disability Trust Funds* (Washington: Government Printing Office, 1995), p. 133.

10. These figures are based on the *Economic Report of the President*, 1995 and 1997, Table B-47. The average labor productivity growth rates are based on the index of output per hour of all persons, and the average real compensation growth rates are based on the index of real compensation per hour.

11. The geometric mean rate of return was 8.1 percent. For each of the years 1970–93, we calculate the after-tax rate of return on private-sector (for-profit) capital by solving for r in the economywide asset accumulation equation, At = At–1(1+r) + Yt – Ct – Tt. Here, At stands for the capital stock in period t (excluding nonprofit organizations); Yt includes aggregate labor income, private and government employee pension benefits, veterans' benefits, workers' compensation, and government purchases; Ct represents aggregate personal consumption expenditures; and Tt stands for aggregate tax payments net of transfers. The data for At were taken from Federal Reserve System, *Balance Sheets for the U.S. Economy—1945-94,* and data for the rest of the variables are those reported in Bureau of Labor Statistics, "National Income and Product Accounts," *Survey of Current Business,* various issues.

12. The report is available at . . .

13. See Krzystof Ostaszewski, "Privatizing the Social Security Trust Fund? Don't Let the Government Invest," Cato Institute Social Security Paper no. 6, January 14, 1997.

14. Those calculations assume a 1.2 percent rate of growth in future benefits per capita, a 6 percent discount rate for calculating the present value of future benefits, and an 8 percent return on private capital. Future Social Security benefits are discounted at a 6 percent rate to capture the uncertainty associated with future taxes and transfers.

15. Note that the relationship between cutoff ages and the fraction of privatized contributions required to finance existing obligations in Tables 1 and 2 is not monotonic in assumed rates of return. The lack of a simple relationship appears to be a general property of the generational accounting exercise that involves present values of earning, tax, and benefit flows, which in turn depend on demographics, age-earning profiles, and so forth.

16. See, for example, Laurence Kotlikoff, "Simulating the Privatization of Social Security in General Equilibrium," National Bureau of Economic Research Working Paper no. 5776, September 1996; or Olivia Mitchell and Stephen Zeldes, "Social Security Privatization: A Structure for Analysis," *American Economic Review* 86, no. 2 (May 1996): 363–67.

17. Kotlikoff.

18. Because benefit payments do not rise proportionately with contributions, the system implicitly contains an element of progressive taxation. In addition, benefits for wealthier recipients are taxed explicitly.

19. We use OASDI taxes and benefits to calculate our results. Hence, under our proposal, disability and survivors' benefits would be paid to older generations as under the existing system. Young generations shifted to the new plan would be required to finance those payments out of their privatized OASDI portfolios.

20. Technically, for a standard type of "utility function" and the empirical distribution of rates of return to capital averaged over periods of, say, 10 years, the expected utility of $1 of investment in private capital exceeds the utility of a certain 2 percent return from Social Security, even for utility parameterizations that imply significant risk aversion.

21. The value of government spending financed by annual Social Security surpluses was calculated by subtracting projected annual benefit payments plus administrative costs from the sum of payroll tax contributions and revenue from taxation of benefits. This calculation produces positive numbers through the year 2012. The numbers were taken from *1996 Annual Report of the Board of Trustees of the Old-Age and Survivors Insurance and Disability Insurance Trust Funds* (Washington: Government Printing Office, 1996), Table III.B3. Detailed data provided by the Social Security Administration.

22. See, for example, Peter Diamond, "Privatization of Social Security: Lessons from Chile," National Bureau of Economic Research Working Paper no. 4510, October 1993.

23. Olivia Mitchell, "Administrative Costs in Public and Private Retirement Systems," National Bureau of Economic Research Working Paper no. 5734, August 1996.

24. The expense ratios reported by Mitchell do not include commissions, or "loads."

Thomas N. Bethell

 **NO**

What's the Big Idea? There's more than one solution for Social Security. Here are nine ways to keep the system solvent

The Social Security Debate boils down to one key question: Can the current system handle the retirement of the baby boomers—the nearly 77 million Americans born from 1946 through 1964—and still be in good shape for the generations that follow?

Today the system is taking in more than it spends. If nothing is done in the meantime, that situation will be reversed around 2018—some 10 years after the oldest boomers turn 62 (the age of first eligibility for benefits).

Although estimates vary, Social Security should have sufficient funds to pay full benefits until sometime between 2042 and 2052. But rather than cash in the bonds held by the system's trust funds—which would require the government to raise taxes, borrow money or cut budgets because lawmakers have been tapping the funds to cover other expenses— many experts agree that it would be better to take steps soon to keep the system solvent.

The debate about creating private savings accounts is actually a distraction because, as President Bush has acknowledged, the accounts would do nothing to shore up Social Security's balance sheet. Money siphoned off to fund the accounts would have to be replaced in order to continue paying the benefits promised to those already retired or approaching retirement. There's little disagreement that carving private accounts out of Social Security would make balancing its books much harder.

So what would help? Social Security actuaries and Congressional Budget Office analysts agree that the system could be kept solvent for the next 75 years—longer-range forecasting is meaningless—if two changes were made immediately: Raise the combined employer-employee payroll tax rate from the present 12.4 percent to about 14.3 percent—that's a 15 percent hike. Or cut benefits by about 13 percent.

No one, of course, is suggesting such changes. But the numbers are useful in showing that Social Security doesn't face an unbridgeable financial gap, let alone bankruptcy. Revenues and expenses over the next 75 years are projected to be quite close: Social Security's trustees anticipate a shortfall equal to less than 2 percent of payroll (total taxable earnings).

Experts and politicians have floated many ideas about how to close that gap. Here are nine ways to increase revenue and trim costs.

Raising Revenue

Raise the cap

In 1983 Congress agreed on a goal of taxing 90 percent of all wages in covered employment. Under present law, earnings above a specified cap—which rises as average wages rise and is currently set at $90,000—are not taxed. But incomes of the nation's highest earners have risen much faster than those of lower-income workers, with the result that about 15 percent of total earnings now goes untaxed. Many experts advocate taxing more of those high-end earnings, and Bush hasn't explicitly ruled it out.

Former Social Security Commissioner Robert M. Ball proposes lifting the cap gradually so that by 2045 it will once again capture 90 percent of all covered earnings. "This isn't a new tax," he notes. "It simply restores a policy already set by Congress—so it should attract bipartisan support."

The change would affect only about 6 percent of all taxpayers, but the increased net revenues would cut the projected shortfall by about 32 percent—or up to 40 percent if phased in faster.

A variation on this theme has been suggested by Sen. Lindsey Graham, R-S.C., who favors a "doughnut hole" approach: taxing earnings up to the present cap, exempting earnings up to a specified level above that, then taxing the highest earners of all. That way, he says, upper-middle-class earners wouldn't be saddled with increased taxes. Graham would use the increased income to help meet the multi-trillion-dollar costs of transitioning to a system that includes private accounts.

Increase the payroll tax rate

Economists Peter Diamond and Peter Orszag would very gradually increase workers' contributions and matching employer taxes from 12.4 percent of payroll to about 15 percent over 70 years.

Here's one way to think about the idea: Would you be willing to pay a 21 percent increase in premiums over several decades to maintain an insurance policy that protects you against lost earnings from disability, pays benefits upon your retirement as long as you live, and pays benefits to your survivors when you die? If the answer is yes, then this is an idea worth keeping on the table. It's estimated that such a payroll tax increase could eliminate 100 percent of the long-term revenue shortfall.

On the other hand, the payroll tax is already high. Pushing it higher could be too hard on lower-wage workers. And Bush has said he would consider just about any idea "except running up the payroll tax rate."

Raise taxation of benefits

It's often said that Social Security wastes billions paying benefits to affluent retirees who don't need any help. As one Washington reporter put it, "My mom says her Social Security checks just cover the payments on her Jaguar."

The fairest way to fix this problem, some believe, is not to deny benefits to people who do well in life—that would penalize success—but to increase the taxation of benefits so that higher-income beneficiaries would make a greater contribution to keeping the system solvent. This change would reduce the shortfall by about 10 percent.

Preserve some of the estate tax—and dedicate it to Social Security

The estate tax is being reduced in stages. Instead of being phased out entirely, as Bush proposes, it could be kept at the level set for 2009, when only estates valued at $3.5 million or more ($7 million for a couple) will still be taxed. Rep. David Obey, D-Wis., among others, proposes such a plan. At that level, he notes, only one-half of 1 percent of all estates will be taxed. Doing away with the tax completely, he argues, would mean "a huge bonanza for those who are already the most fortunate in our society—at the expense of other taxpayers." This change would reduce the shortfall by about 27 percent.

Make Social Security universal

About 30 percent of all state and local government employees are not covered by Social Security. Many experts suggest that newly hired employees be brought into the system and share the obligations and the benefits. But some public employees would object, worrying that they might end up with less protection; and some state and local governments would be reluctant to pay their share of the payroll tax. So it's unclear whether this idea could gain political traction. Ball would give state and local governments five years to modify their employment benefit plans. Making the system universal would reduce the shortfall by about 10 percent.

Invest some of the trust fund in indexed funds

By law the Social Security trust funds are invested in government bonds. Putting a portion into broadly indexed stock market funds could yield higher returns. Risks would be lower, because Social Security could ride out market swings far better than individuals, who might have to retire when the value of their account is down.

Several members of Social Security's 1994-96 advisory council have proposed investing 15 percent of the trust funds in indexed funds. Canada has adopted direct investment for its version of Social Security, and *Business Week* recently recommended the same thing for the United States, arguing that "it looks increasingly as if the direct-investment approach would be cheaper and entail less risk."

Objections that the government might try to influence the market, either for "political correctness" (buying no tobacco stocks) or to prevent downswings, have lost some force lately because Bush's private accounts plan, at least for now, also calls for having the government manage the funds. Depending on the amount invested, improved returns could reduce the shortfall by 15 to 45 percent or more.

Other ideas to raise revenue include:

- Provide for a small increase in the payroll tax rate 40 or 50 years from now, if needed to maintain a 75-year balance.
- Tap new sources, such as a value-added tax on goods and services.
- Partially fund Social Security from general tax revenues (an idea that could work if there were budget surpluses, but not with today's enormous deficits).

Actuaries agree that Social Security's shortfall would more than disappear if the relatively modest ideas outlined here were adopted. Some ideas aren't likely to generate broad political support, but the math shows that even some selections from this menu could keep the system solvent far into the future.

Trimming Costs

Lawmakers have to worry about more than taking care of Social Security. Medicare faces major funding pressures, as does the federal-state Medicaid health insurance program. So there are arguments for slowing the growth of Social Security benefits.

Any proposal that cuts benefits outright should be approached with caution. Benefits were trimmed when the system's financing was addressed in 1983. As a result, Social Security today provides less retirement income as a percentage of prior earnings than in the past, and the replacement rate, as it's called, will continue to drop. For a medium earner it was 41.2 percent in 2000; by 2030 it is expected to be 36.5 percent. Moreover, the rising cost of Medicare Part B premiums is expected to have the effect of further reducing benefits by an estimated 9 percent on average by 2030. Here are a few cost-trimming ideas:

Adjust the COLA

Social Security's annual cost-of-living adjustment (COLA) increases benefits to keep up with inflation. It protects 48 million beneficiaries whose buying power would otherwise dwindle over time. The COLA is determined by the Consumer Price Index (CPI), a measure that may overstate inflation by failing to fully reflect the purchasing substitutions that consumers make as prices rise.

The Bureau of Labor Statistics has developed a more accurate CPI, and Federal Reserve Chairman Alan Greenspan, among others, suggests adopting it. Although this would produce only slightly smaller COLAs, it would cut the long-term shortfall by about 18 percent. But many beneficiaries think the present COLA isn't sufficient and would consider this an unjustified benefit cut.

Raise the retirement age

The normal retirement age—the age of eligibility for full benefits—is slowly increasing from 65 to 67. (It will reach 67 in 2027, for workers born in 1960.) Workers can still retire as early as 62, but with benefits reduced a fraction of a percent for each month before full retirement age.

One idea is to continue raising the normal retirement age as life expectancy rises. Edward M. Gramlich, a Federal Reserve governor who chaired the 1994-96 Social Security advisory council, is among those favoring this approach. Gradually increasing the retirement age to 70, he says, would make a "huge impact" but would be "hugely controversial" because people would think they had to work longer. Not so, he insists, because people could still retire earlier, although with lower monthly benefits. A "slight cut in the growth of future benefits," he says, is a fair way to deal with the fact that retirees are likely to live longer—and collect more in benefits—than in 1935, when the retirement age was set at 65. Raising the retirement age to 70 would cut the shortfall by about 36 percent.

Index benefits to prices, not wages

Social Security benefits are determined by how long you work, how much you pay in and by other factors, including the general rise in average wages over time. "Wage indexing" has helped lower the proportion of retirees living in poverty from 35 percent in 1960 to 9 percent today.

Bush and others have raised the idea of indexing initial benefits to prices rather than wages. Since prices generally rise more slowly, this would slow the growth of future benefits—as much as 46 percent on average over the next 65 years, according to economists Diamond and Orszag. Cutting benefits that much could have severe consequences. The Congressional Research Service reports that if benefits had been linked to prices rather than wages since 1940, poverty rates among the elderly would be three times as high as they are now, placing a tremendous burden on public assistance programs.

Another idea is to mix both types of indexing, using wage indexing to protect the benefits of lower-earning workers and price indexing to reduce the benefits of higher earners. Greenspan has reportedly explored this idea with Graham. A major drawback, however, could be that if the returns on their contributions to Social Security are reduced too much, higher earners would have a strong motivation to oppose Social Security entirely.

One of the reasons why Social Security has worked well for 70 years is that most people feel the system is fair. Social Security has always paid comparatively higher benefits to lower-earning workers, who might otherwise end up on welfare even after paying into the system throughout their working lives. But few people—except perhaps those opposed to the idea of social insurance—have felt betrayed by its redistributional structure. They may not fully understand how the system's machinery works (very few people do), but they believe it produces basically fair outcomes.

For that reason alone it's important not to rush into anything. Most Social Security experts agree that the system isn't in crisis. There's ample time, they say, for the country's leaders to choose wisely from the available options and come up with a broadly acceptable solvency plan.

POSTSCRIPT

Is Privatizing Social Security Good Business?

Why the sudden push for "privatization" of Social Security? Critics of all privatization plans object that the entire suggestion amounts to no more than using suspect figures to justify handing Wall Street brokers a few trillion dollars in Social Security funds to play with, always collecting fees as the securities change hands. Advocates for the elderly, especially, are deeply suspicious of plans to hand over their money to people that they do not trust. As this issue matures, we will have to track the performance of Social Security funds and the capital markets, to find out which system is more likely to serve us well in the future. One of the greatest advantages to this controversy is that it will force us to pay more attention to the career of the money that our government holds for us.

Suggested Reading

To follow up on the subject, consider the following source:

Charles R. Morris, "Gambling Our Future: Should Wall Street Control the Economy?" *Commonweal,* November 3, 2006, pp. 8–11.

ISSUE 6

Should the States Regulate Appropriate Business Behavior?

YES: Eliot Spitzer, from "Business Ethics Regulation: The 'Ownership Society'," *Vital Speeches of the Day* (January 31, 2005)

NO: Alan R. Yuspeh, from "Strengthening Ethics and Compliance Programs," *Vital Speeches of the Day* (April 8, 2005)

ISSUE SUMMARY

YES: Eliot Spitzer, former attorney general of the state of New York, presents a convincing case that the business community has never cooperated in, let alone initiated, any attempts to provide the public with clear understanding of how they work, or safeguards to prevent fraud and systematic injury to the public interest; there is no expectation that anything but regulation will improve business behavior.

NO: Alan Yuspeh has dedicated a good portion of his career to the voluntary initiatives that corporations have undertaken to improve transparency, compliance with existing law and regulation, and ethical behavior on the part of business executives; he is convinced that major ethical reforms can indeed result from the voluntary efforts of the private sector.

$\mathbf{W}$e know, with certainty, that it is possible for private for-profit firms to engage in systematic programs of deceit, concealment, fraud, lies, and theft: Enron is still the standard bearer for a very black chapter in the history of American business. We also know that simply insisting that each company have an ethics program, usually implemented by the drafting of a code of ethics and posting it throughout the company, will not suffice to ensure good behavior; Enron had a long and well-drafted code of ethics.

What is this argument really about? As with so many of the controversies in this volume, we must start with the vastly increased complexity, volume, distance, and anonymity of the current business scene, in contrast to the eighteenth-century origins of market capitalism. Adam Smith (and Benjamin Franklin, for that matter) argued for the usefulness of business in creating human virtue—in encouraging, indeed demanding, faithfulness, industry, honesty, thrift, and the practice of doing good for one's neighbor. They reasoned that in the towns they knew, each merchant's reputation depended on his history of quality manufacture and fair dealing with suppliers and customers, and his prosperity, in a competitive system, depended on such a reputation. On the micro level, no storekeeper could survive if he cheated his customers; honesty was the best policy. On the macro level, the business community and the market system as a whole would not survive unless the citizens could generally count on its honesty and fairness. If merchants turned out to be hostile to the public good, after all, the citizens would simply establish another economic system, one that would keep to the law and serve them well. Therefore, in their own interests, markets would always be transparent and truthful, especially in contrast to their historical precedents, which were monopolies controlled by political power.

Smith's faith is touching, but his certainty that honest behavior will prevail does not seem to be borne out by our own recent experience of fraud, corruption, theft, and deception. When markets are remote, digital, and impossible for the citizen to understand, when "offshore" is the location of our telephone information centers, clothing manufacturers, and the bank accounts of the people who have figured out the system, the temptation on the part of the insiders to gather fortunes at the expense of the outsiders must be overwhelming. But the practical demands of the system are the same, and here Spitzer and Yuspeh are in complete agreement: if business, the market, does not clean up its act, and regain the trust of the people, the whole system of market capitalism is doomed. Where fraud and corruption prevail, investors will not invest, customers will not buy, no one will trust a contract, and the entire system of securities exchange will collapse. Just as in Smith's time, market capitalism is built on trust, and business dies without it.

That conceded, the approaches to restoring trust differ radically. One approach, here represented by Spitzer, would save capitalism by regulating it vigorously from the seats of public authority. Seeing elected authority closely monitoring the markets (while the courts bring to justice the Malefactors of Great Wealth, as Roosevelt called them), ensuring that the people's financial experts keep tabs on the experts hired by the wealthy, the people will believe once more that markets are honest. The other approach, taken by Yuspeh, is that it is so obviously in the market's interest to preserve honesty and transparency, that government regulation is not necessary. What is necessary is a well-understood set of guidelines for ethical behavior—not a code to hang on the wall, but ingrained practice overseen by senior executives dedicated to the preservation of honesty. The businessmen know what honesty is; once the bad apples are gone from the barrel, business will be able to take care of itself internally.

Yes, but they won't, time after time, argues Spitzer, with much history and logic on his side. Will the future be like the past? Are we bound to an endless cycle of business arrogance followed by government restriction, just in order to keep our market system going? Reflect, as you read these selections, on possible causes of this destructive cycle. Is there a fundamental flaw in the notion of free markets?

YES

Eliot Spitzer

Business Ethics Regulation: The "Ownership Society"

Thank you very much for that kind introduction. I noted with interest that Hank McKinnel will be your speaker next week. Hank, the CEO of Pfizer, once introduced me to an audience of CEO's. Hank, who is a wonderful guy and great CEO, came up to the podium and said very seriously: "Eliot, we want you to know that 99 percent of the folks here are good, ethical, hard-working people."

So I went up to the podium and I said: "Hank, thank you very much for that reminder. I know that's true, but I'm not worried about the 99 percent – I'm worried about the 1 percent. Who are they?"

I'm not sure my joke had the desired effect on that particular audience. I thought it would be a funny way to begin, but there were more than a few groans. So, to dig my way out of that hole, I explained I am the 63rd Attorney General of the State of New York, which is something I became aware of only when I was sworn in a few years ago. I felt I should know who my predecessors were, so I looked it up and, low and behold, Aaron Burr was once the Attorney General of New York. So I said to Hank and to the assembled group of CEO's: "Hey, if you think I am hard to deal with, imagine how hard it could have been."

I have never challenged anyone to duel. Not yet, anyway.

What I want to do today is throw out a few facts to frame a political debate. It is an enormously important debate, and it relates to a critical issue – which is government's role in regulating and defining the parameters of appropriate business behavior. The facts that I want to begin with are, I think, beyond dispute: certain elements of the business community are pushing back hard against the effort to impose disclosure obligations, transparency and ethical behavior.

First, they are objecting to the Sarbanes-Oxley act, and objecting to the S.E.C.'s effort to mandate disclosure and certain behavior patterns. The business leadership is saying: "Enough, we got the lesson. Now back off." Second, the U.S. Chamber of Commerce, which views itself as the preeminent business lobbying group, is going to court to challenge the S.E.C.'s capacity to issue regulations relating to mutual funds, board behavior, accounting rules and other rules that the S.E.C. believes are essential to ensure integrity in the capital markets.

Third, the President of the Chamber of Commerce, in a rather direct attack on the cases that my office has brought, has said recently that he thinks we are targeting individuals for what he calls "honest mistakes." He said this in the context of my Office's investigation of the insurance industry. You should know that my office today settled with the nation's largest insurance broker, Marsh, and that as part of the settlement the company made certain comments regarding its own actions. I'll come back to that in a moment. Fourth, there has been an enormous effort sponsored by some in the business community to preempt the states and my office in particular. The goal of this effort is to prevent us from bringing the types of cases that we have been bringing for the past number of years.

Now, what's this all about? Well, it's a debate about the role of Government in defining the boundaries of appropriate business ethics, defining what it means to participate in our economy and what the expectations are for our business leadership and also who is supposed to enforce those boundary lines. One of the interesting things about this debate is that everybody invokes the same heroes. In this regard, everybody harkens back to Alexander Hamilton and Teddy Roosevelt. These are the two icons, the two individuals whom we all embrace and say they really understood what government should do. They understood how the economy should function. They understood how to help the private sector generate the wealth that we so desperately want.

Now the interesting aspect of this is that when Teddy Roosevelt was running for office in 1904, 100 years ago, he wasn't a favorite of the business community. In fact, when Roosevelt attacked the Cartels and when he attacked what he regarded as improper behavior, he met with staunch opposition from the business community. He was reviled by the business community. So the irony is that those who now invoke him, if they actually looked back on what he said and did, and looked back on what their predecessors in the business community said about him, if they did that, perhaps they would rethink their holding him out as an icon.

I listened recently to Roosevelt's recorded speeches, the few that are available on tape. I was stunned by remarkable things that he was saying and you would be, too. He was incredibly forceful in describing the failure of ethics in the business leadership and perverse effect on our economy of the Cartels that he was pursuing. Now today, 100 years later, nobody disputes that what he did was not only beneficial to the economy, but was absolutely necessary. In fact, if he had failed to attack the Cartels, failed to attack the illegal behavior, failed to open up the economy to permit true competition, then we would not have experienced the enormous growth in our economy that came in the years that followed.

I would suggest to you that we are in the midst of a similar debate today. No, I'm not comparing myself to him. As they say: Hubris is terminal. What I am saying is that the debate today is akin to what it was 100 years ago. On one side, there is an element of the business leadership that is cloaking itself in the language of the free market, but which really wants to preserve an ossified system. On the other side, there are those who—I would suggest—really understand the markets and what it takes to generate wealth. They understand that government must step in every now and again to define the boundary lines and ensure that there is indeed integrity, transparency and fair play.

Now what I want to do is run through a few of the cases that we have made in my office. I want to lay out the facts and then ask what was the response of the other side? How did those who pretend to be the voice of the free market, who pretend to be advocates of competition and capitalism, how did they react when there was evidence, overwhelming evidence of illegality and impropriety?

The first case was the analyst case. Analysts on Wall Street were distorting and misrepresenting their true opinion of stocks in order to encourage folks to buy stocks. There was an inherent conflict of interest in the business structure of the major investment houses. By hawking the stocks and giving "strong buy" ratings, they could persuade issuing companies to bring underwriting business to their employers, the investment banks. This was ultimately a much more lucrative stream of income than what was generated from small investors. So they subverted their obligation to give honest advice to the investing public to their desire to get the underwriting business. As a result, we saw overwhelmingly positive reports on all sorts of companies that never should have been taken out into the marketplace in the first instance. And we had a bubble.

My office began to reveal the evidence of this problem and it was rather vivid evidence in the form of e-mails. And one e-mail was from a star analyst named Jack Grubman, who made an observation that really captured the problem. He said this of his profession: "What used to be viewed as a conflict of interest is now viewed as a synergy."

Think about that. They had so rationalized their world view that the duty to deliver an honest opinion was all but forgotten. They said: "Hey, we can make money on both sides of this transaction!" And that is exactly what they did.

We exposed it with the help of those e-mails, and we were negotiating with one of the major companies, trying to resolve the case in a way that would produce some meaningful reforms, and the lawyer for the other side said something to me that was very revealing and true. He said: "Eliot, be careful. We have powerful friends."

He was correct. The existing system has many powerful friends because the status quo always has powerful friends. Those who benefit from the status quo never want change.

But knowing this, what was I to do? Of course, I had no choice but to file the lawsuit. I mean what was I going to do at that point. Should I back down and say: "Oh, I didn't know you had powerful friends. Now you tell me, if you had only told me that last week we wouldn't be here."

So we filed the case and then the lawyers for the company come into my office and what do they say? Now all of you in this room know high-priced lawyers. You know what they're supposed to say. They say: "you don't understand the sector. You're taking the evidence out of context. You don't really mean it, we're really nice guys." That's what high-priced defense lawyers always say.

But, interestingly, they didn't say any of that. No, they came to my office and said: "Eliot, you're right. But we want you to know that we're not as bad as our competitors."

Now how is that for a defense? Even in an era of moral relativism, it just doesn't work. But here's the interesting thing: they were telling the truth. They clearly weren't as bad as their competitors. We found that out and that's what led to the global deal in which every major investment bank signed on.

They were right in a more subtle way. Every one of the investment banks knew what the other banks were doing. But what always struck me was the fact that rather than getting together and saying: "You know what? There's a problem here. This is behavior that we really aren't proud of." Instead of doing that and elevating their standards through self regulation or a discussion about what proper standards should be in the industry, everyone of the banks sank to the lowest common denominator.

And the fact that they were saying: "We've got to be as devious as our competitors in how we take advantage of it," just reinforced in my mind the notion that we had to step in and do something. So we did. But what happened next was even more fascinating.

I called some of the other regulators in and proposed some ideas to remedy the problem, but the other regulators said to me: "No, we can't do that."

Even though they were simple ideas, things that were ultimately made part of the global deal, they said it couldn't be done. I asked why and they said: "Because the industry won't like it."

I looked at them quizzically. "Who cares whether they like it or not? It needs to be done."

But this was the mind set of the regulatory community. Specifically, it was the view of Harvey Pitt, who was the head of the S.E.C. at the time. Harvey was a fine lawyer, but I don't think he understood his job. He was aware of this problem. He actually convened a meeting of the CEO's of the major investment houses, along with the chairman of the New York Stock Exchange. He called them together for the express purpose of addressing the problem of structurally-flawed analytical work that was being distributed to ten of millions of Americans. But what did he say to them? He said it wasn't his problem and he left it to the industry to address.

Here was something that went to the core integrity of the Marketplace. Tens of millions of investors were investing based on knowingly-wrong analytical work, and he said: "It's not my problem."

That was terrible. That shouldn't have happened. But what is worse is that when the self-regulatory bodies that were supposed to do something about it did absolutely nothing. And then the S.E.C. under Harvey Pitt went up to Capitol Hill to support a pre-emption bill that would have prevented my office and other state regulators from looking into the problem in the first place.

Harvey Pitt wouldn't do anything about the problem, but he would support a bill to place handcuffs on those who wanted to investigate.

Now the obvious harm from this scandal is that millions of Americans were investing based on bad advice. The other problem that is less often thought about is the misallocation of capital that resulted. If you were to go to AT&T and say: "Do you remember that year when WorldCom was getting all of those wonderful analytical reports and everybody was saying that WorldCom was the future?"

They remember it all too well. AT&T and other companies couldn't compete with their numbers, and now we know why: Those numbers were a fraud. So, it's not just that investors were hurt, companies that were trying to compete for capital, that were reporting honest numbers, that weren't playing the game in the same devious way, those companies were at a competitive disadvantage and consequently had trouble getting access to capital that they needed. And yet what did the government, those who pretend to speak for the free market do? They did nothing except try to put handcuffs on us.

The mutual fund scandals are the second set of cases that I want to mention. It was a similar story. We revealed a significant problem, actually, a trio of problems: timing, late-trading and fees that were driven higher by the failure of boards simply to pay attention and do what they were supposed to do.

What was the response? Once again, the S.E.C. ran to the Hill and supported a preemption bill. When we tried to say to the mutual fund companies that the failure of board members to live up to their fiduciary duty had generated higher fees to the tune of hundreds of millions of dollars a year from one company alone, the S.E.C. disagreed with us and said that we couldn't get into the issue. They said it was price fixing.

Well, it had nothing to do with price fixing. It was saying to Boards of Directors: "Live up to your fiduciary duty. Understand whom you represent and what you have to do to provide integrity in the marketplace."

But, again, where had the S.E.C. been as this enormous scandal in the mutual fund industry unraveled. The answer is nowhere. This was another one of the scandals that was out there and nobody was doing anything about it.

The Wall Street Journal editorial page attacked us for actually daring to get into this sector, and trying to unravel the massive conflicts of interest that existed. Keep in mind that seventy billion dollars a year is what the mutual fund companies derived from fees. Seventy billion a year! And if fees are ten to twenty percent higher than they should be, which is a conservative estimate, think how much it is costing investors every year. These are enormous numbers.

Next is insurance. And some of you may know, we settled with Marsh this morning. It's a settlement that is wonderful in many respects: It's $850 million dollars and all of it, all of it, is going back to customers. In addition, there is new leadership at the company and there is an entirely new business model predicated on disclosure and transparency so that those who buy insurance in this nation will no longer be victimized by contingent payments that drove premiums up by a significant margin.

This is a significant step forward, but, again, what was the response of the Chamber of Commerce? The head of the chamber said that the leadership of Marsh had made "honest mistakes."

I would note that these "honest mistakes" have already produced six guilty pleas, with more to come very shortly, and many more down the road. These "honest mistakes" involved bid rigging and outright deceit and fraud.

But Marsh, to its credit, is now a new company and I think this is really a turn for the better. They issued a statement today as part of the settlement, apologizing, acknowledging that the actions of the individuals, their employees and others at other companies were "unlawful and shameful". Those were their words, not mine.

There was a wonderful column in the Wall Street Journal a couple of weeks ago written by some industry apologist. He said the mistake of these CEO's was not to realize that in the post Enron era, bid rigging is unacceptable.

You don't need to be an antitrust scholar to know that bid rigging was unacceptable even before Enron. But there it is again, so-called voices of the free market defending frauds as honest mistakes and making excuses for criminal actions like Bid-rigging. But they aren't the voices of the free market; they are the voices of ossification and stagnation.

Now let me make one footnote to the insurance cases: The President of the United States, whom we all respect, is out there attacking problems that drive insurance premiums higher. And, yes, there are a multitude of problems. But I have not heard a single word from the White House saying: "maybe, just maybe, premiums are higher because the insurance companies formed an illegal Cartel."

Remember that six insurance executives at three companies have pled guilty so far, and we are just beginning. The evidence is clear. The record of misconduct is clear. But not a word, not a single word about it from the administration. Everybody else and everything else is a causative factor. But not the corruption that is rife in the industry. It's corruption that touches every line of insurance, every line, and we will keep going until we expose all of it.

Another case that we made was the Paxil case. Not to bore you with details, but Paxil was a drug that was being prescribed off label for adolescents who suffered with depression. Glaxosmithkline, the company that makes it, was saying to the world that it was safe and efficacious. But the problem was that they had done five studies, and one of the studies found that Paxil was marginally better than a placebo. The other four studies found that it was either no better than a placebo, or that it generated suicidal tendencies in adolescents.

But did Glaxo tell people that? Did they reveal this danger associated with the drug? No, they didn't. And if you or I were a parent of an adolescent who had been prescribed this drug or we were doctors considering whether or not to prescribe it, we'd want that information.

So we sued Glaxo. We sued them not to say: "take this drug off the market." We sued them on the theory that the information, the clinical testing data should be revealed to the public. We said simply: "create a website, post the relevant data so that people will have a full array of information and they can make informed judgments."

After some push back in which they again said "You don't understand the market," Glaxo gave in. They agreed to full disclosure and established a website to reveal clinical trial data. Forest labs has agreed to do the same thing and other pharmaceutical companies may follow suit because it makes sense.

But where has the F.D.A. been on this issue? The answer is nowhere. There has been only silence. To us and to the Medical Journals and to doctors and parents, it was simply a matter of decency, disclosure and integrity. Yet this F.D.A. has not said a word about revealing this critically important data so that doctors can make informed judgments.

Now back to my favorite editorial page. The Wall Street Journal wrote an editorial saying that I should back off because, and I quote, "The system is working exactly as it should."

But a system that denies doctors and patients critically important information about the known side-effects of a drug cannot be working as it should. No way. And yet the *Journal*, as the paragon of honesty and integrity in the free marketplace, said the old system was working exactly as it should. Ridiculous. Flat out ridiculous.

The last case I want to mention relates to predatory lending. Let me tell a short story. There was a fellow from Rensselaer County—and for those of you who are unfamiliar with New York, it is a wonderful place just east of Albany. Thirty years ago, this poor fellow took out a 25-year mortgage. There were automatic deductions from his checking account for years and years. He really hadn't paid attention. He'd been divorced and the mortgage had been bought and sold by a couple of companies—securitized as we all know these things are. Time passed, but one day he woke up and he said: "Wait a minute. Why am I still paying on that? Why are they still deducting money from my checking account?"

It was a fair question. So he called the bank, but the bank, based in Texas, gave him the brush off. Worse than that, they told him he would have to pay or they'd foreclose on his house. Then he got a lawyer and the lawyer called the bank and the bank gave the lawyer the brush off, too. So then the lawyer called my office. And we called the bank and said: "Look, it was a 25-year mortgage and he has made 30 years of payments. How is that possible?"

What did we hear back from the bank? Well, they left a voice mail message on an assistant attorney general's phone. The message was: "We don't need to answer your questions anymore. The O.C.C. has told us we can ignore State Attorneys General."

The O.C.C. is the office of the comptroller of the currency, a division of the treasury department that regulates banks. The O.C.C. was indeed telling nationally-chartered banks that they didn't have to respond to state regulators. Why? Because the O.C.C., in an effort to get banks to move their charters from state-chartered status to federally-chartered status had offered the banks preemption from basic state laws, including those governing predatory lending. Yes, as bizarre as it sounds, that's what the O.C.C. is doing.

Now giving the O.C.C. the benefit of the doubt, perhaps you'd say: "Well, maybe the O.C.C. will aggressively pursue cases of predatory lending and otherwise step in to protect consumers."

Well, the O.C.C. says that it's doing that, but it's not. In fact, it can't because the agency doesn't have the manpower. We have more enforcement personnel in New York State alone than the O.C.C. does nationwide. And rarely have they made consumer protection cases. Think about it: does anyone with a consumer problem call the O.C.C.? Do people really say: "Let's call the comptroller of the currency because he's on our side! He'll get it done." I don't think so.

But state Attorneys General have been doing these cases for decades. It's what the A.G's traditionally do. But the O.C.C wants to preempt them. And why? Why is the O.C.C. doing this? Well, their preemption move is all about freeing the banks of state regulatory oversight, which is terrific for the banks, but not very good for customers like the fellow from Rensselaer County.

A postscript: as a result of a lawsuit brought by our office against the Texas bank and against the O.C.C. the fellow kept his home and eventually received a refund of more than $9,000.

Now, as I noted, my office has been attacked for not understanding the markets, for over-reaching, for being unfair to CEO's, and I make two points in response:

First, not once has the other side been able to say that we were wrong on the facts. Not once. And that's the reason companies settle so quickly with our office and acknowledge improprieties. That's what Marsh did today. That's what Merrill Lynch did. And Goldman Sachs. And CSFB and others. And yet those who supposedly speak for the free market refuse to acknowledge that we've been right in these cases. Instead, they recede into a shell of ossification—pretending that these issues should not have been addressed in the first place.

And this raises the second point: does anyone out there really believe that the market was better off with those problems before we revealed them? Does anybody want to go back to an era of conflicted research? Of late trading and market timing of mutual funds? Of contingent commissions and bid-rigging in the insurance business? Of secret clinical trials of drugs? Of unaccountable mortgage institutions? Does anybody want to do that? No, of course not. Even those who kicked back the most can't say they want to go back to those practices and those days.

The reality is that the market survives only because problems are revealed and confronted aggressively. And this has led me to the rule that Teddy Roosevelt advanced and which I have come to live by, which is that only government, at the end of the day, can enforce rules of integrity and transparency in the marketplace.

Remember that comment—"We're not as bad as our competitors." It was correct. Business, in many cases, will descend to a lowest common denominator. And if we believe that the market depends upon integrity and fair dealing, then government must step in to make sure that the rules are honored.

Now there are two corollaries to this: the first is that self regulation failed utterly. I say that with real disappointment. We've gone through, in many respects, a legitimate era of deregulation where an overreaching government bureaucracy has been pulled back. And we were told: "Don't regulate us. We will regulate ourselves."

But in not one of the instances where my office has uncovered rampant fraud has a self-regulatory entity stood up to say: "Hey, we have a problem here. Let's do something about it." And by that I mean not only the New York Stock Exchange or the other securities self regulators, but also the leading industry bodies, such as the Investment Company Institute. Did the I.C.I. say: "We have a problem here?" No, the I.C.I. was professing the purity of the mutual fund industry even after these problems were revealed.

I'll get to the second corollary by means of a quick story, not a terribly flattering story about me. My family was sitting at the dining room table a couple of weeks ago and I turned to my 15-year-old, and those of you who have teenage daughters know that every now and then you try to start up a conversation with them and you meet with utter, abject failure. So this was one of those moments, and I turned to her and I said: "Elyssa, honey, tell my your favorite word. Think about it, what would it be if you had to choose?"

Yes, I know this was a lousy effort on my part at communication. I admit it. Well, she looked at me and she rolled her eyes and said: "Oh dad, cut it out. I don't have a favorite word, but you do and I know what it is."

I was taken aback and I said: "Really, what do you think is my favorite word?

"It's two words, dad: fiduciary duty."

Pathetic, right? But here's the point: there has been a dramatic failure to adhere to notions of honest dealing and fiduciary duty in every sector we've looked at. That was true with investment banks, mutual funds, insurance agents and pharmaceutical companies. The failure to adhere to these concepts of integrity is the thread that runs through everything that we have seen.

So let me now ask a few questions of those who pretend to be the voices of the free market:

First, how much capital has been mis-allocated by virtue of what has been done? How much capital would have gone into IRA's and 401ks, had there not been the bubble that was created in part by the analysts' hype and which resulted in enormous losses? How much shareholder equity has been diluted because CEO's have given themselves not only enormous options which are to a great extent unjustified in my view, but also change of control provisions? What possible justification can there be when the ratio of CEO compensation to ordinary employee compensation has gone from 41 to 1, twenty years ago, to 530 to 1, today?

Now there are other rules that we have discerned over time that relate to why and when the government should step in. These involve externalities and core values. Because I want to move to the question and answer period, I will not go into this other than to make one very quick observation.

Why does government have to pass laws relating to discrimination and the minimum wage? The answer is because the marketplace alone simply won't get us there. If you ask yourself this question: before the civil rights statutes of the mid-1960's, had the market alone begun to eliminate discrimination based on race or gender? No, it hadn't. Giving government the right to enforce a core value, which is that there should not be discrimination, is what changed the system. Do we believe that someone who works a forty-hour week should be able to live at the poverty line or higher? We do, but if we didn't have a minimum wage would that be the case. No, it wouldn't be and that is why there is this consensus that these laws are appropriate and important.

I am not going to go on at length about these issues. Let me just conclude with one observation: these issues are more than an abstraction. They affect real people. Whether it is the people whose money was lost, the people who were given an improper prescription drug, or the businesses that couldn't afford to get insurance because impropriety drove up premiums, real people are affected.

We are going through a debate now relating to the privatization of social security. I would ask people this final question: do you trust an administration that failed to protect investors?

If this administration had addressed the flaws in some way, I might be more sympathetic to their approach. But they are still saying that the system does not need to be fixed. And they're still fighting reform.

So now they say: "Go ahead. Take your savings, your safety net, and put it into the system."

Well, where would we be if those who are retiring had their money in Enron and WorldCom? Where would we be?

Remember that question as I now conclude my remarks with one final thought: as a lawyer, I can tell you that the only thing worse than not making your best argument, is having the other side steal it from you. In this regard, President Bush has embraced what he calls the "ownership society." He claims that his administration is making it possible for the middle class to save and invest and succeed. Well, when I hear that, I say to myself: "No, that is not right at all."

It was the Democratic Party historically that did so much to create the middle class. And it has been the Democrats who have acted to protect middle class investments through the years. We are the ones who understand that government has to enforce the rules of integrity to protect small investors and honest corporations alike. We're looking out for them, not the other side. As I said, the Republicans stole the message in the last election. Hopefully, my party will wake up to that fact and not let it happen again. Hopefully, protecting the middle class, ensuring integrity in the markets and advocating a true ownership society will be a bigger part of our message in the future. Thank you so much for listening to me. I appreciate your patience.

Alan R. Yuspeh

Strengthening Ethics and Compliance Programs

I will be very honest with you. I accepted Frank Daly's invitation to be a part of this program with a good deal of uncertainty as to whether it was something I was comfortable doing. When Frank called, I asked myself if I felt that I had learned enough in my 22 years of working in this field so that sharing my thoughts with you would be a good use of your time this morning. I will leave that for you to judge, but I have tried my best to pull together some observations that I hope are insightful and may be of use to you in your work when your return home.

One other housekeeping matter. I have sometimes been uncomfortable with creating prepared remarks. It seemed to inevitably lead to a lack of spontaneity in presentation. But I've changed my mind about that, at least in some circumstances. Frankly, I thought if I were going to take this large block of your time, I owed you the effort to make these remarks as thoughtful as I could. So I have committed them to writing, and I trust you'll forgive me for reading my text. For those of you who wish to have parts of this presentation for later reference, I understand that EOA will post the text on its website, and we'll do the same on the HCA website.

What I propose to do today is to share with you my primary observations about some aspects of how ethics and compliance programs in large organizations should be approached. These comments are based on my personal experience with a number of ethics and compliance programs in large organizations, as well as my service since October 1997 as a senior vice president and the chief ethics and compliance officer for the Hospital Corporation of America, or HCA. For those of you not familiar with HCA, it owns and operates about 190 hospitals; it has about 190,000 employees; and it has revenues approaching $25 billion and is 80th in the Fortune 500. There are within HCA some other healthcare facilities, including ambulatory surgery centers, freestanding imaging centers, and some physician practices. These are certainly partners in our organization, so when I refer intermittently to hospitals, I use it as a shorthand for our entire team of healthcare providers, some of whom work in other than hospital settings.

I have divided these comments into three general subject areas. I'd like to begin by discussing some suggestions about basic approaches to the position of chief ethics and compliance officer in a large organization.

From there, I'd like to move to some comments about the day-to-day operation of ethics and compliance programs. And I'll conclude with a few more general remarks. To make it easier for you to follow, I have numbered my ten observations. I should also note that we have tried to be particularly transparent about our ethics and compliance efforts at HCA. Thus, you will find at our website, . . . a large volume of information about our program, including the text of all of our compliance policies.

I'd like to begin with some thoughts about the kind of position that many of us are privileged to hold.

My first observation – The chief ethics and compliance officer, or ECO, should want to be seen as the leader of a business function in the company and not as an internal police officer. I hope that this observation is not unduly controversial, though it may be. I have found increasingly that one can be far more effective as an organization ECO if he or she is seen as trying to make a sincere contribution to the business success of the enterprise. As a practical matter, this means that one should have an in-depth understanding of the business or businesses involved. The ECO should like the business, find it interesting, and be engaged with all aspects of it.

In a role like the one we play, we should be just as dedicated as any other member of senior management to the success of the organization. Our role is to ensure that this success is based on a model of integrity and exemplary business conduct. People who do the kind of work we do must believe that such an environment or atmosphere has a profound impact on organizational success.

There are some in jobs like ours, I suspect, who think that this ethics and compliance role necessitates being adversarial in tone to those operating the business. I would not be surprised if some in this field delight in finding some glitch or error, thinking that such discoveries justify their existence. It is, of course, part of the responsibility of someone leading an ethics and compliance effort to deal with misconduct when it occurs.

I think we need to aspire to accomplish something in our roles that is larger in vision. Put most simply, we need to be part of the group in an organization that creates a culture that causes individuals to want to do the right thing. Discovering and correcting misconduct is a part of our responsibility, but arguably only a small part. Being integral to the effort to help that organization be successful because of a sound ethical foundation should be our purpose.

My second observation – Relationships are critically important. The role of an ECO within a large organization is easily misunderstood. The most effective way to avoid that is to have personal relationships with as many individuals throughout the organization as you can. It is important to know those who lead your business units and to maintain close and open professional relationships with your colleagues at headquarters.

While it is not really a topic of this presentation, I want to mention in passing that there appears to be at least some increase in the willingness of large corporations to have someone on the senior management team as the ECO. As to my point about relationships, it is obviously easier to develop effective working relationships with the senior corporate staff if they are your peers.

A part of this relationship building within a large organization is a willingness to engage in personal diplomacy on behalf of the ethics and compliance program. The more that you can spend time visiting local operations and become engaged with those who are leaders at all levels of the organization, the greater the likelihood that people will understand you, understand ethics and compliance, and understand what you are really trying to accomplish.

The other reality of relationship building is that the ECO will have to rely on the efforts of many individuals in the organization who are not a part of the ethics and compliance department in order to be successful. You will have to rely on local ethics and compliance officers, technical experts, the Legal Department, the Internal Audit Department, and others; and thus you will have to build effective working relationships with all of these individuals.

I would also caution that it is sometimes a challenge of leadership to ensure that those who work with you directly are conveying the tone and approach that you think is desirable. I am privileged to have in the Ethics and Compliance Department at HCA a talented, dedicated team. I admire every member of that team. Most members of this team deal in some way with those in our facilities. I know that each person has his or her own style as to how to conduct these interactions. I try to discuss with our team the kind of approach I've shared with you today so that we have a shared vision within our department of what we're trying to do.

My third observation – There is no room for ego in doing this job well. This responsibility in a large organization is one that needs a certain amount of visibility for one to be effective. But it should always be clear where one accepts such visibility that it is not an exercise in self-aggrandizement. People need to trust the ECO in every way, including in knowing that his or her actions are never borne out of a desire to appear important within the organization.

At this point, I'd like to move to some observations that have to do with the operations of an ethics and compliance program.

My fourth observation – Innovation is a challenge! I think one of the most significant challenges faced in any ethics and compliance program is keeping the program fresh, finding new initiatives, and discovering even better ways of doing things. I know that all of us value continual improvement and trying to do work that is distinctive.

There are endless opportunities for innovation. Some innovation may relate to the content of annual activities. For example, with our annual code of conduct refresher training, we have varied the format. We have done professionally acted vignettes on videotape, television quiz shows using computer software, professionally acted longer dramatic scenarios (and yes, it was set in an emergency room), and knowledge maps of our hospitals with more complex scenarios. Next year, we will have completely new content in this training through collaboration with our HR Department related to its diversity initiative.

While on the subject of training, some innovation may relate to new types of training or ways to manage training. Early on in our program, we identified the need to have an innovative learning management system as a way to manage compliance training and to deliver intranet based courses. The system is quite robust and has helped improve training generally in our facilities, in many areas beyond compliance. Another example is our addition of a refresher training course for hospital ethics and compliance officers that we launched this year. The program consisted of somewhat complex case studies and was very well received.

Innovation may also relate to a new way to measure performance. After a number of years, we recognized that notwithstanding various auditing and monitoring efforts, we lacked a means of ensuring that our full set of policies and procedures had been implemented in each hospital. So we developed the concept of a compliance process review, and we have found this highly successful in comforting ourselves that hospitals were implementing the large volume of compliance policies they were sent. The reviews involved a meeting between someone in our Department and the hospital ECO at the hospital. We have a lengthy checklist to support this process. We positioned this review as less of an audit and as more of a tutorial for the local ECO, though there is a "grade" given to the ECO at the end of the process. We have found this innovation to have been well received and valuable.

Another opportunity for innovation is with regard to new lines of business or new business activities. I would caution here that one of the challenges for any ethics and compliance program is keeping up with changes in an organization. You and your team simply need to keep your eyes and ears open to what's going on that's new. But when you see a new line of business or a new type of activity, you need to be proactive by asking if this might pose ethics or compliance risk issues. We all know from practical experience that if we wait for the phone to ring in such circumstances, there will probably be only bad news. You'll almost certainly have to consult with those doing the work to understand these new developments, of course. Reacting to these changes may be some of the most important innovations you can make.

My fifth observation - There must be individuals at each local business unit to deliver the ethics and compliance program. If a part-time approach is used for these duties, there must be some assurance of sufficient engagement by the local ECO. My view of the role of the corporate ethics and compliance department is that it is the architect of the program, the creator of policy, and the developer of resources. Someone who has the leadership responsibility in each location must assure the implementation at a local level. In some instances, depending upon the size and nature of the organization, this should be a full time position. For example, in a highly diversified corporation where the local ethics and compliance officer is inevitably developing a large body of business-specific material, it is almost certainly a full-time job.

At HCA, where we have one predominating business, we have found that in many instances this role can be a supplemental assignment, because all of the program design has been done at headquarters. I would hasten to add, however, that increasingly our hospitals on their own initiative are devoting more resources to this effort, including in some instances appointing full-time hospital ethics and compliance officers. Needless to say, we are delighted with this additional voluntary emphasis. We bring newly appointed hospital ethics and compliance officers to Nashville for orientation, and we have an extensive guidebook that sets forth their duties. We seek to assure ourselves that notwithstanding the part-time nature of these duties for many local ECOs, those assigned to perform this role are engaged and performing satisfactorily. The success of the local ECO program is reflected in part by a decision of our division presidents, individuals who oversee about 15 hospitals, to create division ECOs as part of their staffs.

My sixth observation – There must be a system to routinely solicit and consider field input. I think one of the greatest challenges of ethics and compliance programs is to ensure that they are not developed in an "ivory tower" but rather reflect the practical realities of daily operations in the field. We have tried in several ways to do this. Perhaps the single most important effort is the creation of an "ECO Steering Committee." This committee consists of one hospital ECO from each of our twelve divisions, all division ECOs, and a handful of others. We look to this group to help ensure that all of our efforts reflect practical day-to-day operational realities in the hospitals. The group meets once a year in person, but we routinely solicit advice through e-mail and conference calls. The practical value of the information received has been enormous.

In a similar fashion, we have an Ethics and Compliance Policy Committee that approves all new compliance policies for HCA. The membership of this committee includes a number of technical experts, but it also includes three hospital CEOs. We look to these individuals to advise on the practicality of new policies or policy changes. We are constantly focused on trying to achieve our ethics and compliance objectives in a way that makes sense operationally and not in a way that throws molasses in the gears of the machinery.

My seventh observation – There must be an effective utilization of technical expertise. We have designated about 30 vice presidents throughout our headquarters as Responsible Executives, individuals who are responsible for HCA's approach in a particular area of compliance risk. For example, one of our HR vice presidents is responsible for compliance with employment laws, such as the Fair Labor Standards Act. Our design and construction vice president is responsible for environmental compliance. Our corporate secretary is responsible for our compliance with securities regulations. We have created a guidebook for these Responsible Executives explaining how they are to perform their duties as part of the HCA Ethics and Compliance Program and how they interface with me. We have adopted this system because it seemed to us to be wasteful to hire additional technical expertise when it already existed. But we needed some definition of how those technical experts connected to our formal Ethics and Compliance Program.

While this system is a sensible one, I think, one of the greatest challenges for the chief ethics and compliance officer is trying to develop sufficient expertise in the range of compliance risk areas so as to be "value added" to the work of these individuals. I have no magic formula for doing that, other than constantly reading and visiting with these individuals in order to build my own knowledge base. As a practical matter, engagement with each Responsible Executive will depend on how significant the compliance risk area is and how much internal control exists in the area outside of the Ethics and Compliance Program. I am always trying to judge if I should be more engaged with particular Responsible Executives and am always striving to build my own knowledge base so that I have a better sense of what questions to ask of those individuals as we discuss compliance efforts in their areas.

My eighth observation – Ensuring that all operational leadership is engaged is very difficult. A large challenge of ethics and compliance programs is ensuring that operational leadership at all levels has really bought in and takes it seriously. In an effort to accomplish this at HCA, we have published a Supplement to our Code of Conduct called the Supplement for Leaders. This booklet is addressed to everyone with leadership responsibility and tries to elaborate on how those responsibilities should be executed. We encourage our hospital leadership teams to review this periodically. The booklet has self-assessment tests in it as well as summaries of the parts of our ethics and compliance program.

In addition to this Supplement for Leaders, we have in the last several years been creating a different kind of Code of Conduct refresher training for our hospital leaders. They are given scenarios that are more reflective of complex issues and the type of managerial decision-making that occurs at each hospital. While I would encourage any large organization to use means such as these to engage operational leaders, I would also encourage you to be mindful of where there may be pockets of resistance to what you are doing. In a large organization, it is likely that the enthusiasm for ethics and compliance efforts will vary somewhat depending on the type of responsibility one has and in some instances depending upon the geographic location or business unit affiliation. There are varying reasons for this. For example, if you have an extensive ethics and compliance approach to sales practices, you may find that the sales force feels impeded and is thus somewhat antagonistic to what you are doing. Others may feel much less intrusion. When you discover a business unit or a location or a group of employees that appears to be less enthusiastic than others about what you are doing, I would encourage you to approach those individuals in order to try to understand and address their concerns. As a practical matter, we can often learn a good deal from our critics.

At this point, I'd like to shift to some broader observations about ethics and compliance efforts.

My ninth observation – You need to have senior management who in a very intuitive way buy into this kind of effort. They must be willing to speak out about this, and their commitment must be unambiguous. One would think that this goes without saying, but daily for years now we have read about senior management of major corporations who clearly didn't meet this relatively straightforward test. Though I've made it the ninth of my observations due to the structure of this presentation, it probably should be first in importance. The tone at the top is the single most important factor in whether a corporate ethics and compliance officer can succeed. If those at the top of the organization are not fully committed to integrity, fairness, sound values, high business conduct standards, and—at a very minimum— obeying the law, there will be many others who get the message and follow their lead.

Let's be honest with one another. It is possible for a corporate ethics and compliance program to be mere window dressing. Even Enron had a code of conduct that looked pretty good. In a post Sarbanes-Oxley world, compliance consulting has become a cottage industry. In fact, any of us could probably go into any organization and create the trappings of an ethics and compliance program. The question is, of course, whether the elements of such a program are implemented in such a way as to have a truly profound effect on conduct. It's even possible to have a high level ethics and compliance officer who might be mostly ornamentation, if he or she either permits it or lacks support internally to be anything other than that.

The bottom line here is that all of the codes of conduct and compliance policies one can write will simply be paper on the shelf unless the senior leadership of the organization wants to make the articulated principles a real part of daily business operations. I have been very fortunate in my role at HCA, because for the almost eight years I have been there, I have had constant, unwavering support from every operational leader in the company for what we were trying to do in terms of organizational integrity. The Company's co-founder and then CEO, Dr. Thomas Frist, created the position I hold. Many of you who heard our current CEO, Jack Bovender, speak at the EOA annual meeting in Nashville a few years ago commented to me afterwards that they had never heard a more sincere or committed endorsement of the work we ethics and compliance officers do. If you don't have that kind of buy-in from operational leadership, I don't know how you ultimately succeed.

I would be remiss if I failed to mention that we have also had enormous support from our HCA Board of Directors in what we are doing in this area. We have a Board committee on ethics, compliance and quality of care that meets five times a year and is completely informed about every aspect of our Ethics and Compliance Program. The Committee knows everything we are doing; it understands every single task that appears in an eight-page long annual work plan presented to it. And all of the results of our auditing, monitoring, compliance process reviews, and employee surveys are shared with the Committee.

I would add one other thought as part of this observation. I think it is essential that senior management in any organization resist the temptation to regard the ethics and compliance program as on "autopilot." Some of these programs are now considered to be mature programs. By mature, we mean fully developed and fundamentally complete in terms of the essential elements of the program. With a mature program, it is that much more important that the underlying messages about organizational values be constantly refreshed. In any large organization, people join and people leave. There is endless information competing for the attention of those in the organization, and if some theme is suddenly absent from the messaging, it may be forgotten very quickly. Moreover, it takes only a single person with bad instincts or bad judgment or bad motives to tarnish the reputation of thousands of others in an organization. There are EOA members in attendance today who know that their organizational reputation has been put into question because of the improper acts of a single person. There is no autopilot for the kind of work we do. We need the help and attention of those who lead the organization on a regular basis to make this work. We need them to regularly communicate their own commitment to proper business conduct, in order to avoid even a single person thinking that the commitment has diminished.

My tenth observation – There must be an appreciation of true ethical dilemmas faced by an organization and how they should be resolved. The largest warning sign of problems is some industry-wide practice that appears critical to success that makes no ethical sense. I've not discussed at any length in these remarks the need to identify and address those areas of legal compliance risk. I think by now that goes without saying. But I've said before and I'll say it again now, if individuals go to work each day and their goal is simply to complete the day without being indicted, they haven't set the bar very high. Achieving legal compliance is difficult as a matter of effective administration, but it shouldn't be difficult as a matter of choice. Most well managed corporations set out to obey the law.

But identifying and addressing ethical dilemmas is more difficult. Because without legal standards to guide certain actions, you need to find an ethical compass, and you need to do it when your competitors may not do it at all or may have an ethical compass not calibrated quite as finely as yours is. The truly effective ethics officers will be the ones who can be forces in their organizations to identify the really hard ethical issues and to get approaches to those that reflect high-minded values.

If you are doing the kind of work we do, and you see a wide-spread business practice that makes no ethical sense, well—if you can't get it changed, I think I would try to find work elsewhere. There are a number of industries that have been shown over the last several years to have major ethical lapses. Two highly visible recent examples relate to the research practices of securities firms and the referral practices of insurance brokers. The greatest contribution we can make to our organizations when we find some practice that simply makes no ethical sense is to find a way to elevate the concern so that individuals at the top of the organization will ask themselves, "what are we doing, why are we doing it, and how can we change it." And the most unacceptable statement that can be made in the course of such a conversation is "everyone does it." If it's fundamentally wrong—if it's dishonest, if it's unfair, if it's a misrepresentation, if it's misleading—then the fact that "everyone does it" doesn't make it one bit more palatable. I hope that there aren't other cases of industry-wide practices that by any reasonable standard are unethical, but if there are, I think it would be wonderful if people in this room found them and saw that they got fixed.

I regret that I have not been able to cover every aspect of the work each of us does. For example, all of us operate hotlines or ethics lines and know how challenging that work is. Though the calls we receive tend to be largely matters of personal unhappiness, responding meaningfully to these is important to HHC. There are many elements of ethics and compliance programs that I have not discussed this morning because of time limitations, not because these parts of what we do are insignificant.

I would leave you with three final thoughts. First, the amount of bad business conduct reported in the press over the last several years has been enormous. It leaves one to wonder what the state of business ethics in America is today. I am not certain that anyone can answer that question authoritatively. But those of us who work daily in the trenches certainly see evidence that whatever the baseline may be, we're on an upward improvement slope. What do I look at to judge that? Well, for starters, we're here. A lot of life, we all learn, is simply showing up, so your being at this kind of meeting is important evidence of commitment. Your presence here is also an indication that the Ethics Officer Association remains robust and energetic, and that's a good sign. What are other indicators? From what I read in the business press, every audit committee of every large publicly held corporation is busier than ever, and that's a good sign. As for each of our own companies, my informal conversation shows no decline at all in attention to the work we do. In fact, in many cases, the attention to our work may actually be increasing. Another piece of good news is that yesterday, a group of nine healthcare group purchasing organizations issued a press release announcing the creation of an industry ethics initiative for those nine organizations that account for more than 80% of the volume of supply purchasing done through GPOs. Others will be welcome to join. We are proud that the GPO founded by HCA, Health-Trust Purchasing Group, is a founder of this industry ethics initiative. A primary organizer of this effort has been Premier, and its ethics officer, Megan Barry, has been a dedicated and visible EOA member for years. To my knowledge, this is the first formalized industry ethics initiative since the defense industry initiative started in 1986. That is a very positive sign. This initiative will be distinctive in that it is focused not only on business ethics generally but also on the best business practices in this field, practices that promote competition, ensure that new technologies are considered, avoid conflicts of interest, are sensitive to the needs of disappointed bidders, and deal appropriately with the administrative fees historically paid by suppliers to GPOs. So there are encouraging indicators about business ethics generally.

My second concluding thought is that good indicia of success in your program is how certain you are that someone in your organization would do the right thing where basic integrity and fairness is implicated. At the end of the day, this to me is the single best test as to whether the ethics and compliance program has achieved its real promise. If someone in your organization is faced with a decision that implicates integrity and fairness, will he or she do the high-minded thing, the right thing, even if there are significant business costs to doing it and significant business pressures that make it difficult to do? Will this person do the right thing, even if the likelihood of an expedient action being detected is small? An ethical culture has really taken in an organization when the issue of whether or not something problematic will be discovered is not even part of the decision-making process. If you see people in your organization who routinely pass this test, then you have succeeded in the culture-building exercise I envision. If you see people who fail it, well—you still have work to do.

Third, most individuals who are ethics officers have at least some compliance duties, and many of us are ethics and compliance officers. One of our greatest challenges, I think, is to avoid letting the endless detail of our compliance duties overwhelm our ethics duties. We fully understand that compliance work requires attention to detail. That is inevitable because the law itself is enormously detailed. One of my concerns at HCA is that the leaders in our facilities will become so focused on the details of following the privacy laws or the physician relationship laws or the "you have to see everyone in the emergency room" laws that they will think it's all we care about. Of course, we expect them to observe those laws. But just as importantly, we expect them to create an ethos, an atmosphere, a climate, a culture—whatever word you wish to use—in each HCA hospital whereby everyone who works there lives out the expectations in our Code of Conduct about how we treat our patients, how we treat physicians who practice in our facilities, how we treat government regulators, how we treat payers, how we treat suppliers, and how we treat each other. This is the area in which our work is never done. It is the area in which there is always greater challenge. But living these values we articulate, especially when they involve tough choices, is fundamental to these ethics and compliance programs that are our life's work. Because if we can achieve the full potential of these efforts, we will not only have helped organizations obey the law, but we will have also made an important contribution to business success and to ensuring that articulated obligations to each and every stakeholder group are met. That is what we should aspire to do, and that is why our work truly matters.

POSTSCRIPT

Should the States Regulate Appropriate Business Behavior?

There's a fascinating historical footnote buried in these selections. Eliot Spitzer was attorney general in New York State, home of Wall Street and the most powerful business community in the United States, during the presidential administration of George W. Bush, one of the most business-friendly administrations in the history of the country. Spitzer took on criminals of fabulous wealth during a time when they had powerful friends in Washington. He had the business community doing everything in its power to frustrate and thwart his efforts to reform their practices in his own state, while its friends in Washington did everything in *their* power to preempt the states and limit the power of the state judiciaries. Some of the flavor of the battle comes through in his talk. The conflict was accompanied by an ongoing rhetorical war, in which he was attacked and vilified from the central platforms in the land, by the highest officers. He survived the war in good form and good humor, ran for governor, and won. What does this tell us about the inherent limits on the autonomy of the markets?

ISSUE 7

Is Wal-Mart a Good Model for Retail Sales?

YES: Sam Walton with John Huey, from *Made in America* (Doubleday, 1992)

NO: George Miller, from "Everyday Low Wages: The Hidden Price We All Pay for Wal-Mart," http://edworkforce.house.gov (February 16, 2004)

ISSUE SUMMARY

YES: America loves Wal-Mart, and no one loved it better than Sam Walton, who founded it with a very clear idea of what the American consumer wanted and what had to be done to get a disparate workforce working together. His book is the best place to catch the spirit that informs the company, and the best argument for Wal-Mart's determination to get affordable goods into the hands of the American consumer.

NO: George Miller takes a look at the other side of Wal-Mart—the treatment of the workers, the effects of a monopsony on the suppliers, and (his constituents' chief concern) its effects on the community. He wonders if the taxpayers can continue to support this very expensive guest.

In 1945, as World War II drew to a close, Sam Walton bought a variety store that wasn't making any money and figured out how to cut costs until it did. Then he bought another store and did the same thing. For the most part, he wasn't very cagey about what he was doing; he set up his corporate headquarters in the least expensive part of the least expensive state in the union, he scouted all over the country and the world to find saleable goods at the lowest possible price, and he didn't mark them up very much; he put his new "big-box" stores out in the country where the other stores didn't bother to go but where he knew that there was a commodity-hungry customer base. He advertised the lowest prices in the country for all consumers, and on the whole, he succeeded in making them happen.

As a business plan, it surely worked. Customers reacted positively: they flocked in for the lower prices, they loved the staff, which was trained to be really helpful and cheerful, and the huge volume made for enormous sales income.

Yet the parsimonious image doesn't seem to fit with certain other facts about the company. One would think that such low prices, even with correspondingly large sales, would predict lower profits—yet on its $250 billion annual sales, Wal-Mart made over $10 billion in profits in 2006, twice as much as the next 15 retailers combined. Nor are the top executives ignored: Wal-Mart's compensation committee arranged to have its CEO paid over $15 million in compensation in 2006, then, afraid they were neglecting him, added a $22 million stock bonus for meeting revenue targets. Nor does the family plow its money back into the company: by now, Sam Walton's widow, John Walton's widow, and the three surviving children together are worth more than $90 billion, exceeding the combined net worth of Bill Gates and Paul Allen, the two founders of Microsoft.

The low prices seem to have two sources—the continual squeeze on suppliers, who must cut the amount they charge Wal-Mart by a certain percentage every year, regardless of the effect on quality, and the equally severe pressure on the workforce. The Wal-Mart workers are paid less than equivalent workers anywhere in the United States, are often forced to work "off the clock"—they must punch out, then return to work until a set task is done, or be fired—are often relegated to "part-time" status (32 hours a week or less) to remove the possibility of benefits, and are punished severely for any attempts to join a labor union.

While the customers, in short, may be happy, the effect on all the other stakeholders in the enterprise is not as cheerful. The workers are glad enough to have jobs, but their pay contributes very little to the local economy. As Miller points out, the big-box stores, huge islands in a sea of parking lots, destroy the country's soil and forests, blocking off watercourses and causing other environmental damage. They also draw off customers from the traditional downtown area, threatening stores and their landlords alike. Tax revenue often becomes problematic for the town.

Yet the advantage to the consumer is undeniable, and the stores continue to spread, here and abroad, to the general approval of the communities into which they move. The Wal-Mart controversy is actually part of a much larger identity crisis within the nation. What is an American? Is the American a consumer, interested in personal material acquisition? Or a worker, part of a profession, serving the economic good of the country? Or maybe a citizen, concerned primarily for the good of the community as a whole? Somehow, all three? Which is more valuable to the American: to be able to hold a dignified job, to be able to buy commodities at a very low price, or to support the local community? Remember, as you read the following selections, that your personal answer to that question may determine your position, not only on the next Wal-Mart fight in your own town, but on the economic future of the country as a whole.

YES

**Sam Walton with
John Huey**

Made in America

Hello, friends, I'm Sam Walton, founder and chairman of Wal-Mart Stores. By now I hope you've shopped in one of our stores, or maybe bought some stock in our company. If you have, you probably already know how proud I am of what is simply the miracle that all these Wal-Mart associates of mine have accomplished in the thirty years since we opened our first Wal-Mart here in northwest Arkansas, which Wal-Mart and I still call home. As hard as it is to believe sometimes, we've grown from that one little store into what is now the largest retailing outfit in the world. And we've really had a heck of a time along the way.

I realize we have been through something amazing here at Wal-Mart, something special that we ought to share more of with all the folks who've been so loyal to our stores and to our company. That's one thing we never did much of while we were building Wal-Mart, talk about ourselves or do a whole lot of bragging outside the Wal-Mart family—except when we had to convince some banker or some Wall Street financier that we intended to amount to something someday, that we were worth taking a chance on. When folks have asked me, "How did Wal-Mart do it?" I've usually been flip about answering them. "Friend, we just got after it and stayed after it," I'd say. We have always pretty much kept to ourselves, and we've had good reasons for it; we've been very protective of our business dealings and our home lives, and we still like it that way.

But as a result, a whole lot of misinformation and myth and half-truths have gotten around over the years about me and about Wal-Mart. And I think there's been way too much attention paid to my personal finances, attention that has caused me and my family a lot of extra trouble in our lives—though I've just ignored it and pretty much gone about my life and the business of Wal-Mart as best I could.

None of this has really changed. But I've been fighting cancer for a while now, and I'm not getting any younger anyway. And lately a lot of folks—including Helen and the kids, some of our executives here at the company, and even some of the associates in our stores—have been fussing at me that I'm really the best person to tell the Wal-Mart tale, and that—like it or not—my life is all wrapped up in Wal-Mart, and I should get it down right while I still can. So I'm going to try to tell this story the best I'm able to, as close to the way it all came about, and I hope it will be almost as interesting and fun and exciting as it's been for all of us, and that it can capture for you at least something of the spirit we've all felt in building this company. More than anything, though, I want to get across once and for all just how important Wal-Mart's associates have been to its success.

This is a funny thing to do, this looking back on your life trying to figure out how all the pieces came together. I guess anybody would find it a little strange, but it's really odd for somebody like me because I've never been a very reflective fellow, never been one to dwell in the past. But if I had to single out one element in my life that has made a difference for me, it would be a passion to compete. That passion has pretty much kept me on the go, looking ahead to the next store visit, or the next store opening, or the next merchandising item I personally wanted to promote out in those stores—like a minnow bucket or a Thermos bottle or a mattress pad or a big bag of candy.

As I look back though, I realize that ours is a story about the kinds of traditional principles that made America great in the first place. It is a story about entrepreneurship, and risk, and hard work, and knowing where you want to go and being willing to do what it takes to get there. It's a story about believing in your idea even when maybe some other folks don't, and about sticking to your guns. But I think more than anything it proves there's absolutely no limit to what plain, ordinary working people can accomplish if they're given the opportunity and the encouragement and the incentive to do their best. Because that's how Wal-Mart became Wal-Mart: ordinary people joined together to accomplish extraordinary things. At first, we amazed ourselves. And before too long, we amazed everybody else, especially folks who thought America was just too complicated and sophisticated a place for this sort of thing to work anymore.

The Wal-Mart story is unique: nothing quite like it has been done before. So maybe by telling it the way it really happened, we can help some other folks down the line take these same principles and apply them to their dreams and make them come true.

. . . For all my confidence, I hadn't had a day's experience in running a variety store, so Butler Brothers sent me for two weeks' training to the Ben Franklin in Arkadelphia, Arkansas. After that, I was on my own, and we opened for business on September 1, 1945. Our store was a typical old variety store, 50 feet wide and 100 feet deep, facing Front Street, in the heart of town, looking out on the railroad tracks. Back then, those stores had cash registers and clerk aisles behind each counter throughout the store, and the clerks would wait on the customers. Self-service hadn't been thought of yet.

It was a real blessing for me to be so green and ignorant, because it was from that experience that I learned a lesson which has stuck with me all through the years: you can learn from everybody. I didn't just learn from reading every retail publication I could get my hands on, I probably learned the most from studying what John Dunham was doing across the street. . . .

I learned a tremendous amount from running a store in the Ben Franklin franchise program. They had an excellent operating program for their independent stores, sort of a canned course in how to run a store. It was an education in itself. They had their own accounting system, with manuals telling you what to do, when and how. They had merchandise statements, they had accounts-payable sheets, they had profit-and-loss sheets, they had little ledger books called Beat Yesterday books, in which you could compare this year's sales with last year's on a day-by-day basis. They had all the tools that an independent merchant needed to run a controlled operation. I had no previous experience in accounting—and I wasn't all that great at accounting in college—so I just did it according to their book. In fact, I used their accounting system long after I'd started breaking their rules on everything else. I even used it for the first or six Wal-Marts.

As helpful as that franchise program was to an eager-to-learn twenty-seven-year-old kid, Butler Brothers wanted us to do things literally by the book—their book. They really didn't allow their franchisees much discretion. The merchandise was assembled in Chicago, St. Louis, or Kansas City. They told me what merchandise to sell, how much to sell it for, and how much they would sell it to me for. They told me that their selection of merchandise was what the customers expected. They also told me I had to buy at least 80 percent of my merchandise from them, and if I did, I would get a rebate at year-end. If I wanted to make a 6 or 7 percent net profit, they told me I would have to hire so much help and do so much advertising. This is how most franchises work.

At the very beginning, I went along and ran my store by their book because I really didn't know any better. But it didn't take me long to start experimenting—that's just the way I am and always have been. Pretty soon I was laying on promotional programs of my own, and then I started buying merchandise directly from manufacturers. I had lots of arguments with manufacturers. I would say, "I want to buy these ribbons and bows direct. I don't want you to sell them to Butler Brothers and then I have to pay Butler Brothers 25 percent more for them. I want it direct." Most of the time, they didn't want to make Butler Brothers mad so they turned me down. Every now and then, though, I would find one who would cross over and do it my way.

That was the start of a lot of the practices and philosophies that still prevail at Wal-Mart today. I was always looking for offbeat suppliers or sources. I started driving over to Tennessee to some fellows I found who would give me special buys at prices way below what Ben Franklin was charging me. One I remember was Wright Merchandising Co. in Union City, which would sell to small businesses like mine at good wholesale prices. I'd work in the store all day, then take off around closing and drive that windy road over to the Mississippi River ferry at Cottonwood Point, Missouri, and then into Tennessee with an old homemade trailer hitched to my car. I'd stuff that car and trailer with whatever I could get good deals on—usually on softlines: ladies' panties and nylons, men's shirts—and I'd bring them back, price them low, and just blow that stuff out the store.

I've got to tell you, it drove the Ben Franklin folks crazy. Not only were they not getting their percentages, they couldn't compete with the prices I was buying at. Then I started branching out further than Tennessee. Somehow or another, I got in touch by letter with a manufacturer's agent out of New York named Harry Weiner. He ran Weiner Buying Services at 505 Seventh Avenue. That guy ran a very simple business. He would go to all these different manufacturers and then list what they had for sale. When somebody like me sent him an order, he would take maybe 5 percent for himself and then send the order on to the factory, which would ship it to us. That 5 percent seemed like a pretty reasonable cut to me, compared to 25 percent for Ben Franklin.

I'll never forget one of Harry's deals, one of the best items I ever had and an early lesson in pricing. It first got me thinking in the direction of what eventually became the foundation of Wal-Mart's philosophy. If you're interested in "how Wal-Mart did it," this is one story you've got to sit up and pay close attention to. Harry was selling ladies' panties—two-barred, tricot satin panties with an elastic waist—for $2.00 a dozen. We'd been buying similar panties from Ben Franklin for $2.50 a dozen and selling them at three pair for $1.00. Well, at Harry's price of $2.00, we could put them out at four for $1.00 and make a great promotion for our store.

Here's the simple lesson we learned—which others were learning at the same time and which eventually changed the way retailers sell and customers buy all across America: say I bought an item for 80 cents. I found that by pricing it at $1.00 I could sell three times more of it than by pricing it at $1.20. I might make only half the profit per item, but because I was selling three times as many, the overall profit was much greater. Simple enough. But this is really the essence of discounting: by cutting your price, you can boost your sales to a point where you earn far more at the cheaper retail price than you would have by selling the item at the higher price. In retailer language, you can lower your markup but earn more because of the increased volume.

I began to mull this idea in Newport, but it would be another ten years before I took it seriously. I couldn't follow up on it in Newport because the Ben Franklin program was too cut-and-dried to permit it. And despite my dealings with the likes of Harry Weiner, I still had that contract saying I was supposed to buy at least 80 percent of my merchandise from Ben Franklin. If I missed that target, I didn't get my year-end rebate. The fact of the matter is I stretched that contract every way I could. I would buy as much as I could on the outside and still try to meet the 80 percent. Charlie Baum—who was then one of the field men for Ben Franklin—would say we were only at 70 percent, and I would foam at the mouth and rant and rave about it. I guess the only reason Butler Brothers didn't give me a harder time about it all is that our store had quickly gone from being a laggard to one of the top performers in our district.

Things began to clip along pretty good in Newport in a very short time. After only two and a half years we had paid back the $20,000 Helen's father loaned us, and I felt mighty good about that. It meant the business had taken off on its own, and I figured we were really on our way now.

We tried a lot of promotional things that worked really well. First, we put a popcorn machine out on the sidewalk, and we sold that stuff like crazy. So I thought and thought about it and finally decided what we needed was a soft ice cream machine out there too. I screwed my courage up and went down to the bank and borrowed what at the time seemed like the astronomical sum of $1,800 to buy that thing. That was the first money I ever borrowed from a bank. Then we rolled the ice cream machine out there on the sidewalk next to the popcorn machine, and I mean we attracted some attention with those two. It was new and different—another experiment—and we really turned a profit on it. I paid off that $1,800 note in two or three years, and I felt great about it. I really didn't want to be remembered as the guy who lost his shirt on some crazy ice cream machine. . . .

Not many companies out there gather several hundred of their executives, managers, and associates together every Saturday morning at seven-thirty to talk about business. Even fewer would begin such a meeting by having their chairman call the Hogs. That's one of my favorite ways to wake everybody up, by doing the University of Arkansas's Razorback cheer, real early on a Saturday. You probably have to be there to appreciate the full effect, but it goes like this:

> Whooooooooooooooooooooo Pig. Sooey!
> Whooooooooooooooooooooooooooo Pig. Sooey!
> Whoooooooooooooooooooooooooooooooo Pig. Sooey!
> RAZORBACKS!!!!!

And if I'm leading the cheer, you'd better believe we do it loud. I have another cheer I lead whenever I visit a store: our own Wal-Mart cheer. The associates did it for President and Mrs. Bush when they were here in Bentonville not long ago, and you could see by the look on their faces that they weren't used to this kind of enthusiasm. For those of you who don't know, it goes like this:

> Give Me a W!
> Give Me an A!
> Give Me an L!
> Give Me a Squiggly!
> (Here, everybody sort of does the twist.)
> Give Me an M!
> Give Me an A!
> Give Me an R!
> Give Me a T!
> What's that spell?
> Wal-Mart!
> What's that spell?
> Wal-Mart!

Who's number one?
THE CUSTOMER!

I know most companies don't have cheers, and most board chairmen probably wouldn't lead them even if they did. But then most companies don't have folks like Mike "Possum" Johnson, who entertained us one Saturday morning back when he was safety director by taking on challengers in a no-holds-barred persimmon-seed-spitting contest, using Robert Rhoads, our company general counsel, as the official target. Most companies also don't have a gospel group called the Singing Truck Drivers, or a management singing group called Jimmy Walker and the Accountants.

My feeling is that just because we work so hard, we don't have to go around with long faces all the time, taking ourselves seriously, pretending we're lost in thought over weighty problems. At Wal-Mart, if you have some important business problem on your mind, you should be bringing it out in the open at a Friday morning session called the merchandising meeting or at the Saturday morning meeting, so we can all try to solve it together. But while we're doing all this work, we like to have a good time. It's sort of a "whistle while you work" philosophy, and we not only have a heck of a good time with it, we work better because of it. We build spirit and excitement. We capture the attention of our folks and keep them interested, simply because they never know what's coming next. We break down barriers, which helps us communicate better with one another. And we make our people feel part of a family in which no one is too important or too puffed up to lead a cheer or be the butt of a joke—or the target in a persimmon-seed-spitting contest.

We don't pretend to have invented the idea of a strong corporate culture, and we've been aware of a lot of the others that have come before us. In the early days of IBM, some of the things Tom Watson did with his slogans and group activities weren't all that different from the things we do. And, as I've said, we've certainly borrowed every good idea we've come across. Helen and I picked up several ideas on a trip we took to Korea and Japan in 1975. A lot of the things they do over there are very easy to apply to doing business over here. Culturally, things seem so different—like sitting on the floor eating eels and snails—but people are people, and what motivates one group generally will motivate another. . . .

Back in 1984, people outside the company began to realize just how different we folks at Wal-Mart are. That was the year I lost a bet to David Glass and had to pay up by wearing a grass skirt and doing the hula on Wall Street. I thought I would slip down there and dance, and David would videotape it so he could prove to everyone back at the Saturday morning meeting that I really did it, but when we got there, it turned out David had hired a truckload of real hula dancers and ukulele players—and he had alerted the newspapers and TV networks. We had all kinds of trouble with the police about permits, and the dancers' union wouldn't let them dance without heaters because it was so cold, and we finally had to get permission from the head of Merrill Lynch to dance on his steps. Eventually, though, I slipped on the grass skirt and the Hawaiian shirt and the leis over my suit and did what I think was a pretty fair hula. It was too good a picture to pass up, I guess—this crazy chairman of the board from Arkansas in this silly costume—and it ran everywhere. It was one of the few times one of our company stunts really embarrassed me. But at Wal-Mart, when you make a bet like I did—that we couldn't possibly produce a pretax profit of more than 8 percent—you always pay up. Doing the hula was nothing compared to wrestling a bear, which is what Bob Schneider, once a warehouse manager in Palestine, Texas, had to do after he lost a bet with his crew that they couldn't beat a production record.

Most folks probably thought we just had a wacky chairman who was pulling a pretty primitive publicity stunt. What they didn't realize is that this sort of stuff goes on all the time at Wal-Mart. It's part of our culture, and it runs through everything we do. Whether it's Saturday morning meetings or stockholders' meetings or store openings or just normal days, we always have tried to make life as interesting and as unpredictable as we can, and to make Wal-Mart a fun proposition. We're constantly doing crazy things to capture the attention of our folks and lead them to think up surprises of their own. We like to see them do wild things in the stores that are fun for the customers and fun for the associates. If you're committed to the Wal-Mart partnership and its core values, the culture encourages you to think up all sorts of ideas that break the mold and fight monotony. . . .

NO

Wal-Mart Harms Americans

George Miller is a Democratic congressman from California. He is on the House Education and Workforce Committee and also serves on the House Resources Committee. In the following viewpoint Miller criticizes Wal-Mart for preventing workers from organizing unions, violating workers' rights, paying low wages, and making health care unavailable to or unaffordable for its workers. Miller charges that U.S. taxpayers subsidize wages at Wal-Mart because its underpaid employees seek government assistance to help with their housing, food, and medical costs.

As you read, consider the following questions:

1. According to Miller, how do Wal-Mart's wages compare with wages paid to employees in the supermarket industry overall?
2. Who is eligible to enroll in Wal-Mart's health insurance plan, according to the author?
3. What does Miller estimate is the cost to federal taxpayers of one Wal-Mart store?

T he retail giant Wal-Mart has become the nation's largest created private sector employer with an estimated 1.2 million employees. The company's annual revenues now amount to 2 percent of the U.S. Gross Domestic Product. Wal-Mart's success is attributed to its ability to charge low prices in mega-stores offering everything from toys and furniture to groceries. While charging low prices obviously has some consumer benefits, mounting evidence from across the country indicates that these benefits come at a steep price for American workers, U.S. labor laws, and community living standards.

Wal-Mart is undercutting labor standards at home and abroad, while those federal officials charged with protecting labor standards have been largely indifferent. Public outcry against Wal-Mart's labor practices has been answered by the company with a cosmetic response. Wal-Mart has attempted to offset its labor record with advertising campaigns utilizing employees (who are euphemistically called "associates") to attest to Wal-Mart's employment benefits and support of local communities. Nevertheless—whether the issue is basic organizing rights of workers, or wages, or health benefits, or working

From http://edworkforce.house.gov, February 16, 2004.

conditions, or trade policy—Wal-Mart has come to represent the lowest common denominator in the treatment of working people. . . .

Workers' Organizing Rights

The United States recognizes workers' right to organize unions. Government employers generally may not interfere with public sector employees' freedom of association. In the private sector, workers' right to organize is protected by the National Labor Relations Act. Internationally, this right is recognized as a core labor standard and a basic human right.

Wal-Mart's record on the right to organize recently achieved international notoriety. On January 14, 2004, the International Confederation of Free Trade Unions (ICFTU), an organization representing 151 million workers in 233 affiliated unions around the world, issued a report on U.S. labor standards. Wal-Mart's rampant violations of workers' rights figured prominently. In the last few years, well over 100 unfair labor practice charges have been lodged against Wal-Mart throughout the country, with 43 charges filed in 2002 alone. Since 1995, the U.S. government has been forced to issue at least 60 complaints against Wal-Mart at the National Labor Relations Board. Wal-Mart's labor law violations range from illegally firing workers who attempt to organize a union to unlawful surveillance, threats, and intimidation of employees who dare to speak out. . . .

Wal-Mart's aggressive anti-union activity, along with the nation's weak labor laws, have kept the largest private sector employer in the U.S. union-free. . . .

Low Wages

By keeping unions at bay, Wal-Mart keeps its wages low—even by general industry standards. The average supermarket employee makes $10.35 per hour. Sales clerks at Wal-Mart, on the other hand, made only $8.23 per hour on average, or $13,861 per year, in 2001. Some estimate that average "associate" salaries range from $7.50 to $8.50 per hour. With an average on-the-clock workweek of 32 hours, many workers take home less than $1,000 per month. Even the higher estimate of a $13,861 annual salary fell below the 2001 federal poverty line of $14,630 for a family of three. About one-third of Wal-Mart's employees are part-time, restricting their access to benefits. These low wages, to say the least, complicate employees' ability to obtain essential benefits, such as health care coverage. . . .

Off-the-Clock Work

While wages are low at Wal-Mart, too often employees are not paid at all. The Fair Labor Standards Act (FLSA), along with state wage and hour laws, requires hourly employees to be paid for all time actually worked at no less than a minimum wage and at time-and-a-half for all hours worked over 40 in a week.

These labor laws have posed a particular obstacle for Wal-Mart. As of December 2002, there were thirty-nine class-action lawsuits against the company in thirty states, claiming tens of millions of dollars in back pay for hundreds of thousands of Wal-Mart employees.

In 2001, Wal-Mart forked over $50 million in unpaid wages to 69,000 workers in Colorado. These wages were paid only after the workers filed a class action lawsuit. Wal-Mart had been working the employees off-the-clock. The company also paid $500,000 to 120 workers in Gallup, New Mexico, who filed a lawsuit over unpaid work. . . .

Many observers blame the wage-and-hour problems at Wal-Mart on pressure placed on managers to keep labor costs down. In 2002, operating costs for Wal-Mart were just 16.6 percent of total sales, compared to a 20.7 percent average for the retail industry as a whole. Wal-Mart reportedly awards bonuses to its employees based on earnings. With other operating and inventory costs set by higher level management, store managers must turn to wages to increase profits. While Wal-Mart expects those managers to increase sales each year, it expects the labor costs to be cut by two-tenths of a percentage point each year as well.

Reports from former Wal-Mart managers seem to corroborate this dynamic. Joyce Moody, a former manager in Alabama and Mississippi, told the *New York Times* that Wal-Mart "threatened to write up managers if they didn't bring the payroll in low enough." Depositions in wage and hour lawsuits reveal that company headquarters leaned on management to keep their labor costs at 8 percent of sales or less, and managers in turn leaned on assistant managers to work their employees off-the-clock or simply delete time from employee time sheets. . . .

Wal-Mart's Power Brings Responsibility

> It is inconceivable that Wal-Mart, king of counting the financial cost, is unaware of the human cost of wage levels and working conditions in its suppliers' businesses. Wal-Mart's power comes with responsibility to pay just wages. With hundreds of thousands of Wal-Mart employees below poverty-level income, corporate contributions to community and charity are not enough.
>
> *Brain Bolton, Sojourners, February 2004.*

Unaffordable or Unavailable Health Care

Fewer than half—between 41 and 46 percent—of Wal-Mart's employees are insured by the company's health care plan, compared nationally to 66 percent of employees at large firms like Wal-Mart who receive health benefits from their employer. In recent years, the company increased obstacles for its workers to access its health care plan.

In 2002, Wal-Mart increased the waiting period for enrollment eligibility from 90 days to 6 months for full-time employees. Part-time employees must wait 2 years before they may enroll in the plan, and they may not purchase coverage for their spouses or children. The definition of part-time was changed from 28 hours or less per week to less than 34 hours per week. At the time, approximately one-third of Wal-Mart's workforce was part-time. By comparison, nationally, the average waiting period for health coverage for employees at large firms like Wal-Mart was 1.3 months.

The Wal-Mart plan itself shifts much of the health care costs onto employees. In 1999, employees paid 36 percent of the costs. In 2001, the employee burden rose to 42 percent. Nationally, large-firm employees pay on average 16 percent of the premium for health insurance. Unionized grocery workers typically pay nothing. Studies show that much of the decline in employer-based health coverage is due to shifts of premium costs from employers to employees.

Moreover, Wal-Mart employees who utilize their health care confront high deductibles and co-payments. A single worker could end up spending around $6,400 out-of-pocket—about 45 percent of her annual full-time salary—before seeing a single benefit from the health plan.

According to an AFL-CIO report issued in October 2003, the employees' low wages and Wal-Mart's cost-shifting render health insurance unaffordable, particularly for those employees with families. Even under the Wal-Mart plan with the highest deductible ($1,000)—and therefore with the lowest employee premium contribution—it would take an $8 per hour employee, working 34 hours per week, almost one-and-a-half months of pre-tax earnings to pay for one year of family coverage. . . .

Low Wages Mean High Costs to Taxpayers

Because Wal-Mart wages are generally not living wages, the company uses taxpayers to subsidize its labor costs. While [a] California study showed how much taxpayers were subsidizing Wal-Mart on health care alone [$20.5 million in California], the total costs to taxpayers for Wal-Mart's labor policies are much greater.

The Democratic Staff of the Committee on Education and the Workforce estimates that one 200-person Wal-Mart store may result in a cost to federal taxpayers of $420,750 per year—about $2,103 per employee. Specifically, the low wages result in the following additional public costs being passed along to taxpayers:

- $36,000 a year for free and reduced lunches for just 50 qualifying Wal-Mart families.
- $42,000 a year for Section 8 housing assistance, assuming 3 percent of the store employees qualify for such assistance, at $6,700 per family.
- $125,000 a year for federal tax credits and deductions for low-income families, assuming 50 employees are heads of household with a child and 50 are married with two children.

- $100,000 a year for the additional Title I expenses, assuming 50 Wal-Mart families qualify with an average of 2 children.
- $108,000 a year for the additional federal health care costs of moving into state children's health insurance programs (S-CHIP), assuming 30 employees with an average of two children qualify.
- $9,750 a year for the additional costs for low income energy assistance.

Among Wal-Mart employees, some single workers may be able to make ends meet. Others may be forced to take on two or three jobs. Others may have a spouse with a better job. And others simply cannot make ends meet. Because Wal-Mart fails to pay sufficient wages, U.S. taxpayers are forced to pick up the tab. In this sense, Wal-Mart's profits are not made only on the backs of its employees—but on the backs of every U.S. taxpayer. . . .

Short-Sighted Profit-Making Strategies

Wal-Mart's success has meant downward pressures on wages and benefits, rampant violations of basic workers' rights, and threats to the standard of living in communities across the country. The success of a business need not come at the expense of workers and their families. Such short-sighted profit-making strategies ultimately undermine our economy. . . .

Wal-Mart's current behavior must not be allowed to set the standard for American labor practices. Standing together, America's working families, including Wal-Mart employees, and their allies in Congress can reverse this race to the bottom in the fast-expanding service industry. The promise that every American can work an honest day's work, receive an honest day's wages, raise a family, own a home, have decent health care, and send their children to college is a promise that is not easily abandoned. It is, in short, the American Dream.

POSTSCRIPT

Is Wal-Mart a Good Model for Retail Sales?

America is not the land that it used to be. A largely agrarian society in origin, we were a nation of small towns where people were born, lived, worked, worshiped, and died, where all the businesses were independently owned by residents who were full participants in the community. Now we move away, and leave the little towns, in pursuit of the advantages of the "mass society," commuting to work, traveling to entertainment, and picking our homes from all over the country—all over the world, actually. Why should we object to mass society's favorite retail chains displacing the small shops of the past, while our delightfully low prices are financed in part by prison and slave labor in China? Part of our problem is that we want our world to stand still while we move freely through it. The next decades will confront us with many serious choices about our homes and our work. It may be time to learn Chinese.

If the topic of the patterns and forces of jobs and sales in the globalized economy continues to interest you, you may be interested in the following works:

Suggested Reading

Jim Hightower, *Thieves in High Places*, Chapter 10 (New York: Penguin Group, 2003).

Barbara Ehrenrich, *Nickel and Dimed: On (Not) Getting by in America*, a Metropolitan/Owl Book (New York: Henry Holt and Company, 2001).

Tracie Rozhon, "Teaching Wal-Mart New Tricks—Retailing's Goliath Learns to Listen." *The New York Times*, Sunday May 8, 2005 Section 3 pg. 1.

David Hest, "Is Walmartization Ahead?" from *Farm Industry News*, Sept. 1, 2004, http://www.farmindustrynews.com/mag/farming_walmartization_ahead.

ISSUE 8

Does the Enron Collapse Show that We Need More Regulation of the Energy Industry?

YES: **Richard Rosen**, from "Regulating Power: An Idea Whose Time Is Back," *The American Prospect* (March 25, 2002)

NO: **Christopher L. Culp and Steve H. Hanke**, from "Empire of the Sun: An Economic Interpretation of Enron's Energy Business," *Cato Policy Analysis No. 470* (February 20, 2003)

ISSUE SUMMARY

YES: It seems reasonably clear to Richard Rosen that the disastrous collapse of the Enron energy company—accompanied by soaring prices in California, disruptions of the market here and abroad, and accusations of fraud all around—means we need more government oversight.

NO: Not so, say Culp and Hanke; it was the unwise regulation that caused the problem in the first place, and only deregulation will let the market clear up the problems with the industry.

Everyone since Adam Smith has acknowledged that no matter what the virtues of the free market—and they are many—there are areas where the public needs protection. For an obvious instance, the state, to be called a state, must assert and maintain an absolute monopoly on the use of force, not just force that would deprive of life, health, or liberty, but any force at all (there are towns that forbid parents to spank their children). Force, therefore, or the threat of violence, cannot be part of any legal negotiation. For another instance, there are products so dangerous to human health and welfare that by law we forbid them to be sold on the open market under any circumstances, even though a high demand and lucrative trade could be predicted—hand grenades, crack cocaine, and canisters of poison gas come to mind. (After that, there are the flotillas of restrictions on open trade—drugs available only by prescription, bans on the sale of wild or endangered animals or their parts, bans on pesticides that endure in the environment—the list goes on.)

The state creates such restrictions in the exercise of its inalienable "police power," the responsibility to protect the health, welfare, and morals of the people. The exercise of that responsibility in most developed nations includes the provision of a free educational system and free health care for all citizens; the United States, as a matter of policy, has exempted itself from the latter and seems to be aiming at phasing out the former.

At least since the beginning of the twentieth century, state monopoly and regulation have been extended to a large variety of "utilities"—public goods that cannot fall into private hands without putting the public at serious risk of exploitation. These include transportation corridors (including roads, railways, all waterways), communications pathways (airwaves, telegraph lines, telephone services), and all provision of water and energy (heat and light). For most of that period at least a portion of most of those services has been in private hands, but all were subject to the regulation of rates, the regulation of the choice of services to provide and areas to be served, and the expectation that they would serve the public interest (evidence to the contrary could result in government intervention at any time).

Deregulation began as part of the antiregulatory climate during the Reagan administration, during the period when companies were led by the mergers and acquisitions departments. At that time Kenneth Lay took over the Enron company's predecessor and rapidly picked up several more unexciting pipeline companies. He cultivated friends in high places, and furthered his deregulation agenda all through the Clinton administration. (In 1993, for instance, Wendy Gramm, wife of Senator Phil Gramm, ushered a ruling exempting futures contracts from government oversight through the Commodity Futures Trading Commission, which she chaired. Shortly thereafter, she left that post and accepted a position on Enron's board of directors.) Lay, and Enron generally, spent a very large amount of money on contributions to political campaigns, including at least $6 million to federal candidates and parties as well as $1.8 million or more to candidates for state office. Very large contributions went to George W. Bush's presidential campaign. By the time Bush attained the White House, Lay was a close friend ("Kenny Boy," as he was known to the president). Enron was the most persistent and loudest voice for deregulation.

Was it a good idea? In California, deregulation led to skyrocketing prices, draining the state's coffers. Enron made out very well. Is this just free enterprise at work? Would it have all steadied down eventually? There are two sides to this dispute, which were both silenced on October 18, 2002, when Enron officers pleaded guilty to conspiracy to manipulate energy prices in California. Maybe the damage to California was due to regulation, maybe it was due to deregulation, but probably it was due to criminal conspiracies undertaken by criminals under cover of the deregulation agenda. We will have to await a more honest trial of deregulation to discover the public's real best interest.

Ask yourself, as you read these brief selections, what we expect the free market to provide and to refrain from providing, and what we expect government, in the exercise of its police power, to ensure for our common life. The questions are not simple, and there is no national consensus.

YES

Richard Rosen

Regulating Power: An Idea Whose Time Is Back

Ignored in the scandal about Enron's off-the-books deals is the fact that Enron's core businesses—trading and selling energy—made little economic sense. Starting in the early 1990s, Enron claimed it could make electricity generation more efficient through a system to trade more electric power than regulated utilities. To that end, the company urged the Federal Energy Regulatory Commission (FERC) to promote the deregulation of wholesale electric markets.

But whenever there was an opportunity to reduce consumers' electric rates by trading power at the wholesale level, the old regulated electric utilities had always done so. Indeed, most electric utilities had already grouped themselves into "power pools" or other voluntary energy-swapping systems set up to trade power at its cost of production—the cheapest approach for consumers. If we calculate the relative costs of producing and selling electricity, new wholesale traders like Enron could have reduced our national average electric rates by perhaps 1 percent, if that.

So most of the supposed efficiencies of deregulation were already being realized by regulated utilities. To the extent that Enron could reap large profits, it was only by amassing market power, monopolizing transmission lines, and taking advantage of temporary scarcity—thus raising prices and frustrating the whole supposed point of deregulation. Any efficiency gains were more than wiped out by the cost of administering a new, complex trading system pursuing its own quest for profit.

When it lobbied state legislatures and public-utility commissions to deregulate electric utilities, Enron promised to sell retail electricity to all types of customers. Instead, because it was too costly to compete with traditional utilities for small customers, Enron wound up selling retail electricity primarily to large industrial and commercial companies under long-term contracts. Because government takes ultimate responsibility for the power supply, even in states that have deregulated generation, utilities will remain providers of last resort for at least the next few years. Regulated retail rates, meanwhile, have always been a fallback option for large and small consumers. Enron and other similar companies could seldom beat the regulated price.

Ultimately, Enron never made a profit in its retail business. The costs of gaining market share were just too high—and they were probably hidden by some of Enron's now famous off-balance-sheet debt. In some cases, very large customers saved a few percentage points on their electricity bills, but often only until wholesale prices rose, forcing them to turn back to the regulated utilities for the best rates.

The small savings that deregulation might deliver to some customers must be weighed against the higher costs to others—and against the huge risks of overcharges like those seen during the California debacle, well before Enron's collapse. Analysts who deny that Enron was a failure of deregulation, or who paint Enron as just an isolated case of corporate mismanagement, forget that the firm never realized its original promises—even though deregulated electricity sales, at both the wholesale and retail levels, were its primary reason for being.

How, then, should we regulate electricity? Contrary to the current fashion, our old system—state regulation of vertically integrated electric utilities—makes sense. Regulators need to stress state-of-the-art, "least cost" planning for new investments in generation and transmission. Traditional regulation means that utilities charge consumers their costs plus a reasonably low regulated return on equity.

Utilities should be grouped into power pools—like those we've had in the Northeast—in order to make possible economically efficient sharing of their generating plants. Under a regulated system, concentrated market power is a strength, not a threat, because utilities are prohibited from gouging consumers.

It turns out that it is not economically efficient to divide electric-utility services and create an unregulated market for each. We probably don't even need a competitive wholesale power market. Ironically, by the early 1990s many state regulatory commissions were getting quite good at keeping electric rates in check, thanks in part to growing investments in energy conservation. It was the big industrial customers who thought that they could get better deals in a deregulated market for electricity. On the whole, they didn't. While co-generation and other energy-saving technology surely make sense, deregulation doesn't.

Christopher L. Culp and
Steve H. Hanke

 **NO**

Empire of the Sun: An Economic Interpretation of Enron's Energy Business

Executive Summary

The collapse of Enron Corporation has been portrayed as the result of accounting fraud and greed. Not everything that Enron did, however, was wrong or fraudulent. Fraud contributed to the timing of Enron's failure but was not the root cause of that failure. In analyzing Enron, it is critically important to distinguish what Enron did wrong from what it did right.

Enron's basic business strategy, known as "asset lite," was legitimate and quite beneficial for the marketplace and consumers. By combining a small investment in a capital-intensive industry such as energy with a derivatives-trading operation and a market-making overlay for that market, Enron was able to transform itself from a small, regional energy market operator into one of America's largest companies.

Enron contributed to the creation of the natural gas derivatives market, and, for a while, it was the sole market maker, entering into price risk management contracts with all other market participants. Its physical market presence, as a wholesale merchant of natural gas and electricity, placed the Houston-based company in an ideal position to discover and transmit to the market relevant knowledge of energy markets and to make those markets more efficient.

When Enron applied that same strategy in other markets in which it had no comparative informational advantage or deviated from the asset-lite strategy, it had to incur significant costs to create the physical market presence required to rectify its relative lack of market information. The absence of a financial market overlay in several of those markets further prevented Enron from recovering its costs. It was at that point that Enron abused accounting and disclosure policies to hide debt and cover up the fact that its business model did not work in those other areas.

From *Policy Analysis*, no. 470, February 20, 2003, pp. 1–19. Copyright © 2003 by Cato Institute.
Reprinted by permission.

For its innovations, Enron should be commended; for their alleged illegal activities, Enron's managers should be prosecuted to the full extent of the law. But under no circumstance should Enron's failure be used as an excuse to enact policies and regulations aimed at eliminating risk taking and economic failure, because unless a firm takes the risk of failure, it will never earn the premium of success. As was demonstrated in the case of Enron, markets—not politicians—are the best judges of success and failure.

Introduction

By the time the Enron Corporation filed for Chapter 11 bankruptcy protection on December 2, 2001, virtually everyone with a television set knew that things were not as they had once seemed in Houston. How could a company go from a market capitalization of more than $100 billion and being ranked fifth in the *Fortune 500* list to bust within two years? How could a stock that had seen highs of nearly $90 per share become a penny stock in record time? How could the six-time consecutive winner (1996–2001) of *Fortune*'s "most innovative company in the United States" have engineered its own financial destruction? *And more important, what can be done to make sure this never happens again?*

One must be careful, however, when defining "this" in the phrase "make sure this never happens again." Not everything Enron ever did, after all, was illegal, unethical, or even questionable. In fact, what actually caused Enron to fail is still subject to contentious debate. It is clear, however, that Enron did not fail because it was engaged in commercial and merchant commodity businesses.[1] Nor did a "rogue trader" or Enron's use of creative and sometimes-complex financial contracts bring Enron to its knees. Nor, finally, did Enron's corrupt financial activities—concealing its true indebtedness, lining the pockets of select senior managers at the expense of shareholders, hiding major losses, and the like—cause Enron to fail.[2] Enron's financial deception undoubtedly allowed it to remain in business longer than an otherwise similar firm engaged in accurate financial disclosures might have, but that is a question of timing alone and not causality.

This [selection] argues that Enron's ultimate financial failure most likely occurred for the very same reason that WorldCom, Global Crossing, and many other firms periodically have gone bankrupt or run into trouble. In short, those firms all lacked the ability to identify their true comparative advantage. In some cases that meant Enron overinvested in new markets and technologies that never took off; in other cases it simply meant that the company overestimated the value that it could add. But is *that* something that new policies and regulations should strive to ensure "never happens again"? Or, as argued in this study, is this aspect of Enron's failure simply a testimonial to the fact that competitive markets are effective judges of success and failure?

This study begins with an overview of Enron to stress that it was first and foremost an energy business that employed an innovative "asset-lite" strategy that accounted for many of its genuinely successful years. A discussion of those businesses in which Enron failed follows because it is in those areas where Enron departed from the successful asset-lite strategy employed in the energy business. The next section formally frames Enron's asset-lite strategy in the context of competitive economic theory. Standard "neoclassical" economic models do not explain firms such as Enron, and consequently a more "disequilibrium-oriented," or "neo-Austrian," approach is required. The [selection] concludes by considering whether Enron's failure *as a business* either offers lessons for other firms or provides a proscriptive case for greater regulation.

Neoclassical vs. Neo-Austrian Economic Theory

In addition to providing an analysis of Enron's business strategy through the lens of economic theory, this study illustrates the limitations of the traditional neoclassical theory of the price system for explaining entrepreneurship and innovation—terms that, despite Enron's illegal and fraudulent activities in some areas, nevertheless do describe that company in other areas. The neoclassical perspective views markets as existing in a stationary state in which the relevant knowledge about demand and supply is known; market prices are static, or given; and data are available to be used by individuals and firms. In this world without change, there is no need to ask how that stationary state came about. That knowledge simply falls into the category of irrelevant bygones.

Neoclassical economics does, of course, also deal with change. It does so by employing comparative statistics. For example, we can conceive of a quasi-stationary state in which changes in the relevant knowledge in a market are few and far between, and analysis of the full repercussions is dealt with by evaluating and comparing the stationary states before and after changes in relevant knowledge occur. In the neoclassical world, prices act as signposts, guiding consumers to substitute goods for one another and producers to learn which lines of production to abandon or toward which to turn. In this neoclassical conception, the price system acts as a network of communication in which relevant knowledge is transmitted at once throughout markets that jump from one stationary state to the next.

In the neo-Austrian, or disequilibrium-oriented, context, by contrast, the market is viewed as a process that is in a constant state of flux.[3] In consequence, there are no stationary or quasi-stationary states. Indeed, expectations about the current and future state of affairs are always changing because the state of relevant knowledge is always changing. And with changing expectations, market prices are also changing. In consequence, the price system functions as a network for communicating all relevant knowledge. It is also a discovery process that is in continuous motion, working toward creating unity and coherence in the economic system. The speed of adjustment and of the dissemination of knowledge in the price system depends on the scope and scale of the markets, however.

As it relates to the discussion here, the full force of market integration is realized when both spot and forward markets exist. Indeed, the function of forward, or derivatives, markets is to spread relevant knowledge now about what market participants think the future will be. Forward markets connect and integrate those expectations about the future with the present in a consistent manner.[4] Although the future will always remain uncertain, it is possible for individuals to acquire information about the expected future and to adjust their plans accordingly. In addition, they can—via forward markets—express their views about the future by either buying or selling forward. Forward markets, then, bring expectations about the future into consistency with each other and also bring forward prices into consistency with spot prices, with the difference being turned into "the basis."

In a neo-Austrian world, relevant knowledge and expectations are in a constant state of flux. And not surprisingly, spot and forward prices, as well as their difference (the basis), are constantly changing, too. Individuals' ever-changing expectations, therefore, keep the market process in motion. In consequence, disequilibrium is a hallmark of the neo-Austrian orientation. While the neo-Austrian market process is in a constant state of flux, it is working toward integrating and making consistent both spot and forward prices.[5]

As the analysis in this [selection] will demonstrate, the explicit incorporation of neo-Austrian variables such as time, knowledge, and market process into the traditional price-theoretic framework for microeconomic analysis is fundamental to understanding fully the financial and commercial market strategies of a company such as Enron.

Enron's Energy Business

Understanding Enron's business model for its core activities requires a brief explanation of how commodity markets function. The usefulness of many physical commodities to producers (e.g., wheat that can be milled into flour) and consumers (e.g., bread) depends on the "supply chain" through which the commodity is transformed from its raw, natural state into something of practical use. Figure 1 shows a typical supply chain for a variety of commodities.

Figure 1

The Supply Chain

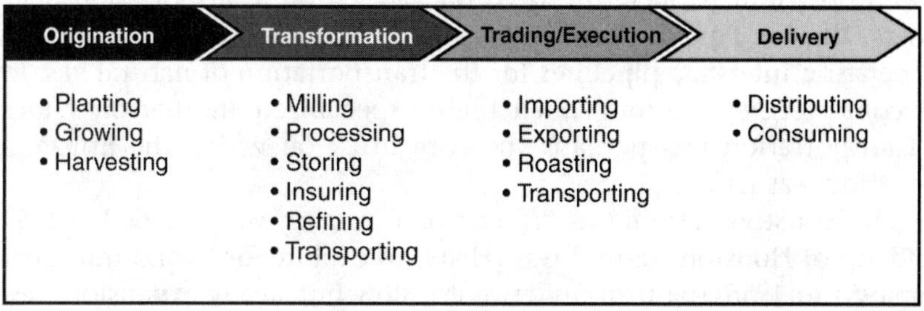

Origination	Transformation	Trading/Execution	Delivery
• Planting	• Milling	• Importing	• Distributing
• Growing	• Processing	• Exporting	• Consuming
• Harvesting	• Storing	• Roasting	
	• Insuring	• Transporting	
	• Refining		
	• Transporting		

When a commodity moves from one part of the supply chain to the next, transportation, distribution, and delivery services are almost always involved. Those services are the glue that keeps the supply chain linked. To put it simply, Enron was a firm that specialized in those transportation, distribution, and transformation services—often called "intermediate supply chain," or "midstream," services. Accordingly, Enron acted as a wholesale merchant. It acquired the latest information about alternative sources of supply and set prices for goods in a process that would maximize Enron's turnover. Enron was therefore an ideal vehicle for the discovery and transmission of relevant knowledge.

In its *2000 Annual Report*, Enron described itself as "a firm that manages efficient, flexible networks to reliably deliver physical products at predictable prices."[6] This involved four core business areas for the firm: wholesale services, energy services, broadband services, and transportation services.

Enron Wholesale Services was by far the largest—and generally the most profitable—operation of Enron Corp. The bulk of that business involved the transportation, transmission, and distribution of natural gas and electricity. On a volume basis, Enron accounted for more than twice the amount of gas and power delivery of its next-largest competitor in the United States.[7] In addition, Enron maintained an active (and, in several cases, growing) market presence in the supply chains for other commodities, including coal, crude oil, liquefied natural gas, metals, steel, and pulp and paper. Enron Wholesale Services' customers were generally other large producers and industrial firms.

Enron Energy Services dealt mainly at the retail end of the energy market supply chains. Enron Wholesale Services' operation might deliver electrical power to a utility, for example, whereas Enron Energy Services might contract directly with a large grocery store chain to supply their power directly.

Enron Broadband was focused on the nonenergy business of broadband services, or the use of fiber optics to transmit audio and video. Capacity on fiber-optic cables is known as "bandwidth." Enron Broadband had three business goals. The first was to deploy the largest open global broadband network in the world, called the Enron Intelligent Network and consisting of 18,000 miles of fiber-optic cable. The second commercial objective in broadband was for Enron to dominate the market for buying and selling bandwidth. Finally, Enron sought to become a dominant provider of premium content, mainly through streaming audio and video over the worldwide web.

Enron's fourth operating division was Enron Transportation Services, formerly the Gas Pipeline Group. Enron Transportation Services concentrated on operating interstate pipelines for the transportation of natural gas, long a core competency of Enron. Albeit highly specialized and narrowly focused, gas transportation was perhaps the core brick on which the Enron Corp. foundation was laid.

The Houston Natural Gas Production Company was founded in 1953 as a subsidiary of Houston Natural Gas [HNG] to explore, drill, and transport gas. From 1953 to 1985, the firm underwent a slow but steady expansion, respectably keeping pace with the gradual development of the gas market.

Natural gas was deregulated in the late 1980s and early 1990s. During that time, supplies increased substantially, and prices fell by more than 50 percent from 1985 to 1991 alone. As competition increased, the number of new entrants into various parts of the natural gas supply chain grew dramatically, and many existing firms restructured.

One such restructuring was the acquisition in 1985 of HNG by Inter-North, Inc. The takeover of HNG was largely the brainchild of Kenneth Lay, who had joined HNG as its CEO in 1984. Working closely with Michael Milken, Lay helped structure the InterNorth purchase of HNG as a leveraged buyout relying heavily on junk-bond finance.[8] Lay wrested the position of CEO of the merged firm from InterNorth CEO Samuel Segnar in 1985.

In 1986 InterNorth changed its name to Enron Corporation and incorporated Enron Oil & Gas Company, reflecting its expansion into oil markets to supplement its gas market presence. By then, most firms active in oil markets were also involved in gas—and conversely—given complementarities in exploration, drilling, pumping, distribution, and the like. With the exception of a brief hiatus toward the end, Kenneth Lay remained CEO of Enron Corp. until the firm failed.[9]

In 1985 the Federal Energy Regulatory Commission allowed "open access" to gas pipelines for the first time. In consequence, Enron was able to charge other firms for using Enron pipelines to transport gas, and, similarly, Enron was able to transport gas through other companies' pipelines.

Around that time, Jeffrey Skilling, then a consultant for McKinsey, began working at Enron. He was charged with developing a creative strategy to help Enron—recall, it had just been created through the InterNorth-HNG merger—leverage its presence in the emerging gas market. Skilling argued that the benefits of open access might well be more than offset by the decline in revenues associated with the general decline in prices and margins that greater competition would bring. Add to that Enron's mountain of debt, and Skilling maintained that Enron would not last very long unless a creative solution was identified.

Skilling argued, in particular, that natural gas would never be a serious source of revenues for the firm as long as natural gas was traded exclusively in a "spot" physical market for immediate delivery. Instead, he argued that a key success driver in the coming era of post-deregulation price volatility would be the development of a "derivatives market" in gas in which Enron would provide its customers with various price risk management solutions—forward contracts in which consumers could control their price risk by purchasing gas today at a fixed price for future delivery, and option contracts that allowed customers the right but not obligation to purchase or sell gas at a fixed price in the future.

Viewed from a neo-Austrian perspective, Skilling was functioning as a classic entrepreneur. Once FERC changed the rules of the game and natural gas became deregulated, Skilling spotted an entrepreneurial opportunity, literally, to develop new forward markets. Once forward markets were introduced, individuals could acquire information and knowledge about the future and express their own expectations by either buying or selling forward.

Moreover, with both spot and futures prices revealed, "the basis"—the difference between spot and futures prices—could be revealed, and a more unified and coherently integrated natural gas "market" could be created. Although such a new setup would not eliminate risk and uncertainty, it promised to allow much more relevant knowledge to be discovered and disseminated, allowing firms to adjust their expectations and plans accordingly and to manage their risk more effectively.[10]

To create that market in natural gas derivatives, Skilling urged Enron to set up a "gasbank." Much as traditional banks intermediate funds, Enron's GasBank intermediated gas purchases, sales, and deliveries by entering into long-term, fixed-price delivery and price risk management contracts with customers. Soon thereafter, other natural gas firms began to offer clients similar risk management solutions. And those producers, in turn, also came to Enron for their risk management needs—that is, to "swap" the exposure to falling prices they created by offering fixed-price forwards to customers back into the "natural" exposure to price increases those producers had before offering their customers fixed-price protection.

Enron acted as a classic market maker, standing ready to enter into natural gas derivatives on "both sides of the market"—that is, both buying and selling gas (or, equivalently, buying and selling at both fixed and floating prices or swapping one for the other). Enron thus became the primary supplier of liquidity to the market, earning the spread between bid and offer prices as a fee for providing the market with liquidity. And in a broader sense, Enron was functioning to spread knowledge about what market participants expected prices to be.

Did that mean Enron was exposed to *all* of the price risks that its trading counter parties were attempting to avoid? No. Many of the contracts into which Enron entered naturally offset one another. True, a consumer seeking to lock in its future energy purchase price with Enron would create a risk exposure for Enron. If prices rose above the fixed price at which Enron agreed to sell energy to a consumer, Enron could lose big money. But that might be offset by a risk exposure to *falling* prices that Enron would assume by agreeing to *buy* that same asset from a producer at a fixed price, thus allowing the producer to hedge its own price risk.[11] Enron was left only with the *residual* risk across all its customer positions in its GasBank, which, in turn, Enron could manage by using derivatives with other emerging market makers, generally known as "swap dealers," or on organized futures exchanges such as the New York Mercantile Exchange.[12]

For a long time, Enron was not merely a market maker for natural gas derivatives—it was *the* market maker. Having virtually created the market, Enron enjoyed wider spreads, higher margins, and more revenues as the sole real liquidity supplier to the market. But that also meant few counterparties existed with which Enron could hedge its own residual risks.

Here is where Enron's physical market presence comes back into the picture. In addition to allowing Enron to discover and reveal a great deal of "local" knowledge, Enron's presence in the physical market meant that it could control some of the residual price risks from its market-making operations.

That could be accomplished because of *offsetting positions in its physical pipeline and gas operations.* Consider, for example, a firm that is buying natural gas in Tulsa, Oklahoma, from a pipeline with a supply source in San Angelo, Texas. If that firm seeks to lock in its future purchase price for gas to protect against unexpected price spikes, it might enter into a forward purchase agreement with Enron, thus leaving Enron to bear the risk of a price increase. But if Enron also *owns the pipeline* and charges a price for distribution proportional to the spot price of gas, then the net effect will be roughly offsetting.

Operating that kind of a gas bank also gave Enron very valuable information about the gas market itself. Knowing from its pipeline operations that congestion was likely to occur at Point A, for example, Enron could anticipate price spikes at delivery points beyond Point A arising from the squeeze in available pipeline capacity. And Enron could very successfully "trade around" such congestion points. Conversely, when prices in derivatives markets signaled surplus or deficit pipeline capacity in the financial market, Enron could stand ready to exploit that information in the physical market.

Gradually, thanks to Enron's role as market maker, the natural gas derivatives market became increasingly standardized and liquid. Accordingly, relevant knowledge was spread more rapidly and the natural gas market became more integrated and coherent. Enron still offered customized solutions to certain consumers and producers, but much of the volume of the market shifted to exchanges like the NYMEX that began to provide standardized gas futures. Nevertheless, Enron's role as dominant market maker left the GasBank well placed to profit from supplying liquidity to those standardized markets, as well as from retaining much of the custom over-the-counter derivatives-dealing business.

The Enron GasBank division eventually became Enron Gas Services, and later Enron Capital and Trade Resources. In 1990 Jeff Skilling left McKinsey to become a full-time Enron employee, and he later became CEO of both EGS and EC&TR. In early 2001 Skilling replaced Lay as CEO of the whole firm, marking the only time in the history of Enron that Lay was not at the helm.

Asset Lite as a More General Business Strategy

When Skilling formally joined Enron in 1990, he maintained that the future success of the firm would be in repeating the GasBank experience in other markets. To accomplish that, Skilling developed a business concept known as "asset lite" in which Enron would combine small investments in capital-intensive commodity markets with a derivatives-trading and market-making "overlay" for those markets. The idea was to begin with a small capital expenditure that was used to acquire portions of assets and establish a presence in the physical market. That allowed Enron to learn the operational features of the market and to collect information about factors that might affect market price dynamics. Then, Enron would create a new financial market overlaid on top of that underlying physical market presence—a market in which Enron would act as market maker and liquidity supplier to meet other firms' risk management needs. As Skilling described it: "[Enron] is a company that makes markets.

We create the market, and once it's created, we make the market."[13] Needless to say, that encapsulates the essence of one of the central roles of an Austrian entrepreneur.

One reason for the appeal of asset lite was that it enabled Enron to exploit some presence in the physical market without incurring huge capital expenditures on bulk fixed investments. Enron quickly discovered that this was best accomplished by focusing on investing in *intermediate* assets in commodity supply chains. In natural gas, this meant that Enron could get the biggest bang for its buck in midstream activities such as transportation, pipeline compression, storage, and distribution. In fact, Enron's Transwestern Pipeline Company eventually became the first U.S. pipeline that was exclusively for transportation, neither pumping gas at the wellhead nor selling it to customers.[14]

Other markets in which Enron applied its asset-lite business expansion strategy with a large degree of success included coal, fossil fuels, and, to some extent, pulp and paper. But after its successful experience with gas, Enron remained much more interested in markets that were being deregulated. Electricity thus became a major focus of the firm in the mid-1990s and was a key success driver for Enron.[15]

Oil and Water Do Not Mix

Throughout its history, Enron's consistent financial and market successes occurred in the energy sector. On more than one occasion, however, Enron tried to expand its business outside the energy area, albeit rarely with any success.

Asset Heavy at Enron International

When it became clear that Kenneth Lay was preparing to turn over the reins in the latter half of the 1990s, an extremely contentious struggle for the leadership of Enron ensued.[16] That occurred in no small part because of the success of Enron GasBank and the power-marketing operations of EC&TR. When the dust settled, Lay named EC&TR CEO and asset-lite inventor Jeff Skilling as the new CEO of Enron Corp. in February 2001. That Skilling would rise to this level, however, was not at all a foregone conclusion. Right up to the announcement date, debates over whose shoulder Kenneth Lay would tap were popular coffee shop banter. Skilling's chief competitor was Rebecca Mark.

In 1993 Mark prevailed upon Lay to establish Enron International, of which she became the first president. Mark did not adhere to an asset-lite strategy. Instead, she pursued an "asset-heavy" strategy of attempting to acquire or develop large capital-intensive projects *for their own sake*. In other words, there was no financial-trading activity overlay component for most of her initiatives. She tried instead to identify projects whose revenues promised to be sizable based purely on the capital investment component with no need for a market maker component. Unlike asset lite, that did not prove to be an area in which Enron Corp. had much comparative advantage.

Water-Trading Rights

The EI operations delved into the asset-heavy water-supply industry. At least here there was some pretense of eventually developing a "water rights trading market," but that possibility was so far down the road that the firm's water investments have to be regarded as largely self-contained capital projects, the largest of which was Azurix and its Wessex Water initiative.

In 1998 Enron spun off the water company Azurix. Enron retained a major interest in the firm, which focused its efforts on water markets in a single purchase—the British firm Wessex Water, for which Enron paid about $1.9 billion. But in this case, deregulation did not help Enron. There was no market-making function and no trading overlay—there was only a British water company serving a market with plummeting prices. (That experience also underscores the fundamentally correct view that Skilling advanced when he was still at McKinsey—namely, that expanding in a deregulating market makes little sense if you are limited to selling a commodity whose price is falling sharply in the spot markets.)

At the same time that the falling prices caused by deregulation in Britain were eating away Wessex's margins, Azurix itself was hit with staggering losses on several of its other operations, mainly in Argentina. In light of that failure, as well as the spectacular failure of EI's Dhabhol, India, power plant project, which may have cost Enron as much as $4 billion, Mark resigned as CEO of Enron International in the summer of 2000. Enron eventually sold Wessex in 2002, about three years after financing its acquisition by Azurix, to a Malaysian firm for $777 million, or $1.1 billion less than it paid for the firm.[17]

The Broadband Black Hole

Like its forays into the water industry, Enron's broadband efforts were plagued with problems from the start. In gas and powermarkets, Enron acquired its physical market presence by investing in assets sold mainly by would-be competing energy companies. It then used those investments to help create and develop a financial market, the growth of which, in turn, helped *increase* the value of Enron's physical investments. But that increase did not come at the expense of Enron's competitors, which in turn were benefiting from the new price risk management market. In broadband technologies, by contrast, Enron's asset-lite effort required the firm to acquire assets not just from competitors but from the *inventors* of the technology. Even then, Enron was paying for a technology that was essentially untested with no guarantee that the "emerging" bandwidth market would bolster asset values. Enron therefore had to pay dearly to acquire a market presence from firms that viewed Enron's effort not as a constructive market-making move but as essentially an intrusive one.

Several other drags on Enron's broadband expansion efforts contributed to its ultimate failure. One was that demand for the technology failed to materialize as expected. Enron is also alleged to have been using the "bandwidth market" to mislead investors—and possibly certain senior managers and directors—about its losses on underlying broadband technologies. On the one hand, Enron was optimistic about the eventual success of the broadband strategy; it "pointed at" significant trading in the bandwidth market. On the other hand, few other market participants observed any appreciable trading activity, and Enron was openly disclosing millions of dollars of losses on its quarterly and annual reports on its broadband efforts. Much of that "market activity" now seems to have come from Enron's "wash," or "roundtrip," trades or transactions in which Enron was essentially trading with itself.[18] To take a simple example, a purchase and sale of the same contract within a one- or two-minute period of time in which prices have not changed will show up as "volume," but the transactions wash out and amount to no real bottom-line profits.

In addition to apparently using wash trades to exaggerate the state of the market's development, Enron was also alleged to have used some of its bandwidth derivatives for "manufacturing" exaggeratedly high valuations for its technological assets. Specifically, Enron and Qwest are under investigation for engaging in transactions with one another that are alleged to have been designed specifically to create artificial mark-to-market valuations. Enron and Qwest engaged in a $500 million bandwidth swap negotiated just prior to the end of the 2001 third-quarter financial reporting period. Many observers would argue that Enron and Qwest were swapping one worthless thing for another worthless thing, given the lack of a market for bandwidth and the lack of *interest* in bandwidth. Nevertheless, both firms apparently used the swaps to justify having acquired a much more valuable asset than the one of which they were getting rid. With essentially no "market," no market prices were available for evaluating the validity of those claims at the time.

The Economics of Asset Lite and "Basis Trading"

Through its investments in the underlying commodity supply chains, the trading-room "overlay" on the physical markets allowed Enron to generate substantial revenues as a market maker. But that was not the only source of profits associated with the asset-lite strategy of combining physical and financial market positions. Specifically, Enron engaged in significant "basis trading." Understanding what that is and when a company might be able to do it profitably is essential for recognizing the differences between businesses on which Enron "made money" and those on which it did not.

To understand the economics of basis trading (sometimes called spread trading), one must first recognize the important finance proposition that commodity derivatives—contracts for the purchase or sale of a commodity in the future—are economic substitutes for physical market operations.[19] Buying a forward oil purchase contract, for example, is economically equivalent to buying and storing oil.[20] In a competitive equilibrium of the physical and derivatives markets, the forward purchase price—denoted $F(t,T)$ and defined as the fixed price negotiated on date t for the purchase of a commodity to be delivered on later date T—can be expressed using the famed "cost of carry model" as[21]

$$F(t,T) = S(t)[1 + b(t,T)]$$

Where $b(t,T)$ $r(t,T) + w(t,T) - d(t,T)$

and $S(t)$ = time t spot price of the commodity to be delivered at T

$r(t,T)$ = the interest rate prevailing from t to T

$w(t,T)$ = the cost of physical storage of the commodity from t to T

$d(t,T)$ = the benefit of holding the commodity from t to T

such that w and d are expressed as a proportion of $S(t)$ and are denominated in time T dollars.

The term $b(t,T)$—the "basis"—is also often called the "net cost of carry," to convey the fact that its three components together makeup the cost of "carrying" the commodity across time and space to the delivery location on future date T. The term $d(t,T)$ that reflects the benefit of physical storage is called the "convenience yield," a concept developed by John Maynard Keynes, Nicholas Kaldor, Holbrook Working, Michael J. Brennan, and Lester G. Telser.[22] The convenience yield is driven mainly by what Working calls the "precautionary demand for storage," or concerns by firms that unanticipated shocks to demand or supply could precipitate a costly inventory depletion.[23] Airlines store fuel at different airports, for example, to avoid the huge costs of grounding their local fleets in the case of a jet fuel outage. Gas pipeline owners store gas to help ensure that there is always an adequate supply of gas in the lines to maintain the flow and avoid a shutdown.

Keynes, Working, and others have observed how the "supply of storage" (i.e., the amount of a commodity in physical storage) is related to the convenience yield and, by extension, to the "term structure of futures prices."[24] That relation defines the economic linkage between derivatives, physical asset markets, and the allocation of physical supplies across time. Specifically, the supply of storage is directly related to the premium placed on selling inventory *in the future* relative to selling spot *today*. When inventories are high, the *relative* premium that a commodity commands in the future vis-à-vis the present is reasonably small; plenty of the commodity is on hand today to assure producers and intermediaries that a stock-out will not occur, leading to a very low convenience yield. As current inventories get smaller, however, the convenience yield rises (at an increasing rate) and the spot price rises relative to the futures price in order to induce producers to take physical product out of inventory and sell it in the current spot market. A high spot price *alone* would not do that. But a high spot price *relative* to the futures price signals the market that inventories are tight *today* relative to the future.

We can now see more meaningfully where cost-of-carry pricing comes from. Namely, it is the condition that must hold in equilibrium to make market participants indifferent toward physical storage or "synthetic storage" using forwards or other derivatives. Here's how it works. Suppose a firm borrows $S(t)$ in funds at time t and uses the proceeds to buy a commodity worth $S(t)$. At time T, the firm is holding an asset then worth $S(T)$ and repays the money loan. In the interim, the firm incurs physical storage costs w but earns the convenience yield d. Table 1 shows the net effect of this physical storage operation.

Table 1

	t	T
Physical Commodity Storage		
Money loan		
Borrow dollars	$S(t)$	-
Repay dollars and interest	-	$-S(t)[1 + r(t,T)]$
Buy and store the asset		
Buy commodity	$-S(t)$	-
Pay storage costs	-	$-S(t)w(t,T)$
Earn convenience yield	-	$S(t)d(t,T)$
Still own the commodity	-	$S(T)$
Net	0	$S(T) - S(t)[1 + r(t,T) + w(t,T) - d(t,T)]$

In turn, a short position in a forward contract involves no initial outlay and has a time T value of $F(t,T) - S(T)$. From the last line of Table 1, it should be clear that physical storage plus borrowing can be used to hedge the short forward contract (or vice versa). The net of the hedged position is then just $F(t,T) - S(t)[1 + r(t,T) + w(t,T) - d(t,T)]$, all of which is known at time t and thus is riskless. If all market participants are price takers and face identical benefits and costs of storage, cost-of-carry futures pricing thus holds purely through the mechanism of arbitrage.

Because not every firm has the same convenience yield or storage costs, however, commodity forward prices are driven to the cost-of-carry expression instead by the dynamics of a competitive equilibrium.[25] To see how it works, suppose the forward purchase price is

$$F° = S(t)[1 + b°(t,T)]$$

where $b°(t,T)$ denotes any arbitrary net cost of carry. All firms for which $S(t)[1 + b(t,T)] < F°$ can earn positive economic profits by going short the forward and simultaneously buying and storing the commodity. They will continue to do this until the forward price falls and $S(t)[1 + b(t,T)] = F°$. As long as any firm can make positive profits from this operation, the selling will continue, until

$$S(t)[1 + b(t,T)] = F*$$

where $F* = S(t)[1 + b*(t,T)]$ and where $b*(t,T)$ denotes the marginal net cost of carry from t to T for the marginal storer. This marginal entrant earns exactly zero economic profits since its own net cost of carry is equal to $b*$.

Things work in the other direction for any firms for which $S(t)[1 + b(t,T)] > F°$. Those firms will go long the forward and then engage in a commodity repurchase agreement (i.e., lending the commodity at time t and repurchasing it at time T).[26] Again, entry occurs until $F°$ exactly equals $F*$ and reflects the marginal basis of the marginal storer.

In the short run, the basis $b*$ thus reflects the marginal cost of carrying an incremental unit of the commodity over time. In the long run, $b*$ will also correspond to the minimum point on a traditional U-shaped long-run average-cost curve.[27] Suppose all firms have b^* below this minimum long-run average cost. In this case, at least one firm will expand output until the marginal cost rises to the minimum average cost and equals the marginal price of the cost of carry and the new b^* will also be reflected in the forward price.

The process by which commodity derivatives and the underlying asset market simultaneously grope toward a competitive equilibrium helps illustrate an important point: namely, the relation between forward and spot prices—the "basis"—is really a "third market" implied by the prices of the two explicit ones.[28] In the example above, the two explicit markets are the spot and forward markets, and the relation between the two implicitly defines *the price of physical storage*. Such "third markets" are also called "basis" or "spread" relations. The implicit market for storage over time is called the "calendar basis or spread," the implicit market for transportation is called the "transportation basis or spread," and so on.

Firms can also use derivatives *based* on *different assets* in order to conduct spread trades to synthesize a third market. Going short crude oil and simultaneously long heating oil and gasoline, for example, is called trading the "crack spread" and is economically equivalent in equilibrium to synthetic refining. Short soybeans and long bean oil and meal are likewise "synthetic crushing." And trading the "spark spread" through a short position in natural gas and a long position in electricity is called "synthetic generation" because the derivatives positions replicate the economic exposure of a gas-fired electric turbine.

A Neo-Austrian Explanation for Basis Trading

Armed with an understanding of how commodity derivatives are priced in equilibrium, we want now to consider the economic rationale for why Enron and firms like it sometimes dedicate substantial resources to "basis trading." We want to recognize what can happen out of *equilibrium*—a state of affairs that typically prevails. Indeed, expectations and relevant knowledge (data) are in a constant state of flux. Accordingly, a neoclassical stationary state—one that treats the data as constant—is of limited use in explaining the market process.[29]

We have seen how equilibrium emerges from the interactions of numerous firms competing to drive prices to their marginal cost. Specifically, suppose b^* reflects the marginal net cost of carry reflected in the prevailing natural gas forward price. This is the price of transportation and delivery in equilibrium. The net cost of carry b^* may only conform to the actual physical and capital costs of carry less the convenience yield for one firm—the marginal entrant into the gas transportation market. Or b^* may be shared by all firms in the short run, but aggregate output may need to adjust in the long run if b^* does not also reflect the minimum average long-run cost of carry. The point is this: the cost of carry reflected in the forward price may or may not be the optimal cost of carry for any given firm at any given time. As is standard in neoclassical microeconomic theory, the price that "clears the market" in the long run will equal the short-run marginal cost for any given firm only by pure coincidence.

Suppose we begin in a situation where $b*$ is the cost of carry reflected in the forward price and is equal to the short-run marginal costs of all market participants at their production optima. Now consider a new entrant into the market and suppose that new entrant is Enron with its large amount of pipelines and strong economies of scale that lead to a cost of distributing and transporting natural gas at some point in time of $b^e < b*$, where b^e is Enron's marginal cost of carry. In this case, Enron can physically move gas across time and space at a lower cost than gas can be moved "synthetically" using derivatives.

By going short or selling gas for future delivery using forwards, or futures, Enron is selling gas at an implied net cost of carry of $b*$. But its own net cost of carry—a cost that is quite relevant to Enron's ability to move the gas across time and space in order to honor its own future sale obligation created by the forward contract—is less. Accordingly, in *disequilibrium*—or, more properly, on the way to equilibrium—Enron can make a profit equal to the difference between its own net cost of storage and the cost reflected in the market.

The reason that that profit is a short-run profit inconsistent with a long-run equilibrium is that Enron's sale of the forward contract drives the $b*$ reflected in forward prices closer to b^e. If Enron is the lowest-cost producer and other firms can replicate its production techniques (i.e., Enron owns no unique resources), ultimately $b*$ will become b^e, which will also eventually approach the long-run minimum average cost of carry. Enron's capacity to earn supranormal profits will vanish in this new equilibrium—in fact, zero economic profits earned by every producer is basically the very meaning of a long-run equilibrium.

Because markets are constantly adjusting to new information, new trading activity, and new entrants, however, it is quite hard to determine when a market actually is in some kind of "final equilibrium resting state," as opposed to when it is adjusting from one state to another. The inevitability of a long-run competitive equilibrium in which profits are not possible thus must be considered relative to the inability of market participants to identify slippery concepts such as "long-run" and "in equilibrium." Strictly speaking, a market is "in equilibrium" as long as supply equals demand. But the term is used here in a more subtle fashion, where "equilibrium" refers to the steady state in which firms earn zero supranormal economic profits in the long run. Accordingly, firms may engage in basis trading to try and exploit the differences in prices reflected in derivatives and their own ability to conduct physical market "pseudoarbitrage" operations that are economically equivalent to those derivatives transactions.[30]

Now consider a situation in which the market is *always* adjusting and never reaches a long-run competitive equilibrium.[31] In this situation, the tendency is still toward the archetypical neoclassical long-run competitive equilibrium, but we never quite get there. Why not? Certainly economic agents are responding in the manner here described, and their behavior should ultimately lead to a steady-state long-run equilibrium. The only reason it does not is, quite simply, that too much is happening at any given moment to make the leap from "short run" to "long run."

In that situation, all firms are always, by definition, inframarginal in some sense of the term. The kind of "pseudoarbitrage" between physical and synthetic storage described above thus can be expected to occur *quite regularly*. And at least some firms will earn supranormal profits quite regularly. Those profits are not riskless, but at least some firms are sure to be right at least some of the time.

Does that mean that physical and synthetic storage are not really equivalent? Technically, it does. But it was never said otherwise. It was only claimed that the two are equivalent in *equilibrium*. When a market is in disequilibrium, what you actually pay to store a commodity physically may well differ from what you actually pay to store it synthetically. But that is not important.

What is important is that, even if new information and other market activities drive a wedge between $b°$ and $b*$, maximizing decisions by firms *always* lead *toward* the convergence of the two prices of storage. Conversely, the price mechanism *never* sends a signal that will lead maximizing firms to engage in physical or derivatives transactions that drive $b°$ and $b*$ further apart. The very fact that maximizing firms are constantly seeking to exploit differences between $b°$ and $b*$ itself is what gives the theory meaning. That the two might never end up exactly equal is not very relevant because, as explained below, information changes before the long-run equilibrium is ever reached.

Asymmetric Information

Now suppose that the net cost of storage is a random variable about which some firms are better informed than others—for example, the impact of supply or demand shocks on particular locational prices, the impact of pipeline congestion on the transportation basis, and the like. Suppose further that we assume a competitive long-run equilibrium *does* hold. Because of the information asymmetry, a rational expectations equilibrium (REE) in which expected supranormal profits are zero in the long run will result. But *expected by whom?*

In that case, firms such as Enron may engage in basis, or spread, trading in an effort to exploit a perceived comparative informational advantage. If a firm owns physical pipelines, for example, it may have a superior capability for forecasting congestion or regional supply-and-demand shocks. That creates a situation quite similar to a market that is out of or on the way to equilibrium—that is, the net cost of carry that the *firm* observes may be *different* from the net cost of carry market participants expect, given the different information on which the two numbers are based. Just as in the disequilibrium case, firms may engage in basis trading to exploit those differences.

In a traditional REE that type of behavior is akin to inframarginal firms attempting to exploit their storage cost advantage relative to the marginal price of storage reflected in forward markets. And as noted, that cannot go on for very long, because the trading actions of the lower-cost firm eventually lead it to become the marginal entrant, thus driving $b*$ to $b°$ for that firm.

The same is true in a REE, where trading *itself* is informative. Every time a well-informed trader attempts to exploit its superior information through a transaction, it reveals that superior information to the market. So, the paradox for the firm with better information is that the firm must either *not trade* based on that information in order to preserve its informational advantage, or it must *give away* its informational advantage while simultaneously trying to exploit it in the short run through trading.

In a study written with the late Nobel laureate economist Merton H. Miller, one of this paper's authors argues,[32] however, that that sort of classic equilibrium assumes that the trading activities of the better-informed firm are, indeed, informative. But what if other market participants cannot see all the firm's trades? And what if the trades are occurring in highly opaque, bilateral markets rather than on an exchange? In this case, better-informed firms can profit from their superior information without necessarily having all of their valuable information reflected in the new marginal price. Anecdotal evidence certainly seems to support this in the case of Enron, given how heavily the firm focused on less-liquid and less-transparent markets.

Why Not Speculate Outright?

Trading to exploit disequilibrium, market imperfections, or asymmetric information is hardly riskless. On the contrary, it can be quite risky. That helps explain why many firms engaged in such trading do so with *relative*, or *spread*, positions in third markets rather than take outright positions in one of the two explicit markets. Suppose, for example, that a firm perceives the "true" net cost of storage of gas to be b^* (which is equal to the firm's own net cost of carry) but that the current net cost of carry reflected in listed gas futures prices is $b' > b^*$. It is a good bet that b' will fall toward b^*. In that case, an outright short position in forward contracts would make sense. But that is *extremely risky*.

A position that exploits the same information asymmetry without the high degree of risk is to go short futures and *simultaneously* buy and hold gas. In this manner, the firm is protected from wild short-term price swings and instead is expressing a view solely on the *relative* prices of storage as reflected in the futures market and storage by the firm itself.

In essence, asset lite is a basis-trading or "third-market" trading strategy in which physical assets are traded vis-à-vis derivatives positions. A physical market combined with the *residual risk* of a market-making function is essentially one big spread trade.

Putting Enron in Context

Reading the marketing and business materials of Enron's energy business lines is eerily similar to reading an example of a firm putting all the theories of basis trading just discussed into practice. And in that sense, Enron was hardly the first firm to leverage its physical market presence into financial- and basis-trading opportunities. Perhaps the best-known example of a firm engaged in the same practice is Cargill.[33] Cargill is the largest private company in the world, with $50 billion in annual sales and 97,000 employees deployed in 59 countries. For 137 years, Cargill has employed an asset-lite strategy that has allowed it to basis trade and manage risks for a wide variety of agricultural commodities, among other things. For the commodities it deals in, Cargill is involved in every link of the supply chains. As a result of its commodity trading, processing, freight shipping, and futures businesses, Cargill has been able to develop an effective intelligence network that generates valuable information. Indeed, via its people on the ground, Cargill knows where every ship and rail car hauling commodities is in real time and what that implies about prospective prices over time and space. By being able to ferret out valuable local information, Cargill has been able to obtain an edge, one that accounts for much of its success.[34]

Basis trading can make economic sense to a firm *ex ante* without making profits *ex post*. The key driver underlying most basis traders' behavior is the *perception* that they have some comparative informational advantage about some basis relation. But perception need not be reality. Markets are, after all, relatively efficient. Indeed, most of the inefficiencies that give rise to profitable trading opportunities can be linked to taxes, regulations, and other institutional frictions that essentially prevent markets from reflecting all available information at all times.

Enron did indeed attempt to focus its efforts on markets riddled with inefficiencies, often created by overregulation, poorly defined property rights, or a slow deregulation process. But that did not mean Enron had a comparative informational advantage in all of those markets.

Structural inefficiencies that prevent prices from fully reflecting all available information are only part of what it takes to run a successful basis-trading operation. The other requisite component is for a firm to perceive itself as (and, it is hoped, actually be) *better informed*. In oil and power, Enron achieved that informational superiority like many other firms do in their own industries—by dominating the financial market. That allowed Enron to develop informationally rich customer relationships that in turn could be extrapolated into superior knowledge of firm-specific supply-and-demand considerations, congestion points along the supply chain, and other important factors.

Now consider, by contrast, a market such as broadband in which Enron was *not* the primary inventor of the technology, *not* the primary buyer or seller of the supply chain infrastructure, and *not* a regular player in the consumer telecommunications arena. The mere existence of market frictions in broadband attracted Enron, but without the requisite information, Enron could not achieve the market dominance required to make asset lite in that market profitable.

Buying Time and the End of Enron

As Culp and Miller explain,[35] firms best suited to the asset-lite kind of strategy that Enron pursued typically require fairly significant amounts of capital—not invested capital assets necessarily but *equity capital* in a financial market sense.

Equity capital is a necessary component of successful basis trading and the asset-lite strategy for several reasons. First, equity is required to absorb the occasional loss inevitably arising from the volatility that basis trading can bring to cash flows. Second, maintaining a strong market-making and financial-market presence requires at least the perception by other participants of financial integrity and credit worthiness. Especially in long-dated, credit-sensitive over-the-counter (OTC) derivatives, financial capital is essential to support the credit requirements that other OTC derivatives users and dealers demand.[36]

Unfortunately, Enron's cash management skills were no match for its apparent trading savvy. Despite being "asset lite," Enron's expenditures on intermediate supply chain assets were still not cheap. Add to this EI's asset-heavy investment programs and a corporate culture under Skilling and Lay that emphasized high and stable *earnings* often at the expense of high and stable *cash flows*,[37] and the net result was financial trouble for the firm.[38]

Enron's Deceptions

Much of the public controversy about Enron focuses on how Enron abused accounting and disclosure policies. In short, Enron's abuses in those areas included the following:

- Using inappropriate or aggressive accounting and disclosure policies to conceal assets owned and debt incurred by Enron through special purpose entities (SPEs);[39]
- Using inadequately capitalized subsidiaries and SPEs for "hedges" that reduced Enron's earnings volatility on paper, despite in many cases being dysfunctional or nonperforming in practice;[40] and
- Allegedly engaging in "wash trades" with undisclosed subsidiaries designed to increase trading revenues or mark-to-market valuations artificially.[41]

At first, Enron's abuses of those structures seem to have been driven more by a desire to manage earnings than by anything else. But as time passed, Enron used aggressive accounting and disclosure policies to "buy time" for itself. Especially as Enron moved into new markets in which its comparative advantage was more questionable (e.g., broadband) or in which Enron's success depended strongly on the rate of government deregulation (e.g., water), Enron's financial shenanigans amounted to "robbing Peter to pay Paul." In other words, as Enron's cash balances got lower and lower, concealing its true financial condition was the only way that Enron could sustain itself long enough to hope that its next big investment program would pay off. That might have worked had Enron stuck to markets in which its success with asset lite was more assured. Unfortunately, as has been argued, the firm's end became inevitable once it decided to start moving into areas that deviated from its core business strategy.

There is also the question of whom Enron was actually deceiving with its accounting and disclosure policies. Over the course of many years, one could argue that Enron seduced investors, monitors (e.g., rating agencies and accounting firms), creditors, and even its own employees into believing that the firm was stronger financially than it actually was through a mixture of aggressive marketing, cultural arrogance, and, in some cases, outright deception. But especially as the end of Enron neared, many institutions had begun to view the company with deepening suspicion.[42] By the time Enron failed, a surprisingly large number of firms dealing with Enron commercially had come to fear that the worst for Enron might lie ahead.[43] In the end, those who seem to have been the most deceived—and for the longest time—were Enron's own employees, who, unlike other firms dealing with Enron, had more cause to be inherently optimistic and were doubtless taken almost completely off-guard.

Conclusion

Enron's main business was asset lite—exploiting the synergies between a small physical market presence, a market-making function on derivatives, and a basis-trading operation to "arbitrage" the first two. Many observers have questioned the wisdom of Enron's asset-lite strategy. Most of the criticisms are hard to address without getting into deeper details of Enron's financial situation. In short, people argue that although asset lite did not require a lot of capital *expenditures* and investments in fixed capital, the strategy *did* require Enron to have a fairly large chunk of equity capital—enough to convince its numerous financial counterparties that it was creditworthy. If indeed Enron was camouflaging its capital structure to hide a massive amount of debt, then Enron probably *was* undercapitalized to exploit asset lite effectively. But that is not a criticism of asset lite—it is a criticism of Enron.

In fact, asset lite has become a very common practice for many firms engaged in energy market activities, especially at intermediate points along the various physical supply chains—transmission and distribution of power and midstream transportation and distribution of oil and gas, to name two. One firm that has been consistently successful at playing the asset-lite game, for example, is Kinder Morgan, founded by Enron's former president Richard Kinder when he left Enron in 1996. Kinder Morgan was started in part by Kinder's successful acquisition from Enron of Enron Gas Liquids, for which he outbid six other firms, including Mobil Oil.[44]

In nonenergy markets, firms such as Cargill have also long practiced their version of asset lite, often going the way of Enron in electricity and becoming asset heavy overtime. The key common denominators are two: the use of a physical market presence to acquire specific information about the underlying market and the use of a financial-trading operation to make markets and engage in basis trading to leverage off that underlying asset infrastructure.

Unfortunately, there is no exact answer to the question of when asset lite and basis trading might work for a firm versus when they might fail dismally. The comparative informational advantage that allows some firms to earn positive economic profits is exceedingly hard to analyze or identify except through trial and error. That process of trial and error is what Austrian economist

Joseph Schumpeter meant by the "creative destruction" of capitalism, and great economists such as Frank H. Knight and Keynes went on to emphasize further that the success or failure of a given firm cannot ever really be predicted. "Animal spirits," as Keynes put it, ultimately dictate the success or failure of a business as much as any other variable.

Economists are uneasy with that notion. As noted earlier, the neoclassical model postulates that markets tend to be "in equilibrium," whereas the neo-Austrian perspective merely argues that markets "lean in that direction." To be in equilibrium implies some steady state of profits resting on an identifiable cost advantage or structural informational asymmetry. But concepts such as "information asymmetry" are completely nontestable. That makes theoretical economists nervous because it means that the success or failure of a firm cannot be related to a defined set of assumptions and parameters *ex ante*. And empirical economists get even more disgruntled because the success or failure of a firm cannot be explained *ex post*.

Nevertheless, that is the state of affairs. Economic theory merely says that firms will strive to exploit perceived comparative informational advantages in disequilibrium situations where prices do not reflect every market participant's information equally. Theory says nothing about firms being correct in their perceived advantages, nor does theory help us pinpoint precisely what those advantages are. Those things are what *the market* is for.

Can Enron's experience be generalized to suggest a "failure" of the theory underlying basis trading? In fact, Enron cannot be generalized at *all*. Looking purely at the firm's *legitimate* business activities, Enron perceived a comparative informational advantage, pursued it, and was wrong. That does not make the underlying economic model wrong, nor even Enron's managers and shareholders. If we could generalize the economic factors that explain why one firm succeeds and another fails, then competition in the open market would serve no purpose. Instead, competition and the market are both judge and jury to a company's perceived informational advantage. And unless a firm takes the risk of failure, it will never earn the premium of success.[45]

There can be little doubt that Enron did a lot wrong. Indeed, where it deviated from its asset-lite strategy, Enron tended to engage in businesses that were unprofitable. In addition, many of the firm's senior managers were basically unethical. But amid all those legitimate criticisms of Enron, we must be careful not to indict everything the firm did. In some instances, Enron got it right. And at a minimum, the firm moved entrepreneurially into new areas and put itself to the ultimate test of the market. Finally, Enron failed that test, but we must at least tip our hats to that part of Enron that was willing to try. Without that spirit of innovation, the process of capitalism would grind to a screeching halt.

Notes

1.   See *Corporate Aftershock: The Public Policy Lessons from the Collapse of Enron and Other Major Corporations*, ed. Christopher L. Culp and William A. Niskanen (New York: John Wiley and Sons, forthcoming 2003), part I.

2.   See ibid., part II.

3.   The Austrian school of economics was developed in the 19th and 20th centuries by a group of principally Austrian economists in response to several noted shortcomings in the neoclassical theory of the price system. The approach adopted here, however, is more properly called *neo*-Austrian. Following Sir John Hicks's use of the term, a neo-Austrian approach recognizes some of the deficiencies of the neoclassical school and seeks to address those problems from a more Austrian perspective. We do not consider, as some do, the pure Austrian school to be a viable stand-alone theory of the price system. Rather than forcing a choice of theories in either/or fashion, the neo-Austrian approach recognizes instead that a little bit of Austrian insight can go a long way toward salvaging the neoclassical paradigm. For an example of this theoretical approach, see John R. Hicks, *Capital and Time: A Neo-Austrian Theory* (1973; reprint, Oxford: Oxford University Press, 2001).

4.   That does not require that forward prices always be unbiased expectations of future spot prices, although they frequently are, especially for physical commodities. But even if forward prices are not unbiased predictors of future spot prices, as in some currency markets, there is still a strong and consistent relation between spot and forward prices—just not an unbiased one. For further discussion of this issue, see Christopher L. Culp, *Risk Transfer: Derivatives in Theory and Practice* (New York: John Wiley and Sons, forthcoming 2003).

5.   For a full elaboration of these concepts, see Ludwig M. Lachmann, *Capital and Its Structure* (Kansas City, Mo.: Sheed Andrews and McMeel, 1978).

6.   See Enron Corporation, *2000 Annual Report*, 2001, cover page.

7.   Ibid., p. 9.

8.   A typical use of junk bonds during this period was providing funds to companies with otherwise questionable access to capital, given their credit risk. Highly leveraged transactions like leveraged buyouts were thus a natural candidate for junk-bond financing.

9.   EOG continued for two decades to spearhead all of Enron Corp.'s exploration and production activities in oil and gas. In 1999, EOG exchanged the shares in EOG held by Enron for its operations in India and China. In so doing, EOG became independent of Enron Corp. and, in fact, changed its name the same year to EOG Resources, Inc. This firm still exists today.

10.   See Lachmann.

11.   For more discussion of these different types of contracts, see Andrea M. P. Neves, "Wholesale Electricity Markets and Products after Enron," in *Corporate Aftershock*; and Barbara T. Kavanagh, "An Introduction to the Business of Structure Finance," in *Corporate Aftershock*.

12.   In the huge interest rate swap market, dealers did essentially the same thing as the Enron GasBank—they used other swaps and futures contracts to manage the *residual* risks of running a dealing portfolio, called a "swap warehouse."

13.   Quoted in Joel Kurtzman and Glenn Rifkin, *Radical E: From GE to Enron—Lessons on How to Rule the Web* (New York: John Wiley & Sons, 2001), p. 47.

14.   See Ronnie J. Clayton, William Scroggins, and Christopher Westley, "Enron: Market Exploitation and Correction," *Financial Decisions* (Spring 2002): 1–16.

15.   See Neves.

16.   See Peter C. Fusaro and Ross M. Miller, *What Went Wrong at Enron?* (New York: John Wiley & Sons, 2002).

17.   Ibid.

18. This can be accomplished in various ways. For examples, see Andrea S. Kramer, Paul J. Pantano, and Doron F. Ezickson, "Regulation of Electricity Trading after Enron," in *Corporate Aftershock*; and Paul Palmer, "The Market for Complex Credit Risk," in *Corporate Aftershock*.

19. Early discussions of the economic rationale for basis, or spread, trading can be found in L. Leland Johnson, "The Theory of Hedging and Speculation in Commodity Futures," *Review of Economic Studies* 27, no. 3 (1960): 139–51; Holbrook Working, "Theory of the Inverse Carrying Charge in Futures Markets," *Journal of Farm Economics* 30 (1948): 1–28; Holbrook Working, "The Theory of Price of Storage," *American Economic Review* 39 (1949): 1254–62; and Holbrook Working, "New Concepts Concerning Futures Markets and Prices," *American Economic Review* 52 (1962): 432–59.

20. See, for example, Jeffrey B. Williams, *The Economic Function of Futures Markets* (New York: Cambridge University Press, 1986); Culp, *Risk Transfer*; and Steve H. Hanke, "Backwardation Revisited," *Friedberg's Commodity and Currency Comments* 8, no. 11 (December 20, 1987).

21. Alternative versions of this rely on different types of discounting and compounding assumptions, as well as allowing certain variables in the equation to be stochastic (i.e., subject to random variation). But the spirit of all versions of the model is well captured by the representation here. See Culp, *Risk Transfer*, for more detail.

22. See John Maynard Keynes, *The Theory of Money*, vol. II, *The Applied Theory of Money* (London: Macmillan, 1930); Nicholas Kaldor, "Speculation and Economic Stability," *Review of Economic Studies* 7 (1939): 1–27; Working, "Theory of the Inverse Carrying Charge in Futures Markets"; Working, "The Theory of Price of Storage"; Michael J. Brennan, "The Supply of Storage," *American Economic Review* 48 (1958): 50–72; and Lester G. Telser, "Futures Trading and the Storage of Cotton and Wheat," *Journal of Political Economy* 66 (1958): 233–55.

23. See Working, "New Concepts Concerning Futures Markets and Storage."

24. See Keynes; Working, "The Theory of Price of Storage"; Culp, *Risk Transfer*; and Hanke.

25. Cost-of-carry pricing for forwards on financial assets, by contrast, is enforced by direct "cash-and-carry" arbitrage because financial assets pay *observable* and *explicit* dividends that are the same regardless who holds the asset. See Culp, *Risk Transfer*.

26. Commodity lending does occur, so this example is in no way unrealistic. See Williams.

27. The classical U-shape is consistent with a production technology that demonstrates increasing returns to scale up to b^* and diminishing returns thereafter.

28. See Williams.

29. For a more general discussion, see John H. Cochrane and Christopher L. Culp, "Equilibrium Asset Pricing: Implications for Risk Management," in *The Growth of Risk Management: A History* (London: Risk Books, 2002).

30. This is pseudoarbitrage because it has the flavor of an arbitrage transaction but is far from riskless.

31. This seems heretical in the neoclassical microeconomic paradigm, but is typical of the notion of "equilibrium" developed by economists in the "Austrian" and "neo-Austrian" tradition, such as Carl Menger, *Principles of Economics* (1871; reprint, Grove City, Pa.: Libertarian Press, 1974); F. A. Hayek, "Economics and Knowledge," *Economica* 4 (1937): 33–54; F. A. Hayek, "The Use of Knowledge in Society," *American Economic Review* 35, no. 4 (1945): 519–30; F. A. Hayek, "The Meaning of Competition," in *Individualism and*

Economic Order (1948; reprint, London: Routledge and Kegan Paul, 1978), pp. 92–107; F. A. Hayek, "Competition as a Discovery Procedure," in *New Studies in Philosophy, Politics, Economics, and the History of Ideas* (Chicago: University of Chicago Press, 1978), pp. 179–91; F. A. Hayek, "The New Confusion about 'Planning,' " in *New Studies in Philosophy, Politics, Economics, and the History of Ideas*, pp. 232–49; Hicks; and Lachmann.

32. See Christopher L. Culp and Merton H. Miller, "Hedging in the Theory of Corporate Finance," *Journal of Applied Corporate Finance* 8, no. 1 (Spring 1995): 121–27.

33. See, for example, Wayne G. Broehl Jr., *Cargill: Trading the World's Grains* (Hanover, N.H.: University Press of New England, 1992).

34. See, for example, Neil Weinberg and Brandon Copple, "Going against the Grain," *Forbes*, November 25, 2002, pp. 158–68.

35. See Culp and Miller, "Hedging in the Theory of Corporate Finance"; Christopher L. Culp and Merton H. Miller, "Metallgesellschaft and the Economics of Synthetic Storage," *Journal of Applied Corporate Finance* 7, no. 4 (Winter 1995): 62–76; and Christopher L. Culp and Merton H. Miller, "Introduction: Why a Firm Hedges Affects How a Firm Should Hedge," in *Corporate Hedging in Theory and Practice: Lessons from Metallgesellschaft*, ed. Christopher L. Culp and Merton H. Miller (London: Risk Books, 1999).

36. See David Mengle, "Do Swaps Need More Regulation?" in *Corporate Aftershock*; and Christopher L. Culp, "Credit Risk Management Lessons from Enron," in *Corporate Aftershock*.

37. See Richard Bassett and Mark Storrie, "Accounting at Energy Firms after Enron: Is the 'Cure' Worse than the Disease?" in *Corporate Aftershock*.

38. Cash flow mismanagement was not always the norm at Enron. Jeffrey Skilling's predecessor Richard Kinder was actually known for being a cash flow "tightwad" and kept the firm's financial health relatively strong during his tenure at the operational helm of Enron.

39. See Bassett and Storrie; Kavanagh; and Keith A. Bockus, W. Dana Northcut, and Mark E. Zmijewski, "Accounting and Disclosure Issues in Structured Finance," in *Corporate Aftershock*.

40. See Bassett and Storrie; and Kavanagh.

41. See ibid.; Neves; Kramer, Pantano, and Ezickson; John Herron, "Online Trading and Clearing after Enron," in *Corporate Aftershock*; and Bockus, Northcut, and Zmijewski.

42. See Bassett and Storrie.

43. See Culp, *Risk Transfer*.

44. See Fusaro and Miller.

45. See Frank H. Knight, *Risk, Uncertainty, and Profit* (Boston: Houghton Mifflin, 1933).

POSTSCRIPT

Does the Enron Collapse Show that We Need More Regulation of the Energy Industry?

The Enron case is in many ways a poor exemplar for any discussion of business activity, since it contains so many activities that were clearly criminal! Had the officers of the corporation been honest men (they were all men except the vice president, Sherron Watkins, who finally blew the whistle on the whole affair), what would we have found out about the operations of deregulated markets in public utilities?

Suggested Reading

For more on the Enron case, and on the energy industry generally, you might wish to consult the following readings:

Michael K. Block, "Energy Deregulation: Moving Ahead Quickly (and Wisely), The Progress and Freedom Foundation (mail@ppf.org).

Peter Behr and April Witt, "Visionary's Dream Led to Risky Business," *Washington Post,* July 28, 2002 (p. A1).

Allan Sloan, "Who Killed Enron?" *Newsweek,* January 21, 2002 (pp. 22–23).

Brian Cruver, *Anatomy of Greed: The Unshredded Truth from an Enron Insider* (New York: Caroll and Graff, 2002).

Kurt Eichenwald with Floyd Norris, "Early Verdict on Audit: Procedures Ignored," *The New York Times*, June 6, 2002 (C5).

Kurt Eichenwald, "Flinging Billions to Acquire Assets that No One Else Would Touch," *The New York Times,* October 18, 2002 (pp. C1 and C9).

Rural Utilities Service, *Connecting Rural America*, RUS Press Releases and Official Statements: 2002. www.usda.gov/rus/index2/press.htm

Internet References . . .

Workplace Fairness

Workplace Fairness is a nonprofit organization that was founded to assist individuals, both employed and unemployed, in understanding, enforcing, and expanding their rights in the workplace.

http://www.nerinet.org

WorkNet@ILR

The School of Industrial and Labor Relations at Cornell University offers this site consisting of an index of Internet sites relevant to the field of industrial and labor relations; a list of centers, institutes, and affiliated groups; and an electronic archive that contains full-text documents on the glass ceiling, child labor, and more.

http://www.ilr.cornell.edu/

WorkNet: Alcohol and Other Drugs in the Workplace

This site of the Canadian Centre on Substance Abuse provides news, databases, bibliographies, resources, and research on alcohol and other drugs in the workplace.

http://www.ccsa.ca/ccsa/

Employee Incentives and Career Development

This site is dedicated to the proposition that effective employee compensation and career development is a valuable tool in obtaining, maintaining, and retaining a productive workforce. It contains links to pay-for-knowledge, incentive systems, career development, wage and salary compensation, and more.

http://www.snc.edu/socsci/chair/336/group1.htm

Executive PayWatch

Executive PayWatch, sponsored by the American Federation of Labor—Congress of Industrial Organizations (AFL-CIO), is a working families' guide to monitoring and curtailing the excessive salaries, bonuses, and perks in CEO compensation packages.

http://www.aflcio.org/corporateamerica/paywatch/

Human Resources: The Corporation and Employees

*W*hat is a just wage—for a worker near the poverty line, or for a multimillionaire corporate executive? What is a just employment policy? What rights does the employer have to limit employee privacy for company interests? And what right does an employee have to denounce an employer publicly for wrongdoing? The limits of employer and employee rights are never fixed, but require repeated examination and balancing.

- Does Blowing the Whistle Violate Company Loyalty?

- Is Employer Monitoring of Employee E-Mail Justified?

- Is "Employment-At-Will" Good Social Policy?

- Is CEO Compensation Justified By Performance?

ISSUE 9

Does Blowing the Whistle Violate Company Loyalty?

YES: Sissela Bok, from "Whistleblowing and Professional Responsibility," *New York University Education Quarterly* (Summer 1980)

NO: Robert A. Larmer, from "Whistleblowing and Employee Loyalty," *Journal of Business Ethics* (vol. 11, 1992)

ISSUE SUMMARY

YES: Philosopher Sissela Bok asserts that although blowing the whistle is often justified, it does involve dissent, accusation, and a breach of loyalty to the employer.

NO: Robert A. Larmer argues, on the contrary, that putting a stop to illegal or unethical company activities may be the highest type of loyalty an employee can display.

The whistleblower is a nearly mythical character—the brave, lonely person who exposes evil in the corporate or governmental bureaucracy. Since the readings are very general, some specific cases might be useful. In a fascinating treatment of the phenomenon, N. R. Kleinfeld portrays five of the early whistleblowers, some of whom have become famous as case studies in business schools across the country. Each one has an interesting story to tell; each claims that if he had it to do over again he would, for he likes living with a clear conscience. But each has paid a price: great stress, sometimes ill health, career loss, financial ruin and/or loss of friends and family. Worst of all is the universal suspicion of anyone who can be characterized as a "snitch" or a "tattletale."

Charles Atchison, for example, blew the whistle on the Comanche Park nuclear plant in Glen Rose, Texas, a power station that was clearly unsafe. It cost him his job, plunged him into debt from which he is still trying to recover, and left emotional scars on his family, but he says he would do it again. Kermit Vandivier, the man who blew the whistle on the B.F. Goodrich Aircraft Brakes scandal, also lost his job; he has a new career as a journalist. James Pope claimed that the Federal Aviation Administration had found in 1975 an effective device that would prevent midair crashes, known as an airborne collision avoidance system, but chose to pursue an inferior device they had had a hand in developing. Mr. Pope was "retired" early by the F.A.A. And A. Ernest Fitzgerald (*The High Priests of Waste; The Pentagonists*), most famous of them all, was an Air Force cost analyst who found huge cost overruns on Lockheed cargo planes being developed for the Air Force. After his revelations, he was discharged from the Air Force, but fought for thirteen years to be reinstated; he was, at full rank, in 1982. The common thread of these hero stories is that when a wrong was seen, and properly reported, the reporters were all demoted, labeled as troublemakers, disciplined, and/or fired even when the evidence was very much in their favor. All of them, incidentally, initially believed in their organizations and acted explicitly out of loyalty. They were sure not only that they were acting in an ethical manner, but that they would be thanked for their efforts and diligence.

Professors Myron and Penina Glazer tell the story of fifty-five whistleblowers, why they did what they did, and what the consequences were for them and their families. The Glazers found their dominant trait to be a very strong belief in individual responsibility. One of the spouses of a whistleblower stated it very clearly: "A corrupt system can happen only if the individuals who make up that system are corrupt. You are either going to be part of the corruption or part of the forces working against it. There isn't a third choice. Someone, someday, has to take a stand; if you don't, maybe no one will. And that is wrong."

The Glazers write that a strong belief in individual responsibility that drives ethical resisters is often supported by professional ethics, religious values, or allegiance to the community. But the personal costs of public disclosure have been high, and the results have been less than satisfactory. In some cases no change in the corrupt system occurred. But the whistleblowers had to re-create careers, relocate, and settle for less money in a new job. For most resisters, the worst part was the devastating months or even years of dislocation, unemployment, and temporary jobs. In a response to a question posed by the Glazers, twenty-one of the whistleblowers advised potential whistleblowers to "forget it," or "leak the information without your name attached," or if you must blow the whistle, "be prepared to be ostracized, have your career come to a screeching halt and perhaps even be driven into bankruptcy." Such outsized punishments must dampen the most heroic. Does it have to be this way?

As you read the debate that follows, think of these cases, and think of others you have known. What would you do if confronted with the challenge to blow the whistle? Then turn it around. How would you react if someone blew the whistle on *you*? Does the role reversal change your weighting of the values at stake in this dilemma?

YES

Sissela Bok

Whistleblowing and Professional Responsibility

Whistleblowing is a new label generated by our increased awareness of the ethical conflicts encountered at work. Whistleblowers sound an alarm from within the very organization in which they work, aiming to spotlight neglect or abuses that threaten the public interest.

The stakes in whistleblowing are high. Take the nurse who alleges that physicians enrich themselves in her hospital through unnecessary surgery; the engineer who discloses safety defects in the braking systems of a fleet of new rapid-transit vehicles; the Defense Department official who alerts Congress to military graft and overspending: all know that they pose a threat to those whom they denounce and that their own careers may be at risk.

Moral Conflicts

Moral conflicts on several levels confront anyone who is wondering whether to speak out about abuses or risks or serious neglect. In the first place, he must try to decide whether, other things being equal, speaking out is in fact in the public interest. This choice is often made more complicated by factual uncertainties: Who is responsible for the abuse or neglect? How great is the threat? And how likely is it that speaking out will precipitate changes for the better?

In the second place, a would-be whistleblower must weigh his responsibility to serve the public interest against the responsibility he owes to his colleagues and the institution in which he works. While the professional ethic requires collegial loyalty, the codes of ethics often stress responsibility to the public over and above duties to colleagues and clients. Thus the United States Code of Ethics for Government Servants asks them to "expose corruption wherever uncovered" and to "put loyalty to the highest moral principles and to country above loyalty to persons, party, or government."[1] Similarly, the largest professional engineering association requires members to speak out against abuses threatening the safety, health, and welfare of the public.[2]

A third conflict for would-be whistleblowers is personal in nature and cuts across the first two: even in cases where they have concluded that the

From *New York University Education Quarterly*, Vol. 11, Summer 1980, pp. 2–7. Copyright © 1980 by Sissela Bok. Reprinted by permission of the author.

facts warrant speaking out, and that their duty to do so overrides loyalties to colleagues and institutions, they often have reason to fear the results of carrying out such a duty. However strong this duty may seem in theory, they know that, in practice, retaliation is likely. As a result, their careers and their ability to support themselves and their families may be unjustly impaired.[3] A government handbook issued during the Nixon era recommends reassigning "undesirables" to places so remote that they would prefer to resign. Whistleblowers may also be downgraded or given work without responsibility or work for which they are not qualified; or else they may be given many more tasks than they can possibly perform. Another risk is that an outspoken civil servant may be ordered to undergo a psychiatric fitness-for-duty examination,[4] declared unfit for service, and "separated" as well as discredited from the point of view of any allegations he may be making. Outright firing, finally, is the most direct institutional response to whistleblowers.

Add to the conflicts confronting individual whistleblowers the claim to self-policing that many professions make, and professional responsibility is at issue in still another way. For an appeal to the public goes against everything that "self-policing" stands for. The question for the different professions, then, is how to resolve, insofar as it is possible, the conflict between professional loyalty and professional responsibility toward the outside world. The same conflicts arise to some extent in all groups, but professional groups often have special cohesion and claim special dignity and privileges.

The plight of whistleblowers has come to be documented by the press and described in a number of books. Evidence of the hardships imposed on those who chose to act in the public interest has combined with a heightened awareness of professional malfeasance and corruption to produce a shift toward greater public support of whistleblowers. Public service law firms and consumer groups have taken up their cause; institutional reforms and legislation have been proposed to combat illegitimate reprisals.[5]

Given the indispensable services performed by so many whistleblowers, strong public support is often merited. But the new climate of acceptance makes it easy to overlook the dangers of whistleblowing: of uses in error or in malice; of work and reputations unjustly lost for those falsely accused; of privacy invaded and trust undermined. There comes a level of internal prying and mutual suspicion at which no institution can function. And it is a fact that the disappointed, the incompetent, the malicious, and the paranoid all too often leap to accusations in public. Worst of all, ideological persecution throughout the world traditionally relies on insiders willing to inform on their colleagues or even on their family members, often through staged public denunciations or press campaigns.

No society can count itself immune from such dangers. But neither can it risk silencing those with a legitimate reason to blow the whistle. How then can we distinguish between different instances of whistleblowing? A society that fails to protect the right to speak out even on the part of those whose warnings turn out to be spurious obviously opens the door to political repression. But from the moral point of view there are important differences between the aims, messages, and methods of dissenters from within.

Nature of Whistleblowing

Three elements, each jarring, and triply jarring when conjoined, lend acts of whistleblowing special urgency and bitterness: dissent, breach of loyalty, and accusation.

Like all dissent, whistleblowing makes public a disagreement with an authority or a majority view. But whereas dissent can concern all forms of disagreement with, for instance, religious dogma or government policy or court decisions, whistleblowing has the narrower aim of shedding light on negligence or abuse, or alerting to a risk, and of assigning responsibility for this risk.

Would-be whistleblowers confront the conflict inherent in all dissent: between conforming and sticking their necks out. The more repressive the authority they challenge, the greater the personal risk they take in speaking out. At exceptional times, as in times of war, even ordinarily tolerant authorities may come to regard dissent as unacceptable and even disloyal.[6]

Furthermore, the whistleblower hopes to stop the game; but since he is neither referee nor coach, and since he blows the whistle on his own team, his act is seen as a violation of loyalty. In holding his position, he has assumed certain obligations to his colleagues and clients. He may even have subscribed to a loyalty oath or a promise of confidentiality. Loyalty to colleagues and to clients comes to be pitted against loyalty to the public interest, to those who may be injured unless the revelation is made.

Not only is loyalty violated in whistleblowing, hierarchy as well is often opposed, since the whistleblower is not only a colleague but a subordinate. Though aware of the risks inherent in such disobedience, he often hopes to keep his job.[7] At times, however, he plans his alarm to coincide with leaving the institution. If he is highly placed, or joined by others, resigning in protest may effectively direct public attention to the wrongdoing at issue.[8] Still another alternative, often chosen by those who wish to be safe from retaliation, is to leave the institution quietly, to secure another post, and then to blow the whistle. In this way, it is possible to speak with the authority and knowledge of an insider without having the vulnerability of that position.

It is the element of accusation, of calling a "foul," that arouses the strongest reactions on the part of the hierarchy. The accusation may be of neglect, of willfully concealed dangers, or of outright abuse on the part of colleagues or superiors. It singles out specific persons or groups as responsible for threats to the public interest. If no one could be held responsible—as in the case of an impending avalanche—the warning would not constitute whistleblowing.

The accusation of the whistleblower, moreover, concerns a present or an imminent threat. Past errors or misdeeds occasion such an alarm only if they still affect current practices. And risks far in the future lack the immediacy needed to make the alarm a compelling one, as well as the close connection to particular individuals that would justify actual accusations. Thus an alarm can be sounded about safety defects in a rapid-transit system that threaten or will shortly threaten passengers, but the revelation of safety defects in a system no longer in use, while of historical interest, would not constitute whistleblowing. Nor would the revelation of potential problems in a system not yet fully designed and far from implemented.[9]

Not only immediacy, but also specificity, is needed for there to be an alarm capable of pinpointing responsibility. A concrete risk must be at issue rather than a vague foreboding or a somber prediction. The act of whistleblowing differs in this respect from the lamentation or the dire prophecy. An immediate and specific threat would normally be acted upon by those at risk. The whistleblower assumes that his message will alert listeners to something they do not know, or whose significance they have not grasped because it has been kept secret.

The desire for openness inheres in the temptation to reveal any secret, sometimes joined to an urge for self-aggrandizement and publicity and the hope for revenge for past slights or injustices. There can be pleasure, too—righteous or malicious—in laying bare the secrets of co-workers and in setting the record straight at last. Colleagues of the whistleblower often suspect his motives: they may regard him as a crank, as publicity-hungry, wrong about the facts, eager for scandal and discord, and driven to indiscretion by his personal biases and shortcomings.

For whistleblowing to be effective, it must arouse its audience. Inarticulate whistleblowers are likely to fail from the outset. When they are greeted by apathy, their message dissipates. When they are greeted by disbelief, they elicit no response at all. And when the audience is not free to receive or to act on the information—when censorship or fear of retribution stifles response—then the message rebounds to injure the whistleblower. Whistleblowing also requires the possibility of concerted public response: the idea of whistleblowing in an anarchy is therefore merely quixotic.

Such characteristics of whistleblowing and strategic considerations for achieving an impact are common to the noblest warnings, the most vicious personal attacks, and the delusions of the paranoid. How can one distinguish the many acts of sounding an alarm that are genuinely in the public interest from all the petty, biased, or lurid revelations that pervade our querulous and gossip-ridden society? Can we draw distinctions between different whistleblowers, different messages, different methods?

We clearly can, in a number of cases. Whistleblowing may be starkly inappropriate when in malice or error, or when it lays bare legitimately private matters having to do, for instance, with political belief or sexual life. It can, just as clearly, be the only way to shed light on an ongoing unjust practice such as drugging political prisoners or subjecting them to electroshock treatment. It can be the last resort for alerting the public to an impending disaster. Taking such clear-cut cases as benchmarks, and reflecting on what it is about them that weighs so heavily for or against speaking out, we can work our way toward the admittedly more complex cases in which whistleblowing is not so clearly the right or wrong choice, or where different points of view exist regarding its legitimacy—cases where there are moral reasons both for concealment and for disclosure and where judgments conflict. . . .

Individual Moral Choice

What questions might those who consider sounding an alarm in public ask themselves? How might they articulate the problem they see and weigh its injustice before deciding whether or not to reveal it? How can they best try to make sure their choice is the right one? In thinking about these questions it helps to keep in mind the three elements mentioned earlier: dissent, breach of loyalty, and accusation. They impose certain requirements—of accuracy and judgment in dissent; of exploring alternative ways to cope with improprieties that minimize the breach of loyalty; and of fairness in accusation. For each, careful articulation and testing of arguments are needed to limit error and bias.

Dissent by whistleblowers, first of all, is expressly claimed to be intended to benefit the public. It carries with it, as a result, an obligation to consider the nature of this benefit and to consider also the possible harm that may come from speaking out: harm to persons or institutions and, ultimately, to the public interest itself. Whistleblowers must, therefore, begin by making every effort to consider the effects of speaking out versus those of remaining silent. They must assure themselves of the accuracy of their reports, checking and rechecking the facts before speaking out; specify the degree to which there is genuine impropriety; consider how imminent is the threat they see, how serious, and how closely linked to those accused of neglect and abuse.

If the facts warrant whistleblowing, how can the second element—breach of loyalty—be minimized? The most important question here is whether the existing avenues for change within the organization have been explored. It is a waste of time for the public as well as harmful to the institution to sound the loudest alarm first. Whistleblowing has to remain a last alternative because of its destructive side effects: it must be chosen only when other alternatives have been considered and rejected. They may be rejected if they simply do not apply to the problem at hand, or when there is not time to go through routine channels or when the institution is so corrupt or coercive that steps will be taken to silence the whistleblower should he try the regular channels first.

What weight should an oath or a promise of silence have in the conflict of loyalties? One sworn to silence is doubtless under a stronger obligation because of the oath he has taken. He has bound himself, assumed specific obligations beyond those assumed in merely taking a new position. But even such promises can be overridden when the public interest at issue is strong enough. They can be overridden if they were obtained under duress or through deceit. They can be overridden, too, if they promise something that is in itself wrong or unlawful. The fact that one has promised silence is no excuse for complicity in covering up a crime or a violation of the public's trust.

The third element in whistleblowing—accusation—raises equally serious ethical concerns. They are concerns of fairness to the persons accused of impropriety. Is the message one to which the public is entitled in the first place? Or does it infringe on personal and private matters that one has no right to invade? Here, the very notion of what is in the public's best "interest" is at issue: "accusations" regarding an official's unusual sexual or religious experiences may well appeal to the public's interest without being information relevant to "the public interest."

Great conflicts arise here. We have witnessed excessive claims to executive privilege and to secrecy by government officials during the Watergate scandal in order to cover up for abuses the public had every right to discover. Conversely, those hoping to profit from prying into private matters have become adept at invoking "the public's right to know." Some even regard such private matters as threats to the public: they voice their own religious and political prejudices in the language of accusation. Such a danger is never stronger than when the accusation is delivered surreptitiously. The anonymous accusations made during the McCarthy period regarding political beliefs and associations often injured persons who did not even know their accusers or the exact nature of the accusations.

From the public's point of view, accusations that are openly made by identifiable individuals are more likely to be taken seriously. And in fairness to those criticized, openly accepted responsibility for blowing the whistle should be preferred to the denunciation or the leaked rumor. What is openly stated can more easily be checked, its source's motives challenged, and the underlying information examined. Those under attack may otherwise be hard put to defend themselves against nameless adversaries. Often they do not even know that they are threatened until it is too late to respond. The anonymous denunciation, moreover, common to so many regimes, places the burden of investigation on government agencies that may thereby gain the power of a secret police.

From the point of view of the whistleblower, on the other hand, the anonymous message is safer in situations where retaliation is likely. But it is also often less likely to be taken seriously. Unless the message is accompanied by indications of how the evidence can be checked, its anonymity, however safe for the source, speaks against it.

During the process of weighing the legitimacy of speaking out, the method used, and the degree of fairness needed, whistleblowers must try to compensate for the strong possibility of bias on their part. They should be scrupulously aware of any motive that might skew their message: a desire for self-defense in a difficult bureaucratic situation, perhaps, or the urge to seek revenge, or inflated expectations regarding the effect their message will have on the situation. (Needless to say, bias affects the silent as well as the outspoken. The motive for holding back important information about abuses and injustice ought to give similar cause for soul-searching.)

Likewise, the possibility of personal gain from sounding the alarm ought to give pause. Once again there is then greater risk of a biased message. Even if the whistleblower regards himself as incorruptible, his profiting from revelations of neglect or abuse will lead others to question his motives and to put less credence in his charges. If, for example, a government employee stands to make large profits from a book exposing the inequities in his agency, there is danger that he will, perhaps even unconsciously, slant his report in order to cause more of a sensation.

A special problem arises when there is a high risk that the civil servant who speaks out will have to go through costly litigation. Might he not justifiably try to make enough money on his public revelations—say, through books or public speaking—to offset his losses? In so doing he will not strictly speaking have *profited* from his revelations: he merely avoids being financially crushed by their sequels. He will nevertheless still be suspected at the time of revelation, and his message will therefore seem more questionable.

Reducing bias and error in moral choice often requires consultation, even open debate[10]: methods that force articulation of the moral arguments at stake and challenge privately held assumptions. But acts of whistleblowing present special problems when it comes to open consultation. On the one hand, once the whistleblower sounds his alarm publicly, his arguments will be subjected to open scrutiny; he will have to articulate his reasons for speaking out and substantiate his charges. On the other hand, it will then be too late to retract the alarm or to combat its harmful effects, should his choice to speak out have been ill-advised.

For this reason, the whistleblower owes it to all involved to make sure of two things: that he has sought as much and as objective advice regarding his choice as he can *before* going public; and that he is aware of the arguments for and against the practice of whistleblowing in general, so that he can see his own choice against as richly detailed and coherently structured a background as possible. Satisfying these two requirements once again has special problems because of the very nature of whistleblowing: the more corrupt the circumstances, the more dangerous it may be to seek consultation before speaking out. And yet, since the whistleblower himself may have a biased view of the state of affairs, he may choose not to consult others when in fact it would be not only safe but advantageous to do so; he may see corruption and conspiracy where none exists.

Notes

1. Code of Ethics for Government Service passed by the U.S. House of Representatives in the 85th Congress (1958) and applying to all government employees and office holders.

2. Code of Ethics of the Institute of Electrical and Electronics Engineers, Article IV.

3. For case histories and descriptions of what befalls whistleblowers, see Rosemary Chalk and Frank von Hippel, "Due Process for Dissenting Whistle-Blowers," *Technology Review* 81 (June–July 1979); 48–55; Alan S. Westin and Stephen Salisbury, eds., *Individual Rights in the Corporation* (New York: Pantheon, 1980); Helen Dudar, "The Price of Blowing the Whistle," *New York Times Magazine,* 30 October 1979, pp. 41–54; John Edsall, *Scientific Freedom and Responsibility* (Washington, D.C.: American Association for the Advancement of Science, 1975), p. 5; David Ewing, *Freedom Inside the Organization* (New York: Dutton, 1977); Ralph Nader, Peter Petkas, and Kate Blackwell, *Whistle Blowing* (New York: Grossman, 1972); Charles Peter and Taylor Branch, *Blowing the Whistle* (New York: Praeger, 1972).

4. Congressional hearings uncovered a growing resort to mandatory psychiatric examinations.

5. For an account of strategies and proposals to support government whistle-blowers, see Government Accountability Project, *A Whistleblower's Guide to the Federal Bureaucracy* (Washington, D.C.: Institute for Policy Studies, 1977).

6. See, e.g., Samuel Eliot Morison, Frederick Merk, and Frank Friedel, *Dissent in Three American Wars* (Cambridge: Harvard University Press, 1970).

7. In the scheme worked out by Albert Hirschman in *Exit, Voice and Loyalty* (Cambridge: Harvard University Press, 1970), whistleblowing represents "voice" accompanied by a preference not to "exit," though forced "exit" is clearly a possibility and "voice" after or during "exit" may be chosen for strategic reasons.

8. Edward Weisband and Thomas N. Franck, *Resignation in Protest* (New York: Grossman, 1975).

9. Future developments can, however, be the cause for whistleblowing if they are seen as resulting from steps being taken or about to be taken that render them inevitable.

10. I discuss these questions of consultation and publicity with respect to moral choice in chapter 7 of Sissela Bok, *Lying* (New York: Pantheon, 1978); and in *Secrets* (New York: Pantheon Books, 1982), Ch. IX and XV.

Robert A. Larmer

 **NO**

Whistleblowing and Employee Loyalty

Whistleblowing by an employee is the act of complaining, either within the corporation or publicly, about a corporation's unethical practices. Such an act raises important questions concerning the loyalties and duties of employees. Traditionally, the employee has been viewed as an agent who acts on behalf of a principal, i.e., the employer, and as possessing duties of loyalty and confidentiality. Whistleblowing, at least at first blush, seems a violation of these duties and it is scarcely surprising that in many instances employers and fellow employees argue that it is an act of disloyalty and hence morally wrong.[1]

It is this issue of the relation between whistleblowing and employee loyalty that I want to address. What I will call the standard view is that employees possess *prima facie* duties of loyalty and confidentiality to their employers and that whistleblowing cannot be justified except on the basis of a higher duty to the public good. Against this standard view, Ronald Duska has recently argued that employees do not have even a *prima facie* duty of loyalty to their employers and that whistleblowing needs, therefore, no moral justification.[2] I am going to criticize both views. My suggestion is that both misunderstand the relation between loyalty and whistleblowing. In their place I will propose a third more adequate view.

Duska's view is more radical in that it suggests that there can be no issue of whistleblowing and employee loyalty, since the employee has no duty to be loyal to his employer. His reason for suggesting that the employee owes the employer, at least the corporate employer, no loyalty is that companies are not the kinds of things which are proper objects of loyalty. His argument in support of this rests upon two key claims. The first is that loyalty, properly understood, implies a reciprocal relationship and is only appropriate in the context of a mutual surrendering of self-interest. He writes,

> It is important to recognize that in any relationship which demands loyalty the relationship works both ways and involves mutual enrichment. Loyalty is incompatible with self-interest, because it is something that necessarily requires we go beyond self-interest. My loyalty to my friend, for example, requires I put aside my interests some of the time. . . . Loyalty depends on ties that demand self-sacrifice with no expectation of reward, e.g., the ties of loyalty that bind a family together.[3]

The second is that the relation between a company and an employee does not involve any surrender of self-interest on the part of the company, since its primary goal is to maximize profit. Indeed, although it is convenient, it is misleading to talk of a company having interests. As Duska comments,

> A company is not a person. A company is an instrument, and an instrument with a specific purpose, the making of profit. To treat an instrument as an end in itself, like a person, may not be as bad as treating an end as an instrument, but it does give the instrument a moral status it does not deserve . . .[4]

Since, then, the relation between a company and an employee does not fulfill the minimal requirement of being a relation between two individuals, much less two reciprocally self-sacrificing individuals, Duska feels it is a mistake to suggest the employee has any duties of loyalty to the company.

This view does not seem adequate, however. First, it is not true that loyalty must be quite so reciprocal as Duska demands. Ideally, of course, one expects that if one is loyal to another person that person will reciprocate in kind. There are, however, many cases where loyalty is not entirely reciprocated, but where we do not feel that it is misplaced. A parent, for example, may remain loyal to an erring teenager, even though the teenager demonstrates no loyalty to the parent. Indeed, part of being a proper parent is to demonstrate loyalty to your children whether or not that loyalty is reciprocated. This is not to suggest any kind of analogy between parents and employees, but rather that it is not nonsense to suppose that loyalty may be appropriate even though it is not reciprocated. Inasmuch as he ignores this possibility, Duska's account of loyalty is flawed.

Second, even if Duska is correct in holding that loyalty is only appropriate between moral agents and that a company is not genuinely a moral agent, the question may still be raised whether an employee owes loyalty to fellow employees or the shareholders of the company. Granted that reference to a company as an individual involves reification and should not be taken too literally, it may nevertheless constitute a legitimate shorthand way of describing relations between genuine moral agents.

Third, it seems wrong to suggest that simply because the primary motive of the employer is economic, considerations of loyalty are irrelevant. An employee's primary motive in working for an employer is generally economic, but no one on that account would argue that it is impossible for her to demonstrate loyalty to the employer, even if it turns out to be misplaced. All that is required is that her primary economic motive be in some degree qualified by considerations of the employer's welfare. Similarly, the fact that an employer's primary motive is economic does not imply that it is not qualified by considerations of the employee's welfare. Given the possibility of mutual qualification of admittedly primary economic motives, it is fallacious to argue that employee loyalty is never appropriate.

In contrast to Duska, the standard view is that loyalty to one's employer is appropriate. According to it, one has an obligation to be loyal to one's employer and, consequently, a *prima facie* duty to protect the employer's interests. Whistleblowing constitutes, therefore, a violation of duty to one's employer and needs strong justification if it is to be appropriate. Sissela Bok summarizes this view very well when she writes

> the whistleblower hopes to stop the game; but since he is neither referee nor coach, and since he blows the whistle on his own team, his act is seen as a violation of loyalty. In holding his position, he has assumed certain obligations to his colleagues and clients. He may even have subscribed to a loyalty oath or a promise of confidentiality. Loyalty to colleagues and to clients comes to be pitted against loyalty to the public interest, to those who may be injured unless the revelation is made.[5]

The strength of this view is that it recognizes that loyalty is due one's employer. Its weakness is that it tends to conceive of whistleblowing as involving a tragic moral choice, since blowing the whistle is seen not so much as a positive action, but rather the lesser of two evils. Bok again puts the essence of this view very clearly when she writes that "a would-be whistleblower must weigh his responsibility to serve the public interest *against* the responsibility he owes to his colleagues and the institution in which he works" and "that [when] their duty [to whistleblow] . . . *so overrides loyalties to colleagues and institutions,* they [whistleblowers] often have reason to fear the results of carrying out such a duty."[6] The employee, according to this understanding of whistleblowing, must choose between two acts of betrayal, either her employer or the public interest, each in itself reprehensible.

Behind this view lies the assumption that to be loyal to someone is to act in a way that accords with what that person believes to be in her best interests. To be loyal to an employer, therefore, is to act in a way which the employer deems to be in his or her best interests. Since employers very rarely approve of whistleblowing and generally feel that it is not in their best interests, it follows that whistleblowing is an act of betrayal on the part of the employee, albeit a betrayal made in the interests of the public good.

Plausible though it initially seems, I think this view of whistleblowing is mistaken and that it embodies a mistaken conception of what constitutes employee loyalty. It ignores the fact that

> the great majority of corporate whistleblowers . . . [consider] themselves to be very loyal employees who . . . [try] to use 'direct voice' (internal whistleblowing), . . . [are] rebuffed and punished for this, and then . . . [use] 'indirect voice' (external whistleblowing). They . . . [believe] initially that they . . . [are] behaving in a loyal manner, helping their employers by calling top management's attention to practices that could eventually get the firm in trouble.[7]

By ignoring the possibility that blowing the whistle may demonstrate greater loyalty than not blowing the whistle, it fails to do justice to the many instances where loyalty to someone constrains us to act in defiance of what that person believes to be in her best interests. I am not, for example, being disloyal to a friend if I refuse to loan her money for an investment I am sure will bring her financial ruin; even if she bitterly reproaches me for denying her what is so obviously a golden opportunity to make a fortune.

A more adequate definition of being loyal to someone is that loyalty involves acting in accordance with what one has good reason to believe to be in that person's best interests. A key question, of course, is what constitutes a good reason to think that something is in a person's best interests. Very often, but by no means invariably, we accept that a person thinking that something is in her best interests is a sufficiently good reason to think that it actually is. Other times, especially when we feel that she is being rash, foolish, or misinformed we are prepared, precisely by virtue of being loyal, to act contrary to the person's wishes. It is beyond the scope of this paper to investigate such cases in detail, but three general points can be made.

First, to the degree that an action is genuinely immoral, it is impossible that it is in the agent's best interests. We would not, for example, say that someone who sells child pornography was acting in his own best interests, even if he vigorously protested that there was nothing wrong with such activity. Loyalty does not imply that we have a duty to refrain from reporting the immoral actions of those to whom we are loyal. An employer who is acting immorally is not acting in her own best interests and an employee is not acting disloyally in blowing the whistle.[8] Indeed, the argument can be made that the employee who blows the whistle may be demonstrating greater loyalty than the employee who simply ignores the immoral conduct, inasmuch as she is attempting to prevent her employer from engaging in self-destructive behaviour.

Second, loyalty requires that, whenever possible, in trying to resolve a problem we deal directly with the person to whom we are loyal. If, for example, I am loyal to a friend I do not immediately involve a third party when I try to dissuade my friend from involvement in immoral actions. Rather, I approach my friend directly, listen to his perspective on the events in question, and provide an opportunity for him to address the problem in a morally satisfactory way. This implies that, whenever possible, a loyal employee blows the whistle internally. This provides the employer with the opportunity to either demonstrate to the employee that, contrary to first appearances, no genuine wrongdoing had occurred, or, if there is a genuine moral problem, the opportunity to resolve it.

This principle of dealing directly with the person to whom loyalty is due needs to be qualified, however. Loyalty to a person requires that one acts in that person's best interests. Generally, this cannot be done without directly involving the person to whom one is loyal in the decision-making process, but there may arise cases where acting in a person's best interests requires that one act independently and perhaps even against the wishes of the person to whom one is loyal. Such cases will be especially apt to arise when the person to whom one is loyal is either immoral or ignoring the moral consequences of his actions. Thus, for example, loyalty to a friend who deals in hard narcotics would not imply that I speak first to my friend about my decision to inform the police of his activities, if the only effect of my doing so would be to make him more careful in his criminal dealings. Similarly, a loyal employee is under no obligation to speak first to an employer about the employer's immoral actions, if the only response of the employer will be to take care to cover up wrongdoing.

Neither is a loyal employee under obligation to speak first to an employer if it is clear that by doing so she placed herself in jeopardy from an employer who will retaliate if given the opportunity. Loyalty amounts to acting in another's best interests and that may mean qualifying what seems to be in one's own interests, but it cannot imply that one take no steps to protect oneself from the immorality of those to whom one is loyal. The reason it cannot is that, as has already been argued, acting immorally can never really be in a person's best interests. It follows, therefore, that one is not acting in a person's best interests if one allows oneself to be treated immorally by that person. Thus, for example, a father might be loyal to a child even though the child is guilty of stealing from him, but this would not mean that the father should let the child continue to steal. Similarly, an employee may be loyal to an employer even though she takes steps to protect herself against unfair retaliation by the employer, e.g., by blowing the whistle externally.

Third, loyalty requires that one is concerned with more than considerations of justice. I have been arguing that loyalty cannot require one to ignore immoral or unjust behaviour on the part of those to whom one is loyal, since loyalty amounts to acting in a person's best interests and it can never be in a person's best interests to be allowed to act immorally. Loyalty, however, goes beyond considerations of justice in that, while it is possible to be disinterested and just, it is not possible to be disinterested and loyal. Loyalty implies a desire that the person to whom one is loyal take no moral stumbles, but that if moral stumbles have occurred that the person be restored and not simply punished. A loyal friend is not only someone who sticks by you in times of trouble, but someone who tries to help you avoid trouble. This suggests that a loyal employee will have a desire to point out problems and potential problems long before the drastic measures associated with whistleblowing become necessary, but that if whistleblowing does become necessary there remains a desire to help the employer.

In conclusion, although much more could be said on the subject of loyalty, our brief discussion has enabled us to clarify considerably the relation between whistleblowing and employee loyalty. It permits us to steer a course between the Scylla of Duska's view that, since the primary link between employer and employee is economic, the ideal of employee loyalty is an oxymoron, and the Charybdis of the standard view that, since it forces an employee to weigh conflicting duties, whistleblowing inevitably involves some degree of moral tragedy. The solution lies in realizing that to whistleblow for reasons of morality is to act in one's employer's best interests and involves, therefore, no disloyalty.

Notes

1. The definition I have proposed applies most directly to the relation between privately owned companies aiming to realize a profit and their employees. Obviously, issues of whistleblowing arise in other contexts, e.g., governmental

organizations or charitable agencies, and deserve careful thought. I do not propose, in this paper, to discuss whistleblowing in these other contexts, but I think my development of the concept of whistleblowing as positive demonstration of loyalty can easily be applied and will prove useful.

2. Duska, R.: 1985, 'Whistleblowing and Employee Loyalty,' in J. R. Desjardins and J. J. McCall, eds., *Contemporary Issues in Business Ethics* (Wadsworth, Belmont, California), pp. 295–300.

3. Duska, p. 297.

4. Duska, p. 298.

5. Bok, S.: 1983, 'Whistleblowing and Professional Responsibility,' in T. L. Beauchamp and N. E. Bowie, eds., *Ethical Theory and Business,* 2nd ed. (Prentice-Hall Inc., Englewood Cliffs, New Jersey), pp. 261–269, p. 263.

6. Bok, pp. 261–2, emphasis added.

7. Near, J. P. and P. Miceli: 1985, 'Organizational Dissidence: The Case of Whistle-Blowing', *Journal of Business Ethics* **4**, pp. 1–16, p. 10.

8. As Near and Miceli note 'The whistle-blower may provide valuable information helpful in improving organizational effectiveness . . . the prevalence of illegal activity in organizations is associated with declining organizational performance' (p. 1).

The general point is that the structure of the world is such that it is not in a company's long-term interests to act immorally. Sooner or later a company which flouts morality and legality will suffer.

POSTSCRIPT

Does Blowing the Whistle Violate Company Loyalty?

Whistleblowers are hard role models. What would you do in their shoes? The corporation, incidentally, is not the only setting for whistles. Would you tell about a friend's drug abuse, cheating on exams (or on his wife), stealing just a little bit of money? How do you weigh the possibility of damage done to the community against the security of your own career (some damage done to many people versus much damage done to a few people)? If you can see nothing but painful consequences all around if you blow the whistle, does that settle the problem—or does simple justice and fidelity to law have a claim of its own, as Ernest Fitzgerald argued? At what point do you decide that you cannot survive as a moral person unless you take action to end an evil that is being concealed—that the value of your own integrity outweighs the certain penalties of honesty?

Should we, as a society, protect the whistleblower with legislation designed to discourage corporate retaliation? Richard De George and Alan Westin, the earliest business ethics writers to take whistleblowing seriously, agree that the best policy is one that precludes the need for such heroics. "The need for moral heroes," De George concludes, "shows a defective society and defective corporations. It is more important to change the legal and corporate structures that make whistle blowing necessary than to convince people to be moral heroes" (*Business Ethics*, 2nd edition, 1986, p. 236). "The single most important element in creating a meaningful internal system to deal with whistle blowing is to have top leadership accept this as a management priority," says Westin, "This means that the chief operating officer and his senior colleagues have to believe that a policy which encourages discussion and dissent, and deals fairly with whistle-blowing claims, is a good and important thing for their company to adopt. . . . They have to see it, in their own terms, as a moral duty of good private enterprise" (*Whistle-Blowing!* 1981, p. 141). He cites Alexander Trowbridge, former secretary of commerce, on the importance of creating the proper organizational climate within the corporation: "It must be one that fosters the development of discipline in response to strong leadership and yet creates an atmosphere in which the individual, when confronted with something clearly illegal, unethical or unjust, can feel free to speak up—and to bring the problem to the attention of those high enough up in the corporation to solve it" (Ibid., p. 142). We need clear policies that permit and encourage the employees to communicate their doubts, and we need to train our managers to be responsive instead of punitive when the doubts are communicated.

206

But these are not enough. "Even the best drafted policy statements and management training programs will not resolve all the questions of illegal, dangerous, or improper conduct that might arise," Westin concludes. "There has to be a clear process of receiving complaints, conducting impartial investigations, defining standards of judgment, providing a fair-hearing procedure, and reaching the most objective and responsible decision possible. Such a procedure has to be fair both to the complaining employee and to company officials if morale is to be preserved and general confidence in management's integrity is to be the general expectation of the work force" (Ibid., p. 143). The company can "establish channels whereby those employees who have moral concerns can get a fair hearing without danger to their position or standing in the company," suggests De George, "Expressing such concerns, moreover, should be considered a demonstration of company loyalty and should be rewarded appropriately" (De George, p. 237). Possibilities for appropriate mechanisms include company ombudsmen, employee advocates, and committees of the board of directors.

Yes, but suppose that *these* are not enough. We run a moral company, we think; we have mechanisms in place to receive and process complaints, we think; but it will still happen that under the pressure of competition, company policies may bend, and the ombudsmen and advocates may become co-opted into the company agenda. At this point, do we as a society have any remaining interest in protecting the whistleblower? Laws are already in place protecting those who expose their companies' illegal activities; but we have always had protections for those who help the authorities bring lawbreakers to justice, so those laws are nothing novel. The question is really, does the society as a whole have any collective interest in the monitoring of private organizations in the economic sphere? And if it does, and it seems that it does, is the legal protection of the whistleblower the appropriate way to express that interest?

Suggested Reading

N. R. Kleinfeld, "The Whistle Blowers' Morning After," *New York Times* Business Forum (November 9, 1986).

Myron Peretz Glazer and Penina Migdal Glazer, *The Whistle Blowers: Exposing Corruption in Government and Industry* (New York: Basic Books, 1989).

David B. Greenberger, Marcia P. Miceli and Debra J. Cohen, "Oppositionists and Group Norms: The Reciprocal Influence of Whistleblowers and Co-Workers," *Journal of Business Ethics*, vol. 6, no. 7 (October 1987), pp. 527–42.

Gene G. James, "In Defense of Whistle Blowing," from William Shaw and Vincent Barry (eds.), *Moral Issues in Business*, 4th ed., pp. 337–46 (Belmont, CA: Wadsworth, 1989).

Editors, "Postscript," *Vanity Fair* (August 1988), pp. 50–62.

Natalie Kandekar, "Contrasting Consequences: Bringing Charges of Sexual Harassment Compared with Other Cases of Whistleblowing," *Journal of Business Ethics*, vol. 9 no. 2 (1990), pp. 151–58.

Rosemary Chalk, "Doing Right on Wrongdoing," *Technology Review* (February/March 1993).

Kenneth Silverstein, "Proposed Whistle-Blowing Law Puts Corporations on Notice" *Corporate Cashflow* (December 1992).

Gerale Vinten, "Whistle Blowing: Corporate Help or Hindrance?" *Management Decision,* 1992.

Marcia P. Miceli, Janet P. Near and Charles R. Schwenk, "Who Blows the Whistle and Why?" *Industrial & Labor Relations Review* (October 1991).

Kenneth Kernaghan, "Whistle-Blowing in Canadian Governments: Ethical, Political and Managerial Considerations," *Optimum*, 1991–1992.

Tim Barnett, Ken Bass and Gene Brown, "Religiosity, Ethical Ideology, and Intentions to Report a Peer's Wrongdoing," *Journal of Business Ethics*, vol. 15, no. 11 (November 1996), pp. 1161–74.

Terry Morehead Dworkin and Janet P. Near, "A Better Statutory Approach to Whistle-blowing," *Business Ethics Quarterly* vol. 7, no. 1 (January 1997), pp. 1–16.

ISSUE 10

Is Employer Monitoring of Employee E-Mail Justified?

YES: Chauncey M. DePree, Jr., and Rebecca K. Jude, from "Who's Reading Your Office E-Mail? Is That Legal?" *Strategic Finance* (April 2006)

NO: *USA Today*, from "E-monitoring of Workers Sparks Concerns," *USA Today* (May 29, 2001)

ISSUE SUMMARY

YES: DePree and Jude argue that employers have a right, indeed a duty, to protect the corporation from legal liability incurred by the careless actions of their employees. Unfortunately, the use of e-mail from the employer's computer can get the company into worlds of trouble, and the company must monitor that e-mail.

NO: There is apparently a substantial body of opinion in the country that e-mail is like other mail, and no one has the right to read it except the writer and the intended recipient. That goes for employers, too.

Is privacy a "right" for the worker? If history is to be our guide, absolutely not. Dictatorial employers of the 19th century had no qualms about making and enforcing rules governing not only job performance but dress and personal behavior on the job; many also had rules for off-the-job behavior. But Americans do not take easily to such governance, and with the advent of organized labor, the freedom of the employer to dictate the employee's life-style off the job almost disappeared. On-the-job requirements also ceased to be absolute; although certain obvious safety rules could be enforced, the pre-sumption was that rules should not be extended beyond necessity, and that necessity had to be job-related.

The last generation's privacy issue turned on the employee's use of rec-reational drugs outside of business hours. Few employees openly snorted cocaine at their desks, but an employee could stay pleasantly elevated all day with doses morning and lunch hour. Employers frowned on such use, partly out of fears of liability should the company's premises be used for drug consumption, or should any product made by the employee turn out badly flawed because of the drugs, but mainly because of the loss of productivity resulting from the impairment and the ever-present threat of drug-induced behavior, bizarre or violent, that would impact the other employees and the workplace as a whole. Drugs were worse than alcohol, if only because any experienced foreman or supervisor can spot drunkenness, which manifests itself in the employee's gait, his speech, and on his breath. But drugs hid themselves, and therefore had to be tested for.

This generation's issue is the monitoring of employee computer use. There are uses of the employer's computer that can raise the same liability issues for the employer as employee drug use: if someone is harmed by the employee's nonbusiness use of the computer on the employer's premises, how shall the employer answer the complaint? The question is not hypothetical: according to the American Management Association, 13 percent of employers who responded to its survey on the subject had had to battle lawsuits triggered by employee e-mail. Of even more concern to employers is inappropriate surfing of the Internet; 65 percent of employers surveyed now use software to block connections to websites whose images have no place in the workplace; similarly, 900 numbers cannot be accessed from office phones. It is also possible to monitor keystrokes—to find out if a secretary, say, is apparently writing more letters than her productivity would indicate. The AMA insists that employers for the most part give the employees fair warning about all monitoring and surveillance, and that it is done with their consent.

Employees understandably object to being watched all the time, down to the least detail of documents stored in their computer files, all e-mail correspondence, and all use of the Web. Of course they "consented," signed a document as they started work, but consent has a strange heft when the alternative is unemployment.

Part of the problem, of course, stems from the semiprivate nature of the cubicle and the sense of invisibility that it conveys. Workplaces traditionally have been open floors for all but the top executives, floors in which work was carried on in full view of everyone, in which the physical products were immediately visible to all, and in which the modes of communication were oral and very audible, or in black and white for several sets of eyes to read before they landed in the company's outgoing mail box. Now the worker seems to have the entirety of the office equipment at his sole command, including the mailroom, and the sense of anonymity is very tempting.

Bear in mind as you read these selections that the requirements that work get done, and inappropriate behavior be avoided in the workplace, have not changed for hundreds of years, and are affirmed by employer and employee alike. But the technology has changed the workplace setting beyond recognition, and many of our previous assumptions about monitoring and freedom will have to be renegotiated.

YES

**Chauncey M. Depree, Jr.,
and Rebecca K. Jude**

Who's Reading Your Office E-Mail? Is That Legal?

Yesterday, as you sat working at your desk, you checked your e-mail and spotted a note from a friend. The message was an off-color joke complete with graphic illustration. Sure, some stick-in-the-mud might find it offensive, but it was awfully funny. So, without thinking, you clicked on the forward button, typed in an e-mail address or two or three, and hit the send button. No big deal, right?

You don't give the e-mail another thought until this morning when a somber supervisor invites you to her office. She hands you a letter of repri-mand along with a copy of the e-mail. She tells you that as a matter of office policy, employee e-mails are monitored. Copies are placed in your file, and, in the event it happens again, she warns that you'll receive a termination letter.

It simply never occurred to you that someone might be monitoring your e-mail. What about your right to privacy?

What Happened to Privacy?

As an employee, the idea of being monitored may trouble you. As an employer, the idea of monitoring employees may be equally distasteful. The right to privacy is so thoroughly ingrained in most of us that we take it for granted—especially in a peaceful environment when we're sitting alone, typing into a computer. We may be lulled into a false sense of isolation and freedom from observation. But even if the technology is available, aren't there simply too many e-mails and too much Internet use to review effectively? After all, the Internet is so big and so anonymous. No one can really track everybody's e-mail or Internet surfing. Besides, it's probably an invasion of privacy and illegal.

Wrong on both counts. To quote Scott McNealy, CEO of Sun Micro-systems, on the issue of Internet privacy: "You have zero privacy anyway. Get over it." McNealy's rather abrupt observation and admonition are particularly true in the work environment.

The simple fact is that monitoring employee e-mail and Internet usage is legal under almost all circumstances. As a general rule, when an employee enters the workplace, an employer may monitor and record communications,

From *Strategic Finance*, April 2006, pp. 45–47. Copyright © 2006 by Institute of Management Accountants (IMA) via Copyright Clearance Center. Reprinted by permission.

including e-mail and Internet use, without any notice to the employee. In *Fraser v. Nationwide Mutual Insurance Co.*, 352 F. 3d 107 (3rd Cir. 2003), the court specifically held that The Electronic Communications Privacy Act, 18 U.S.C.§2701, didn't apply to an employer's search of e-mail stored on its own system.

But in some instances, simple facts tend to beget complicated, counter-intuitive consequences. For example, an employer repeatedly assured its employees that e-mail communications would remain confidential. As it turned out, the assurance wasn't a guarantee that the employees' e-mails wouldn't be used as a basis for discharge. In *Smyth v. The Pillsbury Company*, 914 F. Supp. 97 (ED Pa. 1996), a supervisor e-mailed inappropriate comments to an employee at home, and the employee responded in kind. The e-mails were communicated over the company system. Regardless of the company's assurances, the employee was terminated for communicating "inappropriate and unprofessional comments" via the company system. The Court held that "once plaintiff communicated the alleged unprofessional comments to a second person over the e-mail system that was apparently utilized by the entire company, any reasonable expectation of privacy was lost."

Employee e-mail habits have developed over time, but, as the *Pillsbury* decision exemplifies, employers' practices also can change—sometimes quickly and unpredictably. The Pillsbury case wouldn't be the last surprise for employees. Employers can review e-mail at any time and with lightning speed. Dow Chemical took a "snapshot" of a day's worth of employee e-mails and then systematically sorted through them. Some 254 employees had saved, filed, or sent sexually related, violent, and other inappropriate e-mails. The actual participation and involvement of the employees varied considerably. Dow created a set of criteria so that discipline taken, if any, could be based on each employee's participation. The criteria included offensiveness; what the employee did with the material, such as circulating the materials within Dow; and the frequency of the conduct. Dow discharged 20 employees and disciplined others. The court, although recognizing that Dow was probably employing a union-busting tactic, upheld the company's review and use of its employees' e-mail (*Dow Chemical v. Local No. 564, Operating Engineers*, 246 F. Supp. 2d 602 (SD Texas, 2002)).

Is Monitoring E-Mail and Internet Use Necessary?

Despite the near cultural aversion to intruding on communications, growing numbers of companies and managers record, review, and monitor telephone and computer activities of their employees. According to the American Management Association (AMA) 2005 Electronic Monitoring & Surveillance Survey, 76% of employers monitor website connections, "26% have fired workers for misusing the Internet," and "another 25% have terminated employees for e-mail misuse." Inexpensive software packages facilitate these decisions, and the overriding reason is compelling—it has become a business necessity.

An inescapable consequence of employee e-mail and Internet use is that the employer is responsible for illegal, discriminatory, or offensive communications that are transmitted over the system or viewed by others from a company computer screen. Sexually explicit, graphically violent, or racially inappropriate websites open to view by co-workers may be used to support claims of discriminatory behavior or a hostile work environment. E-mails containing such inappropriate materials that are circulated around the office or forwarded to others have the same effect.

But so there's no misunderstanding, employers and managers can get into just as much trouble with their e-mail as employees. E-mails sent by managers can be used by employees to prove claims of corporate misconduct. For example, the characterization of an employee as "ready for the bone yard" may be evidence of age discrimination. The simple truth is that e-mails containing potentially libelous or defamatory content should *not* be sent or forwarded—even internally. Not only can they easily get away from managers with a click of a button, but they also may become—in a stored capacity on the server or archive—the target of discovery in litigation.

Because e-mails can seem so informal, managers and employees are more likely to say things in them they would never put in a letter. Unlike letters, e-mails can be forwarded over and over to thousands of people with the touch of a button. Impulsive and thoughtless comments can travel the world over. Often overlooked is the liability with regard to foreign laws. Because e-mails can be transmitted anywhere and may then be forwarded practically *ad infinitum*, an employer may be responsible for content based on the laws of the country in which the e-mail ultimately arrives. Electronic communications originating in the company office may have far-ranging legal consequences.

An Easy Prediction and Another Surprise

Some potential liabilities are much better known and may occur with considerable frequency. For example, an employee might use office computers to wrongfully appropriate other people's intellectual property from the Internet, leaving the employer responsible. One of the most popular forms of this activity is file sharing—downloading copyrighted music or movies without payment. Or an employee might copy and paste copyrighted material from someone else's website onto the employer's without the knowledge or consent of any manager or supervisor. The company may be responsible for the copyright infringement.

Other kinds of e-mail-facilitated problems might not be easily anticipated. For example, an employee can enter into a contract with the click of a mouse. This was our firm's first e-mail surprise. An employee took it upon himself to purchase CDs containing copies of documents that we already had in our possession. It was easy. An e-mail arrived asking if he would be willing to share the cost of obtaining copies of documents. All he had to do was return an e-mail agreeing to participate in the project. Seemingly out of the blue, at least from our perspective, a half dozen CDs and an invoice for several thousand dollars arrived at our office. There was no correspondence in the files authorizing the purchase. Ultimately, though, we found a brief e-mail from our employee responding to the inquiry. The reply e-mail simply said "count us in." Of course, the company that provided the service wanted its money. After all, they had spent time and effort preparing the materials for us. We were stuck. If our office had monitored e-mails, we could have caught this and stopped the expensive and wasteful process before the vendor incurred its costs.

From Top to Bottom Line

Even when a company gets lucky and avoids civil or contractual liability, employees will still take time for personal communications, e-mails, and Internet surfing instead of working. This could cost the company a fortune in lost productivity and lost dollars. Time away from work also translates to poor client service. Poor service may lose clients. Consequently, as unappealing as it is, monitoring employee communications is increasingly viewed as a business necessity.

For our firm, a good place to start was to develop a policy to educate employees in the use of company e-mail and the Internet. We believed, as do other employers, that to avoid any potential gray areas in the law, and in the interest of fairness, employers should advise managers and employees of e-mail or Internet monitoring as part of their employment agreement, and it should be included in the employee handbook. We breathed a sigh of relief after we disseminated the policy to all employees and confirmed that everyone understood the importance of compliance.

We weren't so naïve as to believe it would solve our Internet and e-mail problems, but we had no idea just how difficult it would be to change habits. As unbelievable as it may sound, the very next day after the Internet and e-mail policy was communicated, it was completely ignored by a professional employee. He thoughtlessly e-mailed his latest "joke" far and wide, even though it could easily be construed not only as racist but salacious as well. It was forwarded as cavalierly as if he had never read the policy or studied the law. And that's right, he is a lawyer!

E-monitoring of Workers Sparks Concerns

Employee privacy in the United States is under siege as old rules for what employers can and cannot monitor give way to a regime of everyday observation, patchy legal protections and conflicting business priorities.

Software that pours over intimate e-mail correspondences, tracks worker performance or thwarts employee theft has narrowed the realm of privacy for employees in offices, factories, on the road or telecommuting from home.

Three-quarters of U.S. businesses now electronically monitor employees in some fashion, double the rate of just five years ago, according to a recent study by the American Management Association, a New York-based corporate training and consulting group.

Meet the downside of the low-cost, easy-to-use technologies that have powered the technology revolution of recent years.

"As the work has been automated, so also has the watching been automated," said Eric Rolphe Greenberg, director of management studies at the AMA.

"Now that the nature of the work has changed, so also has the nature of the supervision," said Greenberg, the author of the AMA's annual study of electronic workplace monitoring.

Vague policies allow Web and e-mail monitoring software not only to track when an employee views sexually explicit material but potentially any intimate subject. Voice mail retrieval software does the same. Keystroke and screen-capture software can check what you are working on at any moment in time.

Punching the time clock takes on new meaning when every movement can be traced. Field sales representatives have their movements tracked by location-based tracking systems in new wireless phones. Some hospitals now require nurses to wear badges on their uniforms so they can be located constantly.

Managers, business consultants and legal experts say this rise in corporate curiosity is required to keep pace with free-wheeling communications technologies in the Internet age.

Electronic Monitoring Now a Fact of Workplace Life

The AMA's survey of major U.S. firms found that 77.7% now record and review some sort of employee communications and activities on the job.

For example, Internet connections were monitored by 63% of the more than 1,600 companies responding to the survey. Telephone use was tracked by 43%. Computer use such as time logged on or keystroke counts was monitored by 19%. Video surveillance for security purposes was used by 38%.

In addition, the annual survey found that more than a quarter of respondent companies fired people for misuse of company technology and three-quarters have disciplined people.

"People act as if they have privacy protection. They don't stop to think they are under scrutiny," said Stewart Baker, head of the technology law practice at Washington, D.C.-firm Steptoe & Johnson.

"Surprisingly for such a law-happy society, there are few limits on what employers can do in the electronic age with respect to the privacy of their employees," said Baker, a cyber-law expert who was former general counsel of the U.S. National Security Agency.

While federal laws against wiretapping prevent monitoring of employee conversations under most circumstances, there are few limitations on monitoring such things as voice mail, e-mail or Web monitoring—any information that is stored and retrieved instead of directly intercepted, as live phone calls must be.

"Work-place privacy is a contradiction in terms. It's an oxymoron," the AMA's Greenberg said. "I know the illusion of privacy is there, but you are not using your own stuff. The phone, the keyboard, the connections, the job itself—they don't belong to you; they belong to the company, legally."

Most management and legal experts agree that simple prior notice to employees that their activities will be watched give employers wide freedom to monitor. Consultants advise companies to use notice as a way to "get over employees' expectations of privacy," which is an issue of social etiquette rather than a legal one.

Struggle to Balance New Technology, Individual Rights

The Internet has given a powerful window on the world to every office worker with a personal computer and a Web connection. It has also proven to be a powerful distraction, as the spike in usage of sites ranging from eBay to E-Trade during work hours reveals.

The very definition of what is private is up for grabs as lines blur between working hours, personal time and home life. What privacy rights do employees have when working on employer-supplied laptops from home, for example?

Meanwhile, the porous nature of electronic mail communications makes it quick and easy for employees to gossip with friends or business associates outside the organization.

The informality of the medium lends itself to the rapid transfer of a company's trade secrets outside the organization. What they don't send via e-mail angry employees can carry on a floppy disk in their shirt pocket as they walk out the door.

"Employers are much more aware and much more nervous about productivity, legality and security, and these issues are behind the increase," Greenberg said of the spiraling use of monitoring.

But it's a far cry from a century ago when Ford Motor used its Sociological Department to ensure that employees lived "unblemished" personal lives at home, the outgrowth of the intrusive management practices of 19th century industry.

Between productivity issues and competitive threats lie a wasp's nest of potential employer liability if computer systems are not policed for off-color jokes, mean-spirited gossip, or sexual harassment that show a pattern of discrimination.

E-mails and voicemails are frequently the smoking guns in corporate litigation. Standard operating procedure for any plaintiff's attorney in a corporate legal battle is to demand production of electronic records.

Big Brother Does Rest

Still, most monitoring is directed at specific job roles and not done around the clock, Greenberg said.

Because of obvious limitations on time and financial resources the watching is not perpetual and can't be. It mostly consists of keyword searches on Web use and e-mail, just as companies have looked over telephone bills for decades.

"Big Brother is snoozing more often than he's watching," Greenberg said.

POSTSCRIPT

Is Employer Monitoring of Employee E-Mail Justified?

This pair of selections marks a first for this series: while the YES article is from a standard opinion piece from a standard publication, the NO is a contribution from We the People, the general opinion as reported by a news agency. We think that this is significant. It is too early for much official reflection to have taken place on this subject; the technology is new, it changes by the day, the general goals of surveillance remain the same, but the means are very frightening. Technology changes our environment, announces itself, strides forward, and dictates how we will live our lives. (Under surveillance, I may do exactly what I did before, but now I know I am not doing it *in private,* and that changes my perception of what I am doing.) Technology is thought out and intentional. Our reaction to the technology, blindsiding us at least once a week, is inchoate for awhile, expressed as fears, rejections, often turning into legal or political action before it can be fully formulated. Be impressed: We are present at the creation of a controversy that will be with us for a long time.

ISSUE 11

Is "Employment-at-Will" Good Social Policy?

YES: Richard A. Epstein, from "In Defense of the Contract at Will," *University of Chicago Law Review* (Fall 1984)

NO: John J. McCall, from "In Defense of Just Cause Dismissal Rules," *Business Ethics Quarterly* (April 2003)

ISSUE SUMMARY

YES: Richard Epstein defends the at-will contract as an appropriate expression of autonomy of contract on the part of both employee and employer, and as a means to the most efficient operations of the market.

NO: John McCall argues that the defense of the employment-at-will doctrine does not take account of its economic and social consequences and is in derogation of the very moral principles that underlie private property and freedom of contract.

How can there possibly be any objection to freedom? If I want to make a deal with my neighbor, that I will help him move some boxes on Saturday, and he will pay me $20, what could be wrong with that? Suppose I really do a good job moving his boxes. It turns out that he runs an appliance store, and he wants to hire me to move boxes every day. I have the time, the pay's all right, but I have one problem—suppose something better comes along, and I want to up and leave, no offense? Maybe he has a problem, too: there's machinery out there that might make my job unnecessary, and he might want to invest in it next year. So we make a further stipulation: I can leave on thirty days' notice, he can terminate my job on thirty days' notice. We've both bought ourselves more freedom in the future. What's wrong with that?

Note that we don't have to do it that way. I could have said no, I have better things to do Saturday, and no, I don't want to move boxes every day, at least not at that pay. Or, on the other hand, either one of us might be coming off a really bad experience with unreliable bosses or employees, and we might decide to write restrictive terms into the contract—we might make it a five-year contract, with strong penalties on both sides for premature termination, or, as a college professor, I might insist on lifetime tenure in the job before I'll take it. (He might change his mind about hiring me at that point.) If one of those alternatives looks better to us, we can go that way—the law allows us a wide range of freedom in forging our own contracts. But if we choose the first way, what's wrong with it?

Epstein is in the stronger position here, for he only has to say, over and over again, that freedom is good, that autonomy is morally preferable to servitude, and that intelligent people should therefore be free to decide the terms of their own contracts on the basis of their own perceived interests. But the story above is not the situation that raises the questions of just-cause dismissal. The story that raises that question is of the employee who took the job in the shop right out of high school, or in the office right out of college, and has now been a faithful employee for twenty-two years. A new boss comes in and decides that the productivity of the shop is not high enough, or the office doesn't look smart enough, so she fires most of the older employees to hire new young things that will look better and work harder. Should she be able to do that?

The point is, as McCall points out, that after twenty-odd years of work, it doesn't seem fair to be tossed out on your ear with only thirty days' notice, too late in your life to make a new career or, often, even to get another job, after all those years of making it to work through rain and snow, loyalty to the company, assuming that you'd be at the company working hard for the rest of your life. Contract or no contract, it is not in accordance with justice to reciprocate an effective lifetime of labor with a thirty-day termination. When your employer hired you year after year, wasn't he entering into some kind of super-contract with you, that you would always be there for him and he would always be there for you? If your boyfriend hangs out with you for twenty years, you can call yourself married in the common law, and you can get a financial award from the man if he walks out on you. Shouldn't employment be bound by the same presumptions?

Ask yourself, as you read these selections, what you will expect of an employer. If you're doing your job, shouldn't you be allowed to keep it? If times change and the employer wants something else, shouldn't you have the opportunity to upgrade yourself before your employer upgrades for you?

YES

Richard A. Epstein

In Defense of the Contract At Will

. . . **T**he persistent tension between private ordering and government regulation exists in virtually every area known to the law, and in none has that tension been more pronounced than in the law of employer and employee relations. During the last fifty years, the balance of power has shifted heavily in favor of direct public regulation, which has been thought strictly necessary to redress the perceived imbalance between the individual and the firm. In particular the employment relationship has been the subject of at least two major statutory revolutions. The first, which culminated in the passage of the National Labor Relations Act in 1935,[1] set the basic structure for collective bargaining that persists to the current time. The second, which is embodied in Title VII of the Civil Rights Act of 1964,[2] offers extensive protection to all individuals against discrimination on the basis of race, sex, religion, or national origin. The effect of these two statutes is so pervasive that it is easy to forget that, even after their passage, large portions of the employment relation remain subject to the traditional common law rules, which when all was said and done set their face in support of freedom of contract and the system of voluntary exchange. One manifestation of that position was the prominent place that the common law, especially as it developed in the nineteenth century, gave to the contract at will. The basic position was well set out in an oft-quoted passage from *Payne v. Western & Atlantic Railroad:*

> [M]en must be left, without interference to buy and sell where they please, and to discharge or retain employees at will for good cause or for no cause, or even for bad cause without thereby being guilty of an unlawful act *per se*. It is a right which an employee may exercise in the same way, to the same extent, for the same cause or want of cause as the employer.[3]

The survival of the contract at will, and the frequency of its use in private markets, might well be taken as a sign of its suitability for employment relations. But the contract at will has been in retreat even at common law, as the movement for public control of labor markets has now spilled over into the judicial arena. The judicial erosion of the older position has been spurred on by academic commentators, who have been almost unanimous in their condemnation of the at-will relationship, often treating it as an archaic relic that should be jettisoned along with other vestiges of nineteenth-century laissez-faire.[4] . . .

. . . The contract at will is not ideal for every employment relation. No court or legislature should ever command its use. Nonetheless, there are two ways in which the contract at will should be respected: one deals with entitlements against regulation and the other with presumptions in the event of contractual silence.

First, the parties should be permitted as of right to adopt this form of contract if they so desire. The principle behind this conclusion is that freedom of contract tends both to advance individual autonomy and to promote the efficient operation of labor markets.

Second, the contract at will should be respected as a rule of construction in response to the perennial question of gaps in contract language: what term should be implied in the absence of explicit agreement on the question of duration or grounds for termination? The applicable standard asks two familiar questions: what rule tends to lend predictability to litigation and to advance the joint interests of the parties?[5] On both these points I hope to show that the contract at will represents in most contexts the efficient solution to the employment relation. . . .

I. The Fairness of the Contract At Will

The first way to argue for the contract at will is to insist upon the importance of freedom of contract as an end in itself. Freedom of contract is an aspect of individual liberty, every bit as much as freedom of speech, or freedom in the selection of marriage partners or in the adoption of religious beliefs or affiliations. Just as it is regarded as prima facie unjust to abridge these liberties, so too is it presumptively unjust to abridge the economic liberties of individuals. The desire to make one's own choices about employment may be as strong as it is with respect to marriage or participation in religious activities, and it is doubtless more pervasive than the desire to participate in political activity. Indeed for most people, their own health and comfort, and that of their families, depend critically upon their ability to earn a living by entering the employment market. If government regulation is inappropriate for personal, religious, or political activities, then what makes it intrinsically desirable for employment relations?

It is one thing to set aside the occasional transaction that reflects only the momentary aberrations of particular parties who are overwhelmed by major personal and social dislocations. It is quite another to announce that a rule to which vast numbers of individuals adhere is so fundamentally corrupt that it does not deserve the minimum respect of the law. With employment contracts we are not dealing with the widow who has sold her inheritance for a song to a man with a thin mustache. Instead we are dealing with the routine stuff of ordinary life; people who are competent enough to marry, vote, and pray are not unable to protect themselves in their day-to-day business transactions.

Courts and legislatures have intervened so often in private contractual relations that it may seem almost quixotic to insist that they bear a heavy burden of justification every time they wish to substitute their own judgment for that of the immediate parties to the transactions. Yet it is hardly likely that remote public bodies have better information about individual preferences than the parties who hold them. This basic principle of autonomy, moreover, is not limited to some areas of individual conduct and wholly inapplicable to others. It covers all these activities as a piece and admits no ad hoc exceptions, but only principled limitations. . . .

II. The Utility of the Contract At Will

The strong fairness argument in favor of freedom of contract makes short work of the various for-cause and good-faith restrictions upon private contracts. Yet the argument is incomplete in several respects. In particular, it does not explain why the presumption in the case of silence should be in favor of the contract at will. Nor does it give a descriptive account of *why* the contract at will is so commonly found in all trades and professions. Nor does the argument meet on their own terms the concerns voiced most frequently by the critics of the contract at will. Thus, the commonplace belief today (at least outside the actual world of business) is that the contract at will is so unfair and one-sided that it cannot be the outcome of a rational set of bargaining processes any more than, to take the extreme case, a contract for total slavery. While we may not, the criticism continues, be able to observe them, defects in capacity at contract formation nonetheless must be present: the ban upon the contract at will is an effective way to reach abuses that are pervasive but difficult to detect, so that modest government interference only strengthens the operation of market forces.[6] . . .

In order to show the interaction of all relevant factors, it is useful to analyze a case in which the problem of bilateral control exists, but where the overtones of inequality of bargaining power are absent. The treatment of partnership relations is therefore very instructive because partners are generally social and economic equals between whom considerations of inequality of bargaining power, so evident in the debate over the contract at will, have no relevance. To be sure, the structural differences between partnership and employment contracts must be identified, but these will in the end explain why the at-will contract may make even greater sense in the employment context. . . .

The case for the contract at will is further strengthened by another feature common to contracts of this sort. The employer is often required either to give notice or to pay damages in lieu of notice; damages are traditionally equal to the wages that the employee would have earned during the notice period. These provisions for "severance pay" provide the worker with some protection against casual or hasty discharges, but they do not interfere with the powerful efficiency characteristics of the contract at will. First, lump-sum transfers do not require the introduction of any "for cause" requirement, which could be the source of expensive litigation. Second, because the sums are definite, they can be easily computed, so that administrative costs are minimized. Third, because the payments are unconditional, they do not create perverse incentives for the employee or heavy monitoring costs for the employer: the terminated employee will not be tempted to avoid gainful employment in order to run up his damages for wrongful discharge; the employer, for his part, will not have to monitor the post-termination behavior of the employee in order to guard against that very risk. Thus, provisions for severance pay can be used to give employees added protection against arbitrary discharge without sacrificing the advantages of a clean break between the parties. . . .

The contract at will is also a sensible private adaptation to the problem of imperfect information over time. In sharp contrast to the purchase of standard goods, an inspection of the job before acceptance is far less likely to guarantee its quality thereafter. The future is not clearly known. More important, employees, like employers, *know what they do not know.* They are not faced with a bolt from the blue, with an "unknown unknown." Rather they face a known unknown for which they can plan. The at-will contract is an essential part of that planning because it allows both sides to take a wait-and-see attitude to their relationship so that new and more accurate choices can be made on the strength of improved information. ("You can start Tuesday and we'll see how the job works out" is a highly intelligent response to uncertainty.) To be sure, employment relationships are more personal and hence often stormier than those that exist in financial markets, but that is no warrant for replacing the contract at will with a for-cause contract provision. The proper question is: will the shift in methods of control work a change for the benefit of both parties, or will it only make a difficult situation worse? . . .

1. *Administrative Costs.* There is one last way in which the contract at will has an enormous advantage over its rivals. It is very cheap to administer. Any effort to use a for-cause rule will in principle allow all, or at least a substantial fraction of, dismissals to generate litigation. Because motive will be a critical element in these cases, the chances of either side obtaining summary judgment will be negligible. Similarly, the broad modern rules of discovery will allow exploration into every aspect of the employment relation. Indeed, a little imagination will allow the plaintiff's lawyer to delve into the general employment policies of the firm, the treatment of similar cases, and a review of the individual file. The employer for his part will be able to examine every aspect of the employee's performance and personal life in order to bolster the case for dismissal. . . .

Conclusion

The recent trend toward expanding the legal remedies for wrongful discharge has been greeted with wide approval in judicial, academic, and popular circles. In this paper, I have argued that the modern trend rests in large measure upon a misunderstanding of the contractual processes and the ends served by the contract at will. No system of regulation can hope to match the benefits that the contract at will affords in employment relations. The flexibility afforded by the contract at will permits the ceaseless marginal adjustments that are necessary in any ongoing productive activity conducted, as all activities are, in conditions of technological and business change. The strength of the contract at will should not be judged by the occasional cases in which it is said to produce unfortunate results, but rather by the vast run of cases where it provides a sensible private response to the many and varied problems in labor contracting. All too often the case for a wrongful discharge doctrine rests upon the identification of possible employer abuses, as if they were all that mattered. But the proper goal is to find the set of comprehensive arrangements that will minimize the frequency and severity of abuses by employers and employees alike. Any effort to drive employer abuses to zero can only increase the difficulties inherent in the employment relation. Here, a full analysis of the relevant costs and benefits shows why the constant minor imperfections of the market, far from being a reason to oust private agreements, offer the most powerful reason for respecting them. The doctrine of wrongful discharge is the problem and not the solution. This is one of the many situations in which courts and legislatures should leave well enough alone.

Notes

1. Act of July 5, 1935, ch. 372, 49 Stat. 449 (codified as amended at 29 U.S.C. §§ 151–169 (1982)).

2. Pub. L. No. 88–352, 78 Stat. 253 (codified as amended at 42 U.S.C. §§ 2000e to 2000e–17 (1982)).

3. Payne v. Western & Atl. R.R., 81 Tenn. 507, 518–19 (1884), *overruled on other grounds,* Hutton v. Waters, 132 Tenn. 527, 544, 179 S.W. 134, 138 (1915). The passage continues as follows:

    > He may refuse to work for a man or company, that trades with any obnoxious person, or does other things which he dislikes. He may persuade his fellows and the employer may lose all his hands and be compelled to close his doors; or he may yield to the demand and withdraw his custom or cease his dealings, and the obnoxious person be thus injured or wrecked in business.

    81 Tenn. at 519. It should be noted that *Payne* did not itself involve the discharge of an employee for a bad reason or no reason at all. As the last two quoted sentences indicate, the question of the status of the contract arose obliquely, in a defamation suit by a merchant against a railroad. The railroad's yard master had posted a sign that read: "Any employee of this company on Chattanooga pay-roll who trades with L. Payne from this date will be discharged. Notify all in your department." *Payne,* 81 Tenn. at 510.
    The plaintiff Payne claimed that his business, which had been heavily dependent upon the trade of railroad workers, had thereby been ruined. The court held for the defendant on the grounds that (a) there was no defamation implicit in the announcement and (b) the employer's notice to its employees was within its rights because all the contracts with its workers were terminable at will. *Hutton* overruled *Payne,* not on the ground that contracts at will were against public policy, but on an abuse-of-rights theory according to which an employer cannot use his right to discharge employees for the sole purpose of harming third-party interests. The propriety of the *Hutton* theory is a difficult question, but my views tend toward those of the *Payne* court. *See* Epstein, *A Common Law for Labor Relations: A Critique of the New Deal Labor Legislation,* 92 YALE L.J. 1357, 1367–69, 1381 (1983).

4. *E.g.,* Blackburn, *Restricted Employer Discharge Rights: A Changing Concept of Employment at Will,* 17 AM. BUS. L.J. 467, 491–92 (1980); Blades, **Employment at Will** v. *Individual Freedom: On Limiting the Abusive Exercise of Employer Power,* 67 COLUM. L. REV. 1404, 1405–06, 1413–14, 1435 (1967); Blumrosen, *Employer Discipline: United States Report,* 18 RUTGERS L. REV. 428, 428–34 (1964); Feinman, *The Development of the **Employment at Will** Rule,*

2 AM. J. LEGAL HIST. 118, 131–35 (1976); Murg & Scharman, *Employment at Will: Do the Exceptions Overwhelm the Rule?*, 23 B.C.L. REV. 329, 338–40, 383–84 (1982); Peck, *Unjust Discharges from Employment: A Necessary Change in the Law,* 40 OHIO ST. L.J. 1, 1–10 (1979); Summers, *Individual Protection Against Unjust Dismissal: Time for a Statute,* 62 VA. L. REV. 481, 484 (1976); Weynard, *Present Status of Individual Employee Rights,* PROC. N.Y.U. 22D ANN. CONF. ON LAB. 171, 214–16 (1970); Note, *Guidelines for a Public Policy Exception to the Employment at Will Rule,* 13 CONN. L. REV. 617, 641–42 (1980); Note, *Protecting Employees at Will Against Wrongful Discharge: The Public Policy Exception,* 96 HARV. L. REV. 1931, 1931–35 (1983); Note, *Protecting At Will Employees Against Wrongful Discharge: The Duty to Terminate Only in Good Faith,* 93 HARV. L. REV. 1816, 1824–28 (1980) [hereinafter cited as Note, *Wrongful Discharge*]; Note, *A Common Law Action for the Abusively Discharged Employee,* 26 HASTINGS L.J. 1435, 1443–46 (1975); Note, *Implied Contract Rights to Job Security,* 26 STAN. L. REV. 335, 337–40 (1974); Note, *California's Controls on Employer Abuse of Employee Political Rights,* 22 STAN. L. REV. 1015, 1015–20 (1970).

5. The traditional rule has been codified under current California law: "An employment, having no specified term, may be terminated at the will of either party on notice to the other." CAL. LAB. CODE § 2922 (West 1971). Indeed, this should mean, as it now does, that where a contract speaks of "permanent" employment, the presumption should again be that the contract is terminable at will, for all that "permanent" connotes is the absence of any definite termination date. It does not imply one in which there is a lifetime engagement by either employer or employee, especially where none of the subsidiary terms for such a long-term relationship is identified by the parties. The proper rule of construction should be that the contract is terminable at will by either side.

6. Kronman, *Paternalism and the Law of Contracts,* 92 YALE L.J. 763, 777 (1983). The point is especially important in connection with the law of undue influence, where there is a long historical dispute over the relationship between the adequacy of consideration received and the procedural soundness of the underlying transaction. *See* Simpson, *The Horwitz Thesis and the History of Contracts,* 46 U. CHI. L. REV. 533, 561–80 (1979). Nonetheless, paternalistic explanations, whatever their force elsewhere, have little power in connection with employment relations. Indeed, if one thought it appropriate to restrict the powers of workers to make their own decisions during negotiations over the terms of employment, it might follow that restrictions on their right to participate in unions could be justified as well, for in forth instances workers have proven that they often need to be protected against their own folly.

John J. McCall

 **NO**

A Defense of Just Cause Dismissal Rules

I. Introduction

. . . Discussion of business practices often proceeds as if market principles are the only criteria needed in order to assess whether a practice is wise and reasonable. However, purely market-based analyses fail to acknowledge an indisputable fact: all markets operate in a social space that is defined by the moral values of the culture in which they are embedded. An example that illustrates this fact is the difference between U.S. and European practices governing the dismissal of individual employees. If we understand the legal differences between the U.S. and Europe, as well as management's response to those differences, we can see how differences in particular accepted moral norms give a different shape to the marketplace.

In dismissal policy, U.S. law follows a modified Employment at Will (EAW) approach. Corporations have wide discretion in both the procedures and reasons governing an individual employee's termination. For example, except for a handful of reasons identified as illegitimate by statute or past judicial precedent, employers may terminate for any or even for no reason. (Legally prohibited reasons include firings based on race or those in violation of clear public policy.) Employees who successfully press a wrongful discharge case through the courts may stand to recover very sizable awards (in the millions of dollars). However, winning a suit requires that the employee bear the initial burden of establishing that the discharge was for one of the identified illegitimate reasons.

Most European corporations operate in a much different legal environment. There, the legal systems usually mandate a Just Cause approach to dismissal. Under this approach, corporations must notify non-probationary employees of intent to dismiss. They are also significantly limited in the reasons the law will accept as adequate grounds for dismissal. Corporations must supply the employee with the reason for intended dismissal and the employee has the right to challenge the reason, usually in a pre-termination hearing and always before an external, easily accessible, and independent arbiter. Further, the initial burden of proof is on the employer. If, say, an employer wishes to dismiss an employee for poor productivity, the employer must have both clear, previously announced performance standards and evidence that the particular

From *Business Ethics Quarterly*, vol. 13, issue 2, April 2003, pp. 151–153, 161–175. Copyright © 2003 by Business Ethics Quarterly. Reprinted by permission.

employee has failed to meet those standards. If successful, aggrieved employees can receive remedies such as some small multiple of wages or re-instatement (though the latter happens in a very small minority of cases). This Just Cause approach places substantially greater limits on the power of European employers to dismiss a worker.

Legal differences, though, are only part of the difference between the U.S. and European dismissal policies. Interviews I have conducted with executives from across the European Community revealed a strong and almost universal moral endorsement of Just Cause requirements. Senior managers in a wide variety of firms (from small local manufacturers to mega-firms whose products are recognizable in the international marketplace, from large national retailers to EC-wide food distributors) expressed the same sentiment when responding to questions about their attitude towards legally mandated Just Cause: The employee deserves not only an in-house hearing but also an external "court of appeal" where he/she can challenge the reasons for dismissal. Management sometimes mentioned the difficulties encountered under such a system but also often described those difficulties as a cost of doing business, a cost that was required by the moral values to which they were committed.

This commitment seems to extend beyond the few managers that I interviewed. No concerted efforts by business specifically to repeal Just Cause dismissal rules has been part of recent European legal reform. There has been a significant change, however, in that the percentage of temporary and part-time work has grown substantially in Europe over the past decade as regulations governing fixed-term employment contracts have been relaxed. Some attribute this change to corporate desires for a more flexible labor law. There is some truth to this. However, we need to be careful in identifying just what flexibility employers desire. Is it, for example, in rules governing individual dismissal or in rules governing severance in cases of collective dismissals? My interviews found the latter to be more a source of complaint.

In the U.S., on the other hand, corporate lobbying efforts historically have resisted legally mandated Just Cause dismissal rules. Just Cause proposals have been introduced in the legislatures of any number of states over the last decades, but only in the case of Montana has the proposal been enacted into law. While quite a number of large U.S. corporations have adopted internal appeals mechanisms and have promised workers that they will be dismissed only for cause, those systems are voluntary and without the easily accessible external appeals mechanisms available to Europeans. (Non-unionized U.S. workers usually must make their case in the court system, a potentially expensive and daunting proposition.) And recently, many U.S. corporations, in a move to prevent costly wrongful firing suits, are requiring workers to sign waiver statements that indicate acceptance of Employment at Will. Even some corporations that have extensive, voluntarily adopted grievance systems have done this. In the U.S., notwithstanding the common cultural heritage with Western Europe, the traditional emphases on economic liberty, competition, and individualism have given a different shape to the labor market. It would appear, at least at first blush, that the U.S. and Europe have sharply different values that are reflected in how employees are treated.

What are the possible responses for ethicists confronted by circumstances where markets are shaped by such conflicting value assumptions? One response, of course, is to retreat into an easy moral and cultural relativism that views cultural differences as simply brute, irresolvable disagreement. That would be too easy, however. For while some disagreements between cultures may be incapable of rational resolution, others might be settled by careful argument. For instance, it may be that analysis could show that one of the conflicting opinions is inadequate even on the basis of its own foundational assumptions. It is always possible that a given particular normative commitment is not justified by more the fundamental principles of its own value system. To assume, without analysis, that any particular extant cultural norm is coherent with the basic values espoused by the culture is to assume too much.

Another response is available, then, for ethicists who wish to analyze cultural difference. It is to assess the degree to which the specific conflicting judgments of the cultures are (or are not) reasonable given their respective supporting arguments and underlying principles. In the pages that follow, I suggest that such an analysis will find fault with the arguments advanced in the U.S. against Just Cause. I want to argue that, given the underlying principles revealed by those arguments, the U.S. should drop its opposition and, instead, institute Just Cause protections for workers.

Typically, the arguments against Just Cause divide into two broad categories: those based on predicted dire social consequences and those based on individual right claims. For instance, the more *laissez faire* U.S approach is often defended as both a) more productive, and b) required by the rights to property and freedom of contract. I want to argue, however, that: 1) the empirical prediction of productivity losses with Just Cause is not supported by the evidence; 2) the economic arguments based on ideal market analyses are fraught with difficulties; and 3) the appeals to property or contract rights are insufficient to trump the claimed right of employees to freedom from arbitrary dismissal. Accordingly, I will propose that a Just Cause legal regime is preferable to the current U.S. model.

II. Consequences

Consequentialist objections to Just Cause themselves fall into two broad categories. One is associated with practical management and organizational behavior worries; the other comes from the ideal market analyses of law and economics theorists. Both types of argument are substantially speculative and I believe both have serious shortcomings. . . .

A. Market Arguments

. . . The claims that job security provisions are costly to workers themselves can also be challenged. In order to determine whether workers are better off with job security, we need to identify, in the words of a classic jazz tune, "Compared to What?" Even if, for the sake of argument, we accept that there is a wage premium for workers without job security under EAW rules (contrary to some suggestions above), we need to ask whether workers with job security under a legal EAW regime are economically worse off, not only than workers without job security in that EAW system, but also than workers under a Just Cause regime that grants job security as the initial entitlement (Hager, 1991). Under the latter approach, of course, it is management that must buy the right to terminate at will from employees. Once again, the judgment will likely be influenced by what the starting assumptions one makes about the distribution of entitlements.

The previously cited experimental evidence in Millon (1998) about the outcomes of parallel bargaining circumstances where entitlements were reversed is relevant here as well. The evidence cited concerning waivable employment default rules (rules that establish initial legal rules that the parties are free to negotiate around) showed that those persons favored by a default rule do better in negotiations than if the default rule were the opposite. Millon argues that this evidence indicates that workers both with and without job security under a job security default rule will be better off than workers employed at will under an EAW default rule.

Finally, Epstein's argument about the probability of error and the attendant possible harms has fatal flaws. His claim that employer abuse is improbable is discredited by problems noted above. The claim that unfairly dismissed but competent employees are unlikely to suffer serious harm may be an inaccurate description of potential employers' criteria of evaluation. There are reasons for suspecting that an employee who was dismissed, even unfairly, is permanently seen as suspect goods. Additionally, the ease with which even competent employees can find replacement work is overstated. Finally, his appeal to the potential damage to the corporation of large jury verdicts is a red herring, at least as an argument against Just Cause. For, recall that Just Cause policies typically give increased job security for employees in exchange for decreased corporate exposure to the "litigation lottery." For example, in the U.K. there was a limit of £11,000 on unfair dismissal awards (Donkin, 1994). Under Montana's Unfair Dismissal From Employment Act, the maximal award is four times earnings less what one could reasonably have been expected to earn since the termination (Bierman et al., 1993). The potential for large jury awards is irrelevant when assessing the costs of Just Cause.

The preceding theoretical market-based arguments against Just Cause thus fare no better than do those driven by practical management concern for worker productivity. In neither case is there a preponderance of argument to establish that Just Cause damages productivity. And so, these speculative concerns about the potential harmful consequences cannot lead to a rejection of Just Cause.

This final paragraph on the consequential arguments against Just Cause may be an appropriate place to note a tension between the two broad categories of consequential argument we have identified. The motivation argument claimed that workers needed to be motivated by fear of job loss. Such motivation can only be effective if job loss is perceived as both a real possibility and a serious harm. However, some market-based arguments claim that job security provisions are unnecessary and that unfairly dismissed employees are not seriously damaged. But these claims cannot both be true. For if the market already deters abuse, provides for job security, and minimizes the harm of unfair discharge, then the motivational argument loses all force since job loss is unlikely and not harmful. Alternatively, if, as I suspect is more likely, the motivational argument is correct in holding that workers see job loss as a serious harm, then that would disclose the absolute unreality of some of the law and economics objections to Just Cause.

We need now to move to a consideration of the rights based objections to Just Cause policies.

III. Rights

A. Rights Objections

Typically, rights arguments against Just Cause appeal to two members of the generally recognized pantheon of rights—property and freedom of contract (Werhane, 1985; Werhane and Radin, 1999).

Property rights are traditionally understood to involve an owner's entitlement to control goods in specific ways. Owners are entitled, among other things, to possess, to use, to benefit from, to dispose of, and to limit others' use of, benefit from, and access to the thing owned. If we take one's house or car as paradigmatic examples, ownership entitles one to deny access or use rights to others and to revoke previously granted access and use rights. Concretely, I have a right to control who enters my house and a right to ask any guest to leave. Opponents of Just Cause treat corporate property analogously. They argue that owners (or more usually, the agents of owners—managers) retain the right to deny employees further access to the work site, that is, to terminate employment. Legally mandated job security policies are thus unjust interferences with owners' property rights.

The second rights argument against Just Cause sees it as a violation of the right of free individuals to engage in voluntary exchanges with others. By prohibiting contracts with terms that specify employment at will, Just Cause policies interfere with persons' abilities to negotiate for themselves whatever contract provisions they find most desirable. For instance, under some Just Cause regimes, workers may be prohibited from choosing at will employment in exchange for greater income. As such, this second argument claims that Just Cause policies are unjust limits on market agents' freedoms of contract and association (Maitland, 1984; Narveson, 1992; Nozick, 1974). (This claim may not be true, of course. It is possible that Just Cause merely functions as the default interpretation when contracts are silent about dismissal terms, or it could make the job security entitlement one that is waivable by the right holder but only in exchange for at least a statutorily guaranteed minimum consideration.)

B. Method

These arguments are not easily dismissed. The rights they appeal to have powerful rhetorical force, especially in the U.S. But before we accept them as cogent objections, we need to clarify the circumstances of the debate. The debate over Just Cause is a case of conflicting right claims. Management and owners claim rights to property and freedom of contract. Workers claim conflicting rights to freedom from arbitrary and unfair discharge. It is true that the first two rights have existing recognition while, in the U.S. at least, the third is at best what Joel Feinberg calls a manifesto right, one claimed to be supported by good reasons but not yet socially sanctioned. However, its manifesto status is not a reason for allowing property and freedom of contract rights immediately to "trump" job security. For it may be that, on analysis, we decide that our current understanding of rights fails in not recognizing a right to job security.

A more reasonable method for resolving conflicts between rights claims must directly assess the merits of the competing claims. Moreover, a reasonable method will do more than consider the relative importance of the conflicting rights in some general and abstract way. Rather, resolving conflicts between rights requires us to focus on the particular cases where the conflict arises since the conflict between rights typically occurs in defined marginal areas. Recognizing job security rights, for example, will not interfere with conceptions of non-corporate property rights, nor will it impact other aspects of corporate property rights, such as the right freely to sell one's shares in the market.

We can satisfy these requirements for a reasonable assessment of rights conflicts if we ask two questions of each of the competing claims: 1) What are the justifying or foundational reasons for this right (why is it a right)? 2) What harm would be done to those underlying values if we recognized a conflicting right claim and thus marginally constrained the scope of a particular right? Here, for instance, we need to ask what are the foundations of property, freedom of contract, and job security rights, and what harm would be done to those respective values if we denied a right to job security and gave owners the right to terminate at will or, alternatively, if we denied owners that right and instituted a Just Cause policy.

C. Response to Property Objections

What are the foundations of property rights? There is a very clear historical tradition of argument justifying rights to private ownership of property (that is rights privately to control goods, to benefit from them, to exclude others from using them, etc). In the modern period, individual rights to possess property privately have three significant foundations: autonomy, fairness, and utility. First, private control over property has been presented as instrumentally advancing an owner's autonomy by providing her a secure base of material possessions that frees her from over-reliance on the decisions of others. Second, it has been upheld as the only approach that fairly rewards the effort expended or the risk assumed in a productive activity. Finally, it has been urged as providing incentive for people to work and invest, thus raising the total amount of economic production and, in turn, the net standard of living.

Interestingly, the claimed right of employees to job security can be argued to rest on the same grounds: Dismissals can be arbitrary (fairness).

They can damage the worker's ability to gain a wage, and thus make life both less happy (utility) and less within his/her control (autonomy). Workers who are no longer able to rely on secure income will have many significant life choices foreclosed (autonomy). Just Cause, then, can be defended on the same grounds of autonomy, fairness, and utility that are the traditional supports for private property rights.

What harm to these three underlying values would be done if corporations were required by Just Cause rules to extend job security to their workers? Would constraining the scope of an owner's right to deny access to corporate property hamper fairness or autonomy for owners? Would overall social utility be decreased if workers had a right to be free from arbitrary and unfair dismissal?

1. Fairness

First, consider the question about relative impacts on fairness. As was previously noted, property rights, and the associated rights to benefit from and to control goods, are historically justified, in part, on fairness grounds. But fairness, as the parent of any young child will attest, is often simultaneously both an overused and underdefined moral concept. Nonetheless, appeals to fairness can be more reasonably grounded than the simple assertion of "That's not fair!" if clear criteria are available. Criteria for assessing the fairness of a distribution, for example, typically will refer to three considerations: contribution, risk, and/or arbitrariness. Fair treatment requires that allocations of goods (and entitlements over them) be proportional to a person's contribution or risk assumed in creating the goods. It also requires that goods and benefits not be allocated to (or removed from) a person for arbitrary reasons. Since investors bear risk and make a contribution, risk and contribution are intuitively good, not arbitrary, moral reasons for allocating to them rights to privately control corporate property.

However, Just Cause rules do not erase owners' control over corporate property; they merely alter the right to control at the margins. Owners, even under Just Cause, still retain substantial control over assets—they can sell their shares freely; they can collectively dictate to management (with some limits) corporate policy, they retain rights to residual income, etc. This marginal decrease in an owner's control over property under Just Cause seems, whether on grounds of contribution or risk, insufficient to override an employee claim to job security because employees can also point to past contribution and risk as well. In addition, they can assert that they ought not be removed from employment without good cause, that is, for arbitrary reasons. Thus, recognizing an employee claim of dismissal only for good cause simply reduces the owner's marginal control. Moreover, evidence above also suggests that the Just Cause may have small impact on the owner's return/benefit.

Some, of course, will object to this analysis by arguing that the wages paid by the market assure fair treatment of workers (presumably because the wage rate is consensual). In this argument, so long as employees are paid for their past work, they have been fully compensated for their effort, risk, and contributions. They thus have no claim on future employment.

A number of points can be made in response to this argument that wages are full and fair compensation. The assumption (that past wages are adequate compensation for past contribution) may be challenged. Consider, for example, evidence from some analyses of internal labor markets (the labor market as it operates within a firm). These analyses claim that employees are paid less than their marginal contribution to the firm in the earlier years of their career and more than their marginal contribution later in their career (because wages and benefits tend to rise over time in a way that is not based purely on increased productivity). This deferred compensation of the early years is recouped only gradually. Employers can also use the deferral as a mechanism to reduce monitoring costs and to bind a worker to the firm, thus also reducing turnover costs (since a voluntary quit means foregoing deferred wages). Employers reap benefits from this aspect of the internal labor market. However, when an employee is fired without good cause, employers can also opportunistically and unfairly seize the promised future wages. (Blair, 1995; Lazear, 1992; Osterman, 1992; and Weiler, 1990) Thus, it is not necessarily the case that past wages can be assumed to be full and fair compensation for previous contribution. Terminating without good cause may instead be a paradigmatically unfair seizure.

However, even if we assume that the wage already paid is fair compensation for one's past risk and contribution, the issue here is whether terminating a relationship without good cause is acceptable on fairness grounds. It may not be if certain conditions are present. For example, even where pay for past contributions is morally adequate, it is possible that management actions created an expectation of future employment, expectations upon which employees relied. (See, for instance, Kim, 1999 and Singer, 1988, for discussions of ways in which reliance is elicited by particular firms and by economic institutions more broadly. It is worth noting that such reliance has historically been to the firm's advantage, allowing it to secure long term labor and to reduce monitoring costs.) What is fair can be a function not only of wages agreed to but also of promises made (explicitly and implicitly) and of consequent patterns of reliance.

Moreover, the fact that representations upon which employees relied were made by the firm's agents is not the only relevant consideration here. Such representations may be sufficient to raise questions of fairness but they are not necessary. Fairness norms can be implicated as well when, even without clear representations that created reliance, one party has come to depend in basic ways on a relationship or practice. When others crucially depend on and expect continued participation in a cooperative enterprise, it appears patently unfair to abruptly end the relationship without notice and without good reason, an idea we reflect in our common moral assessments of contexts as varied as marriage, housing, and access to traditional routes of public passage through private property. (See Singer, 1989 and Beerman and Singer, 1988 for extended discussions of how these moral assessments are reflected in much of our settled law in areas other than employment.) Thus, giving either party in an employment relationship the power to terminate the relationship without due process and good cause violates commonly held norms of fairness where there is long-standing dependence and expectation. It is especially unfair when one party has the preponderance of power.

The preceding point is merely an instance of a more general point: fair treatment in employment relationships often involves more than consensual monetary exchange. Employees clearly can be paid adequately but nonetheless treated unfairly if subjected to harassment or merely to ridicule. Thus there is clear need to consider when termination, even when past wages were adequate, is compatible with reasonable criteria of fairness. It is presumptively not when corporate actions create expectations of future employment. Dismissal without good reason from one's source of income, from one's social network, and from all the other goods associated with employment would seem to run afoul of this reliance criterion of fairness as well. So, even if past wages were adequate, it is still possible that a dismissal is unfair if it is based on arbitrary reasons.

We have, then, strong reasons for suggesting that firing without good cause, and thus removing a person from a source of income upon which he/she crucially depends, is inherently arbitrary and unfair. We need however to become more precise about what constitutes good cause and whether the set of reasons described as "good cause" is equivalent to the set of reasons accepted under Just Cause policies. It may, of course, be the case that Just Cause rules are more substantively restrictive than merely requiring that dismissal be for morally acceptable, good cause. We can evaluate whether this is the case by identifying the cases where Just Cause rules differ from EAW in the substantive grounds for permissible discharge. Recall that both Just Cause and EAW allow dismissal on grounds of inadequate performance, theft, absenteeism, etc. There are, though, at least three main scenarios where Just Cause is more restrictive than EAW. These are its prohibitions on dismissal for no reason, for personal reasons that are unrelated to productivity, and for the reason that there is a more productive replacement available for a currently adequate employee.

The first and second of these reasons seem to be paradigmatic examples of unfair treatment. Terminating a person's employment for no reason or for purely personal reasons is the epitome of arbitrary treatment. The third reason seems more defensible, however. Maintaining a current employee who merely performs adequately when there are others available who project to be superior performers certainly appears to damage the interests of the firm, as well as the interests of owners and, indeed, of other workers. Dismissing such an employee and replacing him with the predicted superior performer could, from that perspective, be argued as neither arbitrary nor unfair. Under this analysis, cause for termination exists whenever the firm possesses any competitive economic reason for dismissal.

We should reiterate here the previous point about the systemic effects of a firm's labor practices. Allowing the contemplated replacement policy is not a simple exchange of two workers, one for the other. Instead, it alters the entire system of employee relations. As noted above, it is not obvious that the potential gain of the more productive worker is greater than the opportunity costs inherent in adopting this replacement policy. Here, however, the question is not the productivity impact of the replacement but its fairness. At least two serious questions may be raised about the fairness of a policy that allows the replacement of an adequate performer whenever another is available who projects to be superior.

First, we need to ask which persons might be placed at greater risk by allowing such replacement. Arguably, allowing an adequate performer to be replaced would differentially impact more mature workers who might have both higher wages and declining productivity. The removal of longer-term employees whose loyalty has been a benefit to the firm in the past would seem to run counter to notions of fair treatment (for reasons of both contribution and expectation), and would seem to impose unreasonable demands for productivity over the course of a working career. A replacement policy of the sort under discussion here conjures the image of persons (human resources) being used up and disposed of.

Of course, the current American structure is not strict EAW but rather an EAW modified by numerous pieces of employment legislation, legislation that includes a prohibition on age discrimination. Thus, the fact that strict EAW might have this differential impact on mature workers is not to say that current U.S. legal standards would have this impact. This is true enough. But nonetheless, Just Cause would differ from even the modified U.S. version of EAW in that it places the burden of proof in termination on the employer rather than on the employee (as the U.S. law does). This fact is not insignificant given the substantial hurdles faced by plaintiffs under U.S. law and given the attitudinal sea change that would be indicated by adoption of Just Cause policy.

Second, and more importantly, allowing the replacement of an adequate performer has unacceptable implications for ideas about what corporations are entitled to. If we assume that a corporation has set reasonable standards of adequate performance, an open-ended policy permitting replacement of adequate performers essentially entails that employers can threaten dismissal unless ever-increasing productivity demands are satisfied. This demand for optimal, "110%" productivity goes beyond what any partner to an economic relationship is morally entitled. Employers are entitled to reasonable productivity and may morally threaten dismissal if a worker fails to meet that standard. Of course, a necessary condition for a reasonable demand is that a worker could meet it but being able to meet a demand is not sufficient to establish its reasonableness. For a demand to be reasonable, it must be one that can be met, not at any cost, but at a reasonable cost. That is, what is a reasonable demand must be seen in light of what we believe a decent human life to include. Demands that jeopardize goods that are constitutive of such a life are demands that are unreasonable. (Consider, from a wholly different context, Judith Thomson's (1971) analysis of what demands can reasonably be placed on a woman in order for her to avoid having to accept responsibility for pregnancy.) Workplace productivity demands that have seriously damaging impacts on family and social existence are, on any account of a decent human life, demands that are unreasonable. More generally, workplace demands that so exhaust a person's energy or time that other central aspects of life must be neglected are demands that go beyond what a corporation is reasonably entitled to. Given the unavoidable and central role that employment plays in contemporary life, a policy that allows employers to demand ever-increasing productivity under threat of dismissal is an unreasonable policy.

We have, then, grounds for believing that the set of morally good reasons for dismissal map on to that set of reasons for dismissal allowed under Just Cause rules. We can also see that some of the reasons for dismissal allowed under even the limited EAW of the U.S. are reasons that fall outside the set of morally good reasons. And, as argued above, firing without good reasons is arbitrary and, hence, unfair. Thus, the very considerations of fairness that are used in the American tradition to justify private property suggest that corporate property rights be limited by the adoption of Just Cause constraints on dismissal.

2. Autonomy

A private property right justified by appeal to autonomy seems a similarly unlikely candidate for overriding a right to be free from arbitrary dismissal. In Locke's original formulation of the argument, private property gave land-owners some autonomy because it conferred on them an economic independence, especially from the powers of the crown. In the contemporary environment, most workers have whatever measure of economic independence they possess, not from landed estates, but from the security of the income gained by selling their labor on the market. To the degree that income is at risk from job loss, then to that degree workers have lost independence. Arbitrary dismissal, therefore, can substantially damage the ability of a worker to control important aspects of his/her life. On the other hand, precluding arbitrary dismissal through a Just Cause policy does not seriously decrease the degree to which the share-holders' investment in stock provides for economic independence and, hence, does not impact the ability of investors to have control over their lives. (For a more complete version of this analysis of the relation between autonomy, property, and employee rights, see McCall, 2001.)

Of course, someone might argue that Just Cause policies decrease the owner's autonomy and independence because they would decrease value of the investment. That presupposes that productivity and/or profits will decline as a result of job security. As was noted above, that assumption has not been shown to be warranted. But even if stock value or investment income did marginally decline, proponents of job security could respond by arguing that owners are entitled not to maximal return but merely to returns compatible with a requirement to treat others fairly. An invocation of the preceding fairness argument, then, has the potential to blunt even the speculative concern that job security would decrease share value or return.

It should be noted that the preceding analyses have been assuming as a context a moderately large, publicly traded corporation. Analyzing the impact of Just Cause on fairness and autonomy might be different for smaller ventures or ones that are owned by individuals or small numbers of partners. Citibank and the mom and pop corner grocery are at different extremes and may require different policies in practice. Requiring the corner grocer, or for that matter a regular employer of a household worker, to follow the same dismissal procedures as Citibank may more seriously damage the employer's control over his/her life. There may then be an argument for limiting the scope of Just Cause policies to businesses over a certain threshold size. We need to be aware, however, that even in small firms, arbitrary dismissal can still have a devastating impact on the employee and his/her family. Perhaps some mandatory severance but without the procedural requirements would be in order even for the smaller employer. If that were a known requirement, it could be planned for and calculated into the total cost of a person's employment, just as employer Social Security payments already are.

3. Utility

The analysis of the impact of mandated job security on net utility is perhaps less clear, partly because projections about future social consequences are so speculative. But some have claimed, as we have seen, that job security requirements will lower return to investors (thus depressing investment and production), reduce productivity, lower wages for employees, and depress overall employment. A number of points have been made in rebuttal of these charges above. These will not be repeated here. As for the impact on total employment, Just Cause would seem to have little net effect. It does not commit employers to keep workers who are unproductive, nor does it require them to keep workers when there is a downturn in demand. Just Cause may have an impact on the care and speed with which firms select permanent employees but it should not affect total employment levels. (See a similar analysis even for the more costly requirements of severance and restrictions on layoffs in Abraham and Houseman, 1993 and 1994, as well as Houseman, 1990.)

An item to watch, however, is whether Just Cause will increase the incentive of companies to hire temporary workers in order to avoid the process requirements for discharging employees who have completed the probationary period. This would be a significant effect given the income, benefits, and security differences between permanent and temporary work. Recent revisions in European law might provide a test case for this; the evidence is still out. I suspect, moreover, that the evidence of increased use of temporary workers is not clearly due to Just Cause rather than to other, more expensive requirements attaching to treatment of fulltime employees (e.g., other benefits or layoff provisions).

Whether the wages of other workers would decline and thus have an impact on overall utility will depend on whether there really is a wage premium for workers employed at will. This may not be the case since Just Cause appears to have little impact on net corporate income and, therefore, little effect on the employers' wage bargaining stance. Moreover, the evidence cited by Millon (1998) and discussed above makes the assumption of a wage premium problematic. However, if there nonetheless *is* a wage premium and workers under Just Cause are precluded from gaining that premium (which of course would only occur under non-waivable Just Cause rules), a utilitarian justification of Just Cause will depend in part on the benefits and costs of job security to workers, and on the relative size of the employee populations interested respectively in security or the potentially greater income gained without security. Pursuit of these questions will be left for the next section's discussion of freedom of contract.

D. Response to the Freedom of Contract Argument

In order to assess the conflict between freedom of contract rights and rights to job security, we need to ask about the foundations of freedom of contract just as we have asked about the foundations of property and job security rights. Freedom of contract has been defended on grounds of utility in that each person, as best judge of his/her own interests, is also in the best position to optimize the satisfaction of those interests. Allowing each person in the competitive marketplace to determine which goods he/she desires and how much he/she is willing to pay for them will, it is claimed, maximize the net satisfaction of interests.

A second defense of freedom of contract is on grounds of individual autonomy in that freedom of contract will obviously allow persons more direct control over their lives than if the ability to negotiate one's own terms were restricted. For instance, some will argue that employees should have the freedom to choose the job rules they prefer rather than be forced by legal mandates to accept "benefits" they do not wish to have. (Compare Narveson's (1992) argument on mandated worker participation.)

Of course, our commitment to autonomy does not result in absolute freedom of contract, as those in favor of Just Cause will be quick to note. In employment law in particular, we already accept a myriad of limits on the power of parties to set the terms of contracts. Laws governing discrimination, workplace safety, minimum wage, and sexual harassment are just a few instances where we constrain both employers and employees in negotiating contract terms. Since freedom of contract is not equivalent to absolute freedom of contract, the argument against Just Cause is incomplete unless it can show that Just Cause limits are inappropriate while other limits are acceptable. (I do not mean to suggest that all current legal limits on contracts, or even all those just mentioned, must be accepted. Rather, the point is that if one accepts any limits on contracts then one needs to distinguish those from the limits one does not accept. I also take it that a position which rejects all limits is *prima facie* an unreasonable one.)

Some might respond that acceptable limits are ones that are needed to correct for clear market failures. But, the argument continues, there are no clear failures with respect to job security. We have already discussed in Section II the reasons for suspecting that market failures of knowledge, power, and mobility might explain the relative absence of job security provisions in U.S. contracts. To the degree that those points are telling, then this attempt fails to distinguish job security from other market correcting limits on contracts.

However, even if there are no market failures with respect to job security, the response is problematic for other reasons. Not every justifiable limit on freedom of contract exists merely to remedy market failure. It would be odd indeed to claim that Civil Rights protections against discrimination and sexual harassment are responses to classic market failures. Rather, it is more natural to see such laws as expressing the belief that jeopardizing a person's employment for these morally arbitrary reasons is degrading and simply wrong.

So, some limits on contract freedoms can be defended on grounds other than correction of market failures. This is true of job security protections as well. If we accept the preceding fairness arguments, we might use Just Cause limits on employment contracts to underscore social opposition to the serious, avoidable, and arbitrary harms caused by at-will dismissals. Or, if we modeled an autonomy argument on traditional utility analysis, we might construct a "net autonomy" case for Just Cause as follows. Workers dismissed without cause suffer at least temporary loss of income, the stress that comes with that and, in all probability, loss of seniority and firm specific investment. These harms are proportionally greater the more that the dismissal would impact one's future employment applications. All of these economic losses will have serious impacts on the real life choices available to the dismissed worker. There is significant impact, then, on autonomy. The limits caused by job security requirements on the autonomy of other workers who might wish to trade security for increased income are not nearly so great. They merely lose the (speculative) marginal wage increase that might be available under at-will contracts. Moreover, this loss is not a necessary consequence of Just Cause rules. It occurs only when those rules are mandated as un-waivable; they need not be. Constraining freedom of contract, then, might produce more net autonomy for workers than would a discharge at will rule.

So, job security protections may be a rational choice for society either because workers who want them are unable to negotiate for them successfully (the market failure explanation) or because we simply want, as part of a commitment to fairness, institutionally to express an opposition to dismissals without just cause, or because we believe such protections maximize net autonomy.

Finally, we should note the following with respect to utility claims. Some provision prohibiting firing without cause is one of the first demands of union contracts. It would be surprising if unorganized workers somehow desired job security less. More reasonable is the assumption that they desire it but have been unable to secure individually for themselves what organized workers have secured. If this is true and workers generally want security, then perhaps net satisfaction would be also increased by legally proscribed protections against unfair dismissal.

IV. Conclusion

A review of the objections to Just Cause, both on grounds of consequences and rights, reveals them to be seriously deficient. Most seriously, the very foundational values of the rights commonly used in the U.S. to oppose Just Cause suggest, instead, that job security should be pursued. Concerns for fairness and autonomy arguably ought to drive the U.S. toward Just Cause requirements rather than away from them. The American resistance to Just Cause seems unwarranted on its own grounds once one recognizes that the

American system of private property and freedom of contract depend on fairness and autonomy.

There is, however, a reason for resisting the introduction of Just Cause requirements that we have not yet addressed. It may be, despite the rhetoric, that Just Cause policies are simply ineffective at protecting workers from unfair dismissals. That is, while a Just Cause mechanism may be necessary for protecting workers, it may be that it alone is not sufficient. After all, most extant Just Cause policies place significant limits on the compensation available to employees when arbitrators judge them to have been unfairly dismissed. So, some might argue that current Just Cause policies cannot achieve their stated goals because they provide disincentives that are insufficient to deter arbitrary dismissals.

In fact, a survey of the Montana Bar Association completed in 1993 suggests that the Montana Wrongful Discharge from Employment Act may not adequately protect workers. More than half of the attorney respondents claimed that they personally declined to represent a plaintiff in a wrongful discharge suit. Most who said this cited as their reason the inadequate compensation available under the act given the complexity and hours involved in such suits. Perhaps more strikingly, a number of respondents reported that they believed that the act's reduction in liability for corporations had made some corporations more likely to discharge unfairly since they were no longer concerned about large damage awards (Bierman et al., 1993).

It might be that, since punishments under some extant Just Cause regimes, particularly in Montana and the U.K., are relatively small, employers who are not already committed to principles of fair dismissal will have little reason not to discharge without cause. If that is the case, what could the advantage of Just Cause be over the current American approach that at least poses the threat of the litigation lottery? There may still be two reasons for preferring Just Cause. First, a smaller, but highly probable, award for cases of unjust dismissal seems preferable to a litigation lottery where only some unfairly dismissed workers are even eligible for compensation (e.g., if they have been subject to the few unacceptable grounds enumerated under the U.S. approach). Unfairly dismissed workers are treated more equitably as a class and in relation to each other under Just Cause. And, the greater probability of an award might still serve as a disincentive for unjust termination, especially were the maximum awards more generous than those in the U.K. and Montana.

Second, the adoption of a Just Cause approach serves as a statement of public opposition to dismissal without cause. Law, in addition to its deterrence function, can also be a vehicle for educating and for creating or re-enforcing publicly important values. Law can serve the purpose of public notice of society's basic value commitments. The Civil Rights laws of the 1960s may be an historical example of how law can play a role in reshaping extant social norms that are incompatible with the espoused foundational values of the culture. So, while some currently extant Just Cause approaches may not alone guarantee protection for workers against unfair dismissal, properly constructed and publicized Just Cause laws can assist in readjusting a value system so that employers are more likely to be socialized to accept the principles of Just Cause.

This would be a benefit in that it would make American employment practice more adequately reflect the espoused foundational values of its own culture.

Precisely how any U.S. Just Cause protections ought to be codified requires more debate than is possible here. Three distinct possibilities suggest themselves. (See Sunstein, 2001 and 2002, Eastlund 2002, Millon 1998.) One is that Just Cause merely be made the default rule when employment contracts fail to specify dismissal rules. This approach would allow employers and employees to contract around the default rules by adopting specific alternate provisions in the employment contract. Another approach is to make Just Cause the default but also mandate that any opting out of the default rule will provide both for some specified minimum level of compensation and some specific remaining employment protection. A third option would be to follow the lead of most of the industrialized world and to mandate non-waivable Just Cause protections for workers in all firms exceeding a small minimum size. Which of these approaches fits best with the moral values underlying the modern American commitment to private property is a matter for further argument. That argument will have to wait for another article. However, even without that analysis, we can conclude that some Just Cause protections for employees have very strong presumptive support.

Note

I would like to thank George Brenkert for some helpful comments that made this paper more cogent and more clear. I would also like to hold him responsible for any serious argumentative gaffes—but I doubt I can get away with that.

Bibliography

Abraham, Katherine, and Susan Houseman. 1993. *Job Security in America*. Washington, D.C.: The Brookings Institute.

_____. 1994. "Does Employment Protection Inhibit Labor Market Flexibility?" In *Social Protection versus Economic Flexibility*. Rebecca Blank, ed. Chicago: University of Chicago Press.

Beerman, Jack, and William Singer. 1989. "Baseline Questions in Legal Reasoning: The Case of Property in Jobs." *Georgia Law Review* 23: 911.

Bierman, Leonard, et at. 1993. "Montana's Wrongful Discharge from Employment Act: The Views of the Montana Bar." *Montana Law Review* 54: 367.

Blair, Margaret M. 1995. *Ownership and Control: Rethinking Corporate Governance for the Twenty-First Century*. Washington, D.C.: The Brookings Institute.

Donkin, Richard. 1994. "Making Fairness Work." *The Financial Times,* Management Section. September 7, 1994, p. 12.

Dworkin, Ronald. 1977. *Taking Rights Seriously*. Cambridge, Mass.: Harvard University Press.

Eastlund, Cynthia. 2002. "How Wrong Are Employees about Their Rights, and Why Does it Matter?" *New York University Law Review* 77: 6.

Epstein, Richard. 1984. "In Defense of Contract at Will." *University of Chicago Law Review* 51: 947.

Hager, Mark. 1991. "The Emperor's Clothes Are Not Efficient." *American University Law Review* 41: 7.

Houseman, Susan. 1990. "The Equity and Efficiency of Job Security." In *New Developments in the Labor Market.* K. Abraham and R. McKersie, eds. Cambridge, Mass: MIT Press.

Kim, Pauline T. 1997. "Bargaining with Imperfect Information: A Study of Worker Perceptions of Legal Protection in an At-Will World." *Cornell Law Review* 83: 105.

_____. 1999. "Norms, Learning and Law: Exploring the Influences on Workers' Legal Knowledge." *University of Illinois Law Review* 1999: 447.

Lazear, Edward P. 1992. "Compensation, Productivity and the New Economics of Personnel." In *Research Frontiers in Industrial Relations and Human Resources.* D. Lewin et al., eds. Madison, Wis.: Industrial Relations Research Association.

Maitland, Ian. 1989. "Rights in the Workplace." *Journal of Business Ethics* 8: 951.

McCall, John J. 2001. "Employee Voice in Corporate Governance: A Defense of Strong Participation Rights." *Business Ethics Quarterly* 11: 1.

Millon, David. 1998. "Default Rules, Wealth Distribution and Corporate Law Reform." *University of Pennsylvania Law Review* 146: 975.

Narveson, Jan. 1992. "Democracy and Economic Rights." In *Economic Rights.* E. Paul et al., eds. Cambridge: Cambridge University Press.

Nozick, Robert. 1974. *Anarchy, State and Utopia.* New York, N.Y.: Basic Books.

Osterman, Paul. 1992. "Internal Labor Markets in a Changing Environment." In *Research Frontiers in Industrial Relations and Human Resources.* D. Lewin et al., eds. Madison, Wis.: Industrial Relations Research Association.

Singer, Joseph William. 1988. "The Reliance Interest in Property." *Stanford University Law Review* 40: 614.

Sunstein, Cass R. 2001. "Human Behavior and the Law of Work." *Virginia Law Review* 87: 205.

_____. 2002. "Switching the Default Rule." *New York University Law Review* 77: 106.

Thomson, Judith Jarvis. 1971. "In Defense of Abortion." *Philosophy and Public Affairs* 1: 1.

Weiler, Paul. 1990. *Governing the Workplace.* Cambridge, Mass.: Harvard University Press.

Werhane, Patricia. 1985. *Persons, Rights and Corporations.* Englewood Cliffs, N.J.: Prentice Hall.

Werhane, Patricia, and Tara Radin. 1999. "Employment at Will and Due Process." In *Ethical Issues in Business: A Philosophical Approach,* 6th ed. Thomas Donaldson and Patricia Werhane, eds. Upper Saddle River, N.J.: Prentice Hall.

POSTSCRIPT

Is "Employment-at-Will" Good Social Policy?

Ultimately, the rights of Americans are determined by law. In Europe, as McCall points out, the laws are much more protective of the employee than they are in the United States. Epstein and others claim that European-style laws lead to less "efficiency," that is, it is more difficult in Europe for investors to make money quickly. McCall and others argue that we should not be trampling fundamental notions of justice in order to achieve trifles more of efficiency. What do you think?

Suggested Reading

If the subject interests you, you might find interesting the following readings:

Cynthia Eastlund, "How Wrong Are Employees about Their Rights, and Why Does It Matter?" *New York University Law Review* 77:6, 2002.

Paul Weiler, *Governing the Workplace* (Boston: Harvard University Press, 1990).

Edward P. Lazear, "Compensation, Productivity and the New Economics of Personnel," in D. Lewin et al., eds., *Research Frontiers in Industrial Relations and Human Resources* (Madison, WI: Industrial Relations Research Association).

Thomas Donaldson and Thomas Dunfee, *Ties that Bind* (Boston: Harvard University Press, 1999).

ISSUE 12

Is CEO Compensation Justified by Performance?

YES: Ira T. Kay, from "Don't Mess with CEO Pay," *Across the Board* (January/February 2006)

NO: Edgar Woolard, Jr., from "CEOs Are Being Paid Too Much," *Across the Board* (January/February 2006)

ISSUE SUMMARY

"CEOs are paid a lot to face facts, however unpleasant," writes Geoffrey Colvin in *Fortune*, "so it's time they faced this one: The issue of their pay has finally landed on the national agenda and won't be leaving soon." He ticks off the sources of national discontent with the enormous sums (and stocks, etc.) paid to the corporate chiefs: that layoffs continue, that the lowest-paid workers advance only slowly, that Japanese CEOs are paid much less for much more productivity—but mostly, just that paying one person more money than he can ever spend on anything worthwhile for himself or his family, while the world's millions struggle, suffer, and starve, just seems to be wrong.

For the fifth edition of this text (1998), the "No" side of the debate was carried by John Cassidy's 1997 *New Yorker* article, "Gimme." Even then we could not use Colvin's 1992 article. For since Colvin wrote, Cassidy pointed out, chief executive compensation had gone much higher—by a factor of four for the average compensation, up to factors of fifteen and twenty for fortunate individuals. Colvin had clucked at annual compensation from $1.5 million to as high as $3 million a year; Cassidy observed compensation already at the $18 million and $20 million level. For the sixth edition of this text (2000), Cassidy no longer sufficed. Compensation had gone up to $60, $70, $90 million. The reason for the increase is clear enough—stock prices have gone up, shareholder wealth has increased enormously, and for reasons detailed in both of the selections that follow, shareholders wish to compensate management of their companies according to the increase in the price of the stock. Two questions arise immediately: first, if that's the system, what are we to do with compensation "insurance" policies that guarantee the same compensation no matter where the stock goes? Don't those arrangements kind of miss the point? And the second question is, is this right? The shareholders' interests legitimately dictate some aspects of corporate policy, and the salaries have been agreed upon by the legally appropriate parties, but if the result is substantially unjust, should not the people as a whole step in and rectify the situation?

Urgency was added to the issue in the recession that followed the election of George W. Bush in 2000. As the computers rolled in early April of 2001, stocks had undergone a sudden "correction," read, gone very far south, and shareholder wealth decreased substantially. Do we find CEO compensation humbly bowing to the facts of the ROI? Not in the least. "While typical investors lost 12 percent of their portfolios last year [2000], based on the Wilshire 5000 total market index, and profits for the Standard & Poor's 500 companies rose at less than half their pace in the 1990's, chief executives received an average 22 percent raise in salary and bonus." So we found out from a Special Report on Executive Pay from the *New York Times* on April 1, 2001 (First Business Page), and that was no April Fool. Not much had changed in 2005, according to *Forbes,* when Peter Cartwright of Calpine, which runs gas-fired power plants, took home (over the last six years) average annual compensation of $13 million while the ROI of the company over the same period was—7 percent. Average compensation over the last five years for Terry Semel of Yahoo came to $258.3 million; for Barry Diller of IAC/InterActiveCorp, $239.9 million; for William McGuire of UnitedHealth Group, $342.3 million. That last is cause for pause: your health care dollars and mine fuelled that income. We knew the doctors weren't getting rich; now we know who is. You see how these 2005 figures dwarfed those that so bothered Geoffrey Colvin.

This last year, amid accelerating layoffs, our CEOs have done well: the top five earners, led by Richard Fairbank of Capital One at $249.42 million in compensation last year, totaled $878.13 million. Possibly the worst effect of this is not the absolute amount of the compensation of the highest earners (think what the war in Iraq costs, for instance), but the envy effect on all the other CEOs—in Forbes's list of CEO salaries from greatest to least, we are to number 142 before we get below $10 million in annual compensation.

Should the American people step in and claim the right to set limits in the name of justice to the outsized amounts lavished on the fortunate sons of capitalism? That possibility is precisely what troubles Colvin. If CEOs will not regulate their own compensation, Congress and the SEC could surely step in and do a bit of regulating on their own. The prospect is not enticing to the business community. On the other hand, is this not exactly why we have government—so that when private motives get out of hand, the people as a whole can step in and defend their long-term interests?

Bear in mind, as you read the following selections, that the corporation was set up as a private enterprise, literally: a voluntary contract among investors to increase their wealth by legal means. But it is chartered and protected by the state, in the service of the state's long-term interest in a thriving economy. Adam Smith would be pleased; he argued that leaving investors to make money as best they could for their own selfish interests would best increase the welfare of the whole body of the people. The question that confronts us is, at what point do we conclude that the legal means set up for private parties to serve our interests by serving their own have failed in their purported effect and should be modified or revised? Or do we have any right to do that at this point? What do you think?

YES

Ira T. Kay

Don't Mess With CEO Pay

For years, headlines have seized on dramatic accounts of outrageous amounts earned by executives—often of failing companies—and the financial tragedy that can befall both shareholders and employees when CEOs line their own pockets at the organization's expense. Images of lavish executive life-styles are now engraved in the popular consciousness. The result: public support for political responses that include new regulatory measures and a long list of demands for greater shareholder or government control over executive compensation.

These images now overshadow the reality of thousands of successful companies with appropriately paid executives and conscientious boards. Instead, fresh accusations of CEOs collecting huge amounts of undeserved pay appear daily, fueling a full-blown mythology of a corporate America ruled by executive greed, fraud, and corruption.

This mythology consists of two related components: the myth of the failed pay-for-performance model and the myth of managerial power. The first myth hinges on the idea that the link between executive pay and corporate performance—if it ever existed—is irretrievably broken. The second myth accepts the idea of a failed pay-for-performance model and puts in its service the image of unchecked CEOs dominating subservient boards as the explanation for decisions resulting in excessive executive pay. The powerful combination of these two myths has captured newspaper headlines and shareholder agendas, regulatory attention and the public imagination.

This mythology has spilled over into the pages of *Across the Board*, where the September/October cover story links high levels of CEO pay to the country's growing income inequality and wonders why U.S. workers have not taken to the streets to protest "the blatant abuse of privilege" exercised by CEOs. In "The Revolution That Never Was," James Krohe Jr. manages to reference Marie Antoinette, Robespierre, Adam Smith, Alexis de Tocqueville, Andrew Jackson, Kim Jong II, Jack Welch, guerrilla warfare, "economic apartheid," and police brutality, in Selma, Ala., in an article that feeds virtually every conceivable element of the myth of executive pay and wonders why we have not yet witnessed calls for a revolution to quash the "financial frolics of today's corporate aristocrats."

In a very different *Across the Board* feature story published a few months earlier, the myth of managerial power finds support in an interview with one of the myth's creators, Harvard professor Lucian Bebchuk, who believes that the pay-for-performance model is broken and that executive control over boards is to blame. Bebchuk is a distinguished scholar who has significant insights into the executive-pay process, but he greatly overestimates the influence of managerial power in the boardroom and ignores empirical evidence that most companies still operate under an intact and explicit pay-for-performance model. And although he acknowledges in his interview with *ATB* editor A.J. Vogl that "American companies have been successful and executives deserve a great deal of credit," his arguments about managerial power run counter to the realities of this success.

Fueling the Fiction

These two articles, in different ways, contribute to what is now a dominant image of executives collecting unearned compensation and growing rich at the expense of shareholders, employees and the broader community. In recent years, dozens of reporters from business magazines and the major newspapers have called me and specifically asked for examples of companies in which CEOs received exorbitant compensation, approved by the board, while the company performed poorly. Not once have I been asked to comment on the vast majority of companies—those in which executives are appropriately rewarded for performance or in which boards have reduced compensation or even fired the CEO for poor performance.

I have spent hundreds of hours answering reporters' questions, providing extensive data and explaining the pay-for-performance model of executive compensation, but my efforts have had little impact: The resulting stories feature the same anecdotal reporting on those corporations for which the process has gone awry. The press accounts ignore solid research that shows that annual pay for most executives moves up and down significantly with the company's performance, both financial and stock-related. Corporate wrongdoings and outlandish executive pay packages make for lively headlines, but the reliance on purely anecdotal reporting and the highly prejudicial language adopted are a huge disservice to the companies, their executives and employees, investors, and the public. The likelihood of real economic damage to the U.S. economy grows daily.

For example, the mythology drives institutional investors and trade unions with the power to exert enormous pressure on regulators and executive and board practices. The California Public Employees' Retirement System—the nation's largest public pension fund—offers a typical example in its Nov. 15, 2004, announcement of a new campaign to rein in "abusive compensation practices in corporate America and hold directors and compensation committees more accountable for their actions."

The AFL-CIO's website offers another example of the claim that managerial power has destroyed the efficacy of the pay-for-performance model: "Each year, shocking new examples of CEO pay greed are made public. Investors are concerned not just about the growing size of executive compensation packages, but the fact that CEO pay levels show little apparent relationship to corporate profits, stock prices or executive performance. How do CEOs do it? For years, executives have relied on their shareholders to be passive absentee owners. CEOs have rigged their own compensation packages by packing their boards with conflicted or negligent directors."

The ROI of the CEO

As with all modern myths, there's a grain of truth in all the assumptions and newspaper stories. The myths of managerial power and of the failed pay-for-performance model find touchstones in real examples of companies where CEOs have collected huge sums in cash compensation and stock options while shareholder returns declined. (You know the names—there's no need to mention them again here.) Cases of overstated profits or even outright fraud have fueled the idea that executives regularly manipulate the measures of performance to justify higher pay while boards default on their oversight responsibilities. The ability of executives to time the exercise of their stock options and collect additional pay through covert means has worsened perceptions of the situation both within and outside of the world of business.

These exceptions in executive pay practices, however, are now commonly mistaken for the rule. And as Krohe's article demonstrates, highly paid CEOs have become the new whipping boys for social critics concerned about the general rise in income inequality and other broad socioeconomic problems. Never mind that these same CEOs stand at the center of a corporate model that has generated millions of jobs and trillions of dollars in shareholder earnings. Worse, using CEOs as scapegoats distracts from the real causes of and possible solutions for inequality.

The primary determinant of CEO pay is the same force that sets pay for all Americans: relatively free—if somewhat imperfect—labor markets, in which companies offer the levels of compensation necessary to attract and retain the employees who generate value for shareholders. Part of that pay for most executives consists of stock-based incentives. A 2003 study by Brian J. Hall and Kevin J. Murphy shows that the ratio of total CEO compensation to production workers' average earnings closely follows the Dow Jones Industrial Average. When the Dow soars, the gap between executive and non-executive compensation widens. The problem, it seems, is not that CEOs receive too much performance-driven, stock-based compensation, but that non-executives receive too little.

The key question is not the actual dollar amount paid to a CEO in total compensation or whether that amount represents a high multiple of pay of the average worker's salary but, rather, whether that CEO creates an adequate return on the company's investment in executive compensation. In virtually every area of business, directors routinely evaluate and adjust the amounts that companies invest in all inputs, and shareholders directly or indirectly endorse or challenge those decisions. Executive pay is no different.

Hard Realities

The corporate scandals of recent years laid bare the inner workings of a handful of public companies where, inarguably, the process for setting executive pay violated not only the principle of pay-for-performance but the extensive set of laws and regulations governing executive pay practices and the role of the board. But while I condemn illegal actions and criticize boards that reward executives who fail to produce positive financial results, I know that the vast majority of U.S. corporations do much better by their shareholders and the public. I have worked directly with more than a thousand publicly traded companies in the United States and attended thousands of compensation-committee meetings, and I have *never* witnessed board members straining to find a way to pay an executive more than he is worth.

In addition, at Watson Wyatt I work with a team of experts that has conducted extensive research at fifteen hundred of America's largest corporations and tracked the relationship between these pay practices and corporate performance over almost twenty years. In evaluating thousands of companies annually, yielding nearly twenty thousand "company years" of data, and pooling cross-sectional company data over multiple years, we have discovered that for both most companies and the "typical" company, there is substantial pay-for-performance sensitivity. That is, high performance generates high pay for executives and low performance generates low pay. Numerous empirical academic studies support our conclusions.

Our empirical evidence and evidence from other studies have produced the following key findings:

1. Executive pay is unquestionably high relative to low-level corporate positions, and it has risen dramatically over the past ten to fifteen years, faster than inflation and faster than average employee pay. But executive compensation generally tracks total returns to shareholders—even including the recent rise in pay.
2. Executive stock ownership has risen dramatically over the past ten to fifteen years. High levels of CEO stock ownership are correlated with and most likely the cause of companies' high financial and stock-market performance.
3. Executives are paid commensurate with the skills and talents that they bring to the organization. Underperforming executives routinely receive pay reductions or are terminated—far more often than press accounts imply.
4. CEOs who are recruited from outside a company and have little influence over its board receive compensation that is competitive with and often higher than the pay levels of CEOs who are promoted from within the company.
5. At the vast majority of companies, even extraordinarily high levels of CEO compensation represent a tiny fraction of the total value created by the corporation under that CEO's leadership. (Watson Wyatt has found that U.S. executives receive approximately 1 percent of the net income generated by the corporations they manage.)

Well-run companies, it bears pointing out, produce significant shareholder returns and job security for millions of workers.

Extensive research demonstrates a high and positive correlation between executive pay and corporate performance. For example, high levels of executive stock ownership in 2000, created primarily through stock-option awards, correlated with higher stock-market valuation and long-term earnings per share over the subsequent five-year period. In general, high-performing companies are led by highly paid executives—with pay-for-performance in full effect. Executives at low-performing companies receive lower amounts of pay. Reams of data from other studies confirm these correlations.

Why CEOs Are Worth the Money

The huge gap between the realities of executive pay and the now-dominant mythology surrounding it has become even more evident in recent years. Empirical studies show that executive compensation has closely tracked corporate performance: Pay rose during the boom years of the 1990s, when U.S. corporations generated huge returns, declined during the 2001–03 profit slowdown, and increased in 2004 as profits improved. The myth of excessive executive pay continued to gain power, however, even as concrete, well-documented financial realities defied it.

The blind outrage over executive pay climbed even during the slow-down, as compensation dropped drastically. During this same period, in the aftermath of the corporate scandals, Congress and the U.S. regulatory agencies instituted far-reaching reforms in corporate governance and board composition, and companies spent millions to improve their governance and transparency. But the critics of executive pay and managerial power were only encouraged to raise their voices.

It might surprise those critics to learn that CEOs are not interchangeable and not chosen by lot; they are an extremely important asset to their companies and generally represent an excellent investment. The relative scarcity of CEO talent is manifested in many ways, including the frenetic behavior of boards charged with filling the top position when a CEO retires or departs. CEOs have significant, legitimate, market-driven bargaining power, and in pay negotiations, they use that power to obtain pay commensurate with their skills. Boards, as they should, use their own bargaining power to retain talent and maximize returns to company shareholders.

Boards understand the imperative of finding an excellent CEO and are willing to risk millions of dollars to secure the right talent. Their behavior is not only understandable but necessary to secure the company's future success. Any influence that CEOs might have over their directors is modest in comparison to the financial risk that CEOs assume when they leave other prospects and take on the extraordinarily difficult task of managing a major corporation, with a substantial portion of their short- and long-term compensation contingent on the organization's financial success.

Lucian Bebchuk and other critics underestimate the financial risk entailed in executive positions when they cite executives' large severance packages, derided as "golden parachutes." Top executive talent expects and can command financial protections commensurate with the level of risk they assume. Like any other element of compensation, boards should and generally do evaluate severance agreements as part of the package they create to attract and retain talent. In recent years, boards have become more aware of the damage done when executive benefits and perquisites are excessive and not aligned with non-executive programs, and are now reining in these elements.

Properly designed pay opportunities drive superior corporate performance and secure it for the future. And most importantly, many economists argue, the U.S. model of executive compensation is a significant source of competitive advantage for the nation's economy, driving higher productivity, profits, and stock prices.

Resetting the Debate

Companies design executive pay programs to accomplish the classic goals of any human-capital program. First, they must attract, retain, and motivate their human capital to perform at the highest levels. The motivational factor is the most important, because it addresses the question of how a company achieves the greatest return on its human-capital investment and rewards executives for making the right decisions to drive shareholder value. Incentive-pay and pay-at-risk programs are particularly effective, especially at the top of the house, in achieving this motivation goal.

Clearly, there are exceptions to the motivational element—base salaries, pensions, and other benefits, for example—that are more closely tied to retention goals and are an essential part of creating a balanced portfolio for the employee. The portfolio as a whole must address the need for income and security and the opportunity for creating significant asset appreciation.

A long list of pressures, including institutional-investor pushback, accounting changes, SEC investigations, and scrutiny from labor unions and the media, are forcing companies to rethink their executive-compensation programs, especially their stock-based incentives. The key now is to address the real problems in executive compensation without sacrificing the performance-based model and the huge returns that it has generated. Boards are struggling to achieve greater transparency and more rigorous execution of their pay practices—a positive move for all parties involved.

The real threat to U.S. economic growth, job creation, and higher living standards now comes from regulatory overreach as proponents of the mythology reject market forces and continue to push for government and institutional control over executive pay. To the extent that the mythology now surrounding executive pay leads to a rejection of the pay-for-performance model and restrictions on the risk-and-reward structure for setting executive compensation, American corporate performance will suffer.

There will be more pressure on boards to effectively reduce executive pay. This may meet the social desires of some constituents, but it will almost surely cause economic decline, for companies and the U.S. economy. We will see higher executive turnover and less talent in the executive suite as the most qualified job candidates move into other professions, as we saw in the 1970s, when top candidates moved into investment banking, venture-capital firms, and consulting, and corporate performance suffered as a result.

Our research demonstrates that aligning pay plans, incentive opportunities, and performance measures throughout an organization is key to financial success. Alignment means that executives and non-executives alike have the opportunity to increase their pay through performance-based incentives. As new regulations make it more difficult to execute the stock-based elements of the pay-for-performance model, for example, by reducing broad-based stock options, we will see even less alignment between executives' compensation and the pay packages of the rank-and-file. We are already witnessing the unintended consequences of the new requirement for stock-option expensing as companies cut the broad-based stock-option plans that have benefited millions of workers and given them a direct stake in the financial success of the companies for which they work.

Instead of changing executive pay plans to make them more like pay plans for employees, we should be reshaping employee pay to infuse it with the same incentives that drive performance in the company's upper ranks. A top-down regulatory approach to alignment will only damage the entire market-based, performance-management process that has worked so well for most companies and the economy as a whole. Instead of placing artificial limits on executive pay, we should focus squarely on increasing performance incentives and stock ownership for both executive and non-executive employees and rewarding high performers throughout the organization, from top to bottom. Within the context of a free-market economy, equal opportunity—not income equality by fiat—is the goal.

The short answer to James Krohe's question of why high levels of executive pay have not sparked a worker revolution is that the fundamental model works too well. Workers vote to support that model every day when they show up for work, perform well, and rely on corporate leadership to pursue a viable plan for meeting payroll and funding employee benefits. Shareholders vote to support the model every time they purchase shares or defeat one of the dozens of proposals submitted in recent years to curb executive compensation. Rejecting the pay-for-performance model for executive compensation means returning to the world of the CEO as caretaker. And caretakers—as shown by both evidence and common sense—do not create high value for shareholders or jobs for employees.

In some ways, the decidedly negative attention focused on executive pay has increased the pressure that executives, board members, HR staffs, and compensation consultants all feel when they enter into discussions about the most effective methods for tying pay to performance and ensuring the company's success. The managerial-power argument has contributed to meaningful discussions about corporate governance and raised the level of dialogue in boardrooms. These are positive developments.

When the argument is blown into mythological proportions, however, it skews thinking about the realities of corporate behavior and leads to fundamental misunderstandings about executives, their pay levels, and their role in building successful companies and a flourishing economy. Consequently, the mythology now surrounding executive compensation leads many to reject a pay model that works well and is critical to ongoing growth at both the corporate and the national economic level. We need to address excesses in executive pay without abandoning the core model, and to return the debate to a rational, informed discussion. And we can safely leave Marie Antoinette out of it.

Edgar Woolard, Jr.  **NO**

CEOs Are Being Paid Too Much

There's a major concern out there for all of us. I personally am extremely saddened by the loss of the respect that this country's corporate leaders have experienced. We've had a double blow in the last ten years or so. The first one we know way too much about—the fraud at Enron, Tyco, Adelphia, WorldCom, and many others.

The CEOs say there were a few rotten apples in that barrel, and maybe that's the answer—but there are a hell of lot more rotten apples than I would have ever guessed. But that's just the base of one of the issues that has eroded the trust and confidence in American business leaders.

The second one is the perception of excess compensation received by CEOs getting worse year by year. And if directors agree, they can be the leaders in making a very important change. I'd like to deal with it by describing several myths about compensation and trying to undermine them.

Myth #1: CEO Pay by Competition

The first is the myth that CEO pay is driven by competition—and to that I say "bull." CEO pay is driven today primarily by outside consultant surveys, and by the fact that many board members have bought into the concept that your CEO has to be at least in the top half, and maybe in the top quartile. So we have the "ratchet, ratchet, ratchet" concept. We all understand it well enough to know that if everybody is trying to be in the top half, everybody is going to get a hefty increase every year. If Bill and Sally get an increase in their total compensation, I have to get an increase so that I will stay in the top half.

How can we change that?

In 1990, we addressed this issue at DuPont. I became CEO in 1989, and I was concerned about what was evident even then. A 1989 *Business Week* article talked about executive pay—who makes the most and are they worth it: Michael Eisner, $40 million in 1988; Ross Johnson, $20 million; and others. I don't know Eisner, but I know that even fifteen years later he's one of the most criticized CEOs in the country.

What we did at DuPont was go to a simple concept: internal pay equity. I went to the board and the compensation committee and said, "We're going to look at the people who run the businesses, who make decisions on prices and new products with guidance from the CEO—the executive vice presidents—and we're going to set the limit of what a CEO in this company can be paid at 1.5 times the pay rate for the executive vice president—50 percent."

That to me seemed equitable. It had been anywhere from 30 to 50 percent in the past. I said, "Let's set it at 50 percent, and we're not going to chase the surveys." And this is the way DuPont has done it ever since. I think we have tweaked it up a little bit since then, but using a multiple still is the right way to go.

Board members can do this by suggesting that the HR and compensation people look at what's happened to internal pay equity, and seriously consider going in that direction. That will solve this problem in a great way.

Myth #2: Compensation Committees Are Independent

I give a "double bull" to this one. It could be that committees are becoming more independent, but over the last fifteen years they certainly haven't been.

Let me describe how it works: The compensation committee talks to an outside consultant who has surveys that you could drive a truck through and that support paying anything you want to pay. The consultant talks to the HR vice president, who talks to the CEO. The CEO says what he'd like to receive—enough so he will be "respected by his peers." It gets to the HR person, who tells the consultant, and the CEO gets what he's implied he deserves. The members of the compensation committee are happy that they're independent, the HR person is happy, the CEO is happy, and the consultant gets invited back next year.

There are two ways to change that as well. Here's the first one. When John Reed came back to the New York Stock Exchange to try to clean up the mess after Dick Grasso, he made the decision—which I admire him for—that the board was going to have its own outside consultant, one who was not going to be allowed to talk to internal people—not to the HR vice president, not to the CEO.

I'm the head of the comp committee at the NYSE, and when I talk with our outside consultant, he gives us his ideas of what he thinks the pay package ought to be. Then, with the consultant there, I talk to the compensation committee, and we make a decision. I talk to the HR vice president to see if he has any other thoughts, but the committee is totally independent.

The other way to change things is to truly insist on pay-for-performance, which everyone likes to talk about but no one does. Boards pay everybody in the top quartile whether they have good performance or bad performance—or even if they're about to be fired.

Well, I was on a board fifteen years ago, and four CEOs were on the compensation committee, and for two consecutive years, we gave the CEO and the executives there no bonus, no salary increase, and modest stock options, because their performance was lousy those years. After that, they did extremely well, and we paid them extremely well. That's how pay-for-performance should work.

Myth #3: Look How Much Wealth I Created

This one is really a joke. It was born in the 1980s and '90s during the stock-market bubble, when all CEOs were beating their chest about how much wealth they were creating for shareholders. And I'd look to the king, Jack Welch. Jack's the best CEO of the last fifty years, and I've told him this. But he likes to say, "I created $400 billion worth of wealth." No, Jack—no, you didn't. He said that when GE's stock was at 60, but when the bubble burst it went to 30, and it's in the low 30s now. So he created $150 to $200 billion.

But besides the actual figure, there are two things wrong with his claim. Now, I don't care how much money Jack Welch made. God bless him; I think he's terrific. But what did it do? It set a new level for CEO pay based on the stock-market bubble; all the other CEOs were saying, "Look how much wealth I created."

So you've got this more recent high level of executive pay, and then you've got the ratcheting effect in the system. Those things have to change.

Myth #4: Severance for Failing

The last one is the worst of all. Any directors who agree to give these huge severance pay packages to CEOs who fail—Philip Purcell of Morgan Stanley got $114 million, Carly Fiorina of Hewlett-Packard got $20 million—why are you doing that? No one else gets paid excessively when they fail. They get fired; they get fair severance.

All of this is killing the image of CEOs and corporate executives. When it comes to our image, we're in the league with lawyers and politicians. I don't want to be there, and I don't think you do either. We need the respect of our employees and the general public. And there's a lot of skepticism about leaders in politics and in churches and in the military—but we can't have it in the business community, because we're the backbone of the market system that has made this country great and created so many opportunities for people. We can't be seen as either dishonest or greedy.

What can you do about it?

Some of you CEOs need to show leadership and say, "We're going to do internal pay equity." It's easy to get the data, and then you can decide what you think is fair and how much you think the CEO contributes versus the other business leaders who make their companies so strong.

Compensation committees need to seriously consider implementing internal pay equity. Pay only for outstanding performance. Quit giving people money just because Bill and Sally are getting it. Consider going to an independent consultant that deals only with the board while you deal with HR and the CEO.

Last, take a look at stock-option packages. Not just for one year but the mega-grants that built up in the 1980s and '90s. If you've given huge stock-option packages for the last five years, look at their value. There's nothing in the Bible that says that you have to give increased stock options every year. Give a smaller grant; give a different kind of grant; put some kind of limits on.

There are many ways to do it, but it's important to get the system back under control. It's important for our image, for our reputation, for integrity, for trust, and for our leadership in this country.

POSTSCRIPT

Is CEO Compensation Justified by Performance?

In 1992, when Geoffrey Colvin wrote the article bringing the problem of CEO compensation to public attention, he was worried about the country's perception of annual outlays of $1.7 million average total CEO compensation for almost 300 large companies, with pay going up to a whopping $3.2 million annually for the really big companies. By 1995, the CEO of a multibillion-dollar company received an average of $4.37 million in compensation, up 23 percent from 1994. And it got worse from there, with 1996 figures going through the roof: how on earth could Jack Welch, CEO of General Electric, spend the $21.4 million in salary and performance bonuses (and about $18 million in stock options) that he received in 1996, or Green Tree Financial Corporation's Lawrence Coss spend his $102.4 million in salary and bonus (plus stock options worth at least $38 million)? The Business Section of *The New York Times* at the end of 1997 glowed with projected bonuses of $11 billion for Wall Street that year—that was over and above salary, and before stock options. Two years later, Jack Welch was pulling in $68 million. As per the introduction to this issue, the amounts then tripled, quadrupled, into amounts per individual that dwarf the annual health budgets of most of the world. The situation is not correcting itself.

The political impact of these salaries is muted for the present, probably due to the failure of the American left, or liberal political orientation, to find a powerful spokesperson who might gain the confidence of the American people. The moral dimensions of the problem have not changed since the days of the prophet Amos of the Hebrew Scriptures: What right have the rich to enjoy their warm palaces and mansions, dining plentifully on the best food from all the world, while the poor suffer from hunger and cold? But the political dimensions are volatile, and dependent upon the rest of the system to provide context and opportunity. This issue will be with us for a while.

Suggested Reading

For further information on this subject, look into the following:

The Bible: Books of Amos and Hosea, Gospel according to Matthew.

AP dispatch, April 21, Cleveland. "Welch Defends Pay: Ratio Proposal Rejected by Shareholders," *Connecticut Post*, Thursday, April 22, 1999, C1-C2.

Thomas A. Stewart, "CEO Pay: Mom Wouldn't Approve," *Fortune*, vol. 135 (March 31, 1997), pp. 119-20.

Mike Maharry, "AFL-CIO Launches Web Site to Expose CEO Pay Levels." *The New Tribune*, Tacoma, Washington (April 11, 1997).

The New York Times Special Report on Executive Pay, First Business Page (April 1, 2001).

Peter Truell, "Another Year, Another Bundle: Billions in Bonuses Are Expected to Fall on Wall Street," *The New York Times*, Business Day (December 5, 1997), pp. D1-4.

John A. Byrne, "Gross Compensation?" *Business Week* (March 18, 1996), pp. 32–33.

Jack Lederer and Carl R. Weinberg, "CEO Compensation: Share the Wealth," *Chief Executive*, vol. 116, (September 1996), pp. 30–47.

Dana Wechsler Linden and Vicki Contavespi, "Incentivize Me, Please," *Forbes* (May 27, 1991), pp. 208–12.

Frederick Schmitt, "Study Finds CEO Salaries Tracking Performance," *National Underwriter* (October 21, 1996), p. 48.

Peter Passell, "A Theory of Capitalism: Lonely, and Rich at the Top," *The New York Times* (August 27, 1995), p. E5.

Jean McGuire, Sandra Dow and Kamal Argheyd, "CEO Incentives and Corporate Social Performance," *Journal of Business Ethics,* vol. 45, no. 4 (July 2003).

Internet References . . .

Advertising World

Advertising World, maintained by the Department of Advertising at the University of Texas at Austin, links to numerous sites on marketing and advertising. Among the many indexed topics are ethics and self-regulation, consumer interest, public relations, and market research.

http://advertising.utexas.edu/world/

Overlawyered.com

Overlawyered.com explores an American legal system that too often turns litigation into a weapon against guilty and innocent alike, erodes individual responsibility, rewards sharp practice, enriches its participants at the public's expense, and resists even modest efforts at reform and accountability. This page focuses on litigation over auto safety.

http://overlawyered.com/topics/auto.html

The Pew Initiative on Food and Biotechnology

The Pew Initiative on Food and Biotechnology was established as an independent and objective source of information that encourages research and debate on agricultural biotechnology. It is the purpose of this site to provide a resource that would enable consumers as well as policymakers to make their own informed decisions on the subject.

http://pewagbiotech.org

Consumer Issues

*W*hat *does the customer have a right to expect from the maker of the products that he buys? The answer, essentially, is quality and honesty. It sounds simple, but somehow we cannot be sure that the manufacturers are giving us good products and the salesmen are telling the truth about them; the controversies have never ceased.*

- Are Marketing and Advertising Fundamentally Exploitative?

- Is Direct-to-Consumer Advertising of Pharmaceuticals Bad for Our Health?

- Was Ford to Blame in the Pinto Case?

- Should We Require Labeling of Genetically Modified Food?

ISSUE 13

Are Marketing and Advertising Fundamentally Exploitative?

YES: John P. Foley, from "Ethics in Advertising: A Look at the Report of the Pontifical Council for Social Communications," *Journal of Public Policy & Marketing* (Fall 1998)

NO: Gene R. Laczniak, from "Reflections on the 1997 Vatican Statements Regarding Ethics in Advertising," *Journal of Public Policy & Marketing* (Fall 1998)

ISSUE SUMMARY

YES: John Foley summarizes and comments on the report of The Pontifical Council for Social Communications (1997), which charges that advertising can be deceptive, improperly influential on media editorial policy, and often promotes a lifestyle based on unbridled consumption.

NO: Laczniak points out that many of the document's claims are overstated, only partially true, economically naive, and socially idealistic. While sympathetic to its aims, he argues that the Church's contribution to the debate is vitiated by such errors.

In a California Newsreel documentary film on Wall Street, made at the height of merger mania in the 1980s, investment banker Felix Rohatyn is asked his opinion of a contemporary statement by the American bishops on the problems of capitalism and the need to share our wealth with the poor. He was expected, apparently, to attack the bishops as naive, ignorant, and possibly Communists—much as former secretary of the treasury William Simon did, in the next interview. But that was not Rohatyn's reply. Instead, he reflected for a minute, and then suggested that the bishops had spoken well: they spoke out of concern for the poor, and that is what bishops are supposed to do. Who else would do it? Who else but the pastors of the beleaguered flock will recall that not every aspect of our plump economy is good for absolutely everyone? To each economic thrust there is a season. Capitalism is a good system. It helps many people make a living and enjoy a prosperous life. But there are poor people, and they, too, have to be fed. If the Church will not speak out on issues of social justice and of the welfare of those who have not been as fortunate as Felix Rohatyn or William Simon, who will?

If one imagines that the Pontifical Council for Social Communications is trying to tell advertisers how to do their business, their effort must appear ludicrous. They seem to be worried about the possibility that advertisers may be promoting a lifestyle based on unbridled consumption. Of course they are! Your prosperity and mine depend on that unbridled consumption. Lock up those bridles. And the advertisers are accused of causing "people to feel and act upon cravings for items and services they do not need." That's the *point*. If they *needed* those goods and services, we wouldn't have to advertise them, would we? But that of course is not what the council is trying to do. The role of the Church is precisely to point our minds, and our lives, toward possibilities of living that do not make central the pleasurable materialistic styles we have adopted as our own.

Similarly, if we imagine that the council is trying to understand the role of advertising in our capitalist economy, we misread it. What, after all, would we make of an understanding of media (newspapers, magazines, television) as "gifts from God," part of His "providential design" to help people "cooperate with His plan for their salvation"? Is that what the advertising agencies have been doing all these years, and we never figured it out? The council is talking of possibilities outside the capitalist system, possibilities of squiring our energies to goals often forgotten, having to do with a communal life enjoyed for its own sake and for its potential to make us all into better people.

So in many ways Gene Laczniak and the council are talking past each other, toward visions of society that they do not share. But the visions meet on the ground. Advertisers and marketers have to decide every day what sorts of advertising meet the morally minimal criteria of acceptable taste and adequate truth. How can we decide what violates taste (read: what violates human dignity) and what is overly untruthful unless we have some idea of the worth and basic human rights and dignity of the audience that we address? How, for instance, can we decide what should be broadcast in our advertising to young people, especially to young women, about their bodies? How much of our epidemic of eating disorders is to be laid at the door of the advertisers? Can the Church and other moral advisors help to curb this epidemic by formulating sensible guidelines for advertising?

Bear in mind, as you read these selections, that while the exponents sometimes seem to be talking past each other, they present a genuine choice between views of human nature as well as between views of what is desirable in business enterprise. As Archbishop Foley points out, even advertisers want to do the right thing, and are occasionally grateful for suggestions as to how they might do that.

YES

Ethics in Advertising: A Look at the Report by the Pontifical Council for Social Communications

In February 1997, the cabinet-level Pontifical Council for Social Communications at the Vatican released a report on the state of advertising world-wide. To complete its review, the council solicited materials from advertising practitioners and scholars through a variety of venues, including a plea in the trade magazine *Advertising Age.* . . .

A Brief Summary of the Report

The report by the Pontifical Council for Social Communications (1997) is divided into five sections: introduction, benefits of advertising, harm done by advertising, ethical and moral principles, and conclusions. These sections build on one another and overlap in significant ways. A description of each follows, using quotes from the document whenever possible.

The introduction opens with the conclusion that "advertising has a profound impact on how people understand life, the world and themselves, especially in regard to their values and their ways of choosing and behaving" (p. 7). The media are described as "gifts from God" that can be employed to accomplish "his providential design, bringing people together and [to] help them to cooperate with his plan for their salvation" (p. 6). However, the council also "calls attention to moral principles and norms relevant to social communications" (p. 6) that should shape the content, target, and influence of advertising.

The next section, on advertising benefits, is divided into four segments. In the first segment, the council studies the economic benefits of advertising and notes that "advertising can be a useful tool for sustaining honest and ethically responsible competition that contributes to economic growth in the service of authentic human development" (p. 11). These benefits are accomplished in a variety of ways, including "by informing people about the availability of rationally desirable new products and services and improvements in existing ones" (pp. 11–12). The council examines the benefits of political advertising in the second segment and comes to a similar

From *Journal of Public Policy & Marketing*, vol. 17, no. 2, Fall 1998, pp. 313. Copyright © 1998 by American Marketing Association. Reprinted by permission.

conclusion. The primary benefit is educational, "informing people about the ideas and policy proposals of parties and candidates, including new candidates not previously known to the public" (p. 13). In the third segment, the council discusses the cultural benefits of advertising, which comprise "a positive influence on decisions about media content" as well as "motivating [people] to act in ways that benefit themselves and others" (p. 13). The popular culture influence also is recognized as positive because "advertising can brighten lives simply by being witty, tasteful and entertaining" (p. 13). In the fourth and final segment, the council explores the moral and religious benefits of advertising, noting that advertising can deliver "messages of faith, of patriotism, of tolerance, compassion and neighborly service" (pp. 13–14), as well as others. From this perspective, advertising is viewed as essential to effective moral suasion and "a necessary part of a comprehensive pastoral strategy" (p. 14).

Section Three is titled "The Harm Done by Advertising," and it is divided into the same four segments as the previous section. Among the economic harms of advertising, the council includes deceptive advertising, the improper use of influence on media editorial content by advertisers, and the implicit promotion of a lifestyle built on unbridled consumption. It also argues against "brand-related advertising" that drives "people to act on the basis of irrational motives ('brand loyalty,' status, fashion, 'sex appeal,' etc.) instead of presenting differences in product quality and price as bases for rational choice" (p. 16). Furthermore, advertisers are indicted for causing "people to feel and act upon cravings for items and services they do not need" (p. 17).

With regard to the harms of political advertising, the council is concerned that "the costs of advertising limit political competition to wealthy political candidates or groups, or require that office-seekers compromise their integrity and independence by over-dependence on special interests for funds" (p. 18). In addition, political advertising is an "obstruction of the democratic process" when it "seeks to distort the views and records of opponents" or "appeals more to people's emotions and base instincts" (p. 19).

According to the council, the cultural harms of advertising are multifaceted and include "cultural injury done to those nations and their peoples by advertising whose content and methods, reflecting those prevalent in the first world, are at war with sound traditional values in indigenous cultures" (p. 19). Advertisers also are blamed for pressure on the media to "ignore the educational and social needs of certain [market] segments" in favor of editorial content that "attracts ever larger audiences" through the delivery of editorial content that "lapses into superficiality, tawdriness and moral squalor" (p. 20). Furthermore, advertising is blamed for "invidious stereotyping of particular groups that places them at a disadvantage in relation to others," especially the "exploitation of women," which often ignores "the specific gifts of feminine insight, compassion, and understanding" (pp. 20–21).

Finally, the moral and religious harms of advertising include "appeals to such motives as envy, status seeking and lust," or those that "seek to shock and titillate by exploiting content of a morbid, perverse, pornographic nature" (p. 21). The council also finds advertising unacceptable "when it involves exploiting religion or treating it flippantly," or it "is used to promote products and inculcate attitudes and forms of behavior contrary to moral norms," "for instance, with the advertising of contraceptives, abortifacients, and products harmful to health" (p. 22).

The fourth section identifies "moral principles that are particularly relevant to advertising" (p. 25), and three in particular are discussed: truthfulness, the dignity of the human person, and social responsibility. The principle of truthfulness in advertising lobbies against advertisements that are "simply and deliberately untrue" or "distort the truth by implying things that are not so or withholding relevant facts" (p. 25). The principle of the dignity of the human person condemns advertisements that violate our right "to make a responsible choice" or "exploit man's lower inclinations" (e.g., "lust, vanity, envy and greed") (pp. 26–27). This principle is particularly relevant for vulnerable groups such as "children and young people, the elderly, the poor, the culturally disadvantaged" (p. 27). Finally, the principle of advertising and social responsibility criticizes "advertising that fosters a lavish life style which wastes resources[,] despoils the environment[, and] offends against important ecological concerns" (p. 28).

The fifth and final section is the conclusion. Much of this section is consumed with who is responsible for ensuring that advertising is "ethically correct." According to the council, the "indispensable guarantors" of such behavior are advertising professionals who "may be called upon to make significant personal sacrifices to correct [unethical practices]" (p. 34). The council recommends "voluntary ethical codes" before turning to government intervention, and these codes should be updated regularly by the industry, with feedback from "ethicists and church people, as well as representatives of consumer groups" (p. 31).

When all else fails, the government should intervene, especially in areas such as the "quantity" and "content of advertising directed at groups particularly vulnerable to exploitation, such as children and old people. Political advertising also seems an appropriate area for regulation: how much may be spent, how and from whom may money for advertising be raised" (p. 32). Furthermore, "besides avoiding abuses, advertisers also should undertake to repair the harm sometimes done by advertising, insofar as that is possible: for example, by publishing corrective notices, compensating injured parties, increasing the quantity of public service advertising, and the like" (pp. 33–34).

Remarks Made by Archbishop Foley at the 1998 Public Policy Conference

First of all, I wish to express my thanks to Dean Ron Hill of the School of Business Administration of the University of Portland for having arranged this session on ethics in advertising, with a special focus on the document of the same name published last year by our Pontifical Council for Social Communications in Rome. I also wish to thank Professors Brenkert, Laczniak, and Murphy for their generally favorable comments, and also for their constructive criticisms. Such dialogue is exactly what we wanted to happen, not only within the Catholic Church, but also in the advertising and communications industries and in the academic community.

While a number of comments seem to imply that our document will have little or no effect within the advertising community, I must confess that I have been encouraged by the reaction of the advertising community. Not only have I been invited all over the world to comment on this document in various fora of advertisers, agencies, and associations, but the document has been translated into more than a dozen languages and distributed widely, either through advertising associations or the communications committees of bishops' conferences. At a meeting in Geneva of the World Federation of Advertisers, I was even asked to have our Council begin the development of a wider study on ethics in communications, and we are trying to do just that. In fact, I already invoke such ethical norms when I represent the Holy See at the council of Europe to recall that broadcast frequencies should be considered a public trust and should be required to serve the public interest and not merely private commercial interests.

It would be unrealistic, however, to think that our document, which we strove to keep brief, readable, and practical, would result in overnight worldwide conversion. After 2000 years, the world is not yet Christian, and Jesus was (and is) God! If we can get some people all over the world thinking about ethics in advertising, however, using some of the principles which we have articulated, we will consider that some progress had been made.

There were areas into which we did not enter, but well could have entered; for example, the failure in the United States to distinguish when commercial announcements are beginning or ending, so that one can confuse the news or the entertainment program with the advertising message; the use of product placement in films and television programs; [and] the promotion of products connected with programs being shown, so that there is a temptation to use programs which have product tie-ins.

As we know, there are also endorsements of products by famous persons—sometimes apparent endorsements without the knowledge or permission of the person in question. Let me give an example: When I went to Budapest to speak on this same theme, I saw a billboard on the way from the airport showing a yawning Pope saying something in Hungarian, obviously in support of RTL, Radio-TV Luxembourg, one of the continent's largest private broadcasters. I mentioned this in my talk and said that the use of a person's image to sell a product or service without that person's authorization is at least immoral, if not illegal. The head of the Hungarian Advertising Standards Council rose to say that the billboard would be removed, the Ambassador of Hungary to the Holy See called me to apologize, and the president of the RTL later saw me at a dinner and told me that they had canceled that campaign in all of Europe. Occasionally, invoking ethical standards has dramatic results.

I am in favor of advertising, and I am in favor of commercially supported media; after all, I was editor of a newspaper which depended upon advertising for its survival. I am also in favor of ethics in advertising; after all,

I was a Professor of Ethics for 17 years. I am convinced, however, that most people want to do the right thing and that they appreciate some guidance and support, preferably through industry guidelines, and even, if necessary, regulations by public authority to guarantee that they will not be victimized by their competition for being ethical.

Our point is that ethics in advertising serves the truth, the authentic development of the human person, and the healthy progress of society. If that sounds idealistic, so be it; if the Catholic Church cannot articulate an ideal, who can? What is encouraging to me is that so many seem to be hungry to hear such ideals articulated and, as advertising executives might say, in promoting our document, we are meeting a felt need. In this, we are not claiming a monopoly on truth; we are merely trying to articulate a consensus—and I hope that, in large measure, we have succeeded.

Gene R. Laczniak

 **NO**

Reflections on the 1997 Vatican Statements Regarding Ethics in Advertising

In February 1997, the Vatican Pontifical Council for Social Communications issued a 35-page pamphlet, which provides a religion-based commentary on the ethics of advertising. This document is composed of five sections that endeavor to treat the economic, political, cultural, and moral dimensions of advertising as they affect society. Although the thematic tone of the writing is difficult to capture by excerpting a few paragraphs, the following quotations sample the rhetorical sense of the essay:

> On advertising in developing countries: "serious harm can be done them if advertising and commercial pressure becomes so irresponsible that communities seeking to rise from poverty to a reasonable standard of living are persuaded to seek this progress by satisfying wants that have been artificially created" (Section 10).
>
> On the relationship of advertising and the media: "In the competition to attract ever larger audiences and deliver them to advertisers, communicators can find themselves tempted—in fact pressured, subtly and not so subtly—to set aside high artistic and moral standards and lapse into superficiality, tawdriness, and moral squalor" (Section 12).
>
> On the morality of advertising: "Advertising can be tasteful and in conformity with high moral standards, and occasionally even morally uplifting but it can also be vulgar and morally degrading. Frequently it deliberately appeals to such motives as envy, status seeking, and lust. Today, too, some advertisers conscientiously seek to shock and titillate by exploiting content of a morbid, perverse, pornographic nature" (Section 13).

The Vatican essay concludes with the postulation of three ethical principles, which are discussed subsequently. It pointedly calls for greater responsibility on the part of those involved in the advertising industry, especially advertising practitioners. The document states (Section 14), "advertisers—that is, those who commission, prepare or disseminate advertising—are morally responsible for what they seek to move people to do." This pamphlet was distributed in its entirety by the Vatican Office to all Catholic bishops for the purposes of pastoral teaching and reflection. Its explicit target market consists

From *Journal of Public Policy & Marketing*, vol. 17, no. 2, Fall 1998, pp. 320. Copyright © 1998 by American Marketing Association. Reprinted by permission.

of more than 600 million Catholics worldwide, as well as the global advertising community, but it also is intended for all people of goodwill.

The Statement's Fundamental Structure and Method

The Vatican essay takes the form of an analytical commentary on the social implications of advertising. The pamphlet, drawing almost exclusively on Catholic religious sources, logically moves from a statement of purpose to a final explication of principles. It is composed of four parts and 23 sections and runs approximately 35 pages in length.

The bibliographic citations made throughout the essay are scripturally and religiously rooted. The majority of references are to papal encyclicals and the *Catechism of the Catholic Church* (1994). These footnoted sources, in turn, are referenced heavily with additional biblical and doctrinal citations and can be used to examine the full scope of religious teaching that is invoked as a basis for the statements made. This approach to source authority can be expected to receive negative comment in most academic circles. That is, many will argue that, to maximize the credibility and defensibility of the observations made in this document, its tenets should be supported not by sectarian, religious documents but mainly by references to the most current and reputable social science and business literature dealing with the social outcomes of advertising. Such criticism partially misses the point.

. . . [M]ost of the issues raised regarding the possible economic, political, and cultural harms for which the institution of advertising might be responsible have been dissected previously by serious academic analysis (Rotzoll and Haefner 1990). But elaborate discussion of the questions previously raised by advertising should not imply a consensus resolution of the issues. In the mid-1980s, Richard Pollay authored a now-classic article that examines the ever-evolving history of advertising criticism as perceived by significant humanities and social science scholars. Pollay (1986, p. 21) writes in summation, "They see advertising as reinforcing materialism, cynicism, irrationality, selfishness, anxiety, social competitiveness, powerlessness and/or the loss of self respect." As such observations suggest, the power and visibility of advertising breeds ongoing, critical commentary in some sectors of society, but often this criticism raises more issues than solutions. For example, one recent literature review, covering the period 1987 to 1993, found 127 articles published on the topic of advertising ethics alone (Hyman, Tansey, and Clark 1994). That the Catholic Church also might weigh in on this pervasive topic should not be astounding to anyone. Thus, the systematic elaboration of religious values and accompanying citation of supporting writings should be understood as a different and possibly valuable perspective on the impact of advertising in a complex society. For example, Protestant and Jewish academics have drawn on their own religious traditions to offer commentary on addressing and improving business ethics (Camenish 1998; Pava 1998).

The Statement's Likely Impact: Ideal and Actual

The Vatican pamphlet on advertising ethics will receive a modicum of discussion, especially in Catholic circles, given its source and purpose. For example, I already am aware of several faculty, teaching at Catholic business schools, who have incorporated it into classroom discussions that pertain to the social impact of marketing activities. More than likely, it also will be used by some members of the Catholic clergy as an inspiration for homilies or a possible theme in parish programs or youth education efforts that include social reflections. The Vatican essay also can be expected to fall on some sympathetic ears among nonsectarian audiences, especially those searching for novel ideas wherever they can be found. For example, business academics interested in the questions of public policy and social issues certainly would fall into this category. On the balance, however, I believe this statement will not have much visibility or impact, at least not without a concerted effort to publicize (dare I say advertise?) it to upper-level marketing and advertising executives. According to a *New York Times* (Charry 1997) article published approximately 30 days after the Vatican essay on advertising ethics had been released, few high-profile advertising practitioners even were aware of its existence. There is little evidence to suggest that awareness levels regarding the content of the document will increase among the advertising community at any time in the future.

Perhaps more disturbing is my contention that, even if the document comes to the attention of the advertising community, the opinions of the Catholic Church on such matters will not be welcomed. On what basis do I say this? Church leaders systematically have opined on other economic issues on previous occasions (Naughton and Laczniak 1993). These observations, directed at the Catholic laity in general, but at the broader business community as well, have not been received graciously by business. For example, in 1986, the U.S. Catholic bishops published a lengthy, thoughtful pastoral letter titled *Economic Justice for All* (1986). That document attempted to articulate the implications of Catholic social teaching (CST) for the U.S. economy. Specifically, the principles of CST were explicated, and their connections to various managerial issues, such as employment, poverty, and economic development, were laid out comprehensively. In a poll of 2000 randomly selected business executives, reported in *Chicago Studies* (McMahon 1989), the majority of the executives perceived that this Catholic bishops' letter on economics was a political statement, rather than a constructive contribution to the dialogue regarding social justice. This observation was made despite the majority of executives claiming that religious values significantly influenced their business decision making. . . .

As a business professor at a Catholic university, who teaches classes in both competitive strategy and business ethics, I have been asked by corporate executives on several occasions my opinion regarding the standing of the Catholic Church to comment intelligently on economic matters. My standard reply has been to say that Catholic Church leaders probably have at least as much useful to say about "justice" and "fairness" in the operation of the economy as business executives do about the efficient running of universities.

Observations in the Vatican Ethics Statement Likely to Be Attacked

Almost any assertion pertaining to the social role of advertising has a high likelihood of engendering debate. The Vatican statement on ethics in advertising contains several observations that are likely to serve as lightning rods for controversy. Regrettably, a few of these remarks will bolster the position of those in the business community who contend that the clergy lack economic understanding. For purposes of illustration, I focus on three such postulations from the ethics document.

First, in Section 10, the statement criticizes brand-related advertising for often accentuating irrational buying motives by consumers and causing potentially serious, supposedly ethical, problems. This condemnation is blanket and without sufficient illustration. Presumably, unstated examples, such as targeting $180 basketball shoes at the poorest urban youth, would represent such egregious abuse. In these cases, the Vatican and most of us should be outraged appropriately. But, this superficial criticism of branding and brand-related advertising as often leading to product proliferation and irrational consumer choice is also naive. Although branding, at the extreme, has been subject to some marketing exploitation, the benefits of branding are well accepted and key elements in enhancing the social value of advertising (Wilkie and Moore-Shay, in press). Even many severe critics of advertising generally are willing to grant this and admit that branding is one of the net "pluses" of complex marketing systems. Branding enables consumers to accrue a shorthand form of product identification and provides them with a longitudinally consistent indicator of price and quality across product categories. My point here is that such hypercritical analysis of possible advertising shortcomings undermines the credibility of the entire Vatican document.

Second, in Section 11, there is an unfortunate foray into the dysfunctions of political advertising. More than likely, this commentary by the Vatican Office was well intended, given that contemporary political campaigns have evolved away from interpersonal communications campaigns to ones that feature mass communications and often contain destructive negative advertising (Laczniak and Caywood 1987). Nevertheless, political advertising, at least in the United States, remains a protected class of speech that arises from constitutional guarantees. For this reason, political advertising would have best been eliminated in the Pontifical discussion. I say this because, by questioning the ethics of political speech, the church raises a frightening specter. If the Vatican is willing to delimit the sacrosanct area of paid-for political debate, advertising executives will wonder how much else church leaders would want to censor quickly. Such issues would have been better addressed in a separate document on the ethics and morality of modern political campaigns.

Third, in Section 14, the Vatican essay raises a dichotomy that, in my opinion, is far too dramatic. Referencing the media in general, and advertising in particular, the essay portrays media practitioners as facing a forked choice: "Either they help human persons to grow in their understanding and practice of what is true and good, or they are destructive forces in conflict with human well-being." Is human nature really so black and white? Does the Vatican believe that all advertising is either all good or all bad? Such simplistic analysis again undermines the credibility of other useful and valuable insights contained in the essay.

Moral Principles Relevant to Improving Advertising Ethics

The most substantive portion of the document involves the postulation of three principles that should be used to adjudicate the ethics of advertising. According to the Vatican essay, these are the following:

1. A principle of *truthfulness*. It states that, "advertising may not deliberately seek to deceive, whether it does that by what it says, by what it implies, or what it fails to say" (Section 15).
2. A principle of *human dignity*. "There is an imperative requirement" that advertising "respect the human person, his right/duty to make a responsible choice, his interior freedom; all these goods would be violated if man's lower inclinations were to be exploited, or his capacity to reflect and decide compromised" (Section 16). In the explication of this principle, promotions that appeal to lust, vanity, envy, and greed are referenced specifically. In addition, advertising that is directed exploitatively at vulnerable groups, such as children, the elderly, and the poor, is mentioned as particularly troubling.
3. A principle of *social responsibility*. "Advertising that reduces human progress to acquiring material and cultivating a lavish lifestyle expresses a false, destructive vision of the human person harmful to individuals and society alike" (Section 17). Specifically noted in this principle, by way of explanation, are advertisements that encourage lifestyles that contribute to the waste of resources or the despoiling of the natural environment.

Taken together, the worth of these principles is that they cover important, fundamental, and necessary ground. They remind advertisers of their proactive duties to avoid deception and respect persons, particularly those who are vulnerable, and of the special requirement of enlightened stewardship that managers should embrace in constructing responsible marketing campaigns. The principles serve as noteworthy moral commentary in the long-running debate about how advertising is moderated best from a social and public policy standpoint (e.g., Preston 1994).

However, it is also fair to note that most of the issues addressed by these principles have been brought previously to the attention of the advertising community. The sentiment of nondeception covered in the first principle, at least in its basic form (i.e., "do not intentionally deceive"), is included in most existing professional codes of advertising ethics, as well as in the law. For example, "avoidance of false and misleading advertising" is a specific provision of the American Marketing Association code of ethics (Laczniak and Murphy 1993). And regarding the third ethical principle, advertisers long have espoused a high level of social responsibility. For example, the document titled *Standards of Practice of the American Association of Advertising Agencies* begins with the following language:

> We hold that a responsibility of advertising agencies is to be a constructive force in business. We hold that to discharge this responsibility, advertising agencies must recognize an obligation, not only to their clients, but to the public, the media they employ, and to each other . . . unethical competitive practices in the advertising agency business lead to financial waste, dilution of service, diversion of manpower, loss of prestige, and tend to weaken public confidence both in advertisements and in the institution of advertising (quoted in Laczniak and Murphy 1993).

If anything, these three Vatican principles might be faulted as too general. What may be needed more, perhaps, are midrange corollaries that address specific, documentable abuses in the advertising system.

The Professional Responsibilities of Advertising Educators and Practitioners

In the end, whether cleric, layperson, academic, or advertising practitioner, readers are left with the question: What social obligations are incumbent on advertising executives? Clearly, advertisers have some duties to contribute to the common good. The real debate comes regarding how broadly these social requirement parameters should be drawn and how aggressively practitioners should seek to fulfill their professional duties.

References

Camenish, Paul (1998), "A Presbyterian Approach to Business Ethics," in Perspectives in Business Ethics, L. P. Hartman, ed. Chicago: Irwin/McGraw-Hill, 229–38.

Catechism of the Catholic Church (1994). Chicago: Loyola University Press.

Charry, Tamer (1997), "Advertising: Roman Catholic Church Gets Mixed Review on Ads," New York Times, (March 31), Business Section, 1.

Economic Justice for All: Catholic Social Teaching and the U.S. Economy (1986). Washington, DC: National Conference of Catholic Bishops.

Hyman, Michael Richard, R. Tansey, and Jarvis W. Clark (1994), "Research on Advertising Ethics: Past, Present, and Future," Journal of Advertising, 23, 5–15.

Laczniak, Gene R. and Clarke L. Caywood (1987), "The Case For and Against Televised Political Advertising: Implications for Research and Public Policy," Journal of Public Policy & Marketing, 6, 16–32.

_____and Patrick E. Murphy (1993), Ethical Marketing Decisions. Boston, MA: Allyn & Bacon.

McMahon, Thomas F. (1989), "Religion and Business," Chicago Studies, 3–15.

Naughton, Michael and Gene R. Laczniak (1993), "A Theological Context of Work from the Catholic Social Encyclical Tradition," Journal of Business Ethics, 12, 981–94.

Pava, Moses L. (1998), "Developing a Religiously Grounded Business Ethics: A Jewish Perspective," Business Ethics Quarterly, 8, 65–83.

Pollay, Richard W. (1986), "The Distorted Mirror: Reflections on the Unintended Consequences of Advertising," Journal of Marketing, 50 (April), 18–36.

Pontifical Council for Social Communications (1997), Ethics in Advertising. Vatican City: Vatican Documents.

Preston, Ivan L. (1994), The Tangled Web They Weave: Truth, Falsity, and Advertisers. Madison, WI: University of Wisconsin Press.

Rotzoll, Kim and James Haefner (1990), Advertising in Contemporary Society. Cincinnati, OH: Southwestern.

Wilkie, William and Elizabeth S. Moore-Shay (in press), "Marketing's Contributions to Society," Journal of Marketing, forthcoming.

POSTSCRIPT

Are Marketing and Advertising Fundamentally Exploitative?

We live in an age of rapid change in the communications business. We are concerned over the directions that change is taking, and for good reason. How can we assess what proportion of the problems of our society are actually traceable to advertising and the marketing practices of corporations generally? If we find out that there is significant influence—for instance, that ads for diet products and slim fashions, advertised by emaciated supermodels, are indeed influencing young girls to lose their self-esteem and self-confidence, ruin their health with fad diets, and sometimes even starve themselves—what, in this free country, can or should we do about that? Is government regulation the answer? Is industry self-regulation the answer? As citizens and as consumers, you will be part of these serious decisions.

Suggested Reading

To continue the conversation, you might profit from the following works:

Stevan Alburty, "The Ad Agency to End All Agencies," *Fast Company* (December–January 1997), pp. 116–24.

George Brenkert, "Ethics in Advertising: The Good, the Bad, and the Church," *Journal of Public Policy and Marketing*, 17(Fall):325–31 (1998).

Carol Krol, "Pontifical Council Sets Guidelines for Making Ads," *Advertising Age* 68(4):37 (1997).

James E. Liebig, *Merchants of Vision: People Bringing New Purpose and Values to Business* (San Francisco: Berret-Koehler, 1994).

Pontifical Council for Social Communications (1997), Ethics in Advertising. Vatican City: Vatican Documents.

ISSUE 14

Is Direct-to-Consumer Advertising of Pharmaceuticals Bad for Our Health?

YES: Sidney M. Wolfe, from "Direct-to-Consumer Advertising—Education or Emotion Promotion?" *The New England Journal of Medicine* (February 14, 2002)

NO: Alan F. Holmer, from "Direct-to-Consumer Advertising—Strengthening Our Health Care System," *The New England Journal of Medicine* (February 14, 2002)

ISSUE SUMMARY

YES: In this powerful debate, invited by *The New England Journal of Medicine*, two students of current pharmaceutical practices square off: Sidney Wolfe, M.D., of the Public Citizen Health Research Group in Washington, D.C., cites the dangers of overpromoting cures to the consumer.

NO: Alan Holmer, J.D., of the Pharmaceutical Research and Manufacturers of America, also in Washington, insists that more information for consumers can only improve the health of Americans.

$\mathbf{F}$or most of the history of medicine, from Hippocrates to the second half of the twentieth century, the patient has not been invited to participate in the decisions concerning his own care. Once the patient had contracted the services of the physician, the physician formed his own conclusions about the diagnosis of the patient's condition, its treatment, and the prescription of regimen and pharmaceuticals (however those may have been defined at the time). There is a work in the Hippocratic corpus, in fact, *The Decorum,* in which the physician, while treating the patient, is advised "to perform all this quickly and adroitly, always concealing from the patient what you are doing." The patient is to be told nothing of the diagnosis or prognosis, "for much harm has come from this in the past." Of patients, it was assumed that they knew little of the conditions of their bodies, and that they knew even less about treatments and drugs. All the patients needed to do was to follow the doctor's orders. As for the reasons for those orders, there was no point in trying to explain within the compass of a visit what it had taken the physician four years of medical school to learn.

The prevailing doctrine on sharing information with patients followed the Hippocratic author exactly: patients need to be cheered with optimistic forecasts that would set their minds at rest, for if they heard bad news they would surely take a turn for the worse. Medical ethics, then, which forbids the physician to "do harm" to the patient, required deception and concealment.

Naturally, the same ethic was applied to any drugs that might be prescribed. The physician was to give the patient the medicine, or prescribe it for the local pharmacist, with the same cheery optimism evidenced in the treatment to that point: the patient was assured that the medicine would surely help their condition, whether or not the physician felt any such confidence.

The consumer movement of the 1960s and 1970s produced different patients and eventually, different physicians. Informed consent became the rule in medicine: the physician had to tell the patient everything that a reasonable patient might want to know about the treatment proposed, especially about its risks, or risk liability if anything went wrong. Consumers were also asking hard questions about the cars and food that they bought; it was only a matter of time before they started asking about the medications they bought at the pharmacy. Especially as drugs became more expensive, consumers wanted to know what they were really buying, and soon, whether there might be a less expensive alternative—a knockoff or generic version of the medicine. It was an earth-shaking change: a culture that had tamely bought Bayer for headaches and Phillips for constipation all through the century suddenly discovered supermarket brands and many other choices. Pharmaceutical companies became understandably concerned for their future.

Advertising was not new to the pharmaceutical industry. Drug reps had gone from physician's office to physician's office promoting their brands, sometimes using highly suspect means to get the physician to prescribe them. But direct-to-consumer advertising was very rare. It has been legal for some time, as long as adequate provision was made for disclosing risks and contraindications, but the FDA tended to be very strict about what constituted "adequate provision"—until the 1997 FDA guidelines that simplified and clarified the methods of creating an acceptable marketing campaign. Since then, the ads have blanketed TV land, extolling the virtues of brand X and the wondrous relief it will bring to the suffering viewers, but always concluding "ask your doctor if brand X is right for you."

Is this right? Note that the placebo effect cuts two ways in DtC advertising: First, if the drug is in fact right for the patient's condition, and the physician prescribes it, the TV aura will do most of the work of the physician in boosting the confident hope of the patient that will lead to healing. It can speed the work of the drug and shorten the patient's illness. But second, if the drug is not in fact right for the patient's condition, and the physician refuses to prescribe it, the patient leaves the office half convinced that whatever the physician did prescribe is inferior to the drug he has already convinced himself he needs, and the TV aura will have a *negative* placebo effect, retarding the effectiveness of the treatment adopted. It may simply drive the patient to another physician who might be more cooperative.

Bear in mind, as you read these selections, that the practice of medicine is very old, and this controversy, like the medicines around which it swirls, are very new. Where, in this field, does consumer choice really fit? Do the advertisements really convey enough information to constitute informed consent? Should the ads be banned—or voluntarily foregone by the pharmaceutical industry?

YES

Sidney M. Wolfe

Direct-to-Consumer Advertising— Education or Emotion Promotion?

During the past two decades, there has been an irreversible change in the nature of the doctor–patient relationship. Patients are seeking much more medical information and are actively participating in decisions affecting their health. Intruding into this trend has been the rise of direct-to-consumer promotion, which, in its initial thrust, bypasses primary care doctors and other physicians. Although increased access by patients to accurate, objective information about tests to diagnose and drugs to treat illnesses is an important advance, confusion arises when commercially driven promotional information is represented as educational. Two articles in this issue of the *Journal* address the direct-to-consumer promotion of medical products and services. Rosenthal et al.[1] describe the resources allocated to direct-to-consumer advertising of prescription drugs, as compared with other forms of promotion. Lee and Brennan[2] examine issues arising from the direct-to-consumer marketing of high-technology medical screening tests. These articles raise several questions. Is direct-to-consumer advertising educational or emotional? How often is it misleading? Is enforcement by the Food and Drug Administration (FDA) of advertising regulations adequate? What can be done to neutralize the negative effect of this type of advertising?

In an excellent review of direct-to-consumer promotion, Mintzes stated that "the question is not whether consumers should obtain information about treatment options; the question is whether drug promotion—whose aim is to sell a product—can provide the type of information consumers need."[3] Addressing the issue of pharmaceutical advertising more generally 30 years ago in the *Journal,* Ingelfinger[4] argued that "advertisements should be overtly recognized for what they are—an unabashed attempt to get someone to buy something, although some useful information may be provided in the process." He suggested that such advertising should be divested of its "pseudo-educational character."

Serious deficiencies have been documented in the educational value of advertising for prescription drugs. In a survey of 1872 viewers of television advertisements, 70 percent thought they had learned little or nothing more

From *The New England Journal of Medicine,* vol. 346, no. 7, February 14, 2002, pp. 524–526. Copyright © 2002 by Massachusetts Medical Society. Reprinted by permission.

about the health condition requiring treatment, and 59 percent thought they knew little or nothing more about the drug being advertised.[5] Another study found that whereas many advertisements provided information about the name and symptoms of the disease for which the drug was being promoted, few educated patients about the success rate of the drug, the necessary duration of use, alternative treatments (including behavioral changes) that could improve their health, or misconceptions about the disease to be treated. The average number of "educational codes" (i.e., specific learning points relating to a medical condition or a treatment) present in the advertisements was only 3.2 out of a possible 11.[6]

None of these deficiencies should be surprising in the light of the characterization of advertising by the Canadian economist Stephen Leacock as "the science of arresting the human intelligence long enough to get money from it." Leacock also thought that, for the purpose of selling, advertising "is superior to reality."[7] An advertisement, aimed at the marketers of pharmaceutical products, from an agency that creates drug advertisements provides some revealing insights about how the process works. The promotional material describes the hippocampus as the "prescription-writing center of the brain"— the part that "processes information by connecting new concepts with the parts of the brain where gut instincts are formed, areas that influence emotional behavior and form memories." The advertising agency asserts that its "communications are focused on making the hippocampus respond positively to your product . . . [by demonstrating] how your product is superior and unique."[8] An executive of a company that focuses on direct-to-consumer advertising commented that "consumers react emotionally, so you want to know how they feel about your message and what emotional triggers will get them to act. . . . We want to identify the emotions we can tap into to get that customer to take the desired course of action."[9] Another article, describing problems the drug industry has had in adapting to direct-to-consumer marketing, said that companies "are overly focused on communicating rational attributes to customers. But consumers often choose a product on [the basis of] emotional attributes. . . . How an emotional appeal fits into fair balance in advertising prescription drugs under the requirements and approval process of FDA is not clear."[10]

Patients have dangerous misperceptions about direct-to-consumer advertising. According to one study, a substantial proportion of people incorrectly believed that only the safest and most effective drugs could be advertised directly to consumers and that the FDA required that it be allowed to review advertisements before they were published.[11] According to another study, consumers rated the safety and appeal of drugs described with an incomplete statement of risks more positively than similar drugs described with a more complete statement of risks.[12]

Defenses of direct-to-consumer advertising by the pharmaceutical industry inevitably mention that the real gatekeeper is the doctor, since only the doctor can write a prescription. Even Rosenthal et al. state that doctors will only write a prescription for a drug when they are "familiar with it and comfortable prescribing it."[1] Although it is beyond the scope of this editorial, it is important to examine studies assessing the accuracy of sources of information that physicians use to learn about new drugs or devices. There is evidence that many drug advertisements are not balanced or accurate,[13, 14] and duped gate-keepers may not adequately resist patients' exhortations to write a prescription.

Since a ban on the advertising of pharmaceutical agents is incompatible with the First Amendment, much stricter control by the FDA of misleading advertising is necessary. Although expenditures for the promotion of drugs increased from $11 billion in 1997 to $15.7 billion in 2000 (Fig. 1), there was a significant decrease in the number of actions taken by the FDA to enforce advertising regulations—from 139 letters of warning to companies or notices of violation in 1997 to 79 in 2000 and an estimated 73 in 2001. The FDA is grossly understaffed for this important oversight function: the entire Division of Drug Marketing, Advertising, and Communications has had only 28 to 30 employees since 1997 (Abrams T: personal communication). A further handicap for the FDA is that it lacks the legal authority to impose civil monetary penalties on companies, even when they repeatedly violate the law. An editorial in a December

Figure 1

FDA Actions Enforcing Drug Advertising Regulations and Drug-Industry Expenditures for Promotion.

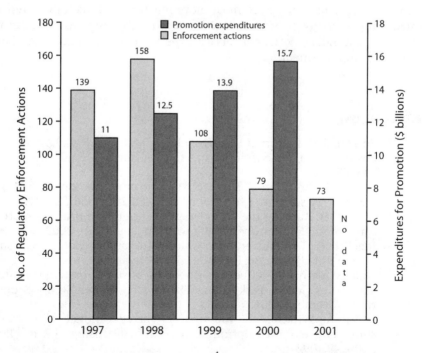

Data on promotion are as reported by Rosenthal et al.[1] Data on enforcement actions (warning letters and notices of violation) are from the FDA Web site.[15] FDA enforcement data for 2001 were extrapolated from data for the first 11 months.

2001 issue of *Business Week* commented that "pharmaceutical company advertising on TV promotes high-priced new drugs with marginal improvement over cheaper generic versions. The FDA should crack down harder on misleading ads."[16] In the realm of screening with the use of computed tomography, analyzed by Lee and Brennan,[2] enforcement is beginning to occur. The FDA recently sent a notice of violation to a company, CATscan2000, for illegally promoting screening for heart disease in asymptomatic people: this form of technology has not been approved for such screening.[17]

Beyond increased enforcement by the FDA, the issue of better information for patients must be addressed. The irritation felt by many physicians when patients approach them after seeing a direct-to-consumer advertisement may derive from the fact that such advertisements, with their powerful, emotion-arousing images and frequently unbalanced information on safety and effectiveness, mislead patients into believing that drugs are better than they actually are. There is a hollow ring to the statement by Pharmaceutical Research and Manufacturers of America president Alan Holmer that "direct-to-consumer advertising is an excellent way to meet the growing demand for medical information, empowering consumers by educating them about health conditions and possible treatments."[18]

The education of patients—or physicians—is too important to be left to the pharmaceutical industry, with its pseudoeducational campaigns designed, first and foremost, to promote drugs. Public Health Service agencies such as the National Institutes of Health and the FDA, along with medical educators in schools and residency programs, must move much more forcefully to replace tainted drug company "education" with scientifically based, useful information that will stimulate better conversations between doctors and patients and lead to true empowerment.

References

1. Rosenthal M. B., Berndt E. R., Donohue J. M., Frank R. G, Epstein A. M. Promotion of prescription drugs to consumers. N Engl J Med 2002; 346:498–505.
2. Lee T. H., Brennan T. A. Direct-to-consumer marketing of high-technology screening tests. N Engl J Med 2002;346:529–31.
3. Mintzes B. Blurring the boundaries: new trends in drug promotion. Amsterdam: HAI-Europe, 1998. (Accessed January 25, 2002, at . . .)
4. Ingelfinger F. J. Advertising: informational but not educational. N Engl J Med 1972;286:1318–9.
5. Understanding the effects of direct-to-consumer prescription drug advertising. Menlo Park, Calif.: The Henry J. Kaiser Family Foundation, November 2001.
6. Bell R. A., Wilkes M. S., Kravitz R. L. The educational value of consumer-targeted prescription drug print advertising. J Fam Pract 2000; 49:1092–8.
7. Leacock S. The garden of folly. New York: Dodd Mead, 1924:122–31.

8. Wolfe S. Drug advertisements that go straight to the hippocampus. Lancet 1996;348:632.
9. Why Rubin-Ehrenthal sticks exclusively to DTC accounts. Medical Marketing and Media. September 1999:136–46.
10. Liebman M. Return on TV advertising isn't a clear picture. Medical Marketing and Media. November 2001:81–4.
11. Bell R. A., Kravitz R. L., Wilkes M. S. Direct-to-consumer prescription drug advertising and the public. J Gen Intern Med 1999;14:651–7.
12. Davis J. J. Riskier than we think? The relationship between risk statement completeness and perceptions of direct to consumer advertised prescription drugs. J Health Commun 2000;5:349–69.
13. Stryer D, Bero L. A. Characteristics of materials distributed by drug companies: an evaluation of appropriateness. J Gen Intern Med 1996;11:575–83.
14. Wilkes M. S., Doblin B. H., Shapiro M. F. Pharmaceutical advertisements in leading medical journals: experts' assessments. Ann Intern Med 1992;116:912–9.
15. Center for Drug Evaluation and Research. Compliance activities: warning letters and notice of violation letters to pharmaceutical companies. Rockville, Md.: Food and Drug Administration, 2002. (Accessed January 25, 2002, at . . .)
16. How to control drug costs, simply. Business Week. December 10, 2001.
17. Letter to CATscan 2000 President/CEO Gina Johnson. Rockville, Md.: Food and Drug Administration, January 3, 2002.
18. Holmer A. F. Direct-to-consumer prescription drug advertising builds bridges between patients and physicians. JAMA 1999;281:380–2.

Alan F. Holmer

 **NO**

Direct-to-Consumer Advertising— Strengthening Our Health Care System

It has been almost five years since the Food and Drug Administration (FDA) issued guidelines clarifying the agency's broadcast requirements for the advertising of specific pharmaceutical agents directly to consumers on television.[1] Previously, most direct-to-consumer advertising had been confined to newspapers and magazines. We think this expansion to television has been a positive step.

Does direct-to-consumer advertising strengthen or weaken the physician–patient relationship? Physicians should and do remain in control of prescribing medicines. As the article by Rosenthal et al. in this issue of the *Journal*[2] makes clear, pharmaceutical companies recognize this fact by directing a large proportion of their promotional activities toward physicians. Moreover, survey data consistently show that when patients ask a physician to prescribe a specific medicine that has been advertised directly to consumers, many receive a different medicine or an alternative, nonpharmaceutical treatment. Among respondents to an FDA survey who said advertisements had caused them to talk with a physician and ask for a particular drug, about half said their doctor recommended a nondrug therapy or a different medicine.[3]

We disagree with the assertion that direct-to-consumer advertising bypasses physicians. The purpose of this advertising is to encourage patients to talk to their physicians about their medical conditions and treatment options. In fact, every television advertisement for a prescription drug must include the message that viewers should ask their physician or pharmacist about the product. Such discussions are beneficial—to the patient, who gains a better understanding of the physician's recommendation for treatment, and to the physician, who gains a better understanding of the patient's needs. In the FDA survey, most patients who had been prompted by direct-to-consumer advertising to discuss a drug with their doctor stated that their doctor welcomed the question (81 percent), discussed the drug with them (79 percent), and reacted as if the question were an ordinary part of the visit (71 percent).

The physician–patient relationship is strengthened, not weakened, when, as surveys show, direct-to-consumer advertising prompts a patient to talk with a physician for the first time about a previously undiscussed condition. A 1999

From *The New England Journal of Medicine*, vol. 346, no. 7, February 14, 2002, pp. 526–528. Copyright © 2002 by Massachusetts Medical Society. Reprinted by permission.

survey by *Prevention* magazine found that since 1997, as many as 24 million Americans had been prompted by a direct-to-consumer advertisement to talk to a doctor about a medical condition they had previously not discussed.[4] This type of advertising also adds to the information available to patients about the risks, side effects, and treatment profile of a particular drug. For example, 82 percent of the respondents to the FDA survey[3] reported seeing information on risks or side effects in direct-to-consumer advertising, and 81 percent reported seeing information on who should not take a drug.

Moreover, direct-to-consumer advertising appears to encourage compliance with physician-prescribed treatment regimens. Lack of compliance is a critical problem in achieving efficacious medical care. In the 2000 *Prevention* survey,[5] 22 percent of consumers said direct-to-consumer advertising made it more likely—whereas only 3 percent said it made it less likely—that they would take their medicine regularly; 33 percent of respondents to the 1999 survey reported that such advertising had reminded them to refill a prescription.[4] A study by Pfizer and RxRemedy from June 2001 found that the percentage of patients with diabetes, depression, elevated cholesterol levels, arthritis, or allergies who continued with therapy after six months was substantially higher when the patient asked for a medicine after being prompted by direct-to-consumer advertising than when the patient was given a prescription for a medicine without such prompting.[6]

Direct-to-consumer advertising is concentrated among a few therapeutic classes. These classes include agents for the treatment of conditions whose symptoms are easily recognized by consumers (such as arthritis, seasonal allergies, and obesity), agents for the treatment of chronic diseases that are often undiagnosed (such as high cholesterol, osteoporosis, and depression), and agents for the enhancement of the quality of life (such as those for skin conditions or hair loss). These advertisements may help consumers to recognize symptoms and encourage them to seek appropriate care.

What accounts for the emergence of direct-to-consumer advertising? Patients are turning to the growing volume of publicly accessible health care information. Dr. Nancy Ostrove, deputy director of the FDA's Division of Drug Marketing, Advertising, and Communications, Center for Drug Evaluation and Research, has argued that direct-to-consumer advertising of pharmaceuticals "is consistent with the whole trend toward consumer empowerment" and has asserted her belief that "there is a certain public health benefit associated with letting people know what's available."[7] In keeping with this trend, direct-to-consumer advertising is used throughout our health care system: managed care organizations, hospitals, and doctors all advertise to consumers. Unlike other health care information, direct-to-consumer advertising of drugs is subject to intense scrutiny by FDA regulators, who evaluate it for accuracy and balance.

In today's health care marketplace, there are numerous financial factors that influence the delivery of medical care. There are payment incentives that are linked to patterns of prescribing and dispensing of medications, formularies that are typically structured at least partially on the basis of financial considerations, and variable cost-sharing arrangements with patients for certain types of medicines. In the light of these strategies designed to influence decisions about the medicines that patients receive, the provision of information to patients about their treatment options through direct-to-consumer advertising is a healthy development that helps balance the system. With so many parties using such financial incentives and encouraging patients to assume increased responsibility for their medical care, it is surprising that the transmission of FDA-regulated information to consumers has engendered controversy.

Direct-to-consumer advertising does not affect the prices of drugs[8]: price increases of drugs are the least important factor contributing to the increase in pharmaceutical spending. In 2000, price inflation accounted for approximately one fifth of the growth.[9] Such advertising may increase the rate of use of prescription drugs by prompting the treatment of patients for previously untreated conditions and by improving compliance with treatment among those with known conditions. If so, this increase is a positive development. The proper use of prescription drugs is often the most effective and least expensive form of health care. Ostrove testified to a Senate subcommittee in July 2001 that there is no evidence that direct-to-consumer advertising is increasing inappropriate prescribing,[10] and an unpublished industry-supported study on cholesterol-lowering statins, which are the subject of a substantial amount of direct-to-consumer advertising, found no tendency toward less appropriate prescribing as the rate of use increased.[11] As John Calfee of the American Enterprise Institute has observed, "On the whole, increases in drug utilization seem to be driven primarily by the fact that health care organizations, physicians, and patients find many of the newer drugs to be extremely valuable. In fact, there is strong evidence that many of the most effective drugs are underused, rather than overused."[12]

Direct-to-consumer advertising is clearly here to stay. Given this reality, physicians must, as Rosenthal et al. note, "develop strategies for helping their patients evaluate this information and make appropriate and informed choices about treatment."[2] With such a diversity of treatment options available for acute and chronic diseases, patients need the guidance that only a trusted health care professional can provide. The health care system is stronger as a consequence. Direct-to-consumer advertising does not replace the physician–patient relationship; its purpose is rather to encourage an informed discussion between patient and physician.

References

1. Center for Drug Evaluation and Research. Guidance for Industry: consumer-directed broadcast advertisements. Rockville, Md.: Food and Drug Administration, August 1999. (Accessed January 25, 2002, at . . .)
2. Rosenthal MB, Berndt ER, Donohue JM, Frank RG, Epstein AM. Promotion of prescription drugs to consumers. N Engl J Med 2002;346:498–505.
3. Center for Drug Evaluation and Research. Attitudes and behaviors associated with direct-to-consumer (DTC) promotion of prescription

   drugs: main survey results. Rockville, Md.: Food and Drug Administration, 1999. (Accessed January 25, 2002, at . . .)
4. Year two: a national survey of consumer reactions to direct-to-
   consumer advertising. Emmaus, Pa.: Rodale, 1999.
5. International survey on wellness and consumer reactions to DTC
   advertising of Rx drugs. Emmaus, Pa.: Rodale, 2000.
6. Drug ads help people take their medicines. New York: Pfizer, November
   29, 2001. (Accessed January 28, 2002, at . . .)
7. Stolberg SG. The Nation: ads that circumvent doctors: want a new
   drug? Plenty to choose from on TV. New York Times. January 23,
   2000.
8. Manning R, Keith A. The economics of direct-to-consumer advertising
   of prescription drugs. Economic Realities in Health Care Policy
   2001;2(1):3–9.
9. Pharmaceutical industry profile 2001: a century of progress.
   Washington, D.C.: Pharmaceutical Research and Manufacturers of
   America, 2001.
10. Teinowitz I. DTC regulation by FDA debated; agency says it has no
    evidence ads prompt unnecessary prescriptions. Advertising Age.
    July 30, 2001:6.
11. Calfee J, Winston C, Stempski R. Statin drug advertising effects. Pre-
    sented at the University of Chicago Conference on the Regulation of
    Medical Innovation and Pharmaceutical Markets, Chicago, April 20–21,
    2001.
12. Calfee JE. Public hearings on direct-to-consumer advertising of
    prescription drugs. Testimony before the Senate Subcommittee on
    Consumer Affairs, Foreign Commerce, and Tourism, Committee on
    Commerce, Science and Transportation, Washington, D.C., July 24,
    2001:2–3.

POSTSCRIPT

Is Direct-to-Consumer Advertising of Pharmaceuticals Bad for Our Health?

It is worth noticing that the disagreements between Wolfe and Holmer go well beyond the single issue they are discussing. They disagree most on the nature of human autonomy—on whether consumers should be allowed, even encouraged, to make mistakes that may hurt them, *by the health care system, of which the FDA forms a part, and by the business community, the economic engine of the country.* Consumers have often made less-than-optimal choices, and the economic system, viewed as an extension of the rights of the citizen, certainly permits these choices. It is the duty of the storekeeper, as a citizen, to respect the autonomy of the consumer. But we have also always insisted that our professionals have a different duty to the people, because of their expertise: they have a duty to deep their clients/patients from harm, and to oppose any economic regimes that systematically harm the citizens in professional areas. Well, where is our duty to the health care consumer, the buyer of pharmaceuticals? Is he (analytically) closer to the doctor's patient, or to the storekeeper's customer? Can the physician, in an increasingly competitive insurance-driven profession, be counted on to hold the line against patient demands that stem from inappropriate advertising? How much do we care if he cannot?

Suggested Reading

If you want to pursue the subject, you might consider the following readings:

Meredith B. Rosenthal, Ernst R. Berndt, Julie M. Donohue, Richard G. Frank and Arnold M. Epstein, "Promotion of Prescription Drugs to Consumers," *The New England Journal of Medicine,* 346(7): 498–505 (February 14, 2002).

Thomas H. Lee and Troyen A. Brennan, "Sounding Board: Direct-to-Consumer Marketing of High-Technology Screening Tests," *The New England Journal of Medicine,* 346(7): 529–31.

Jeffrey M. Drazen, Lead Editorial: "The Consumer and the Learned Intermediary in Health Care," *The New England Journal of Medicine,* 346(7): 523–24 (February 14, 2002).

ISSUE 15

Was Ford to Blame in the Pinto Case?

YES: Mark Dowie, from "Pinto Madness," *Mother Jones* (September–October 1977)

NO: Ford Motor Company, from Closing Argument by Mr. James Neal, Brief for the Defense, *State of Indiana v. Ford Motor Company*, U.S. District Court, South Bend, Indiana (January 15, 1980)

ISSUE SUMMARY

YES: Mark Dowie's article broke a new kind of scandal for American manufacturing, alleging that Ford Motor Company had deliberately put on the road an unsafe car—the Pinto—in which hundreds of people suffered burn deaths and horrible disfigurement. The accusations gave rise to a series of civil suits and one criminal proceeding, in which Ford was charged with criminal homicide.

NO: James Neal, who was chief attorney for the Ford Motor Company's defense against the charge of criminal homicide in connection with the burn deaths, persuaded the jury that Ford could not be held responsible for deaths which were actually caused by others—the driver of the van that struck the victims, for example—and which resulted from Ford's patriotic efforts to produce a competitive small car.

Some cases in business ethics become "classics" in their own time. By 1980 we were considering "the Pinto Case" in our classes, wondering how safe "safe" had to be where the automobile was concerned, wondering how much management might be held accountable for, wondering if criminal penalties were appropriate for respectable businessmen, no matter what they or their product might be doing. This is arguably not the Pinto Case's own time. Almost thirty years have passed since the accident and what followed from it. But we still teach the case. We still don't know how "safe" a vehicle has to be; we still don't know how much responsibility for product failures to assign to corporations, and what the appropriate way might be to force a corporation to take that responsibility. The doubts remain, and the case retains its interest.

There is no doubt about the case that occasioned the criminal prosecution. Three girls died horribly in an automobile accident on August 10, 1978.

They had stopped their car, a 1973 Ford Pinto, on U. S. Highway 33 near Goshen, Indiana, and were about to get under way again when they were struck from the rear, at high speed, by a van with a possibly impaired driver. The car immediately burst into flames, and the girls had no chance to escape the accident before the flames reached them.

The van driver should have been watching where he was going. Beyond that obvious comment, what was wrong with the car? Why did it burst into flames so quickly? Mark Dowie, general manager of business operations of the magazine *Mother Jones*, had argued a year earlier that there was a great deal wrong with the Ford Pinto. He had put together the story printed here from data obtained for him by some very disaffected Ford engineers. The data suggested that the Pinto had been rushed into production without adequate testing; that it had a very vulnerable fuel system that would rupture with any rear-end collision; that even though the vulnerability was discovered before production, Ford had hurried the Pinto to the market anyway; and that successful lobbying thereafter had prevented the government regulators from catching up with them and requiring a safer gas tank.

Most suggestive from the public's point of view was a document supplied by one of the engineers, an estimate of the probable costs of refitting valves to prevent fire in a rollover accident. It was a cost-benefit analysis that placed a dollar value on a human life, estimated the probability of fatal accident, estimated the amount of money needed to settle a lawsuit for loss of life, estimated the amount of money needed to do the refitting so that there would not be that loss of life—and concluded that it was more economical to let the people die and settle the suits afterward. For sheer bottom-line-oriented cynicism, the document was unparalleled in the history of business enterprise, and Ford Motor Company will never live it down.

When reading these selections, pause to enjoy not only the interesting case, but also the finely directed passion of the contestants. Mark Dowie's trenchant prose is a fine example of investigative reporting, muckraking at its best. And nothing can compare with the superb lawyering of James Neal. Who is to blame for anything, if you are a lawyer? Not your client! Anything else! Blame the van driver, marijuana, the government, professors, the service station, the highway, the society at large, anything, but not your client. Then ask yourself: does Neal give the wealthy corporation an unfair advantage in such proceedings? Does the public have the money to hire such advocates? Would you have that kind of money? The jury had a difficult task of sorting out the situation: Was this deliberate malfeasance by Ford? Was it a series of unlucky decisions made in good faith? Or was this just a very unfortunate accident?

Do we know what constitutes sufficient reason to attribute "responsibility" to any person, company, or set of conditions? What kinds of risks do we assume when buying a car, or a motorcycle, or a can of tuna fish? For what is the manufacturer responsible? Should we be willing to assume more risks in the enormously competitive market that prevails among small automobiles? Does the product liability suit unjustly cripple American efforts to compete in highly competitive industries? Is this something we should worry about?

YES

Mark Dowie

Pinto Madness

One evening in the mid-1960s, Arjay Miller was driving home from his office in Dearborn, Michigan, in the four-door Lincoln Continental that went with his job as president of the Ford Motor Company. On a crowded highway, another car struck his from the rear. The Continental spun around and burst into flames. Because he was wearing a shoulder-strap seat belt, Miller was unharmed by the crash, and because his doors didn't jam he escaped the gasoline-drenched, flaming wreck. But the accident made a vivid impression on him. Several months later, on July 15, 1965, he recounted it to a U.S. Senate subcommittee that was hearing testimony on auto safety legislation. "I still have burning in my mind the image of that gas tank on fire," Miller said. He went on to express an almost passionate interest in controlling fuel-fed fires in cars that crash or roll over. He spoke with excitement about the fabric gas tank Ford was testing at that very moment. "If it proves out," he promised the senators, "it will be a feature you will see in our standard cars."

Almost seven years after Miller's testimony, a woman, whom for legal reasons we will call Sandra Gillespie, pulled onto a Minneapolis highway in her new Ford Pinto. Riding with her was a young boy, whom we'll call Robbie Carlton. As she entered a merge lane, Sandra Gillespie's car stalled. Another car rear-ended hers at an impact speed of 28 miles per hour. The Pinto's gas tank ruptured. Vapors from it mixed quickly with the air in the passenger compartment. A spark ignited the mixture and the car exploded in a ball of fire. Sandra died in agony a few hours later in an emergency hospital. Her passenger, 13-year-old Robbie Carlton, is still alive; he has just come home from another futile operation aimed at grafting a new ear and nose from skin on the few unscarred portions of his badly burned body. (This accident is real; the details are from police reports.)

Why did Sandra Gillespie's Ford Pinto catch fire so easily, seven years after Ford's Arjay Miller made his apparently sincere pronouncements—the same seven years that brought more safety improvements to cars than any other period in automotive history? An extensive investigation by *Mother Jones* over the past six months has found these answers:

- Fighting strong competition from Volkswagen for the lucrative small-car market, the Ford Motor Company rushed the Pinto into production in much less than the usual time.

From *Mother Jones*, vol. 2, no. 8, September/October 1977, pp. 18–32. Copyright © 1977 by Mark Dowie. Reprinted by permission.

- Ford engineers discovered in pre-production crash tests that rear-end collisions would rupture the Pinto's fuel system extremely easily.
- Because assembly-line machinery was already tooled when engineers found this defect, top Ford officials decided to manufacture the car anyway—exploding gas tank and all—*even though Ford owned the patent on a much safer gas tank.*
- For more than eight years afterwards, Ford successfully lobbied, with extraordinary vigor and some blatant lies, against a key government safety standard that would have forced the company to change the Pinto's fire-prone gas tank.

By conservative estimates Pinto crashes have caused 500 burn deaths to people who would not have been seriously injured if the car had not burst into flames. The figure could be as high as 900. Burning Pintos have become such an embarrassment to Ford that its advertising agency, J. Walter Thompson, dropped a line from the end of a radio spot that read "Pinto leaves you with that warm feeling."

Ford knows the Pinto is a firetrap, yet it has paid out millions to settle damage suits out of court, and it is prepared to spend millions more lobbying against safety standards. With a half million cars rolling off the assembly lines each year, Pinto is the biggest-selling subcompact in America, and the company's operating profit on the car is fantastic. Finally, in 1977, new Pinto models have incorporated a few minor alterations necessary to meet that federal standard Ford managed to hold off for eight years. Why did the company delay so long in making these minimal, inexpensive improvements?

- Ford waited eight years because its internal "cost-benefit analysis," *which places a dollar value on human life,* said it wasn't profitable to make the changes sooner.

Before we get to the question of how much Ford thinks your life is worth, let's trace the history of the death trap itself. Although this particular story is about the Pinto, the way in which Ford made its decision is typical of the U.S. auto industry generally. There are plenty of similar stories about other cars made by other companies. But this case is the worst of them all.

The next time you drive behind a Pinto (with over two million of them on the road, you shouldn't have much trouble finding one), take a look at the rear end. That long silvery object hanging down under the bumper is the gas tank. The tank begins about six inches forward of the bumper. In late models the bumper is designed to withstand a collision of only about five miles per hour. Earlier bumpers may as well not have been on the car for all the protection they offered the gas tank.

Mother Jones has studied hundreds of reports and documents on rear-end collisions involving Pintos. These reports conclusively reveal that if you ran into that Pinto you were following at over 30 miles per hour, the rear end of the car would buckle like an accordion, right up to the back seat. The tube leading to the gas-tank cap would be ripped away from the tank itself, and gas would immediately begin sloshing onto the road around the car. The buckled gas tank would be jammed up against the differential housing (that big bulge in the middle of your rear axle), which contains four sharp, protruding bolts likely to gash holes in the tank and spill still more gas. Now all you need is a spark from a cigarette, ignition, or scraping metal, and both cars would be engulfed in flames. If you gave that Pinto a really good whack—say, at 40 mph—chances are excellent that its doors would jam and you would have to stand by and watch its trapped passengers burn to death.

This scenario is no news to Ford. Internal company documents in our possession show that Ford has crash-tested the Pinto at a top-secret site more than 40 times and that *every* test made at over 25 mph without special structural alteration of the car has resulted in a ruptured fuel tank. Despite this, Ford officials denied under oath having crash-tested the Pinto.

Eleven of these tests, averaging a 31-mph impact speed, came before Pintos started rolling out of the factories. Only three cars passed the test with unbroken fuel tanks. In one of them an inexpensive light-weight plastic baffle was placed between the front of the gas tank and the differential housing, so those four bolts would not perforate the tank. (Don't forget about that little piece of plastic, which costs one dollar and weighs one pound. It plays an important role in our story later on.) In another successful test, a piece of steel was placed between the tank and the bumper. In the third test car the gas tank was lined with a rubber bladder. But none of these protective alterations was used in the mass-produced Pinto.

In pre-production planning, engineers seriously considered using in the Pinto the same kind of gas tank Ford uses in the Capri. The Capri tank rides over the rear axle and differential housing. It has been so successful in over 50 crash tests that Ford used it in its Experimental Safety Vehicle, which withstood rear-end impacts of 60 mph. So why wasn't the Capri tank used in the Pinto? Or, why wasn't that plastic baffle placed between the tank and the axle—something that would have saved the life of Sandra Gillespie and hundreds like her? Why was a car known to be a serious fire hazard deliberately released to production in August of 1970?

Whether Ford should manufacture subcompacts at all was the subject of a bitter two-year debate at the company's Dearborn headquarters. The principals in this corporate struggle were the then-president Semon "Bunky" Knudsen, whom Henry Ford II had hired away from General Motors, and Lee Iacocca, a spunky Young Turk who had risen fast within the company on the enormous success of the Mustang. Iacocca argued forcefully that Volkswagen and the Japanese were going to capture the entire American subcompact market unless Ford put out its own alternative to the VW Beetle. Bunky Knudsen said, in effect: let them have the small-car market; Ford makes good money on medium and large models. But he lost the battle and later resigned. Iacocca became president and almost immediately began a rush program to produce the Pinto.

Like the Mustang, the Pinto became known in the company as "Lee's car." Lee Iacocca wanted that little car in the showrooms of America with the 1971 models. So he ordered his engineering vice president, Bob Alexander, to oversee what was probably the shortest production planning period in modern automotive history. The normal time span from conception to production of a new car model is about 43 months. The Pinto schedule was set at just under 25.

. . . Design, styling, product planning, advance engineering and quality assurance all have flexible time frames, and engineers can pretty much carry these on simultaneously. Tooling, on the other hand, has a fixed time frame of about 18 months. Normally, an auto company doesn't begin tooling until the other processes are almost over: you don't want to make the machines that stamp and press and grind metal into the shape of car parts until you know all those parts will work well together. *But Iacocca's speed-up meant Pinto tooling went on at the same time as product development.* So when crash tests revealed a serious defect in the gas tank, it was too late. The tooling was well under way.

When it was discovered the gas tank was unsafe, did anyone go to Iacocca and tell him? "Hell no," replied an engineer who worked on the Pinto, a high company official for many years, who, unlike several others at Ford, maintains a necessarily clandestine concern for safety. "That person would have been fired. Safety wasn't a popular subject around Ford in those days. With Lee it was taboo. Whenever a problem was raised that meant a delay on the Pinto, Lee would chomp on his cigar, look out the window and say 'Read the product objectives and get back to work.' "

The product objectives are clearly stated in the Pinto "green book." This is a thick, top-secret manual in green covers containing a step-by-step production plan for the model, detailing the metallurgy, weight, strength and quality of every part in the car. The product objectives for the Pinto are repeated in an article by Ford executive F. G. Olsen published by the Society of Automotive Engineers. He lists these product objectives as follows:

1. TRUE SUBCOMPACT
   • Size
   • Weight
2. LOW COST OF OWNERSHIP
   • Initial price
   • Fuel consumption
   • Reliability
   • Serviceability
3. CLEAR PRODUCT SUPERIORITY
   • Appearance
   • Comfort
   • Features
   • Ride and Handling
   • Performance

Safety, you will notice, is not there. It is not mentioned in the entire article. As Lee Iacocca was fond of saying, "Safety doesn't sell."

Heightening the anti-safety pressure on Pinto engineers was an important goal set by Iacocca known as "the limits of 2,000." The Pinto was not to weigh an ounce over 2,000 pounds and not to cost a cent over $2,000. "Iacocca enforced these limits with an iron hand," recalls the engineer quoted earlier. So, even when a crash test showed that that one-pound, one-dollar piece of plastic stopped the puncture of the gas tank, it was thrown out as extra cost and extra weight.

People shopping for subcompacts are watching every dollar. "You have to keep in mind," the engineer explained, "that the price elasticity on these subcompacts is extremely tight. You can price yourself right out of the market by adding $25 to the production cost of the model. And nobody understands that better than Iacocca."

Dr. Leslie Ball, the retired safety chief for the NASA manned space program and a founder of the International Society of Reliability Engineers, recently made a careful study of the Pinto. "The release to production of the Pinto was the most reprehensible decision in the history of American engineering," he said. Ball can name more than 40 European and Japanese models in the Pinto price and weight range with safer gas-tank positioning. Ironically, many of them, like the Ford Capri, contain a "saddle-type" gas tank riding over the back axle. *The patent on the saddle-type tank is owned by the Ford Motor Co.*

Los Angeles auto safety expert Byron Bloch has made an in-depth study of the Pinto fuel system. "It's a catastrophic blunder," he says. "Ford made an extremely irresponsible decision when they placed such a weak tank in such a ridiculous location in such a soft rear end. It's almost designed to blow up— premeditated."

A Ford engineer, who doesn't want his name used, comments: "This company is run by salesmen, not engineers; so the priority is styling, not safety." He goes on to tell a story about gas-tank safety at Ford.

Lou Tubben is one of the most popular engineers at Ford. He's a friendly, outgoing guy with a genuine concern for safety. By 1971 he had grown so concerned about gas-tank integrity that he asked his boss if he could prepare a presentation on safer tank design. Tubben and his boss had both worked on the Pinto and shared a concern for its safety. His boss gave him the go-ahead, scheduled a date for the presentation and invited all company engineers and key production planning personnel. When time came for the meeting, a grand total of two people showed up—Lou Tubben and his boss.

"So you see," continued the anonymous Ford engineer ironically, "there *are* a few of us here at Ford who are concerned about fire safety." He adds: "They are mostly engineers who have to study a lot of accident reports and look at pictures of burned people. But we don't talk about it much. It isn't a popular subject. I've never seen safety on the agenda of a product meeting and, except for a brief period in 1956, I can't remember seeing the word safety in an advertisement. I really don't think the company wants American consumers to start thinking too much about safety—for fear they might demand it, I suppose."

Asked about the Pinto gas tank, another Ford engineer admitted: "That's all true. But you miss the point entirely. You see, safety isn't the issue, trunk space is. You have no idea how stiff the competition is over trunk space. Do you realize that if we put a Capri-type tank in the Pinto you could only get one set of golf clubs in the trunk?"

⚬⟨◉⟩⚬

Blame for Sandra Gillespie's death, Robbie Carlton's unrecognizable face and all the other injuries and deaths in Pintos since 1970 does not rest on the shoulders of Lee Iacocca alone. For, while he and his associates fought their battle against a safer Pinto in Dearborn, a larger war against safer cars raged in Washington. One skirmish in that war involved Ford's successful eight-year lobbying effort against Federal Motor Vehicle Safety Standard 301, the rear-end provisions of which would have forced Ford to redesign the Pinto.

But first some background:

During the early '60s, auto safety legislation became the *bête-noire* of American big business. The auto industry was the last great unregulated business, and if *it* couldn't reverse the tide of government regulation, the reasoning went, no one could.

People who know him cannot remember Henry Ford II taking a stronger stand than the one he took against the regulation of safety design. He spent weeks in Washington calling on members of Congress, holding press conferences and recruiting business cronies like W. B. Murphy of Campbell's Soup to join the anti-regulation battle. Displaying the sophistication for which today's American corporate leaders will be remembered, Murphy publicly called auto safety "a hula hoop, a fad that will pass." He was speaking to a special luncheon of the Business Council, an organization of 100 chief executives who gather periodically in Washington to provide "advice" and "counsel" to government. The target of their wrath in this instance was the Motor Vehicle Safety Bills introduced in both houses of Congress, largely in response to Ralph Nader's *Unsafe at Any Speed.*

By 1965, most pundits and lobbyists saw the handwriting on the wall and prepared to accept government "meddling" in the last bastion of free enterprise. Not Henry. With bulldog tenacity, he held out for defeat of the legislation to the very end, loyal to his grandfather's invention and to the company that makes it. But the Safety Act passed the House and Senate unanimously, and was signed into law by Lyndon Johnson in 1966.

While lobbying for and against legislation is pretty much a process of high-level back-slapping, press-conferencing and speech-making, fighting a regulatory agency is a much subtler matter. Henry headed home to lick his wounds in Grosse Pointe, Michigan, and a planeload of the Ford Motor Company's best brains flew to Washington to start the "education" of the new federal auto safety bureaucrats.

Their job was to implant the official industry ideology in the minds of the new officials regulating auto safety. Briefly summarized, that ideology states that auto accidents are caused not by *cars,* but by 1) people and 2) highway conditions.

This philosophy is rather like blaming a robbery on the victim. Well, what did you expect? You were carrying money, weren't you? It is an extraordinary experience to hear automotive "safety engineers" talk for hours without ever mentioning cars. They will advocate spending billions educating youngsters, punishing drunks and redesigning street signs. Listening to them, you can momentarily begin to think that it is easier to control 100 million drivers than a handful of manufacturers. They show movies about guardrail design and advocate the clear-cutting of trees 100 feet back from every highway in the nation. If a car is unsafe, they argue, it is because its owner doesn't properly drive it. Or, perhaps, maintain it.

In light of an annual death rate approaching 50,000, they are forced to admit that driving is hazardous. But the car is, in the words of Arjay Miller, "the safest link in the safety chain."

Before the Ford experts left Washington to return to drafting tables in Dearborn they did one other thing. They managed to informally reach an agreement with the major public servants who would be making auto safety decisions. This agreement was that "cost-benefit" would be an acceptable mode of analysis by Detroit and its new regulators. And as we shall see, cost-benefit analysis quickly became the basis of Ford's argument against safer car design.

Cost-benefit analysis was used only occasionally in government until President Kennedy appointed Ford Motor Company President Robert McNamara to be Secretary of Defense. McNamara, originally an accountant, preached cost benefit with all the force of a Biblical zealot. Stated in its simplest terms, cost-benefit analysis says that if the cost is greater than the benefit, the project is not worth it—no matter what the benefit. Examine the cost of every action, decision, contract, part, or change, the doctrine says, then carefully evaluate the benefits (in dollars) to be certain that they exceed the cost before you begin a program or—and this is the crucial part for our story—pass a regulation.

As a management tool in a business in which profits matter over everything else, cost-benefit analysis makes a certain amount of sense. Serious problems come, however, when public officials who ought to have more than corporate profits at heart apply cost-benefit analysis to every conceivable decision. The inevitable result is that they must place a dollar value on human life.

Ever wonder what your life is worth in dollars? Perhaps $10 million? Ford has a better idea: $200,000.

Remember, Ford had gotten the federal regulators to agree to talk auto safety in terms of cost-benefit analysis. But in order to be able to argue that various safety costs were greater than their benefits, Ford needed to have a dollar value figure for the "benefit." Rather than be so uncouth as to come up with such a price tag itself, the auto industry pressured the National Highway

Table 1

What's Your Life Worth? Societal Cost Components for Fatalities, 1972 NHTSA Study

Component	1971 Costs
Future productivity losses	
Direct	$132,000
Indirect	41,300
Medical Costs	
Hospital	700
Other	425
Property damage	1,500
Insurance administration	4,700
Legal and court	3,000
Employer losses	1,000
Victim's pain and suffering	10,000
Funeral	900
Assets (lost consumption)	5,000
Miscellaneous accident costs	200
Total per fatality: $200,725	

Here is a chart from a federal study showing how the National Highway Traffic Safety Administration has calculated the value of a human life. The estimate was arrived at under pressure from the auto industry. The Ford Motor Company has used it in cost-benefit analyses arguing why certain safety measures are not "worth" the savings in human lives. The calculation above is a breakdown of the estimated cost to society every time someone is killed in a car accident. We were not able to find anyone, either in the government or at Ford, who could explain how the $10,000 figure for "pain and suffering" had been arrived at.

Traffic Safety Administration to do so. And in a 1972 report the agency decided a human life was worth $200,725. (For its reasoning, see [Table 1].) Inflationary forces have recently pushed the figure up to $278,000.

Furnished with this useful tool, Ford immediately went to work using it to prove why various safety improvements were too expensive to make.

Nowhere did the company argue harder that it should make no changes than in the area of rupture-prone fuel tanks. Not long after the government arrived at the $200,725-per-life figure, it surfaced, rounded off to a cleaner $200,000, in an internal Ford memorandum. This cost-benefit analysis argued that Ford should not make an $11-per-car improvement that would prevent 180 fiery deaths a year. (This minor change would have prevented gas tanks from breaking so easily both in rear-end collisions, like Sandra Gillespie's, and in rollover accidents, where the same thing tends to happen.)

Ford's cost-benefit table [Table 2] is buried in a seven-page company memorandum entitled "Fatalities Associated with Crash-Induced Fuel Leakage and Fires." The memo argues that there is no financial benefit in complying with proposed safety standards that would admittedly result in fewer auto fires, fewer burn deaths and fewer burn injuries. Naturally, memoranda that speak so casually of "burn deaths" and "burn injuries" are not released to the

Table 2

$11 vs a Burn Death: Benefits and Costs Relating to Fuel Leakage Associated With the Static Rollover Test Portion of FMVSS 208

Benefits

Savings: 180 burn deaths, 180 serious burn injuries, 2,100 burned vehicles.

Unit cost: $200,000 per death, $67,000 per injury, $700 per vehicle.

Total benefit: 180 × ($200,000) + 180 × ($67,000) + 2,100 × ($700) = $49.5 million.

Costs

Sales: 11 million cars, 1.5 million light trucks.

Unit cost: $11 per car, $11 per truck.

Total cost: 11,000,000 × ($11) + 1,500,000 × ($11) = $137 million.

From Ford Motor Company internal memorandum: "Fatalities Associated with Crash-Induced Fuel Leakage and Fires."

public. They are very effective, however, with Department of Transportation officials indoctrinated in McNamarian cost-benefit analysis.

All Ford had to do was convince men like John Volpe, Claude Brinegar and William Coleman (successive Secretaries of Transportation during the Nixon-Ford years) that certain safety standards would add so much to the price of cars that fewer people would buy them. This could damage the auto industry, which was still believed to be the bulwark of the American economy. "Compliance to these standards," Henry Ford II prophesied at more than one press conference, "will shut down the industry."

The Nixon Transportation Secretaries were the kind of regulatory officials big business dreams of. They understood and loved capitalism and thought like businessmen. Yet, best of all, they came into office uninformed on technical automotive matters. And you could talk "burn injuries" and "burn deaths" with these guys, and they didn't seem to envision children crying at funerals and people hiding in their homes with melted faces. Their minds appeared to have leapt right to the bottom line—more safety meant higher prices, higher prices meant lower sales and lower sales meant lower profits.

So when J. C. Echold, Director of Automotive Safety (which means chief anti-safety lobbyist) for Ford wrote to the Department of Transportation— which he still does frequently, at great length—he felt secure attaching a memorandum that in effect says it is acceptable to kill 180 people and burn another 180 every year, *even though we have the technology that could save their lives for $11 a car.*

Furthermore, Echold attached this memo, confident, evidently, that the Secretary would question neither his low death/injury statistics nor his high cost estimates. But it turns out, on closer examination, that both these findings were misleading.

First, note that Ford's table shows an equal number of burn deaths and burn injuries. This is false. All independent experts estimate that for each person who dies by an auto fire, many more are left with charred hands, faces and limbs. Andrew McGuire of the Northern California Burn Center estimates the ratio of burn injuries to deaths at ten to one instead of the one to one Ford shows here. Even though Ford values a burn at only a piddling $67,000 instead of the $200,000 price of life, the true ratio obviously throws the company's calculations way off.

The other side of the equation, the alleged $11 cost of a fire-prevention device, is also a misleading estimation. One document that was *not* sent to Washington by Ford was a "Confidential" cost analysis *Mother Jones* has managed to obtain, showing that crash fires could be largely prevented for considerably *less* than $11 a car. The cheapest method involves placing a heavy rubber bladder inside the gas tank to keep the fuel from spilling if the tank ruptures. Goodyear had developed the bladder and had demonstrated it to the automotive industry. We have in our possession crash-test reports showing that the Goodyear bladder worked well. On December 2, 1970 (*two years before* Echold sent his cost-benefit memo to Washington), Ford Motor Company ran a rear-end crash test on a car with the rubber bladder in the gas tank. The tank ruptured, but no fuel leaked. On January 15, 1971, Ford again tested the bladder and again it worked. The total purchase and installation cost of the bladder would have been $5.08 per car. That $5.08 could have saved the lives of Sandra Gillespie and several hundred others.

❧

When a federal regulatory agency like the National Highway Traffic Safety Administration (NHTSA) decides to issue a new standard, the law usually requires it to invite all interested parties to respond before the standard is enforced—a reasonable enough custom on the surface. However, the auto industry has taken advantage of this process and has used it to delay lifesaving emission and safety standards for years. In the case of the standard that would have corrected that fragile Pinto fuel tank, the delay was for an incredible eight years.

The particular regulation involved here was Federal Motor Vehicle Safety Standard 301. Ford picked portions of Standard 301 for strong opposition back in 1968 when the Pinto was still in the blueprint stage. The intent of 301, and the 300 series that followed it, was to protect drivers and passengers *after* a crash occurs. Without question the worst postcrash hazard is fire. So Standard 301 originally proposed that all cars should be able to withstand a fixed barrier impact of 20 mph (that is, running into a wall at that speed) without losing fuel.

When the standard was proposed, Ford engineers pulled their crash-test results out of their files. The front ends of most cars were no problem—with minor alterations they could stand the impact without losing fuel. "We were already working on the front end," Ford engineer Dick Kimble admitted. "We knew we could meet the test on the front end." But with the Pinto particularly, a 20-mph rear-end standard meant redesigning the entire rear end of the car. With the Pinto scheduled for production in August of 1970, and with $200 million worth of tools in place, adoption of this standard would have created a minor financial disaster. So Standard 301 was targeted for delay, and, with some assistance from its industry associates, Ford succeeded beyond its wildest expectations: the standard was not adopted until the 1977 model year. Here is how it happened:

There are several main techniques in the art of combating a government safety standard: a) make your arguments in succession, so the feds can be working on disproving only one at a time; b) claim that the real problem is not X but Y (we already saw one instance of this in "the problem is not cars but people"); c) no matter how ridiculous each argument is, accompany it with thousands of pages of highly technical assertions it will take the government months or, preferably, years to test. Ford's large and active Washington office brought these techniques to new heights and became the envy of the lobbyists' trade.

The Ford people started arguing against Standard 301 way back in 1968 with a strong attack of technique b). Fire, they said, was not the real problem. Sure, cars catch fire and people burn occasionally. But statistically auto fires are such a minor problem that NHTSA should really concern itself with other matters.

Strange as it may seem, the Department of Transportation (NHTSA's parent agency) didn't know whether or not this was true. So it contracted with several independent research groups to study auto fires. The studies took months which was just what Ford wanted.

The completed studies, however, showed auto fires to be more of a problem than Transportation officials ever dreamed of. Robert Nathan and Associates, a Washington research firm, found that 400,000 cars were burning up every year, burning more than 3,000 people to death. Furthermore, auto fires were increasing five times as fast as building fires. Another study showed that 35 per cent of all fire deaths in the U.S. occurred in automobiles. Forty per cent of all fire department calls in the 1960s were to vehicle fires—a public cost of $350 million a year, a figure that, incidentally, never shows up in cost-benefit analyses.

Another study was done by the Highway Traffic Research Institute in Ann Arbor, Michigan, a safety think-tank funded primarily by the auto industry (the giveaway there is the words "highway traffic" rather than "automobile" in the group's name). It concluded that 40 per cent of the lives lost in fuel-fed fires could be saved if the manufacturers complied with proposed Standard 301. Finally, a third report was prepared for NHTSA by consultant Eugene Trisko entitled "A National Survey of Motor Vehicle Fires." His report indicates that the Ford Motor Company makes 24 per cent of the cars on the American road, yet these cars account for 42 per cent of the collision-ruptured fuel tanks.

Ford lobbyists then used technique a)—bringing up a new argument. Their line then became: yes, perhaps burn accidents do happen, but rear-end collisions are relatively rare (note the echo of technique b) here as well). Thus Standard 301 was not needed. This set the NHTSA off on a new round of analyzing accident reports. The government's findings finally were that rear-end collisions were seven and a half times more likely to result in fuel spills than were front-end collisions. So much for that argument.

By now it was 1972; NHTSA had been researching and analyzing for four years to answer Ford's objections. During that time, nearly 9,000 people burned to death in flaming wrecks. Tens of thousands more were badly burned and scarred for life. And the four-year delay meant that well over 10 million new unsafe vehicles went on the road, vehicles that will be crashing, leaking fuel and incinerating people well into the 1980s.

Ford now had to enter its third round of battling the new regulations. On the "the problem is not X but Y" principle, the company had to look around for something new to get itself off the hook. One might have thought that, faced with all the latest statistics on the horrifying number of deaths in flaming accidents, Ford would find the task difficult. But the company's rhetoric was brilliant. The problem was not burns, but . . . impact! Most of the people killed in these fiery accidents, claimed Ford, would have died whether the car burned or not. They were killed by the kinetic force of the impact, not the fire.

And so once again, as in some giant underwater tennis game, the ball bounced into the government's court and the absurdly pro-industry NHTSA began another slow-motion response. Once again it began a time-consuming round of test crashes and embarked on a study of accidents. The latter, however, revealed that a large and growing number of corpses taken from burned cars involved in rear-end crashes contained no cuts, bruises or broken bones. They clearly would have survived the accident unharmed if the cars had not caught fire. This pattern was confirmed in careful rear-end crash tests performed by the Insurance Institute for Highway Safety. A University of Miami study found an inordinate number of Pintos burning on rear-end impact and concluded that this demonstrated "a clear and present hazard to all Pinto owners."

Pressure on NHTSA from Ralph Nader and consumer groups began mounting. The industry-agency collusion was so obvious that Senator Joseph Montoya (D-N.M.) introduced legislation about Standard 301. NHTSA waffled some more and again announced its intentions to promulgate a rear-end collision standard.

Waiting, as it normally does, until the last day allowed for response, Ford filed with NHTSA a gargantuan batch of letters, studies and charts now arguing that the federal testing criteria were unfair. Ford also argued that design changes required to meet the standard would take 43 months, which seemed like a rather long time in light of the fact that the entire Pinto was designed in about two years. Specifically, new complaints about the standard involved the weight of the test vehicle, whether or not the brakes should be engaged at the moment of impact and the claim that the standard should only apply to cars, not trucks or buses. Perhaps the most amusing argument was that the engine should not be idling during crash tests, the rationale being that an idling engine meant that the gas tank had to contain gasoline and that the hot lights needed to film the crash might ignite the gasoline and cause a fire.

Some of these complaints were accepted, others rejected. But they all required examination and testing by a weak-kneed NHTSA, meaning more of those 18-month studies the industry loves so much. So the complaints served their real purpose—delay; all told, an eight-year delay, while Ford manufactured more than three million profitable, dangerously incendiary Pintos. To justify this delay, Henry Ford II called more press conferences to predict the demise of American civilization. "If we can't meet the standards when they are published," he warned, "we will have to close down. And if we have to close down some production because we don't meet standards we're in for real trouble in this country."

ᐧᐤᐧ

While government bureaucrats dragged their feet on lifesaving Standard 301, a different kind of expert was taking a close look at the Pinto—the "recon man." "Recon" stands for reconstruction; recon men reconstruct accidents for police departments, insurance companies and lawyers who want to know exactly who or what caused an accident. It didn't take many rear-end Pinto accidents to demonstrate the weakness of the car. Recon men began encouraging lawyers to look beyond one driver or another to the manufacturer in their search for fault, particularly in the growing number of accidents where passengers were uninjured by collision but were badly burned by fire.

Pinto lawuits began mounting fast against Ford. Says John Versace, executive safety engineer at Ford's Safety Research Center, "Ulcers are running pretty high among the engineers who worked on the Pinto. Every lawyer in the country seems to want to take their depositions." (The Safety Research Center is an impressive glass and concrete building standing by itself about a mile from Ford World Headquarters in Dearborn. Looking at it, one imagines its large staff protects consumers from burned and broken limbs. Not so. The Center is the technical support arm of Jack Echold's 14-person anti-regulatory lobbying team in World Headquarters.)

When the Pinto liability suits began, Ford strategy was to go to a jury. Confident it could hide the Pinto crash tests, Ford thought that juries of solid American registered voters would buy the industry doctrine that drivers, not cars, cause accidents. It didn't work. It seems that juries are much quicker to see the truth than bureaucracies, a fact that gives one confidence in democracy. Juries began ruling against the company, granting million-dollar awards to plaintiffs.

"We'll never go to a jury again," says Al Slechter in Ford's Washington office. "Not in a fire case. Juries are just too sentimental. They see those charred remains and forget the evidence. No sir, we'll settle."

Settlement involves less cash, smaller legal fees and less publicity, but it is an indication of the weakness of their case. Nevertheless, Ford has been settling when it is clear that the company can't pin the blame on the driver of the other car. But, since the company carries $2 million deductible product-liability insurance, these settlements have a direct impact on the bottom line. They must therefore be considered a factor in determining the net operating profit on the Pinto. It's impossible to get a straight answer from Ford on the profitability of the Pinto and the impact of lawsuit settlements on it—even when you have a curious and mildly irate shareholder call to inquire, as we did. However, financial officer Charles Matthews did admit that the company establishes a reserve for large dollar settlements. He would not divulge the amount of the reserve and had no explanation for its absence from the annual report.

Until recently, it was clear that, whatever the cost of these settlements, it was not enough to seriously cut into the Pinto's enormous profits. The cost of retooling Pinto assembly lines and of equipping each car with a safety gadget like that $5.08 Goodyear bladder was, company accountants calculated, greater than that of paying out millions to survivors like Robbie Carlton or to widows and widowers of victims like Sandra Gillespie. The bottom line ruled, and inflammable Pintos kept rolling out of the factories.

In 1977, however, an incredibly sluggish government has at last instituted Standard 301. Now Pintos will have to have rupture-proof gas tanks. Or will they?

⟡

To everyone's surprise, the 1977 Pinto recently passed a rear-end crash test in Phoenix, Arizona, for NHTSA. The agency was so convinced the Pinto would fail that it was the first car tested. Amazingly, it did not burst into flame.

"We have had so many Ford failures in the past," explained agency engineer Tom Grubbs, "I felt sure the Pinto would fail."

How did it pass?

Remember that one-dollar, one-pound plastic baffle that was on one of the three modified Pintos that passed the pre-production crash tests nearly ten years ago? Well, it is a standard feature on the 1977 Pinto. In the Phoenix test it protected the gas tank from being perforated by those four bolts on the differential housing.

We asked Grubbs if he noticed any other substantial alterations in the rear-end structure of the car. "No," he replied, "the [plastic baffle] seems to be the only noticeable change over the 1976 model."

But was it? What Tom Grubbs and the Department of Transportation didn't know when they tested the car was that it was manufactured in St. Thomas, Ontario. Ontario? The significance of that becomes clear when you learn that Canada has for years had extremely strict rear-end collision standards.

Tom Irwin is the business manager of Charlie Rossi Ford, the Scottsdale, Arizona, dealership that sold the Pinto to Tom Grubbs. He refused to explain why he was selling Fords made in Canada when there is a huge Pinto assembly plant much closer by in California. "I know why you're asking that question, and I'm not going to answer it," he blurted out. "You'll have to ask the company."

But Ford's regional office in Phoenix has "no explanation" for the presence of Canadian cars in their local dealerships. Farther up the line in Dearborn, Ford people claim there is absolutely no difference between American and Canadian Pintos. They say cars are shipped back and forth across the border as a matter of course. But they were hard pressed to explain why some Canadian Pintos were shipped all the way to Scottsdale, Arizona. Significantly, one engineer at the St. Thomas plant did admit that the existence of strict rear-end collision standards in Canada "might encourage us to pay a little more attention to quality control on that part of the car."

The Department of Transportation is considering buying an American Pinto and running the test again. For now, it will only say that the situation is under investigation.

Whether the new American Pinto fails or passes the test, Standard 301 will never force the company to test or recall the more than two million pre-1977 Pintos still on the highway. Seventy or more people will burn to death in those cars every year for many years to come. If the past is any indication, Ford will continue to accept the deaths.

According to safety expert Byron Bloch, the older cars could quite easily be retrofitted with gas tanks containing fuel cells. "These improved tanks would add at least 10 mph improved safety performance to the rear end," he estimated, "but it would cost Ford $20 to $30 a car, so they won't do it unless they are forced to." Dr. Kenneth Saczalski, safety engineer with the Office of Naval Research in Washington, agrees. "The Defense Department has developed virtually fail-safe fuel systems and retrofitted them into existing vehicles. We have shown them to the auto industry and they have ignored them."

Unfortunately, the Pinto is not an isolated case of corporate malpractice in the auto industry. Neither is Ford a lone sinner. There probably isn't a car on the road without a safety hazard known to its manufacturer. And though Ford may have the best auto lobbyists in Washington, it is not alone. The anti-emission control lobby and the anti-safety lobby usually work in chorus form, presenting a well-harmonized message from the country's richest industry, spoken through the voices of individual companies—the Motor Vehicle Manufacturers Association, the Business Council and the U.S. Chamber of Commerce.

Furthermore, cost-valuing human life is not used by Ford alone. Ford was just the only company careless enough to let such an embarrassing calculation slip into the public records. The process of willfully trading lives for profits is built into corporate capitalism. Commodore Vanderbilt publicly scorned George Westinghouse and his "foolish" air brakes while people died by the hundreds in accidents on Vanderbilt's railroads.

The original draft of the Motor Vehicle Safety Act provided for criminal sanction against a manufacturer who willfully placed an unsafe car on the market. Early in the proceedings the auto industry lobbied the provision out of the bill. Since then, there have been those damage settlements, of course, but the only government punishment meted out to auto companies for noncompliance to standards has been a minuscule fine, usually $5,000 to $10,000. One wonders how long the Ford Motor Company would continue to market lethal cars were Henry Ford II and Lee Iacocca serving 20-year terms in Leavenworth for consumer homicide.

 **NO**

Closing Argument by Mr. Neal

If it please the Court, Counsel, ladies and gentlemen:

Not too many years ago our broad American Industry straddled the world like a giant.

It provided us with the highest standards of living ever known to man.

It was ended, eliminated, no more. Now it is an Industry weakened by deteriorating plants and equipment, weakened by lack of products, weakened by lack of manpower, weakened by inadequate capital, weakened by massive Government controls, weakened by demands on foreign oil and reeling from competition from foreign manufacturers.

I stand here today to defend a segment of that tattered Industry.

One company that saw the influx of foreign, small-made cars in 1967 and '68 and tried to do something about it, tried to build a small car with American labor that would compete with foreign imports, that would keep Americans employed, that would keep American money in America.

As State's witness, Mr. Copp, admitted, Ford Motor Company would have made more profit sticking to the bigger cars where the profit is.

That would have been the easiest way.

It was not the way Ford Motor Company took.

It made the Ford to compete. And this is no easy effort, members of the jury.

As even Mr. Copp admitted, the Automobile Industry is extremely regulated.

It has to comply with the Clean Air Act, the Safety Act, the Emissions Control Act, the Corporate Average Fuel Economy Act, the Safety Act, and OSHA as well as a myriad of Statutes and Regulations applicable to large and small businesses generally, and, again, as Mr. Copp admitted, it now takes twice as many Engineers to make a car as it did before all the massive Government controls.

Nevertheless, Ford Motor Company undertook the effort to build a subcompact, to take on the imports, to save jobs for Americans and to make a profit for its stockholders.

This rather admirable effort has a sad ending.

On August 10, 1978, a young man gets into a van weighing over 4,000 pounds and heads towards Elkhart, Indiana, on a bad highway called "U.S. 33."

He has a couple of open beer bottles in his van, together with his marijuana which he may or may not have been smoking. . . .

From U.S. District Court, South Bend, Indiana, State of Indiana v. Ford Motor Company (January 15, 1980).

As he was cruising along on an open stretch of highway in broad daylight at at least 50 to 55 miles per hour, he drops his "smoke," ignores his driving and the road, and fails to see a little Pinto with its emergency flashers on stopped on the highway ahead.

He plows into the rear of the Pinto with enormous force and three young girls are killed.

Not the young man, but Ford Motor Company is charged with reckless homicide and arraigned before you.

I stand here to defend Ford Motor Company, and to tell you that we are not killers. . . .

Mr. Cosentino gave you the definition of "reckless homicide" as "plain, conscious and unjustifiable disregard of harm, which conduct involves substantial deviation from acceptable standards of conduct."

This case and the elements of this case, strictly speaking, involve 40 days, July 1, 1978 to August 10, 1978, and the issue is whether, during that period of time, Ford Motor Company recklessly, as that term is defined, omitted to warn of a danger and repair, and that reckless omission caused the deaths involved. . . .

[I]n my opening statement, I asked you to remember nine points, and I asked you to judge me, my client, by how well or how poorly we supported those nine points.

Let me run through briefly and just tick them off, the nine points, with you, and then let me get down to discussing the evidence and record with respect to those nine points.

One, I said this was a badly-designed highway, with curbs so high the girls couldn't get off when they had to stop their car in an emergency.

Two, I said that the girls stopped there with their emergency flashers on, and this boy in a van weighing more than 4,000 pounds, with his eyes off the road, looking down trying to find the "smoke," rammed into the rear of that Pinto at at least 50 miles an hour, closing speed.

And by "closing speed," I mean the differential speed.

That is Points 1 and 2.

Point 3, I said the 1973 Pinto met every fuel-system integrity standard of any Federal, State or Local Government.

Point No. 4, I said, Ford Motor Company adopted a mandatory standard dealing with fuel-system integrity on rear-impact of 20 miles per hour moving-barrier, 4,000 pound moving-barrier, and I said that no other manufacturer in the world had adopted any standard, only Ford Motor Company.

Five, I said that the Pinto, it is not comparable to a Lincoln Continental, a Cadillac, a Mercedes Benz or that Ascona, or whatever that exotic car was that Mr. Bloch called—but I did say No. 5, it is comparable to other 1973 subcompacts.

No. 6, I said that . . . we would bring in the Engineers who designed and manufactured the Pinto, and I brought them from the stand, and they would tell you that they thought the Pinto was a good, safe car, and they bought it for themselves, their wives and their children to drive.

No. 7, I told you that we would bring in the statistics that indicated to us as to our state of mind that the Pinto performed as well or better than other subcompacts.

And, No. 8, I said we would nevertheless tell you that we decided to recall the Pinto in June of 1978, and having made that decision for the reasons that I—that I told you I would explain, we did everything in our power to recall that Pinto as quickly as possible, that there was nothing we could have done between July 1, 1978 and 8-10-1978, to recall the Pinto any faster.

And finally, No. 9, I said we would demonstrate that any car, any subcompact, any small car, and even some larger cars, sitting out there on Highway 33 in the late afternoon of August 10, 1978 and watching that van roar down that highway with the boy looking for his "smoke"—any car would have suffered the same consequences.

Those are the nine points I ask you to judge me by, and let me touch on the evidence, now, with respect to those nine points. . . .

The van driver, Duggar, took his eyes off the road and off driving to look around the floor of the van for a "smoke."

Duggar had two open beer bottles in the car and a quantity of marijuana.

Duggar was not prosecuted for reckless homicide or for possession of marijuana, even though his prior record of conviction was:

November, '73, failure to yield right-of-way;

April, '76, speeding 65 miles an hour in a 45 mile an hour zone;

July, '76, running stop sign;

June, '77, speeding 45 in a 25 zone;

August, '77, driver's license suspended;

September, '77, driving with suspended license;

December, '77, license suspended again.

Mr. Cosentino, you got up in front of this jury and you cried.

Well, I cry, too, because Mr. Duggar is driving, and you didn't do anything about him with a record like that except say, "Come in and help me convict Ford Motor Company, and I will help you get probation."

We all cry.

But crying doesn't do any good, and it doesn't help this jury.

The big disputed fact in this case regarding the accident, ladies and gentlemen, is the closing speed. The differential speed, the difference between the speed the Pinto was going, if any, and the speed the van was going.

That is the big disputed fact in regard to this accident.

And whether the Pinto was stopped or not is relevant only as it affects closing speed. . . .

Mr. Duggar testified—I guess he is great about speed, because while he's looking down there for his "smoke," he knows he is going 50 miles per hour in the van.

But he said he was going 50 miles per hour at the time of impact, and he said the Pinto was going 15.

But here is the same man who admits he was going at least 50 miles per hour and looking around down "on a clear day," trying to find the "smoke" and looked up only to see the Pinto ten feet ahead of him.

Here is a witness willing to say under oath that the Pinto was going 15 miles per hour, even though he had one-sixth of a second—one-sixth of a second to make the judgment on the speed.

Here is a witness who says he had the time to calculate the speed of the Pinto but had no time even to try to apply brakes because there were no skid marks.

And here is a witness who told Dr. Galen Miller, who testified here, that—told him right after the accident that in fact the Pinto was stopped.

And here was a witness who made a deal with the State.

And here was a witness who's not prosecuted for recklessness.

And here is a witness who is not prosecuted for possession of marijuana.

So the State's proof from Mr. Alfred Clark through Mr. Duggar is kind of a smorgasbord or a buffet—you can go in and take your choice.

You can pick 15—5 miles per hour, if you want to as to differential speed, or you can take 35 miles per hour.

And the State, with the burden of proof says, "Here," "Here," "Here. I will give you a lot of choice."

"You want choices? I will give you choices. Here. Take 5. Take 15. 10, 15, 20, 25, 30, 35."

Because, ladies and gentlemen of the jury,—and I'm sure you are—the alternatives the State offers you are closing speeds of anywhere from 5 miles—on the low side—to 35 miles on the high side as a differential speed in this accident. . . .

Mr. Toms, the former National Highway Traffic Safety Administrator, told you that in his opinion the 20 mile per hour rear-impact moving-barrier was a reasonable and acceptable standard of conduct for 1973 vehicles.

Why didn't Ford adopt a higher standard?

Mr. MacDonald, a man even Mr. Copp—do you remember this? Mr. Mac-Donald sitting on the stand, the father of the Pinto, as Mr. Cosentino called him—and he didn't deny it.

He says, "Yes, it is my car."

Mr. MacDonald, a man even Mr. Copp—on cross examination I asked him, I said:

"Q Mr. Copp, isn't it a fact that you consider Harold MacDonald an extremely safety-conscious Engineer?"

And he said:

"A Yes, sir."

Mr. MacDonald, that extremely safety-conscious Engineer, told you he did not believe a higher standard could be met for 1973 cars without greater problems, such as handling, where more accidents and death occur.

Mr. Copp, let's take the State's witness, Copp.

Mr. Copp admitted that even today, seven years later, the Federal Government Standard is only 30 miles per hour, 10 miles higher than what Ford adopted—voluntarily adopted for itself for 1973.

And Mr. Copp further testified that a 30 mile an hour would be equivalent only to a 31.5 or 32 mile car-to-car.

So, ladies and gentlemen of the jury, Mr. Cosentino tells you about, "Oh, isn't it terrible to put these cars out there, wasn't it awful—did you know?"

Well, do you know that today, the—today, 1980 model cars are required to meet only a 30 mile an hour rear-impact moving-barrier standard? 1980 cars.

And that that is equivalent to a 32 mile an hour car-to-car, and yet Ford Motor Company, the only company in the world, imposed upon itself a standard and made a car in 1973, seven years ago, that would meet 26 to 28 miles an hour, within 5, 6 or 7 miles of what the cars are required by law to meet today.

Mr. Cosentino will tell you, frankly, the cars today, in his judgment, are defective and he will prosecute.

What a chaos would evolve if the Government set the standard for automobiles and says, "That is reasonable," and then Local Prosecutors in the fifty states around the country start saying, "I am not satisfied, and I am going to prosecute the manufacturer."

Well, Mr. Cosentino may say that the standard should be 40.

The Prosecutor in Alabama may say, "No, it should be 50."

The Prosecutor in Alaska may say, "No, it should be 60."

And the Prosecutor in Tennessee—they say—you know, "I am satisifed—I am satisfied with 30," or, "I think it should be 70."

How can our companies survive?

Point 5, the 1973 Pinto was comparable in design and manufacture to other 1973 subcompacts.

I say again, ladies and gentlemen, we don't compare the Pinto with Lincolns, Cadillacs, Mercedes Benz—we ask you to compare the Pinto with the other three subcompacts.

Let's take the State's witnesses on this point first.

Mr. Bloch—Mr. Cosentino didn't mention Mr. Bloch, but I don't want him to be forgotten.

Mr. Bloch and Mr. Copp complain about the Pinto, and that is easy.

Let's descend to the particulars. Let's see what they really said.

Well, they complain about the metal, the gage of the metal in the fuel tank; you remember that?

And then on cross examination it was brought out that the general range of metal in fuel tanks ranged between twenty-three-thousandths of an inch and forty-thousandths of an inch.

That is the general range. Twenty-three-thousandths on the low to forty-thousandths on the high, and lo and behold, what is the gage of metal in the Pinto tank?

Thirty-five-thousandths.

And Mr. Bloch admits that it is in the upper third of the general range.

And they complain about the bumper on the Pinto.

And, remember, I said we would show that the Pinto was comparable to other '73 subcompacts.

They complain about the bumper, but then they admit on cross examination the Vega, the Gremlin, the Colt, the Pinto and the Toyota had about the same bumper.

And they complain of a lack of a protective shield between the tank and the axle, but they admitted on cross examination that no other 1973 car had such a shield, and Mr. Copp admits that there was no significant puncture in the 1973—in the Ulrich accident caused by the axle, and you remember I had him get up here and say, "Point out where this protective shield would have done something, where this puncture source we are talking about—" and you remember, it is so small—I can't find it now.

So much for the protective shield.

And then they complained about the insufficient rear structure in the Pinto, but they both admit that the Pinto had a left side rail hat section and that the Vega had none, nothing on either side, that the Pinto had shear plates, these plates in the trunk, and that neither the Vega, the Gremlin or the Colt or Toyota had any of these.

And the Vega used the coil-spring suspension, when the Pinto had a leaf-spring, and that was additional structure.

I am not going through all those—well, I will mention one more thing.

They talked about puncture sources, there is a puncture source there, puncture source here, but on cross examination, they end up by admitting that the puncture sources on all subcompacts have about the same—and in about the same space. . . .

Mr. MacDonald testified, "Yes, I thought the Pinto was a reasonably safe car. I think the '73 Pinto is still a reasonably safe car, and I bought one, I drove it for years for myself."

Mr. Olsen—you remember little Mr. Frank Olsen?

He came in here, has his little eighteen-year-old daughter—he said, "I am an Engineer responsible for the Pinto. I think it is a safe car. I bought one for my little eighteen-year-old daughter, and she drove it for several years."

And Mr. Freers, the man who Mr. Cosentino objected to going over the fact that he was from Rose-Hullman, and on the Board of Trustees there—Mr. Freers said, "I like the Pinto. I am an Engineer responsible for the Pinto, and I bought a '73 Pinto for my young son and he drove it several years."

And then Mr. Feaheny says, "I am one of the Engineers responsible for the Pinto, and I bought one for my wife, the mother of my six children, and she drove it for several years."

Now, when Mr. Cosentino tried to say there was something phoney about that—he brought out their salaries.

And I—I don't know how to deal with the salary question.

It just seems to me to be so irrelevant, like some other things I am going to talk about in a minute that I am just going to simply say, "It is irrelevant," and go on.

But he said to these people—he suggested to you, suggested to these people, "Well, you make a lot of money, you can afford better than a Pinto."

Like, "You don't really mean you had a Pinto?"

And Mr. Feaheny says, "Yes, I could afford a more expensive car, but, you know, I—all of us, we have been fighting, we come out with something we thought would fight the imports, and we were proud of it, and our families were proud of it."

Do you think, ladies and gentlemen of the jury, that Mr. MacDonald was indifferent, reckless, when he bought and drove the Pinto?

He drives on the same roads, he has the—subject to the same reckless people that Mr. Cosentino didn't prosecute.

Do you think that Mr. Olsen was reckless and indifferent when he gave a Pinto to his eighteen-year-old daughter, a '73 Pinto?

Do you think that Mr. Freers was reckless when he gave one to his young son? . . .

Finally, ladies and gentlemen—not "finally," but Point No. 8: Notwithstanding all I have said, Ford Motor Company decided on June 8th, 1978, to recall the Pintos to improve fuel systems and did everything in its power to recall it as quickly as possible.

This is really what this case, I guess, is all about, because that period of time involved is July 1, 1978 until August 10, 1978.

And the Court will charge you, as I said, the elements are whether we recklessly failed to warn and repair during that period of time.

And whether that reckless omission, if any, caused the deaths.

And you may ask—and I think it is fair to ask—why recall the Pinto, the '73 Pinto, if it is comparable to other subcompacts, if statistics say it is performing as well as other '73 subcompacts?

And if Ford had a standard for '73 that no other manufacturer had?

And Feaheny and Mr. Misch told you why.

The Federal Government started an investigation. The publicity was hurting the Company.

They thought the Government was wrong, but they said, "You can't fight City Hall."

"We could fight and fight and we could go to Court and we could fight, but it's not going to get us anywhere. If we can improve it, let's do it and let's don't fight the Federal Government."

Maybe the Company should not have recalled the '73 Pinto.

Douglas Toms did not think, as he told you on the stand under oath, that the '73 Pinto should have been recalled.

He had information that the Pinto did as well as other cars;

That Pinto fire accidents equaled the total Pinto population or equaled the percentage of Pinto population to all car population.

And Mr. Bloch, on the other hand, says, "All of them should be recalled."

He said, "The Pinto should have been recalled."

He said, "The Vega should have been recalled."

He said, "The Gremlin should be recalled."

And he didn't know about the Dodge Colt.

Nevertheless, the Company did decide to recall the Pinto. And they issued widely-disseminated Press Releases on June 9, 1978.

It was in the newspapers, TV, radio, according to the proof in this case.

And thereafter the Government regulated what they did in the recall.

That is what Mr. Misch told you.

He said, "From the time we started—June 9, 1978—to August 10, Mr.—the Federal Government regulated what we did."

Now, Mr. Cosentino is prosecuting us.

And the Federal Government has regulated us.

Mr. Misch said, "The Federal Government reviewed what kind of Press Releases we should issue, what kind of Recall Letter we should issue, what kind of a Modification Kit that they would approve."

Even so—it is undisputed, absolutely undisputed that we did everything in our power to recall as fast as possible—nights, days, weekends.

And notwithstanding all of that, the first kit—the first complete kit was assembled August 1, 1978.

And on August 9, 1978, there were only 20,000 kits available for 1,600,000 cars.

And this was not Ford's fault. Ford was pushing the suppliers, the people who were outside the Company doing work for them.

And Mr. Vasher testified that he got the names of the current owners from R. L. Polk on July 17;

That the Ulrich name was not among them;

That he sent the Recall Letter in August to the original owner because he had no Ulrich name.

Now,—and he said he couldn't have gotten the Ulrich name by August 10.

Now, Mr. Cosentino said, "Well, the Ulrich Registration was on file with the State of Indiana and it is open to the public."

Well, Ford Motor Company doesn't know where these 1,600,000 cars are. It has to use R. L. Polk because they collect the information by the VIN Numbers.

If Ford Motor Company went to each state, they would go to fifty states and they would have each of the fifty states run through its files 1,600,000 VIN Numbers.

And Mr. Vasher, who is the expert in there, said it would take months and months to do that.

And, finally, ladies and gentlemen, the Government didn't approve the Modification Kit until August 15, 1978.

But the State says that we should have warned—we should have warned 1973 Pinto owners not to drive the car.

But the Government never suggested that.

Based on our information, and confirmed by the Toms testimony, our cars were performing as well—or better than—other '73 subcompacts.

As Mr. Misch so succinctly stated, "We would have been telling the Pinto owners to park their Pintos and get into another car no safer—and perhaps even less safe—than the Pinto." . . .

Well, we submit that the physical facts, the placement of the—the placement of the gasoline cap, where it is found, the testimony of Levi Woodard, and Nancy Fogo—demonstrate the closing speed in this case was at least 50 to 60 miles per hour.

Mr. Copp, the State's witness, testified that no small car made in America in 1973 would withstand 40 to 50 miles per hour—40 to 50 rear-impact. No small car made in America in 1973 would withstand a 40-plus mile per hour rear-impact.

The Dodge Colt would not have; the Vega could not have; the Gremlin would not have; and certainly even the Toyota would not have.

Mr. Habberstad told you that no small car—and some big cars—would have withstood this crash.

And he established by the crash-tests you have seen that the Vega could not withstand 50;

That the Gremlin could not withstand 50;

That the Toyota Corolla with the tank over the axle could not withstand 50;

And that even a full-sized Chevrolet Impala cannot withstand 50 miles per hour.

If it made no difference what kind of car was out there, members of the jury, how can Ford Motor Company have caused the deaths? . . .

I am not here to tell you that the 1973 Pinto was the strongest car ever built.

I'm not here to tell you it is equal to a Lincoln, a Cadillac, a Mercedes—that funny car that Mr. Bloch mentioned.

I'm not here to tell you a stronger car couldn't be built.

Most of us, however, learn early in life that there is "no Santa Claus," and, "There's no such thing as a free lunch."

If the public wanted it, and could pay for it, and we had the gasoline to drive it, Detroit could build a tank of a car—a car that would withstand practically anything, a car that would float if a careless driver drove it into the water.

A car that would be invulnerable even to the "Duggars" of the world.

But, members of the jury, only the rich could afford it and they would have to stop at every other gasoline station for a refill.

I am here to tell you that the 1973 Pinto is comparable to other '73 subcompacts, including that Toyota, that Corolla with the tank over the axle.

I am here to tell you it was not designed by some mysterious figure you have never seen.

It was designed and manufactured by Harold MacDonald, Frank Olsen and Howard Freers.

I am here to tell you these are the decent men doing an honorable job and trying to do a decent job.

I am here to tell you that Harold MacDonald, Frank Olsen, and Howard Freers are not reckless killers.

Harold MacDonald is the same man, State's witness, Copp, called an "extremely safety-conscious individual."

Frank Olsen is the same "Frank Olsen" Mr. Copp said was a "good Engineer."

And Howard Freers is the same "Howard Freers" Mr. Copp said was a "man of honesty and integrity."

I am here to tell you that these men honestly believe and honestly believed that the 1973 Pinto was—and is—a reasonably safe car—so safe they bought it for their daughters, sons and family.

Do you think that Frank Olsen believed he was acting in plain, conscious, unjustifiable disregard of harm?

When he bought a '73 Pinto for his eighteen-year-old daughter?

Or Howard Freers, when he bought one for his young son?

I am here to tell you that the design and manufacture of an automobile is not an easy task;

That it takes time to know whether a change in one part of the 14,000 parts of a car will or will not cause greater problems elsewhere in the car or its performance.

I am here to tell you that safety is a matter of degree;

That no one can say that a car that will meet a 26 to 28 mile per hour rear-impact is unsafe and one that will meet a 30 to 32 impact is safe.

I am here to tell you that if this country is to survive economically, it is really time to stop blaming Industry or Business, large or small, for our own sins.

I am here to tell you that no car is now or ever can be safe when reckless drivers are on the road.

I am here to tell you that Ford Motor Company may not be perfect, but it is not guilty of reckless homicide.

Thank you, members of the jury.

And God bless you in your deliberations.

POSTSCRIPT

Was Ford to Blame in the Pinto Case?

Well, is Ford guilty? The jury said no, but the larger issue remains open: how shall we allot responsibility, where many factors combine to bring about an injury?

Consider the following: Ford Motor Company obeyed the law, but the law was not all it should have been. The reason it was not is that the Ford Motor Company spent a great deal of money lobbying Congress to put obstacles in front of new and higher legal safety standards, in order to be able to sell the Pinto for a lower price and thus increase its market share and yes, its profits. Is not the government, through its agencies, just as guilty as Ford for not fulfilling its role as protector of the consumer?

What was the government's duty at this point? To protect those consumers of the automobile? To protect the workers in the Ford Motor Company factories? To protect the American manufacturers against further encroachments from foreign competition? Does government have some absolute duty in these cases, or are our legislators asked only to bring about the greatest good for the greatest number? How would they have done *that*, in this case? Three girls aren't very many. Could it not be shown that all the people who innocently and safely enjoyed their Pintos at the lower cost outweigh, in their happiness, the enormous unhappiness of the very few who got burned? Or is that the sort of thinking that we take ethics courses to learn not to do?

Ford Motor Company found new structural allies when the criminal negligence case was brought against it. Under our Constitution, the legal system joins in to protect the defendant in these cases. When we enter the courtroom, and The People stand at the bar training all Its accusatory weight against an individual, the traditions weigh in heavily on the side of the individual—and in general, that is as we want it to be. It seems odd that the same traditions apply when the "individual" is one of the largest corporations in the world. If you are very large and rich, you can hire lawyers like James Neal, who knows how to discount every bit of evidence against his client, how to introduce every piece of evidence in favor, and then also knows how to discredit witnesses, how to argue by suggestion, and above all how to deflect attention from his client's wrongdoing. His facts are correct, his presentation is inherently plausible—*of course* the driver of the van was at fault—and his style is immensely entertaining. Could The People hire such a lawyer? Not on your life.

Have we lost perspective on risk? We know how to make a safe car. We build it like a tank and rig it to go no faster than 30 miles per hour. But no one would buy it. So we make unsafe cars that people will buy—lighter, faster, more likely to crumple and burn in an accident. Is this trade-off acceptable to a trading nation that is used to making choices? Or should we be more diligent about eliminating the last threats to safety?

Suggested Reading

For more information regarding the Pinto case and its subsequent effects, try some of the following readings:

Lawrence A. Benningson and Arnold I. Benningson, "Product Liability: Manufacturers Beware!" *Harvard Business Review* 53(3): 122–32 (May–June 1974).

Richard DeGeorge, "Ethical Responsibilities of Engineers in Large Organizations: The Pinto Case." *Business and Professional Ethics Journal* 1(1): 4–14 (Fall 1981).

Richard A. Epstein, "Is Pinto a Criminal?" *Regulation* (March–April 1980), pp. 16–17.

Niles Howard and Susan Antilla, "What Price Safety? The 'Zero-Risk' Debate." *Dun's Review* (September 1979), pp. 47–57.

Alvin S. Weinstein, *Products Liability and the Reasonably Safe Product: A Guide for Management, Design and Marketing* (New York: John Wiley & Sons, 1978)

Mark B. Fuller and Malcolm S. Salter, "Ford Motor Company (A)," (Boston: Case Study, Harvard Business School, 1982), p. 4.

ISSUE 16

Should We Require Labeling for Genetically Modified Food?

YES: Philip L. Bereano, from "The Right to Know What We Eat," *Seattle Times* (October 11, 1998)

NO: Joseph A. Levitt, from Statement before the Health, Education, Labor, and Pensions Committee, United States Senate (September 26, 2000)

ISSUE SUMMARY

YES: The consumer's interest in knowing where his food comes from does not necessarily have to do with the chemical and nutritional properties of the food. Kosher pastrami, for instance, is identical to the nonkosher product, and dolphin-safe tuna is still tuna. But we have a real and important interest in knowing the processes by which our foods arrived on the table, Bereano argues, and the demand for a label for bioengineered foods is entirely legitimate.

NO: Levitt points out that as far as the law is concerned, only the nutritional traits and characteristics of foods are subject to safety assessment. Labeling has been required only where health risks exist, or where there is danger that a product's marketing claims may mislead the consumer as to the food's characteristics. Breeding techniques have never been subject to labeling, nor should genetic engineering techniques.

How much weight can a little label bear? We have seen a profound change in the function of the label over the course of the last century. At first, the label, if such there was, said only what the container contained and the brand name. "Carter's Little Liver Pills." "Argo Cornstarch." With advances in packaging, the labels became more attractive, brighter, eye-catching, and began to carry marketing claims. That was the label's purpose: to sell the product, by featuring a trusted brand name (logo, trademark) and an advertisement for the product, in a design aimed at capturing attention.

Poisons, of course, had to be labeled as such, to warn consumers to use them carefully—and to warn off the vulnerable. Remember the frightening skull and crossbones?

The consumer movement changed all that. Calling upon the police power of the state (the right and obligation of the state to protect the health, safety, and morals of the citizens), the Food and Drug Administration began requiring labels to fulfill serious informational functions. Now actual weights have to be listed on the package, a list of ingredients in order of weight must appear on any complex product, and the real nutritional content has to be listed in a plainly visible uniform panel on the back of the package (even for little candy bars). Even nonfood items have labeling requirements; garments and bedding must state the materials from which they are made, and bedding labels must warrant that those materials are new.

Those who would like genetically modified foods to be labeled as such do not conceal their interest in the same agenda. They would like to see all GM foods (corn, for instance) and all processed foods containing GM ingredients (vegetable oil, for instance) labeled as such, so that consumers will be worried by the labels, so that eventually GM foods will be taken off the market. In the light of the general profitability of GM foods, it seems politically more feasible to get a labeling requirement than a prohibition. Besides, in some polls, up to 70 percent of consumers have said that they would want to know if the product they bought was genetically modified. Who could object to full information about a product, the process by which it was produced as well as its content, being given to the consumer?

As it turns out, there are many objections. One is the sheer mass of effort required to sort out foods that contain GM products (practically ubiquitous at this point), especially processed foods like cereals and bake mixes. More important, whether or not a label designates a difference in a product, the consumer must assume it does, and must assume, unless there is proof to the contrary, that it designates a dangerous difference. There was no doubt as to the intention or the effect of the requirement of labeling for tobacco products. There is every reason to think that a required label, "Contains Genetically Modified Products," would be read as a skull and crossbones.

Not every political agenda justifies labeling, after all. How would we react to a request to label as such all boxes of tampons or sanitary pads that were packed by African Americans? Suppose we could come up with a survey that showed that up to 70 percent of white women in a particular area would want to have that information. Would that influence our reaction? Ask yourself, as you read the following selections, just what political agenda or secondary purposes we want attached to the police power of the state. Is the demand for "labeling" justified or not?

YES

Philip L. Bereano

The Right to Know What We Eat

"I personally have no wish to eat anything produced by genetic modification, nor do I knowingly offer this sort of produce to my family or guests. There is increasing evidence that many people feel the same way."

—Prince Charles, London Telegraph, June 8, 1998.

Genetic engineering is a set of new techniques for altering the basic makeup of plants and animals. Genes from insects, animals and humans have been added to crop plants; human genes have been added to pigs and cattle.

Although genetic-engineering techniques are biologically novel, the industry and government are so eager to achieve financial success that they say the products of the technologies are pretty much the same ("substantially equivalent") as normal crops. Despite the gene tinkering, the new products are not being tested extensively to find out how they differ and to be sure that any hazards are within acceptable limits.

These foods are now appearing in the supermarkets and on our dinner plates, but the industry and government have been vigorously resisting consumer attempts to label these "novel foods" in order to distinguish them from more traditional ones.

The failure of the U.S. government to require that genetically engineered foods (GEFs) be labeled presents consumers with quandaries: issues of free speech and consumers' right to know, religious rights for those with dietary restrictions, and cultural rights for people, such as vegetarians, who choose to avoid consuming foods of certain origins.

The use of antibiotic-resistant genes engineered into crop plants as "markers" can contribute to the spread of antibiotic-tolerant disease bacteria; this resistance is a major public-health problem, as documented by a recent study of the National Academy of Sciences. Some genetic recombinations can lead to allergic or auto-immune reactions. The products of some genes which are used as plant pesticides have been implicated in skin diseases in farm and market workers.

The struggle over labeling is occurring because industry knows that consumers do not want to eat GEFs; labeled products will likely fail in the marketplace. However, as the British publication The Economist noted, "if Monsanto cannot persuade us, it certainly has no right to foist its products on us." Labels would counter "foisting" and are legally justifiable.

The Government's Rationale

In 1992, the government abdicated any supervision over GEFs. Under Food and Drug Administration's rules, the agency does not even have access to industry information about a GEF unless the company decides voluntarily to submit it. Moreover, important information on risk-assessment questions is often withheld as being proprietary, "confidential business information." So "safety" cannot be judged in a precautionary way; we must await the inevitable hazardous event.

According to a former FDA official, the genetic processes used in the development of a new food are "NOT considered to be material information because there is no evidence that new biotech foods are different from other foods in ways related to safety."

James Maryanski, FDA biotechnology coordinator, claims that whether a food has been genetically engineered is not a "material fact" and FDA would not "require things to be on the label just because a consumer might want to know them."

Yet a standard law dictionary defines "material" as "important," "going to the merits," "relevant." Since labeling is a form of speech from growers and processors to purchasers, it is reasonable, therefore, to interpret "material" as comprising whatever issues a substantial portion of the consuming public defines as "important." And all the polls show that whether food is genetically engineered falls into such a category.

Last May, several religious leaders and citizen groups sued the FDA to change its position and to require that GEFs be labeled.

Process Labels

Some government officials have said that labeling should be only about the food product itself, not the process by which it is manufactured. Yet, the U.S. has many process food labels: kosher, dolphin-free, Made in America, union-made, free-range (chickens, for example), irradiated, and "green" terms such as "organic."

For many of these products, the scientific difference between an item which can carry the label and that which cannot is negligible or nonexistent. Kosher pastrami is chemically identical to non-kosher meat. Dolphin-free tuna and tuna caught by methods which result in killing of dolphins are the same, as are many products which are "made in America" when compared to those made abroad, or those made by unionized as opposed to nonunion workers.

These labeling rules recognize that consumers are interested in the processes by which their purchases are made and have a legal right to such knowledge. In none of these labeling situations has the argument been made that if the products are substantially equivalent, no label differentiation is permissible. It is constitutionally permissible for government rules to intrude slightly on the commercial speech of producers in order to expand the First Amendment rights of consumers to know what is of significant interest to them.

Substantial Equivalence

In order to provide an apparently rational basis for its refusal to exercise regulatory oversight in this regard, the U.S. government has adopted the industry's position that genetically engineered foods are "substantially equivalent" to their natural counterparts. The FDA ignores the contradictory practice of corporations in going to another government agency, the Patent Office, where they argue that a GEF is novel and different (in order to justify receiving monopoly protection).

"Substantial equivalence" is used as a basis for both eliminating regulatory assessment and failing to require labels on GEFs. However, the concept of substantial equivalence is subjective and imprecise.

Most genetic engineering is designed to meet corporate—not consumer—needs. Foods are engineered, for instance, to produce "counterfeit freshness." Consumers believe engineered characteristics such as color and texture indicate freshness, flavor and nutritional quality. Actually the produce is aging and growing stale, and nutritional value is being depleted. So much for "substantial equivalence."

The Precautionary Principle

Consumers International, a global alliance of more than 200 consumer groups, has suggested that "because the effects (of GEFs) are so difficult to predict, it is vital to have internationally agreed and enforceable rules for research protocols, field trials and post-marketing surveillance." This approach has become known as the "precautionary principle" and has entered into the regulatory processes of the European Union.

The principle reflects common-sense aphorisms such as "Better safe than sorry" and "An ounce of prevention is worth a pound of cure." It rests on the notion that parties who wish to change the social order (often while making money or gaining power and influence) should not be able to slough the costs and risks onto others. The new procedure's proponents should have to prove it is safe rather than forcing regulators or citizens to prove a lack of safety.

Look Before You Eat

For GEFs, labeling performs important functions in carrying out the precautionary principle. It places a burden on industry to show that genetic manipulations are socially beneficial and provides a financial incentive for them to do research to reduce uncertainty about the consequences of GEFs.

Democratic notions of free speech include the right to receive information as well as to disseminate it. It is fundamental to capitalist market theory that for transactions to be most efficient all parties must have "perfect information." The realities of modern food production create a tremendous imbalance of knowledge between producer and purchaser. Our society has relied on the government to redress this imbalance and make grocery shopping a fairer and more efficient—as well as safer—activity.

In an economic democracy, choice is the fundamental prerogative of the purchaser.

As some biologists have put it, "The risk associated with genetically engineered foods is derived from the fact that, although genetic engineers can cut and splice DNA molecules with precision in the test tube, when those altered DNA molecules are introduced into a living organism, the full range of effects on that organism cannot be predicted or known before commercialization. The introduced DNA may bring about unintended changes, some of which may be damaging to health."

Numerous opinion polls in the U.S. and abroad in the past decade have shown great skepticism about genetic alteration of foods; a large proportion of respondents, usually majorities, are reluctant to use such products. Regardless of whether they would consume GEFs, consumers feel even more strongly that they should be labeled.

In a Toronto Star poll reported on June 2, 98 percent favored labeling. Bioindustry giant Novartis surveyed U.S. consumers and found 93 percent of them wanted information about genetic engineering of food.

Alice Waters, originator of the legendary Berkeley restaurant Chez Panisse and recently selected to organize a new restaurant at the Louvre in Paris, has said, "The act of eating is very political. You buy from the right people, you support the right network of farmers and suppliers who care about the land and what they put in the food. If we don't preserve the natural resources, you aren't going to have a sustainable society."

However, the U.S. government has been resisting attempts to label GEFs. Despite the supposed environmentalist and consumer sympathies of the Clinton-Gore administration, the government believes nothing should impede the profitability of biotech as a mainstay to the future U.S. economy.

The administration's hostility to labeling may also be coupled to political contributions made to it by the interested industries.

Regulation and Free Speech

The government is constrained by the First Amendment from limiting or regulating the content of labels except for the historic functions of protecting health and safety and eliminating fraud or misrepresentation.

The American Civil Liberties Union has noted that "a simple distinction between noncommercial and commercial speech does not determine the extent to which the guarantees of the First Amendment apply to advertising and similar communications relating to the sale or other disposition of goods and services."

Supreme Court decisions have warned against attaching "more importance to the distinction between commercial and noncommercial speech than our cases warrant." Can the government prohibit certain commercial speech, such as barring a label saying "this product does not contain genetically engineered components"?

In several recent cases, the Court has restricted government regulation of commercial speech, in effect allowing more communication. The First Amendment directs us to be skeptical of regulations that seek to keep people in the dark for what the government perceives to be their own good. Thus, it would be hard to sustain the government if it tried to prohibit labeling foods as "free from genetically engineered products," if the statement were true.

In 1995, the FDA's Maryanski took the position that "the FDA is not saying that people don't have a right to know how their food is produced. But the food label is not always the most appropriate method for conveying that information." Is it acceptable for a government bureaucrat to make decisions about what are appropriate methods of information exchange among citizens?

The government and the industry suggest that labels on GEFs might amount to "misrepresentation" by implying that there is a difference between the genetically engineered and nongenetically engineered foods. It is hard, however, to understand how a truthful statement can ever amount to a "misrepresentation." (And of course, they are different, by definition.)

The first food product bearing a label "No GE Ingredients," a brand of corn chips, made its appearance this summer.

Some states have laws creating a civil cause of action against anyone who "disparages" an agricultural product unless the defendant can prove the statements were based on "reasonable and reliable scientific" evidence.

A Harvard analysis suggests that "at stake in the dispute about food-safety claims is scientific uncertainty in an uncertain and unpredictable world. Agricultural disparagement statutes are supposed to regulate the exchange of ideas in that gray area between science and the public good. The underlying approach of these statutes is to regulate speech by encouraging certain kinds of exchanges and punishing others. . . ."

According to the ACLU, "these so-called 'veggie libel' laws raise obvious First Amendment problems and threaten to chill speech on important issues of public concern." Consumers Union argues that "such laws, we believe, give the food and agriculture industry the power to choke off concerns and criticism about food quality and safety."

Such enactments did not prevail in the suit by Texas cattle ranchers against Oprah Winfrey and her guest Howard Lyman (of the Humane Society) for their on-air conversations about "mad-cow disease" possibilities in the United States. The lawsuit was widely seen as a test of the First Amendment constitutionality of such state statutes, although the case was actually resolved on much narrower grounds.

Consequences of Regulation

As Prince Charles noted in his essay, "we cannot put our principles into practice until there is effective segregation and labeling of genetically modified products. Arguments that this is either impossible or irrelevant are simply not credible."

Nonetheless, the biotech industry (and many governments, including our own) make the argument that it is impossible to keep genetically engineered foodstuffs separate from naturally produced ones. However, the same industries actually require rigorous segregation (for example, of seeds) when they are protecting their monopolies on patented food items.

Although it undoubtedly has related costs, the segregation of kosher food products from non-kosher ones, for example, has been routine in this country for decades. The only difference for GEFs appears to be one of scale, not technique, in monitoring the flow of foodstuffs, spot-testing and labeling them appropriately.

In Support of Mandatory Labeling

Can the government mandate commercial speech—for example, requiring GEFs to bear a label proclaiming their identity?

The government does require some label information which goes beyond consumer health effects; not every consumer must need mandated information in order for it to be required by law. These requirements have never been judged an infringement of producers' constitutional rights. For example:

- Very few consumers are sensitive to sulfites, although all wine must be labeled.
- The burden is put on tobacco manufacturers to carry the surgeon general's warning, even though the majority of cigarette smokers will not develop lung cancer and an intended effect of the label is to reinforce the resolve of nonconsumers to refrain from smoking.
- Labeling every processed food with its fat and calorie analysis is mandated, even though vast numbers of Americans are not overweight or suffering from heart disease.
- Irradiated foods (other than spices) must carry a specific logo.
- Finally, the source of hydrolyzed proteins in foods must be on a label to accommodate vegetarian cultural practices and certain religious beliefs.

These legal requirements are in place because many citizens want such information, and a specific fraction need it. An identifiable fraction of consumers actually need information about genetic modification—for example, as regards allergenicity—as the FDA itself has recognized in the Federal Register, and almost all want it.

Foods which are comprised, to any but a trace extent, of genetically altered components or products should be required to be labeled. This can be justified in some instances on scientific and health grounds, and for other foods on the social, cultural, religious and political interest consumers may have in the processes by which their food is produced.

Consumers' right to know is an expression of an ethical position which acknowledges individual autonomy; it is also a social approach which helps to rectify the substantial imbalance of power which exists in a modern society where commercial transactions occur between highly integrated and well-to-do corporations, on the one hand, and atomized consumers on the other.

We should let labeled GEFs run the test of the marketplace.

Statement of Joseph A. Levitt

Introduction

Mr. Chairman and members of the Committee, thank you for giving the Food and Drug Administration (FDA or the Agency) the opportunity to testify today on its regulatory program for foods derived from plants using the tools of modern biotechnology—also known as genetically engineered, or bioengineered, foods. I am Joseph A. Levitt, Director of FDA's Center for Food Safety and Applied Nutrition (CFSAN). Within FDA, CFSAN oversees bioengineered plant products or ingredients intended for human consumption. Our Center for Veterinary Medicine oversees bioengineered plant products used as or in animal feed, as well as bioengineered products used to improve the health or productivity of animals (including fish).

We believe it is very important for the public to understand how FDA is regulating the new bioengineered foods being introduced into the marketplace and to have confidence in that process. To that end, I appreciate this opportunity to describe our policies and procedures to the Committee and to the public.

First, let me state that FDA is confident that the bioengineered plant foods on the U.S. market today are as safe as their conventionally bred counterparts. This conclusion was echoed by a report by the National Resource Council of the National Academy of Sciences which stated, "The committee is not aware of any evidence that foods on the market are unsafe to eat as a result of genetic modification." Since FDA's 1994 evaluation of the Flavr Savr tomato, the first genetically-engineered plant food to reach the U.S. market, FDA has reviewed the data on more than 45 other products, ranging from herbicide resistant soybeans to a canola plant with modified oil content. To date, there is no evidence that these plants are significantly different in terms of food safety from crops produced through traditional breeding techniques.

The topic of bioengineering has generated much controversy, particularly about whether these foods should be labeled or not. As I discuss in more detail later in my testimony, FDA held three public meetings on bioengineered foods late last year, the second one of which I chaired. We wanted to hear the views from all, and importantly, we wanted to discuss and obtain feedback on ways in which information on bioengineered foods could be most appropriately and helpfully conveyed.

From U.S. Senate Health, Education, Labor, and Pensions Committee. The Future of Food: Biotechnology and Consumer Confidence. Hearing, September 26, 2000. Washington, DC: U.S. Government Printing Office, 2000.

Partly in response to information gained from the public meetings and comments received by the Agency, FDA announced on May 3, 2000, that it will be taking steps to modify our current voluntary process for bioengineered foods to establish mandatory premarket notification and make the process more transparent. Further, we will be developing guidance for food manufacturers who wish voluntarily to label their products regarding whether or not they contain bioengineered ingredients. To ensure that the Agency has the best scientific advice, we also are adding experts in this field to our foods and veterinary medicine advisory committees. FDA is taking these steps to help provide consumers with continued confidence in the safety of the U.S. food supply and to ensure that the Agency's oversight procedures will meet the challenges of the future. The proposed notification rule and draft guidance are currently under development. . . .

Legal and Regulatory Issues

FDA regulates bioengineered plant food in conjunction with the United States Department of Agriculture (USDA) and the Environmental Protection Agency (EPA). FDA has authority under the Federal Food, Drug, and Cosmetic (FD&C) Act to ensure the safety of all domestic and imported foods for man or other animals in the United States market, except meat, poultry and egg products which are regulated by USDA. (Note that the safety of animal drug residues in meat and poultry is regulated by FDA's Center for Veterinary Medicine.) Pesticides are regulated primarily by EPA, which reviews safety and sets tolerances (or establishes exemptions from tolerance) for pesticides. FDA enforces the pesticide tolerances set by EPA. USDA's Animal & Plant Health Inspection Service (APHIS) oversees the agricultural and environmental safety of planting and field testing of bioengineered plants.

Bioengineered foods and food ingredients must adhere to the same standards of safety under the FD&C Act that apply to their conventionally-bred counterparts. This means that these products must be as safe as the traditional foods in the market. FDA has broad authority to initiate regulatory action if a product fails to meet the standards of the FD&C Act.

FDA relies primarily on two sections of the FD&C Act to ensure the safety of foods and food ingredients:

1. The adulteration provisions of section 402(a)(1). Under this post-market authority, FDA has the power to remove a food from the market (or sanction those marketing the food) if the food poses a risk to public health. It is important to note that the FD&C Act places a legal duty on developers to ensure that the foods they market to consumers are safe and comply with all legal requirements.
2. The food additive provisions (section 409). Under this section, a substance that is intentionally added to food is a food additive, unless the substance is generally recognized as safe (GRAS) or is otherwise exempt (e.g., a pesticide, the safety of which is overseen by EPA).

The FD&C Act requires premarket approval of any food additive—regardless of the technique used to add it to food. Thus, substances introduced into food are either (1) new food additives that require premarket approval by FDA or (2) GRAS, and are exempt from the requirement for premarket review (for example, if there is a long history of safe use in food). Generally, foods such as fruits, vegetables, and grains, are not subject to premarket approval because they have been safely consumed over many years. Other than the food additive system, there are no premarket approval requirements for foods generally.

In 1992, knowing that bioengineered products were on the horizon, FDA published a policy explaining how existing legal requirements would apply to products developed using the tools of biotechnology (57 FR 22984; May 29, 1992; "Statement of Policy: Foods Derived from New Plant Varieties"). The 1992 policy was designed to answer developers' questions about these products prior to marketing to assist them in meeting their legal duty to provide safe and wholesome foods to consumers. The basic principle of the 1992 policy is that the traits and characteristics of the foods should be the focus of safety assessment for all new varieties of food crops, no matter which techniques are used to develop them.

Under FDA policy, a substance that would be a food additive if it were added during traditional food manufacturing is also treated as a food additive if it is introduced into food through bioengineering of a food crop. Our authority under section 409 permits us to require premarket approval of any food additive and thus, to require premarket review of any substance intentionally introduced via bioengineering that is not generally recognized as safe.

Generally, substances intentionally introduced into food that would be reviewed as food additives include those that have unusual chemical functions, have unknown toxicity, or would be new major dietary components of the food. For example, a novel sweetener bioengineered into food would likely require premarket approval. In our experience with bioengineered food to date, however, we have reviewed only one substance under the food additive provisions, an enzyme produced by an antibiotic resistance gene, and we approved that one. In general, substances intentionally added to food via biotechnology to date have been well-characterized proteins and fats, and are functionally very similar to other proteins and fats that are commonly and safely consumed in the diet and thus are presumptively GRAS.

In 1994, for the first bioengineered product planned for introduction into the market, FDA moved deliberately, following the 1992 policy. We conducted a comprehensive scientific review of Calgene's data on the Flavr Savr™ tomato and the use of the kanamycin resistance marker gene. FDA also held a public meeting of our Food Advisory Committee (the Committee) to examine applicability of the 1992 policy to products such as the Flavr Savr™ tomato. The Committee members agreed with FDA that the scientific approach presented in the 1992 policy was sound and that questions regarding the Flavr Savr™ had been addressed. The Committee members also suggested that we remove unnecessary reviews to provide an expedited decision process on the marketing of bioengineered foods that do not raise substantive scientific issues.

In response, that same year, FDA established a consultative process to help companies comply with the FD&C Act's requirements for any new food, including a bioengineered food, that they intend to market. Since that time, companies have used the consultative process more than 45 times as they sought to introduce genetically altered plants representing ten different crops into the U.S. market. We are not aware of any bioengineered food product on the market under FDA's jurisdiction that has not been evaluated by FDA through the current consultation process.

Typically, the consultation begins early in the product development stage, before it is ready for market. Company scientists and other officials will meet with FDA scientists to describe the product they are developing. In response, the Agency advises the company on what tests would be appropriate for the company to assess the safety of the new food.

After the studies are completed, the data and information on the safety and nutritional assessment are provided voluntarily to FDA for review. The Agency evaluates the information for all of the known hazards and also for potential unintended effects on plant composition and nutritional properties, since plants may undergo changes other than those intended by the breeders. Specifically, FDA scientists are looking to assure that the newly expressed compounds are safe for food consumption, there are no allergens new to the food, no increased levels of natural toxicants, and no reduction of important nutrients. They are also looking to see whether the food has been changed in any substantive way such that the food would need to be specially labeled to reveal the nature of the change to consumers.

Some examples of the information reviewed by FDA include: the name of the food and the crop from which it is derived; the uses of the food, including both human food and animal feed uses; the sources, identities, and functions of introduced genetic material and its stability in the plant; the purpose or intended technical effect of the modification and its expected effect on the composition or characteristic properties of the food or feed; the identity and function of any new products encoded by the introduced genetic material, including an estimate of its concentration; comparison of the composition or characteristics of the bioengineered food to that of food derived from the parental variety or other commonly consumed varieties with special emphasis on important nutrients, anti-nutrients, and toxicants that occur naturally in the food; information on whether the genetic modification altered the potential for the bioengineered food to induce an allergic response; and, other information relevant to the safety and nutritional assessment of the bioengineered food.

It should be noted that if a plant developer used a gene from a plant whose food is commonly allergenic, FDA would presume that the modified food may be allergenic unless the developer could demonstrate that the food would not cause allergic reactions in people allergic to food from the source plant. If FDA scientists have more questions about the safety data, the company either provides more detailed answers or conducts additional studies. Our experience has been that no bioengineered product has gone on the market until FDA's questions about the product have been answered.

Labeling

Labeling, either mandatory or voluntary, of bioengineered foods is a controversial issue. Section 403 of the FD&C Act sets labeling requirements for all foods. All foods, whether derived using bioengineering or not, are subject to these labeling requirements.

Under section 403(a)(1) of the FD&C Act, a food is misbranded if its labeling is false or misleading in any particular way. Section 201(n) of the FD&C Act provides additional guidance on how labeling may be misleading. It states that labeling is misleading if it fails to reveal all facts that are "material in light of such representations (made or suggested in the labeling) or material with respect to consequences which may result from the use of the article to which the labeling or advertising relates under the conditions of use prescribed in the labeling or advertising thereof or under such conditions of use as are customary or usual."

While the legislative history of section 201(n) contains little discussion of the word "material," there is precedent to guide the Agency in its decision regarding whether information on a food is in fact material within the meaning of 201(n). Historically, the Agency has generally limited the scope of the materiality concept to information about the attributes of the food itself. FDA has required special labeling on the basis of it being "material" information in cases where the absence of such information may: 1) pose special health or environmental risks (e.g., warning statement on certain protein diet products); 2) mislead the consumer in light of other statements made on the label (e.g., requirement for quantitative nutrient information when certain nutrient content claims are made about a product); or 3) in cases where a consumer may assume that a food, because of its similarity to another food, has nutritional, organoleptic, or functional characteristics of the food it resembles when in fact it does not (e.g., reduced fat margarine not suitable for frying).

FDA does not require labeling to indicate whether or not a food or food ingredient is a bioengineered product, just as it does not require labeling to indicate which breeding technique was used in developing a food plant. Rather, any significant differences in the food itself have to be disclosed in labeling. If genetic modifications do materially change the composition of a food product, these changes must be reflected in the food's labeling. This would include its nutritional content, (for example, more folic acid or greater iron content) or requirements for storage, preparation, or cooking, which might impact the food's safety characteristics or nutritional qualities. For example, one soybean variety was modified to alter the levels of oleic acid in the beans; because the oil from this soybean is significantly different when compared to conventional soybean oil, we advised the company to adopt a new name for that oil, a name that reflects the intended change.

If a bioengineered food were to contain an allergen not previously found in that food, information about the presence of the allergen would be material as to the potential consequences of consumption of the food. If FDA determined that labeling would be sufficient to enable the food to be safely marketed, the Agency would require that the food be labeled to indicate the presence of the allergen.

FDA has received comments suggesting that foods developed through modern biotechnology should bear a label informing consumers that the food was produced using bioengineering. While we have given careful consideration to these comments, we do not have data or other information that would form a basis for concluding under the FD&C Act that the fact that a food or its ingredients was produced using bioengineering is material within the meaning of 201(n) and thus, is a fact that must be disclosed in labeling. Hence, we believe that we have neither a scientific nor legal basis to require such labeling. We are developing, however, draft guidance for those that wish voluntarily to label either the presence or absence of bioengineered food in food products.

Public Outreach

Although FDA is confident that its current science-based approach to regulating bioengineered foods is protecting the public health, we realized we had been quietly looking at and reviewing these products and making decisions related to their safety while the public was largely unaware of what we were doing. When trade issues erupted last summer with Europe—and in the World Trade Organization meetings in Seattle—it raised public concern that there might be safety issues with these foods.

New technologies typically raise complex questions—scientific, policy, and even ethical. In light of the newness of this technology and the apparent concern, FDA held the three public meetings I previously mentioned. The public meetings had three purposes: to determine whether there were any new scientific or labeling issues that the Agency should consider; to help the public understand FDA's current policy and become familiar with what we are already doing; and to explore the ways in which information on bioengineered foods could be most appropriately and helpfully conveyed.

FDA asked specific questions on both scientific and safety issues as well as about public information issues. We heard from 35 panelists and over 250 additional speakers in the three meetings. More than 50,000 written comments have been submitted.

What did we learn at these meetings?

First and foremost, no information was presented that indicates there is a safety problem with any bioengineered food or feed now in the marketplace.

In general, we heard support for strengthening FDA's premarket review process for bioengineered foods, in varying degrees. Views on labeling were very strong and much more polarized. Overall, we heard from many points of view that FDA needs to take additional steps to increase consumer confidence in these products.

As to specific concerns, there were four basic points of view:

1. One group was concerned primarily with anything that could possibly harm the environment, with food safety being a secondary concern.

2. A second group was concerned about the possibility that there might be unknown long-term food safety problems, despite the absence of any scientific information that would support the existence of such problems.
3. A third group said they were not so concerned about food safety—they would eat bioengineered foods—but still wanted to know what technologies and ingredients were involved in producing their food.
4. A fourth group speaking for developing countries, said they need this technology and do not want it limited or taken away.

New Initiatives

As I mentioned, FDA announced on May 3, as part of an Administration initiative, that we will be taking steps to strengthen the premarket notification program for bioengineered foods. We also intend to provide guidance to food manufacturers who wish voluntarily to label their products regarding whether or not they contain bioengineered ingredients. Our goal is to enhance public confidence in the way in which FDA is regulating bioengineered foods. We want the public to know, loud and clear, that FDA stands behind the safety of these products.

As part of this initiative, we will be proposing regulations to make it mandatory that developers of bioengineered plant varieties notify FDA at least 120 days before they intend to market such products. FDA will require that specific information be submitted to help determine whether the foods pose any safety or labeling concerns. The Agency will be providing further guidance to industry on the scientific data needed to ensure that foods developed through bioengineering are safe for human consumption. To help make the process more transparent, the Agency has made a commitment to ensuring that, consistent with information disclosure laws, consumers have access to information submitted to FDA as part of the notification process and to FDA's responses in a timely fashion.

The proposed rule on premarket notification and the draft labeling guidance are both high priorities for the Agency, and we intend to publish each of these later this fall. Both will provide a full opportunity for public comment before final policies are established. Let me assure you that when we come to a decision regarding these matters, FDA will operate in an open, transparent manner so that the public can understand our regulatory approach and continue to provide us with feedback about its impact. As a scientific organization we are comfortable with debate over complex scientific issues, and welcome the discussions that have occurred at public meetings to date. It is important that the public, including the scientific community, clearly understand FDA's policy on bioengineered foods.

Additional Activities

Before closing, let me briefly describe a few other activities of Agency involvement in the food biotechnology subject area. In our May 3 announcement, FDA stated our intention to augment our food and veterinary medicine advisory committees by adding scientists with agricultural biotechnology expertise. FDA will use these committees to address over-arching scientific questions pertaining to bioengineered foods and animal feed. More specifically, I am restructuring the Food Advisory Committee so that it will contain several special focus subcommittees. One of those subcommittees will have scientists with expertise in bioengineering, and will focus on issues pertaining to food biotechnology.

As I am sure you are aware, the National Academy of Sciences has formed a new standing Committee on Agricultural Biotechnology. FDA has participated in several of its meetings, including one just last week, on September 18, in which two FDA experts made presentations. We think the work of this committee is very important. We are formalizing our relationship with it, particularly with regard to exploring what the potential is for any unknown long-term health effects to result from consumption of bioengineered food.

FDA is actively participating in the work of the U.S. Codex Committee on food labeling, which is considering issues on policies for possible labeling of foods derived using bioengineering. In addition, FDA is participating in the newly formed "Ad Hoc Committee on Foods Derived from Biotechnology." This committee is especially important because its initial focus is to develop principles and guidelines for the evaluation of the safety of bioengineered foods. FDA is providing an international leadership role in this committee to develop harmonized policies for assessing the safety of bioengineered food.

Let me comment briefly on the recall announced by Kraft Foods this past Friday. FDA commends Kraft Foods for acting responsibly in light of testing showing the possibility that the products contained a bioengineered protein that had not been approved for human consumption. This reinforces the importance of FDA, EPA and other interested parties to be vigilant in assuring that the rules pertaining to bioengineered foods are being fully adhered to. FDA's investigation is continuing in this case.

Mr. Chairman, thank you again for the opportunity to address these issues. I am happy to answer any questions you might have.

POSTSCRIPT

Should We Require Labeling for Genetically Modified Food?

William Safire, a journalist often amused by popular trends in the use of the English language, at one point titled his weekly essay "Franken-: A Terrifying New Prefix is Stalking Europe." His point was not that many European nations, acting in fear, have banned or restricted the import of genetically modified foods, but that language had evolved to express that fear. "Franken-," from Mary Godwin Shelley's nineteenth-century book *Frankenstein,* has come to characterize the product of any human "tampering" with nature that displeases the speaker. The fact that we have modified breeds of plants and animals for centuries, in fact millennia, through selective breeding or other methods of assisting evolution, tends to get lost in the scuffle. The language helps the scuffling.

Labeling is another way to use language to affect policy. It simply is not politically neutral to attach a label to something, especially when on our usual understandings, it should not need one. Every required addition to the labels on our food has been made in response to a public agenda, usually concerning public health, but occasionally (as in the case of the tuna and the pastrami) concerning public causes that have nothing to do with the quality of the food. Do we want genetically engineered products to follow that route?

Suggested Reading

If you would like to think further on this topic, you may profit from the following:

Michael Fumento, "Crop Busters," *Reason* (January 2000). This article criticizes opponents of genetically engineered foods.

Kristi Coale, "Mutant Food," *Salon* (January 12, 2000). This article looks at how a lawsuit filed against the Food and Drug Administration reveals FDA internal doubts of genetic engineering safety.

Jon Luoma, "Pandora's Pantry," *Mother Jones* (January/February 2000).

Frederic Golden, "Who's Afraid of Frankenfood?" *Time* (November 29, 1999).

Food and Drug Administration Biotechnology Home Page. This FDA site explains federal policies on bioengineered foods.

U. S. Department of Agriculture (USDA) Biotechnology home page. This site answers frequently asked questions about biotechnology and provides information on regulatory oversight of biotechnology.

Center for Food Safety, International Food Information Council, Greenpeace: Biotechnology and Better Foods and Industry-supported web site.

Internet References . . .

U.S. Business Cycle Indicators Data

This site leads to the 256 data series known as the U.S. Business Cycle Indicators, which are used to track and predict U.S. business activity. The subjects of the data groups are clearly listed.

http://www.economagic.com/bci-97.htm

Voice of the Shuttle: Postindustrial Business Theory Page

This site links to a variety of resources on many subjects related to business theory, including restructuring, reengineering, downsizing, flattening, the team concept, outsourcing, business and globalism, human resources management, labor relations, statistics, and history, as well as information and resources on job searches, careers, working from home, and business start-ups.

http://vos.ucsb.edu/browse.asp?id=2727

Society, Religion, and Technology Project

This is the home page on patenting living organisms of the Society, Religion, and Technology Project (SRT) of the Church of Scotland. It provides a simple introduction to the issues involved, other SRT pages on patenting, and links to related pages.

http://www.srtp.org.uk.patent.shtml

Global Objectives

*O*ur business is increasingly carried on in distant waters and foreign villages. The corporation of the future is a global enterprise, difficult to track, avoiding the jurisdiction of any national government. What sorts of ethical obligations attend their operations? Are there products we should not buy because of the way they were manufactured? Are there products we should not sell because of their potential to cause harm to the citizens of other lands (who willingly buy them)?

- Are Multinational Corporations Free from Moral Obligation?
- Should Patenting Life Be Forbidden?

ISSUE 17

Are Multinational Corporations Free from Moral Obligation?

YES: Manuel Velasquez, from "International Business, Morality and the Common Good," *Business Ethics Quarterly* (January 1992)

NO: John E. Fleming, from "Alternative Approaches and Assumptions: Comments on Manuel Velasquez," *Business Ethics Quarterly* (January 1992)

ISSUE SUMMARY

YES: In the absence of accepted enforcement agencies, there is little probability that any multinational corporation will suffer for violation of rules restricting business for the sake of the common good. Since any business that tried to conform to moral rules in the absence of enforcement would unjustifiably cease to be competitive, it must be the case, Velasquez argues, that moral strictures are not binding on such companies.

NO: Velasquez's logic is impressive, replies Fleming, but conditions on the ground in the multinational corporation are not as he describes. Real corporations tend to deal with long-term customers and suppliers in the goldfish bowl of international media exposure and must adhere to moral standards or lose business.

In three ways this issue is not what it seems.

First, to hear Velasquez tell it, it seems to be an issue between the hard-headed realists of Hobbesian persuasion—those who realize that business is business and the bottom line is all that really counts—and the liberal idealists, who'd like to think that high moral thoughts really influence world affairs. Velasquez concludes, very regretfully, that a Hobbesian realist, knowing all the worst about human nature, must acknowledge that moral obligations simply do not apply in the absence of moral community. Yet Fleming does not answer in the tone of lofty idealism, but in that of the practitioner who has to keep an enterprise afloat from day to day. Realism and hardheadedness seem to have switched sides in the course of the debate, apparently;

realistically, the only way to serve the bottom line is by (tolerably) moral behavior. Velasquez, it now appears, is the lofty idealist, sacrificing moral principles at the altar of an abstract egoism that could never be put into practice on the multinational scene.

Second, to hear Velasquez tell it, right action is on trial: can morality justify itself with regard to profit? Can we show that acting for the common good will not damage the profit picture or detract from the increase in shareholder wealth? For if not, we will have to forego morality. Fleming appears to answer Velasquez's question in the affirmative: yes, we can show that right action is compatible with (in fact necessary for) the health of the bottom line and the corporate enterprise in general. But in reality, his answer goes much further than that. It is not the behavior that is in question, but the theory— not the conclusions of the syllogism but the major premise. For if Fleming is right, the major premise of Hobbesian capitalism—that the sole social responsibility of business is to increase its profits, as Milton Friedman put it so succinctly—is simply incorrect, or unworkable. For any activity that might be expected to follow from the injunction to serve the bottom line and increase profits, activity in total disregard of the moral persuasions of all others in your society, is not only morally wrong on some eternal scale but also self-defeating: business will plunge and the shareholders will be left with valueless promises. So the theory—not, in this reading, a normative theory, but an empirical generalization about the way things happen in fact—fails to predict the data. It is a flawed theory, and needs, based on this reading, to be replaced.

Third, to hear both Velasquez and Fleming tell it, the dispute is over human behavior—both about the way humans *will* behave and the way they *should* behave—in business situations. But both of them condition their predictions and advice on the nature of the international business community. Fleming is claiming centrally that the international business scene is not at all as Velasquez thinks it is—strangers interacting in strange lands, on a one-time basis only—but is a place of custom, regular habits, and familiar people, where memories are long, word gets around, and tolerance for being taken advantage of is very short. It sounds like a small town. And indeed, that is what the world is coming to be.

Ask yourself, as you read these selections, how international dealings differ from domestic dealings. Does it stretch the imagination to consider folks abroad rather like the folks at home, after getting used to time zone changes and differences in manners? What are the real controls on human behavior—enforcement of laws or the simple social expectations of peers and colleagues?

YES

Manuel Velasquez

International Business, Morality and the Common Good

During the last few years an increasing number of voices have urged that we pay more attention to ethics in international business, on the grounds that not only are all large corporations now internationally structured and thus engaging in international transactions, but that even the smallest domestic firm is increasingly buffeted by the pressures of international competition. . . .

Can we say that businesses operating in a competitive international environment have any moral obligations to contribute to the international common good, particularly in light of realist objections? Unfortunately, my answer to this question will be in the negative. . . .

International Business

. . . When speaking of international business, I have in mind a particular kind of organization: the multinational corporation. Multinational corporations have a number of well known features, but let me briefly summarize a few of them. First, multinational corporations are businesses and as such they are organized primarily to increase their profits within a competitive environment. Virtually all of the activities of a multinational corporation can be explained as more or less rational attempts to achieve this dominant end. Secondly, multinational corporations are bureaucratic organizations. The implication of this is that the identity, the fundamental structure, and the dominant objectives of the corporation endure while the many individual human beings who fill the various offices and positions within the corporation come and go. As a consequence, the particular values and aspirations of individual members of the corporation have a relatively minimal and transitory impact on the organization as a whole. Thirdly, and most characteristically, multinational corporations operate in several nations. This has several implications. First, because the multinational is not confined to a single nation, it can easily escape the reach of the laws of any particular nation by simply moving its resources or operations out of one nation and transferring them to another nation. Second, because the multinational is not confined to

Manuel Velasquez, "International Business, Morality and the Common Good", *Business Ethics Quarterly*, vol. 2, no. 1, January 1992, pp. 41-43. Copyright © 1992 by Business Ethics Quarterly. Reprinted by permission.

a single nation, its interests are not aligned with the interests of any single nation. The ability of the multinational to achieve its profit objectives does not depend upon the ability of any particular nation to achieve its own domestic objectives. . . .

The Traditional Realist Objection in Hobbes

The realist objection, of course, is the standard objection to the view that agents—whether corporations, governments, or individuals—have moral obligations on the international level. Generally, the realist holds that it is a mistake to apply moral concepts to international activities: morality has no place in international affairs. The classical statement of this view, which I am calling the "traditional" version of realism, is generally attributed to Thomas Hobbes. . . .

In its Hobbsian form, as traditionally interpreted, the realist objection holds that moral concepts have no meaning in the absence of an agency powerful enough to guarantee that other agents generally adhere to the tenets of morality. Hobbes held, first, that in the absence of a sovereign power capable of forcing men to behave civilly with each other, men are in "the state of nature," a state he characterizes as a "war . . . of every man, against every man." Secondly, Hobbes claimed, in such a state of war, moral concepts have no meaning:

> To this war of every man against every man, this also is consequent; that nothing can be unjust. The notions of right and wrong, justice and injustice have there no place. Where there is no common power, there is no law: where no law, no injustice.

Moral concepts are meaningless, then, when applied to state of nature situations. And, Hobbes held, the international arena is a state of nature, since there is no international sovereign that can force agents to adhere to the tenets of morality.

The Hobbsian objection to talking about morality in international affairs, then, is based on two premises: (1) an ethical premise about the applicability of moral terms and (2) an apparently empirical premise about how agents behave under certain conditions. The ethical premise, at least in its Hobbsian form, holds that there is a connection between the meaningfulness of moral terms and the extent to which agents adhere to the tenets of morality: If in a given situation agents do not adhere to the tenets of morality, then in that situation moral terms have no meaning. The apparently empirical premise holds that in the absence of a sovereign, agents will not adhere to the tenets of morality: they will be in a state of war. This appears to be an empirical generalization about the extent to which agents adhere to the tenets of morality in the absence of a third-party enforcer. Taken together, the two premises imply that in situations that lack a sovereign authority, such as one finds in many international exchanges, moral terms have no meaning and so moral obligations are nonexistent. . . .

Revising the Realist Objection: The First Premise

. . . The neo-Hobbsian or realist . . . might want to propose this premise: When one is in a situation in which others do not adhere to certain tenets of morality, and when adhering to those tenets of morality will put one at a significant competitive disadvantage, then it is not immoral for one to like-wise fail to adhere to them. The realist might want to argue for this claim, first, by pointing out that in a world in which all are competing to secure significant benefits and avoid significant costs, and in which others do not adhere to the ordinary tenets of morality, one risks significant harm to one's interests if one continues to adhere to those tenets of morality. But no one can be morally required to take on major risks of harm to oneself. Consequently, in a competitive world in which others disregard moral constraints and take any means to advance their self-interests, no one can be morally required to take on major risks of injury by adopting the restraints of ordinary morality.

A second argument the realist might want to advance would go as follows. When one is in a situation in which others do not adhere to the ordinary tenets of morality, one is under heavy competitive pressures to do the same. And, when one is under such pressures, one cannot be blamed—i.e., one is excused—for also failing to adhere to the ordinary tenets of morality. One is excused because heavy pressures take away one's ability to control oneself, and thereby diminish one's moral culpability.

Yet a third argument advanced by the realist might go as follows. When one is in a situation in which others do not adhere to the ordinary tenets of morality it is not fair to require one to continue to adhere to those tenets, especially if doing so puts one at a significant competitive disadvantage. It is not fair because then one is laying a burden on one party that the other parties refuse to carry.

Thus, there are a number of arguments that can be given in defense of the revised Hobbsian ethical premise that when others do not adhere to the tenets of morality, it is not immoral for one to do likewise. . . .

Revising the Realist Objection: The Second Premise

Let us turn to the other premise in the Hobbsian argument, the assertion that in the absence of a sovereign, agents will be in a state of war. As I mentioned, this is an apparently empirical claim about the extent to which agents will adhere to the tenets of morality in the absence of a third-party enforcer.

Hobbes gives a little bit of empirical evidence for this claim. He cites several examples of situations in which there is no third party to enforce civility and where, as a result, individuals are in a "state of war." Generalizing from these few examples, he reaches the conclusion that in the absence of a third-party enforcer, agents will always be in a "condition of war." . . .

Recently, the Hobbsian claim . . . has been defended on the basis of some of the theoretical claims of game theory, particularly of the prisoner's dilemma. Hobbes' state of nature, the defense goes, is an instance of a prisoner's dilemma, and *rational* agents in a Prisoner's Dilemma necessarily would choose not to adhere to a set of moral norms. . . .

A Prisoner's Dilemma is a situation involving at least two individuals. Each individual is faced with two choices: he can cooperate with the other individual or he can choose not to cooperate. If he cooperates and the other individual also cooperates, then he gets a certain payoff. If, however, he chooses not to cooperate, while the other individual trustingly cooperates, the noncooperator gets a larger payoff while the cooperator suffers a loss. And if both choose not to cooperate, then both get nothing.

It is a commonplace now that in a Prisoner's Dilemma situation, the most rational strategy for a participant is to choose not to cooperate. For the other party will either cooperate or not cooperate. If the other party cooperates, then it is better for one not to cooperate and thereby get the larger payoff. On the other hand, if the other party does not cooperate, then it is also better for one not to cooperate and thereby avoid a loss. In either case, it is better for one to not cooperate.

. . . In Hobbes' state of nature each individual must choose either to cooperate with others by adhering to the rules of morality (like the rule against theft), or to not cooperate by disregarding the rules of morality and attempting to take advantage of those who are adhering to the rules (e.g., by stealing from them). In such a situation it is more rational . . . to choose not to cooperate. For the other party will either cooperate or not cooperate. If the other party does not cooperate, then one puts oneself at a competitive disadvantage if one adheres to morality while the other party does not. On the other hand, if the other party chooses to cooperate, then one can take advantage of the other party by breaking the rules of morality at his expense. In either case, it is morally rational to not cooperate.

Thus, the realist can argue that in a state of nature, where there is no one to enforce compliance with the rules of morality, it is more rational from the individual's point of view to choose not to comply with morality than to choose to comply. Assuming—and this is obviously a critical assumption—that agents behave rationally, then we can conclude that agents in a state of nature will choose not to comply with the tenets of ordinary morality. . . .

Can we claim that it is clear that multinationals have a moral obligation to pursue the global common good in spite of the objections of the realist?

I do not believe that this claim can be made. We can conclude from the discussion of the realist objection that the Hobbsian claim about the pervasiveness of amorality in the international sphere is false when (1) interactions among international agents are repetitive in such a way that agents can retaliate against those who fail to cooperate, and (2) agents can determine the trustworthiness of other international agents.

But unfortunately, multinational activities often take place in a highly competitive arena in which these two conditions do not obtain. Moreover, these conditions are noticeably absent in the arena of activities that concern the global common good.

First, as I have noted, the common good consists of goods that are indivisible and accessible to all. This means that such goods are susceptible to the free rider problems. Everyone has access to such goods whether or not they do their part in maintaining such goods, so everyone is tempted to free ride on the generosity of others. Now governments can force domestic companies to do their part to maintain the national common good. Indeed, it is one of the functions of government to solve the free rider problem by forcing all to contribute to the domestic common good to which all have access. Moreover, all companies have to interact repeatedly with their host governments, and this leads them to adopt a cooperative stance toward their host government's objective of achieving the domestic common good.

But it is not clear that governments can or will do anything effective to force multinationals to do their part to maintain the global common good. For the governments of individual nations can themselves be free riders, and can join forces with willing multinationals seeking competitive advantages over others. Let me suggest an example. It is clear that a livable global environment is part of the global common good, and it is clear that the manufacture and use of chlorofluorocarbons is destroying that good. Some nations have responded by requiring their domestic companies to cease manufacturing or using chlorofluorocarbons. But other nations have refused to do the same, since they will share in any benefits that accrue from the restraint others practice, and they can also reap the benefits of continuing to manufacture and use chlorofluorocarbons. Less developed nations, in particular, have advanced the position that since their development depends heavily on exploiting the industrial benefits of chlorofluorocarbons, they cannot afford to curtail their use of these substances. Given this situation, it is open to multinationals to shift their operations to those countries that continue to allow the manufacture and use of chlorofluorocarbons. For multinationals, too, will reason that they will share in any benefits that accrue from the restraint others practice, and that they can meanwhile reap the profits of continuing to manufacture and use chlorofluorocarbons in a world where other companies are forced to use more expensive technologies. Moreover, those nations that practice restraint cannot force all such multinationals to discontinue the manufacture or use of chlorofluorocarbons because many multinationals can escape the reach of their laws. An exactly parallel, but perhaps even more compelling, set of considerations can be advanced to show that at least some multinationals will join forces with some developing countries to circumvent any global efforts made to control the global warming trends (the so-called "greenhouse effect") caused by the heavy use of fossil fuels.

The realist will conclude, of course, that in such situations, at least some multinationals will seek to gain competitive advantages by failing to contribute to the global common good (such as the good of a hospitable global environment). For multinationals and rational agents, i.e., agents bureaucratically structured to take rational means toward achieving their dominant end of increasing their profits. And in a competitive environment, contributing to the common good while others do not, will fail to achieve this dominant end. Joining this conclusion to the ethical premise that when others do not adhere to the requirements of morality it is not immoral for one to do likewise, the realist can conclude that multinationals are not morally obligated to contribute to such global common goods (such as environmental goods).

Moreover, global common goods often create interactions that are not iterated. This is particularly the case where the global environment is concerned. As I have already noted, preservation of a favorable global climate is clearly part of the global common good. Now the failure of the global climate will be a one-time affair. The breakdown of the ozone layer, for example, will happen once, with catastrophic consequences for us all; and the heating up of the global climate as a result of the infusion of carbon dioxide will happen once, with catastrophic consequences for us all. Because these environmental disasters are a one-time affair, they represent a non-iterated prisoner's dilemma for multinationals. It is irrational from an individual point of view for a multinational to choose to refrain from polluting the environment in such cases. Either others will refrain, and then one can enjoy the benefits of their refraining; or others will not refrain, and then it will be better to have also not refrained since refraining would have made little difference and would have entailed heavy losses.

Finally, we must also note that although natural persons may signal their reliability to other natural persons, it is not at all obvious that multinationals can do the same. As noted above, multinationals are bureaucratic organizations whose members are continually changing and shifting. The natural persons who make up an organization can signal their reliability to others, but such persons are soon replaced by others, and they in turn are replaced by others. What endures is each organization's single-minded pursuit of increasing its profits in a competitive environment. And an enduring commitment to the pursuit of profit in a competitive environment is not a signal of an enduring commitment to morality.

John E. Fleming

Alternative Approaches and Assumptions: Comments on Manuel Velasquez

Introduction

I feel that Professor Velasquez has written a very interesting and thought-provoking paper on an important topic. His initial identification with a "strong notion of the common good" raises the level of analysis to a high but very complex plane. The author introduces the interesting and, from my view, unusual *realist objection* in the Hobbsian form. After a rigorous analysis of this concept Professor Velasquez reaches what I find to be a disturbing conclusion: "It is not obvious that we can say that multinationals have an obligation to contribute to the global common good. . . ." He then finishes the paper with a strong plea for the establishment of "an international authority capable of forcing everyone to contribute toward the global good."

It would be presumptuous of me to question the fine ethical reasoning that appears in the paper. I am impressed with its elegance. However, in a topic of this complexity I would like to think that there might be alternative approaches and assumptions that would lead us to a different conclusion. The presentation of such alternatives will be the path that I will take, examining the conceptual and empirical underpinnings of the argument from a management viewpoint.

The Model of a Multinational Corporation

The profit-maximizing, rational model of a multinational corporation presented in the paper is consistent with traditional economics and serves as a useful approximation of the firm from a theoretical viewpoint. But it falls somewhat short in less than purely competitive environments and was never intended to describe the decision processes of actual managers. Empirical studies of firms can lead to a profit-sacrificing, bounded rational model. The importance of profit is still there, but the stockholder does not get all the benefits. Other stakeholders are considered and rewarded. Out of all this can come the important concept of corporate social responsibility, which can

John E. Fleming, "Alternative Approaches and Assumptions: Comments on Manuel Velasquez", *Business Ethics Quarterly*, vol. 2, no. 1, January 1992, pp. 41–43. Copyright © 1992 by Business Ethics Quarterly. Reprinted by permission.

include such topics as concerns for the environment and for host country governments.

I also find the faceless and interchangeable bureaucrat a poor model for business executives, particularly the chief executive officers of large corporations. Many of these individuals have a personal impact on the organization, including such areas as business ethics and corporate responsibility. There are also important behavioral aspects of management, such as pride in the firm and corporate culture, that are fertile soil for the nurture of ethics.

Most large American multinational corporations have codes of ethics and some have well-developed programs concerned with ethical behavior worldwide. A number of these firms emphasize that their one code of conduct applies everywhere that they do business. At the GTE Corporation its vision and values statements have been translated into nine different languages and distributed to all its employees to ensure this world-wide understanding of how it conducts its business. This is a far cry from the situational ethics described in the model used by Professor Velasquez.

Model of the International Business Climate

The planning and decision environment of the managers conducting international business is different from that described in the paper. There is the very real problem of a lack of an overarching global government and enforceable laws for the international arena. Nevertheless, there are other very strong restraining forces on companies that prevent the "state of nature" (or law of the jungle) described in the paper. For example, the national governments that do exist influence the ethical behavior of companies acting within their boundaries and beyond. The Foreign Corrupt Practices Act of the United States has set a new standard of behavior in the area of bribery that dictates how American companies will behave worldwide. The financial practices of large banks and securities markets have added major constraints to global corporate behavior. There are also a number of regional and functional organizations in the areas of trade and monetary issues that provide limitations to managerial decision making.

The decisions of multinational executives are also constrained by such factors as public opinion and the pressures of special interest groups. In this area the media also plays a strong role. Examples of these forces are the actions of interest groups that forced marketing changes on infant formula manufacturers and the strong "green" movement that is affecting business decisions throughout many parts of the world. My own view is that considerable progress has been made in the area of limiting the manufacture and release of chlorofluorocarbons. This is a very complex issue involving tremendous social and economic changes that are far more critical, widespread and controlling than the profits of the producing companies. Even with the existence of an enforcing government there is no guarantee that the problem would be solved speedily. An example in point is the acid rain problem of the United States.

Model of the Prisoner's Dilemma

From the standpoint of managerial decision making the Prisoner's Dilemma model does not simulate a situation that is frequently found in international business. An executive generally would not be negotiating or making mutually beneficial decisions with competitors. I would see the greatest amount of effort of multinational decision makers devoted to the development of repeat customers. Such an accomplishment comes about through solving customer problems with better product/service at a lower cost. An emphasis on efficiency and excellence is a far more effective use of executive time than questionable negotiations with a competitor. I believe that the weakness Professor Velasquez identifies in the Prisoner's Dilemma model as a one-time event with competitors applies even more to negotiations with customers.

The author also points out a major weakness of the model in the signaling of intent that goes on between individuals. He then states that this same signaling is not found to any great extent between companies. I would disagree with this thought. An important part of corporate strategic planning is analyzing market signals. United States antitrust forbids direct contact between competitors on issues relating to the market. But there is no limitation on independent analysis of competitive actions and the interpretation of actions by competitors. When Kodak introduced its instant camera, both Kodak and Polaroid watched the other's actions to determine whether it signaled detente or fight.

Conclusion

For the reasons enumerated above I tend to question the models and assumptions that Professor Velasquez has used in his ethical analysis. And, with these underpinnings in jeopardy, I also tend to question the tentative conclusion of his moral reasoning as it relates to the managerial aspects of international business. I feel that multinationals *do* have a strong obligation to contribute to the global common good.

POSTSCRIPT

Are Multinational Corporations Free from Moral Obligation?

As we write, international business has sunk into a sea of troubles: the once-booming Asian economies seem to have gone into self-destruct mode, movie stars and athletes spend air time defending their products from accusations of exploitation and sweatshop abuses, trade in securities has gone global and gone wild. What are the possibilities for the comprehensive set of international laws, guidelines, and the committees to enforce them, as suggested by Velasquez?

Is national sovereignty an idea whose time has come, gone, and gone south? While boundaries between peoples—which may or may not correspond to anyone's idea of settled "national" boundaries—are the subject of violent disputes worldwide, while the economy goes global with blinding speed, unable to recognize any national boundaries at all, can we say that national boundaries make any sense at all? But then, how would we know what each central government controls? What is the reason for the centrality of national sovereignty?

We have, as Velasquez mentions, international conventions on certain subjects—ozone-depleting substances, for example. But on more immediate, and expensive, environmental issues, agreement is hard to reach and harder to monitor (witness the recent global warming conference in Kyoto).

Suggested Reading

For further exploration of this issue, read any of the following:

Ashay B. Desai and Terri Rittenburg, "Global Ethics: An Integrative Framework for MNEs," *Journal of Business Ethics*, vol. 16, no. 8 (June 1997), pp. 791–800.

Kevin T. Jackson, "Globalizing Corporate Ethics Programs: Perils and Prospects," *Journal of Business Ethics,* vol. 16, nos. 12–13 (September 1997), pp. 1227–35.

Thomas Donaldson, *The Ethics of International Business* (New York: Oxford University Press, 1989).

W. Michael Hoffman, Ann E. Lange, and David A. Fedo, eds., *Ethics and the Multinational Enterprise* (New York: University Press of America, 1986).

"Corporate Ethics: A Prime Business Asset." A Report of the Business Roundtable, 200 Park Avenue, Suite 2222, New York, NY 10166, (1988).

Thomas Friedman, *The Lexus and the Olive Tree* (New York: Simon and Schuster, 1999).

ISSUE 18

Should Patenting Life Be Forbidden?

YES: Jeremy Rifkin, from "Should We Patent Life?" *Business Ethics* (March/April 1998)

NO: William Domnarski, from "Dire New World," *Intellectual Property Magazine* (January 1999)

ISSUE SUMMARY

YES: Jeremy Rifkin, a persistent critic of unreflective support of "scientific progress," fears that genetic engineering extends human power over the rest of nature in ways that are unprecedented and whose consequences cannot be known. He urges a halt to research along these lines, especially that research whose aim is no more than profit for the company that "owns" the results.

NO: William Domnarski, an intellectual property lawyer, finds the patenting of genes or genetic discoveries no different than patenting any other ideas. The purpose of patents is to reward and encourage useful invention, and there is no doubt that the modifications we introduce to the genetic material of plants and animals are useful to feed a starving world.

T here is an apocryphal story that at a meeting of a gentlemanly scientific society of the seventeenth century, one of the members proposed a toast to the next scientific discovery, to which another of the members immediately added a fervent wish "that it may be of no use to anyone." The story illustrates well the ambivalence of scientific research that informs this issue.

Why do we seek knowledge? A sufficient reason might be that the Lord created our minds, and a fascinating world to study, and that in seeking wisdom and insight into the ways of nature we honor our creator and raise our minds closer to the divine mind. Something of that sort seems to have informed Aristotle's praise for the life of contemplation in the tenth book of the *Nicomachean Ethics*. But Francis Bacon, an early seventeenth century philosopher of science, suggested another reason altogether: "The end of our foundation is the knowledge of causes, and secret motions of things; and the enlarging of the bounds of human empire, to the effecting of all things possible." Knowledge is power, and the reason we pursue knowledge is to increase the power of human beings. It was the mission of science to expand the domain of human understanding precisely so that in knowing all things, we might do all things.

Shall we pursue knowledge of the genetic factors in animal and plant life, including possibly knowledge of the human genome? As we reflect on the problem, Monsanto Inc. is going forward with genetically engineered agricultural plant germ lines for export. Europe has firmly said, no genetically modified organisms (GMOs) on our tables, and in many places farmers have refused to grow them. Already a controversy has exploded in the grocery market: may GMOs grown without fertilizers or pesticides be labeled "organic"? Enthusiasts point out that GMOs, because they are better plants, often don't need any fertilizers or pesticides, so that should make organic farmers and their customers very happy. Critics point out that the reason they don't need chemical fertilizers or pesticides is that they have the bug repellent and heaven only knows what other chemicals engineered into their skins.

Why is Monsanto investing all this time and money to develop new lines of plants? One obvious reason is to make money. But if they are going to make money, they have to have patents on the new seeds they develop, or they will immediately be outflanked and undersold by similar firms that can duplicate their seeds without all the expensive investment. So patents are necessary in order to protect the enterprise. Meanwhile, Monsanto claims that all it wants to do is provide more food for a hungry world, a goal that we can only applaud, and that it needs the protection of patents to keep up the good work.

Where is technology taking us in this case? Can we separate out the genuine altruism (they really do want to feed the world) from the scientific curiosity (a universal human motive) from the selfish desire to make a very large amount of money very quickly?

Bear in mind, as you read these selections, that you are looking at a real cutting edge issue. For most of biotechnology, we don't even know the empirical consequences ten years down the road—that's how recent the science is. Should we calculate costs versus benefits, as far as they may be known? Or should we adopt the precautionary principle, and put off all introduction of this technology (where it has not altogether taken over already)? Shall we allow the entrepreneur inventor to reap the fortunes associated with a good patent or two on the most recent developments? Or shall we decide that life in all its forms is sacred, not open to private claim or profit?

YES

Jeremy Rifkin

Should We Patent Life?

A handful of companies are engaged in a race to patent all 100,000 human genes. In less than a decade, the race will be over. The genetic legacy of our species will be held in the form of private intellectual property. The genes inside your cells will belong not to you, but to global corporations. Welcome to the world of the biotech revolution.

While the 20th century was shaped by breakthroughs in physics and chemistry, the 21st century will belong to the biological sciences. Scientists are deciphering the genetic code, unlocking the mystery of millions of years of evolution. Global life science companies, in turn, are beginning to exploit these new advances. The raw resources of the new economic epoch are genes—already being used in businesses ranging from agriculture and bioremediation to energy and pharmaceuticals.

By 2025, we may be living in a world remade by a revolution unmatched in history. The biotech revolution raises unprecedented ethical questions we've barely begun to discuss. Will the artificial creation of cloned and transgenic animals mean the end of nature and the substitution of a bio-industrial world? Will the release of genetically engineered life forms into the biosphere cause catastrophic genetic pollution? What will it mean to live in a world where babies are customized in the womb—and where people are stereotyped and discriminated against on the basis of their genotype? What risks do we take in attempting to design more "perfect" human beings?

At the heart of this new commercial revolution is a chilling question of great ethical impact, whose resolution will affect civilization for centuries to come: *Should we patent life?* The practice has already gotten a green light, through a controversial Supreme Court decision and a subsequent ruling by the Patent and Trademark Office in the 1980s. But if the question were put directly to the American people, would they agree? If you alter one gene in a chimpanzee, does that make the animal a human "invention"? If you isolate the gene for breast cancer, does that give you the right to "own" it? Should a handful of global corporations be allowed to patent all human genes?

On the eve of the Biotech Century, we do still have an opportunity to raise ethical issues like these—although the window is rapidly closing.

Reprinted with permission from *Business Ethics*, PO Box 8439, Minneapolis MN 55408. 612/879-0695. www.business-ethics.com

We've only completed the first decade of a revolution that may span several centuries. But already there are 1,400 biotech companies in the U.S., with a total of nearly $13 billion in annual revenues and more than 100,000 employees. Development is proceeding in an astonishing number of areas:

At Harvard University, scientists have grown human bladders and kidneys in laboratory jars. Monsanto hopes to have a plastic-producing plant on the market by the year 2003—following up on the work of Chris Sommerville at the Carnegie Institution of Washington, who inserted a plastic-making gene into a mustard plant. Another biotech company, the Institute of Genomic Research, has successfully sequenced a microbe that can absorb large amounts of radioactivity and be used to dispose of deadly radioactive waste. The first genetically engineered insect, a predator mite, was released in 1996 by researchers at the University of Florida, who hope it will eat other mites that damage strawberries and similar crops.

At the University of Wisconsin, scientists have genetically altered brooding turkey hens to increase their productivity, by eliminating the "brooding" instinct: the desire to sit on and hatch eggs. Other researchers are experimenting with the creation of sterile salmon who will not have the suicidal urge to spawn, but will remain in the open sea, to be commercially harvested. Michigan State University scientists say that by breaking the spawning cycle of chinook salmon, they can produce seventy-pound salmon, compared to less than eighteen pounds for a fish returning to spawn. In short, the mothering instinct and the mating instinct are being bred out of animals.

With genetic engineering, humanity is extending its reach over the forces of nature far beyond the scope of any previous technology—with the possible exception of the nuclear bomb. At the same time, corporations are assuming ownership and control over the hereditary blueprints of life itself. Can any reasonable person believe such power is without risk?

Genes are the "green gold" of the biotech century, and companies that control them will exercise tremendous power over the world economy. Multinational corporations are already scouting the continents in search of this new precious resource, hoping to locate microbes, plants, animals, and humans with rare genetic traits that might have future market potential. Having located the desired traits, biotech companies are modifying them and seeking patent protection for their new "inventions."

The worldwide race to patent the gene pool is the culmination of a 500-year-odyssey to enclose the ecosystems of the Earth. That journey began in feudal England in the 1500s, with the passage of the great "enclosure acts," which privatized the village commons—transforming the land from a community trust to private real estate. Today, virtually every square foot of landmass on the planet is under private ownership or government control.

But enclosure of the land was just the beginning. Today, the ocean's coastal waters are commercially leased, the air has been converted into commercial airline corridors, and even the electromagnetic spectrum is considered commercial property—leased for use by radio, TV, and telephone companies. Now the most intimate commons of all—the gene pool—is being enclosed and reduced to private commercial property.

The enclosure of the genetic commons began in 1971, when an Indian microbiologist and General Electric employee, Ananda Chakrabarty, applied to the U.S. Patents and Trademark Office (PTO) for a patent on a genetically engineered microorganism designed to consume oil spills. The PTO rejected the request, arguing that living things are not patentable. The case was appealed all the way to the Supreme Court, which in 1980—by a slim margin of five to four—ruled in favor of Chakrabarty. Speaking for the majority, Chief Justice Warren Burger argued that "the relevant distinction was not between living and inanimate things," but whether or not Chakrabarty's microbe was a "human-made invention."

In the aftermath of that historic decision, bioengineering technology shed its pristine academic garb and bounded into the marketplace. On Oct. 13, 1980—just months after the court's ruling—Genentech publicly offered one million shares of stock at $35 per share. By the time the trading bell had rung that first day, the stock was selling at over $500 per share. And Genentech had yet to introduce a single product.

Chemical, pharmaceutical, argribusiness, and biotech startups everywhere sped up their research—mindful that the granting of patent protection meant the possibility of harnessing the genetic commons for vast commercial gain. Some observers, however, were not so enthused. Ethicist Leon Kass asked:

> "What is the principled limit to this beginning extension of the domain of private ownership and dominion over living nature . . . ? The principle used in Chakrabarty says that there is nothing in the nature of being, not even in the patentor himself, that makes him immune to being patented."

While the Supreme Court decision lent an air of legal legitimacy to the emerging biotech industry, a Patent Office decision in 1987 opened the floodgates. In a complete about-face, the PTO ruled that all genetically engineered multicellular living organisms—including animals—are potentially patentable. The Commissioner of Patents and Trademarks at the time, Donald J. Quigg, attempted to calm a shocked public by asserting that the decision covered every creature except human beings—because the Thirteenth Amendment to the Constitution forbids human slavery. On the other hand, human embryos and fetuses as well as human genes, tissues, and organs were now potentially patentable.

What makes the Supreme Court decision and Patent Office ruling suspect, from a legal point of view, is that they defy previous patent rulings that say one cannot claim a "discovery of nature" as an invention. No one would suggest that scientists who isolated, classified, and described the properties of chemical elements in the periodic table—such as oxygen and helium—ought to be granted a patent on them. Yet someone who isolates and classifies the properties of human genes can patent them.

The European Patent Office, for example, awarded a patent to the U.S. company Biocyte, giving it ownership of all human blood cells which have come from the umbilical cord of a newborn child and are being used for any therapeutic purposes. The patent is so broad that it allows this one company to refuse the use of any blood cells from the umbilical cord to any individual unwilling to pay the patent fee. Blood cells from the umbilical cord are particularly important for marrow transplants, making it a valuable commercial asset. It should be emphasized that this patent was awarded simply because Biocyte was able to isolate the blood cells and deep-freeze them. The company made no change in the blood itself.

A similarly broad patent was awarded to Systemix Inc. of Palo Alto, Calif., by the U.S. Patent Office, covering all human bone marrow stem cells. This extraordinary patent on a human body part was awarded despite the fact that Systemix had done nothing whatsoever to alter or engineer the cells. Dr. Peter Quisenberry, the medical affairs vice chairman of the Leukemia Society of America, quipped, "Where do you draw the line? Can you patent a hand?"

⚜

The life patents race is gearing up in the wake of government and commercial efforts to map the approximately 100,000 human genes that make up the human genome—a project with enormous commercial potential. As soon as a gene is tagged its "discoverer" is likely to apply for a patent, often before knowing the function of the gene. In 1991, J. Craig Venter, then head of the National Institute of Health Genome Mapping Research Team, resigned his government post to head up a genomics company funded with more than $70 million in venture capital. At the same time, Venter and his colleagues filed for patents on more than 2,000 human brain genes. Many researchers on the Human Genome Project were shocked and angry, charging Venter with attempting to profit off research paid for by American taxpayers.

Nobel laureate James Watson, co-discoverer of the DNA double helix, called the Venter patent claims "sheer lunacy." Still, it's likely that within less than ten years, all 100,000 or so genes that comprise the genetic legacy of our species will be patented—making them the exclusive intellectual property of global corporations.

The patenting of life is creating a firestorm of controversy. Several years ago, an Alaskan businessman named John Moore found his own body parts had been patented, without his knowledge, by the University of California at Los Angeles (UCLA), and licensed to the Sandoz Pharmaceutical Corp. Moore had been diagnosed with a rare cancer and underwent treatment at UCLA. A researcher there discovered that Moore's spleen tissue produced a blood protein that facilitates the growth of white blood cells valuable as anti-cancer agents. The university created a cell line from Moore's spleen tissue and obtained a patent on the "invention." The cell line is estimated to be worth more than $3 billion.

Moore subsequently sued, claiming a property right over his own tissue. But in 1990, the California Supreme Court ruled against him, saying Moore had no such ownership right. Human body parts, the court argued, could not be bartered as a commodity in the marketplace.

The irony of the decision was captured by Judge Broussard, in his dissenting opinion. The ruling "does *not* mean that body parts may not be bought or sold," he wrote. "[T]he majority's holding simply bars *plantiff*, the source of the cells, from obtaining the benefit of the cell's value, but permits *defendants*, who allegedly obtained the cells from plaintiff by improper means, to retain and exploit the full economic value of their ill-gotten gains."

⋯⟨◉⟩⋯

A battle of historic proportions has also emerged between the high-technology nations of the North and the developing nations of the South, over ownership of the planet's genetic treasures. Some Third World leaders say the North is attempting to seize the biological commons, most of which is in the rich tropical regions of the Southern Hemisphere, and that their nations should be compensated for use of genetic resources. Corporate and governmental leaders in the North maintain that the genes increase in value only when manipulated using sophisticated gene-splicing techniques, so there's no obligation to compensate the South.

To ease growing tensions, a number of companies have proposed sharing a portion of their gains. Merck & Co., the pharmaceutical giant (often considered a leader in social responsibility), entered into an agreement recently with a research organization in Costa Rica, the National Biodiversity Institute, to pay the organization a paltry $1 million to secure the group's plant, microorganism, and insect samples. Critics liken the deal to European settlers giving American Indians trinkets in return for the island of Manhattan. The recipient organization, on the other hand, is granting a right to bio-prospect on land it has no historic claim to in the first place—while indigenous peoples are locked out of the agreement.

Such agreements are beginning to meet with resistance from countries and non-governmental organizations (NGOs) in the Southern Hemisphere. They claim that what Northern companies are calling "discoveries" are really the pirating of the indigenous knowledge of native peoples and cultures. To defuse opposition, biotech corporations are seeking to impose a uniform intellectual property regime worldwide. And they've gone a long way toward achieving that with the passage of the Trade Related Aspects of Intellectual Property Agreements (TRIPS) at the Uruguay Round of the General Agreement on Tariffs and Trade (GATT). Sculpted by companies like Bristol Myers, Merck, Pfizer, Dupont, and Monsanto, the TRIPS agreement makes no allowance for indigenous knowledge, and grants companies free access to genetic material from around the world.

Suman Sahai, director of the Gene Campaign—an NGO in New Delhi—makes the point, "God didn't give us 'rice' or 'wheat' or 'potato.'" These were once wild plants that were domesticated over eons of time and patiently bred by generations of farmers. Sahai asks, "Who did all of that work?" Groups like his argue that Southern countries should be compensated for their contribution to biotech.

Still others take a third position: that neither corporations nor indigenous peoples should claim ownership, because the gene pool ought not to be for sale, at any price. It should remain an open commons and continue to be used freely by present and future generations. They cite precedent in the recent historic decision by the nations of the world to maintain the continent of Antarctica as a global commons free from commercial exploitation.

⟿⟐⟾

The idea of private companies laying claim to human genes as their exclusive intellectual property has resulted in growing protests worldwide. In May of 1994, a coalition of hundreds of women's organizations from more than forty nations announced opposition to Myriad Genetics's attempt to patent the gene that causes breast cancer in some women. The coalition was assembled by The Foundation on Economic Trends. While the women did not oppose the screening test Myriad developed, they opposed the claim to the gene itself. They argued that the breast cancer gene was a product of nature and not a human invention, and should not be patentable. Myriad's exclusive rights to such a gene could make screening more expensive, and might impede research by making access to the gene too expensive.

The central question in these cases—Can you patent life?—is one of the most important issues ever to face the human family. Life patenting strikes at the core of our beliefs about the very nature of life and whether it is to be conceived as having sacred and intrinsic value, or merely utility value. Surely such a fundamental question deserves to be widely discussed by the public before such patents become a ubiquitous part of our daily lives.

The biotech revolution will force each of us to put a mirror to our most deeply held values, making us ponder the ultimate question of the purpose and meaning of existence. This may turn out to be its most important contribution. The rest is up to us.

William Domnarski

 **NO**

Dire New World

With an authorial voice that only a conspiracy maven such as Oliver Stone could love, Jeremy Rifkin is back, this time to warn us about the dangers inherent in our idea of so-called "progress," as Rifkin puts it.

Rifkin—the president of the Foundation of Economic Trends and the author of many books on economic trends relating to science, technology, and culture—is especially worried about the implications of the biotech century that will not wait two years to begin. It's here now, and unless we heed Rifkin's warnings and keep ourselves from temptation by agreeing with him that progress is too fraught for mischief to be acceptable, we'll end up in a genetically polluted world in which genetic discrimination reigns—though you will be able to go down to your local laboratory when the time comes to be fitted with that new vital organ you've had cloned in the expectation that you might need it.

The advances in genetic engineering in medicine—to say nothing of the advances in plant genetics—have been staggering. Now knowing most of the code, we can identify and even act on various types of diseases and disabilities before birth. We have added a range of new treatments in which genetically engineered cells are introduced into the body to take hold and combat disease. Alzheimer's disease and Parkinson's disease are not on the verge of being conquered, but we are closer to victory than ever because of genetic research.

But where some see the advances that genetic engineering has produced, Rifkin sees a new wave of eugenic zealots eager to use our genetic makeup as even more revealing of our true nature than the SAT.

Ripped from the Headlines

Rifkin relies primarily on national news magazines and newspapers t[o] sketch both the developments in and the predictions for various aspects [of] this scientific revolution, and, in that sense, his story is one ripped from th[e] headlines. His persistent complaint is that journalists fail to present ba[l]anced coverage because of a delight in describing the often dazzling possib[le] uses of the technology at issue. What's left out, he argues, are the myri[ad] ethical issues that coalesce around the question of whether progress, [it]self, is a good thing.

Trying to interpret the scientific breakthroughs that are changing the way we think of both ourselves as individuals and the dominant species on the planet, Rifkin details seven strands of what he calls the new operational matrix of the biotech century. It's not the evil that men do that outlives them; it's the mischief that computers and genetic research can get us into when they are spliced together that we need to worry about.

Four strands of the biotech century's matrix encompass recombinant DNA techniques; the wholesale reseeding of the planet with genetically enhanced and devised plants; gene mapping; and computers that can probe and manage the vast genetic resources of our bodies and our planet. The other strands include the ideological, philosophical, and cultural structures supporting the new research and its application.

In Rifkin's view, the courts are primarily to blame for this state of affairs because they have allowed for the patenting of genetically altered cells, thus creating a slippery slope that we will be unable to negotiate. Going further, however, he argues that a new cultural context has emerged that favors the new biotechnologies. Underpinning all of this is a new cosmological narrative that sees evolution as an improvement in information processing, rather than as a random process of selection winnowing its way through passive natural elements.

They Know Not What They Do

Rifkin complains that the scientists know not what they do, unwittingly creating Frankensteins at every turn. He objects that their sheer ability to do something seems to them justification enough to just do it. They are too little concerned with the collateral effects of genetic engineering.

It's clear that Rifkin is writing for an audience already persuaded by his general thesis and by his credentials as a prophet of doom. And he wants us to know that he was right in all the predictions on genetic engineering that he began making 20 years ago. But the world still hasn't caught on to the issue as he has framed it—that progress is generally bad—so he's back for more hectoring. What Rifkin does not want to accept is that as a culture we desire and embrace progress.

The press does not seem guilty of the one-sided reporting that Rifkin ascribes to it. Recently, for example, *The New York Times* featured two reports on a new technique in genetic engineering that allows scientists to take embryonic human stem cells before they have distinguished themselves as the type of cell they will be, such as a brain cell or heart cell; the technique then coaxes those cells to morph into the type of cell that is needed. The result is that heart cells can be grown and then used to heal the heart when it fails—all rather heady—or should I say hearty—stuff.

The use of such new cell technology has been condemned by some because it comes perilously close to infringing on our notion of what constitutes an individual. As opponents see it, there is a great difference between using stem cells from miscarried fetuses, which a spokesperson for the Catholic Church finds acceptable, and using cells derived from pre-implantation embryos that were created in fertility clinics. To use the latter cells is to use humans for research, the opponents stress.

Annoying Disingenuousness

One senses, however, that Rifkin would not have been satisfied with the coverage that the ethical issues received, because the heart of the story emphasizes that scientists are all but dancing with excitement over this new technology. There is, at the core of Rifkin's book, an annoying disingenuousness. He poses himself in a neutral posture that pretends to provide us with the information we need to decide if this biotech century is for us; at the same time, Rifkin urges us to think that the problems created by the new technologies outweigh the possible benefits.

Two lines of reasoning in particular show how, despite his good intentions, Rifkin seems out of touch with reality, at least as it is defined by law. The first is the supposed exploitation of indigenous peoples by agribusiness and pharmaceutical companies that search the world, especially the world in the southern hemisphere, for new plants that yield new drugs or new strains of foodstuffs. The indigenous peoples, the argument goes, have done all the work in cultivating the plants over time, which makes the genetic manipulations of the big companies a negligible contribution at best, certainly not one entitling them to patent protection and profits. What Rifkin does not want to acknowledge is that patents are hard earned and necessary for research to continue. Rifkin wants a world that does not privilege the capacity of science to make productive what otherwise wouldn't be. His is a politically correct world, blissfully ignorant of law's contribution to society.

The second and perhaps more revealing line of misguided reasoning is Rifkin's unwillingness to accept patent law for what it is. The Supreme Court has recognized that the distinction is not between living and inanimate things, but between products of nature, whether living or not, and human-made inventions. Rifkin's argument is that scientists cannot be said to create anything patentable because the life they manipulate was already there. That is a narrow and misguided view of both the law and of what scientists do. The law sides with progress; Rifkin sides against it. What Rifkin cannot accept is what Justice William O. Douglas wrote in *The Great A&P Tea Co. v. Supermarket Corp.*, 340 U.S. 147 (1950)—30 years before the celebrated oil-eating bacteria case of 1980: That the inventions that most benefit mankind are those that "push back the frontiers of chemistry, physics and the like."

As his book makes all too clear, Rifkin does not want to explore the frontier. He wants to circle the wagons and hold off, through the pouting in his book, that which cannot be held back. Those concerned with the ethical implications of genetic research are with us and are heard. That we as a society want to search the frontier should not be dismissed, as Rifkin so keenly wants to dismiss them, as ignorant, selfish or misguided.

POSTSCRIPT

Should Patenting Life Be Forbidden?

In general, we in the United States have adopted the cost-benefit approach to problems with new products. If we cannot foresee the consequences of a new technology, we tend to make an educated guess about the benefits of all kinds, another educated guess about probable costs of all kinds, and balance the one against the other. Engineered seeds seem to have the potential to increase crop yields, cut labor costs, and not inconsequentially, lower the use of fertilizers and pesticides. Those are benefits. As for costs, well, we don't know, there might not be any. So go ahead with the new life forms, and allow the companies the patents they need to make them profitable.

On the other hand, in Europe, the custom is to use the precautionary approach toward new technology. If we don't know what the costs might be, try the seeds in a small controlled area for a long time and see what the costs are. If we don't like them, kill the technology. Only after the seeds are proven safe over generations will we make them publicly available.

Suggested Reading

Which approach do you think is better for such new technologies? If you want more to read on the subject, consider the following:

Lester R. Brown, "Struggling to Raise Cropland Productivity," *State of the World 1998* (New York: Norton, 1998).

Charles C. Mann, "The Brave New World of Science and Business," book review in *Foreign Policy* (December 1998), p. 113.

Mae-Wan Ho, *Genetic Engineering: Dream or Nightmare?* (Bath: Gateways Books, 1998).

G. Tyler Miller, *Living in the Environment*, 11th ed. (Belmont, CA: Brooks/Cole Publishing, 2000).

Internet References . . .

FAQs about Free-Market Environmentalism

Sponsored by the Thoreau Institute, this site lists and answers frequently asked questions about free-market environmentalism. It is the Institute's position that a free-market system can solve many environmental problems better than more government regulation can.

http://ti.org/faqs.html

Pennsylvania Department of Environmental Protection

This home page of the Pennsylvania Department of Environmental Protection monitors environmental responsibility.

http://www.dep.state.pa.us

Rainforest Facts

This Rainforest Facts site contains statistics on the rain forest as well as information on rain forest products, worldwide rain forest protection efforts, the tropical timber industry, and more.

http://www.pbs.org/tal/costa_rica/rainfacts.html

Environmental Policy and Corporate Responsibility

T here is a powerful new initiative to enlist business in the enterprise of saving the natural environment, a direction that traditionally private enterprise has left to the government and the NGOs. How should the corporation respond to this new set of demands on its resources?

- Do Environmental Restrictions Violate Basic Economic Freedoms?

- Is Bottling Water a Good Solution to Problems of Water Purity and Availability?

- Should the World Continue to Rely on Oil as a Major Source of Energy?

ISSUE 19

Do Environmental Restrictions Violate Basic Economic Freedoms?

YES: John Shanahan, from "Environment," in Stuart M. Butler and Kim R. Holmes, eds. *Issues '96: The Candidate's Briefing Book* (Heritage Foundation, 1996)

NO: Paul R. Ehrlich and Anne H. Ehrlich, from "Brownlash: The New Environmental Anti-Science," *The Humanist* (November/ December 1996)

ISSUE SUMMARY

YES: John Shanahan, vice president of the Alexis de Tocqueville Institution in Arlington, Virginia, argues that many government environmental policies are unreasonable and infringe on basic economic freedoms. He concedes that environmental problems exist, but denies that there is any environmental "crisis."

NO: Environmental scientists Paul R. Ehrlich and Anne H. Ehrlich, whose 1974 book *The End of Affluence* first outlined the consequences of environmental mismanagement, argue that many objections to environmental protections are self-serving and based in bad or misused science.

Which would you think is more important, if you had to choose: Profitability in the corporation, yielding return on investment to the shareholder, good products reliably supplied for the customer, a tax base for the public sector, jobs for the workers, and, in short, the fundamentals of American life? Or the protection of the natural environment, protection of our fragile ecosystems for the generations to follow us? This is not an easy choice to make, and it confronts our legislatures on a daily basis.

Take pesticides, for example. They form a profitable part of the chemicals manufacturing industry all by themselves, precisely because they increase agricultural production, by orders of magnitude, wherever they are used.

On the other hand, as Rachel Carson pointed out in 1962 (*Silent Spring,* Houghton Mifflin), pesticides don't know enough to poison only crop-eating insects. They poison every living thing that consumes them. They poison the insects that eat the crops, the predator insects that used to keep the crop-eaters' numbers under control, the birds that eat the insects that fall to earth, the fish that eat the insects that land in the water (or that live in the water into which the spray falls, or is washed), and us who eat the fish. When it poisons the birds, their eggs no longer are viable, and the species starts to die out. Which is more important—the present profits of the industry and the present low prices in the vegetable aisle, or the future of the birds? What do you say? What would your grandchildren say?

Since the 1960s, successive administrations in this nation have attempted, with more or less enthusiasm, to adopt regulations that will limit economic freedoms in order to protect the environment. As our knowledge of ecology has increased, so have the regulations, and predictably, so have the objections to them. It seems that every plant manager, every developer, and even every homeowner, bumps into environmental regulations every time they turn around—or try to get something done to improve the value of their property or enterprise. We have as a very close national memory, that America was founded for freedom: the freedom to do what you want to do without monarchs and bishops hovering over you telling you how to think and what you can and cannot build. All this regulation rankles.

Where will this controversy end? Compromise is the great American tradition, but it is no compromise for the environmentalists. If you want to save a stretch of open space for future generations, and I want to build a sub-division on it, I will argue that we must compromise, and you let me build on half of it. But now that half is gone for good. What timber harvester would not gladly accept a compromise that gave him 90 percent of the forest, leaving only 10 percent to be preserved? He would happily promise that he would never ask for any more. But the great redwood forests of the Pacific Northwest are more than 90 percent gone, and the lumbermen want more.

Are there ways that humans can live harmoniously with nature, profiting from relationships that mimic those that existed prior to the Industrial Revolution (only smarter)? The Rocky Mountain Institute has published a powerful argument that such relationships are entirely possible, and even more economical than the business arrangements we have now. (See *Natural Capitalism,* by Amory and Hunter Lovins and Paul Hawken, Rocky Mountain Institute 1999.)

Ask yourself, as you read these selections, which orientation toward the environment is likely to result in a stronger world in the next generation. John Shanahan's selection is from the Heritage Foundation's 1996 *Candidate's Briefing Book,* supplying arguments for conservative candidates to help them get elected; the Ehrlichs insist that the environmental crisis is very real, and that the "brownlash" opponents of environmentalism are peddling worthless ideology in the face of the facts.

YES

John Shanahan

Environment

The Issues

Americans want a clean, healthy environment. They also want a strong economy. But environmental protection is enormously expensive, costs jobs, and stifles economic opportunity. On the other hand, before government stepped in, robust economic activity such as manufacturing led to a deteriorating and unhealthy environment. The challenge is how to achieve both a strong economy and a healthy environment. After all, what Americans actually want is a high overall quality of life.

Three decades ago, as people perceived that their quality of life was beginning to deteriorate, they began to support aggressive policies to reduce pollution. These policies frequently failed to live up to their sponsors' claims; they also became increasingly and unnecessarily expensive. But the environment did improve, especially in the early years. Now, however, Americans are becoming aware that many of these policies are unreasonable and that, even when they work, they result only in small improvements at a heavy cost in jobs and freedom. Americans also are beginning to recognize that there often is no sound scientific basis for assertions of environmental harm or risk to the public. The pendulum finally has begun to swing the other way.

Conservatives, like Americans generally, have no wish to return to the days of black smoke billowing out of smokestacks. But they do believe common sense can be brought to bear in dealing with the environment: that it is possible to protect the environment without sacrificing the freedoms for which America stands. Conservative candidates and legislators therefore should stress the following themes:

Examples of regulatory abuse It is important to show that "good intentions" often are accompanied by oppressive, senseless regulations.

An ethic of conservation Candidates need to explain that conserving or efficiently using natural resources is not in dispute. The debate is over how best to do this: through markets or through government controls.

Economic freedom Candidates need to point out that many government "solutions" to environment problems conflict with basic economic freedoms.

From *"Environment,"* in Stuart M. Butler and Kim R. Holmes, eds, Issues '96: The Candidate's Briefing Book (Heritage Foundation, 1996). Copyright © 1996 by The Heritage Foundation. Reprinted by permission. Notes omitted.

Property-based solutions   Candidates need to explain that environmental objectives can be achieved best not by issuing thousands of pages of rules that people will try to circumvent, but by capitalizing on the incentives associated with owning property.

Sound science   Candidates need to argue that we need policies based on sound science, not "tabloid science."

Priority setting   Candidates must explain that not all problems are of the same importance or urgency, and that regulating all risks equally means fewer lives are saved for the dollars spent than would be saved if priorities were set.

The Facts

While pollution levels have fallen dramatically since 1970, most reductions were achieved early and at relatively low cost. From 1970 to 1990, total emission levels fell 33.8 percent. Over the same period, lead levels in the air fell 96.5 percent, and carbon monoxide levels in the air fell 40.7 percent. But reductions have slowed dramatically. . . .

Unworkable Regulations

Environmental regulation does more than just cost too much. Candidates also should use the growing litany of horror stories to demonstrate how ill-conceived environmental regulations, while delivering little benefit, lead to unintended consequences for businesses especially small businesses, which are disproportionately minority-owned and minority-run.

- Larry Mason's family owned a sawmill employing 40 workers in Beaver, Washington. In the mid-1980s, based on harvest assurances from the U.S. Forest Service and loan guarantees from the Small Business Administration, the family invested $1 million in its business. Then, says Mason, "in 1990, the spotted owl injunctions closed our mill, made my equipment worthless, and my expertise obsolete. The same government that encouraged me to take on business debt then took away my ability to repay."
- While the Clean Water Act (CWA) requires a waste treatment facility to submit a simple form stating that a fence restricts access by the public, the Resource Conservation and Recovery Act (RCRA) requires an additional 25 pages detailing the fence design, the location of the posts and gates, a cross section of the wire mesh, and other minor technical matters. RCRA is so wasteful that one plant, whose CWA permit application was only 17 pages long, had to file a seven-foot stack of supporting documents with its applications.
- Ronald Cahill, a disabled Wilmington, Massachusetts, dry cleaner, purchased expensive dry-cleaning equipment to comply with EPA regulations governing the use of trichlorotrifluoroethane (CFC-113). But the EPA levied a tax on all chlorofluorocarbons (CFCs), making

CFC-113 hard to find and extremely expensive. In 1995, Cahill's business went under. Washington, says Cahill, "has put me out of business with excessive taxes and regulations."

Regulatory abuses like these usually are a direct result of the way government bureaucracies attack environmental problems. Typically, these agencies regulate without regard to the cost imposed on individuals and businesses. Yet it makes no sense to issue a regulation for which the burden far outweighs any benefit that might be conferred. In fact, it often is unclear whether there will be any benefit at all because the science on which many regulations are based is so poor.

Also, instead of setting realistic performance standards and giving businesses the freedom to develop innovative ways of meeting them, agencies typically rely on inflexible command-and-control regulations that, for example, specify what technologies companies must use. Since businesses differ in their operating structures, this one-size-fits-all approach rarely leads to cost-effective solutions compared to more flexible and dependable performance standards. Moreover, by eliminating the incentive for companies to seek out these cost-effective solutions, it stifles innovative technologies or techniques that reduce costs. In the end, of course, the consumer is the one who pays.

Perhaps the most troublesome aspect of current environmental policy is the fact that bureaucrats and liberal lawmakers generally consider regulation the only option. Creative solutions shown to be less expensive, more effective, and more respectful of human liberty are rejected out of hand. Instead of setting up a system of incentives to lure businesses into operating with environmental impact in mind, the system relies on punishment regardless of whether this accomplishes the desired goal or creates unintended consequences.

Rejecting Property Rights

Regulations have become increasingly unfair. The Environmental Protection Agency (EPA), Department of the Interior (DOI), Army Corps of Engineers, and other federal agencies operate on the premise that property should be used to satisfy government's needs and objectives without regard to who owns the property or the financial burden imposed on them. It is this mentality that leads government reflexively to reject the creative solutions advanced by free-market advocates, including incentive-based approaches to protecting endangered species. By ignoring property rights, establishment environmentalists, bureaucrats, and liberal legislators also ignore the benefits to be derived from free trade and free markets.

The most unfair and burdensome hardship inflicted by government "regulatory takings" is that property owners are not compensated for their losses. For instance, if an elderly husband and wife spend a large portion of their retirement savings to buy land on which to build their dream home and that land subsequently is designated a wetland, they lose the value of their property as well as their savings. They are stuck with property they cannot use and the government does nothing to reimburse them for their loss. Unfortunately, tales of financial hardship caused by government designation of land as wetland or endangered-species habitat have become common. For instance:

- Bill Stamp's family in Exeter, Rhode Island, has been blocked from farming or developing its 70 acres of land for 11 years, yet has been assessed taxes at rates determined by the land's industrial value up to $72,000 annually. As a result, this fifth-generation farm family may lose its life savings. The government, however, appears unmoved. Stamp relates what one Army Corps of Engineers enforcement officer told him: "We know that this is rape, pillage, and plunder of your farm, but this is our job."
- A small church in Waldorf, Maryland, was told by the Army Corps of Engineers that one-third of its land, on which it planned to build a parking lot, was a wetland and could not be used. Part of this so-called wetland is a bone-dry hillside which almost never collects water. Says Reverend Murray Southwell of the Freewill Baptists, "this obvious misinterpretation of wetland law made it necessary for us to purchase an additional lot [for $45,000, which] has been a heavy financial burden on this small missions church."
- Developer Buzz Oates wants to develop less than 4 percent of the Sutter Basin in Sacramento, California, where an estimated 1,000 giant garter snakes live. But the federal government mandated that he pay a "mitigation" fee of nearly $3.8 million for the 40 or fewer snakes he might disturb: $93,950 per snake. Says Oates, in an age of "depleted [fiscal] resources and deteriorating school infrastructure, this is a very tough pill to swallow."

Hundreds of such stories have surfaced over the past few years, and many analysts suspect that far more are never made public. According to Bob Adams, Project Director for Environmental and Regulatory Affairs at the National Center for Public Policy Research, "the stories we have compiled are just the tip of the iceberg, but many people are simply too scared to come forward or feel powerless against the government."

Ironically, federal agencies and the Clinton Administration argue that it would cost too much money to compensate landowners. Leon Panetta, then Director of the Office of Management and Budget, told the House Committee on Public Works and Transportation's Subcommittee on Water Resources and the Environment on May 26, 1994, that paying compensation for wetlands regulation would be "an unnecessary and unwise use of taxpayer dollars" and a drain on the federal budget.

Property owners counter that regulatory takings are a drain on the family budget. Nancie Marzulla, President of Defenders of Property Rights, points out that "what people don't realize is that these landowners typically are not wealthy and powerful corporations, but normal Americans schoolteachers and elderly couples whose lives are destroyed by stretched interpretations of a single environmental law." Moreover, the federal government already owns about one out of every three acres in the country (with even more owned by state and local governments). If the federal government can afford to maintain one-third of the nation's land, it should be able to pay landowners for regulatory confiscation of their property. If not, maybe it should consider selling the least ecologically sensitive land from its vast holdings to pay for the land it wants.

Lost Opportunities, Lost Lives

Ask the average American how much a human life is worth, and the answer likely will be that "no amount is too much." This is how Congress and federal agencies justify imposing sometimes staggering costs on businesses to reduce the risks of death by infinitesimal amounts. What policymakers fail to understand is that wasting resources in this way means not being able to use them in other ways that might well produce better results and save even more lives.

If lawmakers ever did consider which environmental policies actually save the most lives, they would scrap many existing rules, freeing up resources to be used in other ways. This commonsense approach would lead to regulation that is very different, in its scope and fundamental assumptions, from that which burdens America today. . . .

What America Thinks about the Environment

When asked by the media, pollsters, or politicians, Americans routinely answer that they want a clean and healthy environment. Indeed, the majority of Americans consider themselves "environmentalists." This does not translate, however, into automatic acceptance of the environmental lobby's agenda. Conservative candidates need to make this clear to discourage voters from supporting policies they do not believe in simply because they are portrayed as "pro-environment."

The dichotomy in public opinion shows up in polling data. When respondents are asked general or theoretical questions that involve little personal sacrifice, or that do not identify those burdened, government intervention fares well. In one poll, for instance, 60 percent of respondents agreed that we must protect the environment even if it costs jobs in the community. In another, 72 percent of respondents said they would pay somewhat higher taxes if the money was used to protect the environment and prevent water and air pollution.

On the other hand, when respondents are asked questions that are more specific, that involve greater sacrifice, or that identify the people losing jobs, government intervention is less popular. When respondents are asked to pay much higher taxes to protect the environment, support drops by almost half. By the same token, only one-third would be willing to accept cuts in their standard of living. When asked to pick between spotted owls and Northwest workers who stand to lose their jobs because of efforts to protect the owls, respondents choose jobs by a margin of 3 to 2. . . .

Perhaps the most refreshing change in attitudes in recent years is the recognition that the country can have economic growth and environmental protection simultaneously. Vice President Al Gore has made the point that economic growth and environmental protection are not incompatible. This is true, but only if America's environmental laws are structured correctly to encourage responsible behavior as part of the business decision-making process. Gore advocates stringent command-and-control regulations that are inconsistent with growth and lead to little real gains in environmental protection.

Whenever this question comes up, Americans must be told that the way to promote both environmental protection and economic growth is to allow them to work hand in hand. The government must stop regarding them as mutually exclusive and stop pitting economic freedom against the environment. Laws must be based on, and work with, a free market. Only then can Americans maximize their economic and environmental quality of life.

The Need for Common Sense

Given Americans' ambivalence on the question of environmental protection, it is all the more important for conservatives to approach the issue in a commonsense way. People must understand that environmental protection need not come at the expense of jobs, but will cost jobs if the socialist model of centralized control for protecting the environment is not set aside. It doesn't work. Rather, the country should adopt a reasonable, commonsense approach to environmental protection that is based on:

Freedom with responsibility   Conservatives traditionally have stressed economic growth while ignoring the importance of environmental problems. Thus, they have fought environmentalists step by step and have lost step by step. The reason, while unpleasant, is not complicated. Environmentalists have had the moral high ground, even though they typically have not provided the most beneficial solutions. In short, conservatives have been on the wrong side of an emotional issue.

Two lessons demonstrate why:

- **First,** leftists and the public at large understand that publicly owned goods, free of constraints on usage, will be depleted over time. Garrett Hardin, Professor Emeritus of Human Ecology at the University of California, in his seminal 1968 work *The Tragedy of the Commons* showed that when a good is publicly owned, or "owned" in common, no one has an incentive to conserve or to manage it. In fact, there is a perverse incentive to use the good inefficiently to deplete it. This fact is at the heart of most environmental problems, such as air and water pollution and species extinction.
- **Second,** if there are incentives to conserve resources, people will conserve out of self-interest. People with a vested interest in providing environmental benefits through property ownership or other positive incentives will provide them voluntarily, without coercion.

. . . "Freedom with responsibility for one's actions" should be the conservative message. Responsibility restrains wasteful behavior. Ironically, the old environmentalist slogan "Make the polluter pay" is consistent with this message. But when they say this, conservatives and liberals mean different things. As Al Cobb, then Director of Environment and Energy at the National Policy Forum, has said, "What the environmental lobby means by that phrase is that corporate polluters should be punished severely for any pollution whatsoever. What conservatives mean, however, is that polluters should bear the full cost of environmental degradation, but no more." At the same time, individuals and corporations also should be rewarded for conservation and other environmentally sound practices.

Conservation through property rights   The free market reflects the conservation ethic better than any command-and-control regulation from Washington. A free market can occur, however, only when private citizens engage in trade, and people can trade only what they own: some form of property. Thus, property is the cornerstone of a free market. If property rights are insecure or publicly owned, a market cannot function effectively. Some critics misleadingly call this "market failure," but it is really a failure to use markets and their main engine: property rights. As a result, both environmental protection and personal liberty suffer. A resource that is not owned will deteriorate or be depleted because neither protection of nor damage to that resource is part of the individual's usual decision-making process. Others, however, are still forced to bear the consequences.

Conservative candidates should concentrate on explaining the innovative ways in which property rights can be used to protect the environment. The most efficient method and the most protective of individual rights and freedoms is to enlist self-interest in the service of environmental protection.

Consider [two] examples of how the principle of property rights-based environmentalism works: . . .

- In Scotland and England, the popularity of fishing has burgeoned in recent decades. Property rights to fishing sites have developed as the building block for markets to provide access to prime fishing spots. As a result, many private, voluntary associations have been formed to purchase fishing rights access. In Scotland, "virtually every inch of every major river and most minor ones is privately owned or leased. . . ." Owners of fishing rights on various stretches of the rivers charge others for the right to fish. These rivers are not overfished because it is not in the owner's best interest to allow the fish population to be depleted. Because he wants to continue charging fishermen for the foreseeable future, the owner conserves his fish stock, allowing them to reproduce, and prevents pollution from entering his stretch of the river. If a municipality pollutes the water upstream, the owner of the fishing rights can sue for an injunction. Everyone wins, including fishermen looking for quality fishing with some privacy.
- One group's approach to wetland protection has shown the power of property rights to achieve environmental goals. Ducks Unlimited, a

group consisting of hunters and non-hunters alike, is dedicated to enhancing duck populations. To do this, it has purchased property or conservation easements with privately raised funds. Unlike other groups (for example, the National Wildlife Federation) that began as organizations of hunters and outdoorsmen but later lost much of their original focus and joined forces with the more extreme elements of the environmental lobby, Ducks Unlimited still focuses on protecting duck habitat. In the last 58 years, it has raised and invested $750 million to conserve 17 million acres in Canada alone, an effort which benefits other wildlife as well as ducks. In 1994, it restored or created about 50,000 acres of wetlands. Since Ducks Unlimited itself pays for the habitat it protects, in many ways it embodies the essence of the conservative message: that the market should be allowed to determine the best and highest use of a good or resource in this case, duck habitat.

Unfortunately, property rights are under attack from the environmental lobby. The Fifth Amendment to the U.S. Constitution states, "nor shall private property be taken for public use, without just compensation," but this has been interpreted as protection primarily against the physical taking of property. Most infringements, however, involve federal decrees that deny owners the right to use their property as they see fit, for example, to continue farming. Since the courts have been unclear on the degree of protection property owners should have from such intrusions, legislative protection is needed.

Sound science, not tabloid science   Before issuing regulations to protect health, regulators should ask whether the science behind a measure justifies the often enormous expenditures involved. Unfortunately, however, the federal government often acts in response to strong environmentalist-generated public pressure without adequate scientific justification. . . .

- In 1992, the National Aeronautics and Space Administration (NASA) reported that [the] hole in the Earth's protective ozone layer might open up over North America that spring. This hypothetical hole, which would have been in addition to the annual Antarctic hole, would be caused by chlorofluourocarbons (CFCs), a refrigerant. After widespread media coverage on the threat of CFCs, the White House moved a production ban, scheduled for the year 2000, up to 1996, raising the cost of the ban by tens of billions of dollars. Unfortunately, NASA held its press conference before it had finished the study or subjected it to even cursory peer review. The hypothesized ozone hole over North America never materialized. Nor could it have. According to Patrick Michaels of the Climatology Department at the University of Virginia, "The only way you could produce an ozone hole in the high latitudes of the Northern Hemisphere that resembles what occurs in the Southern Hemisphere (where the ozone hole occurs) would be to flatten our mountains and submerge our continents. Then you would have airflow patterns similar to those that occur in the Southern Hemisphere, and are the ones that are required to create an ozone hole." One would think NASA would know this as well. Now, although

no information other than a thoroughly discredited hypothesis justifies dramatically stepping up the phaseout, the country is redirecting
its limited economic resources at an extra cost of hundreds of dollars
per household because of the ban, which is now in place.

Instead of merely responding to tabloid claims or politically motivated
studies by federal agencies and environmental organizations trying to justify
their budgets, regulations should be based on credible scientific findings open
to public scrutiny. For instance, agencies should use consistent methodologies
to determine risks. Currently, they use different methods. Thus, for example,
risk assessments by different agencies may turn up different answers as to
whether a chemical at a particular dose level causes cancer. Theoretically,
exposure to some level of a chemical could be found to be both deadly and
perfectly safe.

Government assessments also should reveal the assumptions and uncertainties in their analyses. Typically, because of missing data, most studies use
certain assumptions to estimate these uncertainties. These assumptions,
sometimes unreasonably gloomy, usually determine the conclusion reached.
For instance, sometimes an estimate of the likely risk from some chemical is
multiplied thousands, or even millions, of times just to be "conservative." Yet
the analyses used to justify these enormously expensive regulations often are
obscure as to their assumptions. Moreover, the reports rarely reveal the level
of uncertainty involved in arriving at their conclusions.

Whenever regulations that address risks are considered, each agency
should be required to conduct risk assessments if only to aid in intelligent
decision-making that are consistent, that are transparent to public scrutiny,
and that fully detail their assumptions and levels of uncertainty. Moreover,
each study should be reviewed before a regulation is published to ensure that
scientific guidelines are strictly followed. If federal agencies cannot meet even
this very limited standard, it is unconscionable for them to impose costly
standards on others.

The need to set priorities The economy has a limited capacity to absorb
environmental regulations. Simply put, the country cannot afford to eliminate every risk. Thus, there is a trade-off: Attempting to regulate one risk out
of existence may mean that another risk (or other risks) will have to be tolerated. In most cases, the cure is worse than the disease. Misguided and excessive regulation can cost lives, so it is critical that regulators recognize the
costs of their actions. Spending enormous amounts of money to eradicate
small or even hypothetical risks means that those dollars cannot be used in
other productive ways public or private that might be of greater benefit to the
nation.

. . . [I]t is essential that policymakers develop a priority list of environmental problems, based on the extent of the possible risk each appears to pose
and the cost of reducing that risk to acceptable levels. With such a list,
policymakers can know just how much protection is being bought for every
dollar spent. Americans finally will get the maximum environmental "bang

for the buck." Conversely, the federal government will be able to achieve environmental objectives at the lowest cost, and thus with the fewest "pink slips" for American workers.

Is There an Environmental Crisis?

Is there an environmental crisis? The answer is a resounding "No." Certainly the country and planet have environmental problems that need to be addressed. But overall, the environment has been improving. Unfortunately, the public is subjected only to the "Chicken Little" version of the situation, and reports of environmental progress and refutations of environmental alarmists are rarely covered in the press.

In his 1995 book *A Moment on the Earth,* which details many of the improvements that have taken place in the last three decades, *Newsweek* editor Gregg Easterbrook notes that reports of positive environmental developments, such as significantly lower air pollution in major U.S. cities, are buried inside the newspapers. Negative news, meanwhile, gets front-page attention, and the news that is reported often contains numerous misleading "facts."

The truth is that threats to the environment have lessened considerably. Lead has been almost eliminated. Even in Los Angeles, the most polluted city in the country, levels of Volatile Organic Compounds (VOCs) have fallen by more than half since 1970. In other formerly polluted cities, such as Atlanta, the air is now considered relatively clean as VOCs are down by almost two-thirds and Nitrous Oxide is down 15 percent.

In area after area so-called global warming, endangered species, wetlands, pesticides, hazardous waste, and automotive fuel economy, for example, the problem is the same: only rarely are the facts heard by the American people.

Paul R. Ehrlich and
Anne H. Ehrlich

Brownlash: The New Environmental Anti-Science

Humanity is now facing a sort of slow-motion environmental Dunkirk. It remains to be seen whether civilization can avoid the perilous trap it has set for itself. Unlike the troops crowding the beach at Dunkirk, civilization's fate is in its own hands; no miraculous last-minute rescue is in the cards. Although progress has certainly been made in addressing the human predicament, far more is needed. Even if humanity manages to extricate itself, it is likely that environmental events will be defining ones for our grandchildren's generation—and those events could dwarf World War II in magnitude.

Sadly, much of the progress that has been made in defining, understanding, and seeking solutions to the human predicament over the past 30 years is now being undermined by an environmental backlash. We call these attempts to minimize the seriousness of environmental problems the *brownlash* because they help to fuel a backlash against "green" policies. While it assumes a variety of forms, the brownlash appears most clearly as an outpouring of seemingly authoritative opinions in books, articles, and media appearances that greatly distort what is or isn't known by environmental scientists. Taken together, despite the variety of its forms, sources, and issues addressed, the brownlash has produced what amounts to a body of anti-science—a twisting of the findings of empirical science—to bolster a predetermined worldview and to support a political agenda. By virtue of relentless repetition, this flood of anti-environmental sentiment has acquired an unfortunate aura of credibility.

It should be noted that the brownlash is not by any means a coordinated effort. Rather, it seems to be generated by a diversity of individuals and organizations. Some of its promoters have links to right-wing ideology and political groups. And some are well-intentioned individuals, including writers and public figures, who for one reason or another have bought into the notion that environmental regulation has become oppressive and needs to be severely weakened. But the most extreme—and most dangerous—elements are those who, while claiming to represent a scientific viewpoint, misstate scientific findings to support their view that the U.S. government has gone overboard with regulation, especially (but not exclusively) for environmental protection, and that subtle, long-term problems like global warming are nothing to worry about. The words and sentiments of the brownlash are

From *The Humanist* by Paul R. Ehrlich and Anne H. Ehrlich (November/December 1996)

profoundly troubling to us and many of our colleagues. Not only are the underlying agendas seldom revealed but, more important, the confusion and distraction created among the public and policymakers by brownlash pronouncements interfere with and prolong the already difficult search for realistic and equitable solutions to the human predicament.

Anti-science as promoted by the brownlash is not a unique phenomenon in our society; the largely successful efforts of creationists to keep Americans ignorant of evolution is another example, which is perhaps not entirely unrelated. Both feature a denial of facts and circumstances that don't fit religious or other traditional beliefs; policies built on either could lead our society into serious trouble.

Fortunately, in the case of environmental science, most of the public is fairly well informed about environmental problems and remains committed to environmental protection. When polled, 65 percent of Americans today say they are willing to pay good money for environmental quality. But support for environmental quality is sometimes said to be superficial; while almost everyone is in favor of a sound environment—clean air, clean water, toxic site cleanups, national parks, and so on—many don't feel that environmental deterioration, especially on a regional or global level, is a crucial issue in their own lives. In part this is testimony to the success of environmental protection in the United States. But it is also the case that most people lack an appreciation of the deeper but generally less visible, slowly developing global problems. Thus they don't perceive population growth, global warming, the loss of biodiversity, depletion of groundwater, or exposure to chemicals in plastics and pesticides as a personal threat at the same level as crime in their neighborhood, loss of a job, or a substantial rise in taxes.

So anti-science rhetoric has been particularly effective in promoting a series of erroneous notions, including:

- Environmental scientists ignore the abundant good news about the environment.
- Population growth does not cause environmental damage and may even be beneficial.
- Humanity is on the verge of abolishing hunger; food scarcity is a local or regional problem and not indicative of overpopulation.
- Natural resources are superabundant, if not infinite.
- There is no extinction crisis, and so most efforts to preserve species are both uneconomic and unnecessary.
- Global warming and acid rain are not serious threats to humanity.
- Stratospheric ozone depletion is a hoax.
- The risks posed by toxic substances are vastly exaggerated.
- Environmental regulation is wrecking the economy.

How has the brownlash managed to persuade a significant segment of the public that the state of the environment and the directions and rates in which it is changing are not causes for great concern? Even many individuals who are sensitive to local environmental problems have found brownlash distortions of global issues convincing. Part of the answer lies in the overall lack of scientific knowledge among United States citizens. Most Americans readily grasp the issues surrounding something familiar and tangible like a local dump site, but they have considerably more difficulty with issues involving genetic variation or the dynamics of the atmosphere. Thus it is relatively easy to rally support against a proposed landfill and infinitely more difficult to impose a carbon tax that might help offset global warming.

Also, individuals not trained to recognize the hallmarks of change have difficulty perceiving and appreciating the gradual deterioration of civilization's life-support systems. This is why record-breaking temperatures and violent storms receive so much attention while a gradual increase in annual global temperatures—measured in fractions of a degree over decades—is not considered newsworthy. Threatened pandas are featured on television, while the constant and critical losses of insect populations, which are key elements of our life-support systems, pass unnoticed. People who have no meaningful way to grasp regional and global environmental problems cannot easily tell what information is distorted, when, and to what degree.

Decision-makers, too, have a tendency to focus mostly on the more obvious and immediate environmental problems—usually described as "pollution"—rather than on the deterioration of natural ecosystems upon whose continued functioning global civilization depends. Indeed, most people still don't realize that humanity has become a truly global force, interfering in a very real and direct way in many of the planet's natural cycles.

For example, human activity puts ten times as much oil into the oceans as comes from natural seeps, has multiplied the natural flow of cadmium into the atmosphere eightfold, has doubled the rate of nitrogen fixation, and is responsible for about half the concentration of methane (a potent greenhouse gas) and more than a quarter of the carbon dioxide (also a greenhouse gas) in the atmosphere today—all added since the industrial revolution, most notably in the past half-century. Human beings now use or co-opt some 40 percent of the food available to all land animals and about 45 percent of the available freshwater flows.

Another factor that plays into brownlash thinking is the not uncommon belief that environmental quality is improving, not declining. In some ways it is, but the claim of uniform improvement simply does not stand up to close scientific scrutiny. Nor does the claim that the human condition in general is improving everywhere. The degradation of ecosystem services (the conditions and processes through which natural ecosystems support and fulfill human life) is a crucial issue that is largely ignored by the brownlash. Unfortunately, the superficial progress achieved to date has made it easy to label ecologists doomsayers for continuing to press for change. At the same time, the public often seems unaware of the success of actions taken at the instigation of the environmental movement. People can easily see the disadvantages of environmental regulations but not the despoliation that would exist without them. Especially resentful are those whose personal or corporate ox is being gored when they are forced to sustain financial losses because of a sensible (or occasionally senseless) application of regulations.

Of course, it is natural for many people to feel personally threatened by efforts to preserve a healthy environment. Consider a car salesperson who makes a bigger commission selling a large car than a small one, an executive of a petrochemical company that is liable for damage done by toxic chemicals released into the environment, a logger whose job is jeopardized by enforcement of the Endangered Species Act, a rancher whose way of life may be threatened by higher grazing fees on public lands, a farmer about to lose the farm because of environmentalists' attacks on subsidies for irrigation water, or a developer who wants to continue building subdivisions and is sick and tired of dealing with inconsistent building codes or U.S. Fish and Wildlife Service bureaucrats. In such situations, resentment of some of the rules, regulations, and recommendations designed to enhance human well-being and protect life-support systems is understandable.

Unfortunately, many of these dissatisfied individuals and companies have been recruited into the self-styled "wise-use" movement, which has attracted a surprisingly diverse coalition of people, including representatives of extractive and polluting industries who are motivated by corporate interests as well as private property rights activists and right-wing ideologues. Although some of these individuals simply believe that environmental regulations unfairly distribute the costs of environmental protection, some others are doubtless motivated more by a greedy desire for unrestrained economic expansion.

At a minimum, the wise-use movement firmly opposes most government efforts to maintain environmental quality in the belief that environmental regulation creates unnecessary and burdensome bureaucratic hurdles which stifle economic growth. Wise-use advocates see little or no need for constraints on the exploitation of resources for short-term economic benefits and argue that such exploitation can be accelerated with no adverse long-term consequences. Thus they espouse unrestricted drilling in the Arctic National Wildlife Refuge, logging in national forests, mining in protected areas or next door to national parks, and full compensation for any loss of actual or potential property value resulting from environmental restrictions.

In promoting the view that immediate economic interests are best served by continuing business as usual, the wise-use movement works to stir up discontent among everyday citizens who, rightly or wrongly, feel abused by environmental regulations. This tactic is described in detail in David Helvarg's book, *The War Against the Greens:*

> To date the Wise Use/Property Rights backlash has been a bracing if dangerous reminder to environmentalists that power concedes nothing without a demand and that no social movement, be it ethnic, civil, or environmental, can rest on its past laurels. . . . If the anti-enviros' links to the Farm Bureau, Heritage Foundation, NRA, logging companies, resource trade associations, multinational gold-mining companies, [and] ORV manufacturers . . . proves anything, it's that large industrial lobbies and transnational corporations have learned to play the grassroots game.

Wise-use proponents are not always candid about their motivations and intentions. Many of the organizations representing them masquerade as groups seemingly attentive to environmental quality. Adopting a strategy biologists call "aggressive mimicry," they often give themselves names resembling those of genuine environmental or scientific public-interest groups: National Wetland Coalition, Friends of Eagle Mountain, the Sahara Club, the Alliance for Environment and Resources, the Abundant Wildlife Society of North America, the Global Climate Coalition, the National Wilderness Institute, and the American Council on Science and Health. In keeping with aggressive mimicry, these organizations often actively work *against* the interests implied in their names—a practice sometimes called *greenscamming*.

One such group, calling itself Northwesterners for More Fish, seeks to limit federal protection of endangered fish species so the activities of utilities, aluminum companies, and timber outfits utilizing the region's rivers are not hindered. Armed with a $2.6 million budget, the group aims to discredit environmentalists who say industry is destroying the fish habitats of the Columbia and other rivers, threatening the Northwest's valuable salmon fishery, among others.

Representative George Miller, referring to the wise-use movement's support of welfare ranching, overlogging, and government giveaways of mining rights, stated: "What you have . . . is a lot of special interests who are trying to generate some ideological movement to try and disguise what it is individually they want in the name of their own profits, their own greed in terms of the use and abuse of federal lands."

Wise-use sentiments have been adopted by a number of deeply conservative legislators, many of whom have received campaign contributions from these organizations. One member of the House of Representatives recently succeeded in gaining passage of a bill that limited the annual budget for the Mojave National Preserve, the newest addition to the National Parks System, to one dollar—thus guaranteeing that the park would have no money for upkeep or for enforcement of park regulations.

These same conservative legislators are determined to slash funding for scientific research, especially on such subjects as endangered species, ozone depletion, and global warming, and have legislated for substantial cutbacks in funds for the National Science Foundation, the U.S. Geological Survey, the National Aeronautics and Space Administration, and the Environmental Protection Agency. Many of them and their supporters see science as self-indulgent, at odds with economic interests, and inextricably linked to regulatory excesses.

The scientific justifications and philosophical underpinnings for the positions of the wise-use movement are largely provided by the brownlash. Prominent promoters of the wise-use viewpoint on a number of issues include such conservative think tanks as the Cato Institute and the Heritage Foundation. Both organizations help generate and disseminate erroneous brownlash ideas and information. Adam Myerson, editor of the Heritage Foundation's journal *Policy Review,* pretty much summed up the brownlash perspective by saying: "Leading scientists have done major work disputing the current henny-pennyism about global warming, acid rain, and other purported environmental catastrophes." In reality, however, most "leading" scientists support what Myerson calls henny-pennyism; the scientists he refers to are a small group largely outside the mainstream of scientific thinking.

In recent years, a flood of books and articles has advanced the notion that all is well with the environment, giving credence to this anti-scientific "What, me worry?" outlook. Brownlash writers often pepper their works with code phrases such as *sound science* and *balance*—words that suggest objectivity while in fact having little connection to what is presented. *Sound science* usually means science that is interpreted to support the brownlash view. *Balance* generally means giving undue prominence to the opinions of one or a handful of contrarian scientists who are at odds with the consensus of the scientific community at large.

Of course, while pro-environmental groups and environmental scientists in general may sometimes be dead wrong (as can anybody confronting environmental complexity), they ordinarily are not acting on behalf of narrow economic interests. Yet one of the remarkable triumphs of the wise-use movement and its allies in the past decade has been their ability to define public-interest organizations, in the eyes of many legislators, as "special interests"—not different in kind from the American Tobacco Institute, the Western Fuels Association, or other organizations that represent business groups.

But we believe there is a very real difference in kind. Most environmental organizations are funded mainly by membership donations; corporate funding is at most a minor factor for public-interest advocacy groups. There are no monetary profits to be gained other than attracting a bigger membership. Environmental scientists have even less to gain; they usually are dependent upon university or research institute salaries and research funds from peer-reviewed government grants or sometimes (especially in new or controversial areas where government funds are largely unavailable) from private foundations.

One reason the brownlash messages hold so much appeal to many people, we think, is the fear of further change. Even though the American frontier closed a century ago, many Americans seem to believe they still live in what the great economist Kenneth Boulding once called a "cowboy economy." They still think they can figuratively throw their garbage over the backyard fence with impunity. They regard the environmentally protected public land as "wasted" and think it should be available for their self-beneficial appropriation. They believe that private property rights are absolute (despite a rich economic and legal literature showing they never have been). They do not understand, as Pace University law professor John Humbach wrote in 1993, that "the Constitution does not guarantee that land speculators will win their bets."

The anti-science brownlash provides a rationalization for the short-term economic interests of these groups: old-growth forests are decadent and should be harvested; extinction is natural, so there's no harm in overharvesting economically important animals; there is abundant undisturbed habitat, so human beings have a right to develop land anywhere and in any way they choose; global warming is a hoax or even will benefit agriculture, so there's no need to limit the burning of fossil fuels; and so on. Anti-science basically claims we can keep the good old days by doing business as usual. But the problem is we can't.

Thus the brownlash helps create public confusion about the character and magnitude of environmental problems, taking advantage of the lack of consensus among individuals and social groups on the urgency of enhancing environmental protection. A widely shared social consensus, such as the United States saw during World War II, will be essential if we are to maintain environmental quality while meeting the nation's other needs. By emphasizing dissent, the brownlash works against the formation of any such consensus; instead it has helped thwart the development of a spirit of cooperation mixed with concern for society as a whole. In our opinion, the brownlash fuels conflict by claiming the environmental problems are overblown or nonexistent and that unbridled economic development will propel the world to new levels of prosperity with little or no risk to the natural systems that support society. As a result, environmental groups and wise-use proponents are increasingly polarized.

Unfortunately, some of that polarization has led to ugly confrontations and activities that are not condoned by the brownlash or by most environmentalists, including us. As David Helvarg stated, "Along with the growth of Wise Use/Property Rights, the last six years have seen a startling increase in intimidation, vandalism, and violence directed against grassroots environmental activists." And while confrontations and threats have been generated by both sides—most notably (but by no means exclusively) over the northern spotted owl protection plan—the level of intimidation engaged in by wise-use proponents is disturbing, to say the least. . . .

Fortunately, despite all the efforts of the brownlash to discourage it, environmental concern in the United States is widespread. Thus a public-opinion survey in 1995 indicated that slightly over half of all Americans felt that environmental problems in the United States were "very serious." Indeed, 85 percent were concerned "a fair amount" and 38 percent "a great deal" about the environment. Fifty-eight percent would choose protecting the environment over economic growth, and 65 percent said they would be willing to pay higher prices so that industry could protect the environment better. Responses in other rich nations have been similar, and people in developing nations have shown, if anything, even greater environmental concerns. These responses suggest that the notion that caring about the environment is a luxury of the rich is a myth. Furthermore, our impression is that young people care especially strongly about environmental quality—a good omen if true.

Nor is environmental concern exclusive to Democrats and "liberals." There is a strong Republican and conservative tradition of environmental protection dating back to Teddy Roosevelt and even earlier. Many of our most important environmental laws were passed with bipartisan support during the Nixon and Ford administrations. Recently, some conservative environmentalists have been speaking out against brownlash rhetoric. And public concern is rising about the efforts to cripple environmental laws and regulations posed by right-wing leaders in Congress, thinly disguised as "deregulation" and "necessary budget-cutting." In January 1996, a Republican pollster, Linda Divall, warned that "our party is out of sync with mainstream American opinion when it comes to the environment."

Indeed, some interests that might be expected to sympathize with the wise-use movement have moved beyond such reactionary views. Many leaders in corporations such as paper companies and chemical manufacturers, whose activities are directly harmful to the environment, are concerned about their firms' environmental impacts and are shifting to less damaging practices. Our friends in the ranching community in western Colorado indicate their concern to us every summer. They want to preserve a way of life and a high-quality environment—and are as worried about the progressive suburbanization of the area as are the scientists at the Rocky Mountain Biological Laboratory. Indeed, they have actively participated in discussions with environmentalists and officials of the Department of the Interior to set grazing fees at levels that wouldn't force them out of business but also wouldn't subsidize overgrazing and land abuse.

Loggers, ranchers, miners, petrochemical workers, fishers, and professors all live on the same planet, and all of us must cooperate to preserve a sound environment for our descendants. The environmental problems of the planet can be solved only in a spirit of cooperation, not one of conflict. Ways must be found to allocate fairly both the benefits and the costs of environmental quality.

POSTSCRIPT

Do Environmental Restrictions Violate Basic Economic Freedoms?

The dilemmas that face us as we attempt to adjust our lifestyles to the needs of a suddenly threatened environment are the hardest that this generation will know. It is not just that we are being asked to refrain in the future from certain profitable activities in order to preserve some part of the environment, like building hotels on barrier beaches, for instance. We will be asked—told—to cut back on portions of our lives that we have taken for granted. We will be told to stop driving our cars except in direst emergency, cancel travel plans, forget the vacation house, and pay astronomical prices for goods and services that have always been reasonable. We will be told to separate our trash scrupulously, into plastics, glass, metals, paper, and organic waste, and to take it to five different receiving stations for recycling and reusing. Daily life will be poorer, and will take up much more of our time and labor. Most of these burdens will be chosen by us, through democratically conducted elections and legislation. But there will be no real choice, for the alternative may be the death of the biosphere, including its human component.

Suggested Reading

It sounds terrible. But it doesn't have to be. Some writers are optimistic, most currently the Rocky Mountain Institute's Amory and Hunter Lovins and Paul Hawken, who argue, in *Natural Capitalism*, that we have the technology on board now to save the planet and provide Americans *and the rest of the world* with a really pleasant lifestyle. We suggest that you read it. In addition to *Natural Capitalism*, you may profit from consulting some of the following:

J. Baird Callicott and Michael Nelson, eds. *The Great, New, Wilderness Debate* (Athens: University of Georgia Press, 1998).

Joan Iverson Nassauer (ed.), *Placing Nature: Culture and Landscape Ecology* (Washington D.C.: Island Press, 1997).

Ernest Callenbach, Fritjof Capra, Lenore Goldman, Rudiger Lutz and Sandra Marburg, *EcoManagement: The Elmwood Guide to Ecological Auditing and Sustainable Business* (San Francisco: Berrett-Koehler Publishers, 1993).

Christopher Flavin, in "The Legacy of Rio," in *State of the World 1997* (New York: W.W. Norton, 1997). http://www.conservative.org/heritage/

ISSUE 20

Is Bottling Water a Good Solution to Problems of Water Purity and Availability?

YES: Julie Stauffer, from "Water," *Body + Soul* (April/May 2005)

NO: Brian Howard, from "Message in a Bottle," *E: The Environment Magazine* (September/October 2003)

ISSUE SUMMARY

YES: Julie Stauffer presents a good argument for care in the selection and use of drinking water, while recognizing that guarantees are few and far between in the bottled water industry. The commonly available information on bottled water certainly conveys the impression that it is purer and better than mere tap water; all the ads conjure up a vigorous and healthy outdoor lifestyle amid forests, lakes, and pure flowing springs.

NO: Brian Howard argues that bottling water is environmentally disastrous, because of the huge drains on scarce aquifers and the haphazard disposal of the plastic bottles, and that tap water is often superior to bottled in purity.

We are a nation in love with our bottled water. In 2004, Americans spent about $8 billion on bottles of water, some with very sophisticated labels. Why, when tap water is safe? Possibly this is a habit we picked up from the Europeans, who have never considered their tap water fit to drink. (They may be right; the last time I was in St. Petersburg, Russia, I was firmly warned not only not to drink the gray water that emerged from the tap, but to keep my mouth and eyes closed while showering to prevent any contact with mucous membranes.) But with its wide open spaces to filter our groundwater, contamination of the tap water has never really been America's problem; by all accounts and measures and tests, the public water supply in the United States is perfectly fit for all purposes, and until recently, that's what we used it for. Has there been some sudden revelation that American tap water is contaminated, poisoned, whatever?

Apparently not, but that has not stopped the consumer enthusiasm. Bottled water continues to be seen as a healthy product of choice among consumers looking to quench their thirst. Globally, sales have increased a whopping 17.8 percent over the past year. In North America alone, sales have jumped from $8.4 billion to $13.3 billion in a year, accounting for 68 percent of the total growth. In 2004 in the United States, the average person consumed 18.2 gallons of bottled water, an increase of 1.2 gallons per person average over the previous year.

There are three problems with this trend, as the *E* magazine selection points out. First, there are no guarantees on the provenance of the water in the bottle; while your tap water comes from upstate reservoirs in the country, tested and verified, your bottled water company could have its wells in the middle of the landfill. Second, if the water is really being drained from some pure aquifer somewhere, that's water that will be unavailable to local farmers and wildlife. Water does not go to waste, anywhere on earth; it's keeping something alive, and that something is going to have to struggle with a lowered water table if we pump it into plastic bottles and ship it east and west. Third, where do those plastic bottles come from, and where do they go? They start life as scarce petrochemicals (driving up the price of oil), and they tend to end up in the landfills.

Bottled water is not safer or purer than tap water, even its defenders point out. Somewhere between 40 and 70 percent of bottled water is simply the tap water of the area where it is bottled, possibly purified with some mechanical filters. As such, it often contains the same "chemicals" that some aficionados insist they wish to eliminate. This is not all bad; the chlorine in most tap water is crucial for removing lethal pathogens, and the fluorides are really good for the children's teeth. But isn't the whole enterprise sort of pointless? It isn't as though bottled water tasted better, to the extent that pure water can be said to have taste at all; in every blind test we've tried, consumers have not been able to distinguish bottled from tap water. To be sure, the little bottles are enormously convenient. But couldn't we just refill them when we're done?

Ask yourself, as you read these selections, why we do what we do—not just concerning bottled water, but concerning the ten thousand choices we make as consumers every month. How much is style worth? How much is value? How much of our choice depends on market, advertising, pure hype? How much does the environment count in our consumer choices?

YES

Julie Stauffer

Water

We can't live without water—lots of it. The crisp, clear liquid—which makes up about 60 percent of our body weight—carries nourishment to our cells, regulates our body temperature, and helps our kidneys detoxify, among other tasks. Yet water itself may introduce toxins into our systems. So what's the healthiest way to replenish the 10 to 12 cups we lose daily?

A lot of us are wondering: More than one in four Americans are concerned about the quality and safety of their tap water, according to a recent Gallup survey, and tens of millions are reaching for bottled or filtered water instead, creating a billion-dollar business. Is that mistrust justified?

The answer isn't simple. On the one hand, 92 percent of U.S. public drinking-water systems meet federal health standards, which are quite rigorous, though perhaps not updated recently enough. On the other hand, the nonprofit Physicians for Social Responsibility estimates that thousands of people each year get sick because of pathogens in their drinking water, contracting everything from mild stomach upsets to hepatitis. And scientists are only beginning to discover the impact of the many chemicals that find their way into water sources, some of which are not monitored.

Yet there's no need to be alarmed. Taking the worry out of water is a lot simpler than you may think, requiring just a few steps. Most crucial among them: understanding your public water supplier's Consumer Confidence Report and, if necessary, properly filtering your drinking water.

Think of it as tapping into a fresh start. . . .

Fix the Problems

Using a water filter is the easiest and most comprehensive way to clean up your tap water. If you choose to use bottled water, follow our guidelines to pick a good one. At the least, be sure to run your tap for a couple of minutes in the morning to flush out any lead that's accumulated overnight. And never drink or cook with *hot* water from the tap, because hot water dissolves lead far more than cold water does.

Water filters Whether you use a stand-alone jug or an installed system that hooks directly to your tap, make sure your filter meets the standards of the

---

independent American National Standards Institute and National Sanitation Foundation (ANSI/NSF). And remember that different filters remove different contaminants, so read the tiny print on the package before you go to the checkout counter to make sure that your concerns are addressed. Not all water filters remove lead, for example, so if lead is an issue, be sure to buy a filter that has been ANSI/NSF certified to remove lead.

Stand-alone jug filters   Jug filters, the pitchers or small tanks that you fill from your tap, cost about $20 and are by far the most common and affordable option. They're a little more work than installed systems because you must regularly refill and clean the jug as well as change the filter. Keep your filtered water in the fridge to prevent bacteria from growing, and make sure that you replace your filter according to the manufacturer's instructions—don't just rely on the various signaling systems, which can be inaccurate. A filter that's been used too long can actually release all the contaminants it has accumulated back into your water.

Installed filtering systems   These are more convenient than jug filters and they treat larger volumes of water, but they're pricier, running from $200 to $500, including installation. Their filters, too, must be changed regularly. Some systems hook directly to the faucet, while others attach from under the sink. If you plan to buy one of the latter, by sure to pass up any with brass components. Several years ago, the Center for Environmental Health found that brass alloys in a number of under-the-sink filters sold in California leached lead into the water, though all the manufacturers that were implicated agreed to reformulate their filters.

Bottled water   Americans spend more than $8.3 billion a year on bottled water, but what they're drinking may not be any safer or better regulated than tap water. A bottle of water that sports an image of a pure mountain glacier may actually be municipal tap water that has undergone an extra purification process. In fact, 60 to 70 percent of bottled water sold in the United States is exempt from federal regulations because it's packaged and sold in the same state, not crossing state lines. Moreover, if a product is recalled because it fails to comply with federal regulations, it's generally left up to the bottler to voluntarily make the recall.

Follow these tips to choose a safe bottled water:

Check affiliations.   Look for manufacturers that belong to the International Bottled Water Association (IBWA), which requires its members to test their water daily and to have their bottling plants inspected annually by an independent third party. You can find a listing of IBWA member companies on the group's Web site . . .

Scrutinize labels   Labels will reveal the water's source. When a bottled water fails to meet federal regulations, the label must also state that it contains "excessive levels" of the contaminant in question. If you want water that's closer to nature, stick with brands labeled "natural spring water" or "natural mineral water." And make sure the brand's ingredients match your needs. For example, if you're on a salt-restricted diet, choose a water with less than 10 mg of sodium per liter. If you have any questions about what's inside the container, contact the manufacturer. (By agreement, all IBWA members list their phone numbers or addresses on their labels.)

Assess packaging Water in clear bottles made from polyethylene terephthalate tastes better than water in soft, cloudy jugs made from high-density polyethylene plastic. Avoid polycarbonate (the strong rigid plastic used in five-gallon water-cooler jugs) because it can leach bisphenol-A, a potential carcinogen and hormone mimic.

Chances are, your water—whether from the tap or bottled—is perfectly safe. But you won't know for sure until you do a little investigating. In this case, an ounce of prevention is worth a gallon of cure. Given that a woman of average size should consume 64 ounces of liquid a day, the peace of mind gained by doing a little homework could be enormous.

Hot-Button Contaminants

The Environmental Protection Agency's (EPA) Safe Drinking Water Act, now 30 years old, is quite strict. But even so, there are dozens of common drinking-water contaminants it does not cover, and some regulations may be too lax.

These are some of the hot-button contaminants you may want to test for yourself or use a filter to eliminate.

Arsenic
Arsenic, which occurs naturally in rock and soil, is widely recognized as a carcinogen, but it's expensive to remove from drinking water, whether tap or bottled. In 2006, the current EPA standard of 50 parts per billion (ppb) will be changed to 10 parts per billion (ppb). However, scientists believe there is no safe level of arsenic.

Disinfection by-Products (DBPs)
Water suppliers often use chlorine to kill disease-causing bugs. Unfortunately, the chlorination process releases by-products that have been linked to cancers in humans, and chlorinated water has been linked to spontaneous abortions and stillbirths. Another common method of disinfection, ozonation, creates by-products, including formaldehyde and acetaldehyde, that have been linked to cancer. The EPA is considering strengthening regulations for DBPs.

Methyl Tertiary-Butyl Ether (MTBE)
This common gasoline additive, found in the water supplies of 36 states, may cause cancer. There is currently no health standard for MTBE in drinking water, although the EPA is studying the possibility of developing one.

Perchlorate

This rocket-fuel ingredient, which has contaminated hundreds of water sources in California as well as the Colorado River, interferes with the function of the thyroid gland, which in adults can lead to problems with metabolism and in children and developing fetuses can affect brain development. There is currently no national standard for perchlorate in drinking water.

Radon

A naturally occurring radioactive gas that can leach into drinking water from the surrounding soil and rocks, radon increases the risk of lung cancer and cancer of the gastrointestinal tract. The EPA is investigating regulations for radon, but nothing has been finalized.

Bottled-water Breakdown

There are several categories of bottled water, each reflecting the water's source. Check labels to see which type you're buying.

Spring Water

This water comes from an underground source and flows naturally to the Earth's surface. Bottlers can add carbon dioxide to make it sparkling. Some representative brands: Evian, Poland Spring, Dannon, Crystal Geyser, Trinity.

Mineral Water

This is water that contains at least 250 parts per million (ppm) of naturally occurring dissolved minerals such as calcium, magnesium, sodium, potassium, silica, and bicarbonates. Like spring water, it also comes from an underground source and flows naturally to the earth's surface. Some representative brands: Vittel, Perrier.

Purified Drinking Water

A lot of bottled water has been treated by distillation, deionization, or reverse osmosis. The source of the water doesn't need to be named, and it may even be municipal tap water, but the label must say how the water was purified. Some representative brands: Aquafina, Dasani.

Artesian Water

In artesian wells underground pressure is high enough to push the water to the surface once the well is drilled, making it something like spring water. Some representative brands: Fiji, Avita.

Well Water

Wells are underground water reserves that can be pumped to the surface. Typically, bottled well water is sold locally or regionally.

Brian Howard

Message in a Bottle: Despite the Hype, Bottled Water Is Neither Cleaner Nor Greener Than Tap Water

"**Y**ou drink tap water? Are you crazy?" asks a 21-year-old radio producer from the Chicago area. "I *only* drink bottled water." In a trendy nightclub in New York City, the bartender tells guests they can *only* be served bottled water, which costs $5 for each tiny half-pint container. One outraged clubber is stopped by the restroom attendant as she tries to refill the bottle from the tap. "You can't do that," says the attendant. "New York's tap water isn't safe."

Whether a consumer is shopping in a supermarket or a health food store, working out in a fitness center, eating in a restaurant or grabbing some quick refreshment on the go, he or she will likely be tempted to buy bottled water. The product comes in an ever-growing variety of sizes and shapes, including one bottle that looks like a drop of water with a golden cap. Some fine hotels now offer the services of "water sommeliers" to advise diners on which water to drink with different courses.

A widening spectrum of bottled water types are crowding the market, including spring, mineral, purified, distilled, carbonated, oxygenated, caffeinated and vitamin-enriched, as well as flavors, such as lemon or strawberry, and specific brands aimed at children. Bottled water bars have sprung up in the hipper districts, from Paris to Los Angeles.

The message is clear: Bottled water is "good" water, as opposed to that nasty, unsafe stuff that comes out of the tap. But in most cases tap water adheres to stricter purity standards than bottled water, whose source—far from a mountain spring—can be wells underneath industrial facilities. Indeed, 40 percent of bottled water began life as, well, tap water.

A 2001 World Wildlife Fund (WWF) study confirmed the widespread belief that consumers associate bottled water with social status and healthy living. Their perceptions trump their objectivity, because even some people who claim to have switched to bottled water "for the taste" can't tell the difference: When *Good Morning America* conducted a taste test of its studio audience, New York City tap water was chosen as the heavy favorite over the oxygenated water 02, Poland Spring and Evian. Many of the "facts" that bottled water drinkers swear by are erroneous. Rachele Kuzma, a Rutgers student, says she drinks bottled water at school because "it's healthier" and "doesn't have fluoride," although much of it does have fluoride.

Bottled water is so ubiquitous that people can hardly ask for water anywhere without being handed a bottle. But what is the cost to society and the environment?

Largely Self-Regulated

The bottled water industry has exploded in recent years, and enjoys annual sales of more than $35 billion worldwide. In 2002, almost six billion gallons of bottled water were sold in the U.S., representing an increase of nearly 11 percent over 2001. Americans paid $7.7 billion for bottled water in 2002, according to the consulting and research firm Beverage Marketing Corporation. Bottled water is the fastest-growing segment of the beverage industry, and the product is expected to pass both coffee and milk to become the second-most-consumed beverage (behind soft drinks) by 2004. According to the Natural Resources Defense Council (NRDC), "More than half of all Americans drink bottled water; about a third of the public consumes it regularly." While most people would argue that bottled water is healthier than convenient alternatives like sugared sodas or artificially flavored drinks, are the third of bottled water consumers who claim they are motivated by promises of purity (according to a 2000 survey) getting what they pay for?

While the Environmental Protection Agency (EPA) regulates the quality of public water supplies, the agency has no authority over bottled water. Bottled water that crosses state lines is considered a food product and is overseen by the Food and Drug Administration (FDA), which does mandate that it be bottled in sanitary conditions using food-grade equipment. According to the influential International Bottled Water Association (IBWA), "By law, the FDA Standard of Quality for bottled water must be as stringent as the EPA's standards for public drinking water."

However, the FDA is allowed to interpret the EPA'S regulations and apply them selectively to bottled water. As Senior Attorney Erik Olson of the NRDC explains, "Although the FDA has adopted some of the EPA's regulatory standards, it has decided not to adopt others and has not even ruled on some points after several years of inaction." In a 1999 report, the NRDC concludes that bottled water quality is probably not inferior to average tap water, but Olson (the report's principal author) says that gaps in the weak regulatory framework may allow careless or unscrupulous bottlers to market substandard products. He says that may be of particular concern to those with compromised immune systems.

The IBWA urges consumers to trust bottled water in part because the FDA requires water sources to be "inspected, sampled, analyzed and approved." However, the NRDC argues that the FDA provides no specific requirements—such as proximity to industrial facilities, underground storage tanks or dumps—for bottled water sources. That's looser monitoring than occurs at the EPA, which requires more specific assessments of tap water sources

Olson says one brand of "spring water," which had a graphic of mountains and a lake on the label, was actually taken from a well in Massachusetts in the parking lot of an industrial facility. The well, which is no longer used for bottled water, was near hazardous waste and had experienced contamination by industrial chemicals.

According to Olson, the FDA has no official procedure for rejecting bottled water sources once they become contaminated. He also says a 1990 government audit revealed that 25 percent of water bottlers had no record of source approval. Further, in contrast to the EPA, which employs hundreds of staffers to protect the nation's tap water systems, the FDA doesn't have even one full-time regulator in charge of bottled water.

Scott Hoober of the Kansas Rural Water Association says that although municipal system managers have to pay a certified lab to test samples weekly, monthly and quarterly for a long list of contaminants, water bottlers can use any lab they choose to perform tests as infrequently as once a year. Unlike utilities, which must publish their lab results in a public record, bottlers don't have to notify anyone of their findings, including consumers who inquire. The FDA has the authority to ask for a company's data, although test results can be destroyed after two years.

Olson adds, "Unlike tap water violations, which are directly enforceable, if a company exceeds bottled water standards, it is not necessarily a violation—they can just say so on the label, and may be insulated from enforcement." Further, while EPA rules specify that no confirmed *E. coli* or fecal coliform (bacteria that indicate possible contamination by fecal matter) contamination is allowed in tap water, the FDA merely set a minimum level for *E. coli* and fecal coliform presence in bottled water. Tap water from a surface source must be tested for cryptosporidium, giardia and viruses, unlike bottled water, and must also be disinfected, unlike bottled water. Hoober also notes that food products such as "carbonated water," "soda water" and "seltzer water"—in addition to most flavored waters—are held to even looser standards than "true" bottled water.

The EPA concludes, "Some bottled water is treated more than tap water, while some is treated less or not at all." Henry Kim, consumer safety officer for the FDA, asserts, "We want bottled water to have a comparable quality to that of tap water"—which, of course, runs counter to the widely held public belief that bottled water is *better*. The situation is similar in the European Union and in Canada, where there are more regulations on tap than bottled water. That New York restroom attendant would be surprised to learn that her city's tap water was tested some 560,000 times in 2002.

Environmentalists also point out that if a brand of bottled water is wholly packaged and sold within the same state, it is technically not regulated by the FDA, and is therefore only legally subject to state standards, which tend to vary widely in scope and vigor. Coop America reports that 43 states have one or fewer staff members dedicated to bottled water regulation. On the other hand, California enforces strict regulations on bottled water contaminants, and Fort Collins, Colorado tests bottled water sold in town and posts the results online. The NRDC estimates that 60 to 70 percent of bottled water brands sold in the U.S. are single-state operations. Stephen Kay, vice president of communications of the IBWA, says he doubts the percentage is that high.

Kay is adamant that "no bottled water escapes regulation," and he points out that all members of the IBWA (which are responsible for 80 percent of U.S. bottled water sales) must also adhere to the organization's mandatory Model Code. This code does close some of the FDA's regulatory gaps, including setting a zero tolerance for coliform contamination, and it requires members to follow certain standards and undergo an annual, unannounced plant inspection. However, Olson stresses that, except in a few states, this Model Code is not legally binding or enforceable. Members of the much smaller National Spring Water Association follow their own guidelines, and must get their water from free-flowing springs.

One result of such Byzantine bottled water standards has been the widespread use of disinfection to reduce possible contaminants. Although the FDA does not require it, disinfection is mandatory in several states, including New York, California and Texas. However, chemicals commonly used to disinfect water, including chlorine and ozone gas, may react unpredictably, forming potentially carcinogenic byproducts. Opponents also argue that disinfection destroys naturally beneficial bacteria, creating a blank slate. Further, Mark Johnson of bottler Trinity Springs—which taps a spring in Idaho so pure it doesn't need any treatment—concludes, "If you don't disinfect, you must protect the source and increase environmental awareness so the source stays protected."

What's Really in that Bottle?

Even with widespread disinfection, consumer groups have raised numerous warnings about a host of different microorganisms and chemicals that have been found in bottled water. In a four-year scientific study, the NRDC tested more than 1,000 bottles of 103 brands of bottled water. The group concluded, "Although most bottled water tested was of good quality, some brands' quality was spotty." A third of the tested brands were found to contain contaminants such as arsenic and carcinogenic compounds in at least some samples at levels exceeding state or industry standards.

An earlier NRDC-commissioned study tested for hundreds of different chemicals in 38 brands of California bottled water. Two samples had arsenic contamination, six had chemical byproducts of chlorination, and six had measurable levels of the toxic chemical toluene. Several samples violated California's bottled water standards. In a study published in the *Archives of Family Medicine,* researchers at Case Western Reserve University and Ohio State University compared 57 samples of bottled water to Cleveland's tap water. While 39 of the bottled water samples were purer than the tap water, 15 of the bottles had significantly higher bacteria levels. The scientists concluded that although all of the water they tested was safe to drink, "use of bottled water on the assumption of purity can be misguided."

Another area of potential concern is the fact that no agency calls for testing of bottled water after it leaves its initial packaging plant, leaving some to wonder what happens during months of storage and transport. To begin to examine this question, the Kansas Department of Health and Environment tested 80 samples of bottled water from retail stores and manufacturers. All 80 of the samples had detectable levels of chlorine, fluoride and sodium. Seventy-eight of the 80 contained some nitrate (which can cause methemo-globinemia, or blue-baby syndrome, in higher doses), 12 had nitrite, 53 had chloroform, 33 contained bromodichloro-methane, 25 had arsenic and 15 tested positive for lead.

Forty-six of the samples contained traces of some form of the carcinogen (and hormone disrupter) phthalate, while 12 of those exceeded federal safety levels for that chemical. According to Olson, phthalates may leach out of some plastic bottles into water. "Phthalates are not legally regulated in bottled water because of intense industry pressure," says Olson. Although Co-op America concludes that there is little evidence of a link between phthalate exposure from bottled water and any health problems, the group suggests using glass over plastic bottles as a precaution. Similarly, if your office cooler is made of polycarbonate, it may be releasing small amounts of the potential hormone disrupter bisphenol A into the water.

Idaho's Pure Health Solutions, a water purification company, also conducted its own study that concluded certain bacteria grow significantly in bottled water over a 12-day period. Bacteria will normally grow in tap water within a few days if it is kept bottled up at room temperature. Most municipal water managers leave a residual amount of chlorine in tap water after treatment specifically to inhibit the growth of bacteria as the water runs through pipes and sits in tanks.

The IBWA argues that the presence of benign bacteria in bottled water has no bearing on public health, since the treatment processes used by manufacturers ensure the death of any potentially harmful organisms. The group's website claims that there have been no confirmed cases of illness in the U.S. as a result of bottled water. The IBWA does mention an instance in 1994 in the Northern Mariana Islands, in which bottled well water was linked to a disease outbreak. The NRDC argues that no U.S. government agency actively searches for incidents of illness from bottled water.

On the Internet, one can find testimonials and news reports about people who claim to have gotten sick from tainted bottled water. One man writes that he and his fiancee became ill after drinking bottled water in the Dominican Republic. The Allegheny County Health Department in Pennsylvania reports discovering high levels of coliform in bottled water samples that were taken "after a man reported that he became sick from drinking the water."

Misleading Labels

Another complaint commonly levied against the bottled water industry is that many of the myriad product labels are misleading. Not long ago, New York-based artist Nancy Drew began collecting water bottles for a project. She concluded, "In a culture so inundated with images solely designed for promotion and profit, water is the most absurd element to see being used in this context."

Drew's subsequent art views water labels' ubiquitous depictions of pristine landscapes as a stark contrast to the "gluttonous consumption and sense of status that they represent."

The IBWA states, "The labeling requirements ensure that the source and purity of the bottled water are identified and that, if the label is false or misleading, the supplier is subject to civil or criminal sanctions." Even so, the FDA technically requires that bottled water labels disclose only three variables: the class of water (such as spring or mineral), the manufacturer, and the volume. That brand of Massachusetts "spring water" exposed by NRDC was so-named because the source occasionally bubbled up to the surface in the industrial parking lot.

As ABC News put it, "Ad campaigns touting spring-fed or glacier-born H_2O are winning over a population increasingly skeptical of taps and willing to shell out big bucks for what they consider a purer, tastier and safer drink." Water bottlers use product names such as More Precious Than Gold, Ice Mountain, Desert Quench, Pure American, Utopia and Crystal Springs. The Environmental Law Foundation has sued eight bottlers on the basis that they used words like "pure" to market water containing bacteria, arsenic and chlorine breakdown products.

Co-op America advises consumers "to be wary of words like 'pure,' 'pristine,' 'glacial,' 'premium,' 'natural' or 'healthy.' They're basically meaningless words added to labels to emphasize the alleged purity of bottled water over tap water." The group points out that, in one case, bottled water labeled as "Alaska Premium Glacier Drinking Water: Pure Glacier Water from the Last Unpolluted Frontier" was actually drawn from Public Water System #111241 in Juneau. The FDA now requires this bottler to add "from a municipal source" on the label. According to Co-op America, "as much as 40 percent of bottled water is actually bottled tap water, sometimes with additional treatment, sometimes not." So-called purified water can be drawn from any source as long as it is subsequently treated, which leaves some to wonder how that differs from good old tap water.

The number one (Aquafina) and two (Dasani) top-selling brands of bottled water in the U.S. both fall in the category of purified water. Dasani is sold by Coca-Cola, while Aquafina is a Pepsi product. As *U.S. News & World Report* explains, "Aquafina is municipal water from spots like Wichita, Kansas." The newsmagazine continues, "Coke's Dasani (with minerals added) is taken from the taps of Queens, New York, Jacksonville, Florida, and elsewhere." Everest bottled water originates from southern Texas, while Yosemite brand is drawn from the Los Angeles suburbs.

In June, a lawsuit was filed against Poland Spring, the nation's largest bottled spring water company. Poland Spring is a brand of Nestlé Waters North America, which used to be called Perrier Group of America. Nestlé Waters is owned by the Switzerland-based Nestlé S.A., the world's largest food company. Nestlé's 14 other brands of U.S. bottled water include Arrowhead, Deer Park, Aberfoyle, Zephyrhills, Ozarka and Ice Mountain.

The plaintiffs charged that Nestlé duped consumers by advertising that Poland Spring water comes from "some of the most pristine and protected sources deep in the woods of Maine." The lawsuit alleges that ever since the original Poland Spring was shut down in 1967, the company has used man-made wells, at least one of which is in a parking lot along a busy road. "Poland Spring is exactly what we say it is—natural spring water," responded a Nestlé spokesperson.

Mistrusting the Tap

Despite all the hype, the NRDC concludes, "While much tap water is indeed risky, having compared available data, we conclude that there is no assurance that bottled water is any safer than tap water." Scientists at the University of Geneva arrived at the same conclusion, and add that, in 50 percent of the cases they studied, the only difference between tap and bottled water was that the latter contained added minerals and salts, "which do not actually mean the water is healthier." In 1997, the United Nations Food and Agriculture Organization concluded that bottled water does not have greater nutritional value than tap water.

So why do so many of us trust and prefer bottled water to the liquid that is already piped directly into our homes? For the price of one bottle of Evian, a person can use 1,000 gallons of tap water in the home. Americans spend around $10,700 on bottled water every minute, reports Co-op America, and many consumers think nothing of paying three times as much per gallon of bottled H_2O as they do for gasoline.

Kay says the IBWA does not intend to promote bottled water as a replacement for tap water, except maybe during emergencies. "Since bottled water is considered a food product by law, it doesn't make sense to single it out as needing more regulations than other foods," says Kay. He also stresses that IBWA guidelines strictly prevent members from trying to capitalize on fears over tap water, or from directly advertising that their products are more pure than municipal water.

Bottled water's competition is soft drinks, not tap water, says Kay. Karen from Ames, Iowa posted on the 2000days web diary: "In the summer I buy bottled water more often so I'll have something to drink that's not loaded with syrup and stuff."

Some critics have also found it ironic that many people who purchase bottled water end up refilling the containers from a tap. Clearly, some consumers may be more interested in buying the product for its packaging than for the water itself—or they impulsively purchased a bottle where there was no immediate access to a tap.

The Green Response

More and more environmentalists are beginning to question the purpose of lugging those heavy, inefficient, polluting bottles all over the Earth. The parent organization of the World Wildlife Fund, the Switzerland-based World Wide Fund for Nature, argues strongly that the product is a waste of money and is very environmentally unfriendly. Co-op America concludes: "By far the cheapest—and often the safest—option is to drink water from a tap. It's also the most environmentally friendly option." Friends of the Earth says, "We might as well drink water from the tap and save all this waste."

The WWF argues that the distribution of bottled water requires substantially more fuel than delivering tap water, especially since over 22 million tons of the bottled liquid is transferred each year from country to country. Instead of relying on a mostly preexisting infrastructure of underground pipes and plumbing, delivering bottled water—often from places as far-flung as France, Iceland or Maine—burns fossil fuels and results in the release of thousands of tons of harmful emissions. Since some bottled water is also shipped or stored cold, electricity is expended for refrigeration. Energy is likewise used in bottled water processing. In filtration, an estimated two gallons of water is wasted for every gallon purified.

When most people think of bottled water, they probably envision the single-serve plastic bottle, which has exploded in popularity and is now available almost anywhere food products are sold. The WWF estimates that around 1.5 million tons of plastic are used globally each year in water bottles, leaving a sizable manufacturing footprint. Most water bottles are made of the oil-derived polyethylene terephthalate, which is known as PET. While PET is less toxic than many plastics, the Berkeley Ecology Center found that manufacturing PET generates more than 100 times the toxic emissions—in the form of nickel, ethylbenzene, ethylene oxide and benzene—compared to making the same amount of glass. The Climate Action Network concludes, "Making plastic bottles requires almost the same energy input as making glass bottles, despite transport savings that stem from plastic's light weight."

Andrew Swanander, owner of Mountain Town Spring Water, says, "I'm embarrassed and appalled to see my bottled water products discarded on the side of the road." In fact, a considerable number of used water bottles end up as litter, where they can take up to 1,000 years to biodegrade. A 2002 study by Scenic Hudson reported that 18 percent by volume of recovered litter from the Hudson River (and 14 percent by weight) was comprised of beverage containers.

Pat Franklin, the executive director of the Container Recycling Institute (CRI), says nine out of 10 plastic water bottles end up as either garbage or litter—at a rate of 30 million per day. According to the Climate Action Network, when some plastic bottles are incinerated along with other trash, as is the practice in many municipalities, toxic chlorine (and potentially dioxin) is released into the air while heavy metals deposit in the ash. If plastics are buried in landfills, not only do they take up valuable space, but potentially toxic additives such as phthalates may leak into the groundwater. "It's ironic that many people drink bottled water because they are afraid of tap water, but then the bottles they discard can result in more polluted water," says Franklin. "It's a crazy cycle."

Franklin also acknowledges that although her group is a strong advocate of recycling, the very concept may encourage people to consume more plastics. Replacing used water bottles with new containers made from virgin resources consumes energy and pollutes the air, land and water. CR estimates that supplying thirsty Americans with water bottles for one yea consumes more than 1.5 million barrels of oil, which is enough to generate electricity for more than 250,000 homes for a year, or enough to fuel 100,000 cars for a year.

Big Footprint

Despite such a sizable environmental footprint, the push to recycle plastic water bottles has not been as successful as many consumers might like to think as they faithfully toss their used containers into those blue bins. As *Utne* magazine recently reported, "Despite the ubiquitous arrow symbol, only five percent of plastic waste is currently recycled in America and much of that must be fortified with huge amounts of virgin plastic." One limitation is that recycling plastic causes it to lose strength and flexibility, meaning the process can only be done a few times with any given sample.

Another problem is that different types of plastics are very difficult to sort, even though they can't be recycled together. Common plastic additives such as phthalates or metal salts can also thwart recycling efforts as can too high a ratio of colored bottles (such as Dasani's blue containers) to clear bottles. Because of the challenges, many recycling centers refuse to accept plastics. In fact, a fair amount of America's plastic recycling is done in Asia, where laxer environmental laws govern polluting factories and fuel is spent in international transport.

According to a report recently released by the California Department of Conservation (CDOC), more than one billion water bottles are ending up in the state's trash each year, representing enough plastic to make 74 million square feet of carpet or 16 million sweaters. Darryl Young, the director of CDOC, says only 16 percent of PET water bottles sold in California are being recycled, compared to much higher rates for aluminum and glass. "It's good people are drinking water, but we need to do more outreach to promote recycling," says Young.

Franklin says one potential deterrent to recycling may be that water bottles are often used away from home, meaning they aren't likely to make it into curbside bins. Young advises people to ask for recycling bins in retail and public spaces.

Industry analysts point out that demand exceeds supply in the market for recycled PET plastic, which is used in a range of goods from flowerpots to plastic lumber. Franklin says deposit systems, or so-called bottle bills, would go a long way to improving the collection of used water bottles, especially since only half the country has curbside recycling available. But only a few states have bottle bills, largely because of strong opposition from the container, beverage and retail industries (and their front group, Keep America Beautiful). While Kay stresses that the IBWA urges consumers to recycle, he says his organization opposes bottle bills because "food retailers shouldn't have to devote any money-making floor space to storing and sorting recyclables, especially as that may lead to unsanitary conditions."

The WWF says alternatives to bottled water such as boiling and filtering are cheaper and more sustainable in areas that have contaminated tap sources.

Co-op America and CRI advise consumers to fill their own bottles to take with them on the go. Glass doesn't leach chemicals, and sturdy plastics can be repeatedly washed, so consumers don't have to worry about breeding bacteria. For a lessened environmental impact, spring and other specialty waters can be purchased in bulk. But as BBC News concluded, "The conservationists are fighting an uphill battle. The bottled water market is booming . . . and shows no signs of drying up."

Battling the Bottlers

Numerous environmental and social activists have recently begun to put up a fight against the expanding bottled water industry, which they claim threatens local wells, streams, wetlands and ways of life. Bottling companies may pump up to 500 gallons per minute, or even more, out of each well, and many wells run 24 hours a day, 365 days a year. Such operations have drawn intense opposition in Florida, New Hampshire, Pennsylvania, Texas, Michigan and Wisconsin. Many residents of these states depend heavily on groundwater for residential, agricultural and fishery use. In Wisconsin, for example, three out of four homes and 97 percent of municipalities obtain their water from the ground.

"Resistance against water bottlers is a classic NIMBY (not-in-my-backyard) issue," says Kay. The IBWA claims bottlers wouldn't pump aquifers to depletion because that wouldn't make good business sense. But civil engineer and hydrologist Tom Ballestero of the University of New Hampshire cautions that surrounding wells and the environment can be negatively impacted before an aquifer is severely depleted. "The groundwater they are pumping and exporting was going somewhere where it had an environmental benefit," says Ballestero. Geologist David Bainbridge of Alliant International University also points out that there are scant few penalties against users who draw down water tables or deplete aquifers. Due to the long amount of time it takes to naturally replenish aquifers, most scientists consider groundwater a nonrenewable resource.

Much of the opposition to water bottlers has been directed at Nestlé Waters North America, which taps around 75 different U.S. spring sites. A spokesperson for the corporation, Jane Lazgin, says most communities welcome the jobs and revenue brought by bottling operations. Even so, Nestlé lost several bids to set up bottling plants in the Midwest due to intense opposition. Eventually, for its Ice Mountain brand, Nestlé built a $100 million plant capable of bottling 260 million gallons of water a year from an aquifer in Michigan's rural Mecosta County, which is about 60 miles north of Grand Rapids. Nestlé paid around $150 for permits and received substantial tax breaks.

Local activists, mobilized by the newly formed Michigan Citizens for Water Conservation, protested the plant on the grounds that the facility would take too heavy a toll on the surrounding environment and quality of life. Although Nestlé claims it conducted "exhaustive studies for nearly two years to ensure that the plant does not deplete water sources or harm the ecosystem," the activists pointed out that the state has no authority to limit the amount of water that is actually removed.

Three Native American tribes sued the state on the basis that rivers, and ultimately, the Great Lakes, would be affected. Michigan Citizens for Water Conservation and a few local residents also filed a lawsuit, claiming that the Mecosta operations violate state and federal water rights. The controversy became a hot topic during the 2002 gubernatorial election. As *Grist* reported, "Both major party candidates publicly and repeatedly expressed their resolve to modernize state water policy to block other multinational corporations from privatizing, bottling and selling hundreds of millions of gallons of Michigan's groundwater annually across state lines." A ruling on the case is expected soon, and is believed to have far-reaching ramifications.

In Florida, Nestlé angered many people, including the group Save Our Springs, when it took over Crystal Spring, which is near Tampa. The company fenced out the public, which had enjoyed the water for generations. After five years of bottling operations, the spring level has dropped. Some officals are worried, since the spring feeds the source of Tampa's water. Nestlé blames the change on dry spells and local development.

Local residents have also fought Nestlé in rural northeast Texas, where they complain that a well across the street front the company's bottling site went dry five days after Nestlé began operations. Nestlé's Lazgin claims that well dried up because it was old and shallow, and that it was not on the same aquifer as the bottling plant. Critics counter that aquifer geology is a fairly subjective science. The Texas Supreme Court ruled in favor of Nestlé under the state's "rule of capture." Save Our Springs President Terri Wolfe told *The Northwestern,* "The poor people whose wells run dry because of [bottlers] can't afford that water."

What's the Quencher?

A host of environmental groups are joining resource managers in the call for Americans to cut back on bottled water and instead look to tap systems to provide our daily needs. As the NRDC points out, incidents of chemical or microbial contamination in tap water are actually relatively rare. In a recent review of the nation's public drinking water infrastructure, researchers at the Harvard School of Public Health concluded, "Reasonably reliable water is currently available to nearly all 270 million U.S. residents."

Writing in *The Kansas Lifeline,* Scott Hoober expresses frustration on the part of municipal water managers, who are increasingly shackled with negative reputations despite their actual accomplishments. Hoober advises managers sarcastically, "What are you waiting for? Turn a few valves, install a bottling plant and begin to make the big bucks. You could sell your water for half of what the other bottler down the road is charging and still make a bundle. With no meters or mains to maintain, no monthly billing, lower lab bills, why, you could afford a top-dollar advertising campaign telling folks how much better your water is than the stuff that used to come out of the tap."

It's true that tap water does face numerous threats, including possible contamination from the potentially harmful byproducts of chlorination, the specter of pollution and a lack of adequate funding. Stresses from global warming, urban sprawl and population increase also must be factored in, as well as the looming threat of terrorism. The WWF argues that governments should focus their limited energies on repairing current tap water infrastructures and on protecting watersheds from harmful farm, industry and urban pollutants. Many public water supply advocates feel that tax dollars should be paying to deal with tap water's challenges. We certainly need to think twice before handing off the public water trust to private companies that put it in attractive bottles at a high price. CONTACT: International Bottled Water Association, (800)WATER-11, . . . Natural Resources Defense Council, (212)727-2700, . . .

POSTSCRIPT

Is Bottling Water a Good Solution to Problems of Water Purity and Availability?

Ultimately, bottled water is the poster child for the consumer society. Although it is not safer than tap water and it doesn't taste better, it looks neat—makes us feel European, and slim and athletic (runners and cyclists drink water while exercising). But it really is no more exciting than, well, a drink of water. There is damage to the environment, but right at this point of U.S. history, the environment does not seem to be a selling point for the American consumer. (Witness the sales of SUVs and trucks to people who don't need them.)

Suggested Reading

If you want to pursue water further, the following sources might be valuable:

Emily Arnaiz, "Facts About Drinking Water" from *Michigan's Drinking Water* (July 28, 1998), http://www.gem.nsu.edu/gw/bt_wtr.htm.

Arthur von Weisenberger, "Reading Between the Lines of Bottled Water Labels," http://www.botledwaterweb.com/articles/avw-002.htm.

Janet L. Sawin, "Water Scarcity Could Overwhelm the Next Generation," from *World Watch* (vol. 16, no. 4 2003), by Worldwatch Institute, www.worldwatch.org.

Barbara Whitaker, "For Town, Water Is a Fighting Word," from *The New York Times,* (March 23, 2003), p. A23.

ISSUE 21

Should the World Continue to Rely on Oil as a Major Source of Energy?

YES: Red Cavaney, from "Global Oil Production About to Peak? A Recurring Myth," *Worldwatch* (January–February 2006)

NO: James Howard Kunstler, from *The Long Emergency* (Grove/Atlantic, 2005)

ISSUE SUMMARY

YES: Red Cavaney, president and chief executive officer of the American Petroleum Institute, argues that recent revolutionary advances in technology will yield sufficient quantities of available oil for the foreseeable future.

NO: James Howard Kunstler contends that the peak of oil production, Hubbert's Peak, was itself the important turning point in our species' relationship to petroleum. Unless strong conservation measures are put in place, the new scarcity will destroy much that we have come to expect in our lives.

We might begin with the fact that "oil crisis" has become part of our lives in the last half century. Suddenly gasoline prices are higher, there are lines at the gas stations, political commentators suddenly discover international affairs, and a mood of panic pervades the country. Resolutions are made, actions begun, but then the whole crisis seems to peter out. What's happening?

First, is oil "running out"? Since the 1930s, energy prognosticators have used a model called Hubbert's Curve (named for geologist M. King Hubbert, who first projected it), that predicted the end of oil as an available resource. As oil recovery technology has progressed, the curve has been lengthened; Red Cavaney's selection relies heavily on this fact. But the curve is still there, and even a major contraction in the oil supply will have a very significant effect on the way America continues to grow and develop; James Kunstler calls our attention to some of the changes we may expect.

There are two major dimensions to the "oil crisis," both of which affect the business community. The first is a management dilemma, stemming from the interaction of the U.S. economy and a global monopoly: how to control the impact of the decisions of international business consortia in the energy business. Business is all about supply and demand (see the selection by Adam Smith in Issue 1). In the case of petroleum, the lion's share of the supply is controlled by energy consortia who, as Smith would approve, consider their own economic interests first, with the result that they rarely have the interests of the people of the United States as a priority. The logic of economic success for the industry, as all oil producers know, requires that the producers reduce the supply available for purchase, causing the price to rise, for an interval of time that will be limited by the customer's perception that he is spending too much for oil, and has recourse to other methods of obtaining energy—for instance, by developing solar energy as a source of power, or placing restrictions on the amount of gasoline that automobiles sold in the United States can consume in a mile. At that point, production is raised dramatically, oil prices drop precipitously, and as a result, all investments in alternatives to oil consumption are abandoned. After that point, enough time is allowed to elapse so that investments will have been liquidated and the alternative workforce scattered; then the squeeze begins again. American consumers, on this understanding, are at the mercy of a foreign monopoly in complete control of the price of gasoline and heating oil, and would be well advised to use the periods of inexpensive oil to assemble the capital needed to solve the energy problem once and for all. That gathering of capital can only be done by heavy taxation of oil alone, or of all carbon, sufficient to keep the price of oil level for the consumer while the capital accumulates. The American public dislikes taxes in general, and the oil industry dislikes oil taxes even more.

The second dimension is an industry crisis caused by an environmental threat: how to adjust our automotive industry, traditionally the heart and pride of our manufacturing capacity, to minimize the damage done to the environment by the burning of all fossil fuels, especially the burning of gasoline in the use of automobiles and trucks for transportation. Our automotive industry is set up like all the others—to provide a healthy return to the shareholders by producing products that the consumers want and will buy and that yield a high profit margin. That requirement does not well describe small, fuel-efficient cars, but it does describe the large, low-fuel-mileage sport utility vehicles (SUVs), introduced in the 1990s and now flooding our highways. As the American public contemplates images of polar bears stranded on vanishing ice, hurricanes in the Caribbean and expanding deserts in Africa, it becomes increasingly likely that each new administration will insist on conservation measures, starting with the all-too-visible SUVs. How should the automotive industry—and the advertisers, the oil companies, and the consumers—respond?

Bear in mind, as you read these selections, that global business will suffer major disruptions in any initiative to end oil dependence; what advantages might make the sacrifices worth their cost?

YES

Red Cavaney

Global Oil Production about to Peak? A Recurring Myth

Once again, we are hearing that world oil production is "peaking," and that we will face a steadily diminishing oil supply to fuel the global economy. These concerns have been expressed periodically over the years, but have always been at odds with energy and economic realities. Such is the case today.

Let's look at some history: In 1874, the chief geologist of Pennsylvania predicted we would run out of oil in four years—just using it for kerosene. Thirty years ago, groups such as the Club of Rome predicted an end of oil long before the current day. These forecasts were wrong because, nearly every year, we have found more oil than we have used, and oil reserves have continued to grow.

The world consumes approximately 80 million barrels of oil a day. By 2030, world oil demand is estimated to grow about 50 percent, to 121 million barrels a day, even allowing for significant improvements in energy efficiency. The International Energy Agency says there are sufficient oil resources to meet demand for at least the next 30 years.

The key factor here is technology. Revolutionary advances in technology in recent years have dramatically increased the ability of companies to find and extract oil—and, of particular importance, recover more oil from existing reservoirs. Rather than production peaking, existing fields are yielding markedly more oil than in the past. Advances in technology include the following:

Directional Drilling.   It used to be that wellbores were basically vertical holes. This made it necessary to drill virtually on top of a potential oil deposit. However, the advent of miniaturized computers and advanced sensors that can be attached to the drill bit now allows companies to drill directional holes with great accuracy because they can get real-time information on the subsurface location throughout the drilling process.

Horizontal Drilling.   Horizontal drilling is similar to directional drilling, but the well is designed to cut horizontally through the middle of the oil or natural gas deposit. Early horizontal wells penetrated only 500 to 800 feet of reservoir laterally, but technology advances recently allowed a North Slope operator to penetrate 8,000 feet of reservoir horizontally. Moreover, horizontal wells can operate up to 10 times more productively than conventional wells.

Cavaney, R., "Global Oil Production About to Peak? A Recurring Myth," *World Watch Magazine*, January/February 2006, pp. 13–15. Copyright © 2006 by Worldwatch Institute. Reprinted by permission. www.worldwatch.org

3-D Seismic Technology. Substantial enhancements in computing power during the past two decades have allowed the industry to gain a much clearer picture of what lies beneath the surface. The ability to process huge amounts of data to produce three-dimensional seismic images has significantly improved the drilling success rate of the industry.

Primarily due to these advances, the U.S. Geological Survey (USGS), in its 2000 *World Petroleum Assessment,* increased by 20 percent its estimate of undiscovered, technically recoverable oil. USGS noted that, since oil became a major energy source about 100 years ago, 539 billion barrels of oil have been produced outside the United States. USGS estimates there are 649 billion barrels of undiscovered, technically recoverable oil outside the United States. But, importantly, USGS also estimates that there will be an *additional* 612 billion barrels from "reserve growth"—nearly equaling the undiscovered resources. Reserve growth results from a variety of sources, including technological advancement in exploration and production, increases over initially conservative estimates of reserves, and economic changes.

The USGS estimates reflected several factors:

- As drilling and production within discovered fields progresses, new pools or reservoirs are found that were not previously known.
- Advances in exploration technology make it possible to identify new targets within existing fields.
- Advances in drilling technology make it possible to recover oil and gas not previously considered recoverable in the initial reserve estimates.
- Enhanced oil recovery techniques increase the recovery factor for oil and thereby increase the reserves within existing fields.

Here in the United States, rather than "running out of oil," potentially vast oil and natural gas reserves remain to be developed. According to the latest published government estimates, there are more than 131 billion barrels of oil and more than 1,000 trillion cubic feet of natural gas remaining to be discovered in the United States. However, 78 percent of this oil and 62 percent of this gas are expected to be found beneath federal lands—much of which are non-park and non-wilderness lands—and coastal waters. While there is plenty of oil in the ground, oil companies need to be allowed to make major investments to find and produce it.

The U.S. Energy Information Administration has projected that fossil fuels will continue to dominate U.S. energy consumption, with oil and natural gas providing almost two-thirds of that consumption in the year 2025, even though energy efficiency and renewables will grow faster than their historical rates. However, renewables in particular start from a very small base; and the major shares provided by oil, natural gas, and coal in 2025 are projected to be nearly identical to those in 2003.

Those who block oil and natural gas development here in the United States and elsewhere only make it much more difficult to meet the demand for oil, natural gas, and petroleum products. Indeed, it is not surprising that some of the end-of-oil advocates are the same people who oppose oil and natural gas development everywhere.

Failure to develop the potentially vast oil and natural gas resources that remain in the world will have a high economic cost. We must recognize that we live in a global economy, and that there is a strong link between energy and economic growth. If we are to continue to grow economically, here in the United States, in Europe, and the developing world, we must be cost-competitive in our use of energy. We need *all* sources of energy. We do not have the luxury of limiting ourselves to one source to the exclusion of others. Nor can we afford to write off our leading source of energy before we have found cost-competitive and readily available alternatives.

Consider how oil enhances our quality of life—fueling growth and jobs in industry and commerce, cooling and warming our homes, and getting us where we need to go. Here in the United States, oil provides about 97 percent of transportation fuels, which power nearly all of the cars and trucks traveling on our nation's highways. And plastics, medicines, fertilizers, and countless other products that extend and enhance our quality of life are derived from oil.

In considering our future energy needs, we also need to understand that gasoline-powered automobiles have been the dominant mode of transport for the past century—and the overwhelming preference of hundreds of millions of people throughout the world. Regardless of fuel, the automobile—likely to be configured far differently from today—will remain the consumer's choice for personal transport for decades to come. The freedom of mobility and the independence it affords consumers is highly valued.

The United States—and the world—cannot afford to leave the Age of Oil before realistic substitutes are fully in place. It is important to remember that man left the Stone Age not because he ran out of stones—and we will not leave the Age of Oil because we will run out. Yes, someday oil will be replaced, but clearly not until substitutes are found—substitutes that are proven more reliable, more versatile, and more cost-competitive than oil. We can rely on the energy marketplace to determine what the most efficient substitutes will be.

As we plan for our energy future, we also cannot afford to ignore the lessons of recent history. In the early 1970s, many energy policymakers were sure that oil and natural gas would soon be exhausted, and government policy was explicitly aimed at "guiding" the market in a smooth transition away from these fuels to new, more sustainable alternatives. Price controls, allocation schemes, limitations on natural gas, massive subsidies to synthetic fuels, and other measures were funded heavily and implemented.

Unfortunately, the key premises on which these programs were based, namely that oil was nearing exhaustion and that government guidance was desirable to safely transition to new energy sources, are now recognized as having been clearly wrong—and to have resulted in enormously expensive mistakes.

Looking into the distant future, there will be a day when oil is no longer the world's dominant energy source. We can only speculate as to when and how that day will come about. For example, there is an even bigger hydrocarbon resource that can be developed to provide nearly endless amounts of energy: methane hydrates (methane frozen in ice crystals). The deposits of methane hydrates are so vast that when we develop the technology to bring them to market, we will have clean-burning energy for 2,000 years. It's just one of the exciting scenarios we may see in the far-off future. But we won't be getting there anytime soon, and until we do, the Age of Oil will continue.

The Long Emergency

A few weeks ago, the price of oil ratcheted above fifty-five dollars a barrel, which is about twenty dollars a barrel more than a year ago. The next day, the oil story was buried on page six of the *New York Times* business section. Apparently, the price of oil is not considered significant news, even when it goes up five bucks a barrel in the span of ten days. That same day, the stock market shot up more than a hundred points because, CNN said, government data showed no signs of inflation. Note to clueless nation: Call planet Earth.

Carl Jung, one of the fathers of psychology, famously remarked that "people cannot stand too much reality." What you're about to read may challenge your assumptions about the kind of world we live in, and especially the kind of world into which events are propelling us. We are in for a rough ride through uncharted territory.

It has been very hard for Americans—lost in dark raptures of nonstop infotainment, recreational shopping and compulsive motoring—to make sense of the gathering forces that will fundamentally alter the terms of everyday life in our technological society. Even after the terrorist attacks of 9/11, America is still sleepwalking into the future. I call this coming time the Long Emergency.

Most immediately we face the end of the cheap-fossil-fuel era. It is no exaggeration to state that reliable supplies of cheap oil and natural gas underlie everything we identify as the necessities of modern life—not to mention all of its comforts and luxuries: central heating, air conditioning, cars, airplanes, electric lights, inexpensive clothing, recorded music, movies, hip-replacement surgery, national defense—you name it.

The few Americans who are even aware that there is a gathering global-energy predicament usually misunderstand the core of the argument. That argument states that we don't have to run out of oil to start having severe problems with industrial civilization and its dependent systems. We only have to slip over the all-time production peak and begin a slide down the arc of steady depletion.

The term "global oil-production peak" means that a turning point will come when the world produces the most oil it will ever produce in a given year and, after that, yearly production will inexorably decline. It is usually represented graphically in a bell curve. The peak is the top of the curve, the halfway point of the world's all-time total endowment, meaning half the world's oil will be left. That seems like a lot of oil, and it is, but there's a big catch: It's the half that is much more difficult to extract, far more costly to get, of much poorer quality and located mostly in places where the people hate us. A substantial amount of it will never be extracted.

The United States passed its own oil peak—about 11 million barrels a day—in 1970, and since then production has dropped steadily. In 2004 it ran just above 5 million barrels a day (we get a tad more from natural-gas condensates). Yet we consume roughly 20 million barrels a day now. That means we have to import about two-thirds of our oil, and the ratio will continue to worsen.

The U.S. peak in 1970 brought on a portentous change in geoeconomic power. Within a few years, foreign producers, chiefly OPEC, were setting the price of oil, and this in turn led to the oil crises of the 1970s. In response, frantic development of non-OPEC oil, especially the North Sea fields of England and Norway, essentially saved the West's ass for about two decades. Since 1999, these fields have entered depletion. Meanwhile, worldwide discovery of new oil has steadily declined to insignificant levels in 2003 and 2004.

Some "cornucopians" claim that the Earth has something like a creamy nougat center of "abiotic" oil that will naturally replenish the great oil fields of the world. The facts speak differently. There has been no replacement whatsoever of oil already extracted from the fields of America or any other place.

Now we are faced with the global oil-production peak. The best estimates of when this will actually happen have been somewhere between now and 2010. In 2004, however, after demand from burgeoning China and India shot up, and revelations that Shell Oil wildly misstated its reserves, and Saudi Arabia proved incapable of goosing up its production despite promises to do so, the most knowledgeable experts revised their predictions and now concur that 2005 is apt to be the year of all-time global peak production.

It will change everything about how we live.

To aggravate matters, American natural-gas production is also declining, at five percent a year, despite frenetic new drilling, and with the potential of much steeper declines ahead. Because of the oil crises of the 1970s, the nuclear-plant disasters at Three Mile Island and Chernobyl and the acid-rain problem, the U.S. chose to make gas its first choice for electric-power generation. The result was that just about every power plant built after 1980 has to run on gas. Half the homes in America are heated with gas. To further complicate matters, gas isn't easy to import. Here in North America, it is distributed through a vast pipeline network. Gas imported from overseas would have to be compressed at minus-260 degrees Fahrenheit in pressurized tanker ships and unloaded (re-gasified) at special terminals, of which few exist in America. Moreover, the first attempts to site new terminals have met furious opposition because they are such ripe targets for terrorism.

Some other things about the global energy predicament are poorly understood by the public and even our leaders. This is going to be a permanent energy crisis, and these energy problems will synergize with the disruptions of climate change, epidemic disease and population overshoot to produce higher orders of trouble.

We will have to accommodate ourselves to fundamentally changed conditions.

No combination of alternative fuels will allow us to run American life the way we have been used to running it, or even a substantial fraction of it. The wonders of steady technological progress achieved through the reign of cheap oil have lulled us into a kind of Jiminy Cricket syndrome, leading many Americans to believe that anything we wish for hard enough will come true. These days, even people who ought to know better are wishing ardently for a seamless transition from fossil fuels to their putative replacements.

The widely touted "hydrogen economy" is a particularly cruel hoax. We are not going to replace the U.S. automobile and truck fleet with vehicles run on fuel cells. For one thing, the current generation of fuel cells is largely designed to run on hydrogen obtained from natural gas. The other way to get hydrogen in the quantities wished for would be electrolysis of water using power from hundreds of nuclear plants. Apart from the dim prospect of our building that many nuclear plants soon enough, there are also numerous severe problems with hydrogen's nature as an element that present forbidding obstacles to its use as a replacement for oil and gas, especially in storage and transport.

Wishful notions about rescuing our way of life with "renewables" are also unrealistic. Solar-electric systems and wind turbines face not only the enormous problem of scale but the fact that the components require substantial amounts of energy to manufacture and the probability that they can't be manufactured at all without the underlying support platform of a fossil-fuel economy. We will surely use solar and wind technology to generate some electricity for a period ahead but probably at a very local and small scale.

Virtually all "biomass" schemes for using plants to create liquid fuels cannot be scaled up to even a fraction of the level at which things are currently run. What's more, these schemes are predicated on using oil and gas "inputs" (fertilizers, weed-killers) to grow the biomass crops that would be converted into ethanol or bio-diesel fuels. This is a net energy loser—you might as well just burn the inputs and not bother with the biomass products. Proposals to distill trash and waste into oil by means of thermal depolymerization depend on the huge waste stream produced by a cheap oil and gas economy in the first place.

Coal is far less versatile than oil and gas, extant in less abundant supplies than many people assume and fraught with huge ecological drawbacks—as a contributor to greenhouse "global warming" gases and many health and toxicity issues ranging from widespread mercury poisoning to acid rain. You can make synthetic oil from coal, but the only time this was tried on a large scale was by the Nazis under wartime conditions, using impressive amounts of slave labor.

If we wish to keep the lights on in America after 2020, we may indeed have to resort to nuclear power, with all its practical problems and eco-conundrums. Under optimal conditions, it could take ten years to get a new generation of nuclear power plants into operation, and the price may be beyond our means. Uranium is also a resource in finite supply. We are no closer to the more difficult project of atomic fusion, by the way, than we were in the 1970s.

The Long Emergency is going to be a tremendous trauma for the human race. We will not believe that this is happening to us, that 200 years of modernity can be brought to its knees by a world-wide power shortage. The survivors will have to cultivate a religion of hope—that is, a deep and comprehensive belief that humanity is worth carrying on. If there is any positive side to stark changes coming our way, it may be in the benefits of close communal relations, of having to really work intimately (and physically) with our neighbors, to be part of an enterprise that really matters and to be fully engaged in meaningful social enactments instead of being merely entertained to avoid boredom. Years from now, when we hear singing at all, we will hear ourselves, and we will sing with our whole hearts.

POSTSCRIPT

Should the World Continue to Rely on Oil as a Major Source of Energy?

"**T**wixt the optimist and the pessimist, the difference is droll: the optimist sees the donut, and the pessimist sees the hole" (Anonymous). The selections you have just finished represent the optimistic and the pessimistic sides of the "oil reserves conflict" as we know it. There is more to the subject. We might ask the optimist if the availability of oil is really the heart of the question. Burning fossil fuels hurts the earth; should we cut back on our consumption of oil just to save the earth, now, even if oil supplies are abundant? But there is a question for the pessimist, too: granted that our "lifestyles" this minute require lots of oil, does our happiness depend on it, too? What would it be like to live in a way that consumes lots less oil because it consumes lots less of any kind of energy? Outside of the field of business ethics (and sometimes inside it, too) explorations into the notions of "simplicity" and "the simple life" continue. The less consumption-oriented life suggested in these explorations does not seem to be significantly lower in quality than our own—in many ways, it seems better. Should some ambitious entrepreneurs be looking into these possibilities, as the wave of America's economic future? Think about it.

Suggested Reading

In your thinking, you may find the following sources helpful:

Hawken, Lovins and Lovins, *Natural Capitalism* (BackBay Books, 2000)

Newton, Lisa, *Ethics and Sustainability* (Prentice Hall, 2002)

Newton, Lisa, *Business Ethics and the Natural Environment* (Blackwell, 2005)

Contributors to This Volume

EDITORS

LISA H. NEWTON, professor of philosophy and director of the Program in Applied Ethics at Fairfield University. She is author of *Business Ethics and the Natural Environment* (2004), *Wake-up Calls: Classic Cases in Business Ethics,* (2d ed. 2003), and numerous other books and articles in journals of business and health care ethics.

MAUREEN M. FORD is an associate for the Program in Applied Ethics at Fairfield University in Fairfield, Connecticut. She received a B.S. in business management and applied ethics from Fairfield University. Active as a consultant to community agencies, Mrs. Ford is a former president of the YMCA in Bridgeport, Connecticut, and was for several years vice president–secretary for JHLF, Inc., a marketing and consulting firm in Westport, Connecticut.

AUTHORS

DENIS G. ARNOLD received his Ph.D. in philosophy from the University of Minnesota in 1997 and is a past fellow of the National Endowment for the Humanities. His work in ethics and business ethics has appeared in *History of Philosophy Quarterly, American Philosophical Quarterly,* and other publications. Arnold is co-editor with Laura Hartman and Richard Wokutch of *Rising Above Sweatshops: Innovative Management Approaches to Global Labor Challenges* (New York: Praeger, 2004). He teaches philosophy and chairs the legal studies program at Pacific Lutheran University. His current research focuses on the ethical dimensions of global capitalism.

PHILIP L. BEREANO is professor of technical communication at the University of Washington. He is active in the American Civil Liberties Union, the Council for Responsible Genetics, and the Washington Biotechnology Action Council.

SISSELA BOK is a philosopher, author, and teacher who is well known for the books *Lying* (New York: Pantheon, 1978) and *Secrets* (New York: Pantheon Books, 1982).

NORMAN E. BOWIE is the Elmer L. Andersen Chair in Corporate Responsibility at the University of Minnesota, where he holds a joint appointment in the departments of Philosophy and Strategic Management and Organization. He is a frequent contributor to scholarly journals in business ethics. His most recently edited book is *Blackwell Guide to Business Ethics.* His co-edited text *Ethical Theory and Business* is in its sixth edition. He has held a position as Dixon's Professor of Business Ethics and Social Responsibility at the London Business School and has been a fellow at Harvard's Program in Ethics and the Professions.

THOMAS CARR is an assistant professor in the economics department at Middlebury College in Middlebury, Vermont.

CHRISTOPHER L. CULP is adjunct professor of finance at the Graduate School of Business at the University of Chicago, a principal at Chicago Partners LLC, and senior fellow in financial regulation at the Competitive Enterprise Institute.

WILLIAM DOMNARSKI is an attorney in private practice in Minneapolis, Minnesota. His articles have appeared in such journals as *American Scholar* and *Virginia Quarterly,* and he is the author of *In the Opinion of the Court* (Champaign, IL: University of Illinois Press, 1995).

MARK DOWIE is an investigative journalist and a former editor of *Mother Jones* magazine. He is the author of *Losing Ground: American Environmentalism at the Close of the Twentieth Century* (Cambridge, MA: MIT Press, 1996) and coauthor, with David T. Hanson and Wendell Berry, of *Waste Land: Meditations on a Ravaged Landscape* (New York: Aperture Foundation, 1997).

PAUL AND ANNE EHRLICH are environmental writers who are best known for *Healing the Planet: Strategies for Resolving the Environmental Crisis,*

(Boston: Addison-Wesley, 1991) and *Betrayal of Science and Reason: How Anti-Environmental Rhetoric Threatens Our Future* (Washington, D.C. Island Press, 1996). Paul Ehrlich launched a major sector of the environmental movement with his *The Population Bomb* (New York: Ballantine Books, 1971).

FRIEDRICH ENGELS (1820–1895), a German socialist, was the closest collaborator of Karl Marx in the foundation of modern communism. The official Marxism of the Soviet Union relied heavily on Engels's contribution to Marxist theory. After the death of Marx in 1883, Engels served as the foremost authority on Marx and Marxism, and he edited volumes 2 and 3 of *Das Kapital* on the basis of Marx's incomplete manuscripts and notes. Two major works by Engels are *Anti-Duhring* and *The Dialectics of Nature*.

RICHARD A. EPSTEIN is a James Parker Hall Professor of Law at the University of Chicago. He authored "Unconscionability: A Critical Reappraisal" in 1975.

JOHN E. FLEMING is professor emeritus at the University Southern California, where he taught for twenty-four years, serving as the doctoral program director and Management department chairman. Before entering the academic field he worked in industry for fifteen years. His research areas are strategy and business ethics. He has been published in *The Academy of Management Journal*, the *California Management Review,* and the *Journal of Business Ethics*.

JOHN P. FOLEY, an archbishop, is president of the Pontifical Council for Social Communications and Vatican media director for Pope John Paul II.

MILTON FRIEDMAN, U.S. laissez-faire economist, emeritus professor at the University of Chicago, and senior research fellow at the Hoover Institution, was one of the leading modern exponents of liberalism in the nineteenth century European sense. He was the author of *Capitalism and Freedom* and coauthor of *A Monetary History of the United States* and *Free to Choose*. He was awarded the Nobel Prize for Economics in 1976.

ROBERT GOLDBERG is a senior fellow at the Manhattan Institute. He writes for the *National Review*.

KENNETH GOODPASTER earned his A.B. in mathematics from the University of Notre Dame and his Ph.D. in philosophy at the University of Michigan. He taught graduate and undergraduate philosophy at Notre Dame throughout the 1970s before joining the Harvard Business School faculty in 1980, where he taught MBAs and executives, published numerous articles and case studies, and authored several books. In fall 1989, Goodpaster accepted the David and Barbara Koch Chair in Business Ethics at the University of St. Thomas, St. Paul, Minn.

STEVE H. HANKE is professor of applied economics at the Johns Hopkins University, a principal at Chicago Partners LLC, and a senior fellow at the Cato Institute.

GILBERT HARMAN is Stuart Professor of Philosophy at Princeton University. He regularly co-teaches interdisciplinary courses in "The Philosophy and Psychology of Rationality" and "The Psychology and Philosophy of Ethics." He has been co-director (with George Miller) of the Princeton University Cognitive Science Laboratory and is chair of the Faculty Committee for Cognitive Studies. He is author of *Explaining Value and Other Essays in Moral Philosophy* and *Reasoning, Meaning and Mind*, both published by Oxford University Press.

ROBERT D. HAY is university professor of management at the University of Arkansas. He retired in 1990 after 41 years of teaching, research, and service. He is the author of 11 books and numerous articles and cases.

BRIAN HOWARD is managing editor of *E* and turns on the tap when he wants a glass of water.

JOHN HUEY is senior editor of *Fortune* magazine. The former editor of *The Wall Street Journal/Europe* and founding editor of *Southpoint* magazine, he has long reported on the business world and has profiled many of its leading personalities. He lives and works in Atlanta.

GENE LACZNIAK is the Wayne R. and Kathleen E. Sanders Professor in Marketing in the School of Business Administration at Marquette University in Milwaukee, Wisconsin. His research interests include marketing strategy, business ethics, and marketing and society. He has taught executive development classes in Europe and Asia, as well as in the United States. He is coauthor, with Patrick E. Murphy, of *Ethical Marketing Decisions* (Boston: Allyn & Bacon, 1992).

ROBERT A. LARMER, B.A., M.A., Ph.D., is associate professor of philosophy at the University of New Brunswick. His responsibilities include courses in philosophy of religion and ethics. He is the author of various articles in philosophy of religion and of *Water Into Wine: An Investigation of the Concept of Miracle.*

JOSEPH A. LEVITT, Esq. is the director, Center for Food Safety and Applied Nutrition, Food and Drug Administration, Department of Health and Human Services, Washington D.C.

IAN MAITLAND teaches business ethics and international business at the University of Minnesota. He is author of the *Causes of Industrial Disorder* (Oxford, UK: Routledge, 1983) and has published in the *Journal of Business Ethics, Journal of Politics, Academy of Management Review, British Journal of Industrial Relations, California Management Review, Business and the Contemporary World,* and elsewhere.

KARL MARX (1818–1883), student of philosophy and economics and author of *Das Kapital* and the *Communist Manifesto,* 1848.

JOHN McCALL is a professor in the departments of Philosophy and Management at St. Joseph's University. He has also taught at Georgetown University's McDonough School of Business and at the Wharton School of the University of Pennsylvania. He is coauthor (with Joe DesJardins) of

Contemporary Issues in Business Ethics, now in its fourth edition. He has published on welfare reform, corporate responsibility, product liability, and especially on employee rights issues.

MERTON H. MILLER is the Robert R. McCormick Distinguished Service Professor Emeritus of Finance in the Graduate School of Business at the University of Chicago in Chicago, Illinois. He and William F. Sharpe were awarded the Nobel Prize in Economics in 1990 for their pioneering work in the theory of financial economics. He is the author of *Merton Miller on Derivatives.*

JENNIFER MOORE is assistant professor of philosophy at the University of Delaware. She does teaching and research in business ethics and business law and is coeditor of the anthology *Business Ethics: Readings and Cases in Corporate Morality* published by McGraw-Hill.

KEVIN J. MURPHY is an assistant professor at the Graduate School of Management of the University of Rochester, where he teaches economics. A recognized expert in the field of executive compensation, he consults with a wide range of corporations on their practices and has published in the *Journal of Accounting and Economics* and with Michael Jensen in the *New York Times.*

ALLEN R. MYERSON is a writer for the *New York Times.*

LAURA L. NASH is director of the newly formed Institute for Values-Centered Leadership at Harvard Divinity School. In addition to running the institute's programs, she teaches and writes on business ethics, religious values, and corporate culture. She has also been a senior research associate at Boston University's Institute for the Study of Economic Culture. She is the author of *Believers in Business* (Nashville, TN: Thomas Nelson, 1994) and coauthor, with David A. Krueger and Donald W. Shriver, Jr., of *The Business Corporation and Productive Justice* (Nashville, TN: Abingdon Press, 1996).

JAMES NEAL is a lawyer who has served in many mass disaster and product liability cases, including the Ford Pinto suit and the Exxon Valdez environmental suit.

LISA H. NEWTON, program director in Applied Ethics and philosophy professor at Fairfield University, Fairfield, Connecticut.

FRANK PARTNOY is assistant professor of law at the University of San Diego Law School and a recovering bond salesman.

HEATHER L. PEDERSON is a mathematics teacher at the Colorado Springs School in Colorado.

SUNDER RAMASWAMY is chair of the economics department at Middlebury College in Middlebury, Vermont. He is coauthor (with Sanders and Shapiro) of *The Economics of Agricultural Technology in Semiarid Sub-Saharan Africa* (Baltimore: Johns Hopkins University Press, 1996).

JEFFERSON D. REYNOLDS is deputy regional environmental counsel, U.S. Air Force. He earned his J.D. from Hamline University in 1990 and his LL.M. from George Washington University in 1995.

JEREMY RIFKIN is president of the Foundation on Economic Trends and a long-time critic of innovative technology. He is the author of *The End of Work: The Decline of the Global Labor Force and the Dawn of the Post-Market Era* (New York: Tarcher, 1996) and *The Biotech Century: Harnessing the Gene and Remaking the World* (New York: Putnam, 1998).

RICHARD ROSEN is a writer for *The American Prospect.*

JOHN SHANAHAN is vice president of the Alexis de Tocqueville Institution in Arlington, VA.

ADAM SMITH (1723–1790), a Scottish philosopher and economist. Author of *An Inquiry into the Nature and Causes of the Wealth of Nations*, first edition, London, 1776.

ROBERT C. SOLOMON is Quincy Lee Centennial Professor of Business and Philosophy and Distinguished Teaching Professor at the University Texas at Austin. He authored six books in business ethics, *Above the Bottom Line, It's Good Business, Ethics and Excellence, New World of Business, A Better Way to Think About Business,* and *Building Trust* (with Fernando Flores). He has written many articles and essays, and he lectures and consults worldwide for a variety of institutions and corporations.

JULIE STAUFFER, a published author on environmental issues and a contributor to many environmental publications, researched and published a book on water: its pollution in underdeveloped countries as well as in the United States and the scarcity of water worldwide due to pollution.

MANUEL VELASQUEZ is the Charles J. Dirksen Professor of Business Ethics at Santa Clara University. The author of several articles on business ethics, he is also author of *Business Ethics: Concepts and Cases*, 3rd edition (Englewood Cliffs, NJ: Prentice-Hall, 1992) and co-editor of *Ethics: Theory and Practice*, 2nd edition (Upper Saddle River, NJ: Prentice-Hall, 2000). He is past president of the Society for Business Ethics and is currently director of the Santa Clara University Markkulla Center for Applied Ethics.

MICHAEL A. VERESPEJ is a writer for *Industry Week.*

SAM WALTON, founder of Wal-Mart, the largest retailer in the world and considered an undisputed Captain of Commerce, attended college, put together a family partnership, and became a billionaire.

DEBRA WATSON is a writer for *World Socialist Web Site*, www.wsws.org.

ANDREW C. WICKS is assistant professor in the Department of Management and Organization of the University of Washington School of Business. He has a Ph.D. in religious studies, and his interests are in normative business ethics and the connections between medical ethics and business ethics. His articles have been published in *Soundings* and the *Journal of Business Ethics.*

JOSEPH WIELAND is director of the Centre for Business Ethics associated with the German Business Ethics Network. He is also professor of economic and business ethics in Konstanz, Germany. He previously lectured in economics at the University of Witten/Herdecke. His book, *The Ethics of Governance*, is published in Marburg, Germany, by Metropolis.